Harrow boys playing the original version of squash in the yard at Head Master's House, circa 1890. Note the footscrapers and windows that came into play.

Squash

A HISTORY OF THE GAME

James Zug

WITH A FOREWORD BY GEORGE PLIMPTON

SCRIBNER

NEW YORK   LONDON   TORONTO   SYDNEY

SCRIBNER
1230 Avenue of the Americas
New York, NY 10020

SCRIBNER and design are trademarks of
Macmillan Library Reference USA, Inc., used under license
by Simon & Schuster, the publisher of this work.

For information about special discounts for bulk purchases,
please contact Simon & Schuster Special Sales:
1-800-456-6798 or business@simonandschuster.com

Designed by Colin Joh
Text set in Janson

Manufactured in the United States of America

3   5   7   9   10   8   6   4   2

Library of Congress Cataloging-in-Publication Data

Zug, James, 1969–
Squash : a history of the game / James Zug.
Includes bibliographical references and index.
p. cm.
1. Squash rackets (Game)—History. I. Title.
GV1004.Z84 2003
796.343—dc21
2003050458

ISBN 0-7432-2990-8

For Jim and Debbie Zug

CONTENTS

Contents

by George Plimpton

On occasion I drift into a New York club noted for its athletic facilities—four squash courts, a fifth for squash doubles, two court tennis courts (the game played on them is the progenitor of lawn tennis) and one racquets court. In the club library there are hundreds of books on lawn and court tennis and dozens on racquets. There are only a few on squash and most are instruction manuals. One begins, "Squash is an easy game to play badly—it is a difficult game to play well."

This considerable imbalance has been nicely rectified by James Zug's formidable volume on squash.

A quick word about the author. James Zug learned the game as a youngster growing up in Philadelphia, taught by his father who was a two-time national doubles champion. Young Zug played at Haverford and then at Dartmouth where he was captain in his senior year (1991) when the squad was nationally ranked at number five. How good was he? Squash players have a game called the "Indirect," often played on long college squash trips, that helps determine, however speciously, one's relative prowess at the game. Zug's best "Indirect" works out as follows: one year he beat the number two player at Dartmouth who had beaten the one player who had beaten the number one at Penn who had beaten a top pro player who had beaten Mark Talbott who had beaten Jahangir Khan, who was at the time the best player in the world. Ergo.

Zug has continued to play at high levels since college, playing in a Cape Town squash league, coaching juniors in Washington, D.C., and participating in the amateur doubles circuit. He is blessed with a strong literary bent and was once in my employ on behalf of the literary magazine, the *Paris Review*. I cannot resist wondering how much he worked on behalf of quality literature, since to put together this carefully researched volume on squash must have required an unholy amount of time and effort—the kind only undertaken by those with a great passion and love of their subject. I don't begrudge Zug at all. He has produced the definitive book on the game.

I especially enjoyed what he has done because I have relished squash as well. I first learned about "the delicious pleasure of cracking a ball against a wall" at Harvard, where I was able to study the game from the master, Jack Barnaby. He was the peppery and wise coach who succeeded Harry

Cowles at Harvard and for whom squash was a dominating, utterly absorbing obsession. One winter morning four or five of us were traveling to Williams College for a match. We were in Jack's station wagon, and at the wheel Barnaby had been, as always, talking endlessly about squash since our departure. As we passed through a small town near Williamstown, we came up on a traffic light. Jack miscalculated and bumped the car in front. Without the slightest hitch in the flow of his dissertation, he announced, "let!" and went right on talking. I can't recall how the situation with the people in front was resolved (it was the mildest of fender-benders) but I'll always remember Jack's sharp, authoritative "let!" as we hit.

Titans of the game like Jack Barnaby are wonderfully portrayed here. Zug chronicles the Khans, perhaps the most famous family in squash, endowed with a gene that has produced three generations of champions. I remember playing an exhibition match against the patriarch, Hashim, in Detroit where he was the pro at the Uptown Athletic Club. Before a small gallery of people drinking cocktails we played a gentleman's game, the great man keeping the ball in play until out of exhaustion I dumped it in the tin. After the match he did a little show of trick shots, including a display of footwork I could hardly believe. He asked me to stand near the front wall and hold the ball just above the tin. When I dropped it, Hashim, with his rear foot braced against the back wall, sprang forward, reached the ball with his racquet before it bounced twice and tweaked it into the corner.

It would seem that squash players are different from the rest of society, that to contain oneself in a relatively small room and smack a rubber ball about in competition eventually does odd things to one's mental state: The Talbott brothers, Dave and Mark, spoke to each other in an imaginary language made up of English, French, Latin and Tolkein and played exhibitions in full-length dressing gowns and wigs. Eleo Sears, the great Boston Brahmin and squash pioneer, swam in the Atlantic in February.

In this regard no one looms larger than Victor Niederhoffer, surely one of the greatest who ever played. Here is how Zug describes Niederhoffer's first meeting with my friend Jack Barnaby: "In the autumn of 1960, not yet seventeen, Vic Niederhoffer went up to Cambridge as a freshman at Harvard. He joined the freshman tennis team and played number one. That winter he walked into the office of the varsity tennis and squash coach, Jack Barnaby. 'I hear you're a darn good tennis player,' Barnaby said. Niederhoffer agreed and then blurted, 'I'm going to be the best squash player ever.' Then he paused and meekly added, 'Squash is that wall game, right?'"

Here is Zug's little checklist of Niederhoffer's eccentricities: He took off his shoes and wore only socks in his office. The only newspaper he read was the *National Enquirer*. He did not own a television. He took lessons in checkers every Tuesday evening for fifteen years. In the locker room before matches, he kept a sock on his right hand so, he wrote, "that no one would shake my hand and distract me." His footwear at formal occasions was inevitably a pair of mismatched sneakers.

If interested in learning more about Niederhoffer, readers will find that one of the most entertaining parts of the book is the collected notes at the end. There are an astonishing 539 of them, many paragraphs long, all fascinating. Some of the footnotes would seem to require footnotes of their own. Where did Woody Allen and Michael Douglas learn to play squash (note on p. 320)? When will Sam Friedan, Yale's legendary junior varsity star, reappear (p. 327)? Others are priceless set-pieces on their own—Niederhoffer's reaction on having the lights turned off in a Harvard Club court where he was practicing late at night—pitched into what he refers to as a "Pit and the Pendulum" horror. He felt the walls closing in on him as he searched unsuccessfully for the door latch. He eventually leapt up and climbed into the gallery above the court. He summed up his experience: "The only time a player should be left alone on a squash court is with a voluptuous broad."

One of the more practical pleasures of Zug's book is that our knowledge of the game will be increased immeasurably. I never knew that the squash court was brought to this country by James Potter Conover, more popularly known as Jay, a master at the New Hampshire preparatory school St. Paul's. As squash players know, for seventy-five years the American version of the game was played on a court smaller than its English counterpart—two and a half feet narrower and the ball harder and faster. Zug finally uncovers the true reasons why we had the smaller court, belying my favorite rumor that the larger English court would not fit in the boat bringing the game over from England. I never knew the details of the hearings that led to the smaller courts being legislated out of existence—a decree that forced American schools, universities and clubs to pony up millions of dollars to change their courts to the contours of the larger size. I never knew that the *Titanic* had a squash court (larger size), and that a man named Archibald Gracie, who was saved, had an appointment to play squash on Monday morning, April 15th, with the professional Fred Wright, who went down with the ship a few hours earlier. I never knew the drop shot was popularized by Harry Cowles around 1914—adding a dimension to the game that until then was dominated by players who hung far back in the court as they did in the game of racquets and cease-lessly hammered the ball. Or that Germain Glidden, a fine portrait painter, used his 1937 national champion trophy as a repository for his paint brushes. From my own playing days, I remember the U.S. Naval Academy at Annapolis was a perennial squash force but I never knew that its dedication to the game was such that in 1965 a squash court was built on the U.S. submarine tender *Simon Lake*.

One measure of Zug's assiduous research is that he has turned up and listed (scores and all) just about every match of consequence of the twen-tieth century. I exaggerate, but not much. I half-expected to find the score of my losing match against Tom Kempner (see note, p. 310) which decided the match in Yale's favor in 1949. There were so many lets that Seymour Knox, Sr., a Yale man (see note p. 303), was installed as a referee. Some of my desperate, exhausted appeals were ignored, which to this day I attribute to Knox's understandably strong bias against Harvard. You can-not imagine my pleasure in dropping this item of complete inconsequence into the foreword to this important book.

Squash

Schoolboys created the game out of three simple things. They swung crude racquets shaved off at the handle. They hit gray rubber balls, sticky, misshapen, punctured, smelling of brimstone. They battered stone walls stippled with windows, ledges and pipes. Three items were the sole prerequisites, and a century and a half later it is the same: a bat, a ball and a wall.

Squash breeds zealots. People fall in love with the game to the point of obsession. Something about it captures the imagination. Each of the tripartite aspects of squash is so basic and so uncomplicated that the love runs pure and deep. Time does not leaven the passion. Decades later a squash player can instantly retrieve the memory of that first day he connected on the sweet spot of a racquet and drove a squash ball hard into a wall.

The bat, as a racquet used to be called, is the chief tool of the squash tradesman. At first it was a sawed-off bamboo stick. As the game grew in sophistication, it became a hoop of second-growth white ash, bent by steam, strung with gut and red silk cord, with a pillowy calfskin grip at one end and the stern admission on the side: Squash Racquet Not Guaranteed. Prossers. Wright & Ditson. Spalding. Bancroft. Snauwaert. Cragin. Feron. Unsquashable. Manta. Slazenger. Dunlop. Wilson. Head. Prince. Today racquets are made from high modulous graphite, hyper carbon and titanium. They swoosh through the air with oversized heads, with a powerscoop shaft, microfilament, eighteen-gauge nylon Ashaway strings and a cushion-fit faux-leather grip. The bat is long and light, but capable of delivering satisfying force upon the ball.

King Arthur obtained Excalibur from a beautiful woman who stood sentry at the shores of a lake in which the sword was submerged; a squash player's relationship to his weapon is equally shrouded in the mists of romantic myth. It is a scythe you swing in a white field, a rapier that cuts to the quick, a rifle for a soldier, a hammer for a carpenter. You envelop your bat in a fetishistic aura. You pamper it. You kiss it after a lucky shot. You grip and regrip it, winding wafer-thin blue ribbons around the handle, tying them off with a red stick of tape. You bandage the head with protective tape. You tap it against the wall before you serve, like a blind man touching the sidewalk with a cane. It gives your bearings. You string and restring, and you straighten the strings in between points like a master weaver. You are loath to let someone borrow it. You are superstitious and save a magical racquet for crucial matches. You stick it first into your squash bag when you go away for a tournament. When you come back, you stash it head down in your locker. Squash is a tough sport. Racquets split and crack. Players retire. Memories fade into the back corners of the mind. When your racquet finally breaks, you do not throw it away. You bury it in an upstairs closet to be found by a grandchild. What was this, Grandpa? This, you say as you again heft the glorious weight and swing it whistling through the air and ponder a life not guaranteed, this was my squash racquet.

The ball the schoolboys originally swatted was a globe of vulcanized India rubber pierced with a hole. At the turn of the twentieth century, it became a gutta-percha ball, then the Hewitt, the black Seamless, the Cragin green diamond, the revolutionary blue Merco seventy-plus, the Slazenger fuchsia ball, and now the black Dunlop Revelation Pro XX Yellow Dot. The ball has always been small and quick, an effulgent moonrock flashing and floating through the white space of the court. It cruises like a nuclear pinball. It ricochets like bees shaken in a jar. It darts like a scared serpent. And then it dies upon command. Like the faddish board game from the 1970s, squash is the Othello of games: It takes a minute to learn but a lifetime to master.

The walls were originally made of stone quarried from the earth. They did not enclose as much as draw a line across nature. They were open to the clouds, the spitting rain and golden bars of sunlight. Now squash is inside. The court is a cage. You run on a floor made from northern maple ,with the unpainted boards set on edge for speed. Lights dangle from a fluorescent ceiling. The four walls, constructed of gypsum plaster and concrete or high density composite panel, are incapable of causing distraction or prompting reverie. They are niveous and functional. The only interruptions are a few firehouse-red lines and a piebald, carbon smear pockmarking the walls with the signature fingerprint of squash. The walls are Piet Mondrian in an unhappy mood, meant to be played upon.

Squash saturates the senses. There is the burnt perfume of heated rubber, the tangy admixture of sweat, dust, stale air and wood, the unexpungable odor of ego on display. There is a woolly thirst on the tongue after the most exhausting hour of the day. There is the sight of two people moving so fluidly, in such close proximity and in such a state of ecstasy that it appears they are dancing. There is the Euclidean violence of the dark ball careening from white wall to white wall in combinations only physicists and the gods can explain, and at a speed faster than you can drive a car.

Sound defines the game. The ball makes a schlooping hiss as it comes off hair-thin strings stretched to thirty pounds per ounce. Sneakers squeak on the floor like a disgruntled aviary. Players grunt and gasp and moan at errors. In between points they wipe their hands along the wall as if they are painting with sweat. Above all there is the distinctive *phlap* of rubber meeting wood. This is squash—the ball closing upon itself as it slams into the front wall, then opening again as it rebounds back. It is a stuttering, metronomic incantation, as intimate, steady and comforting as a heartbeat.

Meshed together in the alchemy of squash, the bat, ball and the wall produces beauty and truth. The Holy Grail of the game is perfect length. You try to propel the ball so it glides along the side wall and dies against the back wall. The walls are your enemies. They push your drives back into the center of the court, spin your cross-courts too sharply, kick out your drop shots, repel your advances. You are helplessly in love. Again and again you come back. You aim and hit, hoping the ball will hug the wall, perhaps gently graze it like a lover brushing her lips against your skin. You hit a slow, whispering shot. You hit an electric, ardent shot. It is all the same. No matter how beautiful your stroke, the truth is that you cannot achieve perfect length. You adopt the mien of a monk. You practice alone. You grow pale from the hours spent under artificial lights. You punish yourself with arm-aching drills. You crack one rail after another. You rake a ball that rushes past the side wall like a locomotive on a downhill run and crashes into the back corner, unplayable, stuck to the wall like wallpaper and say, "good length." But you never say, "perfect length." Such a thing does not exist.

Good length is a part of the dialogue of squash. You can rehearse for hours, snap off a hundred shots, one after another, videotape a stroke, repetitively groove your swing until your hand twitches in your sleep, but in a match, like in romance, you can only control your half of the flirtation. A match involves two people. As with all the best games, there is no clock, no limit but what you create. To beat an opponent, you might proceed by indirection, as in sailing. You might throw in inspired combinations of tacks when you sense the wind shifting, when your opponent is tiring or becoming exasperated or growing angry. You might proceed by a golflike pattern: long drives followed by chipped wedges, then a short, putting dropshot.

SQUASH

You might play basketball and go for a winner from three-point range or dash up for a tomahawk dunk. You might take a technique from crew and try to row through your opponent on the home stretch of the fifth game by exceeding his power output. You might play chess. Squash is a culminative game. You pile up tiny victories, you employ tactics, you hunt for psychological advantages, you retreat with the Sicilian defense. Whatever you do, an opponent answers back. You have to react to him. The conversation is rapid fire, elliptical, maddeningly addictive, improvisational, close to the bone. Unlike tennis, there is no net separating you and your opponent in a squash court. You jostle and bump right up against him. You touch his sweat. You hear his heaving lungs exhaling air. You smell his fear or exultation and, if you are not careful, you might absorb it. Squash is the Stockholm syndrome at a hundred miles per hour.

If squash is literature, it is poetry. Its lines are short but heavy with meaning. It condenses and concentrates, distills and refines. It exposes your character like an X ray exposes your bones. It is madness in an unpadded cell. The term for the spectator bleachers at a squash court is the gallery, and squash, seen from above, is like an Impressionism art show. It is something aesthetically soft and engrossing on display. The bodies blur. The racquets flash. The seismic thumps of the ball seem attractive. But, down on the ground, it is murder in the court.

At heart squash is boxing with sticks and a piece of rubber. The same sweet science of pugilism, minus the neutral corners, controls the game. You have a thousand cubic feet of territory to claim. You come out strong. You probe for weaknesses. You jab with boasts and lobs. You circle in a fight for the center of the court. You clinch with the hand-push when caught going the wrong way. You rope-a-dope with attritional drives to the back corners. You swing haymaker volleys into the nick. You tire. You find a second wind. You slump on a stool in between games, sucking on water, toweling off sweat. You go for the knockout drop at match point in the fifth. You shake hands, you hug and you exit together, bound forever by the crucible of the contest. Outside the winter fugue of snowfall and early darkness is playing but, inside, you are as bright and warm as a fire.

The stories of the history of squash are told in locker rooms, galleries and the club bar—the contemporary equivalents of the ancestral campfire. They are passed down from player to player and generation to generation with a focus on the extraordinary. People tell of the three times when the national championship was decided by the slimmest of margins: a winner-take-all point in a tiebreaker in the fifth game. Or when an avatar of soft-ball brilliance arrived on our shores. Or those streak-breaking matches in Boston in 1920, Mexico City in 1975 and Cleveland in 1982. Or that month when a Brooklyn girl swept through a triple crown of the national juniors, national intercollegiates and national singles. Or that Monday in November when one of our own beat the best player in history. People talk of less-obvious legends. They recount the eccentric club upstate, the superstitions of the local champion, rumors of the aging veteran's psycho-logical warfare and the inevitable hilarity of a late tournament weekend evening.

In writing the story of squash in the United States, I have tried to find a narrative equipoise between retelling the legends of the game and explaining the quotidian circumstances from which they rose. Much of what follows necessarily concerns champions. They pushed the game to its highest level of excellence. They represented their club, their city and sometimes their country. I have also tried to recover the biographies of those left at the margins of the historical record—weeknight hackers, C players, juniors, tournament directors, the many fanatics who lived off the East Coast seam and, most of all, women. The game of squash has sur-vived and prospered because these rank-and-file, unheralded people logged countless chilly hours in the gallery watching matches, billeted players, picked up officials at the train station and held up the bar after midnight. They form the marvelously obsessive and jovial backbone of the game. Allison Danzig, who wrote the only other history of the game in his magisterial 1930 book *The Racquet Game*, responded to this bifurcated story by listing the names of men and women who played the game in each city. I trust this is no more clumsy.

In marching to the beat of chronology, I have endeavored to incorporate the sweep of larger issues into the inevitable recapitulation of tournaments and personalities: the ephemeral life of squash tennis, the emergence of intercollegiate squash, the creation of the weekend tournament circuit, the Merion dynasty, the herky-jerky sashay of the game across the country, the commercial club liberation, the rise and fall of the professional tour and the arrival of a single international standard of squash. Only doubles stood outside this narrative and deserved its own separate chapter toward the end of the book. There are a hundred doubles courts in the United States, hardly a blip on the radar screen of singles squash with its four thousand courts. Besides its different court, the four-handed game has its own ball, rules, circuit of tournaments, aura and practitioners.

SQUASH

The unique thing about a squash ball, unlike almost any other sports ball, is that it has no life of its own. It needs to be warmed up. It needs to be hit to have energy. It needs a player. This, in the end, is a biography of the people who have played the game of squash.

CHAPTER ONE

The Joints Trembled on the Spit

Since time immemorial, ball games have been a balm to the human condition. Man has always wanted to throw, catch and hit. An Egyptian tomb built five thousand years ago depicts four women tossing a ball. Homer tells of a ball game in the *Odyssey*. Four different ball games were popular in Rome at the time of Christ. The Visigoths played a complicated sport similar to football. When the Spanish arrived in Mexico, they found the Aztecs playing a game with rubber balls that bounced high into the dusty air.

In medieval France boys played in the narrow streets of their villages. Some pastimes involved slapping balls along the awnings or roofs that lined the street, or into shop and door openings. Rules depended on local geography. In the thirteenth century these street games migrated up the hills to cloistered monasteries. Every Lenten season young brothers strung a fishing net across the middle of their courtyards and patted a ball back and forth with their gloved hands. In time ecclesiastical strictures loosened and the monks played all year. Their divertissement grew in complexity. The balls—a patch of leather with dog hair sewn inside, later cloth stuffed with soil, sawdust, sand or moss—bruised and cut hands. Monks added webbing to the gloves, then extended their hand by picking up a stumpy stick, a branch of a tree or a shepherd's crook. At the end of the fifteenth century, the Dutch invented the racquet: a wooden paddle with the finely braided gut of a sheep twisted through a hole at one end.

Because the European aristocracy entrusted monasteries for the education of their sons, this quiet game had its own missionaries when the boys returned to their parental estates. They built their own courts. Now called tennis, this game for bored monks became in effect the national sport of a dozen European nations. In 1580 the Venetian ambassador to Henri III of France walked around Paris counting tennis courts: he stopped at eighteen hundred. In 1598 Sir Robert Dallington, secretary to the English ambassador to France, wrote: "Ye should have two Tennis Courts for every one Church through France. Methinks it also strange, how apt they be here to play well, that he would thinke they were borne with Rackets in their hands, even the children themselves manage them so well, and some of their women also, as we observed at Blois. There is one great abuse in this exercise, that the Magistrates do suffer every poore Citizen and Artificer to play thereat, who spendeth that on the Holyday at Tennis, which he got the whole weeke for the keeping of his poore family. A thing more hurtful than our Ale-houses in England."

The English extricated themselves from the saloons long enough to play tennis themselves. Oxford had a half-dozen courts, Cambridge ten. Charles II loved his daily game so much that he kept a bed for himself at his personal court. Shakespeare mentioned the game in numerous plays. (Today there is sometimes confusion about tennis and lawn tennis. As played by Tilden, Navratilova and Sampras, lawn tennis was invented in 1873 in Great Britain as an outdoor version of real tennis. Only recently has lawn tennis dropped its first appellation—until the early 1970s, for instance, the national governing body of the new game in America was the U.S. Lawn Tennis Association. Over the course of the twentieth century, the traditional version has had to slowly adapt to calling itself real tennis or royal tennis or, as it is now called in America, court tennis.)

Despite the reports of eighteen hundred courts in Paris alone, tennis was never truly a game for the masses. Many of the courts, which were enormously expensive recreations of a monastery's courtyard, were private. Gangs of gamblers inundated the others, and made swindling and violence the order of the day. In 1606 Caravaggio, the tempestuous Italian painter, disemboweled a man at a tennis court in Rome. The sport had a byzantine scoring system and obscure vocabulary: hazard, chase, penthouse, tambour and grille. Furthermore, the kings of Europe, beginning with Philippe IV of France in 1292 and Edward III of England in 1365, constantly issued prohibitions against play, as they found their soldiers practicing their backhands more than their archery. Slowly tennis retreated to an aristocratic redoubt. By the end of the seventeenth century, it was most often played at royal palaces like the Louvre, Falkland, Fontainebleu and Hampton Court.

The English—for whom one feels tennis never truly lost its taint as a French diversion—took the racquet into their own hands. In the early eighteenth century, prisoners at the Fleet, London's notorious debtor's jail, created an outdoor ball game. It was called racquets and it was brutally simple: hitting a ball against a wall. The ball and racquet were derived from tennis, but the game lacked all the pretense of the game of kings. With no back walls, one or two side walls and no roof, racquets was a delightfully elemental combination of speed and finesse. The ball, unsqueezable, was made from wound cloth and was similar to a golf ball; the racquet looked like a stretched tennis bat.

The Fleet was an atypical jailhouse. Prisoners had free run of taprooms, chandler shops, a bake house, kitchens and whistling shops offering gin, whiskey and rum. If a prisoner posted a small fee, he could leave the prison and take lodgings within the Fleet district, which was a mile and a half in length. To work off their debts, the incarcerated took employment at the Fleet market, local theaters or at the many publishing houses and printing presses nearby (the Fleet was known for its writer prisoners). Detained clergymen, outside the bounds of the London bishop, performed "Fleet marriages"—cheap, quick and without the necessary banns and licenses. Locals were more or less free to enter and leave the prison, bands of smugglers headquartered themselves in cells and unescorted women visited in such droves that the Fleet was considered the most active brothel in London. In its seven-hundred-year existence, the Fleet did not hear a single roll call.

The daytime action was in the Fleet's back courtyard. Called the *bare*, it was a ground covered with paving stones and bounded by two stone walls, one of which was the rear facade of the four-story Bartholomew Fair, where the poorer prisoners lived. Every Christmas the Fleet prisoners elected their own racquet master, the keeper of the court. Charles Dickens, whose father was imprisoned at the Marshalsea debtors jail for fourteen weeks, wrote of a visit to the Fleet in *The Pickwick Papers*: "The area formed by the wall in that part of the Fleet in which Mr Pickwick stood was just wide enough to make a good racket court; one side being formed, of course, by the wall itself, and the other by that portion of the prison which looked (or rather would have looked but for the wall) toward St. Paul's Cathedral. Sauntering or sitting about, in every possible attitude of listless idleness, were a great number of debtors . . . some were shabby, some were smart, many dirty . . . a few clean . . . lolling from the window which commanded a view of the promenade were a number of persons, some in noisy conversation with their acquaintance below, others playing at ball with some adventurous throwers outside; and others looking on the racket players, or watching the boys as they cried the game." There, in the midst of this Rabelaisian life, began the game of racquets.

Due to the uniquely permeable nature of the Fleet, racquets spread like a wild fire in a dry forest. Another London prison, the King's Bench, soon had four courts and an equally active social life. One King's Bench racquet master named Hoskins (who altered the game from eleven to fifteen points) made so much money from giving lessons and supplying balls and racquets that he supported a family of seven. In 1820 a prisoner at the King's Bench, with typical jailhouse bravado, crowned himself world champion. "The King's Bench Prison at that period was one continued scene of gaiety and dash—indeed it was like any thing else but a place of confinement," wrote Pierce Egan in 1832. "The promenade, almost every evening, was a complete picture of *le beau monde*. It exhibited some of the most elegant dressed females of the kingdom, the finest, nay, fashionable women who felt not the slightest reproach by visiting their unfortunate friends in 'durance vile.'" Hundreds of racquets courts dotted the towns and villages of nineteenth century Great Britain. The game was as common as cricket or football. Men found it a pleasant distraction after a hard day's work, and most courts were yards connected to taverns, coffeehouses and alehouses.

By choice or accident, they sometimes left their racquets at home and instead played another ball-and-wall game, fives. Named for the five fingers of the hand, this ancient version of handball was a slower game than racquets. Fives grew so popular at English public schools that the two leading forms of the game derived their standards from the quirky spots on campus where the boys played. Eton fives emerged from the mossy drainpipes outside the school chapel at Eton. It had a court twenty-five feet and three inches by fourteen feet, with many buttresses and hazards. Rugby fives was created at Rugby School, where the sport of rugby football also was started. It had an unadorned court twenty-eight by eighteen feet, with side walls that sloped toward the back wall and a two-and-a-half-foot tin on the front wall. In 1819 William Hazlitt penned an exquisite obituary of John Cavanagh, an Irish fives champion.* Hazlitt noted the fives courts on St. Martin's Street (where the owner charged half a crown a head for spectators at a Cavanagh match), another near Rosemary Branch, and the one at Copenhagen House where Cavanagh often wagered dinners. "The wall against which they play is the same that supports the kitchen-chimney," he wrote of one fives

* "It may be said there are things of more importance than striking a ball against a wall—there are things, indeed, that make more noise and do as little good, such as making war and peace, making speeches and answering them, making verse and blotting them, making money and throwing it away," Hazlitt famously wrote about fives players. "He who takes to playing at Fives is twice young. He feels neither the past nor the future in the instant. Debts, taxes, domestic treason, foreign levy, nothing can touch him further. He has no other wish, no other thought, from the moment the game begins, but that of striking the ball, of placing it, of *making* it."

court, "and when the walls resounded louder than usual, the cooks exclaimed, 'Those are the Irishman's balls,' and the joints trembled on the spit." The company was decidedly mixed, as Hazlitt reported. "The fault of these places is that the company is not sufficiently select, and that a gentleman who is fond of the game (and all are fond of it who can play at all) are there compelled to join a miscellany of very respectable persons no doubt, but not of the highest grade of society."

Wanting peace from the complaints of a thousand scullery maids, Britons started building racquets courts, as opposed to just playing in a convenient corner of a yard or alley. These courts were unadorned, roofless affairs, usually boasting just one or two stone walls and a paving stone floor. In Ireland it was the style to have sloping side walls, while in England the court usually consisted of merely a front wall. In London a number of racquets courts became known for their social swirl, gambling and daily set of matches: the Oval, Belvedere (the oldest court in London), Tufnell Park, Yorkshire Stingo, Eagle Tavern, White Conduit House, the Oxford & Cambridge on Chalk Farm Road, the Bull and an establishment run by an old, one-eyed man named Powell who had lost an eye playing racquets.

Inclement weather, always a factor in soggy Great Britain, drove players toward a court with a roof. In 1830 the Royal Artillery built the first known covered racquets court at its Woolwich depot. The Marylebone Cricket Club, the home of cricket, built one in 1844 next to its tennis court at Lords, and in 1853 Prince's Club opened its historic doors with seven covered racquets courts painted white or a very pale green. Soon an elaborate cultural and sporting divide existed between the open and closed court games: Open courts were sixty feet by forty, played to eleven points, usually involved doubles and often were frequented by a mix of characters; closed courts were usually fifty feet by thirty-two, scored to fifteen, were mostly for singles and were restrictive in membership.

Following flag and florin, racquets spread to the colonies. The first racquets court in Canada was created in Halifax in the 1770s; in India in 1821; Australia in 1847. In 1793 Robert Knox, a Scot, put up the first racquets court in America on Allen Street, between Hester and Canal, in lower Manhattan. A few years later the Allen Street court had a rival nearby that was called, due to the predominant profession of its membership, the Butcher's Court.

On a steep knoll ten miles northwest of London lies an icon of elite English education, Harrow School. In the 1800s Harrow boys, like all public school students, played racquets. It was not what we would consider a varsity sport. At the time Harrow fielded organized teams for just football, cricket and relay races. Much of the afternoon, especially for younger boys unable to make the varsity eleven, was spent casting around for other amusements. There was toozling—throwing stones at birds, a pastime that meant a severe flogging if discovered by a master—and there were organized fistfights, which did not incur punishment if held on the milling ground, a grassy stretch of lawn where it was also legal to smoke.

Above the squalor of the milling ground was Old Schools, a three-story hall built in 1615, and the heart of Harrow. The chief racquets court at Harrow was in the schoolyard that surrounded Old Schools on three sides. One special nook of the schoolyard was called the Corner. It had two good side walls and a front wall with a buttress that dropped the ball straight down and a waterpipe that sprayed it in all directions. The Sixth Formers (seniors) claimed the Corner as their territory. "In those days we played racquets in the schoolyard," wrote Charles Roundell, class of 1848. "The Sixth Form against the school building, with the wall of the milling ground at the back, the Fifth Form on the wall opposite the school steps, the Shell (a class for first-year boys) in the corner to the right. The Sixth and Fifth Form games, owing to their different local conditions, differed much in character. In the Sixth Form game it was compulsory to serve on the big chimney, backhanders from Leith's Wall being also compulsory, and a principal feature of the game; but a return backhander from the milling-ground wall was not compulsory, but optional. Some of the happiest hours of my school life were spent on the Sixth Form ground."

In 1850 Harrow constructed two open-air racquets courts in a steeply pitched apple orchard below the milling ground. Although the bill came to £850, and they were as fine as most other racquets courts, Harrovians found them appalling. One, like a soldier with an amputated leg, had a missing side wall, the other had a back wall that rose a mere three feet above the ground, and both had floors made from rough stone. Unsatisfied, William Hart-Dyke, class of 1856, got involved. In 1862 Hart-Dyke won the racquets world championship (he was the first champion not to have learned the game in prison). Unable to countenance such decrepit courts at his alma mater, he formed a committee of Harrow alumni to raise money. In the autumn of 1864, Hart-Dyke built, at a cost of £1,600, a covered racquets court. The court, still playable today, was opened on Saturday, 20 January 1865 with a doubles match between Hart-Dyke & V. E. Walker and two racquets professionals from the Victoria Club in Torquay, Day & Ponten.

Weak arms and bullying seniors were the mother of the invention of squash. Harrovians were fixated on racquets. Court time at Old Schools and on the new courts below the milling ground was as rare and precious as a hot bath for upperclassmen; it was nonexistent for younger boys. They had to be content to play in the tiny, stone-walled yards at their boarding houses or in village alleys. The yards and alleys, like the Corner, boasted peculiar hazards: water pipes, chimneys, ledges, doors, footscrapers, wired windows and fiendishly sloping ground. Split-second decisions and speedy hand-eye coordination were essential. Racquets, with its long, heavy bat and bullet-hard ball, was a difficult game for an inexperienced, undermuscled Fourth Former to learn in such cramped conditions. With typical English flair, the young boys at Harrow invented something new. Rubber initially came into use in Europe in the 1820s, with the Macintosh coat the first mass-produced rubber object, but it was not until the 1840s that men like Charles Goodyear solved rubber's notoriously unstable qualities and began making objects out of rubber. To play their new game, Harrow boys used a special, thick rubber ball punctured with a hole and sawed-off racquet. This bastardized version of racquets was called "baby racquets" or "soft racquets" or "softer."

The mystery of how baby racquets morphed into modern squash was not solved until December 1923, when the *Times* of London printed a succession of letters to the editor from Harrow alumni. The first correspondent recalled playing baby racquets in the house yards and the various hazards on the walls. Mark Fenwick, class of 1877, wrote in to mention that the cold, damp winter weather made it a pleasant game. Long after graduating, Fenwick continued to buy his squash balls from "Judy" Stevens, the racquets coach at Harrow. "Our old squashes were rather smaller than a Fives ball," added a third alumnus. "They used to make splendid water-squirts in the early 'sixties." In a careful description of the yard at Head Master's House, R. Stewart-Brown noted "play was nearly all backhanded, and a very powerful stroke was thus developed. It was a splendid game, requiring great activity and good sight, as the ball could be made to hit the various projections and openings by a skilful player and come off at all angles or drop dead." The greatest letter, in length and gravity, came from a Scottish judge and viscount in the House of Lords, Dunedin, class of 1868. The school's racquets champion his senior year and "keen on squash," Dunedin described the dormitory yards and other colorfully named spots in the town of Harrow where baby racquets was a daily event: Monkey's, Bradley's, Vanity Watson's, Butler's and Young Vaughan's. He noted that Eton fives, with its many obstacles, "took on fairly well" after the 1865 courts were opened, but Rugby fives, with its plain court, was scorned by Harrovians. "The Rugby courts did not, I know, have half-a-dozen games of fives played in them," wrote Dunedin. "They obviously invited the familiar squash, and were immediately appropriated for that purpose." From Hart-Dyke at Lullingstone Castle in Kent came the final letter on the subject. Sir William, long retired from his forty-one-year tenure in the House of Commons, wrote to the matter so consistently covered on page five of the *Times*. He claimed that he had built the Rugby fives court with squash in mind: "These, I can well remember, I intended for play with a racket and indiarubber ball. I fully agree with Lord Dunedin that these courts obviously invited the familiar squash, and from that sprung the idea of the Harrow squash court."

Almost by accident, Hart-Dyke had built the first squash courts. Cutting up the old Fifth Form racquets court, he put in four Eton fives courts and three Rugby fives courts. So, this was the scene: On some wintry day in January 1865, two young Harrow boys walked into a Rugby fives court with their gray rubber ball and sawed-off racquets and played the first official game of squash.

In the early days at Harrow, squash was looked upon as nothing more than a set of simple instructions for little engineers. One apprenticed at squash before graduating to racquets. "The game is very and deservedly popular," E. O. Pleydell-Bourverie wrote of squash in 1890. "Familiarity with the flight of balls generally and with the handling of a racquet is thus acquired and if the player feels drawn in that direction—and those who become proficient at the softball game usually do—he proceeds to a regular racquet court, where it takes him a comparatively short time to adapt the knowledge and skill he has acquired to the requirements and the rapid flight of the orthodox racquet ball." At times, it was not a pretty sight, as one observer, M. C. Kemp, recorded in the 1880s: "Rather can the casual spectator, strolling through the courts, complain that young players too often are content to make their early efforts with racquets well-calculated to damp their incipient zeal. Racquets with but few strings unbroken, with great holes, through which a ball will often vanish, or more ignominious still, get stuck, are too frequently seen in the hands of the young. What fun, I wonder, can they imagine they derive from the game under such conditions? And yet they look serenely happy, and repeat regularly the performance, destined to wiser eyes and older heads to end in disappointing failure!"

Serenely happy, Harrovians loved their new game. They continued to play in the yards and the Rugby fives courts every afternoon. Harrow shops sold new and used balls. There was a good deal of carry-over in rules from the yards: One always served from the right side of the court first, owing to the fact that such was the custom at the Corner, because it had no right wall. The squash ball in the 1880s, remembered Stewart-Brown, was "a soft, thin rubber one, with or without a hole, and cost fourpence. Sometimes a smaller black 'bullet' was used, but this was too fast." Scoring, like racquets, was to fifteen, with only the server eligible to increase his total. In 1880 Harrow built four new fives courts; in 1889 two more; in 1891 six more—but now, these fives courts were built for squash.

Why was the game called squash? For years it was thought to be ono-matopoeic, that a rubber ball smashing against a stone wall sounded like *ssss-Qua-sshhh*. But why not call it *sklinkle*, *skibble* or *slomp*? The word squash was formed from the Latin *exquasser* meaning "to shake out." It first appeared in English in 1565 and meant "to press into a flat mass." (The vegetable gourd, like butternut or acorn squash, comes from the Narragansett Indian word *askutasquash*.) Historically squash had a number of definitions: to crush or squeeze; to go to ruin; a type of lemonade; the unripe pod of a pea; and a social or literary gathering. Squash also meant a large crush of people. A squash in soccer was a group of players bunched closely around the ball. It was the last definition that related to an odd custom at Harrow. In the nineteenth century, Harrow used the schoolyard outside Old Schools for a procedure known as squash. Each winter the student body elected a cricket keeper, a boy in charge of ordering balls, bats and wickets and arranging matches. "The ostensible object of the election was to secure self-government to the boys in their games," wrote J. G. Cotton Minchin, class of 1868. "This was the ostensible object, but the real object seems to have been to give the majority an opportunity of wiping out old scores against unpopular boys. As soon as he had declared for whom he voted, a general melee took place, and the unhappy elector [voter] was kicked, cuffed, and hustled by all his form fellows. The delights of 'squash' were not reserved for boys personally unpopular, but were afforded in ample measure to the boys of any unpopular house, and of course to all home boarders. . . . So serious was the hustling at 'squash' that many boys used to declare themselves candidates for the sole reason of divesting themselves of their electoral privileges. There certainly never was a suffrage with more unpleasant consequences to those who exercised it." One example of the fear squash generated can be seen in an April 1847 letter written by Augustus J. C. Hare to Charles S. Roundell: "To-day was Election Day, commonly called Squash-day, (Oh, how glad I am it is over), the day most dreaded of all others by the little

The oldest of nine children, Ja[y] become the father of Americ[a] impulses, he was hardy, unrem[?] tional yet innovative. Raised in[?] gling boy's academy in rural [?] from which he graduated in 18[?] lor's degree at Columbia. He liv[?] returning to teach at St. Paul's,

Conover formed the arche[?] ordained Episcopalian priest; in[?] of Henry Coit, the first rector o[?] new chapel). He later wrote tw[o?] *ity in Education*. One St. Paul's h[?] alistic" and a victim of "unworl[d?] taught by him and knew him [?] wrote in 1934, "was of medium[?] lete of great strength, quicknes[s?] ies and nineties owed him a [?] thought of] providing healthy [?] tastes or whose physical develo[?] more vigorous competitions. . [. .] School, he thought it undesirab[le?] in the afternoon writing Latin[?] conceived the idea of having L[?] walking round the pond." Con[?] jumper, he was the first man at[?] than his height. He led Columb[?] fencing club at St. Paul's. He wa[?] cricket was one of the most p[?] three—a critical spot—for the

boys, when they got squ
out. . . . As your name i:
cricket keeper; and as yo
you, while your party tri
hour (without exaggerat
schoolboy democracy ass
sport those young boys ir

Harrow also had a sc
spelling of the word rac
Some say it originated fr
German *racken*, "to stret
old Saxon word used to d
Latin for the wrist or ank
Ball, Bat and Bishop: The
root: "'Racquet' comes f
wound around the hand
quet," wrote Henderson,
lic Library. "This Arab
perhaps accounts for the
finally reached England.
called it a *racquette* or :
weapon, used a variety of

By the nineteenth cent
able. A short street near F
ck, but D'Israeli used *cqu.*
With the advent of lawn t
accepted spelling. In 1878
lished his classic book *Ai*
favor of *ck*. Although *cqi*
Charles Arnold published
erning body of English :
Racquets Committee—M
manently tilted the scale

At Harrow there was
newspaper, on 1 Februar
the game had been establ
quets. They had no inferi
and no need to clarify its
racquets. Harrovians felt
game but rather invente

1887 he built a toboggan slide on a steep hill above the lower pond and spent many winter evenings schussing with students along the black ice.

History, though, remembers the good reverend for a visit he made to Montreal during the 1880 Christmas holidays. A skating enthusiast, Conover saw a version of ice hockey at a winter carnival and brought home rules, hockey sticks and a wooden block an inch thick covered with leather, soon to be called a puck. Ice hockey was barely known in the United States, so St. Paul's was regarded as the birthplace of hockey in America. While in Canada, Conover also played racquets at the St. George Street court in Montreal. He had played a fair amount of racquets while studying at Columbia and, in 1878, joined the Racquet Court Club, which had a racquets court at its clubhouse at Twenty-sixth Street and Sixth Avenue. Playing the game again, Conover reacquainted himself with the delicious pleasure of cracking a ball against a wall. He decided that St. Paul's should have a court.

It took two years and another visit to Montreal to hire a contractor, but in January 1883, St. Paul's finished its racquets building. Placed on the edge of the woods behind the main schoolhouse, near the Lower School Pond, the barnlike facility, as Conover wrote, "has no pretensions to beauty and grace of outline." Built from maple and birch and painted dark red, it was about sixty by fifty feet, with a steeply pitched, seventy-foot roof, to keep snow from accumulating and blocking the sun coming through a skylight. Inside were a spacious vestibule heated by a new stove, with a carpeted dressing room partitioned off on one side and a modest gallery above. The pièce de résistance was two wooden racquets courts, painted white and made entirely of maple. Each court was rather small. At the time there were no regulations for a racquets court, but the sixty feet by thirty courts at Prince's Club in London were becoming the standard. The few courts in America varied in size and often had wooden floors, whereas cement was the norm in England. The building cost $2,800. Conover formed a Racquet Club to pay for it and to encourage play. Thirty-five students paid fifty dollars each to join. Most of the boys, like a young Jack Morgan, composed solicitous letters home to parents begging for the extra allowance. "Of course," wrote Jack in 1883 to his mother when he wanted to join the club, "if Papa thinks it is too expensive a luxury there is nothing more to say." Papa granted permission, his mother sent the money and Jack became an avid racquets player before going to work for Papa, known to the world as J. P. Morgan. Besides courting the sons of famous financiers, Conover secured donations totaling over a thousand dollars from, as he termed it, "some friends of the School and a few 'lovers of the game,'" including a number of Racquet Court Club members in New York like William Travers and Stuyvesant Rutherford, the president and vice president of the club. Conover ordered two hundred dollars worth of racquets and balls from Arthur Pearson in London, but they were detained for months at the Customs House in New York.

Racquets did not inspire the St. Paul's boys the way it did at Harrow. The courts were awkwardly lit—by windows on just one side and by one dirty skylight—and what sunlight did arrive produced glare and shadows due to the white walls. After a winter of blacking balls to ensure they were visible against the walls, Conover repainted the walls black and left the balls white. Over the summer of 1883, the walls and floor warped in the seasonal humidity and had to be replaced. In 1884 the fencing club moved its boxes of equipment into the racquet building, "so that the members can fence while awaiting their turns to play" racquets, the school newspaper said. In 1887 a reporter noted that Mr. Morley, the cricket coach, stored his stock of cricket, baseball and tennis goods for sale in a racquets court.

Undaunted, Conover pressed on. He staged a series of tournaments each winter and began to crown school champions (his son Dick won the championship in 1889). One of the tournaments was the Lenten Tournament, which ran from Ash Wednesday to Easter, with one round each week and a prize going to the boy who won the most games. Other tournaments were handicapped according to ability or age. Each Christmas holiday, the school held a tournament at the Racquet Court Club in New York. Malcolm Gordon, class of 1887 and longtime master at St. Paul's, later wrote that he played racquets every morning after chapel with various masters or with Mr. Morley. "Jay Conover at times would come in and show us the real game. His playing was a treat to us. He could have given Foster or me one hand and three aces and have won. But old Morley's foxy service and cat-like quickness made Conover do his best." Pier mentions the racquet building in his history of St. Paul's: "There were many who through the opportunity offered by the school Racquet Court found healthy exercise and enjoyment in playing a lively and exciting game." He should know. In 1889 one student named A. S. Pier played the greatest number of games of a student during the winter season, 181.

As at Harrow, racquets at St. Paul's led to squash. In November 1884 Conover built four open-air squash courts on the east side of the racquets building. That month the school newspaper reported that "the 'Squashball' courts are ready for play. They are open to all who pay the dues of $1 a year." The ball was a black rubber ball with a hole in it. The four courts, thought of by Conover as "a little village of courts peopled with lovers of tennis, raquettes, fives and hand-ball," lacked back walls. "It is proposed," wrote Conover in the school newspaper, "if the players are incommoded with snow, to inclose the ends with wired glass."

In the winter of 1930, Macmillan published *The Racquet Game*. Written by Allison Danzig, a young sports reporter at the *New York Times*, the book covered the history of a number of winter racquet sports, including squash, but failed to mention St. Paul's. Soon after it appeared, a number of old St. Paul's boys contacted Danzig about his ignorance of St. Paul's history. In March 1930 Danzig replied to one letter writer, Malcolm Gordon. He told Gordon he had talked to dozens of St. Paul's men, and none of them had given him any information about racquets or squash. Explaining that he planned a whole chapter on St. Paul's for a new edition of his book (which never appeared), Danzig then asked for help from Gordon: "Unfortunately, my information about these games (squash and racquets) at St. Paul's was totally inadequate. . . . I simply want to do justice to St. Paul's." Gordon, inspired by Danzig's questions, as well as by Arthur Pier who was beginning to put together his history of St. Paul's, researched the history of squash and racquets at his alma mater. As a part of this process, Jay Conover, then seventy-three, retired and living in Rhode Island, wrote a useful letter that contained a priceless paragraph about the squash courts: "I got the proper dimensions from Hyde Clark of Cooperstown, N.Y. Hyde had been educated at Harrow in England where they had such courts, and he and I were at Columbia together and both members of the N.Y. Racquet Club and both enthusiastic for racquets and cricket."

Conover copied more than just the dimensions from Harrow. St. Paul's masters and boys considered racquets the proper senior sport and squash a junior game. The winner of the spring Lenten tournament in squash was automatically enrolled in the Racquet Club, but other boys had to prove themselves skilled enough in squash to graduate to playing racquets. Conover, although loyal to his old college sport of racquets, nevertheless recommended squash for schoolboys. "In such a court, the game is not quite so enticing as where the walls are of brick and the ball solid, like a small base-ball," he wrote in the school newspaper on 30 November 1882, in what was the first squash manifesto. "But the so-called 'squash-ball court' recommended itself to the club for many reasons;—such courts are largely used in English public schools; cost of construction is much less; fewer raquette bats are broken and fewer balls destroyed; fewer heads are cracked and fewer knees and elbows barked;

the danger from being hit by the ball (quite an item among young players) is canceled."

With barked elbows and cracked heads, St. Paul's boys packed up their squash racquets and balls when they left New Hampshire. The first stop on the train was Boston, where they invented a new game, squash tennis.

Squash tennis—basically tennis in a squash court—had an innocuous birth. The customs man innocently instigated the sport. "By some accident, the materials for the game were detained in the custom-house in New York," wrote Jay Conover in the St. Paul's school newspaper in February 1883 just after he had opened his racquets courts, "but tennis racquets were called into requisition, and the game was started." With the arrival of the proper equipment, the schoolboys officially switched to the relatively established forms of racquets. Yet some boys continued their habit of playing tennis indoors, especially in the new squash courts. Lawn tennis, invented just a decade before, was the current rage across America. With all the troubles Conover had with the courts—the warping wood, the drifting snow—it was no wonder boys brought in balls with which they felt comfortable.

On the evening of 29 December 1888, the Boston Athletic Association opened its new clubhouse on the corner of Boylston and Exeter Streets in Back Bay. It was the most luxurious club in America. The nine-story building boasted a billiards room, a running track, a court tennis court, a bowling alley, a Turkish bath, a swimming pool, a dining room that could seat eighty-five and a Rugby fives court. "No new building in Boston has attracted so much attention as that recently opening of the Boston Athletic Association on Exeter Street," wrote one reporter. "Before dressing, the member can receive a rubdown with alcohol, which will prevent his catching cold and will act like a cocktail before dinner." Eleven hundred men from the highest echelons of Boston society joined the BAA that winter, paying a forty-dollar initiation fee and annual dues of thirty dollars. Court tennis, under the leadership of the current world champion, Tom Pettitt, did quite well at the BAA, but fives, despite the promise of a cocktail-like massage, never took hold. A number of St. Paul's alumni introduced their schoolboy games of squash and squash tennis into the otherwise quiet court. Under the direction of James Dwight, the club built another fives court, somewhat larger than the original. In March 1890 the club organized a squash tournament at the court. Richard D. Sears, the seven-time U.S. national lawn tennis champion, was the winner and took home a twin-handled ivory trophy.

But squash tennis was the BAA game of choice, and BAA members soon scattered the seed of squash around Boston. One member, Hollis Hunnewell, an 1886 St. Paul's graduate and the son of the man who built the first court tennis court in America, put up his own squash tennis court at his home Hill Hurst in Wellesley, Massachusetts. The maple-floored court measured thirty-one feet three inches by sixteen feet three inches, with spruce clapboard walls and cedar shingling on the roof. Hunnewell drew up blueprints of his court for his friends to copy. George Wright, the father of lawn tennis great Beals Wright, built a court in a barn on his estate in Dorchester. Wright outdid Hunnewell with a thirty-four-by-nineteen-foot court that boasted a prism glass skylight. Oliver Ames assembled a court at his house in Northeastern, Massachusetts. The Dedham Country and Polo Club erected one in the garden behind its clubhouse on High Street. In 1900 the Newton Centre Squash Tennis Club built a clubhouse with beautiful wooden courts. Other clubs followed: the Oakley Country Club, the Country Club in Brookline and, in 1904, the Tennis & Racquet Club. In 1902 George Morison founded and became the first president of the Massachusetts Squash Association, with the BAA, Newton Centre, TCC and Oakley as founding clubs. The MSA, the first racquet sports league in the country, immediately flourished.

The game's first temple was, however, at Tuxedo Park, nestled thirty-eight miles northwest of New York in the foothills of the Ramapo Mountains. In 1886 Pierre Lorillard, a tobacco magnate, founded Tuxedo as America's first gated community. Lorillard, having sold his Newport mansion, the Breakers, to the Vanderbilts, originally designed Tuxedo as a summer alternative to the usual patrician retreats. However, Tuxedo soon grew into a year-round colony, with a string of mansions, lakes and a golf course dotting the sixteen-hundred-acre park, and an eight-foot-high barbed-wire fence encircling it. (The tuxedo as an outfit took its name from the community; one story of its origin was that Griswold Lorillard, Pierre's son, appeared at a Tuxedo ball in a dinner jacket without tails.) In 1899 Lorillard contracted with an English company to erect an ideal winter playland. Designed by Warren & Wetmore, the copacetic lakeside clubhouse looked like an Italian palace with shimmering white columns and a red roof. Inside it had a Turkish bath, a plunge pool, five dressing rooms, a court tennis court, a racquets court and two squash tennis courts. Robert Moore, the new professional at Tuxedo, put in a six-inch hole a half foot above the tin on the front wall of the squash tennis courts. If you popped the ball into the hole, you won the point. Otherwise, the court set the standard for all future squash tennis courts: thirty-two-and-a-half feet by seventeen, with a fourteen-foot front wall and a two-foot high playline on the bottom of the front wall and twelve-foot side walls painted dark red. A line ran up the middle the whole length of the floor, marking a service line. Scoring was to fifteen, but you scored only when serving. Tuxedo's annual tournament, held first in 1900, was regarded as an informal national championship. After Reginald Fincke, a national racquets champion, won the tournament for the third time in 1907, he retired the trophy according to tradition and the tournament was discontinued.

With the BAA as a nursery and Tuxedo as its juvenile home, squash tennis reached its full height in a remarkably short spurt of time. For the landed gentry, the game was the newest must-have plaything. In 1901 Billy Gardner, a cousin of Isabelle Gardner, built a squash tennis court in his Pleasure Dome, a luxurious winter playground on the campus at Groton School. August Belmont, Herbert Harriman, W. L. Stowe and James Breese built courts at their estates outside New York. Henry Poor ordered a court for his Tuxedo Park estate. William Whitney erected two at his Wheatley Hills home. George Gould built three rosewood squash tennis courts at his casino in Lakewood, New Jersey, including an extrawide doubles court. James Morgan, the father of squash and racquets champion Hewitt Morgan, built a court at his summer place in the Thousand Islands. John D. Rockefeller had one in Tarrytown and one at the Whitehall Club at Battery Place, the latter made entirely of mahogany. Almost overnight courts sprung up in almost every city in America. Leading country clubs like Baltusrol, Short Hills Casino, Morris County Golf Club, Chicago Athletic Association, Merion Cricket Club and the racquet clubs of Boston and New York played the game. In January 1904 the Tennis & Racquet Club opened its facility on Boylston Street in Boston. The T&R had a court tennis court, a racquets court and five squash tennis courts, two that were artificially lit by thirty-six sixteen-candlepower lights. Slazenger, A. G. Spalding and Wright & Ditson started selling squash tennis racquets and balls. In 1901 a dozen balls from Wright & Ditson cost four dollars. The racquet, made especially for the game, was a modified lawn tennis bat, slightly reduced in size, and no longer than twenty-seven inches. In 1911 Spalding sold its racquets for four dollars, but it was a beautiful bat made of ash with a white kid grip and white lamb's gut strings.

If someone mentioned squash during the Teddy Roosevelt administration, they were talking about squash tennis. "Squash, which was comparatively little known a year or so ago, promises to be one of the most popular of this summer's sports, and squash-courts are going up everywhere," reported *Harper's Weekly* on 7 June 1902. "To have your squash-court this summer, if you have any pretensions to style, is as necessary as to have your Ping-Pong table or your automobile. Last summer the game was so much a novelty that the story is told of a family in a fashionable sea-side resort who made their way into the elect through their squash-court, it being the second only of its kind in the place. This year it is even more essential to one's social success."

The *Harper's Weekly* reporter mixed up squash and squash tennis. He wrote that the ball was "usually of India rubber," and yet the racquet was a "light-weight tennis racquet" and the court was marked by a line dividing the floor into two equal spaces. This confusion was amplified by Eustace Miles. An amateur court tennis and racquets champion in England, Miles had played squash and fives at Marlborough College, a school like Harrow. He then lived for a number of years at Tuxedo Park, where he had a house with a small squash tennis court, and he won the 1900 Tuxedo tournament. In 1901 he wrote *The Game of Squash*. The size of a wallet, it had a brushed leather cover with the title almost obscured, as if an explorer had just swept a dirt-covered tomb. Miles conflated squash and squash tennis. He designated squash the British version and squash tennis the American translation. He recommended players choose the small rubber squash ball or the larger squash tennis ball entirely by what sort of court they were faced with (concrete, wood, large, small) and what sort of sport they were training for (court tennis, lawn tennis or racquets). For years many nonsquash players, including editors at American newspapers and magazines, followed Miles in believing the fallacy that squash tennis was the American version of squash.

After the turn of the century, New York dominated the squash tennis world. In 1902 the Racquet & Tennis Club began a club championship on its old fives courts. In 1905 courts opened at the Harvard, Princeton and Columbia Clubs and a year later the Crescent Athletic and Heights Casino built courts at its clubhouses in Brooklyn Heights. The Columbia courts were built in the back of the old Clark mansion on Gramercy Park. In the mansion's stables, Columbia put two courts, one on top of another, each sixteen-and-a-half feet wide. "It was entered by a passageway that went by the bar," wrote Allison Danzig, "where the players found quick relief after their exertions in the court." Both courts had wooden front walls that thundered when the ball struck it. "When we heard the boom," said Ned Putnam, a leading Columbia player, "we knew we were hitting right." In 1907 the Princeton Club, copying Columbia, moved into Stanford White's home on Gramercy Park and built courts in White's old stable. In 1908 Princeton, Columbia and Harvard Clubs and the Height's Casino formed a Metropolitan Squash Tennis League. In imitation of the MSA in Boston, the MSTL scheduled tournaments every weekend throughout the winter, from the Fall Scratch Tournament to the nationals in April.

Steve Feron, formerly the professional at the Racquet and Tennis Club and Rockaway Hunting Club, and by the turn of the century firmly installed at the Harvard Club in New York, was the kingpin of squash tennis. He reigned as world champion of squash tennis from 1902 to 1914. His style of play, full of deft, spinning angles and feathery drop-shots, was considered the epitome of squash tennis beauty. Feron made the Harvard Club, with its three courts including one on the roof, the headquarters for the sport. In March 1911 seventeen clubs sent representatives to the Harvard Club to found the National Squash Tennis Association. The association held its first nationals there a month later. Forty men entered. In the finals Alfred Stillman beat NSTA president John Prentiss, 15–5, 17–15.

Squash tennis fascinated winter racquet sportsmen like Eustace Miles, yet the uninitiated were less enamored. *American Lawn Tennis*, the monthly New York magazine, reported on the first nationals in 1911: "The word 'squash' is not an inspiring one, and the game which it designates is, to the unbeliever, a sort of mild childlike pastime of batting a ball about within four walls and watching the funny bounces it takes. The average man of athletic calibre is inclined to spend his winters at billiards and bridge, waiting for the snow to melt and recounting his out-of-doors exploits of past seasons and predicting an enlargement of fame for the coming summer." But the ball did more than take funny bounces. "Sometimes it will 'inch' and sputtle across the floor like a sixty-horse-power mouse, some times dart out from a corner in quite another direction from that which one might reasonably expect, and again, it will die away softly in that same corner as though it had no more resiliency than a potato."

Unfortunately, the sport proved to have the resiliency of a potato. In 1913 Feron contracted with Spalding to develop a new squash tennis ball. The new Spalding ball, two-and-nine-sixteenths inches in diameter, weighing about 900 grams and wrapped in a knitted, hard-cotton, green cover, was inflated to forty pounds of pressure per square inch. In 1918 the NSTA boosted the pressure to fifty pounds. The game became insanely fast. The three-wall fadeaway, the four-wall boast and the malevolent breadbasket—when the ball flew into three walls before plowing into an opponent's stomach—now rocketed around the court like electrons in a rare element accelerator. "Many critics shook their heads when the ball was speeded up," wrote George M. Rushmore, a Tuxedo player, in 1949. "They said that the beautiful sidewall and angle play and the delicate corner shots would give way entirely to mere straight up and down slugging."

Calm on the surface despite the turbulence underneath, the years between the two world wars were halcyon days for squash tennis. The game contracted to just New York and its sprawling suburbs, as clubs in other cities converted to the game of squash. In 1929 twenty-seven clubs affiliated with the NSTA, and all of them were in the metropolitan area. In Gotham squash tennis trumped squash. The *New York Times, Herald Tribune, Post* and *Sun* reported regularly on squash tennis tournaments and league play. In the *Times's* annual list of champions at the end of December, squash tennis was listed, but not squash racquets. Great squash tennis players were heroes to generations of New Yorkers. Harry Wolf, an amateur at the New York Athletic Club, won eleven national titles in a row. Frank Ward, a professional at the City Athletic Club, succeeded Walter Kinsella as world champion and retired undefeated. George Rushmore remembered Fillmore Hyde, a three-time national champion (and the first literary editor of *The New Yorker*) as a "skinny figure looking as if it would barely hold together, a pair of long white pants flapping around his thin legs. Ghosting around the court on his long legs, Hyde could not only retrieve impossible balls, but his subtle changes of direction and pace and the rhythm of his stroking combined with that indefinable gift, which is called color, packed the gallery whenever he played an important match." Wolf, on the other hand, was too aggressive a player and was even thought to cheat when necessary to win. "There was something too shiny and efficient," wrote Rushmore about Wolf, "and force had too great a hand in it." In 1940 John R. Tunis, a *New Yorker* lawn tennis writer, dreamt up the perfect squash tennis player: "Today the champion must be a combination of Glenn Cunningham, Don Budge and Joe Louis. He darts, twists, turns around completely a dozen times in every rally. He jumps out with catlike movements as he suddenly volleys to the front wall in the hope of surprising his opponent. The champion needs quick reflexes, better than average footwork, a long reach and he should have more than ordinary endurance."

Regardless of the skill of its champions, squash tennis was dying. As the

that proved popular with mem
that Americans of all classes en
field, Illinois: At the moment
President in 1860, he was pla
newspaper's offices. In 1890
stepped, three-and-a-half-stor
it into its clubhouse. It put i
thirty-one-and-a-half and enti
at the Racquet & Tennis Club
$75 per month.

Squash came next. In Dece
racquets professional who rep
entirely of wood, it was perche
the third floor. "To get in an
wrote Danzig, "as the path lea
roof. There was no gallery and
high perch." It measured thirt
bers played an assortment of g
wrote in 1903, "Hand-Fives,
gained dominance on this peti
gent of players, including St. F
Lord (the winner of the first
Wheeler. Throughout the win
determine the best squash play
entered this first adult squash
was George McFadden. The
Scott in the final, which laste
won seventy-four points, Sco
owner of the Philadelphia Phi
matic decision to divide up th
courts. Each new court meas
teen-and-a-half, and were ma
wall. The total cost was $1,50(
for squash tennis, but the dem:
lifted this restriction. Squash v

Nursed perilously by the R
the city. McFadden and three
courts at their homes. Many
other clubs on weekends, and
Racquet Club game. In 1901 tl

years progressed, the style of play deteriorated under the fury of squash tennis's aerial bombardment. Older players dropped out and it was the rare young man who braved the thundering squash tennis ball. No college had a squash tennis team. Picking up squash tennis was simply too difficult. "The absence of a large duffer class was the cause of decline," wrote Rushmore. "The game was all head and no body, and as everyone knows, it is really the duffers and the mediocrities that support the game. No one who was not to a certain degree expert with a racquet could expect to have a decent rally at squash tennis for several weeks, and many novices went a whole winter without being able to keep the ball in play to any extent." Even Robert Moore, one of the founding fathers of the game, repudiated it. In 1920 he left Tuxedo for the Montclair Athletic Club, which he converted from squash tennis to squash. In 1928 Tuxedo demolished its squash tennis courts. In 1930 Danzig tactfully suggested that the NSTA reduce the pressure in the ball: "The game, with a slower ball, would be more ideal for the average player and for the novice, and the general standard of play, it seems to me, would be higher, while the general degree of enjoyment to be derived from the game would be greater. The beginner would acquire a sounder knowledge of the finer points of squash tennis instead of contenting himself with acquiring a kill shot. Too many players merely hammer away at the ball with little idea of where it is going and with the sole intent of overpowering their opponent with speed or trusting to luck or to the walls to make a clever shot for them. As one player said, 'I hit and pray.' While Heaven may be on the side of the heaviest artillery, Napoleon was a fair strategist, too, and knew when to use his cannons."

The nationals were canceled for six years during the Second World War. In the meantime Spalding stopped making squash tennis balls. Players switched to regular lawn tennis balls, but the old-timers were disenchanted with the slower, heavier ball. In 1953 Spalding created a new, twenty-four-pound-pressure green-felt ball that pros blew up with needles, like a soccer ball. Hemorrhaging members, clubs like the Crescent Athletic Club, the Fraternity Club and the 21 Broadway Club closed. A number of men, especially Willard Rice, Rowlie Haines, Jim Prighoff and professionals Johnny Jacobs at the Harvard Club and Frank Lafforgue at the Yale Club, tried to keep it going, but the game seemed hopelessly antiquated: At the first nationals since Pearl Harbor, in 1947, Norman Torrance, the president of the NSTA at age seventy-eight, won a match. League matches resumed in the late forties, but less than a dozen clubs fielded teams. In 1956 the NSTA switched its fifteen-point scoring from

racquets-style score only
red balls, green balls and
a couple of black Magic
the white walls. The fav
ball, found cheaply at Ma

One final burst of hc
Squires sparked a revival.
of winter racquet sports,
players to the 1968 Mex
demonstration sport tou
promotional pamphlet a
partner in the NSTA wa
moved to New York in 1
of a squash tennis exhibit
son. Soon, he was playing
In 1979 Bacallao moved
national champion. In 1
Squires and Pedro Bacall
Club. Squires won.

In the nineties the on
Gary Squires won each t
organize them, even the
emerged in the mid-nine
court size from eightee
bona fide squash tennis c
and now even the adequa
dismantled. You could n
court. Bill Rubin at the Y
players, but the life had g
league or a quorum of clu

In 2001, for the first
champions, the *New Yor*
squash tennis. It was nov
squash court had come ai

While squash tennis was
lowed a more subdued c
gentlemen's club in Phil
Street. The club built a

---

building squash courts; in 1903 they added electric lights. In 1903 Merion Cricket Club started playing squash on its three squash tennis courts. Two city cricket clubs, Philadelphia Cricket in Chestnut Hill and Germantown Cricket in Manheim, erected courts at the same time, as did Huntingdon Valley Country Club in Jenkintown and Overbrook Golf Club near City Line Avenue.

Seven clubs made a quorum. In March 1903 the Racquet Club offered a cup for the winner of an inter-club team competition that ran throughout the month. Merion won it. The Philadelphia Inter-Club Squash Racquets Association, run by Louis Delone of Overbrook, sponsored a Pennsylvania State Championship. In the finals Samuel Boyle of the Racquet Club beat Harold Haines of Merion. In 1904 the leaders of the league, meeting at the Racquet Club, founded the United States Squash Racquets Association, the first national squash body in the world, and elected a president, Tevis Huhn from the Racquet Club. The USSRA, with its grandiose name and a mere seven clubs under its jurisdiction, set the standard squash court measurements at thirty-one feet six inches by sixteen feet three inches. The telltale or playline on the front wall ran from the floor up twenty-four inches and was made out of hammered tin—this made a sound distinguishable from the cement front wall, and gave the telltale a new nickname, the tin. The back wall was supposed to be four-and-a-half feet high. Although the USSRA created rules by which to play the game, each Philadelphia club had its own local interpretations. Some allowed two serves, others one; some made hitting the side wall on the serve a fault or loss of point; others made it a let point or stroke for a player when the ball hit below the knee but not above. Games in squash, like in racquets, were the best two out of three, first to fifteen points, server only scoring. At 13–all one could "set" or choose three or five points for the tiebreaker, and at 14–all one could choose three points; in both cases one could also choose "no set," which meant no tiebreaker and the first player to reach fifteen points was the winner. In 1911 the USSRA changed the scoring rules to best three out of five, and one could score a point whether serving or not.

In 1907 Potter moved the Racquet Club into a brand-new clubhouse on Sixteenth Street. The new facility boasted a court tennis court, a racquets court, five squash singles courts and one new squash doubles court. League squash became a serious event on winter Wednesday evenings. In 1912 Merion, Germantown, Huntingdon Valley, Overbrook and the Racquet Club entered sides in the league, with Germantown and Merion

fielding two. Germantown dominated league play. In 1913 it went undefeated, with a perfect 36–0 record in matches.

In 1907 as a sign of its increasing size and scope, the USSRA organized
the first national championship. Despite its name, the tournament was
played just among Philadelphians. John Miskey, a doctor from Overbrook, was the winner, and he won again in 1908 and 1910. Like most of
the early squash standouts, Miskey was adept at racquets and court tennis.
"In each of these games he had nice style, but he practically wore himself
out in practice," wrote Danzig. "It was nothing out of the ordinary for
Miskey to play an hour in the squash court, then an hour of racquets and
wind up with another hour of court tennis." After Miskey, three Germantown Cricket men won the nationals in the first years, William Freeland
in 1909, Frank White in 1911 and Mort Newhall in 1913.

The nationals became a little more national with new players in Boston
and Baltimore. In 1905 Austin Potter, a member of the new Tennis & Racquet Club, played squash while on a visit to the Racquet Club in Philadelphia. He returned to Boston with squash balls and racquets and played a
match against Ray Speare at the Newton Centre Squash Tennis Club. "It
so appealed to us as a superior and more scientific game (than squash tennis) that we at once recommended its adoption," wrote Speare later. "As
an interesting competitive game with ample opportunity for the thrill of
'earned shots,' a superlative exercising media, economical for the player
and its facilities imposing no large financial burden for the Club to provide and maintain, it surely merits its obvious vogue in this district."
Speare and Potter had gotten religion, but most of Boston kept to their
old ways. At the MSA's annual meeting in April 1907, thirteen representatives of Boston clubs discussed the squash tennis season just completed.
"All present agreed that the game of squash, as it has been played, was
somewhat unsatisfactory," a reporter from the *American Lawn Tennis* magazine wrote. "The game of squash racquets, as it is played in the Philadelphia clubs, was brought to the attention of the company." In the winter of
1907–08, the MSA added "Racquets" to its name, affiliated with the
USSRA and sent a team to the nationals.

Getting up to speed took a few years. Newton Centre and the Tennis
& Racquet Club dominated the squash circles in the Boston area. At the
T&R, Quincy Shaw, a national racquets champion and finalist in the
national lawn tennis championships, won the first state championship in
1908. Other leading players included sportsmen who already knew how
to wield a racquet: Percy Houghton, a Harvard football coach and

national racquets champion, Beals Wright, a national lawn tennis champion and George Fearing, a Harvard rowing star and national champion in both court tennis and racquets. The top Hub player before the war was Constantine Hutchins. A racquets player at the Boston Athletic Association, Hutchins took the state title from Shaw in 1909, held it until 1915 and won it once more in 1921. Hutchins also broke Philadelphia's iron grip on the national title when he claimed it in 1912 and 1914. The former year was a banner one for Boston. It was the only time in ten attempts before 1920 in which it was able to beat Philadelphia and take the national five-man team championship. With that historic victory at the BAA, the arrival of courts at the Union Boat Club in 1910 and the Harvard Club of Boston in 1914 and the start of a squash league in 1914, Boston was the only city besides Philadelphia to build a viable squash program before the twenties.

Crossing the Mason-Dixon Line, squash went south to Baltimore in 1900, when the Baltimore Athletic Club built three wooden squash tennis courts. Two years later the Baltimore Country Club erected squash tennis courts and Green Spring Valley Hunt Club put up an open-air squash tennis court. In 1907 the Racquet Club invited five squash tennis players from Baltimore to Philadelphia to help inaugurate the new clubhouse. Receiving squash balls and racquets, the Baltimoreans practiced for ten days before their trip. After the visit to Sixteenth Street, they returned home, like Austin Potter, with a bag of squash balls and racquets. In 1908 Baltimore sent a squad to the nationals and in 1910 and 1913 the Baltimore Country Club hosted the tournament.

Two other cities, Pittsburgh and Chicago, sent players to the nationals in these inchoate days. In 1906 the Pittsburgh Golf Club put in three squash courts at its clubhouse. By 1912 there was a Western Pennsylvania state championship, held at the Golf Club, and Pittsburgh sent a team to the nationals. Both the Chicago Athletic Association in 1893 and the Illinois Athletic Club in 1906 built squash tennis courts, though both were quite crude—one court at Illinois AC was entered through a trap door in the floor. The CAA eventually added four more squash courts, but one was forty-five feet by twenty-two and was used for squash tennis doubles. In 1909 the University Club of Chicago opened its new clubhouse on Michigan Boulevard with four squash courts. The courts were a melange of styles: The floors were all cement, three had wooden walls, one was painted white and used for squash, two others were painted red and used for squash tennis and the cement court was used for fives. A club squash championship was begun in 1910 and in 1914 Chicago sent a team to the nationals.

The USSRA embraced these new converts. In 1911, for example, Tevis Huhn was president of the association, Ray Speare vice president, Henry Patton of Philadelphia Cricket secretary and treasurer; the executive committee consisted of George Morison of the T&R, Francis Iglehart of the Baltimore Country Club, Bill Freeland and Laurence Fuller of the Racquet Club and F. H. LeBoutellier of Merion. Except for 1910 and 1913 at the Baltimore Country Club and 1912 at the Boston Athletic Association, the nationals were always held in Philadelphia at the Racquet Club in February. First on the agenda was the national teams, a five-man competition between cities. (In 1913 and 1914, Toronto sent a squad.) Philadelphia usually won the national teams with embarrassing ease. In 1913, for example, they beat Toronto 9–1 and Boston 5–0. The individual tournament came at the end of the weekend. Originally, the USSRA restricted the draw to the winners of the various state championships— three or four men.

The sport was quaintly embryonic at the time. In 1916 there were, one newspaper estimated, between fifteen and twenty squash courts in Philadelphia and "few sportsmen outside those enjoying membership in clubs where squash racquets is played have any idea of the game." The USSRA, although it organized the national championships each winter, was an ineffectual body. It promulgated conflicting sets of rules and appeared lost in the slipstream of the churning squash tennis movement. In 1911 Tevis Huhn, the president of the USSRA, came to New York for the founding meeting of the National Squash Tennis Association. He vainly attempted to persuade squash tennis players to join the USSRA instead of creating a new association. John Prentiss and Steve Feron accepted Huhn's invitation to come to Philadelphia, where they played a squash tennis match in the squash doubles court at the Racquet Club against Fred Tompkins and Jock Soutar, the club's professionals. The cement walls suddenly were fluttering with the nap of the tennis ball, and Philadelphians, perhaps annoyed with their court being so sullied, declined to convert to squash tennis. Regardless of the stalemate with squash tennis, aesthetics were important to these squash pioneers, as one wrote in 1916 in the *Public Ledger*: "It is necessary that the squash player develop correct form. Form is of vital importance just as in racquets, golf, etc., and the man who is content to continue to progress in the game with- out trimming the rough edges will shortly find himself sinking into hopeless mediocrity. . . . Cultivate variety in your style of play. You will thus keep your opponent in an uncertain frame of mind. Mix the strong and weak strokes, according to your adversary's position. Let side walls and back wall do their share of the work, and at times you will find a well-placed cut stroke just the feature needed to win the rally. Learn that 'poetry of motion' may be expressed by the squash stroke."

The enduring mystery in the history of squash was why America developed a smaller court and harder ball. Compared with the standard in England, the court in America was two-and-a-half-feet narrower and the ball was larger, heavier and faster. Explanations for the differences in court size and ball, no matter how outlandish, were posited as fact. One romantic idea was that a British squash official traveling to America with the proper blueprints went down with the *Titanic*. Another maritime conspiracist imagined that a softball court would not fit in a ship bringing squash over from England. Some blamed the cold weather in New England. A faster ball and a smaller court made for a better game when it was below freezing and snow drifts were deep along the road. Others thought that it was typical American hard-nosed cussedness. Forever opposed to British ideas, Americans purposely went against the grain and created their own game. John Horry, a British squash administrator, blamed alcohol when he wrote of "an apocryphal tale that an eminent divine who lived near Detroit went to stay with a friend in Canada and was delighted with the squash court at his host's house. Wanting to import the game to the U.S. our divine went down one night to measure the court, but his friend's hospitality had made him careless and he returned to Detroit with the wrong measurements."

In 1904 the USSRA standardized the thirty-one-and-a-half feet by sixteen-and-a-third court. This standard, like the rest of its rules, was not enforced until 1920 when the USSRA reconstituted itself. At a meeting at Germantown Cricket Club, Sydney Clark, a member of the Racquet Club, "was chosen in proper conclave," as the first true president. No vice president, secretary or treasurer joined Clark until three years later, but the executive committee was reformed. Fatefully, Clark agreed to expand the official court dimensions only slightly, to thirty-two feet by eighteen-and-a-half. The width was determined by squash tennis. The first squash courts in America were modeled directly after eighteen-foot wide fives courts. In Great Britain, as the game spread from Harrow, the tendency was to widen the court, but in America squash tennis's popularity boxed squash into a narrower size. In 1920, when the USSRA changed the standard squash court width to eighteen-and-a-half feet, they were consciously keeping close to the squash tennis model. They had no choice, as a majority of their members played squash on what were originally squash tennis courts. England, on the other hand, had no such brake on court width expansion.

Clark clarified other matters. He expanded the nationals into a regular sixteen-man tournament. Some officials wanted to lower the height of the tin to nineteen inches from twenty-four inches, while others argued for a height of seventeen inches, which would produce more opportunities to hit clear winning shots. Eventually, in 1922, the USSRA adopted a seventeen-inch tin (further motions to drop the tin to fifteen or even fourteen-and-a-half inches were voted down). Clark decreed that wood was the material of choice for a squash court. To prevent crowding on the court, Clark instituted a let or "baulk" rule, which gave an opponent the point if you failed to clear properly. The rule, however, was so worded, wrote Jack Barnaby, a Harvard squash coach, that "it implied intentional cheating, so that calling a baulk meant you as referee were almost accusing a player of premeditated dishonorable conduct. Very few were willing to risk the personal animosities and after-the-match locker room confrontations implied by such a ruling, so the rule was conspicuous by the fact that it was almost never invoked." Instead, players drilled balls into the legs and back of an obstructing player or smacked them so hard with the racquet that you could later see the imprint of strings on their skin. (The latter maneuver was called "labeling.") Still, the baulk rule was better than nothing. "Ten years ago because of the comparatively small number of players as well as the lack of clearly defined playing rules and regulations," wrote Dick Cooke, a Boston player, in 1932, "the game was developing along wrong lines. The percentage of players whose sole idea of the game was a fine opportunity for a rough and tumble contest, was far too high. At that time the Baulk Rule had not been conceived and one player could deliberately crowd and hinder his opponent to such an extent that many inferior players were regularly defeating better players, whose conception of the game was entirely different." In the early thirties the USSRA ameliorated the situation by introducing the "English let" rule, which gave you the point if you hit your opponent with the ball. The English let rule further opened up the game.

The ball, however, proved to be the most vexatious issue. In the beginning clubs imported squash balls from Prossers, the London manufacturers, usually via the Spalding sporting goods company. Before the First

World War, Wright & Ditson began producing squash equipment and in 1920 Clark standardized the Wright & Ditson ball. The first regulations on the ball were that it would bounce "three or four feet" when dropped from five feet onto a wooden floor. The USSRA also asked that W&D print a date on each box of balls, "so that stale balls might be avoided." Previously in Boston they had used a so-called rabbit ball, which was more lively. Dick Cooke estimated that the rabbit ball and Boston's higher tin of twenty-two inches made the old game 50 percent physical condition, 20 percent headwork, 15 percent position play and 15 percent stroking; the new Wright & Ditson ball made the percentages much more balanced: 30 percent physical condition, 25 percent headwork, 20 percent position play and 25 percent stroking. "There is no question that this change has meant a longer playing life for the average business man, resulting in a larger field to draw from, and an increased popularity of the game of Squash Racquets." In 1929 at the nationals in Philadelphia, according to USSRA executive minutes, "there was a general sentiment that Wright & Ditson had not showed themselves particularly disposed or capable of making a uniform and satisfactory ball." The Hewitt ball, a pale gutta-percha ball made in Buffalo, became the official USSRA ball. In the thirties the USSRA "approved" a number of balls, including ones by Wright & Ditson, Dunlop and Spalding, but the Hewitt remained the "official" ball. In 1936 the Seamless ball, made by the Seamless Rubber Company in Buffalo and later in New Haven, became official and remained so until the sixties. The Seamless, a hard black ball that flew like a bullet, symbolized squash for generations of players.

The process of standardization varied from country to country. Up north, Canada followed along the same lines as that of the United States, though Canada used another English public school as the model for its courts. In the 1890s a number of British expatriates erected courts at their private estates, especially in Vancouver (although it appears they played more racquets than squash on these courts). The first bona fide court in Canada was built in 1904 at the St. John's Tennis Club in Newfoundland. Sir Leonard Outerbridge, whose two brothers were on the club's building committee, sent the proper dimensions from Marlborough College in England. The dimensions were, again, of a fives court, with no back wall. In 1911 three clubs—the Montreal Racquet Club, the Toronto Racquet Club and the Hamilton Squash Racquets Club—formed the Canadian Squash Racquets Association. It soon standardized a thirty-four by nineteen court (with a twenty-two-inch tin). In 1921 the CSRA made formal application to the USSRA for affiliation and a year later began switching to American standards. Growth in Canada was even slower than in the United States. In 1930 there were fifty-six clubs registered with the USSRA but in Canada there were only thirteen CSRA clubs, all but one in Toronto or Montreal.

Acting as a younger sibling, Canada followed the United States in decisions regarding standardization, although with a fair amount of kicking and screaming. In February 1923 the CSRA voted to drop the tin to fourteen-and-a-half inches, a motion that was defeated in the face of American resistance. A year later the motion was again brought up. Advocates of the lower tin mentioned the squash courts in Quebec City, which had fourteen-inch tins. Again it was voted down. Canada did not switch to the Wright & Ditson ball until 1925 and to the Seamless ball until 1939. It was 1940 before British Columbia changed to the American scoring system, and both Vancouver and Winnipeg, preferring softball, did not convert to the Seamless until 1958. In 1935 the CSRA, under pressure from the Badminton & Racquet Club in Toronto, allowed the American style of dropped side walls to become standard, although it continued to permit a straight side wall. The biggest source of continental friction came from a coat of paint. The United States painted its floors white in order to better see the black Seamless ball. Canada preferred its courts to keep their natural wood color. For decades, although Canada followed America's lead on every other issue, it refused to whitewash its floors, even in the face of heavy lobbying by the USSRA. In 1952 the CSRA finally capitulated and sanctioned painted floors. Only in the 1980s did both countries end the custom of painting the floors of their squash courts.

In Great Britain there were no official standards until 1923. Old Harrovians continued to play squash after walking down the hill one last time. Some built courts in their homes and regularly returned to Harrow to buy balls. In 1883 Vernon Harcourt, Harrow class of 1855, built a squash court as part of a new home on the banks of the Cherwell in Oxford. His ten children learned the game there, as did friends of the Harcourts, and an occasional varsity athlete who saw the potential in squash for keeping fit in the long winter months. The court was thirty-eight feet by twenty, with a tin of thirty inches. The ball could be anything, as Harcourt's son Simon elucidated in 1938: "The black surface of the ball left the mark of its shape on the walls, and very curious shapes they sometimes were, and in consequence we played for many years with a red ball which, in time gave the walls a pleasant pink hue. We also used a ball with a hole in it, probably about the same time that the Bath Club was trying out a similar ball. This ball was very popular with us, as it needed a perfectly-timed shot to get it to the back wall—in other words, there was no waiting for the ball the second time round."

Other early courts ran the gamut. Numerous public schools, especially Elstree, adopted Harrow's game. West End social clubs took it up. The oldest London courts were at Prince's, Queen's Club and the Royal Automobile Club. Queen's first court, built in 1905 and dubbed "the Long Court," was thirty-five feet by eighteen. The RAC's court was exactly thirty-two feet by eighteen-and-a-half, with American markings. In 1935 the club finally built an English standard court and, even after a second renovation in 1948, decided to keep an American court. Marlborough House, a royal residence, also had an American-width court until the mid-thirties. At Lord's the squash court was forty-two feet by twenty-four, with a twenty-eight-inch tin. In Cambridge they divided a sixty by thirty racquets court into three squash courts, each quite tiny. Private residences had even more diversity. Some boys played pickup games in old coachhouses, greenhouses, attics and barns. An in-law of squash enthusiast S. V. P. Weston had a court in Ross-on-Wye with a court-tennis-like buttress on one wall.

In April 1907 the Tennis, Rackets & Fives Association was founded at Queen's, the twentieth-century headquarters of court tennis and racquets. A discussion ensued about two other sports not under the nascent association's official purview—stické and squash—and the association appointed a subcommittee to handle squash. In 1912, when the TR&FA published a handbook on the rules of the sports under its domain, the subcommittee added a short chapter on squash. These rules were interestingly imprecise. The subcommittee was battling a typically British cultivation of eccentricity. Many felt that the whole realm of standardization was inherently wrong, that the true joy of squash was in an idiosyncratic variety of courts, balls and rules. "It seems almost a pity that any attempt should have been made to standardize a game which has always been a nursery for young boys before becoming racket players and magnificent exercise for many business and other players past their prime of activity," G. J. V. Weigall, one of the two Tennis & Racket Association squash subcommittee members in charge of standardization, wrote in the *Times*. Players enjoyed experimenting in situ, as was the wont of most inventing sportsmen. The "best size" for a squash court, according to the TR&FA, was thirty feet by twenty-one, with a nineteen-inch tin. They stated that a court thirty-three by twenty-three, with a twenty-inch tin or a court twenty-nine by nineteen-and-a-half with an eighteen-inch tin "would both be practically as good as the standard size." Cement or stone were preferred to wood for the materials of the court. Moreover, the sub-committee warned, "the great thing to be remembered is that in any court the game depends on four factors—the size, the materials, the height of the play line [the tin], and the ball. Experiments can be made with various kinds of balls and the kind of game they like best. . . . What is required is a fast ball, that bounces well but not too high, and does not fly about: a very small hard solid ball or a medium-size thin rubber hollow ball, without a hole." As far as the rules of play were concerned, the subcommittee again recommended flexibility. Serving could be either allowing one serve only, or having no service line on the front wall or no part of the court where the serve should land or, most delightfully, allowing the man returning the service the right of "refusing a service he does not like." Much as in Philadelphia in 1904, the rules were as flimsy as hot butter.

With such self-imposed doubt, these standards were ignored as much as obeyed. It took twelve years before an official Tennis & Racket Association (they soon dropped fives) standard was decided upon and another year before it was imposed. The model for the committee was the courts at the Bath Club in London. In 1922 Lord Desborough, the president of the Bath Club, built two courts with widths of twenty-one feet. Both had inestimable advantages of outstanding lighting. Bath immediately launched the Bath Club Cup, a three-man London version of the Philadelphia Inter-Club League. During the first year of the league, players contended with six different court sizes and five different kinds of balls. In January 1923 the Royal Automobile Club hosted a meeting of delegates from English clubs where squash was played and the original 1907 sub-committee was transformed into a much more open "Squash Rackets Representative Committee." Two men, Lord Wodehouse and G. J. V. Weigall, were elected to represent squash on the T&RA board and a committee of six was created to look into the matter of the appropriate squash ball. The committee of six met in February 1923 and discussed the merits of four balls then in vogue: the RAC ball, a larger, heavily perforated ball used at the Bath Club, a ball made by the cricket firm Wisden and the "Gradidge's Nigger," the ball used at Queen's. The balls ranged from a twenty-eight gram RAC ball to a thirty-six-and-a-half-gram Bath ball. All four balls, when at a temperature of sixty-eight degrees, bounced between fifty and fifty-nine inches when dropped from a height of one hundred inches (measured from the bottom of the ball). The committee chose the slowest of balls. In 1926 the committee switched from fifteen- to nine-point scoring, still retaining the hand-in, hand-out feature of racquets scoring. The Squash Rackets Association was finally formed in December 1928.

Around the world, notions of what constituted the proper squash ball and court were susceptible to local prejudice and individual opinion, but naturally, Great Britain, with the sun never setting upon its empire, was able to proselytize its version of squash a lot more comprehensively than America. In 1906 the Johannesburg Country Club built an open-air court that was wider than the American size. Four years later South Africa created a national association and eventually, because of significant heat and altitude in many parts of the country, standardized a wide court and slow ball. At one time the Sudan Club in Khartoum had six courts, all unroofed. Government House in Dar es Salaam boasted a fine, open-air court, with a stone floor. In Egypt the courts were open-air, with concrete floors painted yellow or green. In Kenya the Nairobi Club had two English standard courts made from knotless cedar, but the nearby Muthiaga Club had stone floors and American widths. The St. James's Barracks in Port of Spain, Trinidad, had one open-air, concrete-floored court with American width. In Stockholm the first courts were made with walls of powdered marble. In 1913 a racquets court in Melbourne was split into two squash courts. In 1927 the Royal Melbourne Tennis Club built an American-sized court and, four years later, the Atheneum put in a court even wider than the English size. It was not until the early thirties that Australia officially went with the English size. Nearby, New Zealand played in an English court with an American ball, a combination that was not resolved until the mid-thirties. In France the first courts were at the famous court tennis club Societe Sportive du Jeu de Paume, where in the late 1920s, Pierre Etchebaster turned a racquets court into four tiny squash courts, each with a cement floor.

While the United States standardized tentatively in 1904 and permanently in 1920, the English made a half-hearted attempt in 1912, dilly-dallied in 1923 and waited more or less until 1928. An equally damaging problem was not the misfortune of delay, nor the happenstance of difference, but the poison of defenestration. The SRA threw its own standard out the window and began slowing down the ball. While the Bath courts served as the model for English squash, the Bath ball, as large and fast as an American ball, was deemed too much for English sensibilities. The association chose the most inert ball possible and then in a series of incremental changes reduced it even more. Between 1930 and 1934, the association cut the standard ball's speed almost by half, from a bounce of forty to forty-four inches in 1930, to thirty-six to forty inches in 1932, to thirty inches in 1934.

English squash players did not take this wanton attack on the beauty of their game without protest. Throughout the twenties and thirties, many angrily dismissed the new standard balls. It was common opinion that the Bath Club ball with a hole in it was the true squash ball, because it was quick and you could lay it down easily. The slower ball made squash too much a case of prosaic drives and grinding stamina. "In the Amateur Squash Rackets Championships, at the Bath Club, yesterday, one could not help being suddenly possessed of a terrible idea. Squash rackets, at the moment, is merely a matter of keeping fit," began the *Times* of London in December 1923, in its account of the second national championships (the first was played at Lord's in April 1923). "There are those, already, who consider squash rackets to be more interesting than rackets. If, by some extraordinary decline of the sporting spirit, squash rackets should supersede rackets—as lawn tennis has superseded tennis in certain minds— every squash rackets player of the moment will wish that he had never touched the game. In the Bath Club court and with the present standard ball, the astonishingly fit man can beat a master of the game who is not so fit." Appalled by the two-and-a-half-hour final of 1926 British nationals, irate players complained to the ball committee. They continued to violate the committee's decrees by buying nonstandard balls. In 1926 one could obtain in London five different kinds of balls, in either red or black. There was the large Wisden Holer ball, "as used at the Bath Club," three other balls ranging from 1 and 3/8th to 1 and 5/8th inches and then the Royal Automobile Club's small black ball. The ladies championship in 1925 was played with the RAC ball; in 1926 they used the Gradidge Nigger; and in 1927 they chose the Wisden holer.

In the thirties, as the ball slowed and rallies rolled on inexorably, leading officials began to suggest ways of improving the now-boring game. In 1932 Frank Strawson, the president of the Jesters Club, publicly called for a return to the first-to-fifteen scoring system—now, interestingly, called the "American system"—as a way for both players and spectators to keep from falling asleep. In the same year, a national champion, Kenneth Gandar Dower, suggested putting in a buttress in the back left corner that would, like a Harrow drainpipe, send the ball in unexpected directions. Squash needed something: "Ability will tell in the end, but only by a process of *reductio ad prostration*. . . . Two good players cannot make a winning stroke against each other. Each, at the risk of a burst blood vessel, can just return the best the other can do—but only just. . . . One thing is certain—squash rackets has been revolutionised in the last ten years and in the next ten it will be revolutionised still further. Let us hope that by some inconceivable deus ex machina that revolution is in the direction of a shorter rally." The ruckus over standards resulted in a failed coup d'état in 1938. A number of players, led by Ginger Basset and Captain Palmer-Tomkinson, staged a sixteen-man, top-level tournament at Dolphin Square in March, using a faster ball and a seventeen-inch tin, according to American standards. The tournament was a success, and the participants demanded a special general meeting of the Squash Rackets Association in September to approve of the faster ball and lower tin. At the meeting a group of rank-and-file players from the north of England rebelled against what they perceived to be a top-down decision, and asked for one year to experiment with the new ball and lower tin. A few days before the experimentation period was over and a decision was to be reached, German tanks rolled into Belgium. Squash standards instantly became the least of worries.

The ancient Britons who had invented the game found the results of standardization deplorable. One Harrovian after another considered the slow ball a disfigurement of the game they loved. "Now that squash rackets has become so popular, I hope it will be possible to evolve a ball which is fast and yet capable of being killed, and so do away with the interminably long rallies, which are exhausting both to the players and the spectators," wrote Mark Fenwick in the *Times* in January 1924. "As to the merits of the game as played then and now, I cannot expect that the opinion of an old stager, who obviously could not play the modern game, should be of any value," wrote Viscount Dunedin at the end of his letter to the *Times*. "But I permit myself two observations: first, that success in the game of to-day seems to me to depend on activity and endurance, and not on precision of stroke or a nicety of placing; and, second, that the modern game may be anything beautiful that you like to call it, but that most certainly it is not 'squash'."

The American game, to some, had the right sort of standards. In January 1924, to prepare for the first English tour of North America, a number of London players practiced with a Hewitt. "The American ball, however, is very much more like squash rackets as it was meant to be, than anything else played generally in England," reported the *Times*. "Everyone who played with the American ball seemed to like it enormously. Charles Read was absolutely wonderful in the 'cat-and-mouse' sense."

The coda to the sorrowful story of standardization was that even St.

Paul's School made a mistake. In 1914 St. Paul's received a generous donation from Maurice Roche, class of 1905, and built a new eight-court squash facility, with 186 lockers and an oak-paneled lounge. The courts were twenty-one-feet wide. The reason for the aberration was that Roche had hired the London firm H. M. Rootham, which had built the courts at the Royal Artillery Mess in Woolwich. St. Paul's then tore down the old Conover racquets building and, with that, demolished the first squash courts in America. Today we remember Roche by his formal name, Lord Fermoy, and that he was the grandfather of Lady Diana Spencer and great-grandfather to the future king of England. And on the hallowed spot in New Hampshire where squash first was played in America, there is an unmarked field of grass.

CHAPTER THREE

Don't Keep Late Hours

The great dynasty in American squash began with a pique of jealousy. In the 1890s, Harvard men discovered new options for accommodation besides the bleak and uninviting Harvard Yard. The so-called Gold Coast, a series of luxurious private dormitories near Mount Auburn Street, was taking shape. It was instigated in 1892 by Charles D. Wetmore, who financed and designed Claverly Hall. (Wetmore went on to co-design Grand Central Terminal in 1913, as well as the clubhouse at Tuxedo Park.) Claverly boasted fifty-five steam-heated suites, each with a bathtub and a bay window. Following Claverly was Westmorely Court, also designed by Wetmore and built in 1898, with diamond-leaded panes and oak wainscoting, then Apley Court in 1897 and Craigie Hall in 1898.

Into this fray jumped Archibald Coolidge. With one brother acting as lawyer and another as architect, Coolidge, a young assistant professor in Harvard's Department of History and Roman Law, came up with a plan for a five-story building overshadowing Claverly Hall. Wetmore tactfully suggested Coolidge add a ten-foot setback from the road, so his Claverly rooms would receive sunlight. Coolidge said no. Wetmore secretly purchased land on the other side of Coolidge's plot and drew up blueprints for a ten-story building that would block Coolidge's building. The brinkmanship worked, and Coolidge agreed to the ten-foot setback.

In 1898 Randolph Hall opened for business. The building was named for Coolidge's grandmother, Ellen Wayles Randolph, who had been given away in marriage at Monticello in 1826 by her grandfather Thomas Jefferson. It surpassed anything else on the Gold Coast. Designed by Joseph Coolidge (who also designed Byerly Hall in Radcliffe Yard), Randolph spread across its seven-acre lot with Queen Anne turrets, pitched roofs, bay windows, red-brick Flemish gables and an open quadrangle facing historic eighteenth-century Apthorp House. Randolph was meant to re-create an Oxford or Cambridge college, and Coolidge performed the role of the master in residence when he moved into Randolph 4, a first-floor double suite, with an arresting mural done by Edward Renfield adorning the walls. Each of Randolph's fifty rooms boasted every luxury of the era, including electricity, hardwood floors, open fireplaces and good ventilation. They rented for $300 to $650 per year.

In 1908 Randolph drew closer to the Oxbridge model when Coolidge built a large athletic building on the other side of the quad. The facility, designed by Coolidge and Carlson at a total cost of $60,000, had a swimming pool, a court tennis court, a racquets court and two squash courts. For all three sports, these courts were the first of their kind at an American university. Despite the well-appointed galleries that could seat over a hundred spectators and first-class lighting system, the court tennis and racquets courts were also the last.* Racquets gained hardly any adherents besides the Harvard football coach who had been national champion in 1906. Court tennis started off with a bang, with an exhibition between two world champions, Englishman Peter Latham and Jay Gould from New Jersey, but it, too, was dark most afternoons. Squash, though, was a success. A number of students in Randolph Hall took up the sport and in 1915 Randolph Hall entered a team in the local squash league. The number-one player was Hewitt Morgan, who won the Massachusetts state championship in 1917 while still an undergraduate.

Randolph Hall had everything Christ Church or King's College could offer, except a library and a chapel, yet it was still a failure. In part, it was too pricey. On a chilly March night in 1911 a fire gutted the third and fourth floor. STUDENTS DRIVEN FROM BEDS IN FROSTY AIR AT 3:30 A.M., DAMAGE TO BUILDING $25,000—IN FUR COATS OVER PAJAMAS AND BATH ROBES, read the headline in the *Boston Globe*. But only twenty-four fur-coated students were affected by the fire, indicating that half the rooms in Randolph were empty. Harvard began building its own dormitories, with much cheaper rent. When student enrollment at the university plummeted during the First World War, the experiment in private dormitories was doomed. In 1916 Coolidge gave Randolph Hall to Harvard. Although Harvard did not find use for the dormitories at Randolph until it was incorporated into Adams House in 1930, it seized upon the athletic building with vigor. During the war it was used as a gymnasium. In 1919 Harvard tore down the court tennis court. Thirty-two men worked all

---

* The pool at Randolph had a better fate. The 1937 Harvard yearbook reported that, "Many undergraduates develop the dip habit after exercising and ponder, as they loll in the soothing waters, the thought-provoking tradition that here once bathed the famous knees of Ann Pennington."

summer ferrying six tons of pea stone, two kegs of floor nails and hundreds of board feet of North Carolina pine and New Hampshire maple into the building. By wintertime there were eleven squash courts and a new name: the University Squash Courts.

With the new courts came a new Harvard program, freshman physical training, with squash as the preferred winter activity. Upperclassmen joined in, not wanting to let the freshmen have all the fun and soon the courts were booked solid. Harvard reduced playing periods at the squash courts from sixty minutes to forty-five in 1921, to thirty in 1922. When this had no visible effect, Harvard plopped six new courts into the racquets court and refurbished the original 1908 squash courts. Even with these additions, demand was intense. Each morning at a quarter to nine the daily sign-up sheet was posted outside the courts; a skulk of men, usually two or three dozen, was already gathered there in anticipation. Five hundred undergraduates played each week. On Sundays the courts were locked, but that did not prevent some of the five hundred from playing. William Geer, the physical education director at Harvard, explained in a 1923 article in the *Harvard Alumni Bulletin* entitled, "The Most Popular Indoor Game at Harvard," that "there was evidence many Monday mornings that someone had been in the building on the preceding day. At first the damage in the nature of broken windows was attributed to boys not connected with the College, and a report was made to the University police. The policeman assigned to the squash courts the next Sunday had no difficulty in 'capturing' four students who were willing to 'break and enter' a College building in order to have a game of squash." Thereafter, Harvard tried to discourage such shockingly delinquent behavior among its students by opening the building on Sunday afternoons between half past two and six.

Breaking and entering was the least a Harvard man would endure to get some exercise. At the time, there was very little opportunity for athletics in the wintertime. Skiing was unheard of, snowshoeing hardly common. Basketball and ice hockey had yet to enrapture college men. Badminton was considered a woman's game. Wrestling went in and out of vogue. Gymnastics was the old standby, but it involved a farrago of equipment, space and coaching. College students passively suffered through the dark months, huddling near smoky stoves, drinking whiskey and playing cards. Now, as the *Bulletin* wrote, there was a boon to that "long period of hope deferred, which lasts from Christmas to Easter. During this period of hibernation the ground-hog needs a game which he can play without coming out of his hole; hence the great local demand for a snug in-door activity like squash racquets."

In 1922 Harvard entered two teams in the Boston squash leagues. To coach these players Harvard hired Harry Cowles. One needs to understand Tom Pettitt to understand Harry Cowles. An Englishman who epitomized the rags-to-riches potential of winter racquet sports, Tom Pettitt migrated alone to the United States at age sixteen. He was penniless, jobless and without prospects when, in the autumn of 1876, he met a fellow Englishman, Teddy Hunt. The professional at the just-opened Buckingham Street court tennis facility in Boston, Hunt took pity on the sallow-faced bag of bones—Pettitt weighed only ninety pounds—and hired him as an apprentice. Pettitt showed a remarkable aptitude for court tennis. In just six months, he beat Hunt, one of the top ten players in the world. Hunt smartly departed for England and left Pettitt in charge. In the years to come, Pettitt developed a style almost diametrically opposed to the orthodox style of play fashionable in England. While the English cut with fastidiously correct strokes and played the floor, Pettitt smashed the ball mercilessly. He went for openings no matter what the score and hustled after every ball, no matter how hopeless. In 1885 at Hampton Court Palace, Pettitt won the world championship. He held it for five years, survived a challenge in an all-marble court in Dublin and resigned in 1890. In Boston, at the Athletic Association and Tennis & Racquet Club, and in Newport, at the Casino where he coached until his death in 1946, Pettitt cultivated a legendary persona of one of the most skilled players and coaches of all time. He famously played and won matches with his left hand or with the leg of a chair or with a champagne bottle or while wearing roller skates.

In Newport Pettitt taught a boy named Harry Cowles. Born to an English couple, Cowles showed an early predilection for racquet sports. A bit short, even for this era, at five-foot-seven, with coppery skin, black hair and wine-dark eyes, Cowles was a willing student. The old master taught Cowles about the psychology of coaching, about allowing players to exploit their individual skills, however unorthodox, and about generating enthusiasm for the hard work necessary for greatness. ("He takes infinite pains with everyone," wrote two of Pettitt's protégés in 1903. "He infuses his keenness into everyone, so that his Court is going all day long.") After finishing his studies at Rogers High School in 1908, Cowles worked as an assistant for Pettitt at the T&R for two years before returning to help manage the Newport Casino. When the Harvard Club opened its squash courts in 1914, Cowles returned to Back Bay and began working at the club, stringing squash racquets and giving lessons. In 1931 Cowles dedicated his first book, *A Lesson in Squash Racquets*, to Pettitt: "I attribute any success I have enjoyed to having been taught by one of the ablest instructors who ever played games with a racquet. It was under his guidance that I received my training. I believe Mr. Pettitt to have been the greatest man that ever handled a racquet."

At the Harvard Club, Cowles popularized the drop shot. At the time, squash players, as customary in racquets, hung far back in the court and ceaselessly hammered the ball. Cowles instead delicately angled the ball across the long white space to a spot right above the tin. "For immaculate footwork, perfect execution of every shot, total versatility in technique and the power to deceive, this man has never been equaled," wrote Jack Barnaby, a Harvard man who played and coached under Cowles. "He was also as quick as the quickest. No one before or since has used the front wall from deep in the court with such devastating effects as Harry. He seemed able to find the nick with his drop shots from anywhere with both forehand and backhand." Cowles retired from active play once his Harvard job began.

When Cowles arrived at Randolph Hall in the late autumn of 1922, he found the scope to put Pettitt's training into practice. Some of the students were from New York and had been playing squash tennis. Cowles offered to hold two tournaments to see whether squash or squash tennis would be the more popular. Eight men entered the squash tennis tournament, and four of them defaulted before their first match; seventy men entered the squash tournament. With squash confirmed as the sport of choice, Cowles went ahead with his program. "My idea has been to try to teach that type of game best-suited to each individual," Cowles wrote in 1932. "If a boy lacks ability to grasp the fundamentals of a change-of-pace, if he finds himself powerless unless he whales the ball hard, then he should concentrate on that type of play which he can do best." It took a year of constant application and losses in the Boston leagues before Cowles's boys were ready for their rivals in New Haven. In 1924 Harvard played Yale and won. They won the following year and again and again. Most years this inconspicuous version of The Game was a blowout: In February 1931 Harvard thrashed Yale, 5–0, with only one Eli winning a single game. Other colleges never came close to scaring the Cantabrigians, either: for instance, in Harvard's first match against Pennsylvania in March 1929, they left off their top two players and still blanked Penn, 6–0. Under Cowles, Harvard never lost an intercollegiate match.

This statistic had some caveats. Intercollegiate squash at this time was more disorganized than a teenager's bedroom. Some had teams but no courts, others had teams but no coach. Yale's team played squash tennis until 1924 and got their first coach in 1925. There was no college association before 1931. Harvard split their schedule into official and unofficial opponents. In 1937, for example, the varsity had just three official matches (against Yale, Princeton and the Mt. Hope Club in Providence), as well as three unofficial matches (against Purdue, Dartmouth and Penn). Most men had not played before reaching their college campus, while Cowles was able to bring in a number of experienced St. Paul's graduates. Some people whispered that it was St. Paul's, not Cowles, that was responsible for his successful teams. A cursory look at the Crimson ladder turned up a surprising number of SPS boys: Herbie Rawlins, Larry and Beek Pool, Willing Patterson, Odgen Phipps, George Debevoise and G. H. Hartford. The gaggle of St. Paul's players, however, did not amount to a farm system. St. Paul's had no coach, few matches and the boys mostly goofed around on the courts when the ice on the ponds was not good enough for hockey. The SPS courts, although built by an English lord, were so hyperborean that the boys cooked the ball on a radiator to warm it up. "We played the game like tennis, with overspin on the ball," said Willing Patterson who graduated from St. Paul's in 1928. "I learned most of my game from Harry Cowles." The majority of Cowles's charges neither went to SPS nor had even played squash before. Cowles never recruited players (not enough high school teams existed for formal recruitment), but rather made do with who appeared at the Randolph courts in October. Three of the five players on the 1932 championship team played their first game of squash under the watchful eyes of Harry Cowles. Furthermore, Harvard had the best players in the country—full stop. Harvard won the national five-man team tournament five times under Cowles and, from 1925 through 1940, save for three years, only pupils of Harry Cowles won the national singles.

His 1925 varsity was the first besides Philadelphia or Boston to win the national team title. One of the fresh-faced Cambridge men was not finished, and that same long weekend, playing four matches a day, Palmer Dixon won the national singles. (After that year, the USSRA banned players from participating in both the national singles and the national teams, which were held simultaneously over the same weekend until 1988.) Dixon's victory was a tremendous upset. It was the first time that someone that young—a college student—had seized the diadem of national champion. Captain of the varsity, Dixon was just twenty-two years old, a quarter century younger than the previous year's champion. That weekend marked a shift in the nature of squash in the United States. No longer was the game the plaything of hoary men in wintry city clubs. No longer was squash Racquet Sport 101, an introductory course surveying all types of angles, the prerequisite for the graduate-level games of racquets and court tennis. Squash was its own sport.

Palmer Dixon broke trail with a quiet step. Educated at Eton, Dixon was blessed with a foundation of fives and racquets. He played a cerebral, controlled game. He always hit the correct shot at the correct time. Like a possession receiver in football, he strove to keep the ball in play and not make mistakes. He sometimes used the volley as an offensive shot, but he usually was content waiting for an opening. Even in 1932, when Cowles had coached four other outstanding national champions, he rated Dixon as the best of the lot because of his "headwork and reach. He is always cool and collected . . . Dixon places great reliance on his backhand and his shots require lightning brain cells . . . he had indomitable courage, stamina and a confidence in himself, born of an inner glimpse into the principles of the game . . . he had to surmount obstacles by groping into uncharted seas; he worked out things in such a way that I became convinced that here was a player with remarkable brains." One example was in 1924, when Dixon exploited a weakness in Charles Peabody's game—a high, half-lob rail to Peabody's forehand—that no one had seen before. In a way Cowles rated Dixon the best not only because Dixon was his first champion but also because he reminded Cowles of himself. Dixon had been the way Cowles had been with Pettitt: discussing squash for hours, putting on a miner's headlamp and going down to explore the inner workings of the game. While a senior, Dixon published *Strokes and Tactics of Squash Racquets*, the first book solely on American squash. Forty-six pages long, with thirteen photographs, the book was more than a mere undergraduate gewgaw. "Court Position" was one of nine chapter titles. Throughout the book Dixon lauded his mentor. "Coach Cowles' form," explained the caption to one photograph, "in all strokes is nearly perfect." After Cowles died in the late 1950s, Dixon gave Harvard $140,000 to renovate the courts at Harvard, the place where he was taught by the master.

Despite the fact Dixon won the national singles and led Harvard to the national teams in 1925, he did not capture the Massachusetts state title that year. Myles Baker was the surprise winner. Baker was Harvard class of 1922, the son of the ideal Cambridge marriage: a father who was a Harvard professor and a mother who was a dean at Radcliffe. After working for the Red Cross in Greece, he returned to Cambridge in 1924 and entered Harvard Medical School. Many afternoons Baker took a break from dissecting and walked over to Randolph to practice with the new squash coach. Playing league matches for the BAA, he won the state tournament four times. In the 1927 nationals he pushed Dixon aside in the finals. With a wolfish exuberance, surprising quickness and a piercing level of concentration, he leapt around the court intent on winning each point as quickly as possible. Sullied by the fact that the perceived best player in the nation, Herbie Rawlins, was unable to play in the singles because he was playing in the national teams, Baker's victory was not acclaimed. In future years many squash reporters skipped over him in listing Cowles's serried ranks of titlists.

The supreme stylist in Cowles's pack of winners was the next national champion, Herbie Rawlins, Harvard class of 1927. Rawlins was silky smooth, a sleepwalker whose dreams came true. "Rawlins has the game which should be copied because it is flawless and effortless," wrote Cowles. "Rawlins' footwork and racquet work are things of art." His singular strength was an ability to *hold* a stroke, that is, set up and wait and wait until the last moment before cracking a shot. Holding was a crucial technique in controlling the pace of play, in quietly ensuring a proper stroke and in instilling doubt in an opponent about where the ball is going. Holding was the opposite of telegraphing a shot. Playing against Rawlins was like shaking hands with an infant—you had to do all the work.

Rawlins won his first nationals in 1928 at the age of twenty-three. He beat Larry Pool in the semifinals, after being down 2–1, and Baker in the finals, 15–12, 15–13, 16–15. In 1930 he outlasted the Philadelphia duo, Neil Sullivan and Don Strachan, both in four games. Jack Barnaby ranked Rawlins as one of the most fluid players he ever saw: "He used his quickness to set up instantly for every shot, so that he seemed always to wait quite a while before he played the ball. Having a magic touch that made every possible finesse shot from anywhere in the court, as well as a flair for deception that rivaled that of Harry Cowles, his coach, Rawlins played with a maddening smoothness that made any opponent appear clumsy and inept by comparison. He was a total delight to watch in the court, never hurrying, waiting on every shot, controlling the ball with impeccable accuracy, outthinking his opponent continually with double threats and last instant turns of the racquet. . . . He continually persuaded even the best to take a wrong step only to have to reverse themselves violently to go the other way. There is no punishment in the game more severe than this, an isometric wrench as a player fights his own momentum."

Music might supply an analogy for what happened next. Rawlins was the folkie Dylan of the early 1960s, a fresh, imaginative voice following in traditional lines; the brothers Pool were like Dylan going electric at New-port—loud, disturbing and a distinct break with the past. If anyone could prepare the perfect squash curriculum vitae in the twenties, it was the Pools. Born in New York, their father was Eugene Pool, St. Paul's 1891, Harvard 1895 and a surgeon in Manhattan. Nicknamed the "Iron Duke," the elder Pool mounted the heads of moose and caribou he had killed on his waiting room walls. When his sons got into the papers for squash exploits, reporters often mentioned the Iron Duke's cricketing skill and how he "was credited with the longest wallop ever made in cricket in the United States." The boys, three years apart in age, learned squash at the University Club under the direction of George Cummings, the city's lead-ing squash professional. On weekends they played at Piping Rock in Locust Valley, Long Island. After St. Paul's, they came south to Cam-bridge and, under the tutelage of Cowles, developed into world-class players. Both were slim, five foot ten, rippling with muscle—the perfect build for a slam-bam style of squash.

Larry Pool won the Massachusetts state title his senior year at Harvard. Upon moving home to New York, he joined the Harvard Club and cap-tured the nationals the next two out of three years. His style was pure power. He was the first player to hard serve every time he stepped into the serving circle. (Up to that time, the proper serve was a slow, rainmaker lob that, hopefully, trickled off the side wall.) During a point he slashed a flat-faced racquet at the ball with murderous intent, lacing drives down the walls. Drop shots, suddenly, were passé. He occasionally smacked a roll corner or reverse when an opponent insisted on hanging back to handle the Pool heat but, mostly, he swung for the fences. Usually a home run hitter strikes out a lot, but Larry avoided mistakes. "He almost never made errors," wrote Cowles in 1935. "He covered the court so tirelessly that one could hardly hope to wear him down, and he blasted his shots cross-court and down the walls with a speed that seemed rather to increase than diminish as the match went into the fourth and fifth games."

Following in his older brother's footsteps proved daunting to Beekman Pool. He had sandy hair and gray-blue eyes and looked more comfortable outside in the wind than in an aspirin-white court. His freshman year, heralded as the brother of just graduated captain Larry Pool and a St. Paul's champion, Beek made the freshman team (freshmen could not play varsity squash until 1971) but rarely played number one. Beek hopped from sport to sport, stroking the 150-pound freshman crew and playing fullback for his class football team. The gridiron and the river took Beek away from Randolph just enough to keep him from improving, and his only notable win was the Harvard championship his sophomore year, 17–14 in the fifth. During his junior year he languished at the bottom of the varsity, often on the verge of falling off the team. His problem was that he hit harder than his brother. He broke three or four balls a match. His rapacious rails and serves bounded off the back wall and sat up for easy winners.

One afternoon Cowles took Beek's racquet, cut the perfectly good gut strings, slapped the racquet on his stringing vise and threaded cheap silk strings through the grommets. In an instant, Beek was indomitable. The ball still rocketed off his racquet, but the silk cushioned it enough so that it died in the back corners. He jumped to the top of the Harvard team, repeated as Harvard champion and, unseeded, he took the state title. At the 1931 nationals in Buffalo, Donald Strachan smoked him 13–18, 15–12, 15–12, 15–14, but one month later, Beek reversed the result, beating Strachan 9–15, 15–11, 16–13, 15–4 in the finals of the inaugural intercollegiate championships, held in New York. It was a nail-biting match, with Cowles, Larry Pool and the Iron Duke in the gallery. Strachan went up 13–11 in the third game, but Beek survived in the tiebreaker. Then he ran away with it. "The fourth game was a mere demonstration of devastating hitting on Pool's part," reported Stanley Woodward of the *Boston Herald*. "When Strachan was not aced completely he was unable to handle the hurtling ball cleanly and drove into the tell-tale or provided set-ups for further murderous hitting. The final point was a service ball which came off the back wall so fast that it bounded three-quarters of the way back to the front wall. Strachan chased it and hit into the 'tin.'" At the end of the season, Beek was ranked number one in Massachusetts, a phenomenal fact considering he was not even in the top fifteen the previous year.

More than a shimmering facsimile of his brother, Beek brought an added versatility to the usual puissant Pool strokes. Allison Danzig, reporting on the intercollegiates for the *New York Times*, compared the brothers, saying Beek "plays a game of the same pattern as that of his brother, Lawrence. But while he has the same blinding speed of foot and stroke, he has more variety and uses the corner shot much more often." These differences showed during Beek's senior year. He won the Gold Racquets, the premier invitational tournament, in his first attempt, beating Palmer Dixon in the semifinals and Jay Iselin in the finals, the latter match lasting a flurry-filled twenty-five minutes. *The New Yorker* thought that Iselin had capitulated too easily—he double-faulted at 13–11 in the third game, astonishingly, into the tin—and that Pool was eminently beatable: "When Pool is beaten, however, it will be a game like Rawlins' that will do it. Pool coming forward to drive is almost invincible, but Pool backed up against the back wall is a different matter."

No one was able to push him back. Beek took the state title in straight games. At Trinity he beat classmate Willing Patterson in the finals of the second intercollegiates, getting his name engraved on a massive perpetual trophy donated by his father. After struggling for five straining games against Andy Ingraham in the semifinals of the 1932 nationals, Pool walked out onto the court at the Baltimore Athletic Club for the finals. Tom Jansen, who had knocked Larry Pool out of the tournament in the quarterfinals, girded himself for another Pool explosion, but Beek pulled a rabbit out of his hat. During the first dozen points Pool coaxed drop shots and lobs into the corners. He refused to unleash a hard rail. Jansen, caught by surprise, lost the first two games in quick succession, recovered to take the third, but Pool took the fourth with ease. He hit just two tins in four games, a shocking statistic for a hard hitter. Two weeks later, to round the season off, Beek won the Canadian nationals, beating Iselin, 15–12 in the fifth. It was a record-breaking triple crown: the U.S. nationals, the intercollegiates and the Canadian nationals.

Following his brother back to New York and the Harvard Club, Beek lost a brilliant 1932 Gold Racquets final to Neil Sullivan, 18–17 in the fifth. Sullivan's strategy was to try to volley everything he could or otherwise turn and hit balls off the back wall. "It is the peculiar merit of his game that this last shot, which many players use only when they are forced to, becomes an offensive weapon as Sullivan executes it," wrote *The New Yorker*. "The ball finds its way into a front corner, comes out an inch or so above the telltale, and dies on the floor instead of bouncing." Beek recovered to win the 1933 nationals, beating Sullivan in the finals in four games as the back-wall trick failed. The next year Beek lost to Sullivan, 17–15 in the fifth, and never reached the finals again. In 1935 Beek won his third Gold Racquets, becoming the first player to win the prestigious tournament three times. In the finals that cold December afternoon, he beat a Harvard senior named Germain Glidden.

The last great Cantabrigian of the Cowles era, Glidden began his squash career at the Englewood Field Club in New Jersey, then at Exeter and arrived at Harvard in 1932 as proclaimed a freshman as Beek Pool. Glidden was handicapped by a flaw more serious than Beek Pool's uncontrollable power. As with so many other lefthanders, he had a terrible, dead-fish backhand. In the finals of the 1934 intercollegiates, he played a Harvard teammate, Tanny Sargent. Down two games to one, Glidden forced a fifth game, whereupon Sargent bageled him, 15–0. Cowles forced Glidden to revamp his backhand stroke. The years of running on his raw talent were over; a total overhaul was needed. "It is very difficult for a prep school star to accept that he must start all over again, like a beginner, and learn how to play the ball in an entirely new way," wrote Barnaby who assisted Cowles in the long operation. "Improvement was very gradual— everything was strange and against all his well-entrenched muscle habits. . . . it was like chewing granite."

Glidden had such trouble swallowing the hard rock of practice because he was such an instinctual player. He had the finest sense of anticipation ever seen in squash. He knew where the ball was going before his opponent had finished a follow-through; with a corybantic rush of arms and legs, Glidden covered the court like wall-to-wall carpeting. He hovered sometimes five feet in front of the red line, far beyond where other players hoped to roam. In addition to buttressing his weak wing, Cowles forced Glidden to hit the three-wall boast as a regular offensive shot. This was a quick and, in Glidden's case, a relatively safe way to rush an opponent up the court. "Every tough match developed," wrote Barnaby, "not into a grim exchange of basic drives leading up to a weak return and a crisis, but rather into a mad whirling dervish up-and-back scramble—a mess of quick volleys, shots, and nicks that seemed all wrong but was somehow unbeatable."

His junior year Glidden won the intercollegiates, as well as the Massachusetts states. His senior year he did even better. He had gone down quite cheaply to Don Strachan, the national champion, in four games at the Atlantic Coast Championships in late January and was scheduled to face him in the semifinals of the nationals in Hartford. Before the match, Cowles took a nervous Glidden into a side court and after rallying for a few minutes, he told Glidden to hit the tin. "I don't want to hit the tin," said Glidden, surprised at the request. Cowles insisted. "Hit the tin. Hit the tin. Hit the tin. Hit the tin." Glidden did, "hating that terrible sound," he remembered. After a half-dozen resounding bashes into the tin, Cowles said, "Okay, get in there against Strachan and don't hit the tin." The reverse psychology worked and Glidden won the match in three games. Then it was another all-Cowles finals with Glidden facing Andy Ingraham. Glidden won with ease.

Glidden also took his sheepskin in Harvard Yard and moved to New York. In Cleveland for the 1937 nationals, he faced Neil Sullivan in the finals. Sullivan won the first two games and in the fourth had a solid lead,

13–11. "At that point he was serving the ball hard into the side wall where the fast bouncing ball would come at me like a wounded hornet," Glidden wrote later in his autobiography.

>   To prevent this, I stood with one foot over the line on his side. He gave me a surprised look and said, "are you ready?" Then he hit the ball like a bullet to the back wall, about an inch above the floor, for an ace! The cold, clammy feeling of defeat hit the back of my neck. One more point and I would be dead. Terrific rallies ensued. I remember one shot I hit past him which I thought was a winner, but with a flick of the wrist he bounced it off the back wall [the old Sullivan trick from his battles with Beek Pool] to set up a tantalizing lob, which I returned but found myself caught between the ball and the adjacent wall with Neil in total command, standing in the middle of the court. I braced myself against the wall, and, just as he cracked the ball cross court, I flew and with a last split-second dive, retrieved it to later win the point. It was tied at 14–all, which meant Neil had the option of calling for one point or three out of five. The gallery was absolutely tense. "What is your call, Mr. Sullivan?" the referee asked as I was walking back from the front wall after retrieving the ball. I looked at Neil and pointed my finger upward, meaning, "one point," hoping to psyche him into saying, "three." After all he had just won three in a row from 14–11. He looked me straight in the eye and to my disappointment said, "one point." Neil was right to say one point. It was a championship point [for Sullivan], and the odds were in his favor to win one out of four. We had another terrific rally which resulted in a deafening roar from the gallery, as the referee said, "point and game to Mr. Glidden. The games are two–all." I had managed a pick-up drop shot for the ace.

Administering the coup de grâce, Glidden won the fifth game 15–10.

The final pearl in Cowles's necklace was Willing Patterson. Like the Pool brothers, Patterson grew up in an athletic family with a famous cricketing father. After Haverford School and St. Paul's, Patterson went to Harvard and notched the only victory over Beek Pool in Pool's illustrious 1931–32 season when he beat Pool in the final of the Harvard championships. After graduation he played in two nationals, both times losing in the second round. Patterson then went to England for a year, the first American player to go overseas to improve his squash. He got to the finals of the South of England championships in Brighton and reached the third round of the British nationals. He played in a New Year's Eve match in

Dublin (his Irish host woke him on New Year's Day morning after a late evening involving a tour of Dublin night life by throwing an alarm clock through a closed window). His favorite match, nonetheless, was against Amr Bey, the five-time British Open champion. Patterson lost 9–3, 9–4, 9–4, playing "the best squash of my stay in England."

Upon returning to the United States, Patterson began to translate his new skills into tournament victories. Unlike the other Harvard greats who uniformly moved to New York, he returned to Philadelphia. Patterson became a very solid player, both in singles and in doubles—he and Don Strachan reached the finals of the national doubles in 1938. In the mold of English squash, he was a tireless court coverer. "There was nothing extraordinary about his game," remembered Barnaby. "He just had an all-round toughness. . . . As a boxing critic once said about Rocky Marciano, that he wasn't a great boxer, didn't have an impressive style, couldn't hit as hard as some others, and wasn't really fast on his feet—but he beat hell out of everybody who went with him into the ring. Patterson was that kind of player." In 1938 he won his first tournament, the Union Club Invitational in New York, when he upset two-time defending national champion Germain Glidden. Still, he lost in the quarterfinals of the nationals to Hunter Lott, 15–6 in the fifth. In 1939 he again lost in the quarterfinals, to Sherman Howes in three games. In early February 1940, though, he convincingly beat Lott and Charley Brinton to win the Pennsylvania states at Philadelphia Cricket. The next weekend Patterson fulgurated through the draw at the University Club in New York to win his only national title. He beat Stan Pearson, Jr. in four in the quarterfinals and Dick Wakeman in five (after being down 2–1 and 14–all in the fourth-game tiebreaker) to reach his first final. His opponent, Howes, was exhausted, having just survived match balls against Lott in a five-game victory. Yet Patterson had never, in four matches, beaten Howes. In the first game it went to 10–all and then Howes cranked a number of tins. At one point in the second game, Howes collapsed onto the floor in frustration over Patterson's consistency. He recovered to take an easy third game and played gallantly down 14–12 in the fourth, tying the game and putting it into overtime. Patterson, showing great concentration, took the next three points to win the championship. "Where Patterson gets his amazing stamina is a mystery," wrote a newspaperman after the victory. "He looks the least robust of all the leading players. But when their tongues are hanging out and their eyes popping for lack of breath, Willing is still gliding swiftly in pursuit of the ball. . . . Perhaps he got this in England."

Patterson's victory in 1940 was the last time a player coached by Cowles would become national champion; by then, Cowles was living in a mental institution.

The Knute Rockne of squash, Harry Cowles was the first squash genius. He created the prototype of future squash coaches: the excellent player, the genial taskmaster, the quiet technician, the unflappable leader. He also changed the nature of squash in America. Cowles directed Harvard's physical-education program, which trained three hundred new players a year. He molded dozens of varsity-letter winners from complete neophytes. He developed what one former player called "a miniature horde of really competent players," who gave Harvard such legendary depth. Being number six or seven on the ladder in Randolph meant suddenly being an elite player at a club in Boston, New York or Philadelphia. Cowles's men spread across the country like missionaries, diligently spreading the gospel of the rail and boast. Cities like Cleveland, Seattle, Boston and New York depended on Harvard graduates for squash leadership. He coached two future USSRA presidents. One pupil, Steve Wright, reached the semifinals of the British nationals in 1928, the best result ever by an American. The years Harvard did not win the national five-man teams were years when Harvard alumni did. In 1928 and 1929, when New York won the title, three out of five and four out of five of the players, respectively, were Crimson men. He popularized Harvard squash so much that the game became synonymous throughout America as something college men played. Without Cowles, squash might never have emerged from the sleepy leather chair of the city and country club.

Silver, nevertheless, is the standard by which coaches are judged. In fourteen seasons, Cowles laid his hands on a stream of teenagers and trophies appeared. He coached seven national champions, more than any other person in history. He produced five national team winners and four intercollegiate champions. In advertisements for his squash and tennis store, Cowles noted how many "champions" he had trained; the number reached into the hundreds. He was a very original thinker. He corrected Larry Pool's backhand. He strung Beek Pool's racquet with silk. He matched Glidden up with the three-wall boast to bring his style to fruition. At times he watched from the gallery, "with owl-like solemnity," according to one player, but often he would charge into the court to repair a faulty technique. "Coach Cowles was always on the court, teaching us, demonstrating," remembered Beek Pool. "He would always come up to me and rub the lapels on my jacket and say, 'I've got a champion, I've got a champion.' He was a wonderful, gentle, caring man. I don't think anybody said a word of criticism—they just couldn't. He never raised his voice in the years I played for him."

In 1935 Macmillan published *The Art of Squash Racquets* by Harry Cowles. His opening chapter, due to his iron-tight demand for sportsmanship, was titled, "Good Manners in Squash Racquets." He advocated long trousers over the current rage for shorts and, showing a distinct distaste for sophomoric hijinks, added this sartorial comment: "Now and then a player appears in the court with nothing on at all except an athletic supporter. If such a person could but watch himself a single time from the gallery, he would hasten to change his habits." Distilling his years of coaching into a simple formula, he offered "Hints for Those Wishing to Become Champions": "don't smoke; don't drink stimulants; don't keep late hours; practice one-half hour daily, alone; don't be conceited; don't grouch or lose your temper; don't be over-confident; don't let down; don't play with an old racquet, and always have two to use; wearing apparel should be light; concentrate at all times on the game; always be a gentleman." His thoughts on the mental side of the game evolved into a section titled "Temperament":

> It is not often that a player wins if he permits his feelings to get the better of him. Anger, irritation, disgust, or any display of feeling results in a sort of blindness, and the more one yields to it, the more surely one is at an opponent's mercy. One's energy is lost in emotion when it should be concentrated on the game. Anyone who cannot control himself rarely succeeds in controlling a squash ball.
>
> The game is in this sense a test of character, and beyond a doubt the good and bad points in any man's nature will reveal themselves in his game, as surely as the writer mirrors himself in his stories. In this aspect of squash racquets, there is opportunity for anyone to improve himself as well as his game. Indeed, as was said in the first chapter, one's conduct on the court should be every player's first consideration when he sums up his own game. It is only too frequently that a player is prone to associate virtue with victory and preen himself on his ability, without considering the fact that his friends do not judge him by the score. The most important aspect of any match is the spirit that prevails throughout the contest.

In the winter of 1936–37, just as his fifteenth season at Randolph was getting underway, Harry Cowles had a nervous breakdown. He was at a cocktail party in an apartment in Cambridge when he suddenly sprung for the window and tried to jump out. Cowles was committed to McLean, Boston's mental institution, and diagnosed with schizophrenia. Over-working may have triggered his collapse. Forty-eight years old, he ran both the Harvard squash and tennis teams, a double duty that has felled many a coach. He traveled every weekend for eight months of the year with his teams or to monitor an individual player. He owned and operated the Tennis & Squash Shop, at 84 Mt. Auburn Street, just around the corner from the Randolph courts. The shop, still open today under different ownership, was a time-consuming sidelight for Cowles. He also was elected a Worshipful Master of the Cambridge Masonic Lodge, so many of his nights were taken away. The only public announcement made at the time was that "ill health forced him to retire." At Harvard the athletic department scrambled to fill his shoes. Jack Barnaby had worked as Cowles's assistant since 1932 as coach of the freshman squash and tennis teams, and quickly agreed to replace Cowles as interim coach. The season was a disaster. Harvard lost its first intercollegiate squash match, to hated Yale, 6–3.

Cowles suffered mightily for the next two decades. His wife moved to California. He had a frontal lobotomy, recuperated at his daughter's home in Rindge, New Hampshire, and spent the last three years of his life at Chestnut Hill Farm, an institutional work farm in West Newbury, Massachusetts. In December 1958 at the age of sixty-nine, Cowles died in West Newbury. Six people came to his funeral. His wife did not attend. He was buried in Rindge, in a grave marked by a simple flat stone.

His players had not seen him in decades. He occasionally appeared in Cambridge, but he was a blasted figure, speaking in monotones, his soul squeezed out of him. His last public appearance was with some of his greatest players. It was at the Tennis & Racquet Club where he had first worked for Tom Pettitt. In December 1939, Palmer Dixon, Herbie Rawlins, Larry Pool, Beek Pool and Germain Glidden returned to Harvard to play the Harvard varsity. The undergraduates surprisingly won the match, 3–2, with Larry Pool and Dixon winning at numbers four and five. "Following the tournament," reported the *Boston Herald* the next day, "all players gathered at the Tennis & Racquet club to fete Harry Cowles, coach until two years ago, who has just returned to Harvard after a long convalescence." There was a photo accompanying the *Herald* article, just of the five champions. Captioned "Champions Once, But Not Yesterday," all five stood awkwardly facing each other in a semicircle. Dixon was the only man looking at the camera. No one was smiling. Cowles, not pictured, weighed heavily on their minds. It must have been an appalling evening. Getting beaten by an undergraduate never made an alum feel particularly good, but seeing their coach in such bad shape was a brutal blow.

Later they remembered other moments. They remembered him with a tournament in New York that bore his name; after his death it was not renamed the Harry Cowles Memorial, because his players always felt he was with them, alive or dead. They remembered his love for squash. They remembered his loyalty to Harvard, how he turned down offers to coach at other schools for twice the salary. They remembered his brilliant dropshots. They remembered his quiet counsel. They remembered one winter afternoon driving on a windswept back road in New England, five players crammed into Cowles's car, coming home from a match. They were discussing, as undergraduates are apt to do on long Cimmerian drives in the bleak midwinter, theoretical matters relating to squash. The issue this time was mental toughness. It was the Great Depression. Hope was fighting a losing battle to fear. How much courage did a person need? What breaks down determination and endurance? When should one quit when an opponent is clearly better? After a while, the players paused. Glidden turned to Cowles and asked how long a player should battle even if it is hopeless. Everyone went silent. They could hear the murmur of the engine, the clank of the car heater, the susurrous crush of snow under the wheels. Cowles stared straight ahead at the darkening road and said, "You should fight until you're dead."

CHAPTER FOUR

Hollow-Eyed and Squeaky

A court on the *Titanic*, a fanatical prince, a woman who led a winter swim in the Atlantic, a Saturday evening black-tie dinner dance that lasted until Sunday night and Greta Garbo's boudoir—squash was more than a sweaty way of proving, for the thousandth time, the innate superiority of Harvard University. Underneath the front-page agate lay a melange of equally compelling stories.

Squash in America was a man's game. It started at a boy's preparatory school, migrated to all-male city clubs and seemed to require a Y chromosome as it expanded across the country. Contemporary societal norms were one reason. Another was the legacy of squash tennis. Its courts were at male-only cricket and university clubs and at gentlemen's country estates. When the switch to squash came—whether in Boston in 1907 or New York in the twenties—it was mostly just a matter of substituting a slower, smaller ball and a smaller racquet. Squash absorbed squash tennis whole: its court size, its clubs, its circuit of tournaments and, most of all, its aura of masculinity.

For the first quarter of the twentieth century, women's squash was mostly an oxymoron. "Squash is a grand game for ladies, who need exercise if they are ever to be healthy mothers of healthy children," wrote Eustace Miles in 1901. He added, "Ladies are, almost without exception, wonderfully keen on the game." Yet keenness, for procreative reasons or otherwise, was not enough to force open the necessary doors for the distaff. The notable exception was the Colony Club, founded in 1902 on the corner of Thirtieth and Madison in a Stanford White–designed six-story clubhouse. Established in large part by J. P. Morgan's daughter Anne, the Colony Club boasted one squash tennis court.

In 1925 hope flickered on the Boston horizon. Jack Summers, the professional at the Union Boat Club, persuaded the club to allow women to play squash in the mornings when the courts were otherwise dark. Twenty-one wives of members applied and were accepted under these restrictions. In 1926 Union Boat held a ladies tournament, with a dozen entries. Mrs. Homer Albers, as she preferred to be called, and Margaret Howe met in the finals. Howe won, not surprisingly, since her husband Bill was a champion player in Boston and had encouraged her to play. In 1927 Margaret Howe organized a Massachusetts state championship at the club. Sixty women entered the tournament, which Howe won, beating Eleo Sears in the finals. In November 1928 the Harvard Club in Boston granted the privilege of using some of their squash courts in off-peak hours to "ladies of the families of the Club members." This move "caused lengthy debates as to the pros and cons of sharing any part of the Harvard Club with the fairer sex," remembered John Reynolds, the professional at the club. It reminded some of the suffragette movement. "They have exacted their admission to the courts just as inevitably as they did to the balloting booths," wrote Allison Danzig in 1930. "It has not been without difficulty that they have invaded the sanctum of man, but gradually the bars have been let down more and more, and the number of women players has increased remarkably in the past year or two." Many clubs, ranging from Merion Cricket Club in Haverford to Sleepy Hollow Country Club in Tarrytown to Pretty Brook Tennis Club in Princeton, allowed women to step into their male sanctums.

Old-fashioned correspondence led to a women's nationals. In 1926 Mrs. Edgar Arnold in Greenwich wrote a Christmas card to Sarah Madeira in Ardmore and quietly suggested a match between women of Round Hill and Merion. In February 1927 five women from Merion traveled to Greenwich and soundly defeated Arnold's charges at Round Hill. A few weeks later the women reversed the trip and had a match at Merion. On 16 January 1928 the opening round of the first U.S. women's national squash tournament began at Round Hill. There were forty entries. Eleo Sears beat Aurine Boyden in the finals. During the same weekend Boston, New York and Philadelphia played a national team competition. In 1929 the Harvard Club hosted the second nationals. A full draw of sixty-four women competed in the singles—which was not surprising, since on average seventy-five women played daily at the Harvard Club. Despite playing on her home courts, Sears could not defend her title. Margaret Howe overcame Hazel Wightman in the finals, 17–15, 15–12, 15–11, and took home a cup donated by Mrs. George Townshend of Greenwich.

Even in the dark days of the Great Depression, prospects improved for women's squash. A number of women-only clubs built courts: the Chilton Club in Boston and the Cosmopolitan Club and the Junior League in New York (Stephen Feron, Jr., was the pro). A winter circuit sprung up around various state championships, invitationals and the nationals. In 1930, to manage this growing enterprise, Howe, Sears, Arnold, Albers, Mrs. H. Stuart Green, Mrs. M. Frazier, Mary Adams, Mrs. Lothrop Withington and Mrs. Ellwood Beatty organized the U.S. Women's Squash Racquets Association. Affiliated with the USSRA, the USWSRA decided that all sanctioned tournaments were to be best three out of five games, rather than best two out of three games, until the final rounds. Women had played best-of-five-sets finals at the national tennis championships from 1891 until 1902, but the trend more recently was toward making special exceptions for women. "Squash rackets is a game which should appeal to every lady who wishes to keep fit, to retain a youthful figure and to remain supple and comely for years beyond the general allotted span of such attributes," wrote Charles Read in 1929. "One cannot escape from Nature's provisions, and my advice is that a lady should leave a ball untried for if to take it would entail a long run and a quick return to position near the middle line. I also advise that in all other ways she should conserve her strength on every possible occasion." It was this attitude that made the USWSRA's decision rather bold. The association forced squash-playing women to be athletic, which in the long run made their game more of a sport and less of a hit-and-giggle hobby.

One major boon to the women's game was international play. Women in England contemporaneously picked up squash. They held their first national championship in 1922 and in 1932 formed a ladies committee within the Squash Rackets Association, which became the independent Women's Squash Racquets Association. "One of the first things the liberated women did," one journalist wrote, "was to get out of the country." In January 1933 a team of seven Englishwomen sailed for America to inaugurate a yearly competition between England and the United States called the Wolfe-Noel Cup, named after the team's captain, Eliza Wolfe, and the current champion of England, Susan Noel. The tourists fared quite well, winning nineteen of twenty-one matches in team competitions and individual Englishwomen grabbed the Atlantic Coasts and the New York state tournaments. At the Wolfe-Noel match on the cement courts at Sleepy Hollow, the English, without their captain Wolfe who had broken her leg playing mixed doubles a few days before, trounced the Americans, 4–1. The following year Eleo Sears led a team on tour to England. Anne Page, Agnes Lamme and Margaret Howe respectably reached the quarterfinals of the British nationals. At Queen's Club in the Wolfe-Noel match, the United States lost, 5–0, to England. The four top players lost in three abrupt games. Only the fifth string on the U.S. team, Sis Anderson from Plainfield, New Jersey, was able to generate some excitement by taking her match to a fifth game. "It was a 'needle' match," reported a London squash magazine. "Down in the court it was all anxiety and determination; up in the gallery, and especially among the other ladies of the American team, it was anxiety mixed with fear and hope. Only Miss Bowes' toy dog, flying the Stars & Stripes from his collar, remained unmoved, although later no doubt, in the sanctuary of his kennel, he permitted himself one woof of disappointment."

Barking for joy, the United States recorded their first Wolfe-Noel victory, 3–2, at the Harvard Club in Boston in 1935. The following year they lost again, 5–0, in London. In 1937 they won their second victory, 3–2, at the Junior League Club in New York. British women were able to secure the U.S. national title with notable ease. Susan Noel, an actress who had grown up in the shadow of Queen's and drove a double-decker bus during the Second World War, won both the U.S. and Canadian nationals in 1933, at the age of twenty. Three years later Margot Lumb, a small, aggressive left-hander, repeated Noel's double in style, not losing a game in the U.S. nationals. Twice after the war Janet Morgan, a ten-time British champion, also won the American nationals.

Amid these matches, British women taught their American counterparts a number of cross-cultural lessons. "Their effect on American women's squash was immediate and electric," Agnes Lamme wrote in 1937. "They were extremely fast on their feet, had much greater stamina than our women and displayed better style in hitting the ball. Very few lets were called in their matches, for they were quick and generous in giving way in the court. . . . It would be hard to overestimate the advantage American squash gained from being thrust into such fast competition. We had to become faster of foot, we had to improve our racquet work in the rear corners and off the rear walls and we had to develop stamina to keep in the game with the English girls." While touring England, the Americans enjoyed the illicit pleasure of practicing and playing against men. Sartorial taboos were also broken. English players led them away from bulky, full-length dresses. Eliza Wolfe was the instigator of the new outfits. She first wore trousers in 1933. "There was a dreadful commotion," she said in 1953. "I first wore them at Queen's Club and everyone accused me of wearing my son's trousers. Of course, they weren't his. When I went to America, I took a set of coloured trousers with me, and they caused another sensation over there. The Americans liked the idea so much that all my trousers were stolen, and I had to finish the tour in skirts." The

Americans, though, startled the English by perpetuating the American woman custom of wearing colored clothing—even scarves and mittens—as opposed to the traditional all-white tennis outfits. Anne Page compared off-court vices between American and English squash players: "For instance, after they [the English] play, they have tea instead of cocktails. Then, too, they don't seem to go for all-night dancing, with lots of drinking and smoking thrown in. They have great fun with sherry, and do not seem to attack the hard liquors, nor imitate, by smoking, the proverbial chimney."

The haze of smoke and booze and a lack of opportunity soon blew American women back. The national association faltered at first. It did not appoint a president until 1932, did not issue national rankings until the 1950s and had a terrible time raising funds. Restrictions on court times hindered play. Many women failed to train consistently. Some shied away from the competitive side of squash and most never called lets—in a semifinal match at the 1936 nationals between Babe Bowes and Agnes Lamme, it was the middle of the third game before either woman requested a let. The future was always flimsy at most clubs, since a quick decree of its board would immediately lead to their banishment. Playing against or watching men was impossible, either because a club's all-male policy would not be lifted during tournament weekends or because the club's architectural layout meant that the galleries were only accessible via the men's locker room. In the thirties, moreover, badminton became the rage. It was easier to learn than squash and there were no annoying restrictions on access, as the majority of courts were in public gymnasiums. At the 1935 squash nationals in Boston, only a handful of local women entered, and Boston was unable to muster a squad for the national teams. In fact, after Boston's 1928 win in the inaugural national teams, the city would win it just twice more before the 1990s, in 1953 and 1978.

One savior of American squash was Eleo Sears. She relished in violating established protocol. Born to the bluest of lineages, Eleonora Randolph Sears had to-die-for racquet genes—her uncle was Dick Sears, the seven-time U.S. national lawn tennis champion, and her cousins were the Coolidges who built Randolph Hall. Sears won one U.S. mixed doubles and four women's doubles titles at the national tennis championships and was once a finalist in the singles. She was the first woman to play polo astride a horse or fly over water—she once went aloft with the Wright brothers. A fan of the sport of pedestrianism, she could regularly been seen marathon walking along New England's roadsides, often padding from her townhouse on Beacon Street to her estate in Beverly

Farms. When she wanted to go to New York, she eschewed the Merchants' Limited train and walked. She once walked from Los Angeles to San Francisco and, another time, ambled forty-two miles from Fontainebleau to the Ritz Bar in Paris in eight and a half hours. Adept at squash from years playing at her cousins' courts at Harvard, Sears started her career in 1918 beating the best man in Rye, New York. She proceeded to win four state women's titles with an imposing backhand and an impeccable sartorial standard: "Just as big Bill Tilden is the King of tennis, the never failing player of color, so is the famous 'Eleo' Queen of feminine squash players," reported Helen O. Mankin at the 1936 nationals. "Miss Sears was indeed a regal performer. Wearing her hand-crocheted tiara to keep her gray pompadour in place, and a cream-colored wool sweater with long sleeves and full-fashioned black wool bloomers, she hurried about the court endeavoring to make returns." Sears served a record thirteen years as president of the women's squash association and donated hundreds of dollars to support its activities. She led each of the early Wolfe-Noel tours to England as a nonplaying captain and acted as a sort of prodding, impish, determined matriarch to the younger squash players. "She is one of those people who, by sheer force of character and generosity of nature, keep people together and make things go," wrote Susan Noel in 1950. During the 1935 Atlantic Coast Championships in Atlantic City, she interrupted play by dragging the entire tournament to the beach. She then led three other women into the waves. "Photographers and a crowd followed the daring mermaids and marveled at the trim Miss Sears who outshone the group by twice going into the ocean," reported one newspaper. The headline summed up the Sears spirit: SEARS' OCEAN PARTY STOPS SQUASH PLAY: VETERAN LEADS YOUNGSTERS IN FRIGID DIP. Sears promptly dried off, went inside and beat a girl twenty years younger, 15–12 in the fifth.

Margaret Howe, a tall, feisty Bostonian, served as the other founding force for women's squash. She won the nationals three times. She was slow on court, but had a tricky lob serve, reliable low volleys and the rare ability to adjust her game to exploit her opponent's weaknesses. In the fifth game of the finals of the 1934 nationals, Howe came back from a 8–3 deficit to beat Anne Page, 15–10. Three years later she went on court at the Junior League in New York with the 1937 Wolfe-Noel matches tied at 2–all and beat Elizabeth Barrett in four straining games. Her keen interest in squash was particularly evident in the fact that she was the only national champion ever to raise not one but two national champions as daughters.

A vibrant supporting cast surrounded Sears and Howe. Hazel Hotchkiss Wightman, the four-time national tennis champion, was a keen player in the early years and snagged one national title in 1930. As an upstart teenager, Libby Pearson of Germantown Cricket Club was a regular winner of state and invitational tournaments but never managed to take a national singles title to match her one national doubles victory. Ruth Hall, the 1931 winner who married an Englishman and moved to London after her victory, was the first woman to regularly hit the reverse corner, and had, according to Agnes Lamme, "a bewildering soft serve that seemed to disappear among the lights in the ceiling." Lamme herself was probably the finest player of the era never to win the national championship. The longtime treasurer of the USWSRA, Lamme had bad luck in the nationals. In the semifinals in 1936, she lost a 2–1 lead to Babe Bowes, going down 17–16 in the fifth. "She is outstanding in the U.S.A. as a player with the most brilliant touch and sense of courtcraft," wrote Eliza Wolfe in 1937, "and concentrates on playing all the angle shots to perfection." The most colorful character was perhaps Mrs. Louis Bieler of Philadelphia who always wore a pair of vivid orange shorts and her hair in a coronet braid.

Anne Page and Babe Bowes were the queens of the first two decades of women's squash. Page played on the national field hockey team and was a rugged competitor. "She plays like a man," Anne Lytton-Milbanke wrote in 1939, "hitting very hard and being extremely fast on her feet. Moreover, she has a tenacity in a close fight not often met with." Based at Merion, she won the nationals four times, the national doubles twice and five straight Atlantic Coast titles. In the best result ever for an American woman, she reached the semifinals of the British championships in 1939. "She is very high-strung and nervous before she plays," wrote Lamme, "but concentrates so well during her matches and is so determined that her nervousness is not destructive to her while playing. It serves rather to gear her game up to a higher pitch. She hits the ball high and hard, rarely uses the soft serve. . . . She has extraordinary powers of stamina and strength and can get to almost any ball that an opponent can hit. . . . she rarely attempts corner shots in a close match. She volleys more than any other woman."

Bowes, known to all as Babe, was more of a gracile shotmaker. Five years younger than Page, Bowes splashed onto the scene at the age of sixteen when she reached the finals of the 1931 nationals—establishing a record for the youngest person ever to play in the finals. Playing at the

Cynwyd Club under the tutelage of her husband (they lived across the street from the club), she won four nationals and was runner-up five more times. She would have won more times, if not for being ill with the flu one year and spending another with the Red Cross in India. Furthermore, the Second World War threw the USWSRA into such turmoil that the nationals were not held for five straight winters (the men missed just three years), and Bowes was then in her prime. Her breakthrough year came in 1938 when she won the city, state and national titles, beating Page in all three finals. In the nationals that year she went up 2–0, allowed Page to win the next two games and, at 12–all in the fifth game, forced a Page error and smacked two corner drop shots into the nick to win the championship. In the 1941 nationals in Boston, she survived three match points to beat Libby Pearson in the semis, and then in the finals she sent off Barbara Williams, 15–4, 15–10, 15–9, in fifteen minutes. Bowes also reached the quarterfinals of the British nationals in 1936. "Babe Bowes possesses the most perfect style of any American player," wrote Eliza Wolfe in 1937. "She plays angles and drops from every part of the court with amazing accuracy." Tall and stylish, Babe was one of the most sought-after society belles in the East and the fact that she was a squash champion was considered not a drawback but a precious advantage.

On the male side, equipoise was elusive. While Harry Cowles produced his rumbling juggernaut in Cambridge, Philadelphia strove to offer opposition. The early Quaker City leader was Stan Pearson. The youngest of ten children, Pearson graduated from Princeton and returned to Philadelphia to work for Joseph T. Pearson & Sons, his father's box-manufacturing firm. From the beginning of the 1914–15 season until the end of the 1922–23 season, Pearson put together an unmatched period of domination. For those nine winters (play was officially suspended in 1918 and 1919) he never lost a match. He won the last point of every match he played in the nationals—which he won six times (still an unequaled record after eighty years)—in the national teams in which he led Philadelphia to victory five times, in Philadelphia's interleague play or in the Germantown Cricket and Racquet Club's championships. With his saddle shoes and long white flannel trousers, his doughty toughness and his incredibly reliable hands, Pearson simply never lost. The one blemish in this perfect picture came at the 1920 nationals. Charles Peabody, a youthful shotmaker at the Union Boat Club in Boston, upset Pearson in the finals. On the Harvard Club's court one, which had a nineteen-inch tin, Peabody was able to nullify Pearson's hard rails with scintillating corner shots and won in five games.

After retiring following his second three-title skein in 1923, Pearson spent his time at Germantown Cricket Club persuading some of the tennis-playing youngsters to come inside and try squash. One pupil was his son, Stan, Jr. As a junior player Stan, Jr., won three straight Philly Districts tournaments, a leading indicator of future greatness. A top player at Princeton, Pearson won the intercollegiates as a sophomore. In 1941 he captained the team to an undefeated season, with a sweet victory over archrival Yale. He won the 1948 nationals—the only time a son has followed a father in winning the nationals.

Bouncing off the grassy swards at Manheim were "Strawn" and "Sully," two Pearson stalwarts who kept the Philadelphia name in good stead during the Cowles era. The first of a number of national champions to be born in Mexico City, Donald Strachan left Mexico soon after his birth and moved to Germantown. He became a protégé of GCC's most famous son, Bill Tilden, and played more tennis than squash while attending Germantown Academy and the Hun School in New Jersey. His surname was pronounced to rhyme with brawn, and he was a vigorous socializer. He initiated the oft-repeated custom of appearing in the locker-room Sunday mornings before a match still dressed in his Saturday-evening dinner jacket. One reporter, at the 1935 national doubles in Buffalo, noted his bleary eyes and wrote that "If Donny Strachan had only made up his mind which ball to strike at Sunday morning in the semifinals, he and Buddy Walsh might have done better." Despite his off-court proclivities, he granted no quarter on court. "It's all very well to be nice to your opponent before the match," he told a young Philadelphian, "but remember when the door closes behind you on the court, he's a son of a bitch." His backhand was the best the game had ever seen, turbocharged and full of horsepower. He loved the front of the court and gunned for a winner, usually a reverse corner, at the first opportunity. "He was a total pressure player, perhaps the most aggressive the game has known in going for the throat on every stroke," wrote Jack Barnaby. "He played as if he had never heard that conservative phrase, 'keep the ball in play.' Every shot seemed labeled 'death—right now!'. . . . When Don Strachan rolled, it was like a scythe."

Strachan cut his way to fame at the age of twenty as a sophomore at Princeton, when at the 1929 nationals he chopped Jay Iselin, the number-three seed, with ease and then crossed swords with Larry Pool in five tough games in the semifinals before losing. Nine months later he reached the finals of the 1929 Gold Racquet tournament, losing to Ogden Phipps. In 1930 he reached the finals of the nationals, but lost to Herbie Rawlins. The following February Strachan had a whirlwind weekend at the nationals in Buffalo, as he fought with tremendous courage through a thicket of Cowles's champions. In the opening round he almost stumbled against R. L. Debevoise, losing the first game and almost the second before winning in four. In the quarterfinals he ran into Beek Pool with his silk strings and the ball flew wildly. Strachan survived, 13–18, 15–12, 15–12, 15–14. In the semifinals he outclassed the defending champion Rawlins, 15–9 in the fifth. In the finals he faced Larry Pool, who had outlasted Neil Sullivan in the semifinals.

Splitting the first four games, Strachan and Pool went into the boiler room of a fifth and deciding game in the finals of the nationals. Strachan initially handled the heat better and went up, 14–10. Larry fought back and cannoned one serve after another at Strachan. At 14–13 a famous let occurred. Larry hit a sloppy drive that came wide off the back wall. Strachan, perfectly within his rights, backed Larry off and macheted a backhand down the wall. Larry got entangled in Strachan's extended follow-through and was late in getting to the drive which came off the back wall ever so slightly. He held up a left finger in a silent appeal for a let. The referee, surrounded by a breathless gallery, hesitated, then granted the let. They replayed the point, Larry won it and forced a tiebreaker at 14–all. Strachan chose no-set, giving them both championship point. Strachan lost the point. Beek Pool leapt from the gallery into the court and hugged his brother.

It was a cruel, indelible defeat. The first time the nationals had been decided on a double-match point, the match was a classic conversation piece for years to come. Players debated the let, about whether Strachan had really hindered Larry and whether Larry would have gotten to the drive anyhow.

Five weeks later Strachan lost to Larry's leaping brother, Beek, in the finals of the first intercollegiate tournament. Strachan lost the following year in the quarterfinals of the nationals, to Andy Ingraham, after being up two games to one. In 1933 he lost to Beek Pool in three games in the finals. In 1934 hard luck smacked him down again, as he lost to Beek in the semifinals, 15–8, 13–18, 14–18, 15–12, 18–17. In 1935 Strachan shed his bridesmaid dress and stepped up to the altar, beating Beek in the finals at the Pittsburgh Golf Club for his first national title. He won again in 1939. In his forties he went on the wagon and trained hard, reaching the finals of the nationals in 1949—nineteen years after his initial Presidents' Day appearance, establishing a record of male endurance and excellence that has never been matched. The following year he made the finals of the Harry Cowles tournament, meaning that he managed to reach the finals of a major singles tournament in four different decades. Strachan was an outstanding player, but his game was too finely calibrated. He hit with little margin for error. Weighed down by match points, he sometimes crumbled under the pressure. On the U.S. tour of England in 1935, Strachan went up, 2–1, 8–0, in his first round match in the British championships before skidding to a five-game defeat.

Strachan's principal Philadelphia comrade was his childhood friend, Neil Sullivan. Two years older than Strachan, Sullivan also played at GCC and attended Germantown Academy. He went to Lehigh, which did not have a squash team, so he only took squash seriously once he returned to Philadelphia in 1928. From 1929 through 1938, Sullivan reached the semifinals of the nationals every year. Hard luck came with the consistency. His most famous loss was against Germain Glidden in the finals of the 1937 nationals when he squandered four match points. Sullivan perfected what was known as the Germantown shot, a lob hit sharply off the front and side wall. The shot was eventually renamed the Philadelphia shot, so prevalent was it among players from the city of brotherly love. Sullivan was elected to the USSRA executive committee in 1932, and became president in 1949. Much of his leadership came outside the boardroom. Burdened by an startling appetite for food and drink, Sullivan kept up with Strachan's pace. By day both had that wan, cadaverous appearance of squash players who spent too much time inside a thirty-two by eighteen-and-a-half-foot box. A whiskey in the evening brought a touch of color to their faces. "Sullivan, who was champion in 1934, is now achieving a record as a kind of perennial runner-up," wrote *The New Yorker* in March 1937 in a classic paragraph of nudge-nudge, wink-wink, say-no-more. "Built along Babe Ruth's lines, like so many squash players who go from one festive squash weekend to another, he has a great disdain for training, and has decided views about the advisability of getting in some relaxation to offset the pace a conscientious tournament player has to keep up at this time of year."

Neil Sullivan was Strachan's mirror opposite on court. Strachan had the great backhand, Sullivan the great forehand. Strachan was volatile on court. Sullivan was cool as a cucumber. Strachan so intensely focused during his matches he tunnel-visioned, while Sullivan was acutely aware he was being watched. He showboated. He quipped and cackled in between points. He hit trick shots with his triple-jointed wrist. Instead of hustling into the back corners, Sullivan lazily substituted a touch of razzle-dazzle. "Sullivan uses extraordinary methods, most of which he must surely have invented for himself," wrote *The New Yorker*. "After the serve, he is likely to bound heavily to the forecourt and stand there volleying every ball he can lay his racquet on." Before the 1933 nationals, he slyly floated the rumor that he had started training the previous summer to beat Beek Pool. "Even his friends who knew better," wrote *The New Yorker*, "were ready to make, and did make, substantial bets that he would win the title." Sadly, his bluff was called: Sullivan, having survived three match points in the quarterfinals and then a tough four-game semifinal against Andy Ingraham, had nothing left for the final against Pool.

To his credit Sullivan did deny Beek a hat trick by winning the 1934 nationals. In the finals at the Boston Athletic Association, Sullivan courageously recovered after dropping the first two games to Beek, winning the fourth game, 18–16. The last game might have been Sullivan's zenith as a player. Beek raced to a 3–0 lead, but there was no panic, and Sullivan nicked some boasts and jumped to 14–10. Beek demolished his lead with four straight winning shots. At 14–all, Sullivan called set-three and it went to 15–all. Sullivan, determined not to squander a 14–10 lead in the finals against a Pool, as Strachan did three years earlier, hit two consecutive winners to take the title.

With the expansion of the game in the 1930s came a tempest in a teacup about style. Philadelphians were upset, in part, by the fact they were no longer the best. They had built the tabula rasa and tastefully inscribed it with instructions, and now Harvard men, with their smash-mouth game, were spraying graffiti all over it. Some people were horrified to see Beek Pool flogging a hard overhead everytime he served.

Yet, it went both ways. "The Harvard players greatly feared Strachan and Sullivan," wrote Barnaby. "Much time was spent analyzing and planning how to cope with their deadly attacks." Who would want to copy Sullivan's awful footwork or flim-flam trickshots? Moreover, it was not as if all Philadelphians hit powderpuff stuff. Brendon Walsh hit as hard as the Pools—in one Lockett Cup match in 1933, he broke three of his racquets and finally the ball before winning. Still, the Pools had upset the established order. *The New Yorker* quoted a Philadelphian after Beek Pool had won his second straight nationals as saying Beek "had made squash a game in which nothing counted except hard hitting." George

Cummings, the professional at the University Club who had trained both Larry and Beek Pool, wrote, "the drop and angle shot game is superior to hard hitting . . . to play a sound game of squash one has to have a variety of shots and a good change of pace in order not to depend entirely on hard hitting. The greater skill, however, rests with the soft game. Drop and angle shots require more clever head work, proper foot work, dexterous racquet work and perfect timing. In playing a soft game one is less apt to swing wildly as is the case when every ounce of energy is going into every shot. There is nothing more disconcerting than to play squash with a person who swings the racquet clear around his body off both backhand and forehand. . . . Another interesting comment is that the soft game is more pleasing to watch. [Spectators] will marvel at the speed of the hard hitter, but will applaud the player who wins points with cleanly hit drop shots."

A number of people rose to the defense of the Pools. Allison Danzig argued that, "Pool is by far the hardest hitter in the amateur ranks, but there is much more to his game than merely speed. He has a fine change of pace and his drop shots are so effectively disguised that it is almost impossible to anticipate them. In addition, he is a tireless court coverer who gets almost everything and such is his control over his racquet that he can produce finishing shots within inches of the telltale when off balance." Harry Cowles wrote that Beek was a great champion because he had trained himself to not hit hard: "For years he hit with amazing speed but could not keep it within bounds. For long he was a sure prey to the finesse game. By dint of long practice, often alone in the court, he finally succeeded in controlling his shot." Cowles seemed to have forgotten about the strings of silk.

Strachan died young of cirrhosis of the liver in 1969. In March 1949 Sullivan, along with a group of other Philadelphians, boarded a train in Buffalo to return south. Two policemen came onto the train and arrested him on charges of embezzlement. He was convicted of stealing money from his partner Coffin—they ran a stock brokerage—and spent time in jail. Upon release Sullivan moved to Annapolis and became the manager of a small hotel. Sometimes in the winter he wandered into the Naval Academy squash courts and sat quietly high up in the gallery, watching the midshipmen practice. Art Potter, the Navy coach, would stop instructing a pupil and say, "See that man. That's Neil Sullivan. He was once national champion."

Squash had come a long way since its birth in the open-air courts at St. Paul's and its infancy in a dismal box thrust into the rafters of the old Racquet Club of Philadelphia. Between 1900 and 1915, the game expanded at a leisurely pace, but its hold on the passions of its players was tenuous. Squash tennis, that New York game of tennis in a squash court, dominated the cold dark months. Squash tennis players had a national association, a regular circuit of tournaments, an annual yearbook and a sense of possibility. Squash, on the other hand, was hidden away at a few private men's clubs in a handful of cities. Equipment had to be ordered from London. The national association was moribund. It produced no yearbook, had no committees to focus on pressing issues and neglected to arbitrate on rules and equipment. The nationals was a joke, with no more than four men in the draw. There was a likelihood that squash in America might wither on the vine and contract to just a bizarre Philadelphia winter game.

Instead, squash blossomed. In 1921 just four cities sent squads to the national teams tournament, the same as a dozen years earlier. In 1924 nine cities came and by the end of the twenties there were fifteen. Women launched a national championship in 1928, a national association in 1930 and by 1931 ran interclub leagues in New York, Boston and Philadelphia. In 1919 there were no collegiate squash matches. By 1931 there was a men's intercollegiate association with five charter schools and an annual championship. The number of clubs that affiliated with the USSRA jumped from nineteen in 1923 to forty-four in 1928 to sixty-four in 1940. From a winter without more than two tournaments came a fixtures list that oozed across the calendar. The most startling statistics came from Harvard and Yale. By 1940 Harvard had fifty courts on campus, and Yale sixty-seven. In 1937 the *Literary Digest* reported that squash was still on the rise: "No longer laboring under a stigma which, thirty years ago, relegated it in popular opinion to the 'idle rich' classification, squash racquets to-day rates a respected standing as a legitimate non-class sport, and an active American player roster of more than 15,000."

Key factors propelling the growth were two long-lasting competitions. In 1925 a New Yorker, Arthur Lockett, donated a cup for an annual tri-city, seven-man match between New York, Philadelphia and Boston. The Lockett Cup immediately captured the imaginations of the players in the three leading squash metropoles (in 1962 a Ketcham Cup, donated by Treddy Ketcham, was added for doubles). As the tournament proceeded through the years, always played on the second weekend in December, it remained the epitome of East Coast squash. The Lockett Cup, much like inter-club league squash, gave players a taste of team competition and the vital feeling of being a part of something greater than a quiet game after work. It was the shibboleth for any aspiring player. If you played in the Lockett, you were breathing the rarest of squash's breezes.

Even more influential was the rise of international play. In 1922 Henry Lapham, a member of the Boston Athletic Association, donated a trophy for the winner of an annual fifteen-man amateur singles match between the United States and Canada. Lapham owned the Boston Garden, and, although his Bruins rarely brought the Stanley Cup there, he had the pleasure of turning the Lapham Cup into a reasonable facsimile. With layered bands of silver inscribed with the name of every player on a winning side, the Lapham became one of the largest and heaviest trophies in the world. In 1945 Alastair Grant of Montreal donated a cup for a doubles version of the Lapham, traditionally played along with the Lapham. In the first year of the Lapham, Philadelphia and Boston supplied the entire U.S. team, but two years later it was composed of men from six cities. Rotating from city to city, the Lapham-Grant enabled men from less well-visited cities where the nationals rarely if ever came—like Baltimore (1930), Rochester (1942), Providence (1950), Indianapolis (1960), Wilmington (1968) and Portland, Oregon (1971)—to enjoy the fruits of international play. The protocol was to put five top-class players on your team, then five average club players and round it out with five hackers who excelled more at the bar. The result was an exciting, well-lubricated camaraderie. It was a highlight of the winter, and the Saturday evening dinner dance, renowned for its expensive food, dance band and copious amounts of alcohol, had an infamous catalogue of outcomes: one player fell down a flight of stairs and broke his collarbone, another was jailed for drunkenness, a third was sent to bed down an elevator in a laundry basket and once a player was found asleep in a snowdrift. In Rochester one year, the Canadian captain rose at the dinner to offer remarks. He opened his mouth and immediately slid silently under the table, passing out cold. Both the U.S. and Canadian teams spent the next few minutes arguing over whether his own countrymen or his hosts should attend to him. In the end no consensus was reached, and the captain slept peaceably there until the end of the evening.

England, wanting such fellowship, launched a most exhaustingly enjoyable tradition of touring sides when it sent a team over for the third Lapham in 1924. A Tennis & Racket Association squash committee selected four men—Sam Toyne as captain from Queen's, Ginger Basset and Theo Drysdale from the Royal Automobile Club and Timmy Robarts from Bath—with a fifth string found in Bill Macpherson, who was already living in the United States as a graduate student at Harvard. The Englishmen acquitted themselves well, winning nine out of eleven team matches. Timmy Robarts, age forty-six, pulled off an amazing double. He managed to win the Canadian and U.S. national titles, beating Macpherson in the Canadian finals and W. F. Harrity of Philadelphia in the U.S. finals. The Lapham, played at the time with just five men, had an exciting finish. Canada lost to both teams, and United States v. England went to 2–all in matches. The final match featured Ralph Powers against Ginger Basset. Heavily favored after just having beaten the former Canadian national champion, John Chapman, Basset won the first game. But Powers, a defiant competitor, prevailed in the tiebreaker in the fourth and the United States escaped with a 3–2 victory. After the match the Bostonians held a dinner in the Englishmen's honor, with two jazz bands, speeches and over five hundred guests. Sam Toyne wrote, "And it was not easy to realize we were in a prohibition country."

The United States sent a weak team across to England in 1925. The side, consisting of C. S. Clark, Eugene Hinkle, Joe deV. Keefe, H. E. Mills and A. R. Ells, met with disaster, not winning a game, let alone a match, in any of its contests. The British, under the auspices of the Tennis & Racket Association, again toured North America in 1927. They dominated their hosts, winning fifteen matches, losing three and drawing two in twenty matches. In the Lapham they tied with the United States 3–all and won the cup by virtue of a better result against Canada. Failing to replicate Robarts's feat, Victor Cazalet, the English champion, lost in the quarterfinals of the U.S. nationals to Wally Johnson, 15–10 in the fifth. Cazalet did, however, beat Steve Wright of Chicago in the finals of the Canadian nationals in Hamilton. It was perhaps the closest match in top-flight squash history: 17–18, 17–18, 17–16, 15–11, 17–16.

The Jesters Club supplied the next tour. In 1929 a group of schoolboy Rugby fives players in England formed a traveling, all-male, clubhouseless troupe called the Jesters Club. At the time such touring clubs, like the Escorts and the Rump, were common in England. The Jesters added other sports to their repertoire, including court tennis and racquets, but squash soon was the focal point and the Jesters played a quiet, but forceful, role behind many of the game's developments. After the Second World War, the Jesters launched branches in the United States, Canada and South Africa and, later, unofficial chapters in Zimbabwe, Bermuda and Australia. Membership in the Jesters was one of the highest honors a squash player could receive.

In 1934 the Jesters sent their first side over to North America. The team did quite poorly, losing 5–0 in the opening round of the U.S. national five-man teams. Two English Jesters reached the finals of the Canadian nationals, though, and John Gillies lost in the quarterfinals of the U.S. nationals to Robert Grant. The following year the Jesters invited the USSRA to send its best players to tour Britain. In late November 1935 a team arrived in Southampton. Willing Patterson was working in London at the time. A friend from Queen's Club, Clive Robinson, who worked as a salesman for Slazenger, kindly drove him down to Southampton to greet the U.S. touring side. Upon Patterson's suggestion, Robinson brought about thirty English racquets with him to sell to the Americans. On the deck of the ship early that morning, Robinson made his pitch, but to no avail. "Strachan and Sullivan, our two best players, were particularly scornful of the light English bats," remembered Patterson. "Clive was somewhat disappointed, but I told him to be patient. Later that day, after we had been demolished by a club team at the Flying Elephant, near Brighton, Clive sold our team two dozen English racquets." Scorn was amply replaced not by experience alone, as Patterson remembered:

> It was at this match that we first encountered the famous English hospitality. Shorty Knox, our captain, took us aside when we got to Brighton and told us that although we naturally wanted to win as many matches as we could, we were also on a tour of good-will and we should try to do as the English did and make as good an impression as possible. (Another member of the team told me that Shorty had given the same piece of advice every day on the boat coming over.) We had luncheon at the club with a very genial group of six members. They immediately ordered whiskey and soda. We noticed they drank theirs, so we drank ours, not wanting to offend them. The drinks flowed freely, we had three or four more, and soon we were on the best of terms. International relations were at a very high peak. Then we sat down for lunch, with wine, and afterward we had a brandy and other liqueurs and cigars. By that time it was all very friendly and jolly, and we felt as if we owned most of Sussex County. Finally, at around half past three, one of our hosts said, "I say, shall we start?" One by one we were ushered into the court. To our amazement, we had to play an entirely different group of members, six other English gentlemen who were not only younger than the others, but obviously in excellent training, very much on the lean and bony side and looking like they hadn't had a drink since Michaelmas. How Cy Polley won our one match of the day, I'll never know. I can still recall Dick Wakeman's shock when he failed to win a single point.

The rest of the tour was slightly less brutal. They won six out of twelve matches, watched Amr Bey play Jimmy Dear in the finals of the British Open, went to Twickenham to watch the Oxford versus Cambridge rugby match (0–0 final score) and had luncheon with Lords Desborough and Aberdare at the Houses of Parliament. In the third fixture of the trip, Roy Coffin, burdened by a horrible hangover, bent down for a drop shot during the first point of his match. "It was like a slow motion picture," wrote Shorty Knox. "He bent over, but he couldn't straighten up again. Someone in the gallery said he had sprained his ankle, and he drew a lot of sympathy, especially from the females in the gallery, as he hobbled through the rest of the match waving his racquet in the air and hitting the tin as often as possible to ensure a short match."

Besides the often alcoholic accouterments of the Lapham-Grant and Lockett Cups and the international tours, squash boomed because it fit neatly into a new way of life. Society was increasingly busy and rushed. No longer employed in manual jobs, many middle- and upper-class people found themselves chained to a desk all day and to the family home all evening. Squash was one of the few respectable means for the upper class to totally exhaust themselves. The weather never interfered so, if your opponent appeared and the lights stayed on and you had enough balls and racquets, you could play forever or you could play and shower and be home before dinner. Squash rewarded improvement. It asked for a deep reservoir of strategy and refreshed the mind. "A fair percentage of the men who play with some regularity choose to work it in at lunchtime, but for most it is the ideal chaser to a day's work," wrote Herbert Warren Wind, a *New Yorker* golf and tennis correspondent, in 1962. "There are few games like it for engulfing a man totally. He may walk onto the court with his mind still hacking away at the gray edges of some obsessive problem, but squash will elicit his full attention, whether he wishes it to or not. He usually walks off the court a half hour later so absorbed by how the game went that it takes him several minutes to remember the problem that previously was harrying him."

At its root, squash had a sought-after tinge of sporting aristocracy, as it was yoked to racquets and court tennis in America. Court tennis was invented on the streets of French villages and racquets was begun in a London prison and yet by the twentieth century both had become impossibly elite sports. Just eighteen court tennis courts and forty-odd racquets courts were built in the United States, and the thin upper crust of society played on them. Nathaniel Thayer, sponsor of the Agassiz Expedition to

South America, put up half the money for the first court tennis court in the United States. Payne Whitney built two tennis courts, one at his estate in Manhasset, Long Island (the cost in 1915 was a quarter of a million dollars), the other at his winter home in Aiken, South Carolina. Charles Mackay, whose daughter married Irving Berlin, built a tennis court at his estate in Roslyn, Long Island, and dragooned a former world champion, Punch Fairs, to become his private coach.

Squash emerged from this milieu. The sport started as an addendum to court tennis and racquets. Almost all early squash professionals were culled from the ranks of racquets and court tennis. The first book published on squash in America, in 1901, was written by a champion court tennis player; the second was by Fred Tompkins, a court tennis pro at the Racquet Club in Philadelphia. Anglophiles in America loved squash. Following British custom, players continued to wear long flannel trousers even after Bunny Austin shocked Wimbledon by appearing on court wearing pressed Bermuda shorts. (In fact, until the 1980s, players in USSRA-sanctioned tournaments were required to wear all-white clothing.) Squash developed its leitmotiv in America as an elitist sport for all stages of life—St. Paul's, Harvard, the Racquet Club—a theme that replicated the English model of Harrow, Oxford and Queen's. "Many of the most cultured men in England have played squash," merrily reported Allison Danzig in 1930. Royalty stooped to pronounce its blessing, and it was often argued that because the Prince of Wales, later to become Edward VIII, and later still the Duke of Windsor, waved a squash bat instead of a polo mallet that the game developed so quickly. No doubt more than a few people thought that if the game was good enough for the future King of England, it was good enough for them. The prince put in a court at Buckingham Palace and joined the Jesters. He played in the British championships each year from 1924 to 1927, and loved the game so much that he demanded a court be built on the H.M.S. *Renown*, the battlecruiser he sailed with during his stint in the Royal Navy. While on tours of Canada, he often arranged matches against club professionals, sometimes midnight games that helped cure his insomnia. It is unrecorded, however, whether in 1937 anyone made the connection between the King's passion for squash and his decision to give up his kingdom for love.

The efflorescence of a romantic era suffused squash, in part because there had been a squash court on the *Titanic*. It was perhaps the most famous court in history, yet one used for just four days. Almost 900 feet long, the *Titanic* had many amenities for its passengers: a swimming pool, a gymnasium, a Turkish bath and the latest import from Wiesbaden, mechanical bicycles or "electric camels." On the F and G decks, just forward of the boiler rooms and adjacent to the post office sorting room, was a squash court. The walls were made of steel, painted gray, the floor was made from Veitchi flooring compound and an enclosed gallery, with an unsightly wire fence as a protection from errant balls, provided viewing space for about a half-dozen spectators. The professional was Fred Wright, who was twenty-four years old. He signed on for the statutory wage of one shilling, depending for his livelihood on tips. He received some from an American passenger, Colonel Archibald Gracie, who wrote about playing with Wright. Breaking the sabbath, Gracie played squash with Wright before breakfast on Sunday, 14 April 1912. That evening, when the unsinkable ship hit an iceberg, seawater rushed into boiler-room number six, the room right next to the squash court. By midnight the court itself was flooded. Spectators looked in horror at sea water splashing around the court. Gracie bumped into Wright as they scrambled to the lifeboats. Gracie remembered his half-past-seven court the following morning. In a line almost too good to be true, Gracie asked, "Hadn't we better cancel that appointment?" Wright calmly replied, "Yes, we better." Wright went down with the ship and his body was never found.

Maritime and royal disasters aside, the acceleration of squash from a sleepy amusement to a sport played on the *Titanic* occurred without much fanfare. Philadelphia continued to act as a generating force behind the game. The Princeton Club and the Penn Athletic Club built courts at the end of the First World War; the PAC hosted the 1928 and 1941 nationals, which were the only two times the country's major tournament was played in Philadelphia between the world wars.

Boston, after its initial infatuation with squash tennis, fell in love with the Philadelphia game. In 1914 the Massachusetts Squash Racquets Association started an official inter-club league, with six clubs; five more joined in the next years. After the waves caused by Harry Cowles's activities at Harvard washed across the Charles River, these various clubs expanded their facilities and built more courts. Boston was blessed with a number of newspapermen who played the game and helped promote it, especially Frank W. Buxton, editor of the *Boston Herald* and secretary of the MSRA, and George C. Carens, sports editor at the *Boston Evening Transcript*.*

Boston inaugurated, under the guidance of Arthur Bryant of the Union Boat Club, a B league in 1920, a C league in 1924 and even a D league in 1929. These leagues, the first in the country, did much to strengthen the squash community, for they served as training grounds for new players. Harvard, under the direction of Harry Cowles, blanketed the leagues with teams. A favorite Mass SRA event was the Middlesex Bowl, a tournament started in 1922 and held during the Christmas holidays at Harvard's courts. Harvard undergraduates were forbidden from playing in the Middlesex. "The tournament became increasingly popular among Boston Clubs," wrote Dick Cooke, never afraid to mix metaphors, "when the game was so completely dominated by Harvard. The Middlesex Bowl tournament was a 'port in time of storm' for leading Boston players during the years when a beating at the hands of a Harvard Class A player was the regular diet."

Similar trajectories, albeit without the push of Harry Cowles and some-what reluctant newspapermen, could be graphed onto other cities' growth. Besides its three founding clubs, Baltimore had a new force in squash when the Maryland Club built four courts in 1926. A tony all-male club near Charles Street, the Maryland Club hosted the 1928 and 1932 nationals, and its leading player, Harry Baugher, was a top contender at the nationals. Farther south, the nation's capital took up squash via the usual route when in 1921 the Racquet Club in Washington opened four squash tennis courts in its basement. A year later the club switched to squash. The first club squash champion was Dwight Davis, donor of the eponymous lawn tennis cup. The Racquet Club's top player in the twenties was Eugene Hinkle, a Cowles product and captain of the 1925 U.S. tour of England. With Otto Glockler as professional for the club's first forty years, the Racquet Club's most memorable moment was hosting the 1926 nationals. In Chicago the

---

* Carens reluctantly covered squash, as he wrote in 1932: "Squash racquets is a good game to play, but not so good to write about. One reason why few newspaper-men become really enthused about the game is because it is tiresome to watch a vast majority of the matches. Unless one has learned from playing the game that it is quite a stunt to whale the ball so that it lands three or four inches above the tin and that it requires infinite patience and dexterity to master corner shots or to perfect the tech-nique of covering court, the rallies become boresome. I know there are some squash players who will rise up and say I ought to watch more matches, but my answer to them is that I have been watching matches since Charley Peabody was the kingpin in the amateur ranks, and I never have become so excited about occupying a spectator's role that I would be willing to pass up my evening meal for the privilege of squeezing into a draughty gallery."

1920s were a boon decade. Squash at the University Club skyrocketed, and eight other clubs around the Windy City put in courts, including the Racquet Club, which hosted the 1930 nationals. Cleveland squash started in 1904 when the Tavern Club built two squash courts and a racquets court, but it was not until a group of Harvard men, lead by Andy Ingraham, arrived in the twenties, that squash took off. Cleveland's leading professional was Alfred "Scotty" Ramsay, a Scottish soccer player who worked successively at the Cleveland Club, the University Club and the Tavern Club, from 1923 until 1978. St. Louis commenced its squash history in 1907, when the Racquet Club built two squash courts and a racquets court. After Dave Gardiner ran the club for the first four years, Frank Lafforgue took over and worked as the club professional for the next half century. Jack Gordon was the star of St. Louis squash. A Princeton man, Gordon won thirteen University Club of St. Louis championships, and in 1936 he won the city championships with a broken right wrist by playing the tournament with his left hand. Gordon was a bon vivant of the old school. He took a long hot shower before every match and stored a glass of gin outside the court in case he needed a restorative push.

The two cities of most fervent activity away from the eastern seaboard were Buffalo and Detroit. Squash began in Buffalo in 1912 when the Saturn Club erected a squash tennis court. When the club moved in 1921, it switched to squash and put in three courts. That same year the Buffalo Tennis & Squash Club, which had built two squash courts and four squash tennis courts in 1915—but had played squash tennis on all six—also converted to playing squash. The first non-Philadelphian to be president of the USSRA, Lyman M. Bass, in 1925–26, was from Buffalo, and later came the father-son combination of Adrian W. Smith (1933–35) and A. Warren Smith, Jr. (1977–79). The first nationals in America held beyond sniffing distance of salt water was held at the Saturn Club in 1925 (and again in 1931). The city's original star player was Seymour Knox, known to all as Shorty. Both he and his son, Seymour, III, were presidents of the USSRA, the latter becoming one of the chief benefactors for the game. (Seymour, III, also owned the Buffalo Sabres.) In 1924 Shorty organized Buffalo's first team to go to the nationals, and in 1934 started a tri-city team competition for Buffalo, Pittsburgh and Cleveland modeled after the Lockett Cup (it was later named the Knox Cup).

Detroit, which entered the national teams in 1921, first encountered squash in 1902 when squash tennis courts were built by the Detroit Curling & Racquet Club. Squash soon gained sway under professional George Healey, and a half-dozen other clubs erected courts. A unique example was

Linsdale University. Fred Matthaei, a Detroit businessman, built a court in his backyard. Matthaei had a running joke of calling in scores from matches at his home to Detroit newspapers, dubbing his home team Linsdale University (after Linsdale Street where his factory was located). Although the Michigan SRA was founded in 1911, it was not until Jim Standish became its first president in 1928 that it properly organized itself. Standish helped organize the Western championships, an annual tournament that formed the highlight of the season for squash players living west of the Appalachians, and became the first Westerner to serve as USSRA president, from 1937 to 1939. Detroit stunned the squash world by winning back-to-back national team titles in 1942 and 1947. Both teams were known for their scrappy play and their matching white T-shirts—in 1942 they had bright red devils plastered on the chest, and in 1947 a growling lion.

New York, crucial to the development of the game, was the toughest nut to crack, due to its contumacious preference for squash tennis. "Little missionary work was attempted in New York," Danzig wrote of the period before the Roaring Twenties, "for the same reason that the Republican party refused to spend any of its campaign funds during a presidential election below the Mason-Dixon line." The first club to break party ranks was the Racquet & Tennis Club. In 1914 the R&T, perhaps because of interaction with sister court tennis clubs where squash was in vogue, forsook squash tennis. A club championship was started for squash, played on the club's squash tennis courts. In 1918 the club shifted its home from West Forty-third Street to a grand Italian palazzo designed by Stanford White on Park Avenue. There, in the midst of two court tennis courts and two racquets courts, the club put in four eighteen-foot-wide squash courts. After the war Seton Porter, a squash champion at the R&T, persuaded the Rockaway Hunting Club in Cedarhurst, Long Island, to switch from squash tennis to squash. Rockaway had been playing squash tennis since two courts were built there in 1901. Porter hired William Ward, the older brother of Frank Ward, the squash tennis world champion, as squash professional at Rockaway. With these two clubs as impetus, the University Club also switched from squash tennis in 1920, although their first two 1917 courts were finished with glazed cement. After the club installed three more courts in 1923, the University Club became the headquarters for squash in Manhattan.

Arthur Lockett, the leader of the University Club's transition to squash, was emblematic of New York's convoluted winter-sports journey. An Exeter and Harvard graduate, he moved to New York just before the turn of the century and fell deeply in love with squash tennis. After persuading his home club, Montclair Athletic, to install two squash tennis courts, he became club champion. Lockett then switched to the Englewood Field Club, one of the elite country clubs in northern New Jersey, and persuaded the club to install an eighteen-foot-wide squash tennis court, and again became a club champion. After the First World War, Lockett had a conversion on the road to Damascus (or Fifth Avenue) and swung completely over to squash. He pushed the University Club to switch, hired a locker-room boy, George Cummings, as squash professional and characteristically won the new club championship, at the age of forty-five. "He was a seemingly inexhaustible source for trophies in almost every category of local and national competition," wrote Bob Lehman in Lockett's obituary. "His quietly humorous, self-deprecatory talks were highlights of many squash functions."

Squash in New York in the twenties, as one person said, "was as esoteric as Greta Garbo's boudoir." The Metropolitan Squash Racquets Association at the time was "conducted more or less on an informal basis, with only a few member clubs, casual team matches and an association championship played under not too rigid dictates," wrote Ned Bigelow, later the president of the Met SRA. In 1923 the association started a city squash championship, held at the University Club, but only a handful of men played. The winners each year were members of either the Racquet & Tennis, Rockaway or the University—except for one squash tennis player from the Princeton Club who, one suspects, wandered into the tournament by accident. In 1924 New York sent a team to the nationals for the first time, but they failed miserably.

A deluge of Cantabrigians arriving in New York in the late twenties, however, had a tonic effect on the struggling minority of Gotham squash players. The Harvard Club, which allowed squash on just one of its squash tennis courts, built two squash courts in 1927, "to satisfy the demands of players coming down from Cambridge," wrote Danzig. The University Club built three more courts in 1928 and added a doubles court, the first in New York, for a total cost of $85,000. Later the same year Rockaway built five new courts, including a doubles court. A dozen other squash tennis clubs switched and, in the autumn of 1928, the MSRA voted to issue a schedule of league fixtures. Harvard men led the way for the launch of the league, with two in particular, Douglas Debevoise and Perry Pease, serving as vital officers of the association and Palmer Dixon doing much behind the scenes work. It was taken as a sign of things to come when the USSRA awarded the 1929 nationals to New York, which was played at the original squash club in the city, the Racquet & Tennis Club.

*

For squash aficionados, the core of American squash became a series of two-night, three-day tournaments that dotted the winter weekend schedule. The major tournaments of the year—the season-opening Ticknor-Glidden Round-Robin Invitation at the Englewood Field Club in November; the Gold Racquets at Rockaway Hunting Club in December; the William White at Merion in early January; the Woodruff-Nee in mid-January in Washington, D.C.; the Atlantic Coasts in Atlantic City in late January; the Harry Cowles in the Harvard Club in early February; the DeForest-Tyler Invitation at Plainfield Country Club in mid-February; the Charles Hardy Invitation at Apawamis after the nationals; as well as the Canadian nationals and the Montreal Amateur Athletic Association's invitational—usually had a draw of sixteen amateur players invited to the club. The opening round started Friday evening or the first two rounds were played on Saturday. A black-tie dinner dance came on Saturday evening, and the semifinals and finals were on Sunday. During the week players in the United States did not automatically engage in any après match "sixth game" camaraderie but, on the weekend, with work and familial obligations less pressing, a frantic conviviality ensued. The parties escalated so much that in 1950 the USSRA decreed that the official social schedule at the nationals had to be limited to a maximum of two lunches and one evening party. "At the top Eastern tournament level, squash becomes a world of its own," wrote Herbert Warren Wind in 1962, "a pleasant little realm of well-born, well-educated and superbly well-coached amateur sportsmen, the best of whom (Henri Salaun and Diehl Mateer, Jr., for example) are the peers of the best professionals. On winter weekends the amateur squashmen travel a competitive circuit of good squash and good partying. Elsewhere in American sport there is nothing exactly like it, and if it has an equivalent, it is probably to be found in the tenaciously Edwardian climate of the amateur golf competitions in England, where the weekend jousts at Rye, Worplesdon and other ancient haunts are installments of one long, serialized house party. . . . the charm of the squash milieu, is apparent to anyone from the outside or unsneakered world who looks in on a winter weekend tourney of the Eastern circuit. He is instantly in the midst of a bright and good-humored land, one of the last of the authentically Wodehousian vales. . . . Beneath the camaraderie, the 'inside' jokes and the unparched throats, there lies a supernal dedication to squash."

The Atlantic Coast Championships, started in 1930, was a riotous weekend. In 1929 two Quaker families, the Leeds and the Lippincotts, erected two hotels side by side on the boardwalk at the small summer-resort town of Atlantic City. The fifteenth floor at Haddon Hall was, strangely, left unused, so Bob Leeds and Jack Lippincott, the sons of the owners, convinced their fathers to put in two squash courts. The courts were placed back to back, so cramped that there was a minimum of gallery space and only one of the four side walls had regulation boundary markings, but they were the only courts, until the 1990s, on the Jersey Shore. "In the beginning the people in town weren't exactly sure what to make of squash," said Doris Lippincott, the wife of Jack Lippincott. "They thought of it as some sort of Quaker game we had brought in from Philadelphia." The Atlantic Coast Championships was entirely gratis: the tournament, rooms at the hotel, food, cocktails—everything but tips. Because there were only two courts and sometimes a sixty-four men's draw (as well as, at different times, a professional draw, consolation draw, a women's draw, a veterans draw and a seniors draw), the ACC was memorable for its around-the-clock matches. Play commenced Friday afternoon and was continuous through Saturday evening. Very often players had a match at two or four in the morning and found themselves in an amusingly rigorous rotation of swatting squash balls, eating and drinking and nabbing quick naps. Each hotel room had four faucets at the sink, two of which brought forth hot or cold salt water, and more than one late-night reveler tried to quench his thirst out of the wrong faucet. In 1938 Fred Hawthorne in the *New York Herald Tribune* reported on the scene Sunday afternoon: "Ernest B. Humpstone, chairman of the National Umpire's Association, was hollow-eyed and squeaky in the voice at the end of play this afternoon but still on his feet and functioning flawlessly after refereeing eleven matches." Sunday, after the finals, everyone poured themselves into their cars or train compartments and drifted home.

An equally notorious weekend was the Harry Cowles. Begun in 1947 at the Harvard Club of New York by Germain Glidden and Andy Ingraham, the Cowles became the top tournament warmup for the nationals. It grew so popular that a second-class tournament, the John Jacobs, and a veterans draw, the Jack Barnaby, soon accompanied the main event. The matches were intense, and spectators, bundled in overcoats in the cold Harvard Club gallery, were always attentive if not chilled. Cocktails at the Cowles on Saturday evening began around seven. It was a stag evening, unlike other tournaments, so there would be no dancing. Instead, after drinking for an hour, a bagpiper skirled the call for dinner, and the men repaired to the wood-paneled banquet room where oil paintings of illustrious Harvard men peered down from on high. At a head table sat the chairman of the tournament, an honorary chairman, and officials from various squash associations. Remarks were made; a toast to the Queen was given; professionals in attendance were acknowledged; Stew Brauns was thanked for provisioning the wine; Jack Barnaby cheerfully told a Harry Cowles story. Once dinner ended and the cigars came out, the Calcutta began. Groups of men huddled, formed syndicates and "bought" at auction one of the four semifinalists in the tournament. The syndicate with the winning player on Sunday afternoon received 60 percent of the total pool; the runnerup syndicate 30 percent and the Harvard Club took 10 percent for the expenses of the tournament. Very often the betting went into the tens of thousands of dollars.

Of all the house parties, none provided more memories than the Gold Racquets. Begun at the Rockaway Hunting Club in Cedarhurst, New York, in December 1928, it was always known for its top-notch hospitality. The Gold Racquets, like the Atlantic Coasts, was entirely free for players. The Saturday evening black-tie dinner dance became a New York society event on the holiday calendar. "Hazy recollections of the Gold Racquet," ran the musings of one player in 1935. "Honey Humpstone and his falsetto tenor organization, the Agony Quartet, followed afterward by a series of impromptu skits and acts lasting into the wee hours of Sunday. . . . The party continuing at Ray DeVoe's apartment Sunday night. How did everyone get there?" At the Sunday brunch, the Orpheus Club from Philadelphia sang a cappella songs like "Chantez," "Second-Hand Man" and "Waiting For the Robert E. Lee." Often at the Gold Racquets, a player and his wife would go outside for a stroll in between matches. They walked along the fairway at Rockaway. Leviathan jetliners soared overhead preparing to land at Idlewild. Salt water filled the lungs. The cobalt chop of Long Island Sound splashed ceaselessly against the shore. They came back to a clubhouse well-lit against the darkening sky.

The bedrock of squash in America nonetheless was not only the city and country clubs and their boisterous weekend tournaments. It was at St. Paul's and Harvard where many players and supporters learned to love the game. Operating in much the same way as baseball's farm system did for the major leagues, high-school and college squash teams taught thousands of men (and sometimes women) how to play, sending them off into the world with a rich enthusiasm for the sport. Almost every national men's champion from the 1920s onward played in college. The universities and high schools had the capital and willpower to build attractive facilities and retain good coaches. It was a self-replicating cycle: Boys learned the game at Andover or at Dartmouth, went on to play as adults, then sent their boys to their alma maters with a racquet in their trunk. The ethics of squash were imprinted on these young minds. College matches had no referees. Players policed themselves. They learned to shake hands with opponents and respect squash's tradition of sportsmanship. The coach became a central figure in their lives. You invited him to your wedding. You wrote letters, you called, you visited him when he was dying in a nursing home and you went to his memorial service. The hours in the weight room and the endless winter drives to other schools generated a special fellowship. Years later someone might ask, "Oh, where did you play?" in the same vein of, "Where did you prep?" It was a question of identification and the answer meant a great deal.

Not only did these high schools and colleges maintain varsity, junior varsity and freshman teams, they also offered court time to intramural players and the occasional hacker. Squash became an essential accessory for the preppy man. As Herbert Warren Wind described the process, the uninitiated boy might arrive at college and consciously ignore squash his freshman year. "In most cases sheer exposure crumbles his resolve by the time he is a sophomore. Sooner or later, mainly because a court is only a few steps from his room, the agnostic decides to take a whack at the game, just to see what all the talking is about. Five minutes later he is a believer—converted the first time he strikes the ball squarely on the racquet face and watches it dart off the walls." The next day he buys a racquet. Coming home for the holidays, "he steps off the airplane or train accoutered with the emblems of his new station in life, which he hopes will make it clear even to his father, who is meeting him, that he has become a man of taste and attainments. He has on his Shetland jacket, in one hand he holds a copy of Stendhal's *Le Rouge et le Noir* and in the other his trusty squash bat."

Preparatory schools, the feeders for many of these universities, launched squash programs by the score in the twenties. In addition to St. Paul's, there were courts at St. Marks, Brook School, Hun School, Choate, Exeter and Middlesex. Outside Philadelphia, the Haverford School built its first four courts in 1931 in a gymnasium paid for by Joe Ryan, an alum who founded the ski resort at Mt. Tremblant. Episcopal quickly followed and hired as coach Fitz Eugene Dixon, a Huntingdon

Valley champion. Haverford and Episcopal, the two rival Main Line boys' schools, built such powerhouse programs that together they have more national champions as alumni than all other high schools combined. With coaches like Dixon at Episcopal and Charlie Dethier, a twenty-five-year veteran at Haverford, they regularly beat college teams.

A number of top universities besides Harvard created thriving squash programs in the twenties and thirties. In 1926 Princeton built six courts at Dillon Gym. A team did not coalesce until 1930 when Bill White, the professional at Merion Cricket Club, arrived to coach the Tigers part time. The 1931–32 team, Princeton's first with a formal schedule, played Penn once and Yale twice. The following season they had eight matches, including a losing effort against Harvard. In 1924 the University of Pennsylvania, through the efforts of Sydney Thayer, built handball courts under the stands at Franklin Field. Five years later Wally Johnson, a Davis Cup tennis player, became the first coach at Penn. In 1935 Harvard, Yale, Princeton and Penn created a Quadrangular League, a short-lived predecessor to the Ivy League, which was officially formed in 1954. The Massachusetts Institute of Technology and Trinity created teams in 1929, and in the early thirties Amherst, Wesleyan, Dartmouth and Colby built courts. Dartmouth formed a bona fide varsity in 1937 and after one year hired Red Hoehn, a top amateur player who won the Middlesex Bowl in 1938. Cornell, Army, Navy and Michigan fielded teams as well, but the most unusual college program was at Purdue University. Purdue came east every winter to play matches and ran an intercollegiate tournament in Chicago for other teams in the Western Conference (now Big Ten).

Only Yale was able to put up any resistance to Harvard. In 1915 Yale built a couple of squash tennis courts and in 1919–20 formed a team. They played squash tennis for the first five years, switching to squash only in 1924. A year later Yale hired a coach, William Hinchcliffe, and started sending a team to the nationals. It was not until the early thirties that Hinchcliffe copied Cowles and put up a team in the Connecticut state leagues. In 1932 Payne Whitney paid for a skyscraping Gothic cathedral of a gymnasium, in which twenty-six courts were plopped on the fourth floor. A year later John Skillman took over the program from Hinchcliffe. Skillman had grown up in Princeton and had worked as a professional at the Apawamis Club in Rye, New York. An indefatigable volleyer, he won three national professional titles. With his ever-present pipe and gruff demeanor, Skillman was fiercely loved by his players whom he always called "farmer." He might not have been the technician Cowles was, but he had a fine rapport. "Farmer, go out there and get on top of him, I mean that, farmer, stay on top of him," Skillman famously advised his players before every match. The advice worked, for he posted a 452–79 record in forty-one seasons. In 1937 McGraw-Hill published Skillman's book on squash. Skillman issued a list of rules borrowed from Harry Cowles: "Don't smoke, don't drink, don't keep late hours; have your room well ventilated, be sure there is no draught, draughts often cause cold in the muscles; wash your face in cold water just before a match; do not grip the racquet too tightly; keep a light sweater on through the first game; practice your shots while rallying; take notice of the lighting; don't drive an automobile to the tournament." In 1959 Yale became the second college besides Harvard to win the national team championships.

The fabulous disorder of the first years of college squash—with unofficial matches, opponents that varied from Purdue to local clubs and varying numbers of varsity players—saw its first inkling of regulation in March 1931. Ernest "Honey" Humpstone, a Yale alum, president of the Metropolitan Squash Racquets Association and a member at the University Club, conceived the idea of an intercollegiate association. He invited players from six active university squash teams—Harvard, Yale, Princeton, MIT, Penn and Trinity—to play a tournament at the University Club (Penn declined). Beek Pool beat Don Strachan in the finals, but it was at a luncheon meeting following the semifinals at Eugene Pool's home that had a more profound effect on college squash. Led by Humpstone, Pool and a Princeton alum, Edward G. Herendeen, the players formed the Intercollegiate Squash Racquets Association (later called the National Intercollegiate Squash Racquets Association). Beek Pool was elected president, with the other four colleges represented in the executive and an alumni committee to advise the undergraduates. When formal approval for the association came from the individual colleges' athletic departments later that year, Eugene Pool donated a "particularly imposing" cup, as Ned Bigelow tactfully described it, as the permanent trophy for the winner of the intercollegiate nationals. With the establishment of a national association, college squash expanded, as universities built courts and formed varsity teams. Undergraduates ran the association for its first years, which was a blessing and a curse. They learned responsibility, and the president was given a spot on the USSRA executive committee, but the association moved at a leisurely pace. It still had just the five original colleges in its ranks four years after its founding. In 1935 the association expanded the standard college dual match from five men to seven and two years later increased it to nine. In 1942 the association created a formal national team champion based on dual match records throughout the season. In the early fifties the varsity coaches took over the association. Yet another schoolboy activity was now a business.

For three years in a row in the late thirties, the national intercollegiates were the most thrilling tournament in the country. At Merion in 1937, Bernie Ridder was seeded number one. A six-foot-five Princeton bomber, Ridder had gone undefeated in dual matches. He had a mammoth forehand and a blindingly hard serve. Dick Dorson, his Harvard opponent in the finals, was a small, athletic retriever. Ridder blew Dorson away in the first game. In the second, Dorson's corner shots took a little wind out of his sails. Ridder won the game but doubt had crept in. His arm ached and his 2–0 lead did not seem as immaculate as it should. Dorson took the third game. Ridder collapsed on a bench outside the court for the five minute break. Dorson won the fourth. Ridder blasted one final attack in the fifth and the match went to 17–all. Ridder served a cracking line drive that almost nicked. Dorson dug it out, but the ball fell to Ridder's pinwheel forehand. Ridder whipped it. Dorson dove, tipped it back to the front and saw his racquet slither away from him on the floor. The ball was an easy setup to Ridder's backhand, and Dorson, racquetless, was doomed. But Ridder somehow popped the automatic winner into the tin. The following year Ridder again reached the finals. Now captain of the Princeton team, he seemed assured of victory, but on a cold day in Hanover, he again lost, 18–17 in the fifth, to a man he had beaten earlier in the season. This time it was Leroy Lewis from Penn. In 1939 the finals again went to one final point in the fifth. It pitted Kim Canavarro of Harvard against Stan Pearson, Jr., of Princeton. Canavarro, having saved one match point, was serving. He rocketed a hard serve right at Pearson. With no time to get out of the way, Pearson awkwardly flung his racquet at it. The ball ricocheted into the front right corner just above the tin. It was the luckiest shot anyone had seen.

A hoary division between amateurs and professionals stifled development in these years. Professionals existed primarily to train, coach, coddle and serve the amateurs. Many believed that a game should be a game, and those who made a living off it were somehow suspected of immorality, a weak character or at least a lax upbringing. A pro came into a club through a back door and up narrow, dark stairs. He was not invited to the dinner dances. He earned fifty cents for a lesson and fifty cents for stringing a racquet. His office was a dusty, windowless closet.

The amateur-run national association fought fiercely to maintain this imbalance. The executive of the USSRA so regularly debated the division between amateurs and professionals that one year they voted to ban discussion of the issue for the next twelve months. "The amateur eligibility problem was attacked from every angle," recorded the minutes of the executive in 1932. "Everyone agreed that every possible method should be used to make our rules so tightly drawn that squash racquets would continue to be the leading exponent of amateurism." The USSRA adjudicated on such petty infringements as a player writing an article on squash for money—he was allowed to only if, in the words of the committee, "his name be not followed by any title indicating the winning of any squash racquets championship"—and whether another player, Cal McCracken, could appear in a Ballantine Ale commercial. It was not until 1979 that the USSRA invited a pro, Jim McQueenie, to serve on its executive committee. The men—there were no female pros in America until the seventies—had no stage to exhibit their skills, enjoy some competition and earn money. Exhibitions were a rarity and they were made an exhausting four out of seven games. The key step toward advancement—prize-moneyed tournaments open to both amateurs and professionals—was repeatedly denied.

The first bona fide professional tournament, held at the Huntingdon Valley Country Club in 1904, had six entries. George A. Frazier, a member of the Racquet Club of Philadelphia, arranged the tournament. Alfred Ellis beat John Friel, 3–1; both men were squash professionals at the Racquet Club. Nothing much happened in an organized way for another decade. In 1914 Jock Soutar journeyed to Canada to play the best of the north. In a round-robin of squash in Montreal he beat Fred Hawes of the Montreal Racquet Club and G. Bannister of the Hamilton Squash Racquets Club, both 3–0. Soutar, a toby jug of a Scot who had started his career as a junior marker at the racquets court at Prince's, in London, had come over to America in 1907 to work at the Racquet Club of Philadelphia. From 1913 to 1929 he was the racquets world champion. In 1916 the USSRA announced it would recognize the winner of a match between Soutar and Bill Ganley of Boston as the professional squash champion of America. Like Harry Cowles, Ganley started out as an apprentice under Tom Pettitt at the Tennis & Racquet Club and more than once reached the finals of the national open squash tennis championships. The Boston Athletic Association hosted the first leg of the Soutar-Ganley championship in late March 1916. Ganley won, 3–2. On the first of April they played the second leg at the Racquet Club of Philadelphia. Soutar reversed the score, 3–2. The Tennis & Racquet Club in Boston held the playoff a week later. Soutar survived, 3–2, and took home $1,000. Ganley got nothing. Four years later Soutar defended his title against Otto Glockler, a pro in Washington, D.C. In February 1920 Soutar crushed Glockler, 3–0, at the Racquet Club and, a week later, won the first game of their second leg match at the BAA to clinch the title defense. For five more years, no other professionals challenged, and in 1925, after he defeated John Friel, 3–1, at an exhibition at the Racquet Club, Soutar announced he was abdicating his squash throne to devote himself to court tennis and racquets—such was the fervor with which he held his squash title.

Others felt the same way, for no one took over Soutar's position for another five years. In New England, though, a small pro tournament was held concurrently with the 1925 nationals in Buffalo. That tournament compelled a group of Boston pros to form a New England Professional Association and sponsor an annual tournament for their members. Jack Summers, an English-born professional at the Union Boat Club, won the new tournament each year from 1925 to 1930. The association met periodically to discuss pedagogical concerns, and in 1928 it voted to affiliated with the USSRA and become the United States Professional Squash Racquets Association. Eddie Thompson of the University Club in Boston was president and Edgar Patten, who succeeded Summers at Union Boat, was secretary. In 1930 the USPSRA organized its first national tournament, held in Boston. Summers beat Thompson in the finals. A year later twenty-one professionals gathered in Boston and Summers again won and took home a trophy donated by Bill Howe, the president of the Mass SRA. Summers went on to win four titles in total, the last in 1934 at age forty.

The National Professional Squash Racquets Association (it took that name in 1948 and became the North American Professional SRA in 1965) struggled for decades. Membership was as low as twenty-four men in the late fifties, and in 1969 it had just fifty-one members, eleven of whom were from the Toronto Cricket, Skating and Curling Club. One reason for its continuously dolorous state was that the association was as private as the clubs at which these men worked. To join the association you needed to have a teaching job at a USSRA member club, and three other pros had to write letters of recommendation. The giants of the professional corps, men like Lou Ballato at the City Athletic Club or Tommy Iannicelli at Short Hills, had very little contact with the world outside their own club. They spent most of their time stringing racquets and massaging egos.

The pro-only championship, called the U.S. Professionals, was their standard bearer, the one public opportunity at which they could show off their skills. Yet the tournament, run by the NPSRA, was a decidedly minor event in the winter schedule. It received very little support from the USSRA and had a total purse each year of only a few hundred dollars. The tournament moved around the country, often seeking out less obvious climes like Louisville, Denver, Bethlehem or Atlantic City to draw interest. The best pros were Scotty Ramsay, the Scot in Cleveland; Lester Cummings, the pro at the Field Club in Greenwich; Al Chassard, the lithe, swift pro at Saucon Valley and Eddie Reid, a strong tactician at the Hartford Gold Club. The most heroic story came from Jimmy Tully. A southpaw with such touch, observers said, he could peel a blueberry, Tully's father had been a locker-room attendant at Merion and Tully became a professional at the club when he turned eighteen. Just after he won the 1936 U.S. Professionals, he accepted a job offer from the Pittsburgh Golf Club. Soon after his arrival, he was in a car accident and his left arm was permanently mangled. After years of surgery, a bone graft finally took and he regained enough movement in his arm to play again. In 1949 he relinquished a 2–1 lead in the finals of the U.S. Professionals against Eddie Reid, squandered a match point in the fourth and lost the match, 18–15 in the fifth. Two years later, at the age of forty-one, Tully beat Reid and Scotty Ramsey to regain the title he first won fifteen years earlier.

The pro association, in the hopes of bettering its plight, gently advocated tournaments open to both amateurs and professionals, but the USSRA repeatedly rejected the notion. In 1935 the executive voted six to five against allowing a team match between amateurs and professionals. That same year, the Mass SRA sponsored a Boston Open to raise money to send an amateur team to the nationals in Pittsburgh. Five professionals (Summers, Eddie Stapleton, Edgar Patten, Jack Barnaby and Jack White) played alongside ten amateurs. Attendance for the three days of matches at the BAA was so high that the Mass SRA grossed $50 in gate receipts. Three of the four semifinalists were amateurs. Germain Glidden beat Barnaby in five games in the final. In 1938 the Heights Casino in Brooklyn, which had been running a pro-am doubles tournament at the club since 1935, staged an open doubles tournament. The USSRA wrote a letter to the club, objecting to the tournament; the club, in turn, resigned from the association. In 1938 the Downtown Athletic Club in New York ran an open tournament. Both Neil Sullivan and Germain Glidden reached the quarterfinals, and Sherman Howes took George Cummings to five games before succumbing. Jack Summers won it that year, and

Scotty Ramsay beat Lester Cummings in the 1939 final. In 1941 the Nassau Country Club started a pro-am doubles tournament. Played in November each year, the tournament was another rare occasion for pros to make a little money on the weekend.

The problem of open tournaments was exacerbated by what Glidden evinced at the British open—the amateurs were as good as the pros. At the 1932 nationals, Larry Pool beat Wilmington Country Club's pro Dan Martella in an "amateur-professional match" held three hours before the finals. In a "scratch game" at the Harvard Club in New York in 1934, Beek Pool pushed Jack O'Donnell, the pro at the Downtown Athletic Club, to five games on a damp court. In 1934 *The New Yorker* speculated that the best amateur racquet sports talent in the country opted for squash rather than squash tennis because, in the former, one could beat the professionals. "Considerable discussion has been held among our members with reference to the advisability of open tournaments, both National and State," Edgar Patten wrote delicately in a 1932 squash pamphlet. "Possibly the time is not quite propitious for an event of this nature, but the great success of open golf tournaments and the tendency toward these events in tennis circles lead us to believe that the day is not far distant when such an event will be an annual fixture." A few pages away from Patten's article, Dick Cooke predicted that a national open would come in 1934. He was off by exactly twenty years.

CHAPTER FIVE

Send for the Drama Critic

They were winners. They stood with ramrod straight posture. They wore white flannel trousers and cable-knit cotton sweaters, as if they had just come off a cricket pitch for tea. They could be arrogant, flushed with pride and conviction. They had double-barreled names with roman numeral suffixes. They summered in Maine. They grew up on a squash court and could hit a nicking boast blindfolded. They loved the game. They volunteered for committees and handled meetings, discussions, research and correspondence, but they were never one of those helplessly devoted characters who exhibited signs of obsession. They had more USSRA presidents than any other club, and the first two executive directors, serving from 1974 to 2002, were members. They had the most knowledgeable fans and the classiest parties. They had beautiful courts.

Above all, they produced champions. They made Harry Cowles's factory at Harvard look like a cottage industry of sock darning. More male national champions came from this one club than all other clubs combined. Between 1939 and 1967, ten members won the men's nationals seventeen times; between 1934 and 1981 nine members won the men's intercollegiates; four members won the North American Open; three of the best six Americans on the professional hardball tour grew up there. In 1960 members played number one on the varsities of Princeton, Yale, Penn, Trinity, Williams, Amherst and Dickinson. On the doubles court, they were tantamount to automatic victory. Between 1938 and 2002, a club member was on the men's national doubles championship team fifty-two out of fifty-seven times. The club stamped its maroon and kelly green emblem, with a cocked cricket bat swooping down like a hard backhand reverse, on every corner of American squash.

They were the men of Merion.

The *caput mundi* of squash was birthed in 1865, when a band of sixteen young Philadelphians, the oldest of whom was twenty-two, formed a cricket team. They tossed their yorkers and lofted their sixes on a meadow next to the Wynnewood railway station. Over time their team expanded into the Merion Cricket Club, which moved to a fifteen-acre plot in Haverford. Merion added golf; built a clubhouse, which a fire burned down; rebuilt; added bowling and in 1900 erected three squash tennis courts. The magnificently appointed, red-brick clubhouse, designed by Frank Furness, resembled a British country house. It had a grand porch that overlooked the cricket pitch on which they also played croquet and lawn tennis.

Merion excelled in whatever it promoted. It boasted the best cricket players in America. It hosted the national archery championships. It started the Cricket League, the oldest amateur soccer league in the nation. It was home of Anne Townsend, captain of fifteen U.S. field hockey teams. Distinctive for its wicker flagsticks, Merion hosted a number of immortal golf events. In 1930 Bobby Jones completed his Grand Slam on the eleventh hole at Merion. Although Merion spun off its golf affiliate into a separate club in 1942, the two clubs remained closely allied both in spirit and in practice. Merion was a lodestone in the national tennis circuit. Its Pennsylvania Lawn Tennis Championship—along with Newport, Southampton, Seabright and Longwood—formed the heart of amateur tennis in America. Merion's tournament was started in 1894 and, for three Merion members—Bill Clothier, Dick Williams and Vic Seixas—it served as a launching pad toward winning the national tennis championship. Merion hosted the national tennis intercollegiates and the 1939 Davis Cup finals in which, with war being declared in Europe, Australia came back from a 0–2 deficit.

Visiting players stood in awe when they first glimpsed the lustrous turf of the great lawn and the imposing brick castle off Montgomery Avenue. "There was quite a bit to learn at Merion, and not all of it on the court or in the locker room," wrote Billy Talbert, an Ohioan who in 1938 played in the national intercollegiates at Merion on his first visit east. "There was something rich and heady in the atmosphere. Merion was a repository of Philadelphia's Main Line traditions. The clubhouse, the lawns, the people themselves had that patina of society—the tone that comes with social position established and reinforced over a period of generations. It was that special tone of 'Eastern casualness.' In the mellow sunlight of Merion, the girls in their light skirts and cashmeres seemed gayer and prettier; the men in their dressed-down flannels and seersuckers seemed suave and knowing. There was a wonderful sense of leisure being used with good taste and decency. . . . Most of us tennis players came from homes nothing like the great Main Line houses, and from public courts that had little in common with Merion's tailored grass, but they took us in like blood brothers."

At midcentury squash was synonymous with this elite country club anchored in the tony Main Line suburb of Philadelphia. *Sports Illustrated* dubbed it "the Yankee Stadium of squash." "You can usually tell Merion men by their style," wrote Herbert Warren Wind. "There is a classic purity about their shotmaking as they move into the ball with the free arm providing a fluid balance and then whip the ball with a wide, sweeping stroke." They played offensively, always looking to put the ball away quickly and decisively. They were sportsmen on and off the courts, but they were also fiercely competitive. "The squash player will take liberties as long as it is within the rules and the referee lets him get away with it," wrote Victor Niederhoffer, a Brooklyn-born squash champion who spent his career battling Merion giants. "The great gentlemen of Philadelphia squash are at least as vicious as the handball players of my youth. It is true, however, that they may transgress in the gentlemanly fashion of the Englishman rather than like a rattlesnake. In fact, I prefer the direct approach of the handball player. With the rattlesnake you know when they are going to strike. And if you give the rattlesnake half a chance, he will let you live." In 1979 Frank Satterthwaite wrote a squash memoir. With a catchy title, *The Three-Wall Nick and Other Angles*, and a Germain Glidden cartoon on the cover, his book received glowing reviews from magazines like *The New Yorker*. Satterthwaite had learned squash under Tommy Iannicelli at the Short Hills Club and led teams at Exeter and Princeton. He was reared in the inner sanctum of the preppy world, and yet even he was in awe of the Merion aura and mystique. In 1959 as an Exeter schoolboy, he played his first match against a Merion boy, Maurice Heckscher, in the quarterfinals of the annual holiday junior tournament at the Racquet & Tennis Club:

> Maurice was the first Merion player I'd ever played or even seen in action. . . . When I saw him stroke the ball during the warm-up, I got a shock comparable to the jolt a little child might receive when, having recently and proudly mastered stick-and-ball-print script, he catches a glimpse of an older child's tracebook and discovers the superior aesthetics of longhand. . . . I thought I had learned the squash stroke at Exeter: get down to the ball in a crouch that resembles a hunchback looking for a contact lens; tuck the elbow into the belly and keep it there so the backswing is short and follow-through checked at knee height, take a level, open-faced cut at the ball. All of which seemed fine until I caught

a glimpse of the top seed taking his racquet back, head high, and next swooping down to pick the ball up and send it on its way with a long, unfettered follow-through. . . . sometimes he added a stylish little curlicue at the peak of his windup. Very pretty. I say "caught a glimpse of his swing" because his dorsal region was pretty much obstructing my view. He got down to the ball not by going into a crouch but by tilting forward, with the result that his rear end stuck out in a very confident fashion. Almost as if it were on display, like a duck sticking his tail out in water. Certainly he was very much in his element. And I was in over my head.

Satterthwaite, fourth on the Exeter ladder, managed to beat Heckscher and win the tournament. Twenty years later, though, he was still coming to terms with Merion. In *Three-Wall Nick* he described the "classic Merion move" of backing off, the technique of backpedaling into the middle of the court to take a badly hit drive:

> The Merion players back you off with style. Sticking your rear end in somebody's face is not an inherently stylistic maneuver, but somehow the Merion players have managed to convert an essentially silly posture into an art form. Like figure skaters, they tilt their hindquarters gracefully upward as they glide backward. If they bump you, it's, "Sorry, I didn't know you were there." And that's the essence of the Merion attitude. They're not abrasive. They're not overtly aggressive. Not the pushers and shovers. Not the rock 'em, sock 'em sort. No, they keep their cool; they keep above it all. The very opposite of openly confronting their opponents, they ignore their opponent's presence. Their game is to act as if they are on the court all by themselves. They turn their backs. They take their room. They take their time. As in correct ballroom dancing, they move about gracefully but a little archly, with little pauses for dramatic effect. Just before they serve they strike the Merion pose: they lean forward with the back slightly arched and rear end tilting upward, and they hold it, not so that their opponents can get ready, but so that they can reaffirm their artistic control over the moment. Or so it seems. Between points they pad about the court with the quiet confidence that they're playing not a game, but their game.

Flipping the ignition switch on the Merion steamroller was Hunter Lott. He had a problem no coach could fix. He had a voracious forehand, one of the best in the game, which, as Jack Barnaby wrote, "everybody stayed away from it as though it were poison." The antidote was Lott's weak backhand. In tight matches it let him down. A Penn player who grew up across the street from the Cynwyd Club, Lott's nickname was the Master, and his calling card on the doubles court was a loud "Mah Ball" whenever a ball came down the middle. Lott could never push himself over the top in the national singles. Twice he lost to Charley Brinton in the finals. In 1949, at the age of thirty-four, he won his first and only title. His secret to success that year was not in retooling his backhand, à la Glidden under Cowles but, instead, becoming the first player to intentionally hit the double boast. Originally called the bow shot, it was a risky but spectacular shot in which the ball caromed off both side walls before dripping off the front wall. A sure winner if played properly and a sure loser if not, the double boast was like a three-cushion shot in billiards. It was so complicated that *Time* magazine placed an arrow-filled diagram above its article on the 1949 nationals. "I do not approve of this shot," wrote John Skillman in his coaching manual, "because it is mere luck to execute it correctly in play; if it is not played correctly, it is an easy setup." Lott ignored Skillman and, playing on his home courts at Merion, beat a forty-year-old Don Strachan in a bitterly contested finals, 15–12, 15–14, 12–15, 17–14. Satisfied with his breakthrough—he had never beaten Strachan before—Lott did not defend his title in 1950.

Lott's legacy was Merion's junior program. The club had always had fine professionals. Jimmy Tully, Sr. was the first squash coach when the courts were originally built in 1900. Bill White coached at Merion from 1915–55 (with a five-year absence in the early 1930s to start Princeton's squash program). After White retired, Brendan McRory and Jimmy Tully, Jr. ran the Merion program until Joe Coyle appeared in the seventies. Merion members, led by Lott, added an unusual dimension to the usual country club coaching regimen. Initiating what he called his "neighborhood" program, Lott and other veterans spent hours giving informal lessons to young players and playing practice matches. An avuncular presence, Lott imparted a passion for the game that his students forever retained.

The Master's first pupil was a man five years younger than himself, Charley Brinton. After graduating from Penn Charter, Brinton crossed over to Princeton, and, by the time he left in 1942, he was considered as brilliant a player as anyone to emerge from Harvard. Brinton was the consummate stylist. He flowed across the court. He had perfect footwork, perfect strokes and a tiny twinkle in his eyes which were all but covered by his black bushy eyebrows that arched up like dusty Gothic vaults. When asking for a let, he would stop, raise his left index finger and smile wordlessly at the referee. He had a backhand that rivaled Strachan's, a smoothness like Rawlins and a sense of anticipation like Glidden's. "Charley was the ideal champion," wrote Jack Barnaby, the Harvard coach. "Many of his drives were masterpieces, played with pistol shot crispness and so accurate they would glue to the wall after bouncing. . . . Brinton was a great match player. He was capable of a prolonged intensity of concentration, and he never until near the end of the game put all his chips on the table." As a junior and a senior at Princeton, Brinton won the intercollegiates and the nationals—no college player would again win the nationals twice until Kenton Jernigan did so in the 1980s. The Second World War intervened and the nationals were not held in 1943, 1944 and 1945. In 1946 the nationals again went to Brinton twice in a row before Stan Pearson, Jr. displaced him. Brinton's game began to wane, yet he was a force to be reckoned with until the mid-fifties: He won four straight DeForest-Tylers from 1949 to 1952, reached the semifinals of the 1951 nationals before succumbing to Henri Salaun, 15–12 in the fifth and, twice, in 1951 and 1952, reached the finals of the Harry Cowles.

Going from strength to strength, Merion outpaced every other squash club. Many older Philadelphians joined, most notably Roy Coffin and Don Strachan from Germantown Cricket Club and Willing Patterson from Philadelphia Cricket Club. In addition, a number of outstanding homegrown players at Merion gained national prominence: Joseph de V. Keefe, the former USSRA president and member of the 1925 touring team in England; LeRoy Lewis, the 1938 intercollegiate champion; Cyrus Polley, the 1947 veterans champion; David McMullin, the national doubles partner of Brinton; Vic Seixas, the former tennis great and three-time veterans squash champion; Rod Day, Jr.; Mifflin Large, former USSRA president, and Tanny Sargent. After the Second World War, these men guided a gaggle of boys into the heart of a squash dynasty: Sam and Ralph Howe, Claude Beer, Ramsay and Steve Vehslage, Kit Spahr, Jim Zug, Ben and Maurice Heckscher, George and John West, John Hentz, Jimmy Whitmoyer, Bill Morris and Larry Terrell. The Howes, Vehslages and Zugs lived within a block of the club, so Merion was their private playground. The ragamuffins kicked soccer balls, smashed tennis balls on the lawn, bowled, fenced with racquets and tore through the locker room shrieking. They invented a game called Bogle Ball, four or six to a singles court, balls whirling above the whitewashed floor. Acolytes of the hoary veterans, the boys absorbed the subtle rituals in the locker room and the tricks of the trade on court. They played in Merion's junior tournament, the Philadelphia & Districts. They picked up doubles as teenagers, years before most other players tried it out—Sam Howe and Steve Vehslage played in the 1956 national doubles when they were in high school. With nicknames like Sonny and Mo, they luxuriated in an amplitude of possibility.

Merion boys won the first six national junior tournaments. As adults they did even better. Ben Heckscher went to Choate, then to Harvard where he grabbed two intercollegiate titles and went 48–3 in his Crimson career. He won the nationals in 1959 and 1963. Fast on his feet, a good masker of the ball but erratic at times, Heckscher was a worthy successor to the Harvard greats of the Cowles era. He was sometimes viewed as the only Philadelphian who did not look like one, as he rarely played doubles and usually kept his competitive fires damped. One telling incident occurred in the semifinals of the 1963 nationals. After a demanding first game against Vic Niederhoffer, Heckscher took the next two games, which were marked by long, intense rallies. In the fourth, Niederhoffer was gassed and could barely return the ball. At 14–0, Heckscher purposefully double-faulted to prevent a goose-egg 15–0. He won the next point and the match. To some the gesture was a wonderful example of sportsmanship. To others it showed the lack of a killer instinct.

Sam Howe, a tall, hunchy player, played a more typical Merion game. He had such fluid strokes that observers compared his swing to Sam Snead's. He led Yale to its first national inter-city teams title, won two nationals and lost in the finals of three others. His first victory was earth-shattering. He had never won an adult tournament (his only trophy had been from winning the Yale freshman tournament) when he arrived at the Tennis & Squash Club in Buffalo for the 1962 nationals. Unseeded, he sneaked past Charlie Ufford in four games in the quarterfinals and Jim Zug in five in the semifinals to face his training partner Ben Heckscher in the finals. Sam lost the first two games badly, 15–3, 15–7. In the third game, Heckscher went up 9–7—six points from his second title. Sam shuddered at the thought that he was going to be on the losing end of the shortest final in history. Heckscher let up and began hitting fancy shots that tinned rather than nicked. Sam, clutching at any sign of hope, scrambled back from the abyss and won eight of the next ten points. He took the fourth game with ease, as Heckscher rationed himself for the fifth. Heckscher went ahead 7–6. Sam, having spent the winter working on his conditioning, had more life left in his legs despite the fact this was his twentieth game in forty-eight hours. He burst to a 14–9 lead. Now it was his turn to get wobbly. Heckscher gallantly hung in and brought the score to 14–13. Sam hit a winner and finished what many people believed was the greatest upset in the history of the nationals. Sam went on to an illustrious career. In Chicago five years later, he won the nationals without loss of a game. He was one of a handful of players to win every major amateur tournament at least once. His annus mirabilis was 1967. In a feat never repeated, Sam won the U.S. and Canadian national singles and doubles.

Sam almost made 1967 a perfect year, but lost in the finals of the North American Open by two points. His opponent was his younger brother, Ralph Howe. While at Yale, Ralph absorbed the Skillman edict to volley, volley, volley and turned into a player different from his older brother. He loped around the court like a cheetah, rustling in the savanna grasslands of the back corners before pouncing on an easy kill up front. Some compared Ralph to the ultimate up-tempo player, Germain Glidden. But Ralph hit the reverse when Glidden hit the three-wall, and Ralph played the front end of points a lot less furiously, as he loved tossing up soft parabolic serves that seemed to disappear in the lofty ceilings at Payne Whitney. Ralph took two intercollegiates and one national title. His most memorable achievement was a shocking weekend at the 1967 North American Open at the Badminton & Squash Club on Atwater Street in Montreal. He beat the great Mo Khan in the semifinals. Khan, the British and North American Open champion, had never lost to a nonfamily member in America. The wagering in the gallery was not over who would win but how many points Ralph would get in a losing effort (the bets ranged from seventeen to twenty-seven points). Ralph surprised the gamblers by winning, 15–12 in the fifth. The third game was when he really won the match. Down 2–0 in a set-five tiebreaker, Ralph hit what Jimmy Whitmoyer, the USSRA yearbook editor, later described as "the five greatest shots in the history of squash." Five straight times Ralph drove backhand cross-courts into the sidewall nick. In the finals he faced his brother Sam who had outlasted Vic Niederhoffer in an equally epic match. The brothers, both exhausted by their earlier rounds, produced a tense and uneven finish, with Ralph squeaking by, 15–12, 15–13, 5–15, 13–15, 15–13.

Steve Vehslage made even a bigger splash than the Howes as a young player. He won the first three national juniors, and at Princeton he won three straight intercollegiates, the first player to do so. He played an explosive, overwhelming game. If Vehslage saw the moon, he would shoot it. As with the Pools three decades before, the effort to hit hard on every ball demanded a high level of fitness and concentration. This necessary training brought him the national title in 1965 at the Hartford Golf Club, but just as often it led to fatigue and dispirited matches. Vehslage had another, more unusual problem: unexplainably, he passed out if bumped in the head or shoulders. It started when playing soccer at Haverford School. Going for a headball, he bashed into an opponent and was laid out for a few minutes. Between the start of college and 1966, he estimated he had lost consciousness on court about thirty times. He fell like an anchor to the floor, spreadeagled on his back and lay there for two minutes, then regained consciousness and soon returned to normal with no side effects. In the 1965–66 season, Charlie Ufford knocked him out in the New York state tournament, and Bob Hetherington did likewise in the Gold Racquets. Batteries of tests did not lead to an answer for the blackouts. When they became too frequent, he quit.

The archetypal Merion player was Diehl Mateer. It was Mateer who was one-half of the most gripping squash rivalry of the twentieth century. His foil was Henri Salaun. Mateer was based in Philadelphia; Salaun was in Boston, exacerbating the antagonism between the two original squash powers. Mateer was six foot two, heavily muscled, thick-wristed and a tad over 200 pounds, the heavyweight champion; Salaun was five foot six, 135 pounds, a bantam with amazing acceleration. Mateer was the hammer. He lashed his rails at will. You could see his attack coming, but it was so perfectly executed you could do nothing to prevent it. Jack Barnaby said that "getting a point away from him is much like pulling a crooked wisdom tooth." Salaun was the rock. He was the genius retriever, the sniper who mastered the rarely seen soft reverse corner and a shot no one else dared to hit—the offensive lob. Mateer was all sangfroid, coolly taking stock, never ruffled; Salaun was agitated, distracted, apt to complain. Mateer was old-school, the plenipotentiary envoy of the Merion mission, brimming with his Main Line pedigree; Salaun was a minister without portfolio, a solitary French refugee who spun through practice partners like a washing machine. Mateer loved doubles; Salaun never played a day of doubles, because he hated giving up control of his destiny. Mateer retired from competitive singles; Salaun started playing in age-group tournaments and never stopped. Mateer was the alpha male; Salaun was the lone wolf.

Differences defined their rivalry but, underneath, they had a wealth of similarities. Mateer went to Episcopal Academy and played at Merion; Salaun went to Deerfield Academy and played at the University Club of Boston. Both curiously went to universities—Mateer to Haverford College, Salaun to Wesleyan—that did not have a strong squash program. (Haverford did not even have its own courts or team when Mateer was there.) Both were driven athletes. Mateer played twice at Forest Hills; Salaun was an All-American soccer player and regularly ranked in the first ten of New England tennis.

Fourteen when his father joined Merion in 1942, Mateer immediately excelled at squash. He captained his high school team at Episcopal. When he first won the Philadelphia & Districts, over an Episcopal teammate, John Hentz, Mateer was "bundled in a gray sweat suit and Turkish towel, as a precaution against more cold," as one reporter noticed, demonstrating early evidence that he had absorbed that Merion look of cool. Mateer won the intercollegiates his sophomore year, beating the Yale captain-elect Bruce Bayne, in straight sets in the finals at Payne Whitney. He won his first adult tournament in December 1948, when he beat Andy Ingraham and then Carter Fergusson to win the Gold Racquets. In the quarter-finals of the 1949 nationals at Merion, he rushed to a 2–1 lead on Don Strachan by impudently challenging Strachan's backhand. He lost in five but everyone took notice. Groomed by Hunter Lott, Mateer proved adept on the doubles court, and he and Lott began to win the national doubles. In 1950 Mateer was unable to collect his third intercollegiate championship as a senior because it was scheduled in Amherst the same weekend as the national doubles were in St. Louis. A sign of Mateer's precociousness, it was the first time a player had such a conflict. Mateer's decision to play in the national doubles indicated that he was tired of sleepwalking to victory in college matches. He wanted real silver, not the undergraduate substitute.

Expected to immediately start carving his name on the twin-handled Knox Cup for the national singles champion, Mateer went titleless until 1954. He was always the favorite. He won all the major invitationals. He won every other tournament he entered in 1952–53. He was ranked number one in the nation. He was national doubles champion. But he could not win the biggest title. The problem was unsteady nerves, a lack of fitness in long, close matches and a predilection for trying to smash his way through the pressure points. In 1949 he let a 2–0 lead over Don Strachan in the quarterfinals slip away. In 1951 he tumbled to Jack Isherwood, a low-ranked Pittsburgher. Nat Glidden, Germain's older brother, wrote in 1953 of Mateer's slow improvement on a crucial matter: "Where three years ago (as with Isherwood in the nationals) a booming tin shot might have thrown off his confidence and touch, Diehl now accepts the occasional error without loss to his game of more than one point." Still, Nat

Glidden noted, his biggest weakness was "an inflexibility of stroke pro-duction." Mateer did not know how to ease up and spin and cut rather than simply blast the ball.

A couple of players from hitherto unknown lands, Eddie Hahn and Harry Conlon, also stood in the way. The Hahn brothers, Joe, Happy and Eddie, grew up in the Bronx. In the 1920s Joe Hahn, then a physical-education teacher in New York, moved to Sidney Hill, a fitness club in Cleveland. The professional there, Harry Conlon, Sr., taught him squash. In 1932 Joe transferred to Sidney Hill's Detroit operation, the Uptown and Downtown Clubs. He persuaded both his younger brothers, Ed and Happy (Henry) to join him in Detroit. They started playing squash but did not quite get a grip on it. In 1937 Joe entered the Michigan states. "I thought I was quite something with a racquet because I could beat the fat guys at our club," he told a reporter in 1951 with usual Hahn bluntness. He lost in the second round. He soon improved to a first-class level. He took one Canadian nationals, lost five times in the finals of the national veterans and captained the 1942 Detroit side to its historic victory in the national five-man teams. He was effusive, never refused a bet, avoided training at all costs and could imitate any accent or person. Happy moved west to manage the Milwaukee Athletic Club and was a fifteen-time Wis-consin champion. Eddie Hahn, though, had the most memorable career. In 1938 he returned to New York and worked for three years as a police-man in the Bronx. He enlisted in the Army during the war and upon demobilization, returned to Detroit to run with Joe a car dealership. He also took up his brother's game in earnest. In 1947 he captained Detroit to a second national team title. In 1950 and 1951 he became the first non-college-trained player to win the nationals since the early days of squash and also the oldest player, at thirty-seven, to win since Englishman Timmy Robarts in 1924. Eddie also won the Canadian nationals in 1950, beating Joe in four close games in the finals to snatch the first North American double since Beek Pool in 1932. On court "Steady Eddie" had the patience of Job and was considered a pure retriever. Barnaby said he "was like a glacier. He didn't seem to be going anywhere very fast but he always got there." He disconcertingly watched his opponent with his face masked by the head of his racquet, like a prisoner peering through the bars of a cell. With a puckish smile, graying hair, a rumply belly and his legs looking like two fire hydrants, the Methuselah Hahn did not look stylish on the court, but he had a rum runner's wits.

The title went from a Bronx cop to an Air Force flyboy. In 1952 Harry Conlon beat Mateer in the finals. Conlon, the son and namesake of Joe

Hahn's mentor, was as unlikely a national champion as Eddie Hahn. Thin as a spring onion and only nineteen years old, he had a famous trick of turning his head just as he hit a reverse corner to stare, mouth agape, at his opponent. He loved taking the ball off the back wall and hated to volley. "Conlon never uses two words when one will suffice," wrote one reporter. "Loose, limber and tough as an old razor strop, Harry plays the same game, no matter who his foe might be." At age eighteen, playing at the University Club of Buffalo, where his father worked as a professional, Conlon won the Buffalo city championship. Then he abandoned thoughts of squash glory by enlisting in the Air Force. After boot camp in upstate New York and training school in Cheyenne, he landed at Scott Field in Illinois. One day he went into the base's gymnasium looking for a game of basketball and noticed a dusty sign that said SQUASH COURTS. He started to play again and wrangled a weekend furlough to play in a doubles event at the Racquet Club of St. Louis. When he won the tournament, with Homer Dixon of Chicago, Conlon was permitted to train for the Western championships. At the Cincinnati Country Club, he surprised everyone by reaching the finals where he faced Eddie Hahn. It was a barnburner, with Conlon going up 2–0, then 13–12 in the fifth, before whiffing on a hard Hahn serve and tinning two dropshots to lose 15–13. Two weeks later at the nationals, Conlon, wearing his favorite Kennion High School sweater, beat Eddie Hahn in the semifinals in four. Harry, Sr., heard of the victory and flew from Buffalo to New Haven in time to witness the Monday final against Mateer. It was considered one of the roughest in history. Thirteen lets were given in the first game, including six consecutive lets at 8–4 (the referee was Jim Traviss, the president of the Canadian SRA). Mateer was up, 11–3 in the second game, but Conlon scrapped back to 14–all; Mateer chose no-set and luckily won the point. In the fourth Conlon jumped to a 5–0 lead, but Mateer did not panic and again won in a tiebreaker. In the fifth Mateer moved ahead early, but Conlon was not to be denied, winning 15–12, 14–15, 15–11, 16–18, 15–8. The day after his win, he flew back to Illinois. The entire base came out to greet him, with a general, two colonels and a brass band leading the cheers and his squadron carrying him off the tarmac. Conlon thereafter won a couple of invitational tournaments, but never again was a finalist in the nationals. Just once, he had caught lightning in a bottle.

The 1953 nationals were remarkable. No other nationals have matched any of these three statistics: five of the last seven matches went to five games (three of the five went to tiebreakers in the fifth game), the eight quarterfinalists captured a total of fifteen nationals, and both of the finalists were unseeded. For one observer, Stew Brauns, the tournament was "the greatest for sustained excitement and high caliber of play . . . akin to a 1955 Chateau Lafite-Rothschild." Played in the cold courts at the Tennis & Squash Club in Buffalo, the nationals were a vintage that would never appear again. There were twenty entries in the main draw, twenty-two in the veterans and eleven five-man teams, representing cities as far west as Chicago and as far south as Washington, D.C. The six-row gallery at the T&S's main court seated just eighty spectators. In three decades such a small, parochial tournament would look hopelessly antiquated.

Upsets came right at the start. Charlie Ufford, the intercollegiate champion, lost 15–11 in the fifth to Charley Brinton. Showing remarkable stamina, Brinton then went on to push Diehl Mateer to 17–all in the fifth game of their quarterfinal match. On the double-match point, Brinton broke his racquet returning a sizzling Mateer cross-court and tinned the ball. Harry Conlon, the defending champion, beat Henri Salaun, 13–15, 17–16, 15–12, 7–15, 17–14, in the brilliant quarterfinal match before losing to Cal McCracken in three in the semifinals. McCracken, an Englewood Field Club star, astutely figured out Conlon's Achilles heel—a weak volley—and tossed up high, slow lobs that shoved Conlon into the back corners. In the other semifinal in the afternoon, Mateer went up, 12–10, in the fifth game against Ernie Howard, but a couple of lucky mishits and Mateer tins gave Howard an 18–15 win. The finals looked like a sure thing for McCracken, for he had beaten Howard in three games the year before. Howard, a Toronto bond salesman and member of the Badminton & Racquet Club, was no pushover. The first Canadian to win a match at the U.S. nationals, he volleyed like a Yalie and loved long points. "He would dart around the court like a drop of mercury on a sheet of glass," wrote Brauns. Howard went up 2–1. During the five-minute rest period, Ned Bigelow stood up in the gallery and said loudly to the crowd which was filled with Torontoans, "Where is that Canadian money?" There was a rush to place bets, and Jim Traviss was enlisted as bookkeeper. Bigelow looked clever as McCracken evened the match with a 15–10 fourth game. In the fifth, the score leveled at 11–all. Howard won three prolonged, pressure-filled rallies to go to 14–11 but then tinned twice while going for winners. At 14–13 he returned a McCracken serve cross-court, and McCracken knocked it into the tin. Howard became the first Canadian to win the U.S. nationals.

One story lost in the special narrative of the 1953 nationals was that Henri Salaun had failed again. Born in the old Brittany port town of Brest, Henri

Salaun was introduced to racquet sports by his father, who returned from an outing to Roland Garros to build a clay tennis court at the family's summer house. A red-haired youth, lean as a jackknife, Salaun took up tennis with a competitive spirit. In the spring of 1940, though, the slap of the tennis ball was replaced by the boom of artillery fire. Nazi tanks rolled into Brest, and his father was taken prisoner. His mother spied two fishermen, and, ten minutes later, she and her fourteen-year-old son were on a sloop sailing for Plymouth. From there to London, then Halifax, and by August 1940 the young Salaun was living in Boston. Not knowing English, Salaun taught himself by watching movies. He spent two years at Deerfield Academy, captaining the tennis team and playing striker on the soccer team. Henry Poor, the tennis and squash coach at Deerfield, tried to persuade the little French boy that he should quit basketball and try squash. Senior fall, Salaun succumbed to Poor's encouragement, but with an unusual twist. "Henri came to me," Poor remembered, "and said, 'Mr. Poor, I'd like to play squash, but I'd like to do it differently. I'd like to practice individually, just with you for five days. I don't want opponents, just you.' I agreed and for five afternoons we played alone. Then I put him at the bottom of the ladder. Within two weeks, Henri was the best player at Deerfield." At Wesleyan, Salaun played squash for Jim Reid, Sr., and twice was an All-American in soccer. His studies were interrupted by a stint working as an interpreter for the U.S. Army in France—he had become an American citizen in early 1945. After graduating in 1949, he worked at Governor Dummer School, then as a salesman for Bancroft, before starting his own sporting goods business.

Cutting his teeth in earnest after moving back to Boston and joining the University Club, Salaun improved through a procession of sparring partners, whom he liked to play three or four times a week. Unusually for a top player, Salaun chose men not as good as he was, and, if they reached his level, he dropped them for a weaker opponent. He perfected an unorthodox hammer grip similar to Pancho Gonzales's. He ran four miles every morning. Salaun refused to leave the club in the evening until his weight was 132 pounds. He would jog on an indoor track or sit in the steam room or play another match—anything to get the gray standing scale to balance at 132.

In February 1951, after winning a number of winter tournaments, Salaun made it to the finals of the U.S. nationals at the Lake Shore Club in Chicago. Facing the defending champion Eddie Hahn, Salaun broke a string in the fourth game and borrowed a racquet from Roger Bakey, a fellow Bostonian, for the fifth game. "It was strung very tight," Salaun recalled. "They said my racquets were strung like seaweed, but I liked them loose. Bakey's was as tight as a drum and I had trouble controlling it." Eddie jumped to a 9–1 lead. His brother Joe, sitting in the front row of the gallery, sighed and said, "Don't let up, don't let up." Salaun changed his game, went for risky shots and evened the match at 13–all. Eddie called no set. He won the first point, then Salaun grabbed the second. At 14–all, championship point, twenty years after Larry Pool had beaten Don Strachan by one point, Eddie hit a roll corner. Salaun slipped up front to retrieve it and flipped up a lob. Eddie backpedaled, trying desperately to hit it, but it was too high for him. And too high for the court. The ball flew directly into the front row of the gallery and landed, unceremoniously, in Joe Hahn's lap. "I looked up," said Eddie Hahn years later, "and it didn't come down."

Two weeks later, facing Ernie Howard in the finals of the Canadian nationals in Montreal, Salaun again faced a double championship point. This time he prevailed, but the U.S. nationals remained a bugaboo. In 1952 Salaun lost in the quarterfinals to Carter Fergusson. Up 9–6 in the fifth, Salaun crumbled and lost nine straight points. He walked off the court with bleeding knees from diving futilely for Fergusson's reverses. In 1953 Fergusson inflicted an even worse defeat on Salaun. In the finals of the DeForest-Tyler in Plainfield, New Jersey, Salaun won the first two games, 15–11 and 15–5, and was serving for the match at 14–7 in the third. A half hour later he had lost to Fergusson in five—one the most epochal collapses in top-flight tournament history.

Bête noire for the men's tournament circuit, Salaun bathed his game in histrionics. He was notorious for quitting matches before he lost them. Opponents recall that he halted matches incessantly, claiming a litany of physical ailments. When he crumbled to Fergusson at the DeForest-Tyler, it was a pulled stomach muscle at 14–7 that was his excuse for his capitulation. Once, he left the court after the first game of a match and put on a sweater; after the second game, he put on sweatpants. He violated the one-minute rule for breaks in between games. Playing Hashim Khan in the semifinals of the 1963 Canadian Open, he went into the locker room after the first game. Disrobing completely, he took a shower, then changed into entirely new clothes. He did the same thing after the second game. "He lay on his back moaning," recalled Cal MacCracken of a match against Salaun. "I really thought he would never walk again. I thought his leg was permanently injured. It seemed that bad. He got up and said in his heavy French accent, 'I teenk I cahn plaie.' Salaun then got fifteen out of the next sixteen points and beat me easily in the fourth and fifth games."

SQUASH

Eddie Hahn told *Sports Illustrated* in 1958, "When Henri goes down, you never know whether to send for a doctor or a drama critic."

Like two young lions circling each other before their battle for supremacy in the pride, Mateer and Salaun scrapped a number of times early in their careers. They first met in March 1949, in the semifinals of the inter-collegiates at Princeton. Mateer, en route to his second straight title, won handily. A year later, in the 1950 nationals at the University Club in New York, Salaun, playing in his first nationals, reached the second round where he bumped into Mateer. "I hadn't even heard of him," Mateer recalled years later. "I had completely forgotten about the intercollegiates and had no idea who this little Frenchman was." Salaun gave notice, matching Mateer game for game and going up 10–6 in the fifth. Mateer, no longer diffident, smashed through with eight straight points, but not nine to clinch the match. At 14–10, Salaun refused to slink away and sent the game into overtime. In the tiebreaker, Mateer blanked Salaun, winning the game, 17–14, but he was so drained that he abruptly lost his quarterfinal match. In 1952 Mateer beat Salaun in four games in the semifinals of the Gold Racquets. The next weekend Salaun shocked Mateer in the Philadelphia versus Boston match in the Lockett Cup. Mateer was down 2–1 in games, but up 12–6 in the fourth. Letting up a bit to conserve energy for a fifth game, he left Salaun too much room. Salaun took the game, 16–14, and dealt Mateer his only defeat that season besides his loss to Ernie Howard in the nationals.

In 1953–54 matters reached a boiling point. Mateer and Salaun were the two best squash players in the country and were due to prove that point at the nationals. The season saw both in top form. Salaun had won the U.S. Open, the Ticknor-Glidden and the Harry Cowles. At the Ticknor-Glidden, he beat Mateer 15–10 in the fifth game, and at the Cowles he ended Mateer's string of four consecutive victories with a four-game victory. However, Mateer beat Salaun in two titanic matches. In a folderol disguised as the final of the December 1953 Gold Racquets, Mateer controversially beat Salaun in four courts. After a cold week, it was an unseasonably warm December afternoon in Cedarhurst, and a slick film of moisture covered the plaster walls at Rockaway. "By the middle of the first game, the walls were sweating so much we could barely control the ball," said Mateer. After the first game, the players, the referee and the entire gallery moved next door to another court. After the next game, another court. "We played in all four courts," said Mateer. "It was really a ridiculous situation, but you're in there to win. I was able to beat Henri that day because I could hit the ball harder and make it skid." Mateer won the match, 15–11 in the fifth. Salaun was furious. Mateer and others recall that in the locker room he took the Steubenglass bowl he had just received as runnerup and smashed it on the floor. (Salaun claimed he accidentally dropped it.) He never played in that tournament again. At the Thistle Club in Hamilton two months later, they met in the finals of the Canadian nationals and Mateer survived a thriller, 15–13 in the fifth. A power failure interrupted the third game, and Salaun, used to such stoppages, sparked his game in the fourth but could not take the fifth. At the 1954 nationals, eight days later at the Pittsburgh Golf Club, the kettle had been taken off the stove. In an anticlimactic final, Mateer burned through in three easy games.

Five more times they met in the finals of the nationals, creating a rivalry that is unequaled in the history of the nationals. In 1955 Mateer had another banner year. He ran the table to win the Ticknor-Glidden—beating Salaun after being down, 9–6, in the fifth game—the Gold Racquets, the U.S. Open, the Badminton & Racquet's Pro-Am, the Canadian amateurs—beating Salaun 15–7 in the fifth—and the Pennsylvania states. Just as in 1953, his luck ran dry at the nationals. It was Salaun's moment to shake the monkey off his back and win his first national championship. He beat Ernie Howard in the finals, with Mateer slipping in his first match of the tournament to Henry Foster. In 1956 they again met in the finals of the nationals in Hartford. Mateer breezed in three, with Salaun having trouble covering Mateer's boasts. In 1957 in New York, Salaun turned the tables on Mateer in a fantastic four-game final of the nationals at the University Club. Salaun dove six times in the fourth game alone. He beat Mateer again the next year in Annapolis, again in four games. In 1959 Mateer boycotted the nationals at Harvard, claiming that Salaun should be considered a professional because his name was on a Bancroft racquet that he was flogging as a Bancroft salesman. Salaun failed to capitalize on his rival's absence, as the young Ben Heckscher kept the Merion flag flying with his surprising upset of Salaun in the semifinals. Heckscher, having beaten Salaun earlier in the season, had the advantage of playing on his old college courts. Salaun, coming on court after the break with a 2–1 lead, lost his concentration when the referee berated him for taking more than the allotted five minutes. Heckscher snatched the fourth easily. Down 11–4, then 14–8 in the fifth, Salaun made another of his last-minute comebacks, but Heckscher, at 14–13, ended a nail-biting rally with a perfectly placed backhand reverse. "The gallery roared its approval," wrote Ernie Richmond, the USSRA president. In 1960, at the famous snowbound Rochester nationals, Mateer and Salaun again met in the finals. At 10–all in the fifth game, "showtime" in the argot of players, Salaun stumbled. He tinned a risky reverse from a back corner and muffed a volley. Mateer powdered a cross-court winner, then Salaun bungled two more shots to hand his antagonist the victory.

The final pas de deux came in 1961. Every year but one in the last eleven, Salaun or Mateer had been in the final. Each had won three national titles. A fourth title would elevate the winner into the elite of squash history—at that point, only Pearson and Brinton had gone beyond the hat trick. Four hundred people crammed into the innovative galleries at the new Ringe courts at Pennsylvania, "limp with excitement," according to Joe Hahn, with the idea of seeing a sixth Mateer versus Salaun national final. It had been an interesting tournament. Salaun had run easily through the draw, dropping just two games along the way. Mateer, on the other hand, had reaped what Merion had sowed. He had three leg-sapping matches against some of Merion's young Turks, going to four against Ralph Howe and Jim Zug, then the distance, 15–11 in the fifth, against Ben Heckscher in the semifinals. The first game of the finals saw Mateer and Salaun nervously jab for weaknesses. Neither had a lead of more than one point. At 2–all in the 13–all set-five tiebreaker, Mateer broke loose and with cold calculation smacked three straight winners. Salaun raced to a 9–1 lead in the second and won it easily, 15–5. In the third it went to 11–all, and the match pivoted on the next few points. Salaun got streaky and, after a Mateer tin, slapped three consecutive clean dropshots. Mateer was making too many mistakes, fans could see. He looked wan and rueful. He made a total of twenty-seven unforced errors in the match. Salaun had only nine. In the fourth Mateer mounted a last-ditch challenge. He grabbed a 6–1 lead, but Salaun, anxious to avoid a fifth game as he had never won one in the finals of the nationals, tied it up at 7–all and, at 12–all, copped the next three points to win the match. Mateer stared at the floor for a moment, then looked up and embraced Salaun. FINIS TO SALAUN-MATEER SERIES trumpeted the USSRA headline. Mateer, who had been threatening to quit singles for years, announced his retirement to the gallery at the end of the match. With his rival out of commission, the wind somehow went out of Salaun's sails, and he only once more made it to the finals of the nationals.

G. Diehl Mateer, Jr. and Henri R. Salaun. These two names appear more often on the champions boards of more clubs than any other player. They appeared in sixteen nationals finals between the two of them. Like two strands of DNA spiraling together, each was incomplete without the other. Mateer needed the pesky Salaun to draw attention away from his arrogant Merion style. Salaun needed the powerful Mateer to act as a Goliath against his perennial underdog David status. In 1958 *Sports Illustrated* commissioned a New York freelancer, Tom Lineaweaver, to write a cover story leading up to the 1958 nationals. A member of Merion, Lineaweaver naturally had an affinity for Mateer, but he put forth a balanced account of the rivalry: "A Mateer-Salaun match is a sight to see. It is invariably one which by its sheer power and virtuosity time and time again lifts the gallery off its collective seat and drops it back limp. Mateer plays in the classic Philadelphia style. . . . His strokes are sweeping and lovely to watch. His size (6 foot 1, 185 pounds) not only gives him the ability to cover court, but he can hit the ball so hard that spectators wince. He has little to say during a match beyond an occasional 'good shot.'" In comparison, Salaun, Lineaweaver wrote, "is well muscled and as agile as a cat. There are few shots in a squash court that he cannot retrieve, and fewer that he cannot make. His racquet work in controlling the ball is astonishing." The significant difference off court, according to Lineaweaver, was that Mateer had four sons and a daughter and was vice president of his father's manufacturing company. His family and work took his time, and, with a month-and-a-half of doubles tacked on to the end of a squash season, his winters were pretty much a hurried blur. Lineaweaver noted, on the other hand, that "Salaun lives for squash," and, although he helped raise two sons, his life was focused on tournaments. It was not silver he was searching for, because he stuck his trophies in a steamer trunk, but something more intangible. Lupine, ever grasping for victory, Salaun never gave up playing. The year after he lost to Sam Howe in the semifinals of the nationals, he turned forty and started playing in the veterans (forty and over) nationals. He won it that year without losing a game. He went on to win six veterans, five 50+, four 60+, four 65+, four 70+ and three 75+. His only notable loss was in 1975 when, in the semifinals of the veterans at the age of forty-nine, he was up 2–0 against a fit forty-year-old Pete Bostwick and lost, 15–12 in the fifth. The coda to Mateer versus Salaun came, in fact, in the final of the 1971 national veterans at Penn. Playing on the same court as their grand finale in 1961, this postlude made sweet music. According to Bob Lehman, the Met SRA yearbook chronicler, it was "fascinating to the indoctrinated squash aficionado, particularly the lovely fencing at the start. Long, probing shots, testing eye and mobility, were interspersed with sharp or soft short shots, but only when they would seem to produce a point." Before the match Salaun said he would not feed Mateer any high backhand volleys, because Mateer was brilliant at snapping reverse corners off them. Yet all four times Salaun was forced to throw up such a lob, Mateer tinned—a bad sign for the Merion star. At 14–10 in the fifth, Salaun won the last point of the match "on an unavoidable, unfortunate and ironic drive into his opponent's rump."

Mateer was a bit like Babe Ruth, a larger-than-life hero who epitomized an era. Salaun was like Hank Aaron, the steady, somewhat persecuted and misunderstood successor. Mateer won two U.S. Opens to Salaun's one. He twice beat two Khans in a single day: at the 1955 Badminton & Racquet pro-am (beating Roshan and Azam, both 3–2) and at the 1959 U.S. Open (beating Roshan, 3–0, and Hashim, 15–12 in the fifth). He retired from singles at the relatively sprightly age of thirty-two, so people remembered him in his prime, rather than as a septuagenarian still skittering around a court. Mateer moved on to the more genteel doubles court and became the best amateur left-wall doubles player in history. Late in his doubles career he was the sentimental favorite, trying to win the nationals partnered with his sons. One could dismiss the parvenu Frenchman but not the leader of Merion. Mateer's style was hardwired with orthodoxy. Salaun's was all calculated. He trained, he kept in shape, he prepared for matches. In the seventies Salaun was embroiled in a controversy with the USSRA because he slapped his name on some French sneakers he was importing. Calling him a professional, as Mateer had in 1959, the association banned him on the eve of the 1972 nationals, reversed the ban a few months later upon appeal and then in 1975 banned him from sanctioned tournaments for a year. In response, Salaun turned professional, joined the North American Professional SRA and played in its 1976 veteran championships, losing in the semifinals. A year later he was reinstated as an amateur. Salaun, unlike Mateer, volunteered in district squash administration; he ran the Massachusetts Squash Racquets Association in the late sixties and helped direct the 1968 nationals in Boston, which went so smoothly that for one of the first times it made a profit. Salaun's lack of sportsmanship clung to the memory more than anything else. Although his matches with Mateer were quite clean—the 1960 finals in Rochester had just two lets—Salaun's antics with lesser players damaged his reputation. One never wanted to call for a doctor at a squash match, but it was even worse to call for a drama critic.

The cover photograph for *Sports Illustrated*—it was the first and only time the magazine posed a squash player on its cover—spoke volumes about the two men. Mateer was late to the photo shoot at the University Club in New York and did not have time to shave. Dan Weiner, the photographer, posed him leaning against a pockmarked side wall, smiling, confident, his magnificent right arm almost propping up the wall. Salaun, in the foreground, stared with his slanting half-smile as indecipherable as Mona Lisa's, his shirt uncomfortably buttoned and twisted around his ribcage. He casually held his racquet in his left hand—or so it seemed to the hundreds of thousands of people who saw the 10 February 1958, twenty-five-cent issue. But to squash insiders, it was an ugly thumb in the eye of amateur squash. The racquet Salaun posed with was the one he played with, but also the one that he sold for a living, the distinctive Bancroft emblem clearly presented to the camera.

In 1954 squash in America went open and the division between amateurs and professionals slowly began to fade. Ned Bigelow was the instigator. Bigelow, a self-made millionaire and partner at Dillon Read, a banking firm, was not a blustering newcomer, but rather the ne plus ultra of New York squash. He joined the Heights Casino soon after it was founded in 1904, near the end of Montague Street in Brooklyn Heights. Bigelow created the persona, much copied, of the New York squashman: rabidly social, singlemindedly dedicated, sartorially slick, brimming with a Brahmin bearing, quietly at peace in the private club, generous with time and money and an inconsistent subscriber to the ideals of tradition. He was president of the Metropolitan SRA from 1933 to 1936 and served in countless administrative positions thereafter. Nationally, Bigelow became the leading New York representative in the USSRA hierarchy, serving on numerous committees and as vice president from 1935 to 1937; he was denied the presidency of the USSRA, however, because Philadelphians considered him too progressive.

In 1938 Bigelow founded the first open doubles tournament in the country, the Heights Casino Open. An open singles tournament, though, was a different kettle of fish, and it took years before Bigelow was able to hook the USSRA. In 1950 Bigelow ran the nationals, which were held in New York for only the third time in history (as opposed to nineteen times in Philadelphia). The tournament was a rousing success, but there had been an unusually loud outcry among the powerful New York professionals about being banned from entering. In April 1951, a day after he retired from Dillon Read, Bigelow departed on a squash Grand Tour, an eight-month, twenty-two country expedition. He originally had hoped to go on a holiday from squash. "As a matter of fact," he said after his return, "I forgot about squash until I got to India. Then I had a devil of a time thinking about anything else." In a Bombay bank changing money, he over-heard some men talking about squash. He introduced himself. Members of the Bombay Gymkhana, they agreed to show Bigelow their courts. He then went to the Cricket Club of India and met the best professional in the country, Abdul Bari. Stirred by that visit, Bigelow continued to seek out other pros in such hotbeds of squash as Egypt and Pakistan.

At the autumn USSRA executive committee meeting, he reported on his tour and detailed his hopes for some sort of national open tournament. "This concept met with sturdy resistance within the Board," wrote one member, Stew Brauns, "for there were those who believe Amateurs should not compete against Professionals." Bigelow, functioning, as Herbert Warren Wind wrote, "as a sort of Sol Hurok of American squash," had to throw a lot of fishing lines into the water. A number of squash heavyweights, most notably Germain Glidden, fought against an open tournament. Bigelow offered a compromise of a round-robin tournament. Al Chassard, president of the U.S. professional association, thought the round robin was not feasible and feared a regular sixteen-man draw would be too strenuous for his otherwise tournament-poor professionals. Hunter Lott suggested a small tournament with just eight players, as a way to gauge reaction. Bigelow pointed to the Union Boat Club, which had run the Boston Open from 1949 to 1952, and Badminton & Racquet Club in Toronto, which had started a professional-amateur invitation tournament in January 1953. It made no sense to limit the draw of a national open to just eight men when individual clubs were beginning to legitimize open play. Late in 1953, Bigelow elucidated, in bellicose tones, the exact purpose of his tournament: "This First Open Championship is not, as some mistakenly think, to determine whether Professional players are better than Amateurs, or whether Amateurs are better than Professionals. Whether a player is a Professional or Amateur, a Foreigner or an American, is of little consequence. No distinction in the entry list has been made or intended. We have sought only a fast field and we have eliminated many entrants who in our opinion are not today the top flights. Our purpose is to seek out the one best squash player who is available, regardless of his vocation, residence, nationality, color, creed or club affiliation, and hail him as 'The United States Open Champion.'"

On New Year's Day 1954, the first United States Open began at the University Club in New York.

It was not a success. It was much, much more. The tournament changed squash literally overnight. By the finals on Sunday afternoon, four days later, New York was agog about this bat, ball and wall game. The front page of the sports pages of major newspapers, including the *New York Times*, the *New York Herald Tribune, Newark Evening News* and the *Washington Post*, were filled with photographs and articles on the Open. *Newsweek* printed an article. *The New Yorker* ran a "Talk of the Town" piece. Two photographers for *Life* magazine went to extraordinary lengths to get good pictures. According to Bob Lehman of the Met SRA, they were experts on strobe lighting. "With flash bulbs hidden in the ceiling fixtures synchronized by remote control with two automatic cameras concealed behind shatter proof glass underneath the front-wall tin, they got fantastic action shots and expressions that nobody has ever truly seen before." Spectators, despite a tournament ticket price of $23 ($3.45, including taxes, for standing-room spots for the final), jammed the two-hundred-and-fifty-seat gallery at the University Club to capacity each day. Smoking was not permitted in the gallery; neither were women, as per custom at the club, but they were "particularly!" welcomed at a buffet supper on New Year's Day at the Harvard Club. The widow of Honey Humpstone (Honey died just a few weeks before the tournament started) donated silver cups to the winner and runner-up, and Bigelow paid for a permanent trophy. As for the controversial cash given to the professionals, the winner received $500, the runner-up $350, semifinalists $225, quarterfinalists $125 and first round losers $75. The nationals, since 1907 the high water mark of squash in America, was instantly washed away by the Open.

The winner of the first Open was, as Lehman liked to write, "a simon-pure" named Henri Salaun. Professionals had come from all over America and from Egypt, South Africa, Pakistan, England and Scotland, but it was the little French-American who won the tournament. Still, it was not Salaun who was the focus of the *Life* photographers' lenses, but his opponent in the finals, Hashim Khan.

The dream merchants of Hollywood could not make a more romantic story than the rise of Hashim Khan. His childhood was as removed from buffet suppers at the Harvard Club as possible. Around 1914 he was born to the sound of celebratory gunfire in Nawakille, a village near Peshawar in what was then the Northwest Frontier Province of India. (Hashim's haziness about which first of July he was born on was always a source of amusement, and, it was often claimed, without any denial from Hashim, that he had probably been born five or more years earlier.) He was a Pathan. He grew up a day's walk from the fabled Khyber Pass. His father worked as a steward at a British officers' club near his home, where they had tennis courts, pool tables, a racquets court and brick-walled, cement-floored, open-air squash courts placed where two racquets courts had been until 1901. As a child he earned five rupees (about one U.S. dollar), per month as an informal ballboy. At midday under a boiling sun or in the evening the courts were empty, and the ballboys came off the walls and played the officer's game with cracked, discarded balls. Many times a bare-foot Hashim played alone, "Hashim against Hashim," as he later wrote. Sometimes he got a lesson from a young Pathan squash coach at the club. He started playing against officers. He played in racquets tournaments. In 1942 he became a tennis and squash professional at the Royal British Air Force club in Peshawar. With his fifty rupees per month salary, he got married and thought his life was complete.

In 1944 he played in a new tournament in Bombay, the India champi-onships, at the Cricket Club of India where his cousin, Abdul Bari, was a professional. On the BCC's wooden courts he upset his cousin and won the title. He won the next two years as well, but Partition halted the tour-nament. Hashim then won the new Pakistan championships. In 1950 Bari went to England and reached the finals of the British Open. The de facto world championship, the British Open was the Wimbledon of squash, and Pakistan, eager to match India's success, sent Hashim in 1951. The win-ning purse in the British Open was £250, more than a year's salary for Hashim.

In one month he became the world's first squash celebrity. Hashim played in the two customary warmups. First in London he won the British Professionals, beating Bari in five games in the finals. His oppo-nent in the finals of the Scottish Open that followed was Mahmoud el Karim, a captivating Egyptian who had won the past four British Opens. Karim had gloriously languid strokes and was considered a very able suc-cessor to his legendary countryman, Amr Bey. Hashim slaughtered him, 9–2, 9–0, 9–4. Back in London a fortnight later, he again embarrassed Karim in the finals of the British Open, running away from a 5–5 tie in the first game to win, 9–5, 9–0, 9–0, in thirty-three minutes. He ran at such a blinding speed that it appeared Karim was blindfolded and swim-ming through wet concrete. Hashim won the British Open in 1952 and 1953, as well as a score of other tournaments. When he reached America, he had never lost a match.

Hashim Khan was like a meteorite slamming into a somnolent planet. He was unlike any squash champion America had known. He had an unblemished record at an old age; a sparkling, relentlessly upbeat person-ality; purposefully pidgin English; the ability to sleep ten hours every night; a mythical path to glory and a penchant for whimsical moves (he once vanished into the kitchen of a New York restaurant and reappeared minutes later in an apron with a dish he had personally cooked). His style of play was revolutionary. No one had covered the court that effortlessly and with that much velocity. He never sweated or looked troubled. With his thin legs, five-foot-four frame, hint of a potbelly and bald head, he looked nothing like a world-class sportsman. He weighed one-hundred twelve pounds. He choked up on the racquet and swung awkwardly. "The picture he conjured up was of a butcher hacking off a side of beef," Herbert Warren Wind wrote of his backhand, adding he looked like "one of those marginal types who are regularly photographed plunging into icy water in midwinter. . . . He is unbelievably fast, but it is incorrect to say that he moves like a cat. He is not graceful or supple in a feline way. He just moves beautifully, always on balance and always to the right place, and he is always capable of instant recovery or acceleration. Moreover, he is apparently tireless." Hashim might have become the spitting image of Pablo Picasso, but on the court he had no reference point but himself.

By his very presence, Khan forced the whites-only clubs to admit to their courts, ballroom and locker room a man of color and a Moslem. This was no easy task. The Princeton Club in New York once told Hashim and his cousin Roshan, arriving to give an exhibition, to use the club's service entrance. Although there had been the Wolfe-Noel tours since the 1930s, and a U.S. branch of the Jesters Club since 1948, squash communication between North America and the rest of the world had been limited. Khan formed the first of many bridges. He paved the way for other softball champions to come over to America to try and conquer this strange, hard-ball, squash game. It was this cyclical progression of champions—his relatives Roshan, Azam and Jahangir Khan; Geoff Hunt, Rainer Ratinac, Steve Bowditch, Heather McKay, Angela Smith and Sue Cogswell—that contributed heavily to the improvement in coaching technique, to attention to fitness and better stroke production and, most of all, to legitimizing the professional game.

All eyes were on Hashim once he sailed into New York on Christmas Eve. The Pakistani ambassador arranged an exhibition match at Merion Cricket Club with Diehl Mateer. Hashim was surprised at the narrowness of the court and the speed of the ball and had trouble anticipating where to go. In the semifinals of the Open he again played Mateer. The learning curve had steepened. Mateer took the first two games with the ball coming like bullets at Hashim. "Close to that defeat he has never tasted," as the *New York Times* wrote, Hashim solved Mateer's ripping pace and won the match in five games. In the other semifinal, Henri Salaun clobbered

Mahmoud el Karim in what Salaun later thought was his best, pure win: 15–9, 15–1, 15–5. In the final Salaun continued his mastery over the "Old World" players, as the newspapers called them, and he inflicted the first-ever tournament loss upon Hashim, 15–7, 15–12, 15–14. Salaun worked extremely hard in the three games, tracking down every ball and hitting for good length. He aced Hashim three times on serves and ate up Hashim's soft lobs, which did not have pinpoint placement. Although the match only went three games, Salaun was exhausted afterwards and could barely drag himself off the court. "I had to get that point," he said of the 14–all no-set point in the third game, "I was dead tired." He had squandered two match points already and could sense Hashim, as he had done after two games with Mateer, was figuring out how to beat him. He rolled out a corner shot and dripped off the court with a victory.

The following year the field was even faster. Players from seven countries were in the draw. Three men canceled because they could not afford to buy a plane ticket, and a fourth, Abdul Bari, was scratched at the last minute because, on the day before his departure, he collapsed on a court in London and died of a brain hemorrhage. The second Open was further marred when Hashim pulled a groin muscle during a quarterfinal match with Cal MacCracken. Down 2–1, Hashim limped back to win in five but had to default before his semifinal rematch with Mateer. Azam Khan, Hashim's brother, beat Salaun in the semifinals. The finals were an anticlimax. Mateer walloped Azam in three easy games.

Despite American amateurs capturing the opening two tournaments, the following years confirmed what everybody suspected: The Khans were too good. Except in 1959, 1967 and 1975, a Khan would win every Open until the eighties. The family name became synonymous with squash excellence. Azam, who won four British Opens in a row, took a single U.S. Open. A tennis player eleven years younger than Hashim, he had been dragooned into squash when Hashim had needed a training partner. Full of raw talent, Azam shot off his volley anywhere in the court but in an efficient, unflashy way. He played like an accountant, according to Jonah Barrington, steady, methodical and as silent as a little bird. In 1963 a ruptured Achilles tendon effectively ended his career. Roshan, a cousin of Hashim—or, more precisely, the son of the sister of a man who married Hashim's sister—managed to win just one British Open, but in America had his greatest success. Taller, slower and more temperamental than Hashim and Azam, Roshan grew up in Rawalpindi, not Peshawar. He smoked and had a bum right knee. Many observers thought Roshan was the most talented of the first generation of Khans.

Mohibullah was certainly the most charismatic Khan. A nephew of Hashim, Mo reached the semifinals of the 1957 British Open at the age of seventeen. In 1962 he was down 8–1, match ball, in the fourth game of the British Open finals against Abou Taleb, an Egyptian champion. He survived three match points to win the game, 10–8. Down 6–3 in the fifth, he escaped with a 9–6 victory for the greatest comeback in British Open history. A southpaw, he had a suspect backhand and avoided training. But he wielded a choked-up, eye-popping forehand—he sometimes broke new balls during the warmup—had as much foot speed as Hashim and lived a lusty, rich life. Ted Kennedy quipped that Mo came from the Irish part of Pakistan. Mo played every match as if it were the last match of his life. He was the favorite gate attraction of the Khans after Hashim and could capture an audience as well as any vaudeville showman. "He covered the court like a very angry octopus," wrote Rex Bellamy, a British squash journalist. "The place reverberated with crashing and banging and thumping noises. When he hit the tin, there was such an echoing din that one had mental visions of sentries at Wellington Barracks peering apprehensively into the darkness, and ducks in St. James's Park waking up in a dither."

The litany of Khan victories in America awed the New World. In 1956 Hashim and Azam blew past Mateer and Salaun, 3–0, in the semifinals; Hashim beat Azam "in a friendly five" games in the final, according to Stew Brauns. In 1957 Bigelow moved the Open out of the University Club, to Rockaway Hunting Club. Mateer and Salaun again lost in the semis, to Hashim and Roshan. In his first tournament at Rockaway since the notorious 1953 Gold Racquets, Salaun went down hard to Roshan, losing 15–13 in the fifth. Hashim won the tournament. In 1958 Bigelow went further afield and held the tournament in Detroit. Salaun, with a bloodied nose courtesy of Azam's racquet on the fifth point of the match, took a fifty-minute break, struggled and eventually came back from 2–1 down to beat Azam in the semis. Two-and-a-half hours later, he pushed three of the four games into extra points, but could not overcome a surging Roshan. The sixth Open was held in Pittsburgh. Mateer, doing what Salaun could not, beat two Khans in one day. The finals were especially dramatic, as Mateer came back from a 2–1 deficit. In 1960 at the Hartford Golf Club, Roshan outlasted Azam in the longest final in Open history, one hour and fifty minutes. In 1961 in Indianapolis, Roshan dismissed Azam, losing just eighteen points in the finals. In 1962 at the Chalfonte-Haddon Hall Hotel, in Atlantic City, Azam turned the tables and easily beat Roshan. In 1963, back at the University Club in New York, Jim Zug pulled a huge upset by beating Azam, the defending champion. Azam had not come over to the United States early to recalibrate his softball game, and Zug pounced on him in the opening round in five games. Hashim breezed to his last U.S. Open victory that year. In 1964 (Buffalo) and 1965 (Wilmington) Mo beat Hashim in the finals.

The most fascinating aspect of the Khans and their domination of the U.S. Open was their intra-clan rivalry. They were not a monolithic horde of invaders. Each had his own style and personality. One piece of enduring gossip was that an ancient code of tribal hierarchy controlled the results of their matches—Azam never was allowed to beat his older brother Hashim, Mo was forbidden to beat Azam, and so on. The results of their matches often seemed to disprove the gossip and furthermore, because, or despite, these supposed familial prohibitions, their matches were especially ferocious. In the 1957 British Open, Azam smacked Roshan so hard in the face that Roshan lost a half-dozen teeth, and his shirt was soaked with blood. In the finals of the 1957 U.S. Open, Hashim hit Roshan in the right calf so brutally with a cross-court drive that Roshan could barely walk: He lost the next seventeen of twenty points. In the 1962 U.S. Open, Azam smacked Mohilbullah just above the eye with his racquet, forcing a default at 15–11, 15–17, 15–13, 10–5. "Indeed, watching two Khans go at each other in a prolonged rally for a big point in a tight match is something like watching the speeded-up film of an old Keystone Kops sequence," wrote Herbert Warren Wind, "the two wraiths darting in and out of the corners and making a succession of acrobatic 'gets,' each one more fantastic than the one before, as the tempo of their movements and their strokes keeps mounting until the action becomes almost a blur. I have seen few things in sport that can compare with it for sheer velocity and excitement."

In 1966 Bigelow rescued the Canadian Open. Begun in 1956, the Canadian Open never matched the U.S. Open's buzz. The crowds were not as thick and the press coverage not as frenzied. The Khans did not like the Canadian Open's paltry prize money, and the Canadians were not as thrilled by their own professionals being knocked out early in the tournament by rough-riding outsiders. Financially, only two clubs in the country could handle it; a third put it on one year and lost $1,500. Although non-Khans managed to do well at the Canadian Open—Al Chassard reached two finals, Doug McLaggen made three semifinals and Henri Salaun beat Cal MacCracken and Chassard to win it in 1959—the tournament never gained a solid base. Bigelow combined the national opens of the United States and Canada into one grand tournament that was the most prestigious diadem in the Western Hemisphere: the North American Open.

Hashim, Azam, Roshan and Mo—America was never the same. This quartet did not just win a few tournaments and disappear. Hashim, on the invitation of Arthur Sonneborn, a retired electrical engineer, moved to Detroit in 1960 and became the professional at a new club, the Uptown Athletic Club. The club was so rustic it had no pro shop, and Hashim strung racquets on his lap while sitting on a locker-room bench. He stayed there for a decade. With his unmatched squash résumé (seven British Opens, eight Scottish, three U.S., three Canadian and one Australian), Hashim was America's first squash luminary. He went on to win three U.S. Professionals and ten U.S. Professional veterans titles, injecting the formerly obscure tournament with some zest. All year people flew in to Detroit to get a $4, thirty-minute lesson. One local cardiologist took a lesson every single day Hashim was in town. In 1961 Don Leggat, a Hamilton player intent on winning the Canadian nationals, secretly went to Detroit for four hours of lessons per day. Hashim also traveled to obscure outposts of American squash to give much-needed injections of enthusiasm. In 1973 Hashim moved to Denver—where the Rockies reminded him of the mountains of his childhood—to work at the Denver Athletic Club. Mo secured a prime sinecure when he met President John Kennedy during an exhibition at the Pentagon squash courts in 1962. Kennedy invited him to the White House, and, via the intervention of Ted Kennedy, Mo became the head professional at the Harvard Club in Boston in 1964. He stayed there until 1994, when he had a heart attack outside the club's doubles court and died. A sparkling personality, Mo enlivened New England's squash community. The sons of Hashim worked across the continent: Aziz was a professional at the Indianapolis Athletic Club, then in Toronto; Gulmast worked in Toronto; Charlie and Sam worked in St. Louis; and Sharif dominated Toronto. Gul, Mo's brother, worked in Salt Lake City, Portland, Cleveland, Boston, New York and then St. Louis. Even Mahmoud el Karim, the other famous entrant in the 1954 Open, moved to North America and worked for two decades as a professional at the MAAA in Montreal before returning to Cairo.

Hashim, the barefoot boy of the Khyber Pass, is now in his nineties. He continues to serve as the game's elder statesman and he continues to play squash. His legions of friends have always been struck by the fact that Hashim Khan is the happiest man they have ever met.

CHAPTER SIX

A Clam in Mud at Low Tide

Brighton Beach, hard on the Atlantic at the southern end of Brooklyn, was a special neighborhood in the autumn of 1943 when Victor Niederhoffer was born there. Brighton was named for the English resort. At the turn of the century, it was a country retreat for the well-to-do. Lavish hotels, upscale music halls and three racetracks all centered around gambling, which was legal there until 1910. By the time the subway reached Brighton Beach in 1920, it was transforming itself into a working-class, year-round community. Neil Simon, Arthur Miller and Neil Diamond all grew up there. One of Niederhoffer's grandparents moved there because of Great Depression stock losses, another after doctor's orders for a seaside home after a thyroid operation. Niederhoffer's father was well-educated, with degrees from Brooklyn College and Brooklyn Law School and admittance to the New York Bar in 1940, but was unable to find work as a lawyer. So he joined the New York Police Department and patrolled nearby Coney Island on a 4 P.M. to midnight shift. To supplement his salary, he worked as a night watchman and at a printing plant loading the *New York Times* onto delivery trucks.

His eldest son Vic, born exactly nine months after his wedding, fed like a hungry whale on the rich, variegated life of Brighton Beach. During the summers the young boy roamed the beaches, ate knishes and frankfurters on the boardwalk, played competitive checkers and stoop ball, collected empty soda bottles for their two-cent deposit and hustled nickels in quick games of five-card stud. In winter he played racquet sports. It started when his parents went to play paddleball. They strung a net across the shallow end of a drained public swimming pool and deposited their baby son in the deep end. He crawled back toward his parents while they played. When he reached them, after about five minutes of persistent scrabbling across the cement, they picked him up and returned him to the deep end. This Sisyphusian activity did not daunt little Vic. He started playing paddle himself, as well as handball and tennis. He shoveled snow from the Coney Island tennis courts and was good enough to win a city eighteen-and-under tennis championship at age thirteen. Like his father, he excelled at handball, even with its heavy shadow of gambling and cheating. The Niederhoffer home was a bit unusual for a Brooklyn cop. It contained, in its 700-square-foot meagerness, more than ten thousand books. His father eventually earned a Ph.D. in sociology at New York University. In 1960 he retired from the NYPD and became a professor at John Jay College.

In the autumn of 1960, not yet seventeen, Vic Niederhoffer went up to Harvard. He joined the freshman tennis team. That winter he walked into the office of the varsity tennis and squash coach, Jack Barnaby. "I hear you're a darn good tennis player," Barnaby said. Niederhoffer agreed and then blurted, "I'm going to be the best squash player ever." He paused and asked, "Squash is that wall game, right?" Barnaby almost said, "You seem like the biggest horse's ass I ever had the displeasure to meet," but instead he bit his tongue and kindly replied, "I'd be happy to show you what a squash court looks like." Barnaby took Niederhoffer to the Hemenway courts. They looked similar to the handball courts of Brighton Beach. One afternoon a few days later, Barnaby walked through the gallery and spotted Niederhoffer alone in a court, practicing shots with a book opened in one hand. Barnaby went into the court and asked to see what he was reading. It was a British squash manual, written for the softball game. Barnaby explained the difference and quickly shortened Niederhoffer's swing. As the season went on, a curious sort of pedagogy developed. Barnaby explained a particular shot for a few minutes. "I've got the concept," Niederhoffer abruptly said. Barnaby, taking it as a dismissal, left the court, and Niederhoffer practiced the shot alone for a day or two. A couple of days later they moved to another shot. Barnaby stopped Niederhoffer from switching hands and hitting what should have been a backhand with a left-handed forehand—Niederhoffer had played tennis as a youngster with two one-armed forehands. "He's the only player to merit the word 'genius,'" Barnaby later said. "He was extraordinary. He always talked big and always backed it up. He was like Wagner—he knew he was good and didn't bore you with any false modesty."

Fourteen months after marching into Barnaby's office, Niederhoffer took the first tangible step toward his stated goal by winning the national juniors. Unseeded, he beat the sixth, third, second and top seeds, including Howard Coonley in the second round, Frank Satterthwaite in the semifinals and the defending champion, Bill Morris, in the finals. All with the loss of just one game. It was the first time a college sophomore had won the title. Niederhoffer, after not being chosen to go to England on a Harvard-Yale tour his sophomore year, played at the top of the Harvard ladder his last two seasons and captained the team his senior year. Harvard was national champion all three years, but his career rose and dipped like a Brighton Beach roller coaster. Jim Zug, a senior at Princeton, beat him his sophomore year in both their team match and in the intercollegiates. His junior year, he beat Zug in the finals of the Massachusetts states but lost to him in the finals of the Harvard University championships when Zug was at Harvard Business School. In addition, Ralph Howe of Yale beat him both in their team match and in the intercollegiates. The Niederhoffer-Howe matches were the only intercollegiate contests in which a referee was essential. "The court was just too small for two such huge squash egos," wrote Frank Satterthwaite, a Princeton player at the time. "They got into some terrible squabbles. The Yalies claimed that Vic was the perpetrator with his ridiculous calls for lets and prolonged, unsolicited explanations to the referee. But the Harvard view was that Ralph was slow to get out of the way, and that he egged Vic on with subtle hip checks." His senior year, with Howe having graduated, Niederhoffer finally won the intercollegiates, albeit shakily. In Hanover, he lost the first two games of his opening round match against Dartmouth's Whit Foster.

At the portals of the adult world, Niederhoffer announced himself with a shrill voice. In the quarterfinals of the 1963 nationals, he plucked three straight 15–14 games from defending champion Sam Howe to reach the semifinals. There he crashed out to Ben Heckscher in four, losing the final game 15–1. That year he reached the finals of the Middlesex Bowl in Boston, before Henri Salaun, at the time the twelve-time defending champion in that tournament, crushed him without mercy. At the 1964 nationals in Annapolis, Niederhoffer sneaked into the semifinals to face Salaun. That season Salaun had lost just once, to Hashim Khan in five games at the Canadian Open, and had beaten Niederhoffer, 15–1, 15–12, 15–8, in the Harry Cowles. In a prizefighting atmosphere, the referee lost control of the match straight away as both Salaun and Niederhoffer scratched and clawed. Shouts for lets punctuated the cold military air. "It was bedlam," wrote one observer, with bizarre rulings and overrulings and both players ignoring the referee's calls. Salaun escaped: 9–15, 17–15, 15–7, 7–15, 15–12. "I ran out of gas," said Salaun, "and just barely got it back to the garage." The next morning, Salaun scarcely got his engine started and lost in four games to Ralph Howe.

After losing in the finals of the nationals in 1965 to Steve Vehslage, Niederhoffer won the 1966 nationals. At the University Club, he beat his college rival Ralph Howe in the semifinals. Eight lets were called in the first five points, and both players suffered cramps in toes and legs. Niederhoffer prevailed after ninety minutes, 15–12 in the fifth. In the finals, with his father standing on tiptoe in the back row of the gallery, Niederhoffer dropped an opening game to Sam Howe, but gained confidence as they went along, in part because he had never lost to Sam in five previous matches. Sam was up, 13–11, in both the third and the fourth game, but Niederhoffer blew past him and took his first title in four games. NIEDERHOFFER COMES OF AGE, the USSRA headlined its story of the nationals. It looked as if the national champions' list, after seven different winners in the past seven years, was going to settle down into an annual repetition of one name, Victor Niederhoffer.

Instead his name did not reappear until 1972. Niederhoffer, having moved in the summer of 1965 to the University of Chicago to earn his doctorate in economics, found that all six squash clubs in the Windy City did not want him as a member. The clubs—Bath & Tennis, Chicago Athletic Association, Chicago Dearborn, Lake Shore, Racquet Club of Chicago and University Club of Chicago—were private. They allowed Niederhoffer to play at their club as a guest, but none of them had members who were inclined to propose him for membership. He inquired about joining the Lake Shore Club, which was perhaps the leading club in the city and the host of the nationals in 1939 and 1951. Lake Shore refused to take him. It was not as if he was locked out of squash altogether. He had unfettered access to the courts at the University of Chicago. He could also play at the private clubs, but he was shunted to off-peak hours and, as a guest, he could not bring in guests himself. Even if one considered that most of these clubs had waiting lists and complicated membership processes, it was strange that the current national champion could not find a permanent home in his new city. It also demonstrated the inequities of the private club system of squash in the United States.

Niederhoffer claimed he was excluded because he was Jewish. To some extent, he was right. Squash was still very much a Protestant, Christian sport in America. In New York the City Athletic Club, the Lone Star Boat Club and the Harmonie Club, all almost entirely Jewish, had active squash programs, and Jews were members of most of the city's university clubs. The literary agent Mel Sokolow, Glenn Greenberg, the son of slugger Hank Greenberg, and Bob Lehman, the editor of the Met SRA's annual yearbook, were three highly visible Jewish squashmen in New York. The Jewish Center of Buffalo had a strong contingent of players, including Lou Schaefer, the son of a rabbi, who won the Canadian national doubles three times, the last at age fifty-two. But in Chicago the story was different. Among the seven thousand members of the six Chicago clubs, Niederhoffer said, one person was Jewish. A club might have taken an extrapresentable Jew, especially a national champion, but why should a Jew have to be *extra*presentable?

In the spirit of the countercultural sixties, Niederhoffer decided to make a public statement. In the autumn of 1966 he wrote a letter to the USSRA declaring that he would boycott the 1967 nationals unless a Chicago club asked him to join. The ultimatum was edged by the fact that the nationals that February were to be held at Lake Shore. Niederhoffer said he was unwilling to put on a show at a club when he could not be a member there. Meanwhile, he was on a tear, winning tournament after tournament and proving he was indeed the best amateur in the country. The Chicago clubs and the USSRA called Niederhoffer's bluff and did not make a move. Niederhoffer "retired." He did not play in the 1967 nationals, and stayed away from singles tournaments for five years. Sam Howe swept to victory at Lake Shore, with nary a loss of a game, the first time since Diehl Mateer in 1956 that the champion had an unblemished tournament. However, it was a victory with an asterisk. The same for Colin Adair's wins in 1968 and 1971 and Anil Nayar's in 1969 and 1970. They were national champions, and, along with the likes of Larry Terrell, Tom Poor, Frank Satterthwaite, Bob Hetherington, Larry O'Loughlin, John Reese and the Howe brothers, they took the honors each Sunday afternoon at tournaments. With Achilles sulking in his tent, there was the inevitable *what if* attached to their wins. "Like Caesar when he was dead," Niederhoffer told a reporter in 1975, "even in retirement I had an influence on the game. The champions had to say, 'Would I have won if Caesar was alive?'" Caesar he was not, but Niederhoffer reminded some of Muhammad Ali, another athlete who publicly stood up for his beliefs.

Tension between USSRA officials and Niederhoffer was an unspoken reason for his boycott. The problems stemmed from his notorious 1964 semifinal match against Salaun in Annapolis. The USSRA executive committee, meeting at the national doubles in Minneapolis a month later, decided to hold a private meeting with Niederhoffer "to present constructive criticism." In September 1964 Niederhoffer was duly called uptown to Stew Brauns's home on East Sixty-sixth Street in Manhattan. The committee and Niederhoffer analyzed the match in detail. The affair grated on him, the grand panjandrums of squash scolding him for playing the only way he knew how. This anger was reinforced in 1969, when the president of the USSRA, Seymour Knox, wrote to remind him that he must be a member of a USSRA-member club in order to play in any national championship. Thirty years later, though, he came to regret his boycott. "It was a terrible decision," he said. "My game was peaking. I still should have played. I could have won ten straight nationals."

Niederhoffer was the Ty Cobb of squash. The objective was not enjoyment but to prove he could win. He started each game with a hard, crisscross serve. Haranguing, angry histrionics and professorial lectures were the norm. On the stage of a squash court he showed referees a range of facial expressions Marlon Brando would have ransacked a room for: the look of injured innocence, the blank start of a Zen master pondering a koan, the searing pain of an ultramarathoner on his last mile or the quizzical rictus, with his eyebrows flipping up and down like windshield wipers. He never swore but he never smiled. He stopped matches in the nationals to complain of a radio playing or cigarette smoke, even if he was the only one hearing or smelling it. He hit opponents with a drive, and, unlike the Philadelphians who made a big production out of apologizing, he said nothing. He just picked up the ball and went to the server's circle. With that unmuscular, ungainly body and perpetually droopy, half-closed eyes, he looked at any hour of the day as if he had just spent the night battling insomnia. Salaun, for all his roughness of demeanor, was supersmooth during points, but Niederhoffer played without rhythm and never allowed an opponent to groove into a comfortable pace. He played with all the charm of a workman riveting a building. Bob Lehman said he "seems to cover ground at a cross between a lope and a controlled stagger." Niederhoffer fought for every advantage on court, however infinitesimal. One time, when he was up 12–3 in a game, his opponent moved in front of him and Niederhoffer drilled him with the ball for the point. "At 12–3?" the player exclaimed. "At 14–0," Niederhoffer replied.

He cultivated rodomontade eccentricities. In his office he wore socks without shoes. The only newspaper he read was the supermarket tabloid, the *National Enquirer*. He did not own a television. He took lessons in checkers every Tuesday afternoon for fifteen years from a checkers world champion. He and his wife kept separate bedrooms. He eschewed the light conversation and bonhomie of the locker room and kept a sock on his right hand, so, he wrote "that no one would shake my hand and distract me." In between games he poured packets of sugar down his throat for extra bursts of energy. A sartorial train wreck, he cocked a snook at squash's bluebloods by wearing sneakers to black-tie dinner dances. Best of all, the sneakers never matched. Sometimes he brought four brands of sneakers to tournaments, switching them individually as their luck on court or on the dance floor rose and fell. He once carried three racquets to a tournament, labeled 1, 1A and 3. He switched from 1 to 1A as the weekend progressed, keeping 3 in reserve. Herbert Warren Wind, observing this saga, added, "He has not yet figured out to his own satisfaction why there is no No. 2." For tournament matches he wore ratty shirts with food stains splodged on the front. The Northern California SRA, in perhaps the lasting legacy of Niederhoffer's four years in the Bay Area, annually awarded the "Niederhoffer Best Dressed" prize each spring. In the Calcutta at the Harry Cowles tournament, Niederhoffer ignored all the syndicates and bought himself outright. After winning his bid, he would barter some of himself to other syndicates to improve his odds at making money. He was the most unclubbable man in squash.

Practice is what separates the good from the great, and Niederhoffer was a glutton for practicing. Like Salaun, he spent hours thinking about his opponents and tinkering with his game. He had deceptively good anticipation, sharp peripheral vision and quick hands, but it was his restless imagination that brought him victories. He hit alone in the court four out of seven days a week. He perfected his three-wall boasts, no easy matter with the old Seamless ball. In 1978 he calculated that he had practiced or played a match on thirty-five hundred consecutive days. This was at a time when even hard-charging professionals took the summer off. Although the squash demi monde noticed that he seemed rusty and out of shape each September, Niederhoffer's self-abnegating boast struck an ice pick in the heart of his opponents. Keeping his opponents off-balance seemed a large part of the reason for the bizarre personality. Wind dubbed Niederhoffer "an accomplished eccentric." A hint of calculation hovered around his maverick ways. He got control of the situation by making everyone approach him on his terms, sock in hand. He was a screwball, but a methodical, fascinatingly self-aware one. For a generation of players, Vic Niederhoffer was the toughest opponent possible.

In the autumn of 1971 he returned to New York. He had gained twenty-five pounds and had a potbelly, chipmunk cheeks and stovepipe legs. He joined the Harvard Club, a normally routine procedure for a Cantabrigian, but, with his reputation leading before him, Charlie Ufford had to intercede to ensure his acceptance. In his first tournament back, the season-opening Joseph Lordi Memorial at the New York Athletic Club, he slipped past Frank Satterthwaite in the semis in four and finally faced Anil Nayar in the finals.

Anticipation over a Nayar-Niederhoffer match was keen. Nayar was probably the best player India ever produced. He was first coached by Yusuf Khan, a distant relative of the Pakistani clan. At Harvard Nayar humbly asked Barnaby if he could try out for the freshman team. Barnaby asked if he had played squash before. Nayar said, why, yes, that he had twice won the Indian national championship and in 1964 had won the Drysdale Cup, the English junior nationals. "I don't have the red carpet here today," Barnaby said humbly, "but I'll have it tomorrow." Nayar won the intercollegiates three years in a row (although he barely survived his semifinal match in 1969 against Penn's Spencer Burke, winning, 15–14 in the fifth). He won the 1969 and 1970 nationals and would have taken a third in a row if he had not badly sprained his knee skiing over Christmas. He was fast as a Bengal tiger and had an innately sharp court sense. His bread and butter was a forehand cross-court kill, but he ran risks and committed more unforced errors than any other top player.

The finals of the Lordi surprised the pundits. Instead of throwing up junk, off-speed rails, cross-court lobs and unexpected dropshots, Niederhoffer played to Nayar's strength: He hit hard, going toe to toe. Somehow he won the first game. Nayar seemed tentative and gave Niederhoffer a funny glance a few times. Nayar won the second. Before the third Niederhoffer swallowed a couple of packets of sugar, but the quick rush of energy dissipated, and it was clear he was in no shape to go five. He fought hard in the third game, but, at 13–all, Nayar rang the bell with five straight points, and the fourth game was a formality.

A month later at the Gold Racquets, it was a different story. Niederhoffer was fitter. He began a custom of working all day at the office, playing at the Harvard Club from eight to half past nine, returning to the office till after midnight, then sprinting two miles through the ghostly canyons of New York, from his office at Forty-eighth Street and Third Avenue to his home at Eighty-third Street and Madison Avenue, carrying his racquet in his hand. Why the racquet? "To beat off marauders," said Niederhoffer, "to show the cops I'm not a mugger [this was the seventies] and to make my training as specific as possible." This was the routine, seven days a week. At Rockaway it was Nayar versus Niederhoffer in the finals. They split the first two games, as Niederhoffer again played the seemingly suicidal game of hard hitting. Nayar won the third, 15–7. In the fourth, it was again 13–all. Niederhoffer called set three. At 1–all in the tiebreaker, they played a monster point, the rally lasting for well over a minute. Nayar cracked one of his surefire forehand nicks. Niederhoffer dove desperately for it and miraculously dug it out, his head almost scraping the wall. Nayar, totally shocked, dove for Niederhoffer's shot, probably the first time in his career he ever went horizontal on purpose. His desperate stab looked like the clincher, as Niederhoffer was still on the ground. Somehow Niederhoffer volleyed it while still on his knees. The point continued. Both men scrambled back to their feet. Nayar ended the rally with a resounding drive into the tin.

That point effectively decided the incipient rivalry. Niederhoffer won the next point to take the game and cruised in the fifth, 15–8. Six weeks later they met in the finals of the Cowles. Niederhoffer won in three. They never played again. Niederhoffer was king once more. He had broken Nayar by proving that, given a fast-enough pace, Nayar would eventually make mistakes. With Nayar dispatched (he moved back to India that spring for the next decade), Niederhoffer ran away with the nationals four straight calendar years, something no player had ever done. He won the 1972 nationals without loss of a game; in 1973 he beat Jay Nelson and Bob Hetherington, both tough players, in straight games; in 1974 he lost one game; in 1975 he lost none. He was not perfect. He won three of four Gold Racquets and three of four Harry Cowles titles and lost in the semifinals of a Boston Open to Clive Caldwell, 18–15 in the fifth. He also succumbed to Colin Adair in the 1975 Canadian nationals, a loss that goaded him on to victory the following week at the U.S. nationals. "His opponents did little but gasp, sweat and run," Dan Levin wrote in *Sports Illustrated* after the 1975 nationals. "But Niederhoffer seemed to play effortlessly. His shots were not always brilliant, but he patiently waited out long rallies, and his frustrated opponents consistently found themselves in situations where most of their moves were of high risk. And then they were forced to make mistakes which ruined them." Niederhoffer, like no man since Stan Pearson, dominated amateur squash in America.

His only mountain left to climb was the North American Open. To be one of the all-time greats, Niederhoffer needed to win the top prize on the continent. He had a run of mediocre results. He lost to Hashim Khan in the 1964 semifinals. He lost to Mohibullah Khan twice in a row, in the 1965 quarterfinals and in the 1966 finals. In 1967 he beat Sharif Khan in the quarterfinals, 15–9, 14–15, 16–14, 14–15, 17–15, but then lost to Sam Howe in five games in the semifinals. After his boycott, he lost to Sharif in the 1972 finals, sat out a year, then lost to Rainer Ratinac in the 1974 semifinals.

In early February 1975, Daniel came to judgment. At an altitude of seven thousand feet, the scene was the unlikely locale of the Palace Squash Club in Mexico City. Sharif was gunning for his seventh straight Open title. Niederhoffer beat Mo Khan in four and then Juan de Villafranca, the Mexican champion, in the semifinals. In the finals, four hours after beating deVillafranca, Niederhoffer stood little chance of overcoming Sharif. His playing hand bled from a blister, and the thin air had sucked dry his lungs. With his usual calculating precision, he won the first two games, 15–9 and 15–7. He kept the pace moderate, avoided errors and focused on exposing Sharif's backhand, but the strategy exhausted him and Sharif grabbed the third with ease, 15–4. During the second point of the fourth game, Khan slammed into the left side wall going for a Niederhoffer rail. His contact lens came loose and slipped into his lower eyelid. A forty-five minute delay ensued. Niederhoffer recovered during the break, and, after numerous lets and long points, he forced Sharif into two forehand volley errors and took the game, 15–11. He was North American champion.

It was a bravura performance. Niederhoffer was the first amateur to win the North American Open since Ralph Howe had done so in Montreal eight years before, and he would be the last. With his victory three weeks later in the nationals, Niederhoffer was without question the best squash player on the continent.

Much had changed in the thirty years leading up to Niederhoffer's incredible 1975 season. The Second World War had been a wintry time of hibernation for the squash community. Word of the attack on Pearl Harbor reached the squash world on a fuzzy-headed Sunday at the Gold Racquets. Ray Chauncey, the director of the tournament, announced the horrible news at the luncheon just before the finals. "From that moment," reported the 1942 Met SRA yearbook, "squash racquets for most of the players became a peace time luxury."

Most officials canceled their tournaments. The Met SRA held five tournaments in the 1942–43 season. All entry fees and gallery ticket receipts were donated to the Red Cross, and winners received not cigarettes cases or silver cups but Red Cross certificates. Sherman Howes won the 1943 Red Cross Nationals. College coaches like Red Hoehn and a multitude of players joined the armed forces. The USSRA reduced annual dues for its member clubs from twenty-five dollars to five dollars and waived dues for 1942. Women's squash entirely shut down, except for inter-club matches in Philadelphia. The most active squash court in the war was actually not a squash court. Tucked under the Gothic towers of the west bleachers at Amos Alonzo Stagg Field, the University of Chicago's old football stadium, was an old racquets court. Build by Harold McCormick, the court was never popular. In 1942 the Manhattan Project, deep into its program of creating the atomic bomb, needed an enclosed space to build a primitive reactor. It took over the racquets court. On 2 December 1942, forty people sat in the gallery and watched Enrico Fermi split the atom.

After the war there was an element of spring. Renewal, growth and possibility floated in the warm breeze. New gardens sprouted up in hitherto barren places around the United States, yet the core of this racquet-wielding horticulture remained the same. The white, male, upper-class cycle of juniors, colleges and private clubs was the soil in which the game of squash grew.

Junior squash, a neglected corner of the squash field despite the origins of the game in America, slowly brought forth new blooms. In 1932 Merion Cricket Club founded the first junior tournament, the Philadelphia & Districts, which was played usually the weekend before Christmas. For two decades, the Philly Districts, as it was known, was the sole opportunity for boys to play each other in a competitive, individual situation. After the war under the guidance of Ned Bigelow, the Racquet & Tennis Club started an annual Interscholastics Invitational over Easter, and the Princeton Club began a Metropolitan Junior Invitation at Christmastime. In 1956, under the leadership of John Humes, the USSRA improved matters by inaugurating a national junior championship. (Canada started its national juniors in 1948.) The Union Club hosted the first tournament. It had a draw of eight, "several of which had to be coerced into playing," as Darwin Kingsley later wrote. Kit Spahr, the cream of the Merion crop of youngsters and winner of the 1955 Interscholastics Invitational, was seeded number one. In the opening round Sam Howe beat Spahr, 15–10 in the fifth. In the semifinals Sam lost to John Smith Chapman, a Montreal youngster. Steve Vehslage, in the tournament that earned him the sobriquet "The Little Master," as a junior version of Hunter Lott, beat Dick Hoehn from Hanover, New Hampshire, in the semifinals, then outlasted Smith Chapman in the finals, 15–11, 6–15, 8–15, 15–8, 15–11. (Ralph Howe and two boys from Pittsburgh rounded out the draw.) For the finals Mrs. Vehslage came up by train from Philadelphia to watch. The Union Club refused to allow her to enter its all-male club. With speedy thinking, Humes and Treddy Ketcham bundled her up in Enos Curtin's overcoat (he was well over six feet tall) spirited her into the service elevator at the back of the club and deposited her in the gallery of the exhibition court, just so she could watch her son become the first national junior champion.

Merion dominated the junior nationals, with club members winning the first six titles, but other clubs used the tournament as an incentive for its young players. In Pittsburgh, Martin Tressel turned out a number of top players, including Dave and Larry O'Loughlin, Ralph Mason and two-time nationals finalist Bob Hetherington, the lefty Reverend. In 1957 and 1960, Tressel hosted the national juniors. In 1954 a group of boarding schools in the Northeast formed the New England Scholastics Association, a sign that prep-school squash was becoming more than a mere feeder system for college teams. In the early years some NESA schools—Middlesex, Andover, Exeter, Hill and Kent School—hosted the national juniors during the December holidays. A special, if unnoticed anniversary occurred in 1969: eighty-six years after it opened the first squash courts in America, St. Paul's School in Concord, New Hampshire, hosted the national juniors. In the mid-seventies the USSRA bowed to pressure from universities who wanted to host the national juniors for recruiting purposes and to the fact that the tournament was getting too large for a prep school. Thereafter, it has always been held in March on a college campus. The national juniors tapped a potent market. At the sixth edition in 1961, forty-seven players from twenty-three different high schools and colleges competed. College players, able to slip under the nineteen-year-old barrier, often won the tournament in the early years: Jim Zug in 1959, Ralph Howe in 1960, Vic Niederhoffer in 1962, John West in 1963, Jose Gonzales in 1965 and 1966 and Larry Terrell in 1967. In fact, in 1963, only one schoolboy, Terrell, even reached the quarterfinals.

Behind every player is another player who taught them the game. For many Americans, it was their college coach. Intercollegiate squash was a key part of the squash landscape, but it had a bulky system of competition. In 1956 the National Intercollegiate Squash Racquets Association attached a faux team competition to the national intercollegiates that existed only on paper. At the tournament, each player earned a point for his college for each round gained, including in a consolation draw. With a maximum of four players from a college playing in the national intercollegiates, the so-called four-man team trophy was a peculiar honor. The majority of each team that had sweated and strained together for six months were not even present. Depth, the classic college equalizer, meant nothing. In 1965, for example, Harvard went undefeated in dual match play to become the national champion, but, at the national intercollegiates, in large part because Walter Oehrlein of Army and Howard Coonley of Pennsylvania reached the finals, the four-man team standings were: Penn 15, Army 14, Harvard 13. In 1969 the association adjusted the format, allowing six players from each university to play in the tournament. They divided the players into three divisions, according to where they played on their team's ladder. This format actually made things worse. The "team" part was still silly, with the bottom third of each squad banished to their dormitory rooms. The distortion hurt the actual individual tournament. Before 1969 the top four players from every university had the chance to become intercollegiate champion; after 1969 only the top two players could shoot for the championship. In 1987 Jeff Stanley, the towhead star at Princeton, captured the intercollegiates. But such potent players as Joe Dowling, an All-Ivy player from Harvard; Tim Goodale, All-Ivy from Yale; Rob MacKay, All-Ivy from Princeton; Jon Bernheimer, the Ivy League Rookie of the Year from Harvard and three All-Americans—Ashish Kamat from Franklin & Marshall, Terry Spahr (Kit Spahr's son) from Penn and Spencer Wall from Navy—played three or below on their team and thus were relegated to the B division. In 1989 the association finally abandoned this artificial structure. Led by Dartmouth coach Chuck Kinyon, NISRA created two season-ending weekends. First came a national team tournament. They divided the colleges into four divisions (a fifth was added in 1993), and each college played with its usual nine-man squad. The national team championship was now contested, as was customary in the rest of the American squash scene, at an annual weekend. The individual intercollegiate championship was played separately the following weekend, with the top sixty-four players in the country allowed to enter the draw.

These bureaucratic fandangos did not hide the fact that men's college squash was no longer a two-school fight. Harvard and Yale took their share of titles, but a number of other schools elbowed their way to the top. From 1938 to 1962 Red Hoehn coached Dartmouth at its old warren of courts in Alumni Gymnasium, reachable only through the men's locker room. At Princeton Dillon burned down in 1942 and was rebuilt with eighteen hot, low-ceilinged courts—"white sepulchers among catacomb-like corridors," according to the Princeton 1970 yearbook. John Conroy, hailing like Harry Cowles from Newport, was the coach at Princeton from 1939 to 1969. He had one national team title in 1955 and four national intercollegiate champions. In 1969 Princeton built Jadwin Gymnasium, a half-dome, half-cone gymnasium that Herbert Warren Wind said resembled "a Brobdingnagian armadillo." Two floors below ground was a complex of twelve singles courts and a doubles court. Bowdoin, under the direction of four-time U.S. Professional champion Eddie Reid, produced competitive squads. Clarence Chaffee, the coach at Williams from 1937 to 1970 and Ed Serues at Amherst from 1957 to 1987, developed strong programs and many loyal alumni. Williams won the 1958 four-man team tournament, and Serues coached a number of exciting players, including intercollegiate finalist Tom Poor, as well as notable future coaches Frank Cushman and Tom Rumpler. Jack Summers continued at MIT until 1956, followed by Ed Crocker, who coached for twenty-seven years. Doc Marshall led Franklin & Marshall for eighteen years, leading the Diplomats to a number-two ranking in 1987 and producing sixteen All-Americans, including Morris Clothier, Chris Spahr, Scott Brehmen and Tim Long. George Wigton founded Bates College's program in 1970 and coached there for thirty years. In 1957 Dickinson was so enamored of Kit Spahr, the Merion junior star, that it built squash courts and started a team simply because he agreed to matriculate. In the 1950s Fordham launched a squad under coach Bob Hawthorn, and, although it rarely cracked the top ten, it fielded a good squad each winter. Larry Hilbert, Tim Chisholm and Bill Andruss were his most notable products. Andruss reached the finals of the intercollegiates in 1975, won a match at the 1976 British Open and notched a ranking of thirty-four on the world softball tour—still the highest spot ever for an American man. At times Georgetown, the University of Rochester, Rensselaer Polytechnic and Pittsburgh had varsity programs. Some years a lone player from colleges without any team—Roanoke, Waterloo, Wisconsin, Adelphi—would appear at the national intercollegiates and gain points for his innocent alma mater. In the sixties the University of Texas at Austin, with an enormous facility, and Rice started playing each other in grand fashion, with up to fifteen players on a side; twenty years later, UT formed a Rocky Mountain Intercollegiate Association with Colorado College and Air Force Academy. With its mammoth twenty-four-court facility (including four doubles courts), Air Force brimmed with potential.

In the 1950s, Canadian universities began sending their teams south to the national intercollegiates. They started their own national intercollegiate team competition in 1945 and an individual tournament in 1946. In 1947 Peter Landry from McGill became the only man ever to win both the U.S. and the Canadian intercollegiates in the same year (John Smith Chapman won both titles but in different years). The most notable teams were McGill, Sir George Williams and Toronto. In the late seventies, the University of Western Ontario emerged as the most competitive Canadian college squad.

Many college players in the 1950s and '60s came from a St. Grotlesex school. Harvard's 1957–58 varsity ladder ran with the following high school alma maters: Larry Sears (Andover), Gerry Emmet (Brooks), Charley Hamm (Exeter), Henry Cortesi (Milton), Peter Lund (Exeter),

Chuck Poletti (Exeter), Ed Wadsworth (Cohasset), Fred Vinton (Choate) and John Davis (St. Marks). (Cortesi and Davis, despite their prep school backgrounds, did not take up squash until coming to Cambridge.) During every Christmas holiday season beginning in the forties, the University Club in New York hosted an intercollegiate invitational. The later addition of a college freshman invitational at the Racquet & Tennis Club—freshmen were not allowed to play varsity squash until 1971—further accentuated the exclusive nature of squash.

College squash alternated between staid predictability and chaos. From 1955 through 1959, a different team won the title each year. In 1959, two weeks after Yale won the national five-man teams, Harvard beat them 6–3, making a mockery of their hitherto perfect season. In the late 1940s, Yale went on a forty-seven-match tear, going undefeated for five straight years. In the sixties Harvard equaled the Eli with its own forty-seven-win streak. Ten years later, Princeton missed that mark by one, and in the eighties Harvard finally broke the deadlock when it won seventy-two matches in a row—eight straight undefeated seasons. These streaks were not dull triumphs lined up in a row. Harvard's run in the sixties was regularly in jeopardy. With the streak at nine consecutive matches, Yale, which had beaten Harvard the year before 5–4, put the contest to 4–all, then 2–all in the last match and jumped to an 11–6 lead in that fifth and deciding game. John Francis, a sophomore playing number nine, secured the next nine points to silence the Yale home crowd. At twenty wins Harvard traveled to West Point in early December, with four varsity players extremely rusty—having just a week of practice due to the late end of the soccer season. Army found itself with three match points before John Vinton, at number eight, pulled out a win to give Harvard a 5–4 victory. At twenty-three wins, Princeton went up 4–3 and had a score of 14–10 in the fifth of another match. Francis again showed a remarkable ability to tear his team's heart out, thrust it to the gods as an offering then, at the last minute, put it back. Surviving the four match points, he won the fifth game in overtime, again giving Harvard a 5–4 victory. At thirty-eight wins, Penn went up 4–1 in the contest and had a fifth in their grasp, 2–1 in games, 13–9 in the fourth, but Harvard rallied again. Princeton finally stopped the Crimson in their tracks at forty-seven wins, when the Tigers went up to Cambridge and won a thriller, 5–4. Harvard still took the national title that year, when Princeton stumbled against Penn and Yale.

Nail-biting 5–4 scores in dual matches were so often the norm that it was a wonder coaches did not gnaw their fingers into stumps, or "down to the fourth knuckle," as Jack Barnaby at Harvard used to say. In 1953 Harvard and Princeton were tied 4–all. Steve Sonnabend, at number nine for Harvard, fell behind 2–0. He slumped off the court looking for advice. Barnaby told him a total lie: "You've got him now. He's a flash in the pan. Look at that skinny neck. Keep running him and he'll die." Sonnabend went on to win in five games. In 1956 at Yale, Harvard clinched a national title (and an undefeated season) when it again squeaked out a win. Lee Folder, a Crimson senior playing number five, fell behind 2–0. Folder clawed back to even the match at 2–all and 8–all in the fifth before reeling off a string of winners to take the match 15–9. Two years later Yale finally turned the tables when Harvey Sloane, an Eli senior and captain, out-slugged Gerry Emmet, a Harvard sophomore, after the score was tied 13–all in the fifth with the contest knotted at 4–all, thus preserving Yale's undefeated season. In 1970 Penn and Harvard were tied at 4–all and Eddie Atwood trailed 2–0 before winning the last three games for Harvard. In 1987 Yale beat Princeton for the first time in a dozen years when Bill Barker, a senior playing at number seven, dove for a ball at double match point, 4–4 in matches, and managed to barely tip it above the tin. John Musto was the cardiac kid of the last generation of hardball college squash. A New Haven native and Yale class of 1991, Musto played number one all four years for the Eli. In 1990 he was the focus of an attempt by Yale to break a twenty-eight-year drought against Harvard. In their annual late February meeting, this time in New Haven, the score was tied, 4–4. In the exhibition court Musto battled Mark Baker, an Englishman who had just won the Harry Cowles tournament. Baker took the first game and went up, 4–1, in the second game set-five tiebreaker. Musto somehow won the next five points to even the match. He lost the third game, then scrambled to take the next two, the fifth at 15–13, giving Yale its first undefeated season since 1961.

A surprise addition to the exclusive Ivy League club of knuckle-gnawing teams was the United States Naval Academy. With the help of Merion Cricket Club and the Maryland Club in Baltimore, the Academy started a varsity squash team in 1949, and Art Potter, a hard-driving naval officer who had studied at Penn, became the coach a year later. Recruiting a preppy high-school squash star to Navy proved impossible, so every season he taught midshipmen who had never seen a squash court before arriving in Annapolis. Navy men became known for their fight rather than their forehand boasts. Potter's secret was instilling confidence in midshipmen who might ordinarily feel intimidated facing experienced players. "Warm up like a tiger," he instructed in a Navy squash manual. "Give the impression that you are a powerful pounder of the pill." "Stick to the things you do best like your defense hustle and sweat game." "Remember the brigade and the Navy are behind you. Shift your thoughts from the things that are against you to the vast power behind you." His most lasting advice was, "Whatever happens in a match you should always make the Ivy Leaguers deserve every point they win. They naturally figure mid-shipmen to be in better shape so use this and make them work, especially in the first game. In essence, don't be in a rush to lose. Too many times a player is so worried by an opponent's good form, fancy corner and bow shots and reputation that he is satisfied at merely making a 'good show-ing.' When a shotmaker knows the Navy squash player is going to try for every shot, he will hit closer to the tin and this makes more errors."

With the construction of more courts in 1957, Navy had a total of thirty-two courts and a halo of respectability. They hosted the nationals in 1958, 1964 and 1974. They played in Maryland SRA leagues and often took state titles. One top player was John Griffiths, who reached the 1957 intercollegiate finals, taking a game off defending champion Ben Heckscher. A six-foot-four midshipman from Santa Monica, Griffiths dis-covered squash only once he arrived in Annapolis. In 1957 Navy took their best five players to the national teams and beat Providence, New York and Detroit before losing to the Pacific Coast in the finals. Some other teams grouched at Navy's depth and accused them of stacking their lineup so that better men played lower down on their ladder. Others com-plained about the unsporting behavior of the spectators at Navy matches in Annapolis. When opposing teams came to play them, officers ordered battalions of uniformed students into the galleries. The chanting and shouting disturbed many visiting players who were more familiar with tiny galleries of a few teammates, a parent or two, a brace of fraternity brothers and a quietly supportive girlfriend. Playing against a very fit and determined future naval officer with two hundred of his comrades earning "cheering credit" in the stands was a daunting experience. A few coaches felt that the "sweat game" meant nothing more than bad sportsmanship. In 1959 Yale broke off relations with Navy and refused to play them again for seventeen seasons. Harvard likewise took Navy off its schedule for a few years.

Tough luck, it seemed, followed Navy's counterpart on the Hudson River, the United States Military Academy. In 1954 West Point, under coach Leif Nordlie, won four of its first six matches against Harvard and were up 2–1 in two more matches before succumbing 5–4. Russ Ball, 1947, played number-one singles for three years, losing just one dual match and was runner-up in the intercollegiates his senior year (he also was the undergraduate president of the association). Walter Oehrlein was perhaps its best player ever. He won the 1965 intercollegiates, before launching the Air Force Academy's varsity, then working as a professional in Detroit.

Pennsylvania, able to scoop up players who had not been accepted at Harvard, Yale or Princeton, played a beautiful bridesmaid. In 1959 Wally Johnson retired after thirty years at the helm. Stepping into his shoes was a former Marine, Al Molloy, Jr. The son of a longtime pro, Molloy was an amiable red-headed mentor, yet he also had a stubborn, leatherneck disposition. He built up a program that, despite Johnson's reputation, was struggling. Penn had never challenged the top teams and, at Molloy's first practice, only seven men showed up. Upon retiring in 1991, he had a record of 215–101, Penn had won three Ivy League titles and he had coached three national intercollegiate champions. In the course of five different decades, he groomed an impressive list of leading players: Maurice Heckscher, Howard Coonley, John Reese, Palmer Page, Elliot Berry, Stuart Ballard, Joe Swain, Pat Cavanaugh, Brian Roberts, Ned Edwards, Jon Foster, David Proctor and Rudy Rodriguez. For fifteen years, he also ran, with great panache, the Hunter Lott junior tournament. Molloy's chief skill was teaching efficient stroke production and court positioning. Molloy once beat his top player, with the rest of the team watching, by hitting only lobs—proving his point that a fancy Merion offense often hid an inability to handle finesse. In his quiet way, Molloy was a visionary. He was the first squash coach to embrace weight training, to make and market a squash instructional film (in 1973) and to actively recruit overseas players. He was an early proponent of softball. Starting in 1968–69, he regularly took Penn players on tours of England, and his teams practiced with softballs at the beginning of each season.

The colossus of college squash was up in Cambridge. John Morton Barnaby, II, known to everyone in the squash world simply as Jack, arched over the intercollegiate pastures like a wild rainbow. Raised in Oradell, New Jersey, and a graduate of Hackensack High School, Barnaby played behind Beek Pool and Willing Patterson in the famous class of 1932 at Harvard. After graduation, Barnaby started his coaching apprenticeship with Cowles almost by accident. "It was purely a stopgap thing," he said later. "It was the Depression and I needed a job after graduation." Barnaby coached the freshman squash and tennis teams for five seasons. In 1937, days after Cowles had become incapacitated, Barnaby's new team suffered the ignominy of becoming the first Harvard squash side to lose to Yale. The title of national champion went to Yale that year and the next, and to

Princeton in 1939, Yale in 1940, Princeton in 1941 and 1942 and Yale in 1943. In 1938 in a final divorce from the Cowles era, Harvard moved its undergraduate squash program out of thirty-year-old Randolph Hall and up Massachusetts Avenue to Harvard Law School's Hemenway Gymnasium.

During the war all coaching halted at Harvard, and Barnaby did not return to Hemenway until the autumn of 1945. He found an apathetic group of debonair undergraduates who liked to play for fun and did not care about winning. Barnaby turned the program around, but they struggled. That first postwar year Dartmouth beat them 4–1 and 6–1, and Yale crushed them, 9–0, with no player winning more than one game. The next year they won a single match against Yale. In 1950, finally with a team as good as John Skillman's, injuries plagued Harvard: one player badly sprained an ankle; another came down with pneumonia; a third, captain Henry Foster, broke his leg playing football for his house and a fourth, George Plimpton, slipped on an icy doorstep and sustained, as Barnaby described it, "a clay shoveler's fracture of his neck." With a number-seventeen man on the ladder playing in the number nine slot, Harvard lost again to Yale.

Nineteen-fifty-one proved to be the tipping point. Barnaby won his first national intercollegiate team title, Foster won the national intercollegiates and, to top it off, his top players won the national five-man teams in Chicago. Barnaby then blew open the record books. Coaching from 1937 to 1976, he had a record of 355–95. He won seventeen Ivy League titles and sixteen national intercollegiate team titles. Nine of his Harvard players won the national intercollegiates a total of fourteen times. From 1960 to 1976, at the end of his career when his program might naturally be in decline, Barnaby lost just six dual matches. In his last fourteen years, Harvard beat Yale, the last seven coming in 9–0 shutouts. In his final year his team went unbeaten.

His beloved mentor Harry Cowles still reigned supreme. Cowles coached seven future national champions as opposed to Barnaby's four. But if Cowles was Knute Rockne, Barnaby was John Wooden, the midcentury giant leading undefeated teams. Barnaby made squash a religion. He bubbled over with effervescent squash talk. He parried and poked at a subject for hours, laughing, leaping to his feet to demonstrate some shot or even a whole point, pantomiming the faces of players in a long-ago match. For every statement, there was a gesture. "Barnaby mimes a shot with jabs of his forearm and clenches his jawbone so that he looks like a snarling curmudgeon or he beams and claps and says, 'beautiful, by gawd, that's beautiful,'" wrote one reporter in 1976. Bud Collins, the *Boston Globe* sportswriter and bon vivant himself, called Barnaby "the eternal sophomore, in the best sense of the word." At the annual Cowles tournament in New York, he gave a clinic on Thursday evening and spent the rest of the weekend swimming in a flowing conversational tide of former players and friends. He chain drank Coca-Cola and smoked a pack of cigarettes a day, but his tongue never faltered. Barnaby became the jocund archivist for the history of squash. He had played with or coached or watched every good player from the late twenties through the nineties. History for him was a living, breathing animal that tugged him onto his feet. In 1978 he published *Winning Squash Racquets,* the bible of a new generation of squash players, and in the 1980s he penned a monthly column of reminiscences in *Squash News,* which covered his encyclopedic memories of notable players and their famous matches.

Barnaby was perhaps the most egoless great coach who ever lived. He held open practices, allowing players to schedule their own practice times and partners. He banned speeches at the annual team banquet. He attributed all his successes to Harry Cowles. He demanded good behavior and was a keen champion of the intercollegiate custom of refereeless matches. "Sportsmanship," he said, "is maintaining a regard for the other guy's space, whether your ancestors came over on the Mayflower or not." Unlike most coaches who cut their teeth during the Depression, Barnaby adapted with ease to the efflorescences of campus life in the late sixties. "Oh, they're better than they've ever been, in every way," Barnaby exclaimed in December 1970. "Hair? In my day, a guy with long hair was a bad poet. Now everybody has it. So what? The main thing is these kids are better students, more aware, conscientious and concerned. My team works like hell—not too talented this year, but they'll win because they're tigers [the 1971 team went undefeated]. I get a team at the start of a season and tell them the object of the game is fun. The best way to have fun is to get the most you can from the game—that means work and work means winning. If I said squash was really important, they'd laugh at me. We have no illusions about its importance, and we know the world won't go out of orbit if we lose." Harvard did not recruit better players than Yale or Princeton. In fact, Barnaby never formally approached potential players until they arrived on campus, and, even then, he handwrote them a three-page letter inviting them to join the team. He shared his time with every varsity player, knowing full well that his number-nine man counted as much as his number one. "When you're a freshman," he said, "and the Great Head Coach, who's like a tin god, gives you the impression that you're not any good and you'll never be any good, it scorches you, like a drought kills the green grass." They did not have exalted facilities like other schools. Hemenway had peewee galleries filled mostly by aimless law students. Yet, according to Barnaby, there was no holier place in the world.

Although there was no Harvard system, Barnaby's chief revolutionary tenet was to teach finesse early. With the delight of a chess lover—which he was—Barnaby spent hours explaining the concepts behind a shot. His players developed a good squash brain, which was why a John Russell, down in the fifth game of a match that would decide the season, did not wilt under pressure. He regularly brought in champions like Diehl Mateer to spar with his number-one player. Following Cowles's example, Barnaby fielded two or even three Harvard teams in the Boston leagues. He loved the cut and thrust of squash—his *Winning Squash Racquets* had a chapter entitled "The Psychology of Match Play." Barnaby produced some of the great players of American squash. He coached the three Foster brothers, all of whom played number one and captained the varsity. He coached national champions Ben Heckscher, Victor Niederhoffer, Anil Nayar and Peter Briggs. He coached Dave Watts, a six-foot-five power hitter who lost to only one man, Williams's Soapy Symington, in his three years on the varsity. Gene Nickerson, as a freshman, came down with polio, which paralyzed his right hand. Barnaby taught him how to play lefthanded and eventually he gained a spot on the varsity. Jay Nelson played seven on the team but learned to love squash so much he continued to play for years, winning national age-group titles in both hardball and softball.

Above all, he coached Charlie Ufford, arguably the best player never to win the nationals. Ufford won two national intercollegiates and moved to New York after graduation. Six foot six with a famously supple and fast wrist, Ufford moved well for a big man and played a classic finesse game of guile and variety. Superstitious like many players, Ufford never left the court in between games but rather paced across the floor, hands on his hips. Perhaps he needed the break, for hard luck bedeviled his career. He won every major tournament in the country and was the first Harvard man to win the Harry Cowles. In the nationals he was the essence of enduring consistency: nine times he reached the quarters, four more times the semis and once the finals—in 1963 in Detroit, beating Henri Salaun and Ralph Howe, only to lose to Ben Heckscher in four games. A record of fourteen top eight or better finishes in the men's nationals has never been bested. He deserved his nickname of "Ye Compleat Squasher."

Squash in America was born here in November 1884, when Jay Conover built four squash courts on the side of this building on the campus of St. Paul's School.

A 1911 advertisement for squash equipment. The racquets, "not guaranteed," were made from ash and the balls were imported from London.

Four giants of the 1930s relax in a locker room: Germain Glidden, Don Strachan, Neil Sullivan and Beek Pool.

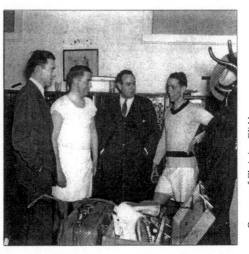

The Brothers Pool: Beek and Larry Pool eye each other before facing off in the 1935 Lockett Cup at the Philadelphia Country Club. Beek won the match in five games.

The iconic squash cartoon of Germain Glidden's "grogs" or squash-playing frogs has been reproduced on tournament programs, T-shirts and even the cover of a book.

A bathing party for polar bears during the Atlantic Coast Championships. Eleo Sears, far left, leads Anne Lytton-Milbanke, Libby Pearson and Esther Daly out of the Atlantic City surf after a February 1935 swim.

For American women in the early years of squash, the Wolfe-Noel Cup competitions between the U.S. and England were the highlights of their careers. This was the 1937 U.S. team before their match at the Junior League Club in New York: Libby Pearson, Margaret Howe, Anne Page, Eleo Sears, Babe Bowes and Agnes Lamme. They won 3–2.

"Remarkable Hashim From Pakistan: Once a Ball Boy in Peshawar, Khan Barely Misses Coup at Unfamiliar U.S. Brand of Squash Rackets" read the headline in a January 1954 *Life* magazine article on the first U.S. Open at the University Club in New York. Hashim, showing his usual agility, was pictured playing Doug McLaggan, a Scottish professional who later became the pro at the University Club. This was the first photograph ever published that was a live action shot taken from the front of a court.

Ralph Morris, courtesy of *Life*

Richard Meek, one of the three original photographers for *Sports Illustrated*, recorded this scene in the University Club gallery at the finals of the 1955 U.S. Open. Squash had opened its doors to pros, but it had not yet abandoned its roots as an exclusive, white, male game.

Richard Meek, courtesy of *Sports Illustrated*

The only time a squash player has appeared on the cover of *Sports Illustrated*, Henri Salaun and Diehl Mateer pose for the 10 February 1958 issue. The two dominating figures of American squash mid-century, Salaun and Mateer faced each other a record six times in the finals of the nationals.

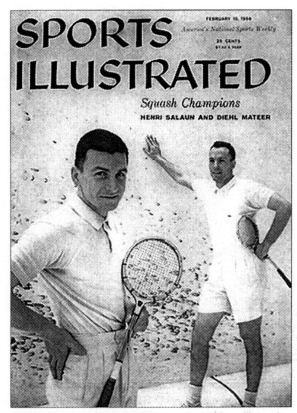

Dan Weiner, courtesy of *Sports Illustrated*

Sixteen national titles were among the many accolades these superb players garnered in their careers. Posing at the Philadelphia Country Club was the 1963 U.S. Wolfe-Noel Cup team: Peggy Howe White, Betty Howe Constable, Jane Austin Stauffer, Ann Wetzel, Margaret Varner and Betty Woll Meade.

Courtesy of USSRA

On his first assignment of his thirty-year career at *Sports Illustrated*, James Drake posed the five 1959 national champions from Merion Cricket Club on the club's great lawn: Ben Heckscher (singles), John Hentz (doubles), Jim Zug (juniors), Diehl Mateer (doubles and open) and Steve Vehslage (intercollegiates). Only Eddie Hahn, who won the 1959 veterans, prevented Merion from a clean sweep of every available men's title that year.

In 1966 Victor Niederhoffer looks up at the gallery with his hangdog eyes as Steve Vehslage lays flattened on the court. Although he grew up in the rough handball scene in Brighton Beach, Niederhoffer did not cause Vehslage's collapse, for Vehslage suffered from an unexplained tendency to pass out when bumped in the shoulders.

Mohibullah Khan, the fierce southpaw who electrified Americans for thirty years before he died outside the doubles court at the Harvard Club in 1994. "He had a flair for the histrionic," wrote Herbert Warren Wind, "an effervescent sense of humor and talent to burn."

Courtesy of Saki Khan

You can call me Al: Two of the leading teachers of the game, Al Molloy, the coach at the University of Pennsylvania, and Al Chassard, pro at Saucon Valley Country Club, chat together at a women's clinic in 1967.

Courtesy of USSRA

Flopping on the floor after smashing a forehand at the 1976 nationals, Gretchen Spruance grimaces as her opponent, Barbara Maltby, moves to the ball. Maltby lost in three straight finals to Spruance, including by one point in the fifth game in 1978.

Women began playing squash in large numbers in the 1970s. This Charles Saxon painting, drawn from an old squash tennis court at the Yale Club, gave a wry look at how the game was evolving. Dozens of public squash clubs sprung up to accommodate this new demand for court time.

Or rather Incompleat. His losses were devastating. As the top seed in the 1961 nationals at Penn, he tumbled in the quarterfinals to former Harvard teammate Dave Watts after squandering a 14–6 lead in the fifth game. Watts won eight straight points, seven of which were clean winners and one was an Ufford error. Ufford called set three at 14–all and went up, 2–1. Watts poked a reverse corner off a lob serve to tie and then aced Ufford on double match point with another bullet serve. Still, Ufford redeemed himself somewhat by winning a classic, 18–17 in the fifth, quarterfinal match at the 1970 nationals, at age thirty-eight, against Colin Adair. This occurred in court two, the same court where he had cratered against Watts nine years before.

As for Jack Barnaby, mandatory retirement in 1976 was a misnomer. Not only did he appear at Hemenway most winter afternoons, but in 1979 he became the head coach of the Harvard women's squash team. For three years, he coached the Crimson women, posting a 28–4 record and winning the Howe Cup in his final year. After winning the clinching match at Yale, Barnaby poured champagne into the silver trophy, drank it with relish and said, "I'm as happy as a clam in the mud at low tide."

Women's squash, as Jack Barnaby so vividly demonstrated, could be invigorating, but, until the 1970s, the United States Women's Squash Racquets Association never fully freed itself from a parlous state of health.

Administratively, the USWSRA and the USSRA acted like an old married couple. They lived separate lives, slept in separate bedrooms and yet still shared a common name. In 1947 Eleo Sears stepped down as president. Although she maintained some involvement until her death twenty-one years later—she won matches at the nationals in her seventies—her retirement allowed a new breed of women to come into power. These women, many of them wives of prominent squash players, built and maintained vis-à-vis the USSRA a complete, if somewhat redundant, set of structures. They wrote their own section in the annual USSRA yearbook, along with other independent associations like the professionals and the colleges, and every five years they printed their own USWSRA yearbook. The association rented office space from the USSRA and set its own fixtures schedule. Its tournaments ran separately from the men's—it was not until 1976 that the U.S. women's nationals was played at the same club on the same weekend as the men's nationals.

There had been serious doubt as to whether women's squash would reappear after the Second World War at all. Only Philadelphia's missionary zeal put that question to rest. Yet the scale of operations in the fifties and sixties was frighteningly small. Forty years after its founding, the USWSRA had barely grown. In 1935 there were, in addition to the national singles and doubles and teams, seven singles, two doubles and two mixed doubles tournaments; in 1968 there were seven singles, three doubles and six mixed doubles tournaments. The USWSRA, with membership hovering around one hundred and fifty, limped along needing more organizational determination. It never declared which squash ball would be the official ball for the year, as the USSRA did. Instead individual tournament directors selected a ball at whim, a custom that often troubled players who had been practicing with a different ball. One continual problem was sustaining interest from players. Women got involved, played for a few years, then dropped away. Few women could raise children, work and swat a ball around a white box. The association condoned the practice of holding tournaments during the week—until the mid-sixties almost every tournament except the nationals started on a Tuesday and finished on a Thursday. Access was a continual problem. There were few public facilities, and the private clubs were indifferent if not hostile to women. "In the States squash is a man's game—and a rich man's at that," Barbara Clement, a leading Philadelphian player and administrator, said while touring England in 1953. "It's an invariable rule that if a woman wants to take up the game she has to have men relatives or friends already in a club."

The women's district associations struggled or thrived in large part because of the issue of access. Three associations—Massachusetts, Philadelphia and Metropolitan—performed yeoman USWSRA work on the local level. In 1939 the Massachusetts association started a series of inter-club matches amongst three participating clubs (Harvard, University and Union Boat) and took over the running of the state championships. In the postwar era, a woman had to be a Sherlock Holmes to discover available courts in Boston. Harvard banned women. MIT allowed women to play if they were connected to the university. YMCAs in Boston and Newton were open. Middlesex School permitted women to play. If you lived in Brookline, you could play at the town courts for one dollar per year. The Baba Lewis Invitational, named after the stalwart Boston player and 1958 national finalist, began in 1971 and was the district's highlight tournament. Betty Baker, Pat Keohane, Laura Farnsworth, Mrs. Robert Potter, Debbie Brickley and Winky Zug were the association's leaders. Every year was a struggle—in 1968 there were ten teams in the local Tuesday night squash league, nearly double the previous year, but only eight women, five from out of state, entered the Massachusetts state championship.

Although founded after the Massachusetts association, the Philadelphia district was the strongest. It had six active clubs in its inter-club (Cynwyd, Germantown, Merion, Philadelphia Country, Philadelphia Cricket and Wilmington Country) and a strong women's doubles league. In the sixties Philadelphia, under Noel Spellman, formed an Evening League "for working gals." Barbara Clement directed a fine junior program. In 1938, six years after launching the boys' Philadelphia & Districts tournament, Merion Cricket Club started a girls' wing of their annual Christmas holiday junior squash weekend. Not surprisingly, until the sixties, only two non-Merion or Cynwyd players, Betty Shellenberger and Barbara Salembier, won the tournament. New adult players were encouraged by the Manheim, a Germantown Cricket Club tournament open to women who had not won an A-level tournament. Mixed doubles was also a cornerstone of the Philadelphia association, which ran its own state tournament and the famous Germantown Invitational Doubles. Founded in 1942, at Germantown Cricket Club, and the predecessor to the national mixed doubles tournament that superseded it in 1969, the Germantown tournament had a Saturday evening dinner dance that was the curtain closer to the Philadelphia squash season. Howard Davis, who had played soccer for Dundee United during the war, helped start it, and he and Peggy Scott Carrott won it eight times in the forties and fifties. The Philadelphia women, with all the activity in their home city, were so blasé about tournaments in other cities that the USWSRA decreed that no woman could be nationally ranked unless she played in at least one tournament outside her home district.

The Metropolitan association did not have such a revulsion toward travel. Because New York City was full of male-only clubs, outlying clubs experienced the most activity. In the five boroughs, only the Riverdale Yacht Club and the West Side YMCA (the former home of the Lone Star Boat Club) were available for female squash players. In 1962 the district held four tournaments, none of which were played in the city, so it was considered revolutionary when the old Columbia Club agreed to host a women's tournament in 1971. Under the leadership of Mary Ellen Johnson, Princeton was the nucleus of the Metropolitan association. It published a periodic newsletter, the *Pumpkin Papers*, that was the closest thing to a national women's squash magazine. The Pretty Brook Tennis Club annually hosted the New Jersey states, one of the oldest and most popular tournaments.

For other areas of the country, personal initiative made a staggering difference. Barbara Clement, from Merion, sparked a revival in Boston when she lived there in the forties. Peggy Scott Carrott, a Germantown Cricket Club star, married a Greenwich man and revitalized that ancient home of women's squash in the early fifties. Mary Knapp was the doyen of Hartford squash. She hosted the 1962 nationals, the first time they were not played in Greenwich, Philadelphia or Boston. In 1968 in Baltimore, Margaret Riehl bought an old gymnasium from a former school called Girls' Latin. She and her husband John put in two squash courts and created the Racquet Club in Roland Park. Within four years, she had persuaded Eddie Shaeffer, the professional at the Maryland Club, to coach the dozens of women she had inspired to learn the game. In 1974 two Baltimore teams went to the Howe Cup and Maryland hosted more than ten women's singles and doubles tournaments that year. Four years later Riehl started a Baltimore Open, with substantial prize money. Riehl went on to become the last president of the USWSRA, from 1975 to 1979, and play a key role in merging the association with the USSRA.

A major focus of the USWSRA was the Wolfe-Noel Cup. In 1949 Eleo Sears revived the competition, which had been played six times during the thirties. It would be played eleven more times before it was discontinued in 1977. Sears's death in 1968, entropy and a changing way of life led to the demise of the Wolfe-Noel—after all, not everyone could pick up and leave for a month and a half every other year—but the main dehabilitating factor was that the U.S. women were dramatically worse than their English counterparts. America never won a single match in the Wolfe-Noel matches in England, while the English managed to win twenty-one matches and three cups in America. Twice in America, the U.S. team barely pulled off heroic wins. In Philadelphia in 1949 with the contest tied at 2–all, Peggy Scott Carrott survived a tough five-game match against Betty Cooke of England to give America the victory. Ten years later at Penn, with the contest tied at 2–all, Betty Howe Constable powered through a four-game victory against Sheila MacIntosh. In 1968 Janet Morgan, the English champion, had to actually coach the Americans during the cup match. At the Lansdowne Club in London in 1953, the United States sunk to its lowest point. The team had such little confidence that they bet amongst themselves that if anyone got seven points in a game she would be thrown into the pool. Peggy Howe managed to reach the magic number in the second game of her match against MacIntosh—

she led 7–2 in the game but hit her serve out and went on to lose in three games. Afterwards, the U.S. team ducked Peggy in the water wearing her squash clothes. In the melee of photographers and onlookers, her twin sister, Betty, who, as the *Times* reported, "was well-beaten by Mrs. G. R. Turner, 9–3, 9–2, 9–2, and she did not deserve her involuntary bath," was also pushed into the pool.

Foamy swims aside, the Wolfe-Noel greatly boosted top-flight American women's squash. The media attention was flattering. In 1957 the BBC broadcast the Wolfe-Noel match over the radio. English newspapers followed the U.S. tour every day, breathlessly reporting on what the women wore, ate or said. "The team brought with them a variety of footwear, including gumboots, fur boats, galoshes and court shoes," one Edinburgh newspaper told its readers in February 1950; the headline to the story declared that Peggy Howe was wearing black tartan panties. Reporters added up the number of children the U.S. team had birthed and gave biographies of the "careerist" women on the team. "Have American women bigger personalities than English women?" another asked after the team did "their hilarious version of a Red Indian squaw dance at a Cheltenham hotel. . . . This has always been and always will be a matter of controversy." "The team has brought on average fifteen dresses, including six ball gowns, and each have ten pieces of luggage," noted the *Evening Standard* in 1953. The ball gowns came in handy because the team had an active social schedule, with champagne dinner parties, receptions with the Lord Mayor of London and teas with the Duke of Edinburgh.

Closer to home, the annual domestic equivalent of the Wolfe-Noel was the Howe Cup, a five-woman national team competition that was launched at the first nationals in 1928. In 1958 the competition was expanded with a B division and ten years later a C division. In addition, in 1968 the women's association invited a team from Canada to participate, which was the first official interaction between women in the two North American squash nations. In 1955 the competition formally split from the nationals to its own weekend, when Gig Griggs, a former Canova model and USWSRA official, donated a permanent trophy, the Howe Cup, named in honor of Margaret Howe and her twin daughters Peggy and Betty.

It made sense to honor the daughters because they were the commanding players in the 1950s. Only three times that decade did someone besides one of the Howe twins capture the nationals. Peggy, a tall, dark-haired woman who was born twenty minutes after Betty, won back-to-back titles in 1952 and 1953 and lost a further three times in the finals. She triumphed in her first year in part because of some inadvertent familial meddling. Janet Morgan, the Englishwoman who won the U.S. nationals with ease in 1949, came over a week before the nationals. In an exhibition at the New Haven Golf Club, Morgan got tangled with Bill Howe, the patriarch of the Howe family, and badly sprained her ankle. At the week-long squash festival at the Harvard Club in Boston—the Howe Cup for two days, the U.S. nationals for five and, on Sunday, the Wolfe-Noel Cup—Morgan hobbled around with her leg in a cast and managed only to play in the Wolfe-Noel, losing quickly to Peggy. With Morgan a non-factor in the U.S. nationals, Peggy flew to victory despite the fact she played all week with a self-inflicted black eye. In the finals the following year, at Merion, Peggy played her sister. Betty had until that season never lost to Peggy, but Peggy was match tough this time. In the first game Betty fought back from a 12–3 deficit to 12–11, but Peggy ran out the game and took the next two, 15–5 and 15–9, to repeat as champion. "We just don't like each other on the squash court. I won't get out of her way, and she won't give me a thing." Peggy told *Time* magazine. "She's like a bulldog. She drives in under an opponent's racket or swings without regard for anything but hitting the ball. I'm daintier. I play a softer game."

Less a bulldog than a tiger, Betty did not seriously play squash until she was twenty-three. A southpaw with an aggressive, enterprising game, she lost in the finals of the 1948 nationals to Babe Bowes in three games and went down fighting in the 1949 semifinals to Janet Morgan in five long games (Morgan beat Peggy easily in three the next day). After winning in 1950, she married Pepper Constable and partially withdrew from competitive squash while having a family. In 1955 when her third child was a year old, she yearned to get back on the court. Living in Princeton, Constable persuaded John Conroy, the Princeton squash coach, to let her play. Conroy put her down on his roster as "B. Constable" and snuck her into Dillon Gym through a back door. The Princeton men, in the warm Dillon courts, provided good tuneups for Constable. It turned out she could beat most of them, and she often smacked balls into the rears of male players who refused to clear for her. Constable set the standard for excellence in women's squash, winning four straight nationals. Constable's last victory came in the finals of the 1959 nationals at Pretty Brook. After winning the match with a forehand rail, she tossed the ball up to her husband and announced her retirement.

An absolute beginner, Margaret Varner, took over her throne. A tall rodeo rider from El Paso, Texas, Varner won the world badminton championship in 1956. She then picked up tennis and reached the finals of the doubles at Wimbledon in 1958. In the winter of 1959, living in Wilmington, she began taking squash lessons at the Cynwyd Club. Varner's first tournament was the 1959 nationals where she upset Janet Morgan in the third round to reach the quarterfinals. The next week, she played number five for the U.S. Wolfe-Noel team and won her match. After Constable retired, Varner won four straight national titles with ease, rarely losing a game as she shellacked the ball with unusual vigor. Varner retired in 1963 and in 1967 she co-authored a squash instructional manual, making her the first American woman to write a book on the sport. She was tough and leathery and had that Texan thousand-mile stare—meeting her gaze was like looking into the lights of an oncoming express train.

With Varner, Norm Bramall cemented his position as the most effective women's coach in history. Bramall, the son of a cotton salesman, coached the varsity tennis team at Haverford College, where he stayed for forty-one years. He also joined the Cynwyd Club and in 1939 took over its squash program. Unlike most clubs, Cynwyd encouraged the wives of members to play. Still the women needed a coach. Cynwyd member Frank Zook coached Babe Bowes privately, and the other women were left to fend for themselves. Bramall was not a radical liberationist—he quit Haverford in 1968 when too many players came to his courts with beards and beads— but he firmly believed in a woman's right to swing a racquet. One rainy day in 1946, he took Jane Austin Stauffer, a woman he was teaching on the tennis court, inside to play a little squash. In 1951 Stauffer beat Betty Howe Constable in the finals of the nationals, 15–12 in the fifth. Steady as a metronome, the five-foot-four Stauffer managed to slip past Constable, who had beaten her in the finals of the nationals the previous year.

Bramall had a magic touch. Five of his seven national champions hit, or missed, their first squash ball with him watching. One was Lois Dilks, who won the nationals in 1954, while a senior at Penn. In the final of the nationals at the Harvard Club in Boston, Dilks beat Peggy Howe, 13–15, 11–15, 15–9, 17–15, 15–12, in a major upset. Peggy, the two-time defending champion, had beaten Dilks in three games earlier in the week at the Howe Cup. Dilks, with a poker face reminiscent of Helen Wills, climbed up to a 12–6 lead in the fifth game and managed just barely to hold on. Another Bramall winner was Ann Wetzel, a beautiful retriever and shotmaker who replaced Varner as national champion in 1964. Before her victory, Wetzel lost a record six times in the finals of the nationals. The ignominious streak started in 1952, when she was twenty years old, and included a disastrous 1957 final when she held two match points against Betty Constable. Despite the losses, Wetzel earned a number of notable titles. In 1961 she beat Varner twice in one month, in the Philly Districts and the Pennsylvania states. Her best win came in 1959 when she finally beat Constable, in eighteen minutes in the finals of the Pennsylvania states, breaking Constable's six-year unbeaten streak. After Wetzel came Joyce Davenport in 1965 and 1969. Davenport, a mercurial player with a cutting reverse corner, went on to dominate veteran squash à la Henri Salaun, winning multiple titles in various age groups. Carol Thesieres, a Germantown Cricket Club lefthander, also trained with Bramall. She won the nationals in 1971 and was runner-up twice more.

More than just a mentor to national champions, Bramall was a leader of women's squash. He coached the 1959 Wolfe-Noel team to a 3–2 victory, its last win in the series. He supported women's doubles and carefully instructed his charges in the mysteries of the four-handed game. Twenty-two times, one of his players was a part of the national doubles champion team. Gail Ramsay won the intercollegiates a record four times—no man or woman has replicated that feat—as well as three national doubles titles and a record seven national mixed doubles, six with her brother Bill. A stream of other players learned to love squash under his direction: Doris Foster, Margaret Osborne duPont, Nancy Huntsberger, Mary O'Toole, Irma Brogan, Judy Michel, Tiny Stevenson, Edith Beatty, Blanche Day and Fran Bottger. Bramall had two mottoes that were etched upon the minds of his players: "The walls are your friends" and "tell them once, make 'em practice it a thousand times."

Betty Meade, a three-time national champion, was the only non-Bramall protégé to emerge from the Cynwyd Club besides Babe Bowes. She did not train regularly with Bramall, as her husband Newt was a strong player. (The Meades won the 1967 national husband-wife tennis title at Forest Hills, beating Larry and Billie Jean King.) In one week in 1968, Meade won the national singles and doubles, both without loss of a game, to become only the fourth woman to win both titles in the same year. Two days after her splendid double, tragedy struck. On a rainy night, her husband pulled over on Lancaster Pike to look at some new cars at a Mercedes-Benz dealership, and another driver plowed into their car. No one was hurt, but all three people got out to inspect the damage. A third car suddenly barreled in and pinned Meade against the trunk of her car. Her right leg had to be amputated below the knee. After a three-and-a-half month stay in the hospital, she returned home with a prosthetic leg. In July she returned to her job; in August she played squash with Richie Ashburn and on Labor Day she and Bob Betson won the Cynwyd Club mixed doubles tennis championship. The next winter she danced at President Nixon's inaugural ball.

Besides the Howes, the other ruling women's squash clan was the Vosters family of Wilmington. Bunny, the mother, who was from Philadelphia, never won the national singles, but she was the most dominant woman in doubles history. Her two daughters ruled the 1970s. Gretchen Spruance won five national singles titles and Gretchen's older sister, Nina Moyer, won two. They played each other in the 1972 finals, with Moyer, as defending champion, winning 15–12, 18–16, 18–13. Spruance was the last truly amateur woman national champion. After losing to her sister, she won the nationals every year she played, taking a year off to have a child. At five-feet-eleven with a very contemporary look—frosted bouffant, rose lipstick and stylish coral-colored gingham pinafore outfits—Spruance had the nickname of the Pink Panther. She epitomized the traditional, well-heeled squash woman. She sewed her own squash dresses, cooked chocolate-chip cookies and sold garden plants part time. A natural talent, she had taken only one lesson in her life and nobody had ever corrected her unorthodox strokes. She dropped her racquet head and slapped at the ball with a limp wrist, reminiscent, at least to one observer, of French tennis star Francoise Durr's groundstrokes. Spruance talked incessantly on the court, had superb balance for a tall person and volleyed very well. Every winter she trained solely by playing one match a day, usually against a man. Never a full-time circuit player, she was often ranked at year's end in the "insufficient data" category, because she had not played in enough tournaments.

The most atypical women of the era was Goldie Edwards. She managed to win tournaments without benefit of coaching or even good practice partners in her home city. A New Zealand professor, she moved in 1962 to the University of Saskatchewan, then to Germany and, in the late sixties, to Pittsburgh. Edwards started playing squash because no one played badminton in the Iron City. Her first attempt was at the University of Pittsburgh where she taught health. Situated above a wrestling room, the courts were hot and the play rough. Although somewhat isolated in Pittsburgh, Edwards reached the finals of the nationals four times (and the semifinals of the 1983 nationals at age fifty-one) and won two Canadian nationals. Her silver came more easily in the age groups, where she won more than twenty-five titles.

In the postwar era, squash trickled west and south, like a coral reef, slowly building outcroppings in new and unusual places. A cursory, if alphabetical, glance at the regional reports in the 1959 USSRA yearbook belied the notion that squash was just played at McKim, Mead & White–designed clubs in the big-three cities. Morrie Fink took another Class C title in the Atlantic City championships. Joe Lacy beat Southey Miles in the finals of Baltimore Country Club's annual handicap tournament, 15–13, 12–15, 12–15, 17–16, 15–13. Seymour Knox came back from 14–7 in the fifth game to beat Bob Scamurra in the Buffalo city championships; his father presented him with his eponymous trophy in the same court where he had won the title thirty-two years before. Chicago had twenty teams from nine clubs playing in its squash leagues. John Blossom, a recent migrant from Detroit, won the Cincinnati city title over Roland Nord, but the result was reversed in the University Club championships. Cleveland had eleven teams in its city league and Holstein "Foxy" Fox reported that membership in the district had increased by 20 percent. Dayton attracted forty-two entries to its city singles championship, which Doug Talbott won in three games. Detroit had almost one hundred players enter the Michigan state tournament; Eddie Hahn won it for the twelfth time. Van Slyck of Hartford beat Audley Clarke of Providence, 15–8 in the fifth, swinging the Connor Cup to Hartford by one match. Indianapolis ended its 1959 season with a bagpiped-and-kilted parade before its league finals. Louisville, with four active clubs led by the Pendennis Club, declared itself to be "the home of fast horses, beautiful women, excellent bourbon and tired but eager squash players." Both semifinals of the Minnesota state doubles tournaments went into overtime in the fifth game, but Carl Hensel & Frank Jevne won the finals in three swift games. The Pacific Coast championships had one hundred and eighty-six entrants. Pittsburgh broadcast the finals of the 1959 U.S. Open live on local television. Rhode Island Hospital won the Providence C league with a 52–8 record. For the first time in five years, Frank Smith did not meet Charles Sherman in the finals of the Rochester city championships. William Schock & David Mesker won both the Missouri state doubles in St. Louis and the Western doubles. Ed Garofalo won his sixth straight Syracuse YMCA championship. Tulsa had a club with a dozen white-shirted players. Cy Borgos emerged from a field of ninety-six to win the Pentagon Officers' Athletic Club championship outside Washington, D.C. William Chambers won his seventeenth consecutive Delaware state title in Wilmington. And, last and probably least, the Worcester YMCA fielded three teams in the Massachusetts SRA leagues and won the B division.

Inter-city tournaments in particular were the highlight of the winter for many districts. The Hahn Cup, launched in 1963, was battled for among Indianapolis, Cincinnati and Louisville; the Knox Cup, started in 1980, was vied for by Pittsburgh, Cleveland and Buffalo; the Browne Cup was decided among St. Louis, Louisville and Atlanta/Charleston; and the Connor Cup, started in 1939, was competed for by Hartford, New Haven and Providence. Many annual home-and-away matches occurred between rival clubs. The Edgemont Country Club in Charleston, West Virginia, started a yearly match with Pendennis in Louisville in 1963; Washington, D.C., and Baltimore fought over the Fitzgerald Cup every year beginning in 1949; Cincinnati and Dayton competed for the Collopy Cup; and the Andrews Cup, a co-ed match between St. Paul's and Minneapolis, was played every year in the 1930s, then revived in the 1980s. Rochester, Buffalo, Hamilton and Toronto played a nine-man team round-robin one day every October. Charleston hosted a seven-city team tournament every winter. Dallas, led by Fred Oman, founded an association in 1957 and spent most of the winter flying to other cities for matches. These weekends were coupled with inter-club competitions like the Lyman Bass Cup in Buffalo and the Ugly Cup in Seattle (for the club that lost the most points in inter-club matches).

The power of these annual events was illustrated by the story of Atlanta squash. Frank Goodman, a Louisville native, first saw squash at a Hahn cup match at Pendennis when he was thirty years old. When he moved to Atlanta in 1960, he found twelve players using the city's only two courts, at the Piedmont Driving Club. Goodman revived the annual Pendennis versus Piedmont match and held matches with clubs in Charleston, West Virginia, Indiana, St. Louis, Lynchburg, Virginia, Oak Ridge, Charlotte and Winston-Salem. He persuaded Hashim and Aziz Khan to come give a weekend of clinics and exhibitions in the late sixties and had Claude Beer, Howard Davis, Treddy Ketcham and Billy Morris fly down to help open Piedmont's new doubles court in the early seventies. Goodman literally created a squash boomtown.

Squash was even more multifarious than anyone in New York could imagine. The Denver Athletic Club, Denver Club and University Club of Denver all claimed their first squash tennis courts to be nineteenth-century vintage, but squash only took hold there after Doug McLaggan arrived. An itinerant Scottish professional, McLaggan had started his career at the Edinburgh Sports Club in 1939, working subsequently in Montreal, London, Chicago and at both the University and Racquet & Tennis Clubs in New York. In 1967 McLaggan moved to the Denver Club and spent many weekends traveling to minor squash outposts to give clinics and exhibitions and prepare the ground for Hashim Khan's arrival in 1973. One strange club was the Bow Brook Club outside Concord, New Hampshire. In 1913 fifteen men bought an old one-room schoolhouse for $900 and turned it into a squash court. The club played matches against the faculties of Dartmouth and Exeter and the Cygnet Club of Manchester. West of the Bow Brook was the Amalgamated Chowder Club in Keene, New Hampshire. Built in 1910 and moved three times, the court has a number of interesting features, including a fire escape reached through a removable front-wall tin. Each autumn the club hosts a New England clam-chowder supper on the court. In 1929 in Rhode Island, the Cranston Print Works put a court with four-inch maple boards on the second floor of an 1864 carriage barn. Its factory workers played during their lunch break. In 1970 George Rowan installed two singles courts and one doubles court in an 1865 Methodist church in North Wales, outside Philadelphia. Dubbed the Church of the Holy Racquet, the Gwynedd Squash Club boasts stained glass windows, a leaky roof and a popular short cut from the ladies' locker room to the doubles court through the men's locker room.

The Northern New Jersey SRA had a number of peculiar member clubs. The players at the Elizabeth Town & Country Club outfitted their gloomy squash-tennis-sized courts with twenty-five-watt light bulbs so that opponents could not see the ball. The Short Hills Racquet Club courts required a ladder to get in and out. Morristown was represented by a private court in an old barn. The owner's dog liked to run away with players' dress shoes during matches. The Sea Bright Racquets Club's locker room was even more curious. Jerry Meyer put a few courts, including a doubles court with a bumpy front wall, into an old apartment building that originally had been a trolley barn, then a grain storehouse. The club's locker room was the apartment of Meyer's eighty-year-old mother. When players went to shower, they passed her, wrapped in a shawl, napping on a couch.

The first club west of the Mississippi to join the USSRA was the Elko Squash Racquets Club in 1937. Newton Crumley, born in a mining camp in Tonopah, Nevada, had learned squash in the Army while stationed near San Antonio and built a one-court club in the Nevada mining town of Elko. In 1955 Crumley moved to Reno and persuaded the local YMCA to build two courts with wood salvaged from a bowling alley. Reno's consummate player was an Army general who played wearing a full-length overcoat.

In a category with fierce competition, the most unusual scene was in

Los Angeles. Squash first appeared there in the 1930s, on an open-air concrete court on the roof of the University Club. Members strung chicken wire across the top of the court to prevent balls from flying out to the street below. Roosting pigeons found the perch delectable. The South Bay Squash Racquets Club in Torrance, the first true squash club in southern California, had six-inch protrusions around the bottom of the walls, which made for some interesting nick shots. In 1956 Stan Woodworth, a Trinity graduate, started a squash team at the Cate School in Captineria and launched the Cate Invitational, the first squash tournament in southern California. The tournament's outdoor cocktail parties were a far cry from the black-tie indoor versions back east, and on-court competition was so casually approached that, one year, three of the four semifinalists never made it back for their Sunday matches. On the entry form Woodworth sent out each winter, he wrote at the bottom, "Remember: It's Just a Game." Observers often referred to this motto as another example of the innate sportsmanship in squash. "People have often complimented me on my 'wisdom,' 'objectivity,' 'good sense' in thus keeping values in perspective, etc., etc.," Woodworth wrote in 1987. "That's all nonsense, of course. When I first put the phrase onto the entry form back in the mid-50s, it was no detached philosophical maxim. It was a desperate plea to bloodthirsty gladiators to refrain from cheerfully assassinating each other with racquet, ball and, yes, fist. . . . In those early years southern California squash was a far cry from the polite preppy little enclave some of us nostalgically (if erroneously) chose to recall from our Eastern past. . . . Los Angeles was more reminiscent of the NHL than that of Merion Cricket Club."

The largest reef in the squash ocean was the Pacific Coast Squash Racquets Association. Like the Western SRA, which included a dozen states west of the Appalachian Mountains, the Pacific Coast gerrymandered more than fifteen U.S. states and two Canadian provinces into its fold. The Pacific Coast championships began in 1940, and, in true West Coast fashion, it was another ten years before players got around to forming an association to govern their championship. Ralfe Miller, a coach at Cal-Berkeley and secretary treasurer until 1965, was the driving force behind the Pacific Coast. The annual championships were a version of the USSRA's nationals, since West Coast players rarely went east for the nationals—in part, because they often found themselves playing the number-one seeds in the first round. The Pacific Coast was a pioneer in crossborder exchanges. Creating their own Lockett Cup events, Seattle annually played Portland for the Old Sitting Bull Trophy, Seattle played Vancouver for the Sir Lancelot Trophy and Seattle, Portland, Vancouver and Victoria all contested the Heussy-Borgendale Trophy. Seattle was blessed when Yusuf Khan, an Indian player distantly related to the Khan clan of Pakistan, moved to the city in 1970. Yusuf was a brilliant coach and helped lead a squash renaissance in Seattle. Multanomah Athletic Club and its dynamic leader, Tom Wrightson, solidified Portland, Oregon. In 1954 the Pacific Coast shocked the Eastern establishment when it managed to win the national five-man team title. Repeated in 1961 and 1974, these victories, along with Mark Alger's victory at the 1981 nationals—the first time a Westerner won the men's nationals—demonstrated the first-class level of play in the Pacific Coasts. Much like when the nationals came to New York in 1929, when the USSRA held the nationals for the first time west of the Mississippi, at Multanomah in Portland in 1979, it was a signal that squash had colonized a new territory

The 1960 Rochester nationals were a perfect example of the do-or-die nature of the obsessed American squashman. A typical February upstate storm hit the Friday morning of the tournament and ruined the best-laid plans of dozens of players. On the New York State Thruway, a skidding truck slammed into Dick Rothschild and Billy Tully's car and sent them into a gully; they waited five hours before a tow truck dragged them back onto the road. Pete Truesdale and Reg Johnson slept on a garage floor. Ned Bigelow, Stew Brauns, John Weeks and Joe Hahn had their flight diverted to Pittsburgh. They took a flight to Erie, another to Buffalo and a train to Rochester. Treddy Ketcham and Paul Steele chartered a helicopter flight, which was canceled when the helicopter was called to rescue stranded motorists. Two men slept on the cold floor of a gas station. Another abandoned a bus and walked through the blizzard. A group of Detroiters driving via Canada bivouacked in their car on the side of the road, running the engine every hour to keep warm. Four Philadelphians circled Rochester for three hours in a plane before returning to Philadelphia. Part of a Buffalo contingent took five hours to reach Rochester by back roads. One man struggled into the Genesee Valley Club Sunday morning. In the end only seven men failed to appear on court for their first-round matches, evincing the Shackleton-like courage and ardor of the squash player going to the nationals.

The stars of squash received all the glory but it was the unsung rank and file that were the game's raison d'être. Carter Fergusson exemplified the squash junkie (or "squnkie") persona. Fergusson, a charming Merion stalwart, made a couple of semifinals in the nationals, won three DeForest-

Tylers and had wins over all the major players in his youth, but it was his role as the Lou Gehrig of squash that makes him memorable. Through 2003 Fergusson played in fifty-six straight nationals, either in the main draw, the teams or an age-group division. It was a study in perseverance. In his senior year at Yale in 1947, he won all thirteen of his matches, playing at number one and led Yale to a 7–0 win over Harvard. In 1948 in his first nationals, he captained the Philadelphia team to victory in the national five-man teams. Then came fifty-five years without a second championship. Another Yalie with grit was Dick Cooley. A leading intercollegiate player, Cooley lost his right arm in the Second World War as a fighter pilot. After the war he stubbornly learned how to play with his left arm and was able to serve by dropping the ball from his mouth. Cooley made it into the top fifteen in the country and, after moving to San Francisco, was a proud member of the 1954 Pacific Coast national team champions. A classic squash conundrum was Bunting Hayden-Whyte, an Englishman who played on the varsity at Whitman College, in Walla Walla, Washington. Every few years thereafter, he materialized at an obscure tournament like the M. Plymouth Shedd Invitational in Minneapolis or the H. H. Bennett Cup in Salt Lake City, often reaching the finals. Hayden-Whyte, a paradelle poet, played barefoot and hit so hard the ball sometimes left little dents in the walls. In 1938 Stanley Galowin, a New York University senior, reached the finals of the New York states. He switched hands during play, thus never hitting a backhand. The Union Boat Club in Boston had its share of squash eccentrics. Lindsay Ware famously brought half the contents of his locker onto the court—briefcases, a sheaf of unstrung racquets, a shoebox with a rabbit's foot. Eddie Bradford, the brother of the governor, played barefoot. Eddie Stapleton, one of the Union Boat pros, played with a wooden leg. Bill Veeck, the underwriter of the 1970 Boston Open, was a fine player who happened to have a wooden leg. The game was especially kind to older players. Connie Saulson was an octogenarian who taught a noon intramural squash class each day at the University of Texas. Howard Wilkins graduated from Yale in 1929 but did not pick up squash until he was fifty. Living in Wichita and flying himself to tournaments in his own plane, Wilkins fell in love with the game, played in his first nationals at age seventy-three and won a number of age group titles. He was a gallery fixture at major professional tournaments well into his nineties and bought a rose for every woman at the annual Jesters' dinner dance. For forty-five years he drove the same car he bought when he first picked up squash, a 1958 Ford Fairlane convertible.

A glass ceiling still loomed over the game. Squash hopscotched across the country by private clubs that were, by definition, uninterested in a mass-supported game. As *The New Yorker* noted in 1974, all the places where squash was played were at clubs that "have membership requirements wholly unrelated to one's enthusiasm for squash (one may have to have attended a certain university, for example) and that charge annual membership fees far in excess of the average worldwide per-capita income. The result has been to give squash the image of a game that is played less by inclination than by right of birth." Squash was an extremely preppy game. "The round-headed bat," wrote Allison Danzig in the *New York Times* in 1966, was "a status symbol." "Until the 1970s, in fact you could tell a true squash player by stripping off his shirt," wrote Bill Mandel, a San Francisco columnist, in 1982. "If an alligator was tattooed on his left pectoral, he was legit." In the *Official Preppy Handbook* ("Look, Muffy, a book for us"), squash was a central accessory. "Squash is such an intensely Prep sport that general competence can be assumed to be part of the average Preppy's talents," announced the book, published in 1980. "You have to be very good to make the varsity squad, but that needn't stop you from playing every day. . . . Though singularly ill-suited for an audience, Preppies nonetheless sit on chilly cement steps to watch two men chase a small black ball around a white box." *Love Story*, the 1970 Oscar-winning film about a preppy Harvard student and his working-class girlfriend, had two squash scenes.

The problem of discrimination had been with squash since its infancy. In 1933 *The New Yorker* broke a story on the ban against Amr Bey. Abdel Fattah Amr, known on the roll of champions as F. D. Amr Bey, was the Egyptian ambassador to the United Kingdom and a Davis Cup player for Egypt. He learned squash at Queen's Club and won six straight British championships. A Jester, he was surprisingly not asked to join the 1934 Jesters tour of America because, as the club historian later wrote, "of the attitude to colour held at that time by many in the United States." The decision not to include Amr, "a small, wiry Egyptian, with a face like a sad mask and a dexterity so pronounced that it give the impression of being no more than harnessed laziness," as *The New Yorker* described him, was a base capitulation to the insidious Jim Crow laws of the American South. It angered many on both sides of the pond. The final match of the tour in New York was, as reported in the *New York Times*, not only played in front of a capacity crowd at the Harvard Club but "sent out on the air by the

National Broadcasting Company on a coast-to-coast hook-up and it was picked up by short wave by the British Broadcasting Company." Willard Rice, chairman of the squash committee of the Harvard Club, gave the play by play, with Don Wilson and Ned Bigelow providing the color commentary. The Jesters lost all their matches that historic night, except for their number one, Edward Snell, who beat Beek Pool, 15–8 in the fifth. It was a shame that the first broadcast of squash on nationwide radio could not have featured Beek Pool and one of the greatest squash players in history, Amr Bey.

Imbroglios like this were commonplace in New York. For years the Metropolitan SRA discouraged clubs from offering "athletic memberships," which to them smacked of professionalism. When the practice grew too blatant, the Met SRA kicked a number of clubs out of its association and refused to allow certain new clubs to become members. Professionalism was just a red herring. Many working- and middle-class men were learning squash, especially at clubs that had formerly used their courts for handball. "There was a feeling that chivalry might give way to roughhouse, body blocks and the like," recalled a squash reporter in 1951. In 1934 the New York Athletic Club launched the Eastern SRA, an association for clubs that were not allowed entrance into the Met SRA, including the Bayside Tennis Club, Block Hall, City Athletic Club, Jackson Heights Squash Club, Mitchell Field Aviators and Crescent Athletic-Hamilton Club in Brooklyn, whose number one player, Murray Vernon, won the league's first championship. The NYAC thrived during its years in the wilderness. Its club championship in 1935 attracted seventy players. Still, the Met SRA's bitter pill was hard to swallow. "They may be bitter over their rejection," editorialized Wallis Merrihew, the editor of *American Lawn Tennis*, in 1934, "from an organization they consider was set up for the good of the game, and also the slight stigma that might be attached to such rejection. There is something of an impugnation of their good sportsmanship which they justifidedly [*sic*] deny and which the conduct of their engagements in any number of other sports belies." Yet Merrihew sided with the Met SRA in this conflict. He argued that the schism was good, that the Met SRA was actually encouraging growth, "by taking a tolerant and even helpful attitude toward new organizations." The Met SRA was oversubscribed. It had its hands full, and its tournaments were "so complicated" due to the many men who entered. People were being melodramatic when they said that the Met SRA should want squash to be played everywhere under all conditions by all people. Merrihew concluded that it was the USSRA's job to sort out the mess.

The Gotham gossip mills continued even after the Eastern SRA merged into the Met SRA in 1946. Tone was important and, more than once, private club officials scolded uncouth players. "I can remember some unnecessarily loud cheering by the members of one club while sitting in the gallery watching a match in which their man was playing," John Humes, Met SRA president, said in 1951, "but that sort of thing is apt to happen once, and never again." People of color were rarely seen. "The MSRA has maintained, despite a facade of hauteur to the superficial observer, a reasonable amount of progress to keep abreast of the spread of squash racquets into less exclusive spheres," concluded an article in a squash magazine in 1951. "The day is not too far off, according to some of the better informed MSRA people, when Negroes, now excluded mainly because of prohibitive construction costs of acceptable courts at Negro athletic clubs, may eventually take their place in the ever-growing MSRA." Subtle and not-so-subtle reminders of prejudice were commonplace. Black players remembered doormen refusing them entrance to clubs, even though they were scheduled to play in a tournament there. Other times, while inside clubs, they were asked by members, who thought them to be waiters, to fetch a cocktail. Steve Simpson was the first prominent black player. He reached the finals of the 1964 national juniors and played varsity at Harvard. Still, it took until 1988 for a black man, Wendell Chestnut at Williams College, to become an All-American in college squash.

If squash was to ever really grow and fulfill its promise, it would have to break the paradigm upon which it was founded. In the spirit of a player like Victor Niederhoffer, who grew up in Brighton Beach and could not get into a private club in Chicago, squash did just that.

It went public.

CHAPTER SEVEN

Sex, Scandal and Celebrities

As with many cataclysmic events, a reformer started the revolution. Paul Monaghan had rich squash credentials. He graduated from Haverford School and the University of Pennsylvania and played at Merion Cricket Club. For his master's thesis in architecture, he designed a sports complex that included squash courts. He gave the model to a bookstore in Haverford. One day in 1954, Hunter Lott walked by the bookstore and saw the model displayed in a window. Knowing that Hill School was contemplating new squash courts, he asked Monaghan if he would help design them. Monaghan agreed. Curious to find new materials for squash court walls, he traveled to plywood mills in Wisconsin, where he heard about an interesting company in the small prairie town of Marshfield. Flying in a single-engine airplane through a snowstorm, Monaghan reached Marshfield and inspected the Doweloc factory. Doweloc produced edge-grain, laminated-maple truck-bed flooring. Monaghan figured that if Doweloc could build maple panels sturdy enough to withstand thirty thousand pounds of bananas, they could probably handle a couple of Hill boys tapping the wall with a rubber ball. Upon returning, Monaghan had Diehl Mateer and Charley Brinton hit balls against a series of panels on Merion's doubles court. Doweloc walls gave solid and consistent rebounds. Monaghan designed Hill's courts using sixty-six prefabricated Doweloc panels instead of the usual two thousand maple strips, which had to be individually nailed into place, sanded and planed. Each court cost twelve thousand dollars, less than half the usual price.

It was a metaphysical storming of the Bastille. No one had ever scientifically researched squash construction materials before. Courts had gone up according to the whims of local contractors, who knew little about boasts and rails. Players always grumbled about courts. The walls cracked. The floors warped. The tin buckled. The door would not stay closed. So few clubs built courts in any given year that there was not enough financial incentive for any industry research and development. It had to come from a player.

Lott introduced Monaghan to the USSRA executive at the 1955 national doubles at Merion. The board asked Monaghan if he would volunteer as a consulting architect for the association. A few of the 1,500 letters and 400 telephone calls he fielded in the next twenty years led to contracts to build courts—his favorite was an underground court below a living room in Midland, Texas—but, mostly, he dispensed free advice. He consulted with a number of construction companies that were developing squash-court building divisions: Powerlock in New Jersey with its "steel-channeled rock maple boards" and a "hot-asphalt backpour technique"; D. B. Frampton in Columbus, who guaranteed its courts for the life of the building; Precision Courts in Cincinnati; American Sports Company in Philadelphia; World Courts outside Boston; Dudley Couglin in New York. In 1958 Monaghan designed the innovative Thomas Ringe courts at Penn. The ten-court complex, with its distinctive two-tiered, wraparound galleries and a glass panel in the tin for photographers, cost $250,000, $100,000 more than if Monaghan had designed a traditional building. Ringe represented a quantum leap in squash court design and was hailed as the finest facility in the world.

Glass was the next step. For decades players had talked about courts with see-through glass walls. John Skillman suggested them in his 1937 book on squash. In 1950 a British tennis magazine reported on the exciting news that a Harley Street doctor had discovered a compound that was opaque on one side but transparent on the other. In the late fifties, the USSRA sent Eddie Reid to Illinois to test handball courts with glass panels. He found it difficult to see the ball if the audience behind the glass was wearing colored clothing. In 1968 Monaghan built eight more courts at the Ringe complex. One court had the first full-length glass back wall in the world. As with many inventions, it took years before people understood the possibilities. The USSRA forbade matches on the court at the 1970 nationals, as they were worried the wall would shatter. A glass back wall eventually led to glass side walls, then a glass front wall. Walls of glass could be moved, making a portable court possible. In recording the action, either with Kodak film paper or an ABC transmitter, a camera could pick out better angles of view. Before glass walls, a spectator had a single, monochromatic perspective: the white, sweat-stained backs of players. It appeared from the gallery as if a mysteriously hypnotic force pulled them, like lead to a magnet, to the front wall where they suddenly recovered their strength, backpedaled, only to be dragged forward again.

The glass wall revealed pained eyes, the grimace of agony after a tin, the lips sucking in breath. They took the game out of the dark oubliette of old-school squash, where courts were perched in the rafter or bowels of clubs, hidden in a crepuscular warren of musty, creaking wood. Everything was now visible.

Emboldened by his glass-wall courts, Monaghan went a step further. He and Barclay White, a real-estate developer who had erected a doubles court in a barn outside Philadelphia, developed the idea of a commercial squash club. In 1973 their company, Squashcon, opened the Berwyn Squash Racquets Club, a complex at the edge of the Main Line, with four singles courts and two doubles courts. A year later Monaghan converted a beer distributor's warehouse in Manayunk, a working-class neighborhood along the Schuylkill River, into a seven-court complex. In 1976 he completed his triad with a four-court facility, Washington Squash Club, in an office building on Washington Square in downtown Philadelphia. Squashcon's facilities were air-conditioned, the first squash courts in Philadelphia cool enough for summer squash. Public high schools fielded teams that played at Squashcon's clubs. Monaghan dreamed of a nation dotted with public courts. "If you're still kicking yourself for not investing in a tennis franchise when tennis was just a gleam in the public's eye, Squashcon offers you a second chance," read one of his advertisements. "A Squashcon franchise in your area represents an opportunity to get in on the ground floor of the next sport to go public, squash."

Harry Saint took Monaghan's project one step further. Monaghan built three facilities in what was thought to be a squash-saturated market. Saint, in building three public clubs in New York, did more than just that. He directly challenged the economic structure of the game in the tightest, most expensive real-estate market in the country. Saint was not from Merion, but he had gone to college down the street at Haverford. After college he had studied for a doctorate in philosophy at the University of Munich, before returning to the States to work in real estate and computers. Caparisoned in monogrammed shirts and suspenders, with his hair slicked back, Saint was a passionate C player whom one magazine described as stepping out of *The Great Gatsby*. He built three facilities in New York: the Fifth Avenue Racquet Club, at Thirty-seventh Street, on the eighth floor of an office building in the shadow of the Empire State Building, the Doral Inn on Lexington Avenue and the Uptown Racquet Club at Lexington and Eighty-sixth Street.

After opening in January 1974, Fifth Avenue boomed. Three-thousand people joined in the first two years, making the $350,000 two-floor, seven-court complex a profitable business—perhaps it was the free coffee. Doral was a different species, a squash-only club located within a hotel. Uptown was the gem in Saint's crown. Designed by the firm Copelin, Lee and Chen, the $1.5 million facility (and a further $1.3 million to originally buy the building) had fourteen courts, including a couple of attractive glass-backed courts and two twenty-one-foot-wide softball courts, along with a sauna, day care for children and a restaurant and bar. Courts could be rented for half-hour time slots, for between six dollars and nine dollars, depending on the time of day (annual dues were a hundred dollars). The *New York Times* hailed the architecture as an example of "splendid urbanism" and Paul Goldberger, a leading critic, added that "the inside moves naturally from the stark whiteness of a customary squash court to a suave white style that calls to mind the spirit of Le Corbusier, with cool white walls, rounded curves and pipe railings." A notorious mix of characters roamed the club, which became a libidinous singles scene: a man who wrote pornographic novels, a number of leggy models and more than a few dedicated players. "Uptown's Super Matchmaker," Aline James, "a personable blonde from Oklahoma," according to a squash magazine, set up games for members and organized round-robins. James's Friday and Saturday evening's co-ed sessions were usually oversubscribed. Squash was sexy. "Play around with a weekend date," suggested a 1978 ad. "Instead of standing in a long line at the movies or that popular disco palace, line up a smashing date to play on Saturday or Sunday. They'll think it's a great idea." For those whose dates did not work out, Saint organized an "insomniacs club" for court time between eleven in the evening and six in the morning. In the summer of 1977, when the city suffered its infamous blackout, twenty-two thousand fans at Shea Stadium were left sitting in the dark, the sixth inning of the Mets-Cubs game suddenly on hold. But at Uptown, two players fetched candles, placed them behind the glass back wall and doggedly went on with their match. Perhaps the most conspicuous match at Uptown appeared on the movie screen in 1979. Woody Allen and Michael Murphy played for a minute and a half on an Uptown court in the film *Manhattan*.

Following Monaghan's and Saint's lead, pay-and-play clubs sprung up everywhere from Los Angeles (The Squash Club International in Torrance) to St. Paul (Commodore) to Dallas (Inwood) to Fort Lauderdale (Players). Saint himself invested in the Capitol Hill Squash and Nautilus Club, a ten-court facility on D Street, in southeast Washington, D.C., just a couple of blocks from the Capitol. The club, patronized by a number of senators and congressmen, was immediately the focal point of Washington squash after it opened in 1982. In Allston outside Boston, Jeff Randall renovated a Pierce-Arrow car warehouse and created The Squash Club, with a chartreuse front door and nine courts glowing under orange trusses. The Concord-Acton Squash Club in historic Concord opened with four courts. Philadelphia had Squashcon, as well as the Uptown Swim and Health Club in the Franklin Plaza Hotel. In 1974 in San Francisco's Bay Area, Alex Eichmann opened the Peninsula Squash Club in San Mateo. The club did so well he opened another in San Francisco, on Harrison Street, in 1981. In Seattle, Yusuf Khan opened Tennis World, an eight-court facility that soon included softball courts. In 1977, just a three-wall boast from the famed Newport Casino, Sam Jernigan put five courts into an old automobile dealership that had been turned into a bowling alley. Dozens of health clubs with racquetball courts built a couple of squash courts to bring in a more discerning clientele: the Downtown Court Club on North Wabash in Chicago put in two squash courts to complement its thirteen racquetball and four tennis courts. The Haddon Hall Racquet Club, the host of the Atlantic Coasts, advertised that, for one dollar, any guest at the hotel could play squash for forty-five minutes. In 1981 Jack Herrick, a Dartmouth graduate and Ohio state champion, and Ham Biggar, a restaurateur and photographer, built Thirteenth Street Racquet Club in downtown Cleveland. With twelve singles courts, a doubles court and six racquetball courts, it was the social hotspot of Cleveland, especially after rumors floated about putting in a co-ed hot tub. Both Biggar and Herrick loved squash and, as one reporter noted in 1979, "a sneaky reason for launching the enterprise was to bring him [Biggar] within proximity of a squash court during working hours." The most licentious public club was in Los Angeles. The Venice Squash Club, which opened in 1972, was in keeping with the bohemian atmosphere of Venice Beach. The roof had gaping holes. The upstairs lounge doubled as a brothel. There was a co-ed sauna and, as one member wrote, "most of the gals used the men's shower, with or without men present." Across the street was Jerry Kilpatrick's welding shop. Kilpatrick, red hair flying down to his waist, came up with a colorful way to dispose of broken squash racquets: he hammered and welded them into a tree stump until he had an enormously spiky squash tree.

New York eventually had eleven commercial clubs devoted primarily to squash, each with wildly different atmospheres. Besides Uptown and Fifth Avenue, the notable facilities were Park Avenue (at Thirty-fourth Street, ten courts, unlimited towels), Park Place (near Wall Street, four courts, telephone number SQUASH-1, antiquated stone-walled locker room, once a newspaper printing plant, now nicknamed the Dungeon), Broad Street (near Wall Street, had one softball court), Lincoln Squash Club (on West Sixty-second Street, designed by Robert A. M. Stern) and Manhattan Squash Club (in the Grace Building on Forty-second Street overlooking Bryant Park, had one doubles court; it was a "slick, clean club where sweaty players wander around among the quiche-eaters," according to the *Village Voice*, but *New York* magazine noted "reports persist that couples have been known to use the courts as trysting places"). Just north of Manhattan appeared Squash/I, a five-court facility in an old trucking warehouse in Mamaroneck, and Southport, with four courts, in Stamford. By the early eighties almost a third of the one-thousand squash facilities nationwide allowed anyone to walk off the street and onto a court.

Populating these courts was a new kind of American. In the 1970s a fitness craze swept the country. With sudden cardiovascular consciousness, couch potatoes, formerly mesmerized by television and the eight-hour casserole, now exercised madly. Jogging became a permanent addiction. Health clubs opened where people lifted and pushed and pulled newfangled Nautilus machines. Time was also an everincreasingly rare commodity. The leisurely three-martini lunch and the longeurs of an afternoon spent dozing at the club with a newspaper vanished. The most economical workout was squash. The intoxication of straining muscles and numbing the mind came in a quick thirty minutes. "This means that harried suburbanites can get in a game at lunchtime or before or after work without biting into a busy schedule," reported the *New York Post* in 1977. Another writer found the game a way to obliterate modern ennui: "Squash is the perfect antidote to some of the dehumanizing effects of our Organization society. The age-old need to vent one's frustrations through violence can be pleasantly and harmlessly satisfied by whacking the little green ball around at tremendous speeds. Squash is an amazing aggressive game (working out may very likely reduce your shrink bills)." Squash was the ultimate mental laxative. The fact that squash was complicated and hard to learn, Harry Saint thought, "attracts neurotic, upper-middle-class people in our society—they like things that are difficult."

More than mere good health drove people to squash. The war in Vietnam and the Watergate scandal shattered the old class structures. American society evolved to such a point that these so-called outsiders—the middle and working classes, women, Jews, hyphenated Americans—could breach the aristocratic gates that barred entry to such previously obscure upper-class sports like squash. "Hardly a game remains that a blueblood can call his own," *Sports Illustrated* sardonically lamented in 1977. "Golf fell to the masses long ago. Court tennis is moribund. The democratization of tennis is almost complete. And now squash. . . . Someday, somewhere, some businessman is going to figure out a way to make 12-meter yacht racing a pastime for the masses and an era will have ended for sure." For many people, learning to play squash was just another lesson in a subtle finishing school before graduating into the upper class. "Women are finding it a good way to meet the nice young men who seem to be squash types. (Squash, you know, is very big at the prestige university clubs, like Harvard and Princeton)," reported the *New York Post* in 1977. An MIT graduate wrote a 1979 article on squash, with "An Upward-Mobility Guide," written for the neophyte who wanted to "adopt the other marks of a bona-fide Eastern Establishment squash player." Suggestions ranged from refraining from outbursts—"breeding will tell"—to cultivating a lockjaw accent and finding an old racquet—"one that looks like Daddy could have used it at Dartmouth (even if Daddy learned taxidermy by mail)."

Racquetball, as much as anything else, engendered the squash boom. In the late fifties, Joe Sobek, the tennis pro at the Greenwich Country Club, created a game called paddle racquets. With racquets made especially for him at the Cragin-Simplex factory in North Attleboro and balls by the Seamless Rubber Company, Sobek popularized his "Greenwich Game" on handball courts. In 1959 Sobek hosted the first paddle racquets tournament on handball courts at a YMCA. Eight years later in Milwaukee, seventy-two players entered the first nationals. In 1969 Bob Kendler, president of the national handball association, took over the sport and renamed it racquetball. It exploded into the consciousness of every American. In 1970, 50,000 played; in 1973, 350,000; in 1975, one million; by the end of the decade, seven million people played racquetball, a figure that dwarfed the country-club world of squash. A professional tour, begun in 1973, expanded so fast that by 1978 it had $250,000 in prize money and sixteen events. One event gave $30,000 to the winner. Marty Hogan, the brash world champion from St. Louis, became a household name.

As squash thrashed in racquetball's wake, the two games raced toward the harbor of public acceptance. Squash, racquetballers claimed, was elitist. Racquetball was a public game. Many of the racquetball courts were new—because the game was new—and had attractive glass back walls in the middle of a health club, not dingy courts in the basement of a club that only a claustrophile would enjoy. Squash was unnecessarily hard to learn, with a tiny ball and racquet head. The squash scene was starchy. Kendler called squash "a lace-pants game." Philadelphia was the capital of squash, while racquetball's heart was in San Diego. In racquetball you could hit the ball anywhere on the front wall and even the ceiling. Squash had the three-wall nick and the Philadelphia shot; racquetball had the crotch shot, the Garfinkle serve and the mercy ball. "Racquetball is like singing in the shower," said Bob Doyle, owner of a racquetball club in Los Angeles in 1977, "it does something for the ego." The better racquetball players dove on almost every point and climbed up side walls like a pro wrestler to launch out for balls. Swearing was commonplace. Rules were meant to be stretched. A four-time national champion, Charles Brumfield, told reporters after losing a tournament in New England, "Next time I've got to be completely obnoxious." Saul Bellow played racquetball. Elvis Presley built a court at Graceland.

For squash players, racquetball was a poor alternative, a game without range or depth for the veteran. It had stumpy racquets, a court with the monotonous measurements of forty by twenty feet and, worst of all, the ceiling was in play. "Virtually anyone with a set of Keds and sufficient motor skills to scratch his nose can play a plausible game immediately," sniffed one player in 1985. Racquetball, moreover, was filled with lunkhead, proletarian types. "Strip away the veneer of the racquetballer, look behind his Las Vegas is for Lovers T-shirt and his recoilless Ektelon racquet and what have you got?" wrote an Edmonton squash player in 1979. "Just an ordinary fellow, four parts real-estate salesman, one part disc jockey and five parts professional football player. But go behind the quintessential squash player, take away the starched whites, his ginger beer and his Dunlop Maxply, and you've got a squash enthusiast, nine parts Bruce Jenner and two parts Salvador Dalí, with just a hint of Machiavelli thrown in for good measure. Squash will never be a sport for the masses—thank God. It would ruin the game if it were." Harry Saint thought racquetball was good for squash: "There's not that much to the game. It's like bubble gum. You can chew all the flavor out of it quickly. I look on every racquetball player as a potential squash player." Tom Jones, a squash promoter, summed up the attitude many had that squash should not hide from its patrician past. He told a *New York Times* reporter, "Whenever you can, mention racquetball and bowling in the same sentence."

The model for public squash came not just from racquetball. In England most towns and villages had public leisure clubs where one could swim, swat a shuttlecock in a badminton court or play squash. Australia also made squash a middle-class sport by building hundreds of public clubs, mostly rudimentary outfits with two courts, a shower and a bar for the all-important post-match beer. In 1964 in Mexico, there was the proverbial one squash court in the country; fifteen years later, Mexico City had over fifteen-hundred courts, many of them public. Canada also went in for pay-to-play facilities. In the summer of 1972, a giant hole appeared on Lombard Street in downtown Toronto. The hole slowly filled with eighteen courts (sixteen hardball, one softball and one doubles). Aziz Khan moved up from Indianapolis to become the head pro at the club, the prosaically named Toronto Squash Club. Anyone who could pay $250 (Canadian) per year could join; five hundred people joined in the first four weeks. By the end of the seventies, Toronto was the squash capital of the world in the eyes of many observers, and this was not because of the Badminton & Racquet Club or the Toronto Cricket, Skating and Curling Club, but because of its public clubs.

A better ball bounced into the picture. Just as with the architecture of squash courts, innovations in the squash ball were slow in coming because no company ever got rich producing balls. Ever since the 1930s, Seamless, the rubber company in New Haven, had a monopoly on squash-ball manufacturing in the U.S, with the Seamless 560 for singles and the Seamless 561 for doubles. But in the early 1960s, new competition emerged from Walter Montenegro. An emigrant from Toledo, Spain, Montenegro parlayed a tiny tennis-racquet-stringing operation in Brooklyn into ownership of Cragin-Simplex, an old tennis-goods company with a distinctive racquet press. Montenegro changed Cragin's focus to squash. He opened a sixty-thousand-square-foot factory in North Attleboro, Massachusetts, and began marketing three lines of squash racquets. Cleverly kowtowing to an influential group, he put the signature and club colors of the many professionals on the handle, including a Mohibullah Khan Personal Model "with built-in power for the incomparable Khan touch," which was adorned with a green Islamic crescent and star.

Montenegro, much like Monaghan, attacked a perennial squash problem almost by accident. The Seamless ball was loaded with carbon (thus staining the walls of squash courts with that distinctive pockmark), had little bounce and was usually troublesome. Half a box of balls played beautifully, the other half was filled with duds. Some broke like eggs, others went clumpy like wet clay. Some got too warm, others stayed ice cold. A conversation with Joe Hahn, a USSRA official, led to Montenegro tinkering with rubber and molds in his Varick Street offices. He gave Hahn bags of balls to test at the New York Athletic Club. In 1961 Cragin issued its diamond balls: the green diamond for regular winter play and the yellow diamond for summer play. Montenegro pushed squash into new worlds, for the diamond balls made it possible to play squash in the warmer months. Squash went from an October-to-March romance to an all-year affair.

Sadly, the green diamond proved to be fungible with the Seamless. It too broke frequently, played inconsistently and often went mushy after a couple of hard games. Throughout the sixties and early seventies, the USSRA sanctioned both the Seamless and the Cragin balls, using whatever was the better product that season. In 1967, for example, the USSRA used the green diamond for the national singles but the Seamless for the national teams, even though both events were on the same courts at the same weekend. Ted Friel, a Philadelphian on the USSRA executive committee, was in charge of the ball, bat and court subcommittee for a decade. Every year he sent in a dolorous report to his colleagues, rife with complaints from players about the Seamless and Cragin balls. "The problem of finding a consistently playing ball which won't break in the first few points of a match continues to plague this Association," he wrote in his 1973 report. "After a decade of jawboning, promises, great expectations and complete frustration, our domestic manufacturers appear no closer to a lasting solution than they ever were. As a result of our Canadian neighbors' experience last weekend, we were forced to eliminate the Seamless ball from our tournament this weekend. The Cragin ball has varied from poor to excellent, and all we can do is hope that we have a decent batch to play with tomorrow." Friel ended his report by mentioning that in October 1972 a number of players and board members hit with a new Australian ball.

Made by Bestobell-Merco in Australia and distributed by Walter Eichelberger, a Cynwyd doubles player, the ball was called the seventy-plus—it was originally meant to be played in temperatures over seventy degrees. Squashcon's 1975 summer league formally field-tested it and players immediately wanted to use it all year long. Without guidance from the USSRA, there was some confusion. During the 1975 Met SRA season, the Cragin, Seamless and seventy-plus were all approved and the selection of ball at league matches was determined by the spin of a racquet. The USSRA agreed with such an indiscriminate method of ball choice. "The sense of the meeting was that we have a wonderful game as played with our standard hardball, and are not yet prepared to go officially soft—not with the 70+ and certainly not with the little-used British soft ball," announced Friel after the February 1977 annual meeting. "The USSRA's position is one of encouraging play of the game with whichever ball one chooses." This sort of waffling at the USSRA would become endemic fifteen years later, when another squash ball change was imminent. Finally, in the autumn of 1977, a year after the men's and women's intercollegiate associations and the professional association had switched, the USSRA adopted the new ball for its tournaments.

The seventy-plus changed American squash as much as the glass back wall. Much smaller and lighter than the Cragin or Seamless, the ball looked similar to the standard softball. The complaints to Friel stopped, more or less, with the seventy-plus. You could open a box and be sure that every one of the dozen would play the same. Neophytes could use a lighter racquet (the old balls required a sturdier frame) and pick up the game twice as fast. The seventy-plus didn't explode off the racquet like the old balls. It was so easy for beginners that many saw the seventy-plus as a response to the challenge of racquetball. Certainly its genesis in Australia had nothing to do with racquetball, but its quick adoption was in part because of the rival game's success. Top players loved the seventy-plus. Instead of a sign of fatigue and desperation, the lob now was an offensive shot; lob serving became an art. The front court was no longer a no-man's land. The roll corner stayed down. The double boast was less risky. "A game that was basically rather a primitive slugging match has become a game with a greater capacity for flair and invention," wrote Adrian Goddard, a British professional at the Downtown Athletic Club in New York, in a 1979 squash manual devoted to the new seventy-plus game. "Squash is no longer raw hacking and a cold shower; you have the time now to throw your opponent the wrong way and dispense with the rugged All-American stuff if it's distasteful to you. The basic units of the hardball game—alley shots and cross-courts—retain their importance, but the 70-plus ball has brought with it some of the characteristics of the International game—the parabolic serve and lob, the straight drop shot, the corner boast, the attacking boast. There is more running, along with more strokes and more time to play them. The 70-plus may be a compromise, but it has a charm all its own."

A final reason for the sudden rise of squash was increased media coverage. A few years before, one was lucky to see a tiny listing of results from the nationals in a newspaper. Now magazines wrote profiles. Newspapers ran articles. Advertisers used squash as a backdrop for copy. "In Jack Daniel Hollow we play horseshoes as serious as you play squash," advertised Jack Daniels. "Of course, we're not ready to challenge anyone in squash. We don't even have a court here in Lynchburg." More books on squash were published in the five years between 1975 and 1980 than in all other periods combined. Squash racquets bulged out of the briefcases and gym bags of commuters, an old-school status symbol that was suddenly cutting edge. Station wagons bore the telltale sign of the suburban squash player—a USSRA bumper sticker: SQUASH IS MY RACQUET. Miles Donald, an Englishman who moved to Austin to teach at the University of Texas and won the Texas championships in 1968, wrote a mystery novel called *Boast*, a riproaring tale with characters modeled on Hashim Khan, Mahmoud el Karim and Jonah Barrington. The villain was a bloodthirsty Rastafarian who had played number one at Cornell.

Squash finally got its own monthly magazine. In the 1920s the USSRA started publishing an annual yearbook, which was the sole reliable source of news. The yearbook had only a few photographs, no prose writing and came out sporadically. Starting in 1955 it began appearing each autumn and slowly grew in size and substance. Essays, reproductions of draws of all national tournaments, rankings, regional reports, advertisements, by-laws of the association, playing rules and lists of members filled each issue until it ran for over two-hundred pages. The yearbook was the definitive publication that every squash player pored over as the next season began. Many districts produced their own yearbooks, which varied in style from mimeographed pamphlets (southern California's was a classic case of illegibility) to glossy newsletters (Philadelphia's *Tell-Tale*) to the regional masterpiece of the Met SRA yearbook. Produced singlehandedly by Bob Lehman from 1949 to 1987, the New York yearbook was a thick, idiosyncratic and delightful paean to the game. A jazz lover, Lehman was a ubiquitous sight in the corner of a gallery, camera and notebook in hand, silk foulard around his neck.

Independent voices did not exhibit such endurance. For years squash magazines had sprung up only to wither away after two years or so. Some had a naked commercial aspect, like Walter Montenegro's *Squash Magazine* while others, like Lowell M. Durham's *Squash Racquets USA*, based in Salt Lake City, suffered from its distance from the heart of the game. In 1977 *Racquet Voice*, a newspaper published by Hank Katten, became the USSRA's first official publication for all members. Katten soon downsized his publication and made it into a typed four-page newsletter. In 1976 Kevan Pickens, a fiery New York veteran player, began publishing *Racquet* magazine, a high-brow, glossy magazine filled with top writers and photographers. Pickens slowly pushed the magazine toward tennis, and, after a few years, *Racquet* magazine was almost devoid of squash coverage.

In April 1978 two advertising agents named Tom Jones and Hazel

White Jones launched a monthly newspaper called *Squash News.* Tom, a Rochester native, was a typical New York squash player. He had played at Williams and joined the Racquet & Tennis Club when he moved to New York. Hazel, his vivacious wife, had grown up in Indianapolis and first encountered squash at a brokerage-firm office party at the Indianapolis Athletic Club where she played doubles in her stockings and cocktail dress. In the late sixties, she moved to New York and, after working at Dean Witter, married Jones and joined his agency. In 1976 John Halpern, the co-owner of Broad Street, asked Tom if he might work as a press agent for a consortium of the public clubs. Tom agreed, but for six months, nothing took. On Saturday 2 July 1977, he got a hit. The *New York Post* ran a full-page article on SQUASH CRAZE PROMISES PROFIT TO CLUB OPERA-TORS with a photograph of Halpern, cigar in mouth, at Broad Street. Within weeks the dam had burst and dozens of magazines and newspapers did stories on the new world of public squash. The clubs thought Jones had done such a good job that they asked about a regular monthly magazine. Tom and Hazel agreed to create one, even though neither had any journalistic experience. A black-and-white tabloid, the first issue of *Squash News* ran sixteen pages, with a dozen photographs and a smattering of advertisements. It cost fifty cents an issue, or five dollars for a year's subscription of twelve issues; another way to read it was to join one of the public clubs in New York, where membership included a subscription. Tom and Hazel traveled around the country, meeting with officials from every district association and asking for a simple deal—if you give us all your news and five dollars per head for each member of your association, we will send them the magazine. By the end of the year, the USSRA made the magazine a benefit of membership.

Squash News helped change the way squash players in America saw themselves. It reached, at its peak, seventeen thousand people per month. Hazel as editor and Tom as publisher officially divided duties, but the lines blurred because the magazine was just a part of their general promotion of the game. They produced four North American Opens, and in 1985, relaunched the United States Open as a softball event. At the core was the magazine, which in its black agate gave the news and the gossip (as well as a tournament entry form) to players in every squash town in the country. "The arrival of a new issue of *Squash News* is a considerable event in the eyes of every squasher," wrote Larry Shames in 1979, "and many a self-respecting businessman has been known to tuck the tabloid inside his *Wall Street Journal,* secretly perusing it on the commuter train when he should be studying those little tables and graphs."

There was a remarkably faddish look to a sport whose players previously hoped to be in the newspaper just three times in their lives—at birth, at marriage and at death. Celebrities of all stripes admitted to being addicted to squash: Zubin Mehta, Tom Jones (the panty-engulfed singer, not the publisher), William Shatner, Eartha Kitt, Phil Esposito, Robert McNamara, William F. Buckley, Perry Ellis, Richard Avedon, Jackie Kennedy Onassis, Strobe Talbott, Kris Kristofferson, Tom Selleck, Joe Frazier, Dick Cavett, John Lindsay, William Weld, Tom Brokaw and Carl Bernstein. Top businessman like George Ball (Prudential-Bache CEO), Brian Dyson (Coca-Cola CEO), George Kellner (hedge-fund giant) and Ivan Boesky all played—Boesky even sponsored the 1986 nationals. In New York the famous often retreated to private clubs: Mort Zuckerman played at Harmonie, Leonard Bernstein at the University Club, John Knowles at the Racquet & Tennis, Dustin Hoffman at the City Athletic Club and Frank Gifford at the New York Athletic Club. The public clubs had their regulars: Alan Alda, Jean Strouse, Yvette Mimieux and Brian DePalma played at Uptown and Paul Simon belonged to the West Side YMCA. Mick Jagger somtimes rocked up to Uptown on Sunday afternoons to play in between concerts, and Roger Daltrey once was caught on film at Thirteenth Street in Cleveland. B-list celebrities gravitated to the game. In 1977 Manhattan Squash hosted a promotional party in which a *Penthouse* cover girl, Cheryl Rixon, played an exhibition against a radio personality, Dick Heatherton. Richie Ashburn, a former outfielder with the Philadelphia Phillies, took up squash and reached the semis of the national seniors in 1978. In the winter of 1977, Tom Seaver, the former New York Mets hurler, took an elbow to the face during a squash match and suffered a broken nose. After his retirement from baseball, Seaver played in a number of pro-am doubles tournaments (he won the 1989 Boston Open pro-am with Clive Caldwell). In 1993 he squared off against John McEnroe as a warm-up exhibition for the finals of the U.S. Professionals. Kareem Abdul-Jabbar and Ivan Lendl had courts at their homes. In the nation's capital, a herd of senators swatted and sweated in a rough, if bipartisan, fashion. John Warner, who with his wife at the time, Elizabeth Taylor, helped open Capitol Hill, once whacked John Chaffee in the face and broke his glasses during a match. Another time, Bob Packwood hit Arlen Specter so hard that he fractured Specter's cheekbone. Packwood later got a broken lip that needed stitches when he was hit by a staff member. After detailing a list of squash-playing senators, a reporter wondered if Jimmy Carter might start playing? "According to a White House spokesman, officials there are sticking to tennis and basketball."

Ordinary players could relate more to Frank Stella. The abstract painter took up squash in the early eighties after hurting his back. He played at Park Place, designed promotional posters and financially supported a number of softball tournaments in New York, including the U.S. Open at the Palladium, which was next door to his studio. Like many players, he had grandiose dreams of squash glory when he first saw a squash court: "When I started playing, I have to admit, I really thought I would become a great player. I really wanted to become a great player. I really hoped I'd become a great player. In art, you can keep getting better, but in squash you hit your level and that's just about it. Curtains. You're finished. I hit my limit at about forty minutes of mediocre playing. . . . I'm too old to be a great squash player. At my best, I'm a D. In fact, I can hardly walk." "I can forget about painting," he once said when yet another reporter asked him about the relationship between art and squash. "A white blank and a ball; you don't know where you are. It's like a snowstorm. . . . I'm not tempted to paint squash scenes. All squash has tempted me to do is break my racket."

Junior players benefited tremendously from the new squash dispensation. The club-based system, based on Merion Cricket Club's modus operandi, became the standard method for young players to enter the squash world. The Cincinnati Country Club started the Cincinnati Juniors in the sixties. Don Mills, a Trinity graduate, arrived at CCC in 1975 and was the coach of many future stars. Outside of Washington, D.C., Geff Fisher ran a bountiful program at Regency Racquet Club in McLean and in 1976 began the National Capitol Juniors, a popular January tournament. Apawamis started a junior tournament in 1972 and built up a solid program. In Rochester Jim and Barbara Stewart organized volunteers to coach at the Genesee Valley Club.

The Heights Casino, however, proved to be the only club to equal the Merion farm system. In 1965 the Heights started its junior program when Fred Weymuller resigned his membership to become a tennis professional at the club. Weymuller, a Heights native who had worked at the *Wall Street Journal*, soon shuttled kids to squash courts because his junior tennis program was oversubscribed. In 1970 he brought his soon-to-be wife Carol into the club, and the young couple started a Sunday afternoon squash league and, in 1974, a morning junior program. In just six years, they produced an amazing generation: Bobby Ankerson, the Boyums, the Claytons, the Deans, the Franks, the MacKays, the McCarthys, the McConnells, Eric Vlcek and Erik Wohlgemuth. In 1977 Heights became the first club to send a group program to the nationals. At the same time, the Weymullers, Geff Fisher and Barbara Stewart persuaded Warren Smith, the president of the USSRA, to create a standing junior committee. The committee set a tournament schedule to avoid conflicts, instituted USSRA sanctioning, encouraged good sportsmanship and added the feed-in consolation feature that ensured each player got a number of matches. In 1978 the Weymullers started the first summer junior squash camp. Soon a number of other coaches started their own. The most longlasting were the Princeton camps, which Bob Callahan started in 1981 and the Harvard camps, which Dave Fish started in 1982. Squash summer camps served not only as a place to improve strokes, but as a way of cementing friendships within the game. Bonds formed on a hot summer day toiling inside on an otherwise deserted college campus lasted well into adulthood.

The commercial clubs supplied the catalyst to the creation of a junior tournament circuit. In December 1974 Paul Monaghan, with teenage sons, decided to launch a junior tournament. He called it the Hunter Lott in honor of the great Merion player and mentor and hosted it at his Schuylkill club. In 1978 Monaghan transferred it to Penn, where Al Molloy directed it. By the early eighties, more than 300 juniors would enter. The Hunter Lott, an early December fixture, ranked second only to the nationals in terms of prestige, and many an afternoon was spent wandering the cavernous galleries at Ringe or staring at the drawsheets taped to the brick wall below the courts.

Following Monaghan's lead, Uptown, Squash/1 and Lincoln Squash started junior programs and tournaments. Plainfield Country Club hosted the Sy Perkins tournament, Choate hosted an Invitational, Mercersburg Academy hosted the Tom Flanagan Memorial and Boston hosted the Holiday Juniors. For prep-school boys the unofficial national schoolboy team championship was a five-man team tournament, held in January at Choate. Begun in 1978, the Choate tournament was the key battleground between Inter-Academic League teams like Episcopal and Haverford, and the New England prep schools.

Women reaped the most benefits from the squash boom of the seventies. A desire for a slenderizing workout and a new attitude toward competition prompted thousands of women to pick up the old gentlemen's game. With child daycare, stay-at-home fathers, flexible work schedules and delayed childbirth all increasingly common phenomena, women had the interest, time and ability to play. "Squash—like brandy and comfortable shoes—has become one of those life-enhancers that women can also enjoy," declared *Savvy* magazine in 1980. The public clubs were completely accessible. Harry Saint specifically advertised for women squash players, prominently noting his daycare facilities. "This is one club where the women's locker and shower facilities are nicer than the men's," he loved to tell reporters. Over a third of the membership at New York commercial clubs was female, which helped fill courts during off-peak hours. In Philadelphia Squashcon ran women-only daylong squash marathons, and in 1978 Schuylkill entered an all-female team into the historic Philadelphia Inter-Club League, the first time since the league was founded in 1903 that women had played official matches. Mixed doubles became increasingly popular. The national tournament, started by the U.S. women's association in 1969 as a replacement for the Germantown Cricket Club's annual tournament, soared in popularity in the late seventies—a record nineteen teams entered the 1978 draw, which was played at Manhattan Squash. Although "squash bunnies"—women using squash purely as a means to pick up men—were not uncommon, the vast majority of women players were as dedicated and obsessed with their sport as men had always been. The public clubs offered new job opportunities for women. Wendy Lawrence started as a professional at Uptown just after her graduation from Vassar in 1974. In 1981 she moved to Capitol Hill to run its squash program. Carole Dicker and Nancy Gengler also worked at Uptown, and Dicker volunteered for almost every administrative position available in New York. Dale Philippi Walker started at Margaret Riehl's Racquet Club in Baltimore, got a job at Newport Squash and in 1981 became coach of the women's team at Yale. Sara Luther worked at the International Athletic Club in Denver. Mariann Greenberg helped run Southport. Ellie Pierce worked for six years at the Printing House, a small public club in the West Village of Manhattan.

Breaking into the private clubs was a little harder. Women had to sue the Harvard Club of New York to be allowed entrance, which was granted in 1975. At the nearby Princeton Club, it took Podie Lynch Milhaupt, class of 1971, to break the squash barrier. The club accepted women members in 1971 but frowned upon women playing squash. Milhaupt and her husband Peter first played late at night. Then a sign went up near the courts cautioning members that women might be present so please refrain from rough language. Eventually Milhaupt and other Nassau women were accepted at the club, but it took a while for male members to break a habit of walking naked into the lounge, which was once an extension of the men's locker room. In 1973 Carol Weymuller became the first woman permitted to play in the Met SRA league, as a D player for the Heights team. That year she also took women from her club to the Princeton Club, then the Harvard Club, for matches. In five years these matches blossomed into a nineteen-team New York City women's league.

In 1981, bowing to pressure from women players, Harry Saint started an E division for tournaments. Hitherto, any beginner was automatically a D player, which itself had only been formally designated in New York in 1966. The E division granted some women a room with a view, although E matches often included them the unattractive combination of extremely frustrated and extremely uncoordinated men as opponents. In 1982 and 1983, Park Avenue won the Met SRA E league. In 1984 Uptown offered not only an E draw at its Chivas Regal tournament, but an EE. "In E people call footfaults on each other, deploy advanced psychological stratagems, bounce off walls or will back the opponent out of position and then call a let," Peter Stephans wrote in summary of the 1983 E league season in *Squash News*. "A player with good technique can be beaten by a willing retriever. Players never know whether they'll face a man, woman or child in their next match, and can't predict if the opponent will be a hot shot from the racquetball world or someone who is unable to hit, throw or even catch the ball. The only factor which can be counted on is competitiveness. Everyone who enters an E tournament is slightly surprised to be in an athletic contest at all. Long forgotten dreams of glory quickly surface, a sense that it's not too late after all."

Progress for women was uneven. In 1977 the USSRA started a junior girls' nationals. In Philadelphia women's squash thrived. In 1976 there were one-hundred-and-nine teams from thirteen clubs playing women's league squash. In New York women finally had a choice of venues but it was still a paltry percentage: As late as 1978, only thirteen of the sixty-two member clubs of the Metropolitan SRA allowed women to play on their courts. On May Day 1979, after almost fifty years of independence, the women's association merged into the USSRA. (In 1985 a "women's division" within the USSRA dissolved, and all women simply became regular members of the USSRA.) At the time of the merger, there were less than one thousand female members of the USSRA.

Collegiate squash for women started in Poughkeepsie. Cal Mac-Cracken's father, Henry, was president of Vassar from 1914 to 1946. Midway through his presidency he built some squash courts, and in 1937 a young woman working in the athletic department, Betty Richey, began a team. Two years later Wellesley built two courts; Smith soon followed, but these schools frowned upon intercollegiate matches, so they never played each other. In 1965 Aggie Bixler Kurtz, Smith class of 1962 and a physical education teacher under Richey at Vassar, organized the first national intercollegiate tournament at Wellesley. Eight college women came that weekend, and a Vassar first-year student, Kit Allabough, who was ranked in the top ten in the nation, won the tournament. Each year the national intercollegiates got bigger: In 1969 fifteen women played at Vassar; in 1971 twenty-five played at Penn; in 1973 forty-seven played at Wesleyan and in 1975 sixty-four women filled a standard draw at Harvard.

The surge in players in the early seventies resulted in part because many universities began accepting women and launching women's squash teams. Title IX, the federal law mandating gender equality in intercollegiate sports, spurred these colleges to add a women's team to their existing men's programs. In 1966 Penn began offering squash for women as a way to fulfill physical education requirements, but initially the women were allowed only to play at nine in the morning. In 1970 Ann Wetzel, the 1964 national champion, started a varsity team at Penn. Radcliffe women also found doors literally shut to them. Until the mid-sixties, women were banned from Hemenway. Then they were permitted on the courts, but only before eleven in the morning, which often meant banging on the front door until a custodian unlocked it. In the early seventies, women were still excluded from the five basement courts, because athletic administrators feared they might be sexually assaulted there. Eventually this rule was relaxed and women's squash at the house that Barnaby built finally was free to prosper. In 1972 Kurtz started the first women's squash team at Dartmouth, but only after she insisted they build a separate entrance to the courts so the women did not have to walk through the men's locker room.

For a number of years, the college women piggybacked onto the adult Howe Cup as a way of having national competition: Vassar played in 1968 in the C division and lost nine out of ten matches, and two years later Delaware and Penn sent teams. In 1972 tournament organizers at the New Haven Lawn Club, tired of including college teams in the regular tournament, ran a separate intercollegiate draw down the road at Yale. Penn came in first, Princeton second and Wellesley-Radcliffe third. At a meeting that weekend, coaches from these three teams and four other coaches, who happened to be at the Howe Cup, decided to hold a separate intercollegiate team tournament. Margaret Howe donated a trophy, and the tournament, begun at Yale in 1973, was named the Howe Cup—nicely causing confusion with the adult inter-city Howe Cup. Eleven teams participated in two divisions that first year. Princeton won the A division.

This result was no surprise because the queen of women's intercollegiate squash was Princeton's coach, Betty Howe Constable. With her upswept hair, adorable dog Anna and fiery enthusiasm, Betty willed her players to excellence. Each December she ran the Princeton Squash Invitational, a tournament for the top sixteen collegiate women in the country and, each February, her team triumphed at the Howe Cup. She coached until 1991 and, in those years, she won the Howe Cup twelve out of nineteen times. With an overall record of 117–16, she had ten undefeated teams. In the late 1970s Princeton posted a record forty-three-match win streak; after Harvard ended that streak with a 4–3 win in 1980, her teams won thirty-two more matches in a row (women's intercollegiate squash consisted of seven-woman teams until 1982, when they switched to nine per side). Wendy Zaharko was her first great star. Another product of Wilmington's excellent women's squash scene, Zaharko went undefeated her sophomore year and won three national intercollegiate titles. Nancy Gengler won the intercollegiates the year after Zaharko graduated. Gengler went on to become a professional at Uptown and a leading player on the women's professional tour. Demer Holleran, Betty's last great player, won three intercollegiate titles. Holleran, with her soft hands and brilliant mind, went on to become one of the great woman players of the century. When she retired in 1991, Betty Howe Constable ended sixty-five years of continuous squash leadership by a woman named Howe.

The whirlwind whipped up the leaves outside and, inside the cozy world of squash, the old guard was forced to look outside their window. Up until the seventies, squash had remained a relatively uncommercialized sport. Professionals, in the Met SRA yearbook, appeared in articles with their names italicized, as if they were a different species. One could still peek through the black-tie facade of tournaments and clubs and see the innocent schoolboy game it was a century ago. Many regional leaders felt comfortable within their own fiefdoms, unbuffeted by the winds of commerce. Encouraging hoi polloi of America into their clubs, their courts and their homes was anathema to many. Herbert Warren Wind best described the ambivalence in 1962: "For all its growth, it remains the great undiscovered game. In one corner of his heart, each devotee, knowing its valid magic, would like to see facilities available for everyone who loves sport; in his mind's eye he pictures inexpensive courts constructed on public playgrounds and affording pleasure for millions. (This is not very different from the prophecy of Capt. Victor Cazalet, the British sportsman of the 1920s, that the day would come when every factory would have squash courts for the recreation of its workers.) At the same time, having seen so much that has been popularized also vulgarized in the process, the devotee, in another corner of his heart, wonders if it wouldn't be best to let squash remain essentially the school and club game it has always been. Just as it is, the atmosphere is sweet to him and a meaningful part of his life."

Part of the hesitation came from the fact that the essence of the game had not changed. A blue-blooded circle—preparatory schools fed the Ivy League, which fed the elite city clubs, which saw their members emigrate to the suburbs and the country clubs, which fed the prep schools—hung on the neck of squash like a dowager's diamond necklace. Oxygen-rich blood poured into the veins and capillaries of squash from the public courts, but the heart of squash pumped out the same leaders and the same Saturday evening frivolity. Despite the open avarice of some people eager to make a buck and the age-old hopes of men and women finding a mate, squash seems not entirely dissimilar to what it was a half century before. To be sure, squash was expanding far beyond its purebred pedigree, but it looked the same. "Squash may not be as exclusive as fox hunting anymore, but it isn't played by dead-end kids either," *Sports Illustrated* said after the 1976 nationals. "The tournament was dominated by Ivies and observed by a mink-coated, tassel-shoed crowd." Squash still had the whitest collars in the national washload.

Squash mandarins wrestled with the new realities. Like an economy or a relationship, squash had to grow or it would die. Ted Friel, in the 1975 USSRA yearbook, attempted to justify the association's embrace, however tentative, of commercial opportunities by arguing that if they did not "control the dialogue between the commercial interests and the players," someone else would: "The ultimate possibility would be the formation of a rival organization which could, for a profit, fill the void left by a national association which ignored the fact that squash can be good for business— and business can be good for squash. Orderly growth, commensurate with the changes being wrought by public facilities and TV, and mindful of the needs of all the parties involved—players, both amateur and professional, clubs, public facilities and potential advertisers or sponsors—is a more viable alternative to the chaos which other sports have experienced in the last two decades." Friel added, "Time alone will be the judge of whether we are acting prudently."

In adapting to a commercial age, the USSRA examined the histories of lawn tennis and golf. After it opened its tournaments to amateurs and professionals in 1968, the modern game of tennis suffered through years of organizational turmoil, with self-interested entrepreneurs and old-school traditionalists battling for control. A combination of money and the determination of trailblazers like Billie Jean King and Arthur Ashe helped spread the game beyond the country club, but a lack of leadership and a missing identity doomed the game to be a mish-mash of conflicting values, personalities and purposes. The players were rapaciously money hungry and poorly behaved. College tennis was no longer a top-flight area of play. The Davis Cup, once the obsession of nations and the equal of a Grand Slam tournament, was page-ten news. Golf, on the other hand, had the mixed blessing of an elitist background but, it learned, despite the corrupting influence of television money, to parlay that into a more unified brand. Fans knew what golf at the higher levels meant. Private clubs hosted the majority of the amateur and professional tournaments. The college system was intact. The Ryder Cup, an approximate version of the Davis Cup, still fascinated fans and players alike. Golf, played by millions of Americans from all walks of life, did not abandon its roots in order to spread its branches.

The USSRA followed golf rather than tennis. It retained control over the game either through its own organization or through personal relationships with the people who were making decisions. Wind thought that someday the nationals would be played on a squash court in the middle of Madison Square Garden and "the old wheelhorses of the USSRA would welcome the phenomenon, would continue to govern the game with their characteristic easy efficiency and would go on enjoying the pleasures of their winter weekends precisely as they always have." That was, more or less, what happened. The game grew but the Gold Racquets still captured the hearts of many players. The men who made a living from squash joined rather than fought the old guard: Harry Saint became president of the Met SRA and was a long-time USSRA executive committee member; Arnold Moss was on the executive of the Met SRA; Ham Biggar ran the USSRA's admissions and ranking subcommittees; Sam Jernigan chaired the development subcommittee; Tom Jones chaired the Olympic subcommittee; Jack Herrick became USSRA president. Members of the Jesters Club, the group of leading male players and administrators that quietly supported squash, could be found inaugurating open tournaments, and public squash clubs. Private clubs hosted the majority of pro tournaments whose players came from the usual schools: The first three amateurs to turn professional went to Harvard (Niederhoffer and Briggs) and Princeton (Satterthwaite); the top American professional players in the eighties had gone to Trinity (Talbott), Penn (Edwards), Princeton (Nimick, Stanley and Page), Harvard (Jernigan and Boyum) and Williams (Zaff); and the top women players went to Penn (McConnell, Maltby and Kelso), Princeton (Holleran, Gengler) and Harvard (Akabane, Hulbert and Edge). The leading lights of squash may have given off the robust glow of something fresh, but it was new wine in old bottles.

The USSRA grew exponentially in the postwar era but still retained its hidebound, insular aura. In 1938 the executive board expanded from five men to twelve, and, after the Second World War, it included at least one person from each of the member districts (twenty-eight in 1980). In 1957 there were eight standing committees beside the executive committee; by the seventies there were twenty committees, ranging from Long Range Planning to Professional Relations to International Affairs. The annual meeting of the executive committee, held at the nationals each February, was still the most important morning in the game each year. The committee, usually a fusty-looking, all-male, all-white group, stood for a formal photograph. Often the meeting would last just ten minutes as most of the work was done in private conversations. It was considered the mark of a progressive organization that it paid for the winner and finalist of the nationals to go to the Canadian nationals. The USSRA only began national rankings in 1951. Three years later, Germain Glidden suggested individual memberships to supplement dues received from member clubs (each member club paid $25 per year to the USSRA.) One-hundred and seventy-nine squash supporters replied to Glidden's initial letter asking for memberships, with 146 joining the USSRA as annual members and 33 opting to pay $50 for a life membership—which came with a free USSRA necktie. Until 1974 the headquarters of the association moved every two years when a new president came into power.

The growth in the game threatened to overwhelm these quaint traditions. Membership in the USSRA jumped from 250 in 1956 to over 1,500 in 1974; member clubs doubled from 70 to 150. In one year alone, 1976, more than a hundred new tournaments appeared on the annual fixtures list. Darwin Kingsley, who was in the midst of his presidency of the association, agreed to become the first paid staff member of the USSRA. Kingsley, Yale class of 1950, whose father and brother had been presidents of the association, was a three-time senior doubles champion and member of Merion who had, according to *Sports Illustrated*, "a flair for plaid and a feel for people." Kingsley, known in the squash world as "PK," moved into a small office in Bala Cynwyd and set about revitalizing the USSRA.

Sponsorship was vital. There was a full-time staff to pay. The landlord needed rent. National tournaments took more money to stage. Sending teams to world championships drained resources. In 1975 Kingsley, Ted Friel and Jim McQueenie traveled to Rhode Island to meet with Bancroft, the leading racquet manufacturer. Bancroft agreed to a three-year contract to sponsor the North American Open, the women's nationals and a Bancroft women's open, as well as help finance the permanent office and junior tournaments. Other key sponsorships involved Coca-Cola, which sponsored the national hardball singles for ten years and Rolex, which sponsored the national softball championships for seven years. In 1977 Kingsley and Ted Friel secured the most significant account, Insilco. Formerly known as the International Silver Company, Insilco was a Fortune 500 company in Connecticut with sixteen subsidiaries producing paint, Rolodexes, high school yearbooks and fiber optics. The USSRA and Insilco created a national tournament for B and C players. Previously left in the slipstream of top players, the intermediate and neophyte players finally got their own tournament to determine a national champion. The Insilco, unlike the regular nationals, was actually a pyramid of local and regional tournaments that culminated in a season-ending grand finale nationals, with all travel and accommodation expenses paid by Insilco. In 1978 at Broad Street, Peter Monaghan, the son of Squashcon founder Paul Monaghan, won the national B title and Ed Bresnitz won the C title—each received the Insilco trophy, a replica of the Peace Cup exhibited at the 1964 World's Fair. Two thousand men, women and juniors played in the tournament. Each year thereafter, thousands more played, and more than two-hundred clubs participated, making each year's edition the largest squash tournament in the world. In 1981–82 Insilco added a D division and began sponsoring the Saturday dinner at the nationals. In the mid-eighties the company paid for Insilco Business Leagues in eight cities, with the winners of each league meeting annually in a grand finals. New York, which had twenty-four teams in its Insilco league, was usually the strongest of these business leagues. The focus on grass-roots amateur play was a tremendous boon to the health of the game.

In 1985 membership in the USSRA flew to three hundred member clubs and eight thousand members. The estimated number of active squash players in America jumped from 60,000 in 1975 to 300,000 a decade later. In 1982, 210,000 balls and 150,000 racquets were sold. Twenty-five thousand people played squash in the greater New York City area in 1974; in 1981 it was at one hundred thousand. Even more apparent was the diffusion of quality players. In 1980 more than 40 percent of all national champions came from Boson, New York and Philadelphia, and in the first six years of the Insilco, ten of the fourteen winners were New Yorkers. In 1984 less than 25 percent of the national champions came from the big three cities and not a single Insilco winner was a New Yorker. Squash, ten years after it went public, was now a national sport.

CHAPTER EIGHT

Box of Rain

They were a different species. They took money to play a schoolboys' game. They spent months on the road, cocooned from society in a hermetic routine of hotel, court and plane. Kids had posters of them on the walls of their rooms. Sponsors lavished them with products. There were about twenty-five men who played the majority of tournaments. They flew together, bunked together, nightclubbed together. They dated each other's college friends. They went to each other's weddings. They squabbled together. Collectively, players of the World Professional Squash Association looked as if they had spent the last decade together at a small, rural boarding school.

The strain of this lifestyle produced some unique inner lives. At the highest level, the players were about the same in ability, and the man who won the last point of a match was the one who was stronger psychologically. Emotional endurance, focus and resiliency were the final arbitrators. Talbott was not the best athlete or best stroke producer or best shooter, but he was the best mentally. Edwards could never beat Desaulniers. Sanchez could never beat Talbott. Binns and Jernigan could never win a tournament. Desaulniers was alone with his fears and Page was an enigma and Boyum wanted to quit and Zaff was driven by the ideal of perfection and Nimick could never believe in himself and Waite could never be fit enough and Caldwell was a clown and Talbott, the leader of the band, seemed almost mystified by the power granted to him.

Squash in the 1980s was a cornucopia of drama. The game soared to its apogee. Junior tournaments regularly had over three hundred entries. The men's nationals topped six hundred. National champions came from Seattle and Mexico City and Newport. Women formed a professional tour. One American, Alicia McConnell, won the world junior title and reached a ranking of fourteen on the international softball tour. Above all, the men's professional tour brought the first hundred years of American squash to a scintillating climax. By making it possible for a player to make a living solely on prize money, sponsorship and exhibitions, the tour liberated players from the shackles of the club. It raised the profile of squash to a new level. Television stations broadcasted matches. Newspapers covered tournaments. Magazines wrote gushing profiles of players. The tour democratized the game as players named Goldstein and Sanchez won tournaments. Yet, the very success of the tour blinded almost everyone to the simple fact that the American hardball game was dying. It was similar to what happens to a tuberculosis victim: In the last manic days, they feel exuberantly healthy. The tour lasted for just fifteen years, and people assumed it would go on forever.

With the growth in sponsorship, commercial courts and raised public awareness, the natural outcome was the development of a bona fide professional squash circuit. Before the 1970s, pro squash was mostly a ramshackle hut on the edge of town. The U.S. Professional, the North American Open and the Heights Casino Doubles were the only three annual tournaments where pros could earn some money. The North American Professional Squash Racquets Association, despite its clumsy name, slowly gained momentum in the early seventies under president Fred Weymuller, and then Jim McQueenie. In 1974 the association had seventy-six registered professionals, although everyone was a teaching professional or a college coach. That year the NAPSRA voted to allow women members. Carol Weymuller, the co-director of squash at the Heights Casino, was the first to join.

NAPSRA's first success came in the city where it started, Boston. After winning the national five-man team title in 1949 and 1950, Boston never again produced a victorious team, and New York took over as the leading rival to Philadelphia. In the sixties the standard of play declined, membership in squash clubs dropped and women's play all but disappeared. In 1970 Boston's squash fortunes suddenly looked good again. Henri Salaun, as usual, cleaned up the national veterans; Anil Nayar, the national champion, had temporarily resisted returning to Bombay and was still living in Boston; Larry Terrell was the latest Harvard undergraduate to win the intercollegiates; and Mohibullah Khan, the charismatic professional at the Harvard Club, was just two years removed from his double win of the U.S. Professionals and the North American Open. Tom Poor, a young schoolteacher with Deerfield and Amherst on his squash resume, had just moved to Boston. Seeing this string of champions, Poor persuaded the Massachusetts Squash Racquets Association to sponsor an open tournament by reviving the old Boston Open. He printed programs by hand and got Mo Khan to recruit some of his colleagues to come play. On the first weekend in November 1970, the Harvard Club restarted the Boston Open. A few squash fans wandered into the club and grudgingly paid for tickets. The finals featured Mo Khan facing his distant cousin Yusuf Khan. Yusuf, a new émigré to Seattle, surprised everyone by beating Mo in three games, despite Mo's racquet sometimes flashing over Yusuf's head. In the consolation, Colin Adair came back from 2–0 to win 15–14 in the fifth against Terrell. Yusuf earned $500. The total prize money was $1,000.

The Boston Open did not adhere to the NAO model of skipping from private club to private club. After another year at the Harvard Club, the tournament moved to Hemenway Gymnasium at Harvard, where the gallery could accommodate a larger number of spectators. Len Bernheimer, a top University Club player just out of Stanford Business School, co-directed the tournament with Poor. Each September they called a number of Boston squash players and supporters to raise funds that paid players' travel and hotel expenses, a per diem for food and prize money. In 1975 Bernheimer and Poor, doubles partners when they got off the telephones, raised the prize money purse to $2,700, with a total budget of $10,000. The following year, knowing that they could not raise any more money privately, they cautiously ventured into the world of sponsorship. Bancroft, the dominant Rhode Island racquet manufacturer, gave $2,000, and the Boston Open became the first U.S. tournament to openly accept sponsorship. In 1974 Poor and Bernheimer broke another taboo when they encouraged players to wear colored, nonwhite clothing. That same year they added to the excitement by holding a consolation draw (which saw the top two seeds, Mo Khan and Rainer Ratinac, meet in the finals, both having lost in the first round) and a battle for third place between the semifinal losers (Poor beat Vic Niederhoffer). In 1975 it was the first tournament to adopt the "green ball," a forerunner to the seventy-plus. In 1976 they enforced the "striker's point rule," which made it a let, not a let point, if a player "turned" on a ball and hit an opponent; the USSRA adopted the rule the following year. In 1977 Poor and Bernheimer expanded the draw to include a sixteen-man qualifying tournament—a first for pro tournaments—with the top-four finishers given slots in the main draw. In 1978 they created a Grand Masters (over forty) event where a number of acclaimed veterans like Henri Salaun, Diehl Mateer, Pete Bostwick and Hashim Khan played as a sort of undercard for the main event. The Boston Open was considered one of the four majors, along with the U.S. Professionals, the Canadian Open and the NAO, but every year Tom Poor greeted each player with the simple phrase, "Welcome to the Big One."

It was therefore at the Boston Open, in November 1975, that Victor Niederhoffer announced he was turning professional. He issued a four-page memorandum detailing his reasons. The *New York Times* ran an article headlined NIEDERHOFFER TURNS PRO TO AID GAME. "I've run out of opponents in amateur squash," he told the *Times*, "so I want to create a professional circuit so glamorous, so exciting and profitable that more youngsters will be attracted to the sport, more players will become expert, more sponsors will join the bandwagon, and squash will ultimately rival tennis and golf in importance and attention." The *Times* added, "Money is not a dirty word to Niederhoffer." Although it was nice to receive some cash for his weekend's work (Niederhoffer estimated that it cost him $5,000 a year to play squash), this move was a leap into the unknown. Risk was something Niederhoffer, as a currency speculator, knew well, but he was no ordinary pro who worked at a club and had time to train. Niederhoffer was keeping his day job. In addition, he was removing himself from the heart of competitive squash. His winter schedule was going to have just three pro tournaments versus a dozen amateur fixtures, and the amateur ranks had as much or more depth of talent. Given his deep desire for competition and his urge to add to his total of national titles after his five-year boycott, it was a courageous move. The move paid off, literally, in Boston, as he took home $1,200 as a finalist. He lost to Sharif Khan, who, angry at his loss in Mexico City, crushed him, 15–1, in the first game of the three-game match.

A few months later Frank Satterthwaite became the second amateur to break ranks and turn professional; at the 1976 Boston Open, a third amateur, Peter Briggs, Harvard class of 1973 and national champion in 1976, turned professional. The NAPSRA was a strange home for them. "At the time," Satterthwaite later said, "Vic and I were the only members who didn't know how to string a racquet. When I first joined, I must say I was afraid that some of the club pros—all of whom were hard working and many of whom had been dedicated to their profession for years—would view me as something of a dilettante, or worse, as someone who was trying to cut into their money." The reaction was the opposite. In 1977 Niederhoffer was elected president of the association, replacing McQueenie, and Satterthwaite was elected to its board. As president of the professional association, Niederhoffer made a series of moves that pushed pro squash to the front of the squash world. He adopted the seventy-plus ball. He allowed nonteaching professionals to become members of the association.

He instituted a "technical foul" rule similar to basketball, in which a referee could subtract two points from a player for unsportsmanlike behavior. In 1978 he added the first qualifying tournament for the North American Open. Most critically, he and Harry Saint grasped the synergy of combining pro tournaments and commercial clubs. The clubs loved the publicity, and access to spectator galleries was easy—there was no smuggling of mothers through service entrances.

It started with the Boodles. The paint was not even dry at Uptown, and Saint was already holding his first pro tournament. Don Smith, a public-relations representative for General Wines Company, approached Stu Goldstein, Uptown's first head pro, and asked him how much first-place prize money it would take to get all the top players to enter a tournament. Goldstein said $500—such was the world view of the U.S. pro at the time. In a few weeks the 1976 Boodles Gin Open was played, and prize money in the inaugural tournament was $8,000, with the winner getting $2,000 more than Goldstein had hoped. In 1977 it reached $10,000 and two years later it was $20,000. The Boodles—"The World's Costliest British Gin"—was more than a reviving shot of alcohol for New York. Saint created a series of side tournaments for women, amateurs, veterans and seniors, so that by 1980 more than 800 people played in one of thirty-one Boodles draws on one massive weekend.

Ironically, Niederhoffer never won the U.S. Professionals or the Boston Open, and, in the all-important North American Open, he never repeated his 1975 victory over Sharif Khan. His only pro victory came in the inaugural Boodles, where he beat Sharif one last time, 3–1. The NAO was a trail of tears after his triumph in Mexico City. In 1976, with the Fifth Avenue Racquet Club sharing matches with the University and New York Athletic Clubs, Niederhoffer played with a sprained ankle and a pulled hamstring. He was also distracted by public relations, arriving late for (and almost defaulting) his semifinal match with Clive Caldwell because of meetings with Bancroft. He lost to Sharif in the finals, winning just fifteen points total. In 1977 he lost in the semifinals to Geoff Hunt and fell badly in the third-place match to a young Tom Page. In 1978 in Toronto, he barely beat Mike Desaulniers, 15–11, 14–15, 5–15, 15–13, 18–17, in the quarterfinals before tumbling to Clive Caldwell in three quick games. In the third-place match against Rainer Ratinac he crashed in three—he tanked the second game 15–0, turning his back to a serving Ratinac at 14–0, with the crowd audibly booing. Niederhoffer continued to provoke the squash establishment. "Squash players may anticipate criticism from snobs who have disdain for our inordinate desire to win," he wrote in the inaugural issue of *Squash News*, countering arguments against a professional tour. "Perhaps the critics have never been exposed to competition in their own lives or are speaking from the lofty plane of an inheritance or the ivory tower of some educational institute." Snubbing squash, he publicly switched to racquetball. He started playing pro racquetball tournaments, winning one in New Haven and beating Marty Hogan in another in Las Vegas. When refereeing the finals of the 1980 Boodles, he insisted on substituting the racquetball term "hinder" for "let." "I felt like Winston Churchill after playing four years of polo in India and then going to war," Niederhoffer told reporters, in his unique style, after playing racquetball. "'That was the real thing,' Churchill said, 'with bullets flying overhead.' That's the way it is with racquetball." In 1979 Niederhoffer did not enter the North American Open. He unofficially retired, gave up the presidency of the NAPSRA and drifted away from squash.

The tour sped on at mach-nine speeds. Clive Caldwell, a bright and ebullient product of Jim Bentley's junior program at the Toronto Cricket, Skating & Curling Club and the recent president of the Canadian Professional Squash Association, took over. Along with Niederhoffer, Caldwell had renamed the tour the World Professional Squash Association (its fifth name in fifty years) and designed the new association's red and white logo. Caldwell took the association's longtime flagship tournament, the U.S. Professionals, and baptized it the WPSA Championships. With the help of Jack Barnaby and Fred Weymuller, he developed an annual training certification conference for teaching professionals. He contracted with Bata to make WPSA sneakers and Spalding to make a WPSA racquet with an oversized head. The CS-120 racquet was a quiet revolution. The USSRA banned the bat from amateur tournaments, but Caldwell was able, as president, to get WPSA approval for the racquet. No other professional player used Caldwell's sword, but the theory of the oversized racquet gained acceptance and by the mid-nineties it was the norm. Critically, Caldwell organized a permanent office. Located at the Toronto-Dominion Centre on Sheppard Street, the office eventually had eight people working there full time under the direction of Bob French. A childhood friend of Caldwell's from Toronto Cricket, French first encountered the tour in 1975. Living in Los Angeles when Mexico City hosted the NAO, he organized a $600 six-man round-robin tournament at the Venice Squash Club for some of the professionals on their way back home. Gordy Anderson beat Sharif in the finals, amid yelling and screaming in the gallery and a woman from Pernod, the sponsor, pouring free drinks. After the success in Venice, French returned east and began building corporate relationships for the WPSA. He pitched professional squash as a classic marketing opportunity. It had a pristine slate—no corporations had been there before, so there was almost no commercialization or brand to overcome. It had its famous demographics—high quality, well-educated people, the sport of businesspeople. And growth was almost inevitable. With Melissa Winstanley, a Yale Club of New York player, as the key staff member, French secured major deals with a number of Canadian subsidiaries of Fortune 500 corporations: Xerox, American Express, World Trust, Ford and Nabisco.

In 1979–80, in the first year of the Caldwell administration, prize money topped $100,000, with twelve tournaments. Prize money doubled each year until it reached over a half-million dollars. The WPSA staged tournaments in twenty-nine cities in the United States and Canada, in the likely hotbeds of New York, Philadelphia, Boston, Montreal and Toronto, but also in the unlikely: Cleveland, Toledo, Guatemala City, Fort Lauderdale, Rochester, Aspen and St. Paul. The private clubs embraced the tour. The Yale Club in New York hosted a new U.S. Open for two years, the University Club of Chicago had the Windy City Open, the Field Club had the Greenwich Open, Apawamis converted its Charles Hardy into an eponymous pro tournament and the Boston Open switched from Hemenway to the University Club. Yet an equal amount of the generating power behind the tour was the commercial clubs, especially the Boodles Open at Uptown, the Mutual Benefit Open at Capitol Hill in Washington and the Cleveland Open at Thirteenth Street. Local promoters secured sponsorship from Desenex, Hefty, Smith Barney, Chase Manhattan, Stouffer's and Moussy. In the late seventies, Spalding sponsored a Grand Prix of six tournaments in the summer, culminating in a major open in Philadelphia in September. Perhaps the most famous new tournament was the Mennen Cup. Trevor Marshall, a Yorkshire-born squash impressario in Toronto, started the Mennen in 1979 as a showpiece event. He invited the best player from eight different countries to enter, tempting them with the most lucrative prize-money purse of any squash tournament in the world. Besides having leading softball stars like Geoff Hunt and Jahangir Khan playing in North America, the Mennen tinkered with the game. One year they played on a twenty-foot court and another year on a twenty-one-foot court, both with a hardball.

Physics was the next thing to conquer. An all-glass portable court was the dream of every squash player. In 1901 in the first squash book ever published, Eustace Miles advocated for a movable court. In 1935 Harrods erected a squash court on the ground floor of its sports department, as a part of Squash Rackets Week at the store. Twice a day, Charles Arnold, the professional at the Bath Club, gave "lecture lessons" on the court which, although not full size, was "extremely efficient for the purpose." In 1973 Paul Monaghan invented a folding, "accordion" court, priced at $8,500. He claimed that two players in two minutes could unfold a regulation-size court that, when closed up, took up less than three feet of space. (It actually took about twenty minutes and was rather awkward.) In 1981 Playcon, a Canadian squash and racquetball construction firm in Kitchener, Ontario, built a glass portable court for the World Open. After the event, Playcon dismantled the court, but it was soon needed. The WPSA Championships was the only major tournament under the tour's control (Bernheimer and Poor ran the Boston Open and the USSRA ran the NAO), and Caldwell decided to make it a glamorous event. In 1982 Bob French persuaded Fleischmann's, the margarine manufacturer, to sponsor the WPSA Championships and host it in the grand ballroom at the Sheraton Centre, a massive hotel and retail complex in downtown Toronto. Playcon resurrected the portable court. Initially, in 1982, it was eighteen-and-a-half-feet wide, with a glass back wall and wood-panel side and front walls. The tongue-and-groove maple floor was screwed directly into the ballroom floor and a gridwork of aluminum beams supported the side and back walls. Although the court was portable, the single glass back wall provided no more spectator capacity than a private club could. To rectify this, Playcon added a glass right wall for the 1983 WPSA Championships and in 1984, a glass left wall. Caldwell also widened the court to a nonstandard twenty feet. This was done to encourage clubs to convert racquetball courts to squash and to make the WPSA tour more accessible to overseas softball players.

The tour court, which the WPSA eventually bought from Playcon for $75,000, delivered a blow to the age-old drawback of squash: It could be plopped down anywhere. The first portable-court event in the United States was, naturally, at the Boston Open. In 1984 Bernheimer and Poor moved their tournament from the University Club to the South End where a unique building stood waiting. Originally a circular art gallery when it opened in 1884—the first painting was a giant four-hundred-by-fifty feet, panoramic canvas depicting the Battle of Gettysburg—the Cyclorama was a rough-and-tumble industrial space. Everything from a car factory to a laboratory where the spark plug was invented to a flower market had been there. In the eighties it was a dilapidated exhibition hall with a Buckminster Fuller–designed black grid hanging from the ceiling—perfect for squash's new image. The Cyclorama was a huge success for the Boston Open. Almost a thousand people, three times the total of the previous year, watched the matches. Publicity was enormous. Other cities followed suit. The Toledo Club, hampered like many private clubs by limited gallery space, decided to bring the tour court to its fourth-floor ballroom. The glass panels were too big for the club's elevators, so Playcon hoisted each panel with a crane through a fourth-floor window. One crew member got frostbite. The WPSA rewarded the club for its perseverance with the 1986 WPSA Championships, then a four-year run of hosting the North American Open. In 1985 Playcon dragged the court three stories down an escalator to put the court on Hunter College's gymnasium floor. In 1986 Penn hosted a tournament on its hockey rink, with the court placed near the blue line. Toronto not only hosted the WPSA Championships at the Sheraton Centre every year from 1981 through 1988 but, in 1985, added a second tour-court event by creating the Canadian Open. Held in the city's convention center and sponsored by Xerox, the Canadian Open became a fourth major for the pro tour. Some years it had more prize money and more spectators per match than any other tournament. In 1989 the WPSA Championships went to New York. Instead of disappearing into a private club, the tournament appeared in full view at the Winter Garden. A one-hundred-and-twenty-foot high atrium adjacent to the World Trade Center, the Winter Garden was an airy space with palm trees, marble floors and room for a thousand spectators.

But this spectacular space was nothing like the 1985 North American Open's locale. Twenty-one years after its beginning, the continent's greatest tournament appeared again in midtown Manhattan. This time it was ten blocks south and a world away from its original home at the University Club. Tom Jones erected the court sideways on the stage at Town Hall, a mammoth fifteen-hundred-seat auditorium at the edge of Times Square. Drakkar, the men's cologne company, sponsored the tournament, and fans could, prompted by six-page ads in major magazines like *Gentlemen's Quarterly*, order tickets by phone via Ticketron. Prize money totaled $75,000, more than double the previous year when it was held at Park Avenue. Thirty-three players battled through a qualifying tournament for eight open spots in the sixty-four man draw. *Sports Illustrated* sent an editor, a writer, a photographer and a reporter to Town Hall. The atmosphere had a touch of Broadway with lights flashing in the lobby to signal the start of a match, but it reminded John Atwood, a *Village Voice* writer, of Madison Square Garden: "With close to one thousand beer-soaked squash nuts cheering, stomping and bellowing like Ranger fans, the place shook with the din. At the conclusion of a full game of such thrills, the crowd would race breathlessly out to the lobby, pushing blindly in the direction of the bar while sputtering excitedly about the play."

Solving the problem of accessible and ample galleries proved much easier than the other stumbling block for professional squash: television. The only way to truly change the dynamics of the tour was to involve klieg lights, pancake makeup and protons whizzing through the ether into cathode ray tubes. The pleasure of squash—a bat, a ball and a wall—was also its pain. It was too difficult to broadcast. The bat flashed through the air so fast it was hard for a viewer to grasp how magical was the player's art, the ball was too small and moved too quickly and the background walls had no texture and not nearly enough distance. Instead of expanding the view, television reduced everything until, as one wag put it, "the players somehow look as if they are strolling about a pocket handkerchief engaging in a leisurely game of (albeit acrobatic) Ping Pong."

The first time squash was televised in America was at the 1959 U.S. Open in Pittsburgh. The early rounds of the Open were broadcast on closed-circuit television and the final, for ninety minutes, went live on local Pittsburgh television. Alcoa ran commercials, Cal MacCracken gave a short demonstration of various squash shots, the Pakistani ambassador to the United States spoke a few introductory words and a sportscaster, Bob Prince, commented upon the match. (Prince yelled "Get a can opener" anytime a player tinned a shot.) The 1967 and 1968 intercollegiates were televised on closed-circuit television. Boston, struggling to dig itself out of the blizzard of 1978, had the unfortunate problem of a sudden withdrawal when it broadcast the nationals. When the finals of the men's championship was canceled due to a last-minute default by Mario Sanchez, viewers of the six and eleven o'clock news watched the less riveting finals of the over-thirty-five's division, between Roger Alcaly and Al Jacobs. In October 1980 local Rochester television screened a taped, one-hour version of the finals of the Northeast Open at the Mid-Town Tennis Club. Tony Glassman, the producer of the show, used four cameras and painted the walls a chocolate beige. Later, Glassman managed to get half-hour tapings of WPSA events shown on the Canadian Broadcasting Company show *The Wide World of Sports*, as well as regular coverage on Rogers Cable. In 1983 Toronto Cricket slapped bright-red tape along all the red lines on its doubles court and succeeded in producing ten hours of cable coverage for its World Doubles tournament. In the United States some promoters, including those at the Toledo Club, persuaded local stations to broadcast a lead-in from a tournament, but the only time squash went national was when Prime Sports Network broadcast a ninety-minute edited show on the WPSA Championships at the Winter Garden. Playcon painted the front wall and floors blue and the game lines yellow and created a new white television ball for the occasion.

The failure to reach the Shangri-La of television-inspired riches was just one of the problems that plagued the tour. The archaic conflict between amateurs and professionals stymied development. Some of the old invitationals, most notably the William White at Merion in 1973, opened their draws to pros, but the USSRA, arguing that it had to focus on amateur matters in order to maintain its tax status with the Internal Revenue Service, declined to lend more than cursory support to the pro tour. Yet it often meddled with the WPSA, and, in 1979, with the help of Jim McQueenie, it set up a Pro Division in the hopes of corralling the professionals under its aegis. The professionals treated it as a fifth column and refused to join, and the Pro Division folded after two years. "The powers that be right now are stunting the growth of the game," said Mike Pierce in 1978. "The pros are up in arms over the people running the game of squash. I think the old guard is slowly being eased out, but they've retarded the growth—not intentionally, but I think their way of thinking has held the game back the last few years." Another battlefield was the Lapham-Grant. The WPSA wanted to add a professional wing to the crossborder bacchanal, but the USSRA refused. In 1983 Caldwell and Alan Rose, the director of the Loews Summit Hotel in Manhattan, created an abbreviated professional version, the Loews Cup. The top five U.S. and Canadian professionals played each other annually in a season-opening contest that was a media bonanza. More than one newspaper called it "the Davis Cup of squash." The players, although no WPSA ranking points were at stake, put on a vigorous show and, almost every year, it came down to a final match.

The tour reached its zenith in the 1984–85 season. It had prize money of $632,000, with $450,000 in nineteen singles events and the rest in doubles tournaments and special draws (veterans, legends and the Loews Cup). In addition to reaching a high-water mark for prize money, the tour had five portable court events that season. Clive Caldwell predicted that, by 1990, the WPSA would have a $5 million tour complete with network television coverage.

Sharif Khan was the starting point of the WPSA tour. He was a holdover from the antediluvian days of professional squash, when there were just three or four tournaments a year and prize money bought you a couple of hamburgers. He first played in the North American Open in 1967. It was a sixteen-man draw played under the traditional eight amateur/eight professional pattern. It was held at a private club. One hundred spectators attended. Total prize money was $1,000. Sharif also played in the 1985 North American Open. It was a sixty-four man draw, with a further thirty-three men in a qualifying tournament. It was played at Town Hall in front of nearly one thousand people and had a purse of $75,000. In between those two points arched the biography of a legend.

The eldest son of Hashim Khan, Sharif was the most intimidating man in squash. He punished the ball. He swore in Pashtun. He swung regardless of how close your face was to his racquet. He gargled with pebbles. He snarled from a mouth hidden under his mustache. His black-coal eyes had a legendary glare. "He worked up a suitable quota of bravura shots and theatrical gestures," wrote Herbert Warren Wind after one tournament. "He roared at himself after a needless error. He popped his large eyes malevolently at an opponent whom he thought had purposely taken too long to clear himself from Sharif's route to the ball. . . . He was not above shouting, 'Come on, Pakistan!' to himself loud enough to let the gallery know he meant to shilly-shally no longer." He looked like Omar Sharif—sad, mysterious and infinitely compelling.

Born in Pakistan and educated at Millfield School in Somerset, England, he won the Drysdale Cup, the English junior national title, at age sixteen. He graduated and moved to Detroit where his father was living. After explaining to his father that he did not want to be an accountant, doctor or engineer or even play cricket for Pakistan, Sharif spent a fortnight learning how to be a club professional. He spent two years at Downtown Athletic Club in Detroit and turned professional at age nineteen. In 1969 he moved to Canada to work at Skyline, a private club in Toronto run by Ralph Gardiner. Anxious to prove himself and discovering he did not relish the racquet-stringing and hobnobbing chores of a teaching professional, Sharif escaped. For six months he toured with Jonah Barrington's traveling circus, which was the origin of the pro softball tour. He reached the semifinals of the 1970 British Open, losing to Barrington in four games.

Hardball proved more pliable. Sharif won nine U.S. Professionals, seven Boston Opens, four Boodles, and he captured the North American Open every year from 1969 through 1981, except for the Mexico City debacle against Niederhoffer in 1975. The victories started in 1969 at the NAO, when Sharif violated the Khan code of respect by upsetting

Mohibullah. Firmly ensconced in the throne of champion, Mo had beaten Sharif in three quick games at the 1968 NAO, an emphatic 15–2 in the third. A year later, at the Cincinnati Racquet Club, Sharif surprised Mo in four games. "He glared at his opponent through wide-open eyes and drove every ball with such smashing power that only another Khan would have been unintimidated," wrote one observer. Although Mo rebounded two months later to beat Sharif at the U.S. Professionals, Sharif's win in Cincinnati marked a changing of the guard, and, except for a tough five-gamer in the finals of the 1973 NAO, Sharif was never seriously troubled by Mo again. He still, however, had to overcome Hashim. In the semifinals of the 1970 NAO, Sharif did what for many sons was the hardest thing to do—beat his father—by surviving a harrowing four-game match.

Sharif hit cruise control, and, except for two momentary bumps against Vic Niederhoffer, he steered a simple course for the rest of the decade. The theory in the seventies was that to beat Sharif you had to stay with him and never give an inch. But Sharif evolved out of his smash-mouth style. In 1974, while his girlfriend was making French fries, hot cooking oil spilled on his legs and hands, and he spent a week in the hospital. He played thereafter with a bit more finesse, pacing himself, only pulling the wide-eyed blasting moves—"King Khanning" the ball—when the game got tight.

Geoff Hunt offered the only roadblock. Hunt won the British Open eight times. In 1977 at the height of his career, he came over to try to win both the British and the North American Opens in the same season. (He had once played a week of hardball as a sixteen-year-old on his way from England back to Australia, reaching the quarterfinals of the Jacobs draw at the Harry Cowles.) He won the William White at Merion, and then he practiced with Peter Briggs and Niederhoffer in New York for four days before returning to Philadelphia. In the first round of the NAO at Penn, Hunt escaped from John Reese, 18–17 in the fourth game. He beat Niederhoffer in four games in the semifinals to earn the right to face Sharif. Having trained for the tournament by working out in Denver with his father—although many suspected this was a Neil Sullivan–like hoax, for he was known to loathe running—Sharif started the match off with stinging hard serves and well-timed three-wall boasts. He won the first game. Hunt won the second as he upped the tempo and hit as hard as Sharif. In the third game, Sharif dramatically changed the pace and tossed up high lobs and soft drops into the corners. For the first time, Hunt was disrupted. Caught out of position, he made reckless errors and gave Sharif the game. In the fourth Sharif motored to a 13–4 lead. Hunt chipped away and, at 14–8, Sharif looked like he had a flat tire. He went for six match-ending three-walls. Five times they kicked out but, the sixth time, at 14–13, Sharif got his nick and the victory. If it had gone to five games, no one doubted that Hunt would have won 15–0.

Bancroft gave Sharif his check that afternoon and, as the WPSA tour stepped on the accelerator, his bank account finally began to match his skills. He took in $60,000 in the 1979–80 season but made more in endorsements of clothing, racquets, shoes and contact lenses—a nod to his famously hypnotic eyes. Yet some people felt that Sharif, age thirty-three in 1975, was also a stumbling block. He demanded appearance money for many tournaments. This mercenary approach was understand-able. He had suffered through some dismal periods: In 1970 he and Jonah Barrington had to literally pass a hat around the gallery in order to get money after they gave an exhibition at the New York Athletic Club, and, after winning the 1971 NAO, he was handed an envelope with fifty $10 bills. Americans, especially after the Miracle on Ice victory of the Olympic ice hockey team in 1980, particularly wanted to see homegrown players on Sunday afternoons. Patriotism, a love of the underdog and a tinge of racism all combined to create an undertow of support for the young Turks who were hacking away at the latest Khan.

Two products of Jim Bentley's junior program at the Toronto Cricket, Skating and Curling Club were the first of the new generation of chal-lengers. Gordon Anderson beat Sharif at least once a season for five straight years, including in the quarters of the 1978 U.S. Professionals, ending Sharif's twenty-six-match winning streak in that tournament. Anderson panzered the ball, especially with a sweeping forehand. His spe-cialty was the double boast, the risky shot that hit both side walls before trickling off the front wall like a butterfly with sore feet. Anderson was an amiable bon vivant, but too erratic on court and never could translate his wins over Sharif into major tournament victories.

His stablemate Clive Caldwell turned professional at age eighteen but, initially, discarded thoughts of victory. "I had no aspirations of being a champion," he said in 1984. "The Khans seemed so dominant fifteen years ago. They were like aliens." Caldwell, though, had a vital combina-tion of brio and endurance. He lost thirty straight times to Sharif before beating him in Detroit in November 1980. Although never a number-one player, Caldwell, with his distinctive thick brow running in a straight line over both eyes, was ranked in the top five of the WPSA for nine years in a row and in the top ten for fourteen straight years. He won four majors. With a playful, anarchic glee, he relished controversy, whether with his

Spalding oversized racquet or a white velour jumpsuit he wore on court in 1978. Like a threshing machine, he constantly worked opponents over with his patient court positioning and methodical shot selection. He delighted audiences and dismayed referees with his acerbic commentary. After a bad call, he would bump his head against the wall like a dolphin unsure of his sonar. "Caldwell was at his political best," wrote one observer at Apawamis in 1984, "and the match took almost as long to discuss as it did to play."

A poster boy for public squash, Stu Goldstein was everything old squash was not: Jewish, middle-class, short, not Ivy League, a full-time professional and left-handed (only three southpaws, Germain Glidden, Mo Khan and Betty Howe Constable, have ever dominated American squash). He grew up in Little Neck, a non-squashy part of Long Island, went to Stuyvesant High and was a nationally ranked table tennis player. He attended Stony Brook, a part of the State University of New York system. Under coach Bob Snider, Goldstein was ranked seventh in the intercollegiates his senior year. After graduation he turned pro in tennis and taught at the Roslyn Racquet Club. In 1974 Harry Saint, casting about for a coach for his Fifth Avenue Racquet Club, hired Goldstein; two years later, when Saint opened Uptown, Goldstein moved there. He did not give many lessons, but focused on his career as a touring pro. He initially had trouble getting his name on draws—the top invitationals were amateur only, and without qualifying rounds he did not get into the few open tournaments. Goldstein blamed the squash establishment. "To this day Goldstein feels there was a conspiracy against him," reported *Sports Illustrated* in 1979. He took out his frustrations on his body. He lifted weights for hours, did forty minutes of yoga each morning and ran ninety miles a week in Central Park, all adding thick strands of muscle to his five-foot-seven frame. Goldstein appeared on court in perfectly tailored Fila shirts, shorts and sweatsuits, new racquets in his hand, his mustache trimmed, his socks pulled high. Goldstein looked like a genuine heir apparent when he knocked out Clive Caldwell and Vic Niederhoffer to reach the finals of the 1977 U.S. Professionals, but Sharif crushed him in the finals. His banner year of 1978—three wins, including the U.S. Professionals, five finals and one semifinal in the nine WPSA tournaments, and a summer playing softball overseas—led to a bandage year in 1979 when, in San Francisco, he slipped on a spot of sweat, wrenched his back and played in just four tournaments. In the 1979 North American Open he squandered a 13–8 lead in the fifth against Gordy Anderson in the semis. In the 1980 NAO, Goldstein pushed Sharif to 15–12 in the fifth, but that was his last great effort. A frontrunner, Goldstein had a brittle game and would too quickly lose confidence if he fell behind. In the semifinals of the 1982 North American Open, as Mark Talbott later described it, "Sharif completely intimidated Stu. He used all his guile and experience. Sharif argued, he bumped and he glared at Stu (as only Sharif could). I knew in my mind that Stu was a better player at the time, but he dismantled Stu 3–1. Stu lost his focus and his game plan and never challenged for another NAO."

It was the bearded mystery man Mike Desaulniers who finally toppled Sharif. Eleven years old when Sharif won his first North American Open, Desaulniers grew up idolizing the man he would one day replace. Desaulniers's father Neil was a president of the Canadian squash association and taught Mike as a child. As a teenager, having beaten most adults in Vancouver, Mike toured Australia, Pakistan and England, getting exposure to the softball game. He won the 1975 Canadian softball championships at the age of seventeen. He went through four epochal years at Harvard in a way that made Jack Barnaby smile: He did not lose a single college match, won three of four intercollegiate titles (he missed his junior year due to an injury to a bone in his right foot, which required surgery) and twice took the U.S. nationals. By winning within one month the U.S. and Canadian nationals and the intercollegiates—all without loss of a game—Desaulniers established himself as the next great thing.

The modern incarnation of Germain Glidden, Desaulniers scurried around the court like a harried commuter late for work. He beat Sharif in the 1980 WPSA Championships but then lost to Caldwell in the finals, 15–2 in the fifth game. At the 1980 NAO, he reached the finals but bowed meekly to Sharif in four unsuspenseful games. In 1980–81, his first year as a pro, he won six events, one less than Sharif. He took the Boston Open without loss of a game, lost to Sharif in the finals of the Boodles (15–6 in the fifth) and beat Sharif in the Minneapolis Open. In Toronto he grabbed the WPSA Championships, after almost stumbling in the opening round to Howard Broun, 15–13 in the fifth. In the finals against Sharif, Desaulniers went up 2–0 and withstood a fierce Sharif comeback to win the fifth game at 15–9. Still, he was unable to complete the coup d'état by winning the North American Open. Sharif survived three tie-breaker games in the quarterfinals and semifinals to reach the finals. His opponent was not Desaulniers or Goldstein, for his younger brother Aziz Khan had dispatched both of them, and Sharif beat Aziz in a breezy three games to take his twelfth NAO. Desaulniers's season ended with a heartbreaking 18–17-in-the-fifth loss to Geoff Hunt in the semifinals of the Mennen Cup. Sharif, in the end, was still ranked number one.

In the 1981–82 season, Desaulniers got the job done. After Thanksgiving, he went on a 28–1 tear, winning seven of eight tournaments. Desaulniers lost in the WPSA Championships in January 1982 to Caldwell, but, at the 1982 North American Open, he erased all doubt. The tournament was held at Cleveland's Thirteenth Street, in a court heated to a hundred degrees by television lighting and a faulty air conditioner. Sharif, playing in his fifteenth consecutive NAO final, won the first game and went up 8–3 in the second. Desaulniers turned on the afterburners and took the game with rapacious strokes. In the third, with Sharif again up 7–6, Desaulniers again upped the tempo and took nine of the next eleven points. He won the fourth 15–9 and hurled his racquet into the air after winning the last point. For the first time since the Johnson administration, there was a new number-one-ranked professional in North America.

The glory of being number one lasted just a few weeks. At the Mennen, he faced Sharif in the finals. While Desaulniers sat sullenly waiting for the match to begin, Sharif bantered with his home-court crowd and warmed up under the hot television lights. Desaulniers looked jumpy and agitated and lost the match, 15–6, 15–5, 15–9, in thirty-seven minutes.

That bitter defeat hung over his neck all summer like a millstone. In the opening tournament of the autumn, in Rochester, Desaulniers lost in the first round to Tom Page. He never reached a final the rest of the season and won just one more WPSA tournament in his career. He tore his hamstring, then needed a hernia operation. Like Vic Niederhoffer, Desaulniers became a commodities trader in New York who maintained a ferocious schedule of work and training. He even went to work for Niederhoffer and soon adopted his boss's cult of eccentricity. He worked too hard. He kept quiet in the locker room and did not revel in the barnstorming fun of the tour. He would rather play guitar with his blues and calypso band, Extended Adolescence. Squash seemed almost painful to him. "I don't love the game for the sake of being on the court," he said. Keeping his hyperkinetic game motoring at such high speeds took a particular high-octane blend of intensity and willpower. Most champions could gut out a victory even if they were not playing well. Desaulniers, somewhat like Steve Vehslage, had such a finely edged game that if he was off form, he mentally could not get back into the match. He played so violently and so rashly that he drove in fifth gear or else stalled. After two regrettable seasons that saw his ranking drop to sixty-three, he returned to the tour in 1984 with a new persona. He shaved his beard, pierced his ear and deliberately took deep breaths and long walks between points. He reached five WPSA finals, including the Canadian Open, and won one, in Denver, but the glory of 1982 was gone. "I don't worry about no.1, and in a way it would be pointless to try to do all over again something I've already done," he told Bud Collins in 1985. "What I'm looking for is a feeling. . . . I just want to play this way, with real joy, not worry about what happens. And when I reach this abandon, I'm at my best. Have I felt this way again? Maybe for a run of five or six points, then my concentration wavers."

Mark Talbott proved to be the enduring successor to the Khan dynasty. Trickster of the double boast, shaman with the soft smile, witch doctor with the whippy legs, smoke from an unlit fire—Mark Talbott enticed and thrilled the squash world. He was a retriever who never hit terribly hard. He had hippie-length hair and a bony body and insisted on wearing protective goggles years before they were mandated. But, for mental toughness, no one—not Larry Pool or Diehl Mateer or Ed Hahn or Hunter Lott—wanted a fifth-game tiebreaker more than Talbott. He was the greatest player in the history of American squash not because he occasionally touched greatness but because in an era of unprecedented competition, pressure and challenge, he was greatness.

He was born with a silver racquet in his hand. His grandfather was a leading Dayton businessman and his grandmother had coined the name Nabisco for her father's National Biscuit Company. Raised in a Dayton house his grandfather had built, Talbott had a squash court in his basement. The court had no door, just a ladder on which you climbed down. His parents had a child-rearing technique of putting three or four of their children in the court with balls and racquets and pulling up the ladder for a few hours.

This time on court paid off. His parents moved to Baltimore when he was thirteen and he started playing tournaments. He appeared in the first issue of *Squash News* as the winner of the 1978 national juniors. After graduating from Mercersburg Academy in central Pennsylvania, Talbott matriculated at Trinity College. He played one match, an informal match against Harvard and took a game off Desaulniers—the only game the Canadian gave up in his college career. Before the end of the semester, however, Talbott dropped out. One December morning he walked across the sloping green lawn to his coach's office and told him he was leaving. He packed his clothes and books into his station wagon, got in the car, slid a Grateful Dead bootleg tape into the stereo and turned his wheels west. He spent the winter working as a lifeguard at the Detroit Athletic Club, where his older brother Dave was the squash pro. Counterintuitively, it was a shrewd move for his squash career. To become the best, a player in his late teens needed to play full time. Going to college, especially in America, meant fraternity parties and late nights in the library and all the other accouterments of the four best years of your life, but it also meant lost years of training.

Talbott, nonetheless, was not thinking squash in particular. In the spring of 1979, he went overseas. He hitchhiked through South Africa for six months, playing squash with members of the South African branch of the Jesters Club. He came back for the Christmas holidays. In January 1980 he went to a tournament at the Edinburgh Sports Club in Scotland. He stayed at the club for four months, giving lessons and playing more softball. In the summer he moved to Toronto and got a job as a pro at Valhalla, a small club outside Toronto. In between stringing racquets and giving lessons, he played softball with Murray Lilley, a New Zealand softballer who was ranked in the top ten in the world. Talbott had played in only one U.S. nationals, in 1979, and had lost in the first round. His future seemed pointing toward softball.

One day Talbott chanced to run into Clive Caldwell. In his usual persuasive way, Caldwell told Talbott about the new hardball tour and encouraged him to play. In September 1980, only twenty years old, Talbott quit his job and joined the World Professional Squash Association. He had a respectable first season, reaching two semifinals in Salt Lake and San Francisco. In March 1981, two weeks before the season ended, the tour came to the Capitol Hill Club in Washington, D.C., and the squash world was turned upside down in three bloodless days. Talbott blew through the draw, beating the four top players on the tour: Clive Caldwell, Stu Goldstein, Mike Desaulniers and Sharif Khan. "To a man, the WPSA tour players predict that Mark Talbott may soon rank as the greatest squash player ever produced in America," reported a normally taciturn *Squash News.* Talbott's first tour victory pushed him up into the top ten in the year-end rankings.

One hundred and sixteen tournament wins followed in the next fourteen years. In the 1981–82 season, when Desaulniers finally toppled Sharif, Talbott won three events and raised his ranking to five. In the 1982–83 season he took seventeen of nineteen tournaments. He was able to do what Goldstein and Desaulniers could not: permanently overcome Sharif. It was not an easy task. In the third game of an early round match against Sharif at the 1980 Boodles, Sharif informed Talbott he would not exit gracefully. As he stroked a reverse corner, Sharif swung with a 360-

degree follow-through that knocked a front tooth out of Talbott's mouth. Talbott, his mother in the gallery, pocketed his tooth, wiped the blood off his mouth and played on. In the fifth game, Sharif smacked Talbott on the forehead with another wild, wheelhouse swing. Talbott won the match and never lost to Sharif again. With the king deposed, Talbott held the number-one ranking for eleven of the next twelve years. He won five North American Opens, five WPSA Championships, four Canadian Opens and three Boston Opens. He won the Windy City Open in Chicago twelve years in a row. He won over 70 percent of the tournaments he entered and reached at least the semifinals 95 percent of the time. He won twenty-three consecutive finals at one stage. He won eight five-game final-round matches after being down 2–0 (three times surviving match points).

"People, in general, are not aware of the skill required to play the game well," wrote Pierce Egan about racquets in 1832, "and, the fact is, the better it is played the more easy it appears." Talbott played a dramatically undramatic game. He was the game's best retriever. In his first years he lacked an offensive punch, his backhand was weak and he depended solely on being a human backboard. "It was hard to tell whether he was the winner or the runner-up—or maybe just some loose-limbed kid who had found his way downstairs from the A semifinals," wrote *Squash News* in 1983. As he reached the top he developed an offense, especially a consistent double boast. He glided across the court like an osprey on the crest of a thermal. Patient to a fault, he loved to go to five games and seemed incapable, no matter how bad his opponent, to get off the court in three games. This was in part because unlike most players, the egoless Talbott adapted his game like a chameleon to the style of his opponent. If he played Sharif, he volleyed more; against Edwards, he counterpunched; with Mendez, he moved up front and shot more. Quietly zealous, he was a brilliant tactician, knowing exactly when to force an opening. Above all, Talbott had the ability to concentrate. He almost never made an error after 10–all. The Sturm und Drang that Sharif Khan employed was absent with Talbott. He was one of the first top players to say, "nice shot," after a point. He cleared so thoroughly players sometimes forgot he was even on the court. He sometimes corrected referees and took points away from himself if he thought his shot was down; twice, in major tournaments, he refused to accept points and lost games as a result. After a point, he flipped the ball to the server, unlike many players who would not help at all in that small, necessary act. He ended the traditional practice of appearance money.

Talbott looked like a follower of the Grateful Dead, which he was—his dream was for Jerry Garcia and Clive Caldwell to sit down and coordinate their tour schedules. He wore a ratty Army jacket. His tea-colored hair dangled around his shoulders. He developed a habit, much copied, of tearing up a towel and wearing a flopping headband. "Slim and long-haired and wearing glasses, Talbott looks frail and vulnerable on the court, like a child of the Sixties," wrote George Vescey in the *New York Times*. "But, instead of singing 'Alice's Restaurant,' he slashes the hard rubber ball at sharp angles, deflating more powerful players with his persistence." Talbott's doghouse was his most famous accessory. Constructed of tongue-and-groove maple planks, the doghouse was originally a squash court at the Detroit Athletic Club that he tore down and reconstructed on the back of a 1978 Ford pickup truck. For his first three seasons on the tour, he was a star yet slept in a brokedown palace.

A minstrel living on the open road, Talbott was still enormously popular with the corporate crowd sponsoring the WPSA. He happily bore the endless round of cocktail parties, dinners, clinics, exhibitions and pro-ams. He satisfied the crowds by entering almost every WPSA event: In his first six seasons he played in one hundred and six tournaments, missing only two. He secured a half-dozen endorsement deals (the joke about his Rolex sponsorship was that Talbott was the last guy actually to wear a watch). He paved the way for the acceptance of eye protection, which was a flashpoint of controversy within hardball squash circles. The Canadian SRA ruled in 1980 that all its juniors had to wear eye goggles. Acrimonious discussion, led by president Herb Gross, followed in the U.S. Reports of incidents of eye damage—Mike Desaulniers took a ball in the eye at the Cambridge Doubles, Tom Rumpler hit Sharif in the eye with a racquet—filtered through the squash community. In 1982 the men's intercollegiate association instituted a mandatory eye-protection rule. In October 1983 the USSRA officially announced all players at any national championship had to wear eye protection. The WPSA never required its members to wear goggles, but they had to in the North American Open after 1986, since the USSRA sanctioned and ran the tournament. Talbott was the first pro player to wear goggles, years before the others did, and he became the early role model for the commonsensical move toward eye safety.

Goggles were not his only squash accessory, especially when his brother Dave was involved. Seven years older and a pro at the Detroit Athletics Club, Dave offered a canvas upon which Mark could splatter his commedia dell'arte personality. Mark wore gorilla masks or a carved-out pumpkin at the DAC's annual Halloween evening black-tie dinner. When Dave took the head coaching job at Yale, he once put Mark in a junior varsity match against a brand-new Connecticut College team of squash neophytes. Another time, Mark wore a dime-store handlebar mustache, strapped two pillows inside a sweatsuit and donned dark sunglasses. Claiming to be Sam Friedan, a bumbling junior varsity player with glaucoma, he played for Yale in its annual Jester Club match. In both matches, Mark strung along his opponents, losing the first two games and barely winning in a fifth-game tiebreaker. Mark's favorite maneuver was to find outrageous outfits for tournament matches against Dave. They would warm up in sweatsuits and then, as the match began, strip off to reveal antique full-length dressing gowns or black-tie dinner jackets or Pilgrim getups with top hats and gray flannel knickers (and "Air Winthrops" sneakers). At a first-round match at the 1983 U.S. Open at the Yale Club in New York, they appeared in boxing regalia—shiny satin boxing trunks and color-coordinated, knee-high socks with tassels—that Mark had bought at Madison Square Garden. A year later they again met at the Yale Club and this time they went white tie: starched shirts, suspenders, bow-ties, cummerbunds and long tails. Mark once asked for a "cufflink timeout." After the match they dried their rented outfits by hanging them out the window of their room on the nineteenth floor of the Loews Summit. When asked by the *Wall Street Journal* why they had switched from the boxing outfits of the previous year, Mark said that they did not want to be too informal at the Yale Club, now that Dave had gotten a job at Yale.

Of all the names on the tour, none was more often placed next to Talbott's each Sunday afternoon than Edward C. P. Edwards. Ned Edwards had more than a passing resemblance to Ted Hughes, the English poet and husband of Sylvia Plath. Growing up on the Main Line and learning squash at Merion, he had been a tempestuous child, small for his age, a prankster and punk, and when he grew into a large man he developed a gentle-giant persona. But, behind the soft-spoken, self-contained exterior, some observers thought, that angry, short kid itched to get out. He struggled against his Merion upbringing and his share of personal obstacles. In college, his sister was electrocuted while taking a bath. He also found out he was a diabetic. "It seems that his disease and background have made him so hard on himself that self-doubt encompasses him," the *Village Voice* reported in 1985. "'There's a dark hole in terms of my athleticism that hasn't been resolved,' says Ned. 'I'm scared that either I don't have the will to win or the stick-to-it-iveness that's necessary to be the best . . . sometimes I have trouble with just being practical on court. I want to feel as though I'm doing something special. I've always felt that not being able to settle in and be comfortable with just competing and being a squash player has been my problem, not so much hitting the ball. I've always had trouble just saying I'm out here to win.'"

Few champions can hit every shot and Edwards was one of them. He became the much-needed foil to Talbott. He was ranked two on the tour for six seasons. The inevitable Sunday finalist, he lost thirty-two times to Talbott in tournament finals—more than double the total of anyone else. In some years he was the only player to beat Talbott, and, for five consecutive years, he was the only player besides Jahangir Khan to beat Talbott in the finals of a tournament. He won four majors. As adept with the sponsors as Talbott, Edwards raised thousands of dollars for the Juvenile Diabetes Foundation for whom he was a national spokesman. On court he was the brawler, while Talbott was the counterpuncher. He moved deliberately in between points, and before serving he held an awkward position for three or four seconds, as if weighed down by a great burden. Nicknamed "The Bear," he was like a caged panther, his strapping physique and mercurial personality too large for the court. When Edwards played well, he dipped into a red-hot core of rage. While Talbott seemed to get stronger as the tournament progressed, almost thriving on the competition, Edwards often got weaker and was sometimes spent by Sunday afternoon.

Some of his matches with Talbott were classics. At Greenwich in January 1985, Talbott was up, 9–1 and 12–5 in the fifth, before Edwards stormed back to push ahead, 3–0 and 4–1, in the set-five tiebreaker. Talbott won the match, when Edwards lost four points in a row, including tinning on double match point. At the 1987 North American Open in Toledo, Edwards beat Talbott 15–14 in the fourth game. Edwards, with a 2–1 lead, went ahead, 14–13, in the no-set tiebreaker. Talbott crunched a backhand rail off a serve for a winner but then whiffed on an Edwards cross-court that skidded on a sweat spot. At the 1988 WPSA Championships, Talbott beat Edwards in a ninety-minute sweat-fest after being down, 2–0. Talbott had been up, 13–9, in the first game and 13–11 in the second, but had been unable to win either game. In the third Talbott survived two match points to win the game, 15–14, before capturing the last two, 15–9 and 15–12. A week later in the finals at Greenwich, Edwards returned the favor. He lost the first two games and then was up, 14–10, in the fifth. Talbott smacked two winners and

Edwards slammed a ball into the tin. At 14–13, Edwards hit a clean backhand rail to escape.

Edwards's finest moment was probably the 1985 Boston Open, when he captured his first major title in desperate fashion. He won two quick games from Steve Bowditch, the Australian bad boy, and was up, 8–0, in the third. His fatal attraction to the tin ended his easy march to victory. Bowditch saved two match points to win the third game, 15–14. In the fourth Edwards again rushed to an early lead, 6–0, only to again get mired in errors and face another tiebreaker, set-five at 13–all. Up 3–0, Edwards gave away five straight points. In the fifth he went up 9–5, and it went to a tiebreaker, no set at 13–all. Edwards plucked the first point to get another match point, a full hour since he last had held one. He immediately tinned a forehand roll corner to set up a double match point for himself and for Bowditch. The point started with Edwards sprinting up to the front to retrieve a Bowditch dropshot, then Edwards sent a stiletto backhand volley drive past a dazed Bowditch for the win.

Kicking around before the inevitable Talbott versus Edwards final were a brace of outstanding characters. John Nimick, known as "Tiny Dancer," was a thick-legged bruiser who often was ranked third on the tour. Raised at Merion and a star at Princeton, Nimick won the 1982 nationals before turning professional. He won four majors and helped run the WPSA for its last six years. Like Edwards he felt conflicted about his background. "I guess the Main Line is still my biggest ball and chain," he said in 1985. "But I feel more and more that I'm divorced from my background. Squash is my way out." Another American who hesitated about his career was David Boyum. A leading junior out of the Heights Casino program, Boyum played a close second fiddle to Kenton Jernigan at Harvard. He dramatically beat Mark Talbott in the first round of the 1985 Boston Open and stayed in the top ten for five years. Still, like Desaulniers, Boyum eyed the real world with increasing avidity. "Being a pro squash player doesn't cut it for me," he told George Bell of *Squash News* in 1987. "This may sound snobbish, but I don't think it's worthy of me." Kenton Jernigan, Boyum's teammate at Harvard, thought otherwise. Jernigan grew up playing at Newport Squash, his father's public club, and became the boy wonder in the mid-eighties. He won the nationals as a freshman in college and two more times before turning pro after college. His game was like a good burgher of Delft—solidly orthodox—but he had a reputation for late-round destruction. He clinched one major, the 1991 WPSA Championships but, until he won in Hartford in 1990, he was known as the greatest player on the tour never to win a WPSA title, having lost previously in nine finals. Todd Binns, the gunslinging southpaw son of Australian great Ken Binns, was the other perennial candidate for that ignominious moniker. Binns took eight years and seven losses in WPSA finals before capturing his first title at the 1991 Canadian Open. His worst loss was at the 1987 Canadian Open when he let an 8–1 fifth-game lead slip away to Talbott, going down 18–14. Greg Zaff, a doughty Williams graduate who was the first man ever to be an All-American in tennis and squash, followed Binns by grabbing his only major at the Canadian Open, in 1990. Jeff Stanley turned professional in the spring of 1989 and had little time to make an impact on the tour before it folded, but he cracked the top ten after one season and won at Newport in 1991. The most exciting late arrival was Gary Waite, a Canadian who displaced Talbott at the number one spot in 1993. Waite played on the softball tours as well, reaching a ranking of eleven. He was the hardest-hitting player on the tour and had a gargantuan appetite for fitness.

Mexico supplied a number of exciting talents to complete the North American tour. At one time, nine Mexicans placed in the top fifty. Marcos, Juan and Jose-Luis Mendez, three brothers from Mexico City, all had top ten rankings. Juan reached three finals and posted wins over every top twenty player but Talbott and Edwards. Marcos had the best career of the three, staying in the top five for three years and winning the last hardball North American Open in 1994. Pepe Martinez reached three finals and Alberto Nunez landed exactly at the number twenty spot in the rankings five times in his first seven years on tour. Mario Sanchez, however, was the leading Mexican player of his generation. Tall, thin, bearded—newspapers always called him "aristocratic"—Sanchez upset every player on the tour at least once. Although he only won one major tournament and had a deflating record against Talbott, Sanchez was as brilliant a player as any on the tour. He was ranked in the top six for ten straight years.

Two tragic WPSA stories came from athletes dying young. Alex Doucas, a young Montreal native, turned pro at nineteen. Emulating Talbott, Doucas and another young Canadian, Brendan Clarke, toured in a Winnebago. Doucas announced his talent by winning the 1984 Mennen Cup qualifying tournament. He beat Edwards in the final, 15–14 in the fifth, making him the first player outside the top twenty to win a WPSA tournament. In June 1989 Doucas drowned in a boating accident on Lac St. Louis near Montreal. He was twenty-four.

Blithely gifted, Tom Page was originally supposed to be what Mark Talbott became. A Merion product like Nimick and Edwards, Page won the inaugural national boys under seventeens in 1973. At age nineteen and a sophomore at Princeton, he had a miraculous season. He grabbed the Gold Racquets and the Harry Cowles (beating his brother Palmer in twenty minutes in the finals) and reached the semis of the North American Open before losing to Sharif Khan, 15–11 in the fifth. After winning just one previous match in the nationals, Page obliterated the draw in the 1977 nationals, losing just one game and becoming the youngest champion since Harry Conlon. Page dropped out of Princeton and turned pro. He beat Aziz Khan, Mario Sanchez, Sharif Khan and Clive Caldwell to win the first tournament he played in, the 1980 Philadelphia Open. He reached the finals of four other draws his first season and was ranked eighth that first season, right above another rookie named Mark Talbott. Built like a halfback, Page suggilated the ball with the hardest backhand in the game. The acme of his career was his quarterfinal encounter with Jahangir Khan at the 1985 North American Open. In the glass court on the stage at Town Hall in front of a thousand screaming spectators, Page went up, 2–1, winning a tense third game 15–14. He lost in five, but it was the highest quality match of the season.

Inconsistent as always, Page did not capitalize on his fine effort. Six days later at the Canadian Professionals at Skyline, he stumbled in the first round to a lower-ranked player, badly tinning at simultaneous match point. Physically impregnable, Page played with a deep stress fracture in his leg one season. After a horrific bicycle accident in Manhattan in October 1986, when he crashed head-on through the windshield of an oncoming taxi, he played tournaments with his jaw wired shut. "Only a mediocre person is always at his best," wrote Somerset Maugham and Page lived up to that maxim. Sometimes he was brilliant, and sometimes he was horrible. With his tousled hair, eye-averting gaze and rudderless aura, he was a bit like Vic Niederhoffer. Niederhoffer's eccentricities were calculated; Page's were involuntary and it was later discovered he suffered from schizophrenia. He died in 2001 at the age of forty-four.

Overseas players ripped apart the strangely functional cocoon of professional squash in North America. Rainer Ratinac, a lanky, six-foot-four, extremely fit Australian of Greek descent, had worked as a fireman in Sydney before joining Jonah Barrington's 1969 traveling circus. He came over to North America in 1972 and, after working in Calgary and Salt Lake City, found a post at the University Club in Chicago. Ratinac reached the finals of four majors. Geoff Williams played in the inaugural Canadian Open in 1985. Having flown in three hours before his match with Gul

Khan, Williams was woefully unprepared. Gul hit him five times alone with his hard serve. Maqsood Ahmed also came and lost as quickly to Sharif Khan. Ross Norman and Chris Dittmar both entered the 1985 North American Open. Norman won one match, but Dittmar lost immediately.

The most notorious interloper on the WPSA tour was Steve Bowditch. A volatile Australian based in West Germany, Bowditch reached the top five on the hardball tour and the top fifteen on the softball tours, a twin triumph only matched by Gary Waite. He never won a WPSA tournament, but he reached two North American Open finals. A notoriously distempered player with the nickname "the Disputatious Digger," Bowditch revolted against the WPSA's strictures. He walked off the court in the semifinals of a 1984 St. Louis tournament, down 15–7, 15–12, 12–3 to Mike Desaulniers, after becoming miffed by referee decisions. He refused to follow the association's dress code requiring collared shirts and pocketed shorts. At the 1985 NAO at Town Hall, he wore a collarless Drakkar T-shirt and gym shorts so tight, one observer said, "the poor guy looked like he could sing the lead in *Aida* out there." John Nimick castigated Bowditch after their second-round match at the 1985 Canadian Open, which Bowditch won in five games, for multiple dress-code violations. Bowditch's adventures on the hardball tour ended in the quarterfinals of the 1987 NAO. Bowditch complained bitterly about wearing eye goggles, which were unknown in softball circles. Down 2–0, 10–4 to Ned Edwards, Bowditch hurled his goggles out of the court and was disqualified.

Jahangir Khan had as great an impact in the U.S. as any overseas player since Hashim Khan. With a first name meaning "conqueror of the world," Jahangir was destined for greatness ever since he was first held by his father, Roshan Khan. A sickly child, he had hernia operations when he was five and twelve years old. In 1979 at age fifteen, he got a place in the qualifying tournament at the world amateurs because a Nigerian entrant did not appear. He won the title. A month later his older brother, Torsham, died of a heart attack on court in Adelaide. Torsham was the heir apparent to Roshan's throne. A top-ten softball player, Torsham had even ventured to the North American Open in January 1979, losing to his cousin Sharif in the quarterfinals. Exactly two years to the day after Torsham died, Jahangir won the World Open in Toronto. For the next five years, seven months and a day Jahangir never lost a softball match. He had thighs like a bear, a drooping mustache and an inexhaustible reservoir of talent and flair. He trained ferociously: a typical day was a ten-mile run, sprints, jump rope skipping, swimming, court drills and a couple of hours playing against a variety of opponents. He loved to lay siege to an opponent, jerking him around and crushing his spirit in marathon opening games. In 1983 he played a two-hour-and-forty-six minute match against Gamal Awad at the Chichester Festival. He won, 9–10, 9–5, 9–7, 9–2. The first game lasted seventy-one minutes—even though Jahangir had an 8–1 lead.

Anticipation was high on a Talbott versus Khan matchup. Jahangir first played hardball in the 1982 Mennen Cup, where he lost to a number of players, including Talbott. In September 1983 at a Chivas exhibition in New York, Talbott and Ned Edwards played Jahangir one match with a softball and one with a hardball. Edwards lost both. Against Talbott Jahangir took the softball easily but lost in the hardball. He faced Talbott a few weeks later in the 1983 World Championships in New Zealand. Talbott, serving on the first point of the match, substituted a hardball and served it as a joke to Jahangir. Both players and the audience laughed; Jahangir went on to win, 9–3, 9–4, 9–0.

Jahangir returned to North America and blitzed the WPSA tour. He won the 1983 Boston Open with ease, strafing Talbott in thirty minutes in the final, 15–8, 15–8, 15–5. Jahangir captured twelve of the last thirteen points of the match in a brutal display of perfection. "He retrieved all but one of Talbott's fabled double boasts, able to reply with feet planted in remote areas ordinarily untouched save for an occasional outstretched racquet," wrote Derrick Niederman in *Squash News*. "Once arrived, his textbook preparation allowed for a deadly dichotomy of purpose. Perfect length along the backhand rail or a stomach-wrenching straight drop, with no time to decipher which. Pick your poison. Suddenly Talbott's own stroke production seemed fragile." In 1984 and 1985, Jahangir won both the WPSA Championships and North American Open. At the 1984 WPSA Championships, Talbott stayed with Jahangir in a tough thirty-four-minute first game before collapsing, 18–14, 15–8, 15–6. Two months later at the North American Open at Park Avenue, Talbott grabbed the first game and was up 8–7 in the second when Jahangir slipped and twisted his knee. After a minute break, play resumed. Something clicked. The match lasted only fifteen more minutes and Talbott won just six more points, as Jahangir streamrolled, 12–15, 15–9, 15–4, 15–1. It was a traumatizing end to the tournament.

There was just one brief respite to the bombardment. In the spring of 1984, Mario Sanchez broke Jahangir's epic win streak by shocking him 15–11, 15–12, 15–9, in the semifinals of the Canadian Professionals at Skyline. Sanchez simply outslugged Jahangir in a strange match made stranger by the fact that only four people were in the gallery. (Talbott beat Sanchez in the finals in three.) In the semifinals of the 1985 WPSA Championships, Jahangir got revenge when he faced Sanchez again. Sanchez jumped out to a 2–1 lead but lost the fifth, 15–0. It was the first fifth-game shutout anyone could remember in professional squash. Jahangir looked as if he was alone on the court. In the finals against Talbott, it took sixty-eight minutes to finish the first two games, the score 1–1. Then, twenty minutes ended it, with Jahangir cruising to a 3–1 win. In Minnesota, he beat Talbott, 15–2, 15–7, 15–3. At the 1985 North American Open, Jahangir survived Tom Page's onslaught in the quarters to win the prestigious title again. He also stormed to victories in the 1985 and 1986 Canadian Opens, the Skyline Professionals, the last Chivas and two Mennen Cups. In total, he played fifteen hardball tournaments and lost just twice. He was squash's Horowitz, a maestro capable of unprecedented skill who could still blast you away with the pure intensity of his artistry. His patience was awesome. "He ignores openings on the court and makes no attempt to serve aces," wrote Peter Stephan in *Squash News* in 1984. "He just keeps the ball in play until his opponent starts to dream of Barcaloungers instead of scraping those perfect rails off the walls."

If Mark Talbott and Jahangir Khan were the quintessential male players of the decade, Alicia McConnell was their female counterpart. Her shining moment came at the age of eighteen in Sweden at the 1980 world junior girls' championships. McConnell, a Heights Casino junior, was wearing the gold medal. For the first time in squash history, the Star-Spangled Banner was played at a world championship. It seemed that women's squash in America was about to soar into bomb-bursting air.

Instead, it was rather a damp squib. The female professionals were never able to ratchet their circuit up enough to sustain a viable tour. There was a dearth of depth in the women's ranks, with the level of play dropping off vertiginously after the top ten. In 1980 a group of women founded the Association of Women's Professional Squash. Mariann Greenberg, a New York professional, was president. AWPS's motto was "Women's Squash—A Game of Growth." Three years later AWPS was renamed the Women's American Squash Association, with Nina Porter as president, and in 1986 a new organization, the Women's American Squash Professionals Association, succeeded WASA. Directed by Pippa Sales, a South African transplant, WASPA had $60,000 in total prize money in its first season. Whatever the alphabet-soup nomenclature, women's profes-sional squash never reached the tipping point of viability. The women's nationals, unlike the men's, had always been open to professionals and was never superseded by any pro tournament. It was still the pinnacle of great-ness. A half-dozen tournaments supplemented it, but, too often, they were played for just three or four years before disappearing. The celebrated Bancroft, for instance, lasted just two years at Uptown before moving to Philadelphia for one final renewal. In 1987 WASPA had just twenty-two playing members. Two years later it had just three tournaments. In 1989, the leading professional player, Alicia McConnell, publicly quit squash. She earned $18,000 in 1987 and $14,000 in 1988, not nearly enough money to support her career as a fulltime professional. Lower-ranked women rarely even broke even with expenses.

Professional women's squash dated from January 1977, when Bancroft sponsored an open at Uptown. As a publicity stunt, Uptown persuaded Jack Dempsey to pull names out of a hat to make the draw. The eighty-one-year-old Manassa Mauler was a bit unsteady, but the event received a lot of publicity. The winner earned $2,000 and the total purse was $6,500. In March 1978, *Viva*, a glossy magazine run by Bob Guccione, the publisher of *Penthouse*, became the first company other than a sports-equipment firm to sponsor a women's tournament, when it ran the $3,500 *Viva* International Open at the Manhattan Squash Club. The Carol Weymuller at the Heights Casino was a favorite tournament. A number of men's professional events attached a women's draw: the Boo-dles, Greenwich, Capitol Hill, Cleveland, the New York Met Profession-als, Rochester, the Boston Open, the WPSA Championships and the Canadian Open. The most extravagant tournament was the Loews. Hosted by Alan Rose at his Loews Summit hotel and the Doral Inn, the Loews began in 1983. It attracted two hundred women playing in a vari-ety of draws. The professional draw often had the highest prize money of any women's tournament ($10,000 in 1987), but the real allure of the Loews was its unusual prizes. The Loews ran a raffle that offered lucky winners free meals at fine restaurants, a reading by a psychic and tickets to Broadway shows; the trophy for each draw's champion was a free, all-expenses paid trip to a beach resort.

The first female pro to win the nationals was Barbara Maltby. Voted the best athlete at Pennsylvania in 1970 for her field hockey and basketball exploits, Maltby did not pick up squash until three years after graduation. Her coach was the legendary Norm Bramall. While Bramall put her through her paces on the courts at Cynwyd, Maltby worked on her fitness with a personal conditioning coach (a volleyball coach at Penn by the illustrious name of Ralph Hippolyte), who designed a routine that included lifting weights. Maltby dedicated herself full time to squash. She got a job teaching at Squashcon in Philadelphia and entered the city's men's B league. Although clearly the leader of a new breed of female players, Maltby could not prove it with a national championship. In 1974 she lost in the semifinals to Gretchen Spruance. In the 1975 finals in Rochester, she stayed on court for an hour and a half but succumbed to hometown favorite Ginny Akabane, 17–15, 16–17, 13–16, 15–11, 15–11. In 1976 at Penn, she lost in the finals to Spruance. She went up 9–1 in the second game and barely held on, escaping, 15–13. She snagged a 6–1 lead in the third, but Spruance plowed through to win, 15–9. Maltby had a 14–10 lead in the fourth and held on, saving a match point to win, 17–16. Spruance bludgeoned her, 15–6, in the final game. The fourth game was particularly rough, with thirteen lets and errant backswings hitting each other's faces. "I hate it when there are so many lets," Spruance said afterwards. "It's disgusting and unpleasant, but the two of us just don't seem to move well, not clearing the way. I guess we're too overanxious." In 1977 after beating Weymuller and Goldie Edwards with ease, Maltby lost to Spruance in the finals in four. In 1978, in front of a vocal hometown crowd at Wilmington Country Club, Spruance again fended off the surging Maltby in an exhilarating final. Even though Maltby had beaten Spruance at a number of events during the season, the nationals jinx seemed firmly in place. Spruance, "garbed in a pink and white checked pinafore with a pink ribbon holding back her blond tresses," according to a USSRA reporter, jumped to a 15–10, 15–5 lead. In the third, she went up 14–6, and some friends in the gallery headed to the bar to celebrate. Maltby never lost hope. Moving deliberately before serving, she survived nine match points to win the third game, 17–16. She took the fourth game, 15–8, from a stunned Spruance, and the crowd reluctantly put down their drinks and filtered back from the bar. In the fifth, Spruance got to thirteen first, but Maltby hung in and evened the score. Spruance chose set-five, and it inevitably went to 17–all. Both players hurtled up front in a mad scramble. Spruance asked for a let. With the tension unbearable, the referee said, a *deus ex gallerie*: "Let point. Game and match, Spruance."

In 1979 Spruance retired, but Maltby did not win her long-sought-after national title. Heather McKay ruined Maltby's chances. Five-foot-six with a face not unlike Julie Andrews, the girl from Queanbeyan, Australia, picked up squash at eighteen. By twenty McKay was world champion. She won the British championships sixteen years in a row. She did not lose a match, after yielding to Fran Marshall in the 1962 Scottish championships, for the rest of her two-decade career. She did not lose a game in a tournament between 1968 and 1977. She won the 1965 British finals in fourteen minutes. She won the inaugural women's World Open in 1976 with the loss of just fifteen points, including four in the final. If she had a weakness, the joke went, it was her service return, which was rusty from disuse. She was, according to Herbert Warren Wind, "vastly aided by a self-critical attitude common to champions; when she plays a batch of loose points, it miffs her." Her crisp strokes reminded Wind of Ben Hogan's swing. McKay was often proclaimed the world's most accomplished athlete.

McKay moved to Canada in 1975 to work, along with her husband, at the Toronto Squash Club. Amid much fanfare, she came to the U.S. and won the 1977 Bancroft Open at Uptown. She beat Gretchen Spruance (listed as "housewife" in the tournament program) in the semifinals in twenty-eight minutes, surviving an errant Spruance swing that caught her in the mouth. McKay won the 1979 nationals, beating Maltby with ease. Ever eager for new worlds to conquer, McKay picked up racquetball in 1979 and became national champion within a year—the only person ever to win both the racquetball and squash nationals.

For Maltby, it was not until 1980, after five straight losses in the finals, that she won her first national title. With Spruance and McKay finally out of the way, she won in straight games, beating Gail Ramsay, another Bramall player from the Cynwyd Club, in the finals. She won it again in 1981, beating Alicia McConnell, a young high-school girl from Heights Casino, in the finals in four games. Maltby, spancelled by knee injuries, then retired from competitive singles and, like McKay, began playing racquetball.

McConnell dominated women's squash as no one had since Betty Howe Constable. At five-foot-eight and one hundred and forty-four muscular pounds with a mane of dark hair cascading around her shoulders, she was, according to *The New Yorker,* "what one of our uncles would call a big package." McConnell carried Maltby's penchant for physical fitness and hard-hitting to a level where hitting a floater against her was like looking into the mouth of a cannon. At age eleven she started playing squash at the Heights Casino, which was two blocks from her home. In 1980 Carol Weymuller took her and four other girls to the inaugural World Juniors in Sweden. McConnell beat Katja Sauerwald of Finland, 9–0, 5–9, 9–4, 9–7, in the finals of the individual tournament. The U.S. girls team came in first, ahead of Sweden, Ireland, Scotland and Finland.

In 1981 she matriculated at Penn and won the nationals, the national intercollegiates and the national juniors, all in the space of one month. With practice partners like Larry Sconzo, a top B player in New York and squash referee gadfly, and coaches like Jon Foster, a professional player, McConnell established herself as an instant genius. Her first few years of playing women were not easy. She lost regularly and badly to Maltby. "It wasn't only that McConnell lost," wrote Marcyellen Burns in *Squash News* after Maltby beat her in the 1981 Boodles. "It was the way she lost—with temper tantrums and a childish display of pouting and even some tears. It was plainly a girl against a mature woman." In 1984 she turned professional at the Boodles (now called the Chivas) and accepted her first place prize of $1,500, after a hasty telephone call to Penn to make sure she could still play college lacrosse. "The Alicia McConnell who easily swept the Chivas field is far different from the tantrum-throwing teenager who made her debut in the Open several years ago," admitted *Squash News*. "Today she is a streamlined, mature young woman, as much in control of her once-fiery emotions as she is of her wide assortment of shots."

Alicia McConnell won seven straight national titles, something no man or woman had ever done. She won them in decisive fashion, losing just five games in the first four years. Toward the end of her reign, she slipped a bit: In 1986 Diana Edge, Nina Porter and Sue Cogswell all extended her to five games, and in 1987 and 1988 she lost a game in the finals to Demer Holleran. But, throughout the eighties, Alicia McConnell was synonymous with women's squash excellence.

Holleran proved to be a worthy successor in the nineties. Eventually she racked up even more national titles than McConnell, winning six in both hardball and softball. Holleran, raised at Merion and the Field Club in Greenwich, had a game similar to McConnell's, except she often substituted patience for power. Quietly competitive and a firm believer in sportsmanship, Holleran was awarded the President Cup in 2000, the first professional woman player ever to receive the USSRA's highest award. Holleran replaced Ann Wetzel as coach at Pennsylvania in 1994 and, for seven years, led the Quakers. In 2000, her varsity won the Howe Cup, the first time a Penn team had ever won the national intercollegiate championship.

Surrounding McConnell and Holleran were a number of women intent on dynamiting a niche for themselves in squash. Nina Porter, from Trinity, had a 2–0 lead against McConnell in the semifinals of the 1986 nationals before falling in five. Mariann Greenberg, a spunky pro at

Southport and Sleepy Hollow, won the Canadian nationals in 1984 and was ranked number two in the U.S. in 1986, at age thirty-nine. Diana Nyad, a marathon swimmer who set the record for swimming around the island of Manhattan, played a fierce game. Ellie Pierce, a redhead rival of Holleran's, won the Carol Weymuller in 1990, as well as two softball national titles. Pierce played on the U.S. national team five times. Gail Ramsay had a successful run after her unprecedented college career. Her best win was a 15–13-in-the-fifth victory over McConnell in Greenwich. In the semifinals of the 1987 Carol Weymuller, Ramsay stretched McConnell to her limit, losing, 18–17 in the fifth. Karen Kelso capitalized on Ramsay's work, demolishing McConnell in the finals in three games. Kelso, a Penn graduate and Heights Casino player, then beat McConnell later that season, becoming one of the few women to beat her more than once a season. Kelso had a rowdy game of hard serves and gritty shotmaking and reached the finals of the nationals four times in a row. Nancy Gengler, a willowy redhead, played number one at Princeton, then became a professional at Uptown. In 1983, in a match covered in *The New Yorker*, Gengler took the first game of the finals of the nationals against McConnell. After losing the second, she went up, 14–12, in the third and barely lost, 15–14. She surrendered the fourth, 15–11. Gengler, although she had just one win over McConnell in fifteen tries, was usually considered along with Kelso as the two best Americans of the era never to win the nationals.

Just like the men, a number of leading overseas women came over to play hardball, led by Marge Zachariah, Sue Newman and Heather McKay who played in the first Bancroft. Angela Smith worked in New York as a professional and coached the national men's team. Heather Wallace moved to Toronto and eventually played for Canada. Julieanne Harris appeared in the mid-eighties in San Francisco. She immediately reached the top of the hardball game, while working as a pro with her husband Bill Lane. Like many Australians, "her glares could seal blister packs," according to *Squash News*. Sue Cogswell, a five-time British Open finalist, worked at Fifth Avenue. Cogswell challenged McConnell more than any other woman in the eighties. Some years she won more tournaments than McConnell, but her career was curtailed in June 1987 after she sustained a back injury in a subway mishap. "I thought women's squash was minor in England," Cogswell bluntly told *Squash News* in 1986, "but it's very nearly invisible here."

The most profound change in the women's game was that it evolved away from the ladylike orthodoxy of earlier generations. Gone were the sherry and long skirts. "It is a game of aggression and intimidation," said Diana Nyad in 1978 in a statement that summed up an era. "And women need to learn that they can go out and push somebody out of their way and hit the fuckin' ball."

CHAPTER NINE

18–16 in the Fifth

It is a Monday evening around seven o'clock, the twelfth of November. The Cyclorama in the South End of Boston shudders with excitement. There is an overflow house, more than nine hundred people, the largest crowd ever to watch a squash match in America. People push along the bleachers and sit in the aisles. It is the final of the 1984 Boston Open, the first portable glass-court tournament in the country.

Facing each other are the two most electric players in the world: Jahangir Khan of Pakistan and Mark Talbott of Dayton, Baltimore, Detroit, Toronto, Atlanta, Marblehead, Florida and Mars. Never before have almost a thousand people gathered in one place at one time simply to see two men swat à ball around a white box. In November 1884 the first squash courts in America appeared in New England, and now, exactly one hundred years later in New England, the game is culminating its long journey.

Jahangir Khan is the rajah of the racquet. He has muscular, hirsute legs and a barrel chest. His shorts have a wide blue stripe around the pocket but, otherwise, he too is following the age-old custom of wearing all white clothing. He looks immensely relaxed. He tattoos the ball against the front wall with powerful, technically perfect strokes. He looks invincible.

Mark Talbott steps out onto the court wearing a white shirt with the Skyline logo on the left breast, white shorts, white socks and a red WPSA headband placed on his forehead above his trademark eye goggles. He warms up with a lazy confidence and he fluidly strokes the red Merco tour-court ball three or four times down the wall before zipping it cross-court. While Jahangir hits, Talbott swings his racquet back and forth, as if brushing off a table. He seems oblivious to any pressure, but there is a lot riding on the match. His brother Dave has driven up from New Haven, his father has flown in from Atlanta and his new coach Ken Binns has flown in from Toronto—all to see if Talbott can do the impossible. Talbott has been disgusted with his lack of resistance against Jahangir, having been blown out in their three previous tilts. He has spent the summer of 1984 training with the sole purpose of overcoming the Pakistani. Normally he fishes, golfs, sees some Dead shows and lollygags around his farm outside Ludlow, Vermont. This summer he hires his first coach, Ken Binns, and works out at the Skyline Club in Toronto with a vengeance. His main goal: to hit the ball harder and more precisely. He has to overcome Jahangir's legendary fitness, strength and perfect length by overpowering him with speed and accuracy. "I had to prevent him from dominating," Talbott says later. "Jake was so strong, so invincible, I had to overwhelm him in order to get him to pop up any loose balls."

Still he struggles through the tournament. He has two overtime games against Gul Khan, goes four tough games against Alex Doucas and is down, 5–2 in the fifth, against Mario Sanchez in the semifinals, before sneaking out a 15–10 victory. Jahangir, on the other hand, is the human tsunami and rolls through the tournament without a hint of trouble.

The match begins, like all sporting events, with a sacramental ritual. Jahangir points to the name on the racquet (his own, in a subtle bit of gamesmanship) that will provide the method of spinning for serve. Mark nods and backs away. He stretches his arms in wide crossing arcs, like a football official motioning for a decline of penalty. Jahangir carefully places the head of his racquet directly on the T in the middle of the court and twirls it like a top. Many players have abiding beliefs in the spinning for serve—who spins, what is used (W or M if a Wilson racquet, P or D for Prince, up or down, rough or smooth) and what to call. The racquet pirouettes in tight rotations and topples over. Jahangir bends over as if the racquet is a lost work of art. He hesitates to pick it up. He tells the result to Talbott and wants Talbott to verify it. Talbott wanders over and glances at the racquet, then releases the ball which he has been holding. Jahangir slowly unbends, picks up the ball with his right hand and his racquet with his left hand, strides confidently to the right serving circle and wipes his hand on the glass wall. Talbott wipes his right hand on his shorts, gives his shoulders a loosening shrug and retreats to the left box. As the prelude to the show, this is a strangely stylized bit of choreography.

"Quiet in the gallery, please," says Derrick Niederman, the referee. "Mr. Khan to serve. Players ready. Play." Niederman, a Yalie and one of the better amateurs in the game, has been one of the refereeing mainstays of the Boston Open since its days in Hemenway Gymnasium at Harvard. He had played in the tournament, losing to Talbott in the opening round. He is known as a fair and diligent referee. There are two side judges,

Mario Sanchez, the Mexican star, and Kirk Randall, the professional at the University Club.

The first point of a match can deflate, encourage or destroy confidence. One of Talbott's advantages is experience serving hardball's high lobs, but it is Jahangir who tosses up a perfectly placed serve. Talbott stabs at it as it skids off the side wall but it is too close and he misses. It bounces off the back wall, and, on his second attempt, he slaps an awful backhand that shoots off the front wall far from the side wall. Jahangir lets the ball come off the back wall, then rifles a rail that almost nicks on the side wall just at the service line. Talbott lunges at it and flicks back another weak return. Jahangir smacks a second vicious backhand rail. In prior matches, Talbott has been sucked into long left-wall exchanges that drain his energy and produce easy winners for Jahangir. The basic problem is Jahangir has the best backhand on the planet; Talbott's is mediocre. In a move that reveals the new Talbott, he ends the sequence quickly, wristing the rail cross-court. Jahangir, so hard to dislodge from the T, cuts it off with his feet still in the middle of the court and pummels it down the right-wall. Talbott, off-balance, manages a low cross court that comes sharply off the left wall. Jahangir turns on the easy ball. It tins.

"Ball down," Niederman says. "1–0, Talbott choice." Jahangir tugs at his shorts. An unforced error from Jahangir? Maybe Talbott has a chance.

The match begins. Jahangir wins the next three points in a row. He ominously tracks down a patented Talbott double boast. He hits a three-wall for a winner. Then, he unnecessarily tins two balls. A pattern emerges. Talbott is stepping into the ball, taking it early and hitting it crisply. Jahangir appears on the defensive, tentative, tight. Talbott hard serves often, trying to discomfort Jahangir. He asks for lets when he is in trouble, and he is in trouble a lot with his accuracy not always congruent with his newfound pace. In one rally, a Jahangir rail comes off the back wall at an unexpectedly sharp angle. Talbott, flatfooted, flips the ball between his legs like a trick artist. The crowd murmurs with astonishment, and Talbott goes on to end the point with a ripping double boast. At 8–3, he spanks another double boast that Jahangir barely reaches, but he muffs Jahangir's easy reply by dumping an open volley into the tin. The gallery groans.

A forty-six stroke point comes next. Talbott almost wins it at the start with a sharp cross-court return of service. A lovely six-stroke exchange of backhand rails follows. It looks like two players drilling in practice. Talbott cracks a forehand volley cross-court that Jahangir barely retrieves. Jahangir winds up on one forehand and swings so violently he hops a little, like a hunter recoiling from a shotgun blast. Three times, Jahangir takes floating balls up front and throws them to the back wall on a rope. Each time they should be a winner, but Talbott digs them out. The point ends anticlimatically with a squibbed Talbott forehand that Jahangir can only wave vainly at, made unplayable by the sidewall. Applause lasts for ten seconds.

It is crucial that Talbott patiently climbs these summits to prove that he can endure the apoxic air of a match with Jahangir. He must not be frightened of long points. And it is equally essential he wins the next point. He cannot collapse coming off the peak. The next point is a second marathon, forty-five strokes—this is how Jahngir breaks his opponents. It ends in a let. They replay the point, and early on Jahangir slugs a backhand into the tin. He is disturbed. He tosses his racquet into his left hand and angrily smacks his right hand against the wall. Talbott hits his first two tins of the match, wins a point on a crisp, perfectly angled backhand volley, then ends a brilliant fifty-one stroke rally by flubbing a backhand straight drop into the bottom of the tin. His 10–4 lead is evaporating.

Jahangir immediately tins a volley, his fifth unforced error of the game. He hits a clean backhand boast for a winner and snips off a classy forehand roll corner. It is now 12–9. Talbott is given an iffy let point. Jahangir stares at the side judges in annoyance. Talbott flips another pinballing double boast and dismisses Jahangir's reply with ease. At 14–9, each player tins a forehand drive. After twenty brutal minutes, Talbott walks off the court ahead.

Seven months earlier, in the first game at the North American Open in New York, Talbott had taken the first game against Jahangir. Now, everyone thinks, the Pakistani champion will again roar back in the second.

After the two-minute break, they warm up. Jahangir nervously kicks out his feet in an effort to get loose. Niederman says, "Time. Quiet in the gallery, please. Mr. Talbott to serve." Then Niederman says, "Just a moment," just as Talbott is about to launch his serve. Cameramen are repositioning themselves, spectators are shuffling past knees and coats to get to their seats. "Again, take your seats quickly please. Stay seated. Mr. Talbott to serve. He leads one game to love. Play." Talbott, not having turned around to face Jahangir, hunches over again. He does his usual pre-serve routine, tapping the ball quickly to the floor, eight or nine times, his racquet no higher than his knee. He serves.

Slashing a forehand cross-court, Jahangir wins the first point. Talbott wins the second point on a tight backhand rail, and then a curious thing happens. Talbott picks up the ball near the front wall and starts to head to the right serving circle, hesitates and walks to the left circle to serve to Jahangir's forehand. Without skipping a beat, Jahangir steps into the other box. "I wanted to break up the rhythm and get Jahangir thinking," Talbott says later. He hits a casual lob serve and in five strokes loses the point on an ungettable Jahangir forehand rail. The next time he comes in, he serves to Jahangir's backhand, but he comes in to Jahangir's forehand repeatedly throughout the rest of the match. At 4–3, Talbott, they play the longest point of the match. It lasts eighty-two strokes and contains sublime shotmaking, gorgeous gets and lovely rails and cross courts suddenly being broken, again and again, by a flurry of stormy drop shots. Four times Talbott is in such trouble he dings his racquet off the left wall in a desperate swipe at the ball. Each player cuts volleys into the nick and pastes rails off balls floating off the back wall. Jahangir hits two boasts and a curling roll corner; Talbott hits five boasts, including a reverse boast, and also one surprising double boast that is a feat of legerdemain. Neither player deserves to lose, so it is poetic justice when the point ends in a let. Talbott wins the replay on a let point.

Still, Jahangir looks more comfortable. He dictates play. He swings with a preternatural grace. He forces Talbott to respond to him and follow his patterns, rather than himself lurching after Talbott's boasts. Talbott wins one point on a boast that nicks, but Jahangir is standing right there, feet ready, racquet cocked. The message is clear: Talbott has to be perfect or else. A couple of bad tins by Talbott and Jahangir bursts ahead from 5–all to 8–5 to 10–7 to 12–9.

Talbott wins the next six points. He slices a forehand cross-court and Jahangir tins an easy backhand volley. At 11–12, Talbott plays through some incidental contact up near the front wall and Jahangir stops. He asks for a let and, when it is not given, he opens the door to complain to Niederman. In an instant he has gone from looking in control to looking for excuses. At 12–all, they play three straight points that end in lets. Talbott serves for a fourth time, a hard serve that sticks to the side wall as it comes out and Jahangir can only swing at air. At 13–12, a Talbott cross-court hooks sharply off the side wall and Jahangir whiffs it. He wrenches away, looking like he had just been bayoneted in the back. He stares at the slightly transparent side wall and loudly slaps his hand against it. Talbott ends the game with a driving volley into the nick.

Mark Talbott is up 2–0 on Jahangir Khan.

It is not going to end quickly, with a three-game Talbott sweep. That is obvious. The first game has been Talbott's, especially with the six Jahangir tins, but the second, although it lasts twenty-two minutes, is a fluke. Talbott tinned five balls and Jahangir ran him ragged. Somehow, a lapse of concentration engulfed Jahangir at the end. It will not happen again.

As if he worries that all his luck will disappear if he stays away too long, Talbott gets back to the court first after the break. Jahangir jumps to a 3–0 lead. Talbott zooms back with a nicking three-wall and then, after three scrappy lets, plays a beautifully constructed point. He hits two boasts, a reverse and a straight drop and ends it with a windmill double boast that Jahangir cannot return. Serving at 2–3, Talbott looks like he might prevent the inevitable onslaught.

Not a chance. In the next twenty-one minutes they play thirty-six points and Talbott wins just eight of them. Jahangir hits the ball with new-found zest. It explodes off his racquet and slides ominously into the nicks. He intercepts Talbott's drives. He is confident and calm. He has seen what he has to do. He knows what is required. He is regal, patient, balanced, infused with the childhood rapture of stroking a ball against a wall.

The point at 2–3 is the harbinger. Talbott lob serves and Jahangir's return is a skimming ball straight to the front wall, an inch above the tin. It dies at the service line, beyond Talbott's reach. Two quick forehand cross-court tins by Talbott are followed by two perfect Jahangir rails, one off each side, that leave Talbott pawing the air. The crowd, wanting a closer match, roars with glee. Talbott hits a double boast and Jahangir smacks it for a winner. Talbott, defensive and out of position, twice hits the ball off the back wall. Jahangir ends the pain with a brutally decisive roll corner. Talbott kicks the ball in disgust. He tins the next service return. Jahangir caresses a slow three-wall and Talbott, in reply, tins as he tries to lay the ball down on a reverse corner. Talbott tries another double and Jahangir again answers with a winner. In four-and-a-half minutes it is 13–2. Salvaging some honor, Talbott hits a pretty backhand straight drop, but Jahangir soon puts him out of his misery with two bullet rails. 15–3.

Donning a new white headband after the five-minute break, Talbott hopes to stem the tide in the fourth game. He continues to take his time while preparing to serve, but during the rallies he looks diminished. He is slow to recover from a shot. He is volleying less. His length has deserted him. His boasts are ending up in the middle of the court. Still, Jahangir is also to blame for Talbott's decline. The Pakistani is hitting harder and tighter and, crucially, is anticipating Talbott's shots better. In the third and fourth game, Talbott hits just one boast that Jahangir does not get. Sometimes Jahangir overruns them he is so quick. He is seeing the ball as if it is a huge, fat tomato. He is hitting untouchable winners. He is wrongfooting Talbott. He is in charge.

Jahangir encounters another curious incident. Talbott takes an easy ball off the back wall and turns on it, sending it cross-court. It catches Jahangir in the cheek near his eye as it flies by. Niederman says, "Play a let." Jahangir puts his hand to his face and walks into the front of the court. Talbott trails him, trying to comfort him. Jahangir bends over in pain and Talbott bends over next to him. Jahangir straightens. Talbott straightens. Jahangir grabs his shirt, daubs his face and bends over again. Talbott sticks his racquet on the floor like a cane and hunches over next to him. Lenny Bernheimer stands up, opens the door and gives Jahangir a towel. Jahangir's coach and cousin, Rahmat Khan, appears. After a minute of ministrations, Jahangir declares himself ready, the group at the door disperses and the crowd applauds.

The stoppage helps Talbott. The next point is a long, solid one. It ends in a let. Another long rally and Jahangir tins on a backhand reverse corner—his first tin since the second game. Talbott gets a lucky bounce off a rail that Jahangir misjudges. Another long point that ends in a let. Jahangir tins immediately on a cross-court. Soon it is 5–4 and Talbott is hanging tough. Then another collapse. 9–4. 11–5. 14–6. 15–7.

"Mr. Khan to serve. Games are two all. Play," says Niederman. After sixty-nine minutes of squash, they are back to where they started. Talbott debates whether to change tactics. No, he decides to stay the course. He will try to outlast Jahangir, crush his will, grind down his spirit. He will try to break him.

Jahangir wins the first point when Talbott tins on a backhand rail. Talbott smacks a double boast and this time Jahangir does not get to it. Talbott hits a double boast from the T, Jahangir reaches it and sends it to the back corner. Talbott half-dives. His legs splay out on the floor like an octopus on the bottom of the sea. He hits a second double, and even though Jahangir is far up in the front he cannot reach it. The audience screams and whistles with delight. A few stand up and pump fists. This is magic. For the first time in three-quarters of an hour, Talbott has a lead. Jahangir tins on a forehand rail, hitting the top of the tin so hard the ball flies out of court. At 3–2, Talbott stumbles as he tries to go around Jahangir to get to a rail. Jahangir helps him up and pats his chest. Talbott rubs his right arm and goes out of the court to get a towel. He then wipes the sweat off the floor where he fell. At no time does he release his tight grip on his racquet—he is tense.

They slowly inch their way toward fifteen. Talbott mishits a lucky winner off a Jahangir boast. It is so lucky he waves an apology at Jahangir. At 4–2, Talbott cannons a hard serve that flies over the back wall into the gallery. It takes three minutes before it is located. Jahangir paces in a circle. Talbott stands at the service circle and tweaks his strings, refusing to look at Jahangir. Talbott is up 5–3 when Jahangir wins five straight points. Twice Talbott fishes for lets and hooks none. He tins a forehand rail. At 6–5, they play the best point of the match. Eighty-five seconds long, it consists of fifty-five magical thrusts and counterthrusts. Talbott slaps eight three-walls, all in hopes of moving Jahangir up and producing an opening. Talbott even dives at one point but all in vain. Jahangir wins the point with a clinging rail.

Ending the five-point slide, Talbott steps forward and neatly smacks two backhand rails. Jahangir tins on a backhand boast. 8–all. They trade points up to 11–all. Every point is a clean winner except for one in which Talbott pops a forehand rail into the tin and one in which Jahangir flubs a forehand boast. Then Talbott, backing up on a forehand, accidentally hits Jahangir with the ball. It is a mistake, but the rules state that the point goes to Talbott. Jahangir is miffed at this unsettling turn of events. He runs his left hand through his hair and looks skyward. He takes the next point with a felicitous roll corner. At 12–all, Talbott hits a boast, Jahangir drops on it, Talbott flings out his racquet and gets caught in front of a sitter. Niederman rightly awards Jahangir a let point.

At 13–12, there comes a controversial point. In the midst of a drawn-out rally, Jahangir digs out a Talbott boast well up front. Talbott, thinking the ball has bounced twice, sticks up his left arm and extends his index finger. After the point ends in a let, the two side judges adjudicate on Talbott's silent appeal. Both call the ball down. Niederman later said that the side judges were probably right. Jahangir disagreed. "I got a bad call there," he later said. "The referees made a mistake and I shouldn't have lost that point."

Regardless, the decision is final and Jahangir, after much strolling about, chooses set-five. After two lets, Talbott follows wildly on a forehand double boast and telegraphs his shot, Jahangir dinks a drop and Talbott ends up laid out on the floor. 1–0. Talbott then horribly tins on a backhand boast. He taps his racquet against his head. *Stupid, stupid.* 2–0. "C'mon, Mark," is heard from a half-dozen spectators.

The match turns. After one hundred minutes, Jahangir collapses. There is no other way to describe it. Here is this champion, this genius, this beautiful, immaculate player, and he folds before our eyes. Talbott has grafted, rope-a-doped, fought through appalling physical deprivation and endured. He has eroded Jahangir's mental strength. He breaks him. Every match reaches this point, where one player breaks. It often happens after a first game or a third game. It very rarely occurs in a fifth-game tiebreaker. Physically, Jahangir is fine. But mentally, he has not faced this sort of sustained pressure in almost four years, since April 1981 when in the finals of the British Open Geoff Hunt scrambled back from a 6–1 deficit in the fourth and final game. He was young then, just seventeen, and as he matured he never again encountered the trauma of a long, tight match. He is not yet twenty-one years-old. He breaks.

It ends astonishingly fast. Jahangir serves. Five strokes into the point, he sends Talbott up to the front with a nice backhand boast. Talbott offers a weak drop that hangs near the left-side wall. Jahangir replies with a cross-court, that inexplicably flies into the tin. 1–2. On the eighth stroke of the next point, he tins a forehand roll corner. 2–all. He takes a deep breath and half punches the side wall. After a quick let, Jahangir tins a forehand reverse corner on the fourth stroke of the rally. In ninety seconds, he has committed three unforced errors. He quickly wins the next point with a cutting backhand boast. 3–3. This impatient shooting is out of character for Jahangir. He has won with depth, with movement, with length, not with desperate shots.

The last great rally comes. In thirty-eight strokes it is like a coda in a symphony, recapitulating all the themes of the evening: boasts hit with élan, rails rocketing down the walls, nibbling rolls, pure athleticism and peerless cunning. It ends, as so many of their great points do, in a let. In the next rally, Talbott quickly scythes a crisp backhand boast. Jahangir rushes forward and slaps a forehand right into the bottom of the tin. It is his fourth tin of the tiebreaker, his eighth of the game. The crowd surges with excitement. Talbott wipes his hand on the floor, trying to pretend he does not have a match point against Jahangir Khan.

He serves a slow, high ball. Jahangir backs up and slaps a backhand rail. It hits the side wall and Talbott powders a rail. It does not have good length and Jahangir strokes a smooth roll corner. Talbott is quickly onto it and pulverizes a forehand cross-court, leaping as he follows through. He is still hitting out. Jahangir sends the ball cross-court, but it lacks depth and Talbott immediately returns it to Jahangir's backhand. The ball spins off the side wall and then the back wall. With plenty of time, Jahangir goes for a three-wall. As Talbott sprints up front, the ball catches the top of the tin.

It is extraordinary. There is silence, as the enormity of the moment hits everyone in the building, and then there is an explosion. Talbott, facing the front wall, hurls his racquet into the air and extends both arms as the racquet falls back into his hands. He turns, shakes Jahangir's hand and talks to him for a few lingering seconds. Jahangir acknowledges the crowd, which is on its feet, howling with glee. Talbott, behind him, raises his arms in triumph. Jahangir picks up the ball and hits it into the gallery. He stands back to let Talbott exit the court, but Talbott insists that Jahangir leave first. As he steps off the court, his arm and racquet raised high, Talbott is engulfed. Doc Talbott hugs him for what seems like an eternity. His eyes are wet like oysters. Bill Austin hugs him. Dave Talbott hugs him. Wave after wave of applause cascades down on Talbott.

It had not been a perfect match. There were too many tins—more than thirty—too many lets—thirty-six in the fifth game alone—and the third and fourth games were too one-sided. Yet it was a masterpiece. It was full of drama and tidal shifts and it was immediately hailed as a breakthrough. Niederman's front-page article for the next issue of *Squash News* began, "In a match destined to assume classic proportions, Mark Talbott defeated Jahangir Khan, 15–10, 15–12, 3–15, 7–15, 18–16, winning his second Xerox Boston Open title and foiling the Pakistani's first major hardball title defense." The touchstone of a generation, the match reverberated throughout the squash world. It was talked about for years. Many thousands of people claimed they were there in the bleachers of the Cyclorama. College teams watched a video of it to psyche themselves up before critical matches. Like an epic heavyweight prizefight, it had a nickname, the Drama in the 'Rama, and it had a memorable storyline: Mark Talbott beat Jahangir Khan, 18–16 in the fifth.

CHAPTER TEN

Bait and Switch

Two-and-a-half feet were the difference.

Hardball and softball were like fraternal twins, sharing the same genetic material, yet having a triflingly altered appearance. On either side of the pond, it was squash. You served a small rubber ball, you circled around the center of the four-walled court, you hoped for good length, you cracked the ball into the nick, you winced at a tin. You said your favorite room in the world was a squash court.

You could adjust almost everything in an instant. The rules were slightly divergent. In America let points were harder to earn. In England you got less time between games. In America you had a referee and two side judges. In England you had a referee and a marker. In America you needed six points more to win a game and you did not have to serve to score a point. Racquets corresponded, American ones weighing a bit more. Balls presented a stickier wicket. The most common term used to describe each game derived from the ball, rather than the size of the court (narrow versus wide court) or where the games were played (American versus international or English). No matter how similar the weight or color or size, the balls were like apples and oranges: both fruits, but tasting different. The American ball bounced faster and was easier to lay down. The English ball hung in the air like a harvest moon. Still, grafting and breeding were always the norm in the squash orchard. The ball had evolved in both America and in England throughout the twentieth century. Between 1923 and 1934, England slowed down its ball by half; in America, in the mid-seventies, the national association adopted the seventy-plus, a new ball that dramatically cut the difference between hard and soft balls. Compromise rules, racquets and balls were all easy leaps of faith.

Thirty inches, the difference in width between a hardball and softball court, was the chasm too far to cross. It was the one adamantine issue that could not be finessed.

SQUASH

In 1904 the United States standardized a court sixteen-and-a-third-feet wide. In 1920 it widened the standard to eighteen-and-a-half feet. In 1923 the English officially adopted a twenty-one-foot-wide court. Difference was originally a good thing. The original joy of squash at Harrow was variety, the waterpipe at Head Master's House and the devilish footscraper at Vanity Watson's. Just like the Greeks retold Homer's *Iliad*, players altered, interpolated, emended and parsed the game to suit their own purposes as it spread. In Nairobi they played on cedar floors, in Stockholm on marble, in Christ Church on a narrow court, in Victoria on a wide court. Squash then grew up. It became more than an outdoor schoolboy pastime, and its serious adult players wanted uniformity rather than waterpipes and footscrapers. Standards were not scorned but revered. Due to Great Britain's sunny empire, every country in the world, except the three North American nations, played softball. The vast majority of courts in the world were softball. The sheer preponderance of numbers would be the final arbitrator. It was clear that the twenty-one-foot court was inevitable.

Except that squash was a game played inside buildings. This meant the horrors of weight-bearing walls, low ceilings, cramped quarters and slews of permitting entanglements. Physically changing the dimensions of the court proved to be such an impossible task that the switch took seventy fractious years.

No one knows the precise moment when the first person came to the awful realization that American squash was different from English squash. The concrete was poured, probably around 1920, when it became clear that the Bath Club court, with its twenty-one-foot wide court, was going to become the model for English squash.

The concrete set on 20 April 1923. In late March, W. S. Greening of Toronto wrote a letter to the Tennis & Racket Association, inviting an English team to tour North America and play in the Lapham Cup. The letter was read out loud on 20 April at the T&RA squash committee's meeting. The committee was favorably inclined to accept but was unable to decide officially, because it was clear from the letter that squash in North America was a different game. The committee met again in July to discuss the matter. This time Eugene Hinkle was in attendance. A New Yorker who had captained the Harvard squash team before graduating in June, Hinkle assured the T&RA that North American squash, though not a perfect copy of the game in England, was a reasonable facsimile and that the tour would be a success.

In March 1924, when the British team returned to England after its North American tour, Lord Desborough hosted a welcoming dinner at the Bath Club. The touring men told of the different standards in North American and strongly advocated that the T&RA form a subcommittee "for the purpose of considering the possibility of bringing the game as played in England and in America into line." The subcommittee, consisting of Captain Palmer-Tomkinson, Captain Jameson, and Theo Drysdale and Ginger Basset from the tour, submitted recommendations in May 1924. Although there was a "strong divergence of opinion" within the committee, they suggested keeping the status quo.

It was a fatal decision. In October 1924 the USSRA sent a letter to London requesting that the English lower their front-wall tins. The English declined. During the 1935 U.S. tour of England, both the U.S. team and their English hosts tried to develop a compromise ball. The Americans brought over several prototypes they had asked Seamless to produce. Willing Patterson promoted these hybrid Seamless balls, as well as a hope that the English would switch back to fifteen-scoring. In 1937 the directors of the Atlantic Coasts Championships in Atlantic City used an English ball at their tournament. In 1954 the Squash Rackets Association asked member clubs to experiment with American scoring, to see if a switch might be countenanced. Each time, there was too much resistance to change.

Touring revealed a simple fact that spelled doom for hardball. It was easier for softball players to pick up hardball than vice versa. The first days in America were a muddle for a Londoner. The heavier, larger ball flew at whirlybird speeds. The court felt crowded. Soon, though, he would become competent and, within a month, might even win the U.S. nationals. For the American overseas, however, what looked quite gentle and agreeable on the first day actually was much more complicated. There was never an American Timmy Robarts or Janet Morgan who arrived in London and three weeks later won the English nationals. The English were not inherently better athletes, but their game demanded a higher level of excellence. Softball required superior concentration. "I recall many a rally in English matches I have played," wrote Willing Patterson in 1936, "when in about the thirtieth or fortieth time the ball was struck, I began to wonder whether we were going to have shepherd's pie or pheasant for dinner, Rhine wine or champagne." You could not simply run on instinct. Softball placed a higher premium on the core aspects of squash—rails, cross-courts and volleys. You had to hit good length and width. You had to have good racquet work, good footwork, good strategic thinking. Softball simply made you a better squash player.

In a genteel version of the Cold War, Americans hoped that either a peaceful coexistence could be maintained or that the Evil Empire of softball squash would come to its senses, realize the errors of its ways and convert to the hardball standards. In 1950 Ned Bigelow established the first formal relationship between the USSRA and the Squash Rackets Association in London, the de facto governing body of softball squash, by becoming a "liaison officer" and organizing two tours of America by British university teams. After Bigelow died in January 1970, Stew Brauns became the U.S. squash ambassador. Brauns was a droll and engaging bachelor. An MIT and Harvard Business School graduate and New York stockbroker, he was Bigelow's right-hand man. He did most of the legwork for the early U.S. Opens as referee and tournament manager. He collected a melange of squash charivari—cufflinks, neckties, programs, draws, books—auctioned off teams in the Calcutta at the Harry Cowles and, by the end of his career, could count over fifty squash administrative positions. In succeeding Bigelow, he faced a vastly more threatening situation.

In the early 1960s rising squash play in South Africa and Australia threatened English hegemony in the softball world. Both countries wanted to host a world championship. Meetings at the 1963 British nationals and the 1966 British Open, as well as letters in newspapers and behind the scenes maneuvering, led to an official launching of the International Squash Rackets Federation at the first world championships in Australia in 1967. Stew Brauns, representing the United States and Canada, attended the initial meeting of the ISRF and immediately confronted a hostile audience—Australia, Great Britain, Egypt, India, New Zealand, Pakistan and South Africa—who did not want to include the foreign game of hardball. Despite Brauns's presence, the ISRF declared softball the only federation game and refused to grant the United States or Canada membership in the new organization. In 1969, after two years of intense lobbying, détente became the new watchword. The ISRF accepted the United States and Canada, retroactively, as founding members and conceded to Brauns a clause in its constitution that said that hardball was, like softball, an official ISRF game (the only federation doubles game was the hardball version). The ISRF was a moribund organization for its first half-dozen years. It had no executive committee, money went missing and, after twelve years in existence, had just twenty-one member countries. Its annual meetings were farcical as the executive ignored its own rules of decision making. Brauns fought hard to revise the federation's constitution and, as chairman of the constitution committee, produced a new draft in 1973. It was rejected, and another version, written by a South African, was approved in 1975. Brauns also tried to develop one internationally acceptable game. "One or two member countries cooperated in this effort," he wrote in 1978, "but the vast majority were apathetic. One important member went so far as to lie to us in official correspondence about non-existent tests of a compromise game." It was naive, he concluded, to hope for a compromise. At one point the United States almost resigned from the association.

As the softball world galvanized itself, started world championships and increased communication, the North Americans became isolated. One chief difference between the last quarter of the century and earlier eras was globalization. International communications became an everyday reality. The fax, the telex and cheaper and clearer long-distance telephone service shrunk distances. Jet planes began flying passenger service in the early sixties, and the week-long crossing of the Atlantic shriveled into a few hours. College teams from England and the United States and pros in New York and London began to exchange tours. The ISRF world championships were disasters for the United States. These were softball events and amateur only until 1980, and American players—notwithstanding Alicia McConnell's win at the first world juniors in 1980—found themselves severely overmatched. Every two years Brauns and other administrators had to pull teeth to get players to go to the world championships, for unlike all other national team members, the U.S. players had to pay their expenses themselves. The 1977 world championships in Ottawa were a glowing example of American ineptitude. The team was slighty long in the tooth—Eliot Berry was twenty-eight, Tom Poor thirty-four and Len Bernheimer and Denis Bourke thirty-five—and no one besides Berry had played much softball. They lost all but one of their matches 3–0 and had a running wager that the man who won the fewest points in a match had to pay for dinner that night. Bourke lost one match 9–0, 9–0, 9–0 in fourteen minutes, paid for dinner and flew home the next day. His comment, upon being asked why he was leaving so abruptly, summed up the experience of Americans abroad in the seventies: "Life is too short to be this unhappy."

For other U.S. teams, the picture was equally bleak. In 1979 in England, the first U.S. women's team came in sixth out of six teams and never finished higher. In 1984 in Canada, the first U.S. junior boys' team came in twelfth out of fourteen. After the stunning win in Sweden in 1980, the U.S. girls usually stayed at the bottom of the top ten. Besides the world championships, another international gathering influenced American squash players. In 1977 the Maccabiah Games added squash as a medal sport. The United States won silver that year, losing to South Africa in the finals, but beating England, Australia and Canada. For national pride alone, a switch to softball was necessary. Americans innately yearned to be world champions.

Softball squash stealthily crept into America in the sixties. Play was scattered and incoherent, mostly involving a few expatriates who had slipped softballs past the customs man. The only formal play was with the Jesters Club who, in honor of their British forebears, played softball at their annual spring weekend. The catalyst for tournament play was, naturally, an Englishman. In December 1968, Quentin Hyder, a psychiatrist and New York Athletic Club member, organized a softball tournament on the NYAC hardball courts. Most of the players were expats living in New York, with three New Zealanders from Toronto filling out the draw. Graham Sharman, an Englishman who was a member of the Heights Casino, beat Dave O'Loughlin of Pittsburgh in the final. In 1972 Hyder opened his tournament to professionals, and Mo Khan beat his cousin Sharif in a five-game final. Soon Hyder added draws for B players, veterans and women.

Softball, once it sneaked inside the house of hardball, instantly began rearranging the furniture. In the spring of 1969, Hyder started a three-man, two-month team softball league and a one-weekend inter-city competition. Each spring thereafter, more clubs and more cities joined in these competitions. In October 1969 Bermuda started hosting a softball tournament, which became an annual pilgrimage for many Americans (Henri Salaun won the first title). In September 1971 the Buffalo Athletic Club sponsored an English Ball Singles Invitational. Ed Jocoy, "using a series of reverse corners," according to one USSRA observer, beat Gary Carr in the finals. In 1974 New York and a small club in the Bahamas, run by Keith Parker, began a home-and-away tournament series. That June Geoff Hunt and Ken Hiscoe gave a softball exhibition at Fifth Avenue. In 1975 and 1976, Park Place, Uptown and Broad Street opened with softball courts, making New York with its four courts the epicenter of softball squash in America (Hyder immediately moved his tournament). In 1977 Sam Jernigan started the Newport Summer Ball Tournament, which a hundred people entered. By the summer of 1981 there were nine softball tournaments—Newport, Boston, Mexico City, Washington, D.C., Los Angeles and four in New York—and numerous summer softball leagues. In New York in 1974, eight clubs entered Hyder's softball league; in 1980, there were forty-four teams; in 1983, seventy-six. In 1982 Uptown started a winter softball league.

While in the seventies and early eighties softball was viewed, as a warm-weather phenomenon in the United States, in Canada, it was a winter game. Canada had closer ties to England, and squash was much less entrenched in Canada—it was mostly a Toronto and Montreal sport into the sixties—so, it was natural for them to switch first. Canada started a national softball championship in 1974 (won by Gordon Anderson). It hosted the 1977 men's world championships and the 1981 women's world championship, which further spurred softball growth in the country. A crucial factor was government funding. In 1976 the Canadian SRA became an official governing body and received $75,000 (Canadian) in grants that year. Between 1976 and 1980, Squash Ontario alone received three-quarters of a million Canadian dollars. All this money was directed toward softball squash, the only version recognized by the Canadian government. By 1980 no one was building new hardball courts in Canada. Hardball continued to be played, and Canada produced a healthy number of the top hardball professionals in the eighties, but Canada was becoming a softball nation.

Unruffled, hardball squash in America sailed onwards on serene waters. The professional tour boomed. Players from overseas, including the conqueror of the world, Jahangir Khan, deigned to enter hardball tournaments. In 1983 the U.S. men's team came in seventh at the world championships. At the 1986 U.S. Open, a softball event, both Mark Talbott and Ned Edwards beat current top ten softballers. Americans believed these were indications we could easily ramp up our softball games when necessary. Hardball, they averred, also had an aesthetic advantage. Spectacular shots like the double boast and the Philadelphia shot made it a wild adventure, while softball was as much fun, one wit wrote, "as whacking a dead mouse around the court with a wet mop." The nine-point scoring especially grated on Americans, who liked instant scoring and double-digit point totals. Americans, with a famously short attention span, would never favor such a subtle sport. The last Maginot line of defense was the sheer magnitude of hardball facilities. By most counts, there were about three thousand hardball courts in America. To tear down these courts and convert to softball would cost millions of dollars.

Troubling riptides roiled under the surface. The physical workout of squash, which was what attracted many people to the game in the first place, was clearly more intense with softball. With the extra room and the longer rallies, one positively oozed off the court in a puddle of perspiration after a match. In addition, schedules no longer held to the rhythms of the seasons. Summer was no longer a time for long holidays, extended camping trips up north, week after week at the shore. People worked harder and wanted to play harder. They dreamt of chasing the endless winter by playing all year, rather than downing their bats after the nationals in March. Women became loyal to softball. They found it easier to learn and less a game of brute power. Technology also skewed neophytes toward softball. In the early 1980s, after a hundred years of ash and bamboo, metal racquets appeared. In September 1982, the USSRA finally approved metal racquets and Head, formerly manufacturers of ski equipment, brought out the Head Competition. This black graphite racquet instantly overwhelmed the wooden Bancroft racquets that had dominated the U.S. squash market since the thirties. The lighter racquets made softball an even more attractive game. One no longer needed a mile-wide swing to hit for good length, and one no longer needed to choke up on the handle, as was customary, to be able to hit good drop shots. With the new racquets, the deathless attritional game of Barrington and Hunt gave way to shorter matches with more shotmaking.

Economically, squash in the United States also had a core problem. The commercial clubs, although successful in raising the profile of the game, were losing money, and money was the point of their existence. Clubs turned their squash courts into exercise rooms for aerobics and yoga or spinning classes or simply moved in some exercise machines. New York's real-estate slump of the seventies, which had enabled investors to build squash clubs, ended in the early eighties and rents skyrocketed. In 1981 Broad Street closed, after less than six years of operation. Manhattan Squash soon became the headquarters for Home Box Office. Fifth Avenue went private, then closed. Uptown changed its name to the Uptown Racquet & Fitness Club and stole one court after another for other purposes; today, it has just four courts. Squashcon disappeared after burning through all its investors' money; Berwyn was bought and is still functioning today, but the Manyanuk facility was turned back into a warehouse and Washington Square became a law firm's offices. By 1995 just five of the original eleven commercial clubs in New York were still in operation.

Once feared as a rival, racquetball damaged hardball squash more by providing a means to add softball courts. Racquetball declined tremendously in the eighties. By installing a glass wall eight feet from the back wall of an otherwise empty racquetball court, adding new boundary lines and a tin, you had a thirty-two-by-twenty-foot court. The Texas Club in Houston pioneered this process and, by the mid-eighties, Playcon was selling court conversion kits for $3,000. In 1984 the USSRA recognized twenty-foot courts as acceptable for USSRA-sanctioned softball tournaments.

Squash's expansion across the United States, forever considered the gold mine for the health of the game, actually dug out lead for hardball. The climate in the South and West was too warm for hardball, even with air-conditioning, and these sun belters found themselves playing softball all year. In the Pacific Northwest, the Pacific Coast association's cross-border nature meant that softball crept south after Canada switched. Yusuf Khan led the movement toward softball in Seattle and eventually ran an eight-court facility, the largest softball club in the country at the time, at the Seattle Racquets Club. In the early eighties a splinter group of San Francisco softball players, led by Malcolm Dutch, formed their own organization. Calling themselves the International Squash Association of Northern California, they sought recognition with the ISRF as a formal U.S. softball squash association. With a base at the Bay Club, which had the city's first softball courts, ISANC did not merge into the Northern California SRA until 1989. The Wisconsin SRA also temporarily split in two, with Madison, a softball city, and Milwaukee, a hardball city, refusing to communicate. Florida, Texas, New Mexico and much of the Midwest played only softball. Houston was a good example. In 1986 the city squash association had thirty hardball members; a year later it had two hundred, but all the new members were softballers. There were by then eighteen softball courts in Houston (many were racquetball conversions) and zero interest in hardball. The weather was certainly a cause for the switch, but so was black gold. With so many overseas oil businessmen visiting or moving to Houston, the demand for softball was too strong to ignore.

In 1981 the USSRA finally grappled with an issue it had formerly treated with benign neglect. President Herb Gross set up a committee to make recommendations. In the spring of 1982, this committee, chaired by Charles Perkins, advised the USSRA to sanction local softball tournaments, create a national softball ranking list and hold an annual national softball championship. In return for these concessions to softballers, the USSRA split the year into two seasons, the summer for softball and the winter for hardball. In September 1983 Baltimore hosted the first softball nationals. The tournament used softball scoring and rules and was played on hardball courts. Almost all of the seventy-three players entered the tournament at the last minute. They were mostly Maryland hardballers who had picked up softball for a summer frolic, as expatriate softballers found it too painful to play their native game on the hardball court. A suffocating heat wave blanketed Baltimore, and the first day of play coincided with the forty-eighth consecutive day of temperatures above ninety degrees. In the finals of the men's draw, Gil Mateer lost to Kenton Jernigan after building a 2–0, 6–1 lead; Alicia McConnell easily swept up the women's title. The softball nationals, despite the sticky conditions, generated a noticeable enthusiasm for the game in America. Washington hosted the second softball nationals, again on hardball courts. The third nationals, chaired by Perkins in Houston, were a breakthrough, for they were played on converted racquetball courts. It was not, however, until 1989 in Seattle that the softball nationals were played on twenty-one-foot courts.

Bickering led to professional softball. The United States Open, in retirement since the amalgamation of the U.S. and Canadian Opens in 1966, had been played in 1983 and 1984 as a hardball tournament at the Yale Club in New York. Howie Rosenthal, the promoter of the new Open, then sold the rights to the tournament name to Tom Jones, and the WPSA and Jones immediately got into an argument about who actually owned the rights. To avoid a messy situation, Jones made the U.S. Open a softball event and held it on the other side of the country on a converted racquetball court at an obscure health club in San Francisco, the Telegraph Hill Club. Nine of the top ten softball pros in the world entered, the International Squash Professional Association sanctioned it and Jones experimented by having a seventeen-inch tin and fifteen-point scoring. (In 1989 men's pro softball squash adopted both changes for all its tournaments.) The Open was a success, despite what Jones called "light applause." In 1986 Jones moved it to Houston to follow up on the recent success of the softball nationals, and a year later he brought it to New York. Frank Stella arranged with a night club, the Palladium, next to his art studio on East Fourteenth Street in Manhattan, to host the Open on its dance floor. With a portable court imported from Europe, the 1987 U.S. Open was as exciting an event as the 1985 North American Open at Town Hall. It put pro softball on the map.

In 1989 following on the success of the Open, Jones launched a series of small professional softball tournaments around the country. Called the Grand Prix, this summer series carpeted America with softball. The first year saw seven tournaments, in the second year, eleven, including the Hyder, in 1991, sixteen, and, eventually, more than twenty annual tournaments with a prize money total of over $150,000. The Grand Prix tournaments offered ISPA ranking points for participants. Originally Jones had imagined that the series would help American players start their ISPA careers, but he underestimated the size and depth of the ISPA tour. Dozens of lower-ranked men, eager to earn precious ISPA ranking points, swamped the Grand Prix. Many future top-ten players, like Anthony Hill, Simon Parke and Peter Nicol, spent formative summers in America playing the Grand Prix. Not only did America see high-quality softball squash with the Grand Prix—especially smaller cities like Pittsburgh and Oklahoma City—but dozens of these players stayed in America once the Grand Prix season finished in the autumn. Most notably, Tony Brettkelly of New Zealand, John Phelan of Ireland and Anders Wahlstedt of Sweden, relocated after their first season and eventually played for the United States in world championships.

Gold became a critical force behind softball. It had been the goal of squash players to play for an Olympic medal since the Games began. In 1986 the International Olympic Committee recognized squash as a sport, and the ISRF launched a formal campaign for its inclusion in the Olympic Games, with the Barcelona Games as the first realistic target. The U.S. squash community, in order to be ready in case squash joined the Olympics, had to get under the USOC umbrella. At the 1988 U.S. Open in Houston, Tom and Hazel Jones; Roger Eady, the head of the ISPA; Bob Kingsley, an assistant director of the USSRA in the Bala Cynwyd office; Tim Bale from Canada and Angela Webber from the Caribbean, held a meeting about the Olympics. Jones reported on what the U.S. Olympic Committee had told him: that squash would only become a USOC sport when it was played at the Pan-American Games, the Olympic-style quadrennial gathering of North, Central and South American countries. To get into the Pan-Am Games, squash needed a Pan-American squash federation. It took exactly a year to the day after their initial meeting in Houston, but, on 18 November 1989, a dozen western hemisphere nations formed the *Federacion Panamericana de Squash*. Juan Carlos Bravo of Colombia was elected director general. Then, after a year of politicking, ODEPA, the governing body for the Pan-Am Games, approved squash for inclusion as a medal sport at the 1995 Games, to be held in Mar Del Plata, Argentina. Success in joining the Pan-Am Games meant that the USOC officially invited squash into the Olympic family as a Class C, nonmedal sport (along with karate, roller sports, racquetball, bowling and water skiing). Each year, beginning in 1990, $100,000 flowed into the USSRA coffers, money that was used to support U.S. national teams in international softball competitions and junior softball squash in America. The first evidence of the change was a junior Olympic softball championship, played in Atlanta in June 1990 and a three-day softball coaching clinic in September 1990, run by Dardir el Bakary and hosted by Don Mills in Cincinnati. Twenty-seven teaching pros came to sit at the feet of the great Egyptian, who was revered as one of the world's great coaches. The USSRA was now, by its progressive leap toward the Olympics, inadvertently conspiring to destroy hardball.

A tumor at the periphery was one thing, but the cancer of softball, as some traditionalists saw it, had invaded the heart of squash. In Boston a winter softball league, started in 1987–88, was more popular than the old hardball league. In northern New Jersey people also played softball in the winter, and in Washington, D.C., although not a single softball court would be built in the District until 1998, the senators were playing softball. In 1989 the Cynwyd Club built the first softball court in the Philadelphia area and the Loews women's professional tournament switched to softball. In February 1990, the *New York Times*, in an article entitled, "Softball Edging Hardball Among Squash Partisans," reported on the growth of softball in New York. In 1991 the Lapham-Grant added softball to its program.

The canaries in the coal mine of the game, court builders were aware of the impending switch. In 1987 Gordy Anderson's first project for Playcon was to build a court in Steve Green's office building in midtown Manhattan. Green, a real-estate developer, was an avid squash player. The court was twenty-one-feet wide. Anderson realized that the switch to softball was about to occur and that there would be money to be made in replacing old hardball courts. When Anderson was forced to build hardball courts, he tried to ensure that the side walls would not bear weight, so that a conversion to softball courts would be relatively inexpensive. But more and more of his courts were softball.

The numbers were unassailable. In 1988 the USSRA counted twenty-seven softball courts in the country and over a hundred racquetball courts had been converted to twenty-foot wide softball courts. By 1990 there were more than three hundred converted twenty-footers and forty softball courts. In 1991 according to Dunlop/Slazenger, the sale of softballs overtook hardballs for the first time, 58 percent to 42 percent. In 1991 a milestone occurred when the softball nationals had more participants than what was now called the "hardball nationals." Eight years after the first softball nationals, the world had turned upside down.

The World Professional Squash Association was no longer a bulwark to hide behind. In 1985 the WPSA suffered a sudden loss of sponsorship. Boodles, after ten years, ended its sponsorship of its seminal event at Uptown. The Boston Open lost its sponsor at the last minute, when

Xerox pulled out. Fleischmann's, the steady supporter of the WPSA Championships, dropped its sponsorship two weeks before the 1986 edition. In 1985–86 the tour had to cancel five tournaments and reduce prize money in four others. It steadied itself and found new sponsors—the WPSA Championships switched from Fleischmann's to Royal Trust—and the tour had a final burst of success. In 1988–89 it had a total prize money of $547,500 ($385,000 in seventeen events, $95,000 in doubles and $67,500 in special events), and in 1989–90 it had $642,500 (with fifteen singles events; a large part of that prize money went into five "grand master" veteran events sponsored by Pru-Bache). In 1985–86 though, the professional softball tour passed the WPSA in terms of total prize money and soon easily outdistanced its North American brethren. By the end of the decade, it had three times as much prize money, six continents with tournaments and better players. For years the WPSA fought a losing battle with the ISPA for sponsorship dollars, media interest and psychological advantage in North America. The WPSA copyrighted "world ball" for its hardball when the ISPA began calling its ball the "international ball." The Mennen Cup proved to be a particularly nasty battleground. Trevor Marshall and the WPSA disagreed about how his tournament should be run, with the WPSA wanting more hardball stars in the eight-man draw and Mennen refusing to use WPSA rankings as a basis for invitations. In 1983 the WPSA asked Mark Talbott to uphold a boycott of the tournament, which he did, and in 1986 the entire WPSA contingent pulled out of the Mennen at the last minute. The following year Marshall gave up and made the Mennen a softball tournament on a twenty-one-foot court. The ISPA did offer some compromises. It eventually adopted fifteen-point scoring. It lowered the tin from nineteen to seventeen inches. It sought to change the amount of time allowed players between games, giving ninety seconds between games instead of one minute. The ISPA adjustments, although comforting to Americans, were window dressing, small, relatively painless adjustments made only to the men's professional game. The rest of the world, even the women's pro tour association, WISPA, still played to nine points on a court with a nineteen-inch tin. A compromise game was not in the offing.

The WPSA, sensing the turning tide, started holding softball tournaments. In 1985–87 it sanctioned the U.S. Pro Softball at Park Place in New York. Frank Stella designed the tournament poster. In 1989 the Boston Open, one of the tour's majors, added a softball draw to complement the main hardball tournament. In 1990 the WPSA suffered from a second wave of lost sponsorship. Key firms like Xerox did not renew their contracts. For some companies, it was a case of cold facts: They were not getting enough return on their investment. For others, the recession of the early nineties tore away the extra digits on the balance sheet that were hitherto easily tossed to squash. New companies were not willing to jump into the vacuum. The pro tour often needed a squash-playing chief executive officer in order to entice a company to sponsor a tournament, as the simple economics of the game—at most a thousand spectators, meager television and print media exposure—made sponsorship more of a goodwill gesture than a prudent move. With softball seen as the next new thing, hardball squash was viewed as about to go extinct. The excitement of the "Drama in the 'Rama" faded. Jahangir Khan last played in the U.S. at the Boodles in New York in October 1985. The old guard, led by Mark Talbott, seemed to never lose. Relentless American neophilia meant that some people found it boring to watch Talbott play Edwards again. Aesthetically, hardball looked less attractive than it had ten years before. With the advent of the graphite racquet, warmer courts, increased weightlifting and better nutrition, players hit the ball too hard. Rallies were shorter. Hard serves threatened to decapitate opponents. Some of the Mexican professionals rifled rails so bullet-fast that they aimed to nick it off the back wall. This so-called "Mexican drop shot" was certainly interesting, but it did make a mockery out of the core of traditional squash, good length. What happened to squash tennis after Stephen Feron introduced his new ball was beginning to happen to hardball squash: It was getting too fast. There also was the nagging inferiority complex for Americans about the tour. Fans wondered why Mark Talbott and Ned Edwards were not the best in the world. Many people shook their heads in wonder when they read what Geoff Hunt said after spending a month playing hardball tournaments in 1976–77: "Despite the matches I've been playing, I will be out of shape for the international game."

The hardball pros started playing softball to prepare for hardball tournaments. Mark Talbott and Jeff Stanley trained on a converted racquetball court in Rhode Island all of the summer of 1990. Ned Edwards and Kenton Jernigan practiced with a softball before the WPSA Championships at the Winter Garden in 1989. More than one supporter of the tour wondered why they were playing hardball if they knew softball was a better game. In February 1992 the Boston Open went under because of a lack of sponsorship money. In April 1992 the tour switched the WPSA Championships to softball and renamed it the Tournament of Champions. Since 1930 it had been the cornerstone of the professional calendar and now just three North American men—Gary Waite, Marcos Mendez and Mark Talbott—were eligible to enter. For decades, softballers had argued that diversity was good for the American squash community. Now, in a sad reversal, the WPSA had to employ the same reasoning. "We have a smorgasbord of choice," wrote John Nimick. "Let's not make it a one-dimensional Parris Island chow line."

On New Year's Day 1993, thirty-nine years to the day after Ned Bigelow had effectively launched the hardball tour with his U.S. Open, the World Professional Squash Association underwent its seventh change in name. The WPSA amalgamated with ISPA to become the Professional Squash Association. The merger was complementary. The ISPA was in debt, the WPSA solvent. The ISPA had a solid worldwide tour, a handful of portable glass courts and a good base in the heartlands of the softball game: Australia, Asia, Egypt and Great Britain. The WPSA had access to the future of squash: America. John Nimick became the executive director of the PSA and Jack Herrick joined the board.

Within the USSRA, the most strident voice for change in the early nineties came from the junior committee. Founded in the late seventies and comprised mostly of parents and coaches of active junior players, the committee had long advocated the benefits of softball. The major summer camps for youngsters started using the softball full time. The directors of leading junior programs, like Don Mills, Fred Weymuller and Bill Lane, were proponents of switching. Weymuller led a summer squash tour of Australia in 1979 and coached the first two U.S. boys' teams at the 1984 and 1986 world championships; Mills lead junior trips to Australia in 1986 and 1988 and Scotland in 1987. Such trips had resulted in a deep undertow pulling junior squash away from hardball shores. In 1986 the Heights Casino started the Baird Haney, a softball tournament named after a former professional at the club who died tragically in a car accident. The earliest junior softball tournament, the Haney had eighty players in its first year. In 1991, in light of such interest, the junior committee persuaded the USSRA to allow it to schedule a few sanctioned softball tournaments in the autumn rather than in the prescribed summer months. In December 1991, seeing how the children had enjoyed the few extra months of softball, the junior committee voted to continue the experiment for a second season in 1992–93 and make the entire 1993–94 season softball only. Two months later, the USSRA executive committee voted down this gradual change at its annual meeting. Instead, the USSRA formed a committee chaired by Yale professor Ted Marmor. In June 1992 Marmor handed in a ten-page report. It called for a continuation of the split season, arguing that the United States should still support both versions of squash. Applying separate-but-equal status to the two games, as the history of twentieth-century race relations proved, was an unpalatable and unworkable solution. The Canadian experience was not instructive. Canada attempted to maintain two games and hardball hung on for fifteen years. Without the infusions of cash, new courts and younger players, it endured a slow, horrible death. Canada was not big enough to support two different kinds of the game. Why would the United States be any different?

The USSRA was in a bind. Schools and clubs had a substantial investment in their hardball courts, which would have to be changed. Furthermore, in 1989, the USSRA launched a five-year endowment campaign that raised $1.5 million. It did not want to risk alienating the very people—mostly old-guard hardballers—who were opening up their wallets. It was less controversial to hide behind the mantra of "letting the market decide." Much like the indecision surrounding the adoption of the seventy-plus ball fifteen years before, the USSRA decided to wait and see.

Lasell Gymnasium, Williams College, Williamstown, Massachusetts, 28 February 1993. The fortieth annual championship weekend of the New England Interscholastic Squash Association was an unlikely place for the squash world's version of the Tennis Court Oath. But, on a cold Sunday morning in the Berkshires, twenty-nine preparatory school coaches sat in an undecorated room near the Williams squash courts and vowed to topple the ancien régime.

Representing thirty boy squash teams from schools of the St. Grotlesex variety, the NEISA held a singular niche in the squash world. Although few of its boys in recent decades had gone on to squash stardom, it had attractive facilities, supportive alumni and still politely churned out hundreds of experienced squash players. There were 142 boys from twenty-nine schools at Williams. Ned Gallagher, the president, opened the meeting with a report on recent developments in the conflict between hardball and softball. He then moved to change the NEISA's by-laws to require a two-third's vote of members, rather than a simple majority, in any vote on switching to softball. The motion passed with ease. Malcolm MacColl, the chair of the USSRA junior committee and a guest at the meeting (his son played at Andover) gave the coaches the official USSRA line about sticking with hardball. The coaches examined the situation from all sides. Three NEISA schools had, within the previous six months, built softball courts: Taft had five, St. Paul's had three and Andover had one. In addition, St. George's used Newport Squash and Kingswood-Oxford used Trinity College. After two hours of discussion, Gallagher asked for a roll call vote. Twenty-two coaches voted to switch to softball, seven to keep hardball. With the new by-law requiring a two-thirds majority, the vote swung on just a single vote. One-hundred-and-nine years before, a prep school started squash in America, and, now, an association of prep schools changed it forever.

The dominos immediately began to fall. The girls of New England prep-school squash switched the following weekend. The women's college squash association then changed but not without contention. In March 1992 at its annual meeting, the U.S. Women's Intercollegiate SRA formed a committee on softball. The committee, chaired by Herb Bunker, a Bates College coach, sent a questionnaire to all twenty-six USWISRA member colleges. The coaches of the six Ivy League colleges with women's teams circulated a four-page letter supporting a switch to softball, noting that rallies among women players using a softball lasted longer and that new players found the game more encouraging. Bunker's committee, however, submitted its recommendations to the USWISRA in an eight-page memorandum entitled "It Ain't Broke—So Don't Fix it!" On 5 March 1993, USWISRA voted to switch. Its constitution, unlike the NEISA, allowed for a simple majority to change to softball.

With both the preparatory schools and women's colleges in its pocket, the junior committee again asked the USSRA if it could switch to softball. This time the executive committee agreed, and the 1993–94 season was officially softball only. Not a single junior hardball tournament was scheduled. The women's division of the USSRA announced in May that the Howe Cup, to be held in Baltimore in September, would be softball. In October 1993, 628 players entered the softball nationals, besting the 1987 hardball nationals record of 576. Everyone was playing softball. Except men's college squash.

Since Harry Cowles's days at Harvard, men's college squash had been at the forefront of change in America. The National Intercollegiate Squash Racquets Association had been the first association to require protective eyewear, the first to adopt the seventy-plus ball and the first to abandon it for the Slazenger fuchsia ball. However, giving up hardball was too catastrophic.

Institutional lethargy lately seemed imbued in the association. The major squash powers, especially the Ivy League colleges, with their Friends of Squash funds, fantastic facilities, long-tenured coaches and administration support, often had different agendas than the small colleges with struggling programs. The usual Harvard-Yale-Princeton triumvirate dominated. In 1983 Harvard pulled off a clean sweep: It won the national intercollegiate team title; the national intercollegiate six-man team title; the national five-man teams; a Harvard player (Kenton Jernigan) won the national intercollegiates; another player (David Boyum) won the Harry Cowles; and its top two players, Jernigan and Boyum, reached the finals of the national amateurs, with Jernigan winning 3–0. Expansion in the college ranks, a key aspect in the overall paradigm of squash in America, never materialized behind this juggernaut. More than one-hundred-and-fifty colleges had squash facilities and no varsity team.

NISRA battles with the softball invasion were a microcosm of the conflict in America. In the eighties some coaches, especially Paul Assaiante at West Point, had pushed for a spring softball tournament, and in 1991 he hosted an NISRA softball tourney. In January 1992 Bob Callahan, the Princeton squash coach since 1980, wrote a four-page letter on Princeton letterhead to his fellow NISRA coaches. In his first sentence, he dropped a bombshell: At the association's annual meeting at the national intercollegiates in February, he would offer a motion to switch to softball. To justify his actions, he mentioned everything from the evolution of juniors toward softball to the Pan-Am Games to the historic role of men's college squash as a leader. Stapled to the end of the letter was an informal ballot with eight different choices for the upcoming season, which coaches were to rank in order of preference, and a space at the bottom for "your own scenario or comments." In February 1992 the men's intercollegiate coaches met at Yale. Some wanted to promote both games. Others wondered about the viability of playing softball on a hardball court. No consensus could be reached. Dave Brown, the NISRA president, reconstituted the association's ball committee to look into the matter and make recommendations for the following February.

A schism occurred. The ball committee broke into two factions, one behind Bob Callahan, which supported softball, and the other, led by Dave Talbott, the coach at Yale, which wanted to retain hardball. One cause for their different approaches was a home-field advantage. In 1992 at a cost of $135,000, Callahan converted seven hardball courts in old Dillon Gymnasium into five softball courts. Talbott, on the other hand, was hamstrung by the cumbersome tower of Payne Whitney. There was no room to build separate courts, and tearing down existing courts would be difficult because in 1988 Yale spent three quarters of a million dollars renovating its courts. Over the next year the ball committee struggled with key issues like the unpalatable alternative of playing softball at off-campus clubs while waiting for softball courts to be built and the inevitable difference between wealthy programs and the more beleaguered ones—the former would build quicker than the latter and might refuse to play a college that had only hardball courts.

In November 1992 the association organized a coach's softball clinic at Penn, concurrent with the second annual intercollegiate softball championships, to teach coaches the subtleties of softball. A week later Yale held the annual Ivy League scrimmages and, for the first time, used a softball for the matches. In December 1992 Ted Marmor wrote to all NISRA coaches appealing for a vote for hardball at its February 1993 meeting. "It is extraordinarily unwise to contemplate a drastic change in the American game of squash," Marmor wrote, "when the bulk of our physical capital is most appropriate for hardball and the great majority of squash's most devoted players—and especially those who have supported the USSRA most generously with their funds and time—want to see hardball continued to be played vigorously." Marmor reiterated the USSRA's proposal of a split season, with a national intercollegiate softball tournament around Thanksgiving. In early February 1993 the ball committee sent out a ballot offering three proposals: a softball season, with the visiting team being allowed to select the venue; a split season, with a fall softball term and a winter hardball term; or a hardball season. In late February 1993, a week before Gallagher's men stormed the ramparts, the NISRA tabulated the votes: thirteen for hardball, eight for softball and six for the split season. For the 1993–94 season, men's college squash was to remain hardball. They had gone to the brink and backed away.

The following year saw the complete capitulation of the rest of the hardball squash community. The men's college game, formerly in the van, was being left behind while it engaged in a debilitating haggle over a fait accompli. Straw ballots on the softball issue, mailed in October 1993, recorded a volte-face: twenty-three for softball, eleven for hardball. At the end of the month, Princeton hosted the third annual NISRA softball tournament, and in November the Ivy League scrimmage again was a softball event. At a coaches' meeting that weekend, an informal show of hands indicated an overwhelming level of support for a switch to softball. In January 1994 the ball committee wrote up another set of ballots. The results, with each ballot signed by the college's athletic director, were twenty for softball, thirteen for hardball. With thirty-three possible votes, two more votes were needed to make the change.

Politicking for the February 1994 meeting grew desperate. Dave Talbott wrote a long letter to all NISRA coaches, while Bob Callahan made a series of phone calls to athletic directors, including a conference call with Ivy League athletic directors. John Nimick, as executive director of the new PSA, wrote an open letter to college coaches and athletic directors, declaring an affinity for softball and softball courts. In a last ditch effort to keep men's college squash from the guillotine, USSRA president Alan Fox wrote to all NISRA coaches and college athletic directors: "While the USSRA is very supportive of the softball game, we would prefer to see both games made available to our constituencies, rather than have one game 'mandated' or voted out of existence. It would be our preference for the NISRA to continue to operate under a 'split' season which affords the players the opportunity to play both games." He concluded by saying that the voters needed to "recognize that yours is an important decision, not only for the future of collegiate play, but for the future of the game of squash in the U.S. Recognize that you have choices."

In late February 1994, on the fourth floor of Payne Whitney, the NISRA again met to discuss softball and again they could not make the switch. Callahan announced the twenty-to-thirteen split in favor of softball. Three coaches said they had misunderstood the ballot. Dan Hammond, a coach at Bowdoin, offered a motion (signed by his athletic director) to reconsider the vote. The motion was successful and the meeting adjourned. In March coaches received a ballot asking if they wanted to reconsider the October 1993 ballot. A majority of coaches (twenty-two to six) agreed to a reballot. Before the reballot deadline, more lobbying from both hardball and softball factions ensued. Some coaches tried to bring in more colleges to further swing the vote. Alan Fox sent another letter asking athletic directors to educate themselves on the ramifications of their votes. At six o'clock in the evening on 14 April 1994, a new vote was tabulated. This time two coaches switched sides. By the margin of one vote, men's intercollegiate squash switched to softball.

Cartoonish shilly-shallying over the last stronghold of hardball did not blind most squash leaders to the basic fact that the kingdom was in tatters. On 21 January 1994, Alan Fox wrote a letter to "Hard Ball Enthusiasts" to ask for guidance and support in organizing a committee devoted exclusively to the promotion of hardball. It was a letter inconceivable ten years earlier. It was a letter admitting the demise of hardball.

Two finals matches defined the end. On Thursday 23 February 1994, in New Haven, Harvard played its annual dual match against Yale. The two teams had the oldest rivalry in intercollegiate squash, dating back to 1923, and their sixty-fifth meeting was to be their last with a hardball. Yale went up 4–1 but, the contest, like so many previous ones, went to 4–all. The decider was between the number three players, Jamie Dean for Yale and Tal Ben-Shachar for Harvard. It was rather symbolic. Dean was a senior from New York. He had grown up playing hardball in the fabled Heights Casino program. His brother had played at Yale. Ben-Shachar was from overseas (Israel) and had grown up playing softball. Dean rushed out to a 2–1 lead, but Ben-Shachar fought back and the match, inevitably, went to 13–all in the fifth. Ben-Shachar called set-five. It took fifteen minutes to complete the tiebreaker. Dean went up 3–0, then 4–2. Ben-Shachar tied it up at 4–all. Serving from the left circle on simultaneous NISRA championship point, Ben-Shachar put up a soft lob serve. Dean cranked his forehand return into the middle of the tin. In an instant, it was over. Harvard mobbed Ben-Shachar. Yale helped a disconsolate Dean off the court.

On 21 January 1996, Mark Talbott played in the last official professional hardball tournament, the Rolex Greenwich Open at the Field Club. The $7,500 tournament was a quiet adjunct to the professional doubles tournament held at the club. Without fanfare, Talbott lost in the quarterfinals Saturday morning to Anders Wahlstedt, 15–13, 13–15, 15–10, 10–15, 15–10. Gary Waite beat Wahlstedt in the finals. There was no ceremony, no formal acknowledgment of the fact that hardball was now, finally, history.

CHAPTER ELEVEN

The Infinitely Greater Game

Americans love squash doubles. We love the court's attenuated expanse of white with red trim, a gleaming ocean liner plowing through the winter seas. We admire its deliciously infinite panoply of shots: the high-flying Philadelphia shot, the stupefying skid lob boast, the ankle-twisting reverse corner, the feather-floating drop, the gut-wrenching double boast, the skyscraping lob, the astonishing reverse volley three-wall. We delight in the fact that the game's most loyal players are octogenarians. We feel a frisson in the leaping, last-ditch lunge for a ball sucked by gravity to the floor twenty feet away. We enjoy the pleasant, equitable sight of mixed doubles. We like four-handed strategy. Youth is never served on the doubles court. There are no manuals to read on doubles. You have to just play. Above all, we love doubles because it means two; team spirit; confrere in victory, comrade in defeat; first man and second man; your ball; I'll cover those cross-courts over your head; thanks for bailing me out; yesssssssssssssss PARTNER. In January 1937 an English squash magazine wrote of the opening of a doubles court in London: "It is magnificent, and it makes Squash seem an infinitely greater game even if one merely contemplates the empty court. There is no doubt at all that doubles at all games are infinitely superior to singles if only because they introduce that element of team spirit and combination which are so essential to sport. With the introduction of doubles there should really be no limit to the playing life of the happy Squash player."

Four players, standing in feel-my-breath proximity to one another in the middle of the court, bash a little rock at each other. The angles and combinations, the volcanic spray of drives, volleys and drop shots, cloud the newcomer's eye. To the initiated, doubles is clarity. The two right-wall players circle each other throughout the point, as do the left-wall players. The unspoken rule in squash doubles is that if one team is striking the ball, the other team, especially the opposing player on the other wall, is allowed to stand in front. Therefore, both the right-wallers and the left-wallers constantly revolve around each other. It is like two gears in a machine, like two couples dancing a graceful waltz, like two pinwheels blowing in a hurricane wind.

Doubles works because of limitations. This oversized box of 22,500 cubic feet is 138 percent bigger than a hardball singles court, but it is exactly the right amount of space. Creativity is constrained by the laws of gravity and physics. Parabolas of drives, tangents of drop shots, swirling cosines of caroms are all predictable. Within one point (many rallies last more than thirty or forty strokes) the momentum can shift a dozen times as players dig themselves in and out of trouble. The usual pattern consists of the right-wall player cannoning drives and the left-wall player sniping off shots. Hunter Lott was power, Diehl Mateer was finesse; Maurice Heckscher was power, Mike Pierce was finesse. That is why the mid-1990s Canadian combination of Gary Waite and Jamie Bentley, two of the hardest-hitting doubles players in history, was so lethal. It was power and power, and their two-year unbeaten streak was a testament to turning the dictum upside-down. However, Waite & Bentley (the left-wall player is traditionally listed first) won not just because of their overwhelming force, but because both men could hit very good drop shots and did so all the time. "All of the greatest doubles champions have been shot makers rather than retrievers," wrote three-time national doubles champion Victor Niederhoffer in 1979. "Diehl Mateer, who won the doubles titles on eleven occasions, is probably the greatest left court player. He goes for winners at least once in four hits. Jim Zug is probably the greatest right court player. Again, his ratio of attempts for winners to drives is phenomenally high."

Doubles calls for the sharpshooter, Dirty Harry with a Dunlop trigger-finger. The doubles court had all that tempting room up front. Power will always succumb to finesse in doubles. "The essence in doubles," continued Niederhoffer, "is to place your team in an area where it's impossible for your opponents to go for the point with a high percentage shot." This cat and mouse game is what makes four-handed squash so fascinating. In doubles as in all other racquet sports, consistency and patience are the watchwords. Keep the ball in play. Wait for mistakes and unforced errors. Squash doubles tips its hat to the person willing to shoot.

Like squash singles, the game of squash doubles was invented by an Englishman. In 1907 the court tennis professional at the Racquet Club of Philadelphia was Fred Tompkins. At the time his family was a noted name in the ancient sport of court tennis. His great-grandfather had kept the tennis court at Merton College, Oxford; his grandfather was world champion from 1862 to 1871 and his father had managed the court at Brighton. Before coming to Philadelphia in 1904, "Pop" Tompkins had coached court tennis at Prince's Club and Stratfield Saye and racquets in Malta and Ireland and was, therefore, intimately knowledgeable about racquet sports. The youngest of seventeen children, he also knew something of the essence of doubles—sharing.

In the autumn of 1907, the Racquet Club switched clubhouses. It put in five squash singles courts, a court tennis court and two racquets courts on the fourth floor of its new building. Next to the stairs leading down to the locker room was an unused space. It was much too large for another squash singles court, and no club west of London needed a third racquets court. Tompkins knew exactly what to do. "Why, you have just the right amount of space," he told the club managers, "to build a court for that grand old English game of squash doubles." The Racquet Club, ever attuned to things Anglo, agreed to put in a doubles court. Tompkins paced out an enclosure forty-five-feet long and twenty-five-feet wide, laid down some cement walls, shoved four men inside, gave them a dark ball and told them to hit it as hard as they could.

Doubles had a shaky infancy. Finding sufficient room for a court nearly twice the size of a singles court was not easy. The doubles court at the Racquet Club was not exactly a perfect showcase for the new sport, with a low ceiling that made lobbing a risky maneuver. In 1923 Germantown Cricket Club built a court, but a beam ran right above the middle of the court. Lobbing there was even more fraught with danger than at the Racquet Club. Two years later Merion Cricket Club built its first court, but it was considered not of standard size until it was remodeled in 1950. In 1928 doubles came to New York, as both the University Club and Rockaway Hunting Club built courts. In 1930 the Heights Casino in Brooklyn, under the eye of president Ned Bigelow, cleared away four bowling alleys in the basement of the club to make room for a new doubles court. In the process they uncovered a mammoth boulder that they buried below the front of the court.

In 1930 the USSRA changed the scoring system from racquets style— only the server can score—to regular fifteen-point scoring, and in 1933 Neil Sullivan led a successful campaign to lower the official height of the tin in a doubles court from nineteen to seventeen inches. Finding a standard ball was a chore. "There is nothing entirely satisfactory," the USSRA secretary wrote in 1932. "There is no official ball but many different makes and types in use throughout the country, which makes it very difficult to standardize." Eventually Spalding produced a red-dot black ball that became the standard ball until Seamless took over in the late thirties.

Arthur Lockett started the first doubles tournament in January 1929 at the University Club. Ernest Jonklaas & Howes Burton of Rockaway Hunting Club won the eponymous cup. The Gold Racquet Invitational, held at Rockaway in Cedarhurst, Long Island, inaugurated an "Informal Doubles" in December 1930 that served as a consolation for players who had lost in the first round of the singles. A year later Greenwich Country Club and the Field Club in Greenwich, Connecticut, started a third doubles tournament, the Invitation Doubles Championship. On the last weekend of January 1931, Roy Coffin & Neil Sullivan, both Germantown Cricket Club players, won the sixteen-team Greenwich Invitation, beating Ray DeVoe & Don Nightingale in the finals. Thirty-two players from sixteen different clubs in four different cities came to the tournament, evincing a diversity in a game thought to be as Philadelphia-based as cheese steaks and the Liberty Bell. In February 1931 the national singles in Buffalo had a casual doubles draw. In 1932 Coffin & Sullivan repeated their win at Greenwich, topping Prescott Bush (the father and grandfather of future U.S. Presidents) & Stape Wonham in the finals. In 1933 the USSRA, seeing a growing seriousness among doubles players, annointed the Greenwich tourney as the national championship. Coffin & Sullivan, as usual, won the inaugural tournament, thrashing Spuggy Haskins & Robert Goodwin in three games, 15–6, 15–8, 15–12. In 1934 the Racquet Club of Philadelphia hosted the nationals. "The final, held on Sunday, March 18, and played before a packed gallery of about two hundred, was productive of the finest doubles play that has been seen this year at least," one reporter wrote of the match between Coffin & Sullivan versus Perry Pease & Wonham. "The Philadelphians won in three close games. Although there was little to choose between the four players, Sullivan's genius for bringing off winners from many positions, because of his great versatility, gave the defenders a slight edge." In 1936, after taking his fourth title in a row, Sullivan mislaid the permanent trophy and had to pay for a new one.

The wave of excitement carried doubles to the shores of the birthplace of singles. In 1935 three courts were laid out following USSRA specifications at the St. John's Wood Squash Club and Ladies' Carlton Club in London and the Edinburgh Sports Club in Scotland. In addition, Prince's Club tore down a racquets court and created a nonstandard cement doubles court, fifty-four feet by thirty. Balls were imported from the U.S.

Carlton Club member Hugo Fleury, who had won the inaugural Gold Racquets doubles title, and the two sets of U.S. national champions from England—Anne Lytton-Milbank & Judy McKechnie in 1935, and Betty Cooke & Janet Barret in 1937—keenly advocated doubles. Starting in 1937, the Squash Rackets Association held a national doubles tournament. It was won by W. B. Scott & Roy McKelvie, the latter the legendary squash and tennis reporter. Don Butcher, a top professional player, was always on the winning side of the national pro champions, in part because he was the head professional at St. John's Wood, which had the most active doubles court. Dreams of international competition were soon realized, as England and Scotland played an annual Test match against each other in doubles.

The Battle of Britain killed doubles in England. Both St. John's and Ladies' Carlton were blitzed and destroyed, and, at the same time, Prince's closed its historic doors. In Edinburgh the court remained intact but rarely was used for doubles. It did see one particularly noteworthy event: In 1950 the United States beat England in doubles, the only time the United States has beaten England in a squash contest in Great Britain.

Doubles in America carved itself a notable niche in the winter fixtures schedule. During the main part of the winter, there were only a few doubles tournaments. The season opened Thanksgiving weekend in Buffalo, with an invitational at the Tennis & Squash Club. The Gold Racquets had a limited draw because, if you played in the singles draw at Rockaway, you could not play in the doubles. Merion Cricket Club added an invitational doubles to its William White weekend in January 1962, replacing the University Club in New York's Lockett Cup doubles tournament. Not to be confused with the tri-city Lockett Cup (played the second weekend in December), the doubles Lockett Cup usually had a strong draw because there was no singles tournament that early in January. After Lockett died in 1957, his doubles tournament declined as players disliked University Club rules that forbade female spectators from the gallery. In 1959 the club switched to a handicapped member-guest format. Eighteen teams entered and the club, as Bob Lehman noted, "relented to the extent of admitting damsels for am and pm Sunday matches."

For most of the second half of the century, doubles had a distinct season. After the national singles finished in mid-February, players picked up their heavier bats, donned their white flannel trousers and played a breakneck five-week season. In the leadup to the national doubles in late March, four men's tournaments predominated, with club, city and state championships usually extended over the course of weeks or months. The first weekend after the national singles was the Heights Casino Open, then the Greenwich Invitational, the Baltimore Invitation Doubles and, finally, the Canadian nationals, the weekend before the U.S. nationals. After the men's season ended with the national doubles, the men joined with women to play mixed doubles tournaments, especially the Germantown Cricket Club extravaganza.

The warmer weather with a hint of spring and the innate camaraderie of doubles combined to make these weekends even more relaxed than the singles circuit. A Philadelphian named Carter Simonin was renowned for his faithful attendance at doubles tournaments, but he would dally so long at the club bar that he sometimes went whole weekends without ever seeing a single game. The Baltimore Invitational Doubles, held at the University Club, was probably the most easygoing. The court was in the loft of a hotel across West Madison Street from the club, with creaky iron circular stairs leading to the gallery. After a weekend-long open bar situated nicely in a singles court, the BIDs closed with a terrapin brunch and cocktails on Sunday afternoon that were so engaging that most visiting players stayed over until Monday. In 1958 the BIDs started an award named after Simonin for notable extracurricular achievements. After a Baltimorean, Southey Miles, won the trophy—a crumpled, gilded beer can on a pedestal—a record five times, it was renamed after him. Joe Hahn won the Miles one year by dislocating his shoulder after, as Bob Lehman wrote, he was "tripped by a drunken chair."

As with singles, amateurs dominated doubles until the rise of the professional tour in the late 1970s. Philadelphia was the center of the sport. It had more courts than any city except Toronto and in most years had an autumn and winter doubles league. Since the nationals began in 1933, only twelve times out of sixty-nine tournaments has the winning men's team not included a Philadelphian. The toughest tournament in the country was often the Merion club championship. Beginning in 1947, Diehl Mateer & Hunter Lott won it nine times in twelve years. In 1959 Mateer finally left the partnership to play with John Hentz. Mateer & Hentz had won the national doubles in 1958 and 1959. They might be national champions, but, at their own club, Mateer & Hentz were not the best team that year. Lott teamed with Jimmy Whitmoyer, and they upset Mateer & Hentz in five games.

New York had, at its height, seven clubs with doubles courts, as well as two of the major tournaments. Since the Harvard Club built a low-ceiling court in 1947, Boston had to make do with just one court. In 1962 Treddy

Ketcham started the Ketcham Cup doubles wing of the inter-city Lockett Cup in an effort to encourage more enthusiasm for doubles in Boston (it first won the Cup in 1981). Nevertheless, both of squash's other major cities regularly felt overwhelmed by Philadelphia's prowess in four-handed squash. New York did produce a brief stretch of success in the fifties, when Germain Glidden, Rich Remsen, Cal MacCracken, Dick Squires, Carl Badger and Jim Etheridge all won national titles. However, Philadelphia returned without fail to claim a share of every title, but eight, from 1960 to 2002. Boston is still waiting for its first doubles champion.

The founding partnership in doubles was Roy Coffin & Neil Sullivan. Coffin was a fine singles player in his own right. He reached three national semifinals and won the national veterans title in 1940. Sullivan had his devastating forehand. Coffin & Sullivan played the inchoate game of doubles at an entirely different level from anyone else. They won the first five national doubles, three Greenwich Invitationals and five Lockett Doubles Cups.

Hunter Lott, the young Merion player, then strode onto the scene. An animated right-waller, Lott teamed up with fellow Philadelphian Bill Slack to win the next five national doubles until the Second World War halted their streak. After the war, Lott brought along his most famous protégé, Diehl Mateer. In 1948 he led their partnership to victory in the Pennsylvania state tournament and they reached the finals of the national doubles. The following year, they won the tournament, making Mateer the first player to win the national doubles while still in college.

Mateer got his first inkling that he could captain his own team in 1951. The day before the national doubles was to start in Pittsburgh, Lott fell violently ill. Mateer, scrambling to find a partner, telephoned a top singles player, Cal MacCracken, at his home in Englewood, New Jersey. Mateer persuaded MacCracken to join with him. The only problem was that MacCracken had never played a competitive doubles match and barely knew where to stand. During the first point of their opening match, Mac-Cracken ended up on the left wall, taking a ball Mateer ordinarily would have hit. "Get over there and stay over there," Mateer shouted. Mac-Cracken retreated to his side and somehow they won their first three matches. On Sunday afternoon they found themselves in the finals play-ing the top-ranked team that year, Germain Glidden & Cliff Sutter. Dur-ing a frenzied melee of a point, a ball squirted cross-court from where Mateer and Glidden were battling. MacCracken instinctually swung at it. "I waded into it and made a beautiful reverse corner to end the point," MacCracken later said. "I felt great, until I realized—aided in no small

measure by the silence and Diehl's icy stare—that I had hit my own partner's cross-court shot, in the finals of the national doubles championships." MacCracken became the first non-Philadelphian to win the
national doubles.

In 1954 Mateer left Lott and put forth a convincing argument that he
was the Jack Nicklaus of doubles. Over the next three decades, he teamed
with eight other partners and won a total of eleven national doubles titles.
A further nine times, he lost in the finals. In a feat of endurance
unmatched by any player, he missed just a single national doubles tournament from 1946 through 1983. He played an aggressive, imaginative
game and constantly went for winners with his scything backhand. Some
of his losses in the finals of the nationals were among the most memorable
doubles matches ever played. In 1967 in Buffalo, going for his third consecutive title with Ralph Howe, Mateer rushed up front to retrieve a ball
at 12–all in the first game. Suddenly he felt a sharp blow to his ankle. He
fell and yelled, "Who hit me?" He had snapped his Achilles tendon. He
recovered to play six times with his sons. Twice he reached the finals with
his son Gil. Their last stab at a father & son victory—something never yet
achieved in men's doubles—was at Merion in 1983, in which they reached
the finals.

The Howe brothers, Sam and Ralph, each won six national titles. They
first did not play together, wanting to prove to the world—and to each
other—that each could become national doubles champion on his own.
Sam won three times with Bill Danforth, the hardy Pittsburgher and
Ralph took two with Mateer. After their string of three straight was broken by two other Merion players, Larry Terrell & Jim Zug, in 1972, they
split up.

Vic Niederhoffer was typically unconventional on the doubles court. In
1967, while living in Chicago and boycotting singles tournaments, he
decided to play doubles. He chose Vic Elmaleh as a partner. Elmaleh, a
forty-eight-year-old City Athletic Club and Heights Casino veteran, was
an able left-waller who had more or less retired from play. Niederhoffer
persuaded Elmaleh to play the right wall in the Johnson. They got to the
quarterfinals before losing in five tight games to Stephen & Ramsay
Vehslage, 18–16 in the fifth. At the 1967 national doubles, the two Vics
reached the quarterfinals, losing to the eventual winners Sam Howe &
Bill Danforth. In 1968 they did better, losing 15–13 in the fifth of the
finals at the Johnson. Three weeks later at the Racquet Club of St. Louis
came one of the most outlandish upsets in national doubles history.
Elmaleh, now a few months shy of fifty, drank gallons of orange juice to

keep hydrated and energized. Niederhoffer placed Elmaleh in front of the red line on the right side, told him not to worry about any balls that flew past him and proceeded to scamper around the court like a scared rabbit. Spectators estimated Niederhoffer covered 75 percent of the court. They had a rough five-game opening round match Saturday morning over local favorites Ted Simmons & Charlie Cella and another five-gamer that afternoon. No one thought Elmaleh would be able to walk Sunday morning, but he covered his 25 percent like a blanket. They went down, 2–0, to Kit Spahr & Jim Zug, but scrambled back to win in five. In the finals, they went up, 2–0, and withstood a furious comeback by Mateer & Ralph Howe, to win, 15–10 in the fifth. They won 251 points and lost 256.

As in men's singles, twice has the men's national doubles championship come down to a single point. In 1964 at the Minneapolis Club, Kit Spahr & Claude Beer were up 2–1 to Sam Howe & Bill Danforth, the defending champions. The long break after the third game gave new life to Howe & Danforth and, in the hot Minneapolis court, Howe began to lay down his reverse corner. In a tense fifth game, Howe & Danforth jumped to 14–12, but Spahr & Beer evened the score at 14–all. After a long consultation, Howe raised his index finger: one point. Daringly, they decided to give their opponents, as well as themselves, a championship point. Soon after the point began, Danforth crushed a forehand cross-court that luckily nicked on the back wall. Spahr, arguably the best doubles player never to win the nationals, dug at the ball in vain. In 1988 in Pittsburgh, the Mateer sons did not garner the same good luck their father had received there thirty-seven years before. Gil & Drew lost to Scott Ryan & Rich Sheppard, 8–15, 16–13, 15–9, 11–15, 16–15. Each team had won the nationals in the past two years, without facing the other, as well as splitting the majority of the invitational tournaments. This match determined who was the best amateur doubles team in the late eighties. Ryan, a Merion veteran aged forty-two, had ruptured his Achilles seven months before, so his presence in the tournament was testimony to his intense will to compete. Ryan & Sheppard went up, 13–8 in the fifth game, but the Mateers, exhibiting the usual Mateer-like grace under fire, came back. At 13–12, a Ryan lob grazed a light fixture. Ryan & Sheppard called set-three. On the first point, Sheppard, the ever-eager twenty-nine-year-old Philadelphia Cricket Club star, hammered a side-wall nick. Drew responded by rifling a perfect reverse. 1–1. Gil, not to be outdone, flicked a gorgeous cross-court from near the front wall. 2–1. With the tension unbearable, Drew flubbed two straight balls into the top of the tin.

Doubles, much more than singles, was an inclusive game. Late bloomers, players from untraditional backrounds, players who did not go to preparatory school or an Ivy League college, tennis stars—all found the doubles circuit amenable to their love for competition and their need for a sport easy on an aging body. Beginning in the sixties, older players were blessed with opportunities to compete. The USSRA started a seniors draw (fifty and over) in 1962, a veterans draw (forty and over) in 1971 and a masters draw (sixty and over) in 1983. These age-group tournaments helped situate doubles as the premier place for mature squash players. The hometowns of national champions ranged well beyond Philadelphia, everywhere from Brunswick, Maine, to St. Petersburg, Florida. Hastings Griffin, a Princeton graduate, won national titles in four racquet sports and still rode his motorcycle to tournaments in his eighties. Treddy Ketcham won a record seven senior doubles titles with four different partners. Cliff Sutter was a tennis great in the thirties who won two Greenwich Invitationals, two Gold Racquets doubles titles and four Metropolitan Doubles. Glidden, at the age of thirty-eight, won his only national doubles title in 1952. In 1955 in Philadelphia, Eddie & Joe Hahn performed a miracle of sorts. Joe, forty-nine years old, and Eddie, forty-five, walked right into the lion's den at Merion and upset Mateer & Dick Squires, the defending champions, in the final, 15–10, 15–14, 6–15, 12–15, 15–5.

Women played in the inaugural national doubles at Greenwich, with Anne Page & Sarah Madeira, Merion Cricket Club players, winning it. Before the Second World War, women spent more time on the doubles court than the singles court. Philadelphia was the home of champions—more than half of all national women doubles titlests had at least one Philadelphian on the team. Louisa Manly-Power was a mediocre singles player with her best result a victory in the Manheim Challenge, a Germantown Cricket Club tournament for B players, but she was the dominant doubles player in the fifties. She won four national doubles titles, two with Barbara Newlin and two with Sylvia Simonin (wife of Carter; did he ever make it to her matches?) and took six Pennsylvania state titles. Ann Wetzel, the one-time national champion, won four national doubles titles with four different partners. Bunny Vosters was the Diehl Mateer of women's squash. She won eleven titles, five with her daughter Gretchen Spruance. The women, ahead of the men, started a senior doubles championship in 1956. (The tournament, unlike the men's age-group tournaments, was played on a separate weekend from the regular women's national doubles.) Still, women's doubles never became a mass game. In 1981, for example, when thousands of women were playing squash, just eight teams entered the women's national doubles, and half of those women were beginners.

Mixed doubles, spearheaded by women, was very popular, especially in Philadelphia. In 1942 Howard Davis and his wife Dorothea launched a tournament at Germantown Cricket Club, which, with a black-tie dinner dance and competitive but mostly harmonious matches, was a genteel way to end the squash season. In 1969 the U.S. Women's Squash Racquets Association co-opted the tournament and made it the national mixed doubles championship. The most intriguing matchup might have been the finals in 1974 at Berwyn. Tom Poor and Mike Pierce, two up-and-coming left-wallers, had diametrically opposed partners: Poor played with Jane Stauffer, a forty-six-year-old woman who had won the national singles seven years before Pierce's partner, a sixteen-year-old Gail Ramsay, had been born.

Monkey doubles was a bizarre outcome of the American love for doubles. In the twenties, with that innate ability to be creative with small spaces, New Yorkers invented a four-handed version of squash in a singles court. The starting point was the 1928 Gold Racquets. A gaggle of galleryites wanted to play squash, but the doubles court at Rockaway was filled. "So they quite naturally played with a doubles ball in a singles court," wrote Bob Lehman in a history of the sport in 1961. "Not being completely insane, they picked up some racquets with broken handles, since four long racquets in a small court would be a short-cut to the emergency ward." In 1929 Tom Byrne, Sr., and Al Molloy, Sr., two young assistant professionals at the old Park Avenue Squash Club, cut a few racquets down for some neighborhood children to use. One evening two other men were in the club and the four of them decided to play doubles in a singles court with the children's racquets. The game, nicknamed monkey doubles due to the primate-like actions of four grown men in a tiny box, soon became popular in New York. Bill Ketcham, Sr., a Rockaway player and Frank Ward, the City Athletic Club professional, were the two leading lights in the early years, and the Harvard, University and Racquet & Tennis Clubs were the most active locales, although, Lehman noted, "it was indulged in mostly under rather suspect conditions, after midnight." In January 1953 the Plainfield Country Club formally organized a tournament among early dropouts at the DeForest-Tyler. Treddy Ketcham and Bob MacLeod, a Dartmouth football star, won the first four years of monkey doubles at Plainfield. Rules were akin to regular doubles, including using a doubles ball. Racquets could have at most a six-inch handle and were most often found from broken bats left outside a court. A front-and-back I formation was considered orthodox. In the seventies monkey doubles appeared at the commercial squash clubs in the guise of mixed doubles. Uptown Racquet Club held a Monkey Doubles Nationals in the spring of 1979, which proved so popular that all summer they ran monkey doubles round robins every Thursday night. Downtown Athletic Club and Fifth Avenue also had regular monkey doubles matches. In the summer of 1979, Newport ran the First Great Flying Sneaker Mixed Monkey Doubles Tournament (FGFSMMDT). Sam Jernigan put four people on a singles court with a softball. The Delaware Junior Doubles tournament, begun in 1986 at Wilmington Country Club, started in 1988 a blind draw monkey doubles for boys and girls who were no longer in the draw. This proved successful and contributed to the popularity of the tournament, which became the national junior doubles in 1991.

Professionally, the game traveled a rocky road for many decades. In 1938 Ned Bigelow started an open championship at the Heights Casino. It was the first doubles tournament that allowed professionals to participate and paid them if they won. A number of notable racquet-wielding geniuses appeared that first year: Vinnie Richards, the lawn tennis star; Frank Ward, the squash tennis champion and Pierre Etchebaster, the court tennis world champion. Until the sixties, the Heights Casino tournament (renamed the Johnson in 1965 after the untimely death of its driving force, David Johnson, Jr.) was the only open tournament, and it struggled to offer enough prize money to entice professionals to enter. For some years, in the forties and fifties, the tournament was not played and for long stretches in the sixties and seventies all-amateur teams won it.

In 1964 Jim Bentley, a pro at the Toronto Cricket, Skating & Curling Club, launched a round-robin pro doubles tournament. In 1972 he moved to the Cambridge Club, a new men's club high above the Sheraton Centre Hotel in downtown Toronto and, after a year's sabbatical, restarted the tournament. With an unusual Thanksgiving Day starting date, a six-team limit, a notorious stag black-tie dinner and Calcutta (more than once members wagered a quarter of a million Canadian dollars), the Cambridge Club created a special ambiance of drama. In 1969 the City Athletic Club in New York, under the hand of Mel Sokolow and CAC professional Lou Ballato, started a pro tournament.

With the Johnson, the Cambridge Club and the CAC as foundation stones, the World Professional Squash Association built a viable circuit of professional doubles tournaments when the hardball singles tour skyrocketed in the eighties. The season's pipecracker was the Canadian Open, sponsored by Xerox and hosted at the Badminton & Racquet Club in Toronto. In 1984, in a nod to its history, the Greenwich Country Club went professional, renamed its Invitational the North American Open and eventually switched to a mid-November date. After the Cambridge Club came the British Columbia Doubles, usually played in early February at the Vancouver Lawn Tennis Club. Capping the season was the Elite Doubles, started in 1982 by Maurice Heckscher at the Cynwyd Club for the top eight teams on the tour. Pro-am events, often held the same weekend as a professional tournament, were especially popular, as the pros could get upwards of $2,000 if they won, and the amateurs, usually club members, had the thrill of playing with the best in the world. Prize money, with solid sponsorship from Mutual Benefit, Xerox and even Bud Light, was substantial. In 1980 the total was $25,000 for three events; in 1987 it was $125,000 for eight events; in 1989 it was $95,000 for six events. Most of the tournaments were between $7,500 and $15,000, with the Johnson traditionally leading the way with an eye-opening $25,000.

In February 1981 Toronto Cricket launched the first World Doubles. Sponsored by Bata shoes and sanctioned by all three North American squash associations and the International Squash Racquets Federation, the tournament was meant to be a global affair. "It was hoped," wrote Bob Lehman, "that teams would enter from Europe and other parts, where the game of doubles is virtually unknown." That hope was dashed, as it was only North Americans who came to Toronto. Still, twenty-two teams vied for the four qualifier spots in the sixteen-team main draw. In the finals Mo Khan & Clive Caldwell beat Peter Briggs & Ralph Howe in four games. Rogers Cable in Toronto broadcast ten hours of coverage from the tournament. The World Doubles ran into sanctioning conflicts with the ISRF and after three years moved to Buffalo in 1985. Unable to resolve the sanctioning problems, the tournament hibernated until 1994, when it was relaunched in Toronto. Held every two years in either Toronto or Philadelphia, the World Doubles became the world's largest squash doubles festival, with a dozen draws and 400 players playing matches around the clock.

In the early years of the professional doubles circuit, many singles champions found traction on the doubles courts. Gordy Anderson, Clive Caldwell and the brothers Desaulniers (Mike and Brad) and Khan (Mo and Gul) won their share of tournaments. Mo, with an intimidating forehand and more than a dollop of Khanian aplomb, was especially tough, but it was the doubles specialist who knew how to cut a skid boast or crack a deathless reverse corner. Peter Briggs, Ralph Howe, Michael Pierce and Maurice Heckscher were men who held down jobs all week and were professional only in that they accepted prize money to cover expenses. Briggs and Howe were renowned singles players; although fine "singlists," as Bob Lehman liked to say, neither Heckscher nor Pierce played an iota of pro singles. Pierce, displaying rare precocity, won the Gold Racquets doubles at the record age of twenty (he remains the only player to win the Gold Racquets doubles in four different decades). Pierce & Heckscher won the U.S. national doubles in 1975 and, a year later, lost to Briggs & Howe in one of the best four-game finals in national doubles history: 15–13, 11–15, 15–14, 16–15. Pierce had uncanny vision on the court and hit the most back-wrenching Philadelphia shots in the game. Heckscher eventually took six Johnsons (a record that stood until Jamie Bentley appeared). He banged the ball quite hard and had a very good sense of positioning. For four years, Pierce & Heckscher were never ranked below number three and were named WPSA Doubles Team of the Year in 1982. Peter Briggs & Ralph Howe stayed in the top four in the rankings all four years they played together. Ralph had a tough lob serve, a knack for timely winners and true versatility: In 1969 he won all six amateur doubles tournaments he entered, playing the left wall in three and the right wall in the other three. Peter Briggs, the unprepossessing portsider, was the greatest of the quartet. In 1984, playing with four different partners, he went undefeated in all six professional events held that season and also won the U.S. Mixed Doubles. He stood far up in the court, well in front of the red line and crushed the ball with his whippy left arm. His battles on the left wall with Pierce were legendary. Pierce stood three or four feet behind him and retrieved and lobbed as only a perfectly schooled Philadelphian can, while Briggs sniped reverses at will.

Pierce & Heckscher's maiden tournament together was in the pit at the Heights Casino in February 1974. Unseeded and unheralded at the Johnson, they won a semifinal match on Sunday morning over top seeds Clive Caldwell & Ken Binns, 15–14 in the fifth. They dropped their first two games, won the next two and went up, 14–11 in the last stanza. Binns slapped a reverse, and two Heckscher errors leveled the match. Pierce & Heckscher boldly called no set. Binns slashed an unbeatable roll corner, but as he turned around, with the gallery in pandemonium, he stuck his thumb on the floor. He had trapped the ball. In the afternoon, two-and-a-half hours later, Pierce & Heckscher faced the unpredictable team of Pedro Bacallao & Vic Niederhoffer. A Cuban-American squash tennis champion, Bacallao played the left wall with a right-wall game—more power than finesse. Tied at 13 in the fifth game, set three was called and Bacallao & Niederhoffer went up 2–1. Then a furious rally ensued. Heckscher dove for a ball and played the next shot while flat out on the floor—all in vain as a couple of strokes later the ball broke. After warming up the new ball, Pierce shoveled a cross-court drop in for a winner. At double championship point, Bacallao lunged at a passing drive and tinned the ball.

The most talked-about match of the era was the finals of the Cambridge Club Doubles in November 1980. It was Briggs & Howe versus Pierce and a surprise partner, Sharif Khan. (Briggs & Howe had survived a double match ball in the semifinals, coming back from 14–5 down in the fifth to beat Mo Khan & Clive Caldwell. Briggs had thrown up junk balls to break Mo & Caldwell's rhythm and they tiptoed through when Mo, brimming as usual with braggadocio, had momentarily gotten distracted.) In the finals Sharif displayed his fierce determination so often seen on the singles court. But his serving was atrocious. He simply put the ball into play, with a nonchalant slap. With over two hundred thousand Canadian dollars in the Calcutta riding on the match, Pierce & Sharif rushed to a two-love lead. Then, Briggs & Howe, summoning another miracle, clawed back to even the match at 2–all. In the fifth, Briggs & Howe went up 14–10 and seemingly had the match in hand, but Pierce reeled off a bunch of sharp reverses and inched the score back to 14–all. Briggs & Howe called no set. The crowd roared with anticipation. Sharif served up a low hard serve that was clearly below the service line. Briggs caught it on his racquet. The crowd exploded, thinking Briggs had blown his return, but the referee called the serve down. After the jampacked gallery returned to their seats, Khan tossed up his second serve. It was another soft, easy lob. Briggs blasted a low reverse for a winner. It was a gutsy, beautiful shot, the kind that Bobby Jones said required "sheer delicatessen."

In the late 1980s, the leading singles players started to give the sport more than a sideways glance, and pro doubles never returned to the days when amateurs ruled. The first twosome to dominate was Ned Edwards & Dave Johnson. Edwards was a strong, bullish player adept on either wall. Johnson, the son of the former great Heights Casino player, was an average singles player who never cracked the top ten but did wonders on the doubles court. Edwards's most memorable match, though, was partnered with Alex Doucas in the 1989 Elite. They survived a three-hour marathon final against Briggs & Talbott. It ended with Doucas rolling out a winning corner shot at 17–all in the fifth. It was Doucas's first win on the pro doubles tour. Two months later, he was dead.

Todd Binns & Tom Page came next and did even better. Binns apprenticed with Gordy Anderson for one season and, after winning the World Doubles, switched to the powerful Page. For three years in a row, they won the WPSA doubles team of the year award. One season, they went undefeated until the seventh and final tournament, the Elite, when Jamie Bentley and Kenton Jernigan surprised them in a five-game final. Other teams managed to win as much as Binns & Page—in 1986–87 they won just three of eight tournaments and seven other teams reached a final— but they brought forth a new style. Using the seventy-plus ball and graphite racquets, Binns & Page changed the nature of professional doubles with their unusual power-and-power partnership. Both delighted in pinballing the ball onto as many walls as possible, trying to handcuff and rattle opponents as much as put the ball away.

The 1990s saw three partnerships predicated upon this new method of play. Kenton Jernigan, the amateur star of the mid-eighties, proved to be a natural on the left wall. Jamie Bentley, the son of junior guru Jim in Toronto, launched his career in the mid-eighties by partnering with Mike Pierce for a season. He soon outpaced his mentor and, after playing with fellow Canadian Alan Grant for two seasons, found his mark with Jernigan. They won in the usual pattern of the right-waller bashing and the left-waller shooting, only that Bentley himself was a fabulous touch player and knew exactly when to ease up on the throttle. They won one world championship, five Johnsons, three Cambridge Clubs, four Elites, two CACs and seven BC Doubles.

In the autumn of 1996 Bentley called Jernigan and said he was switching partners. He broke up his team to get Gary Waite as a partner. Waite, the superfit Canadian, had just finished his first season on the right wall. Bentley moved him to the left wall and they went on a tear. For two straight years, seventeen tournaments and fifty-seven matches, they never lost. They wore black shirts, black shorts and scared opponents with their take-no-prisoners attitude. Hitting the ball harder than any team before, Waite & Bentley were an army with no foe. Their closest win was in the finals of the 1997 Johnson, when Scott Stoneburgh & Anders Wahlstedt took them to 15–13 in the fifth.

In the autumn of 1998, Bentley, by now having established himself as the best right-wall player in doubles history, inexplicably switched partners again. Waite moving to New York to take the head pro job at the University Club, picked up Mark Talbott. A steady tactician, Talbott kept the ball in play while Waite did the bulk of the hard hitting. They managed to win all but a handful of tournaments in their three years together.

In 2000 Talbott retired and Waite brought in his young assistant at the University Club, Damien Mudge. A six-foot-three Australian softballer, Mudge hit the ball even harder than Waite. The two colleagues rampaged through the professional tour. Their first year they won three straight tournaments, lost the fourth, then paused while Mudge recovered from a freakish wrist injury. In 2001–02, they replicated Waite & Bentley by going undefeated all season. They won seventeen ranking tournaments, with just two matches in fifty-three going to five games. It was an extraordinary season for Waite. He also won the nonranking Cambridge Doubles, the U.S. national doubles with Morris Clothier and the World Mixed Doubles with Jessie Chai. In 2002–03 Waite & Mudge's winning streak ended at an extraordinary twenty-four consecutive tournaments

The engine for the doubles tour, the WPSA singles tour, perished in the nineties, but pro doubles survived and even prospered. Doubles had never been dependent on large crowds because the tournaments were at private clubs, with no ticket sales. Private money, freed from obligations to the singles tour and growing rapidly in the nineties' stock-market boom, poured into doubles tournaments. Administration problems, however, plagued the tour. The Professional Squash Association, the world body that ran both the softball singles and the hardball doubles tour beginning in 1993, was focused on Hong Kong, Cairo and London, not New York and Toronto. In 2000, inspired by a $40,000 George Kellner Cup in New York, the hardball players formed a new body, the International Squash Doubles Association. Gary Waite became director and Morris Clothier, the seven-time amateur national doubles champion, led a private fundraising campaign. Prize money, without any significant corporate sponsorship, doubled in two years to $500,000. The Kellner Cup event rose to $100,000 in prize money in its second year. In 2003 Peter Briggs organized a tournament at Apawamis that had a total of $130,000 in prize money, one of the richest squash events ever. The schedule of events expanded from a dozen tournaments to twenty in 2002–03. The number of players' nationalities grew to include Australia, England, Sweden and New Zealand, as a gaggle of retired PSA headliners joined the tour, most notably Brett Martin, an Australian former world number two; Clive Leach, an English former top thirty and Blair Horler, a fireball from New Zealand. A trio of callow Canadians—Viktor Berg, Josh McDonald and Michael Pirnak—jumped into the fray. In 2000 Clive Caldwell, the director of the Cambridge Doubles, teamed six top softballers with six top doubles players. Caldwell's experiment was a success. The crowd at the club loved the unpredictability of the event and it was good exposure for doubles, as the softball players learned first hand about the joys of hardball doubles. A number of them, like Chris Walker, Anthony Hill and Graham Ryding, subsequently played in other ISDA events.

Persuading the top singles players in the world to get on the doubles court did not end the troubles for doubles. Part of the problem was its provincial nature. One of the arguments that doomed hardball singles was that no one outside North America played the game; doubles had the same weakness. The ISDA worked hard to live up to the "international" part of its name. It latched onto any court outside the region—a new one built by a Jester in Tijuana, Mexico, the old 1935 one in Edinburgh. In 1976 the Royal Bangkok Sports Club in Thailand built a USSRA-standard court. The club played its traditional monkey doubles tournament—the Chiengmai Cup, begun in 1910—on the new court with a softball. In the nineties, to compete in the Chiengmai, two other clubs in Asia built hardball courts: the Tanglin Club in Singapore and the Raintree Club in Kuala Lumpur. Waite led a contingent of professional doubles players over to the Chiengmai in the spring of 2001. Despite playing with a softball, Waite & Berg managed to win the tournament.

Softball doubles, however, loomed as a serious roadblock for hardball doubles. In 1986 four members of the Royal Automobile Club traveled to the Lanz Club in Bournemouth. On a court with movable walls (the only one in Britain), they conducted research on what would be the ideal width for a softball doubles court. They added three feet, eight feet, twelve feet to the standard twenty-one-foot court and decided upon twenty-five feet, three inches. In 1988 the RAC constructed two softball doubles courts at its Woodcote Park clubhouse outside London. The builder misread the Bournemouth dimensions and when the plaster and paint was slapped on the brick walls, the width had been reduced to exactly twenty-five feet. Without missing a beat, the RAC proclaimed twenty-five feet the standard softball doubles width, and the World Squash Federation followed suit. With sliding wall technology made common by the German-based court building company ASB, the game slowly spread. In 1997 the first World Softball Doubles Championships were held in Hong Kong. Supposed to alternate with the biannual World Doubles in North America, the Hong Kong tournament was not played again. The biggest showcase was the Commonwealth Games. At both Kuala Lumpur in 1998, and Manchester in 2002, men's, women's and mixed softball doubles were medal events. Few people argued that softball doubles presented a better game. It was interminably slow and, with four people on a thirty-two-foot by twenty-five-foot court, it was almost impossible to produce clear winners. Matches were two out of three games, yet some matches lasted two hours and were jammed with lets. Still, many older players liked softball doubles for the same reasons Americans had been playing for almost a century: the affability of partnerships and the lower impact on the body.

Whether hardball doubles faces the fate of hardball singles is open to debate. Although it is a finer game than softball doubles, hardball doubles has severe limitations. The game is essentially private. The ISDA doesn't play a single event at a public club and out of the hundred courts in the United States only a handful are public. All junior players grow up playing softball, so it will be difficult to persuade a growing majority of players to learn a strange game with a new ball, a new court and new tactics. Today Tompkins's game is in its strongest position ever. But it could reach its sesquicentennial looking like the game of court tennis or racquets—a superannuated relic immensely enjoyed by a tiny cabal of practitioners.

Ham Biggar

Eight-time British Open champion Geoff Hunt watches Gordon
Anderson strike the ball in the 1979 Mennen Cup in Toronto. Hunt
almost became the fifth man to win both the British and North American
Opens, losing in the 1977 NAO finals to Sharif Khan in four close games.

Ham Biggar

Two legends share a laugh at the 1981 WPSA Championships in
Toronto: Heather McKay, who went undefeated for eighteen years,
and Hashim Khan, the game's first international celebrity. Both
players moved to North America to coach.

A portrait of Sharif Khan by Ham Biggar. The first thing you noticed about Sharif, the twelve-time North American Open champion, was his eyes. "Big and dark and brown, they seem to glow, snapping on and off like flashbulbs," wrote Edward B. Fiske. "At crucial points in a match he will turn them defiantly, disconcertingly, on his opponent. 'When he stares you down like that,' says Gordon Anderson, one of the few top pros who has ever taken Sharif's measure, 'it is important to get the next point.'"

Ham Biggar

Ham Biggar

Perfectly attired in his Fila outfits, Stu Goldstein follows through against his rival Sharif Khan. Goldstein was emblematic of the growth of squash in the seventies. He was Jewish, a pro at a public club, and ultra-serious about training. Still, Sharif maintained his status as the number-one player on the continent.

Hugh McClean

The WPSA introduced a portable glass court in 1982. Although painfully rudimentary, with a wooden front wall and view-obstructing struts on the side walls, the court allowed the WPSA to stage tournaments in hockey rinks, auditoriums, gymnasiums, and convention centers, well beyond the private, country-club world.

Tommy Page, the mercurial prodigy from Philadelphia, always played brilliant matches against Jahangir Khan, the ten-time British Open champion. Here they square off at the 1983 Boston Open at the University Club.

Richard Ashley

Courtesy of Sports Illustrated

Avatar of the new pro tour, Mark Talbott rests in his truck that he built from an old Detroit squash court. For three seasons Talbott traveled the North American circuit, sleeping in what looked like a doghouse.

Richard Ashley

The touchstone match of the eighties, the final of the 1984 Boston Open was a classic confrontation between East and West. Mark Talbott survived a thriller against Jahangir Khan, winning 18–16 in the fifth.

Richard Ashley

Richard Ashley

Richard Ashley

Richard Ashley captures the emotions of the final of the 1985 Boston Open. Ned Edwards, the bruising American star, let a 2–0 lead slip away against Australian bad-boy Steve Bowditch. Diving and scrapping, Bowditch climbed back into the match. After squandering three match points, Edwards blasted a volley for a winner at 17–all in the fifth. He exulted à la Bjorn Borg at Wimbledon, while Bowditch appealed in vain for a let.

The two greatest American women: Demer Holleran lashes a rail against Alicia McConnell in 1986. McConnell won the 1980 World Juniors and a spot in the top fifteen on the world softball tour. Holleran has captured more national titles than any man or woman in history.

"In a bitterly contested, four-game, hour-and-a-half battle with much appealing and disputing the officials' decisions," wrote the USSRA yearbook, the trouser-wearing father-and-son Mateers beat Brad Desaulnier and Tom Poor (raking a rail on the right) in the semifinals of the 1983 national doubles at Merion. For Diehl Mateer, an eleven-time champion, it was the last match he would ever win in his storied career at the national doubles.

Richard Ashley

Ned Edwards squares off against John Nimick at the 1989 WPSA Championships at the Winter Garden, a palm-tree studded atrium next to the World Trade Center that survived the September 11, 2001 attacks. In 1992 the tournament switched to softball and was renamed the Tournament of Champions.

Greg Zaff, the first man to be an All-American in squash and tennis, shows his hardball stroke. In 1996 Zaff founded SquashBusters, the first urban youth enrichment program.

Courtesy of USSRA

Spectacular sites for pro tournaments became the norm. In 2002 John Nimick staged the United States Open at Symphony Hall, the century-old home of the Boston Symphony Orchestra.

The future of squash in America is seen in the bright faces gracing the cover of *Squash Magazine* in the summer of 2000, when team members from SquashBusters (Boston) and StreetSquash (New York) played each other in an historic match.

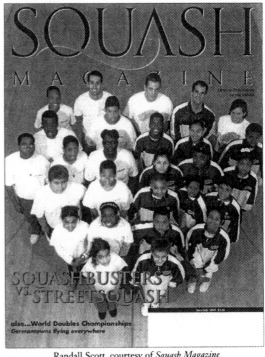

Randall Scott, courtesy of *Squash Magazine*

CHAPTER TWELVE

This Mollycoddled Age

In October 1932 an English squash champion, Kenneth Gandar Dower, offered a pithy forecast on the future of the game: "By 1970 athletes, trained from the cradle and having reached their physical prime between 28 and 32 (and not as I see in my evening paper at 18, as they do to-day) will drug themselves scientifically and make their one great bid for the championship and totter home and die. And I shall come puffing into the auditorium and take my place among 50,000 people and watch the final reflected in the vast mirror in the roof, and mutter something about the age of specialised athletics and tell vacantly that in my day we used to be able to finish off a rally.... I will say that we used to drive all the way to the Bath Club before matches instead of being landed in autogyros on the roof, whereas this mollycoddled age doesn't even seem to try."

The transition to softball was the roughest period for squash since the beginning of the century. In 1989 the USSRA decamped from its original headquarters. After renting office space for eighteen years, it bought, with the help of the Pierce family, an eighty-year-old house on Cynwyd Road. Craig Brand arrived in March 1991 and, at the end of the year, succeeded Darwin Kingsley as executive director. Brand, whose father was a professional badminton player, was a veteran in the sporting goods industry. With the cheerfully efficient help of Anne Farrell and Jean McFeely, two office managers who came to the USSRA in the mid-seventies, he faced a dire situation.

America switched from hardball to softball almost overnight. The bottom fell out of the pro hardball singles tour. In 1991–92 there were ten tournaments, then eight, five and three, and the last professional hardball tournament of the era was staged in January 1996. After four years at the Detroit Athletic Club, the North American Open switched to softball in 1995 and moved to Denver for one year. No sponsorship money appeared, and the most prestigious tournament on the continent disappeared without a trace. The old WPSA portable tour court, the scene of so many classic matches, returned to storage in a truck parked in a yard outside Playcon's offices in Kitchener, Ontario. In 2001, after discovering a bee's nest in the truck, Playcon officials took the court to the dump and destroyed it.

Amateur tournaments ended. It was hard to squeeze a four-round tournament into the usual two days when using a softball. The Harry Cowles stopped after February 1995. The Gold Racquets played four-man hardball round robins until Rockaway built softball courts in 2000, then it switched to a small softball tournament. Inter-city and inter-club matches ceased. Leagues dried up. Except for the continued good health of the Lapham-Grant and the arrival, in 1990, of the Copa Wadsworth, a comparable match between Mexico and the United States, the interlocking latticework of annual team competitions was shattered.

Women dropped hardball altogether, with the last nationals occurring in 1994. Canada, America's traditional sister nation, did likewise. In January 1995 at the Canadian hardball nationals, they held a formal funeral service at the Toronto Cricket, Skating and Curling Club and buried Canadian hardball in one final celebratory weekend.

In the United States, there was no such poetic denouement. In the eighties, disgruntled softballers formed splinter organizations; in the nineties, it was hardball's turn. In 1994 Ted Marmor announced the formation of the American Squash Racquets Association. "It is not inept leadership nor lack of interest, it's just that no organization can easily manage competing objectives," Marmor wrote in ASRA's manifesto. "This is not an angry or splinter group of USSRA dissidents. . . . to the extent that the USSRA is an advocate for the future, the ASRA will be a steward of the past." ASRA's board members, Charlie Baker, Walt Smedley and Scott Ryan, were quickly co-opted into the USSRA's hardball committee and a schism was avoided. Baker soon replaced Dave Talbott as chair of the committee and concentrated on the men's hardball nationals, which continued to decline in numbers. One hundred and seventeen men came to Merion in 1996. In successive years, fewer than one hundred would come. In 2001 the tournament bottomed out with just fifty-six players—six in the main draw. Although the numbers recovered slightly in the next two years, and a few new tournaments made almost a semblance of a winter circuit, it was a false dawn. The only hope was in playing hardball on a wide court, a proposition that was beginning to gain adherents.

Coupled with the shredding of the annually restrung web of tournaments, matches and parties was the psychologically damaging destruction of the old voices of the game. Due to worsening relations with a number of USSRA leaders and a propensity to deliver the magazine late, *Squash News* lost its contract as the membership benefit for USSRA cardholders. In October 1997 *Squash Magazine*, a crisp new magazine based in Seattle and run by Jay Prince, a former Cal-Berkeley player, took over. *Squash News* limped along, but in the spring of 1999 Tom and Hazel Jones abandoned publication. Within months, they sold the rights to the U.S. Open back to the USSRA, halted their Grand Prix circuit of softball tournaments and retired to North Carolina. A quarter century of squash promotion ended with their departure. All the major districts including, most tragically, the Met SRA, stopped printing annual yearbooks. Even the USSRA halted its annual yearbook after seventy annual issues dating back to 1923. After the 1995–96 season, no one had a sense of American squash as a single entity. The lists of former champions were no longer at the fingertips of newer players. The season was played in a vacuum. Who won the Hahn Cup? Was it even played?

Slipping into the past like morning mist on the sea, a number of squash giants passed away during this period of transition. In 1990 on Nantucket, Margaret Howe died at age ninety-three. One of the founding matriarchs of the women's game, she was the final remaining link to the bright days of the twenties. In 1994 Mo Khan died outside the doubles court at the Harvard Club in Boston. He was just fifty-six. Nineteen ninety-six was perhaps the worst year. Seymour Knox, III, died at age seventy. Within a week of each other, Lester Cummings, the last of the Cummings brothers, died in Florida and Lou Ballato died in Rockaway. Both men were in their eighties and had begun their professional careers in New York in the squash tennis days of the early thirties. Al Molloy died in the summer of 2000. In April 2001 Tom Page suffered a massive heart attack on a Manhattan street and died surrounded by strangers. In the autumn of 2001 Eddie Hahn died at age eighty-nine. In February 2002 Jack Barnaby died in Boston at the age of ninety-two. The dozens of players and coaches and administrators who came to these funerals buried a sport, not just a beloved person. "I stood up in front of all these people and saw the whole history of hardball," said Peter Briggs who delivered a eulogy at Page's memorial service. "I saw all these famous faces, players who went back to the thirties and forties, players who had won national titles, every decade, every style of play, every famous match. And it struck me that this service was not just for Tommy, but for the game. Hardball was gone. We were mourning the loss of something greater than one of our most precious friends."

Administratively, it was a disaster. Districts shriveled from hundreds of members to dozens. Membership in the USSRA peaked at over ten thousand in 1989; in 2001 just seventy-five hundred people carried USSRA membership cards. Many former supporters were angry at the loss of hardball. Others, with the overwhelming rush of contemporary life, had no time for a new sport.

Mortar and stone threatened to crush squash as Americans rushed to convert their courts. The numbers changed dramatically between 1993 and 2003: 3,000 hardball courts in America in 1993 dropped to 2,000, and 400 softball (and racquetball conversion) courts rose to 1,500. Three new companies became major players in the growing squash construction industry. Gordy Anderson left Playcon and started his own company. David Carr, the director of the second softball nationals in Washington, D.C., in 1984, launched his own company. ASB, the giant German firm, established a U.S. branch under the management of Sparky Lersch, a Delta Air Lines pilot. These companies thrived on the building frenzy.

Bob Callahan predicted, in the heat of the 1994 men's college softball debate, that 50 percent of active colleges would not be able to convert to softball courts by the end of the decade. He was wrong. With the economy enjoying its biggest peacetime expansion in history, more than 90 percent of colleges with varsity teams switched courts. For some facilities it was almost laughably easy to convert. St. Paul's School, still playing in its 1915 building, had narrowed its courts in the thirties by constructing false walls; now, sixty years later, it simply took out the false walls. For many institutions, it was a ghastly age. The Heights Casino in Brooklyn faced a typical problem. In the thirties, the Heights had converted its squash tennis courts into hardball courts. A load-bearing steel girder was added to support these courts and, in the mid-nineties, an extra $50,000 was needed to remove the girder. Two courts ultimately cost the club $350,000. The Racquet & Tennis and the University Clubs spent more than $400,000 per softball court. Top colleges also threw enormous funds into this new money pit. In Jadwin, Princeton slipped softball courts between the steel beams that supported the old hardball courts. Yale, stuck in its cathedral, contemplated a separate facility to sit in Payne Whitney's parking lot as a way to avoid having to reconstruct its fourth-floor courts. Only after raising $10 million was it possible to renovate the fabled courts. Today, Yale has one of the best squash facilities in the world: fifteen glass-back courts, two of which are three-wall glass and one a four-wall glass with a gallery for three hundred people.

The most melancholic result at many clubs was a strange five- or ten-foot-wide space. It looked like an afterthought or a mixup between contractors, but it was the remnants of a hardball court that had been chopped apart to make way for softball. Clubs put Ping-Pong tables, workout equipment, desks or stretching mats in the space, but nothing could mitigate its sad aura of displacement.

Squash after the switch to softball appeared to be a less quirky, less full-blooded USDA prime-cut American game. Gone were the maverick players and quirky clubs and in their stead was a slightly milquetoast homogeneity. Squash was another victim of fin de siècle globalization. Stan Woodworth, the founding spirit of squash in southern California, wrote of the change: "It's hard to believe that those same rawboned players who in our Dodge City days made John McEnroe look like Helen Wills Moody have now thrown away their tank tops and high-laced Keds and, dressed in white (well, almost white) and carrying three or four racquets, discourse learnedly on the theory of the let point or an 'interesting' match they saw last weekend in Detroit." Squash, outside the East Coast, previously had a wild frontier feel to it and softball had swept that aside and replaced it with an anodyne sameness. The cozy Eastern circuit, that "bright and good-humored land," had disappeared, just as the old clubmen had always feared, but the cause was not the expansion of the game and the influx of the middle-class players but rather the introduction of softball. The assured confidence of the old days was gone. The ten-minute annual USSRA executive committee meeting was now a full-day affair, supplemented with telephone conferences and acres of electronic mail messages. It was a profoundly humbling era. No longer "world champions," Americans were now thrown into the neglected depths of the international squash ladder. At the world team championships, the United States played amongst such unexalted squash nations as Malta and Japan. Even the style of the new game seemed symbolic. Fitness was suddenly paramount. Attritional drives and irritating working boasts had replaced the three-wall and the Philadelphia shot. There was a new vocabulary for softball. The referee, when giving out the score, would add, "Game ball" when a player had a game point and "match ball" when a player could end the match. What piffle, many thought. Did Larry Pool or Gretchen Spruance not know when it was match ball? College squash abandoned its longstanding belief in players' sportsmanship. Women's intercollegiate squash switched, in 1994, to the British standard of a referee and a marker, as well as nine-point scoring. The men added refereeing in 1996, but in a unique manner—each team supplied a referee and both had to agree on awarding a stroke, otherwise just a let could be given. The men, moreover, kept fifteen-point scoring until 2001, when they switched to nine point.

The USSRA instituted a rating system based on numbers rather than the traditional A, B, C and D (and, lest we forget, those E players). To veterans, the old system had a comfortable vagueness to it. The B player could be quite good or quite awful and still be a B. Now he was a 3.5 player with specific playing characteristics, delineated in a ratings' matrix, that separated him from the 3.0 and the 4.0 player: "This player is typically not balanced enough to have a wide selection of shots after a dash to the ball."

Reversing the usual one-way street of globalization, overseas coaches motored into the United States to educate the backward Americans. In 2003 the professionals at most of the elite East Coast clubs—the University, Heights Casino, Union, Racquet & Tennis and Southport in New York, Merion Cricket, Germantown Cricket and Cynwyd in Philadelphia and the Harvard Club in Boston—were softball players from other countries. Famous coaches like Bryan Patterson, Ken Hiscoe, Satinder Bajwa and Craig Thorpe-Clark moved to the United States and assumed powerful positions within the squash community. Pat and Richard Millman, an English couple, converted Squash/I, the commercial club in Mamaroneck, outside New York City, to softball, and began what was soon to become one of the hotbeds of squash for the top U.S. players. In 2002 eleven of the thirty-six men's college coaches, including four of the eight Ivy League squads, had a head coach from another country.

The brightest area of hope were the children. In the summer of 1999 Princeton hosted the boys' world juniors championships, the first world softball tournament ever played in America. Although the tournament lost money for Princeton, it exposed Americans to top junior play. In March 2000 the USSRA hired Stephen Gregg, a Trinity graduate, to oversee all junior activities from Cynwyd Road. Junior membership in the USSRA jumped from one thousand in 2000 to over sixteen hundred in 2002. Tournaments became unmanageably large, and for the 2002 junior nationals (which was now restricted to U.S. citizens) Gregg had to close the draws to the top thirty-two ranked entrants. To encourage younger and lower-ranked players, Gregg launched a FutureStars circuit of second-tier tournaments and a FutureStars national championship. Tom Rumpler, a veteran of Park Avenue Squash, dug roots in Atlanta and produced a number of top juniors. In 2000 Michele Quibell, his prize pupil, won the under-seventeen title at the British Open, the best result ever for an American player at the world's top junior tournament. In 2001 Will Broadbent, a Greenwich boy, won the Australian juniors. In world competitions, U.S. junior teams became part of the elite: The girls team secured a fourth place finish in 2001 and the U.S. boys came in seventh in 2002.

Young players traveled to Europe and Australia to improve their games. By the late eighties, beginning with Yale's Will Carlin, all motivated players spent at least their summers overseas, if not going on the PSA tour full time after graduation from college. Camps like Bryan Patterson's in the south of England became as popular as Princeton's or Harvard's. In the summer of 2002, Ken Hiscoe, Mark Devoy and Julieanne Harris & Bill Lane led six-week junior tours of Australia, New Zealand or Africa. The cost per child was over $6,000. Today, any good college player spends his summers overseas, usually training with a gurulike English coach such as Neil Harvey or David Pearson. The flow of young players went both ways, as dozens of overseas youths matriculated at squash colleges. In 2002 over half the All-Americans in both men's and women's intercollegiate squash were from other countries. Trinity, in particular, thrived on top imports. Its men's team broke Harvard's seventy-two match win streak by going undefeated for ninety straight matches. The Trinity varsity in 2001–02 had one American in its top ten.

The newest goal for the young player was the S. L. Green. In 1990 Steve Green, a New York real-estate developer, gave $100,000 to endow a true men's national championship open to amateurs and professionals. Originally, U.S. residents who had lived in the country for at least four years could play in the tournament but, in 1996, it was closed to just U.S. citizens. In 2001 the last vestige of the artificial boundaries between amateurs and professionals died away when the USSRA opened the men's national doubles. The winners of the nationals were the best players. For professional squash players, the S. L. Green was the pinnacle of the year. Otherwise there was not much of a bona fide pro singles tour. There were three major PSA tournaments on the continent. Each had a spectacular site: The WPSA Championships, now called the Tournament of Champions, was played in Grand Central Terminal amidst the bustle of nearly a half-million daily commuters; the YMG Classic was in a Toronto business district atrium (much like the Winter Garden) and, most wonderful of all, the U.S. Open was played in Symphony Hall, Boston's landmark auditorium. However, these were elite tournaments beyond the reach of American players. There were a scattering of second-tier PSA tournaments: Santa Barbara, Salt Lake City, Rochester, Chicago, Westchester, Greenwich, Detroit and, of course, the Hyder. But they, too, were heavily stocked with overseas players, and no native American could win one. For women, the situation was the same. There were solid WISPA tournaments—the Weymuller at the Heights Casino, Vassar, Seattle, Houston, Salt Lake City—and in 2000 Seattle hosted the women's world open but there was nothing like a viable tour. The biggest news was when top-two tour veteran Natalie Pohrer permanently moved to the United States.

Working-class African-American and Hispanic children provided the most exciting development in the first years of American softball squash. In 1996 Greg Zaff launched SquashBusters. A Boston youth-enrichment program for middle schoolers, SquashBusters focused on academic tutoring, community service, cultural outings and mentoring. The boys and girls practiced squash twice a week at the Harvard Club and played in tournaments and team matches on weekends. In 1999 George Polsky started StreetSquash, a version of Zaff's program based in Manhattan. Polsky, a wry Harvard graduate, used courts at Columbia University and the Harvard Club. In 2001 Julie Williams started SquashSmarts at Drexel University in Philadelphia, and in 2002 Tim Wyant, a former Harvard player, started CitySquash at Fordham. These four programs created hundreds of squash lovers from nontraditional squash communities. Polsky added a high-school component to the standard middle-school program, summer camps and book clubs, so that StreetSquash became a full-body immersion for over one hundred and twenty kids per week. The pinnacle of success for these urban squash programs came in 2003 when SquashBusters opened its own freestanding, eight-court, three-classroom $6 million facility on the campus of Northeastern University.

These youth programs are a symbol of the future of the game, but they also reflect the fact that squash is the same as it was a century and a half ago. Right now, somewhere in America a child is walking onto a squash court. Alone, he picks up a bat and begins to hit a ball against a wall.

ACKNOWLEDGMENTS

Four decades ago I first encountered the game of squash under the loving guidance of my mother in the gallery and my father on the court, and it is to these two people that I offer this book as a token of my gratitude. They have read and commented wisely upon numerous drafts, found photographs, provided useful perspectives and have steadfastly, humorously and abundantly encouraged me, whether life was a series of nicks or a skein of tins.

My family—sisters, cousins, aunts, uncles, grandparents and in-laws—have been adamantine advocates for this project. I thank George Plimpton for writing his wonderful foreword, for introducing me to my literary agent and for perfecting the persona of the racquet-wielding writer. Joseph Regal was a staunch defender throughout many tribulations, including when a fellow passenger on the commuter train discharged the contents of his stomach upon my manuscript. At Scribner, Brant Rumble was a brilliantly consistent and companionable editor, and I am grateful for the contributions of Erin Cox, Daniel Cuddy and Charles Scribner, III. Gerard J. Belliveau, Jr., the librarian at the Racquet & Tennis Club, was an indefatigable research ally, and I recall with fondness the many hours poring through the past in the quiet of that famous library. The librarians at the University Archives at Harvard, Harrow School, especially Rita M. Gibbs, British Library, New York Public Library, University of Notre Dame, especially George Rugg, Butler Library at Columbia University and St. Paul's School, especially David Levesque and Jose Ordonez, kindly pointed me in the right directions.

The North American squash community played a decisive role in developing this history. In interviews, conversations and correspondence spread over the years, the following people have offered their time, their knowledge, their libraries and their memories about the game of squash: Samuel F. Abernethy, Robert Adams, Gordon Anderson, James Ardrey, Chris Arriz, Bill Ashcroft, John Asnato, Paul Assaiante, Richard O. Austin, William A. Austin, Pedro Bacallao, Harold d'O. Baker, Charlotte Barnaby, John M. Barnaby, II, Adrian Battersby, John Beddington, George Bell, Jr., Jamie Bentley, Viktor Berg, Leonard Bernheimer, Eliot Berry, Jack Bickel, Hamilton F. Biggar, III, Todd Binns, Margaret Varner Bloss, G. H. Bostwick, Jr., Don Boyko, Sharon Bradey, General James Bragg, Mac Brand, Richard L. Brickley, Jr., Peter S. Briggs, Charles M. P. Brinton, Dean Brown, Doug Brown, Beau Buford, James J. Burke, Jr., John Burke, Joseph Burns, Scott Butcher, W. Keen Butcher, Clive Caldwell, Mac Carbonell, Bill Carlin, Will Carlin, David Carr, John Cashman, Wendell Chestnut, Patrick Chifunda, Edmund Chilton, Richard Chin, John Churchill, Gaetano P. Cipriano, Morris W. Clothier, Benjamin Chaffee Collier, Betty Howe Constable, Janie Coolidge, Joe Coyle, Steve Crandall, Charles T. Crawford, J. D. Cregan, Richard K. Danforth, Howard Day, Jean De Lierre, Charles Dethier, Charlie Devens, Chris Dittmar, Molly Downer, Scott Dulmage, Nathan Dugan, J. Frederick Eagle, III, John Eaton, Edward C. P. Edwards, Marigold Edwards, Margaret Elias, Steiner Ericson, Wink Faulkner, A. Carter Fergusson, Dudy Fergusson, David Fish, John Flanigan, Ken Flynn, Alan L. Fox, Garrett Frank, Robert French, Ned Gallagher,

Acknowledgments

Lolly Gillen, Germain G. Glidden, Christine Glidden, Zerline Goodman, Don Goodwin, Albert Gordon, Christopher Gordon, Joe Gould, Robert Graham, Mariann Greenberg, Thomas Greevy, F. Hastings Griffin, Jr., Herbert H. Gross, Eric Grossman, George A. Haggarty, Edward T. Hahn, George Haines, John Halpern, Howard Harding, Thomas Harrity, Bob Hawthorn, Shannon Hazell, Benjamin H. Heckscher, Maurice Heckscher, II, James Heldring, T. James Hense, Jr., John F. Herrick, James Hewitt, Larry Hilbert, Jamie Hickox, Marty Hogan, Demer Holleran, Joe Hoopes, Willie Hosey, Ernest Howard, Ralph E. Howe, Samuel P. Howe, III, Francis Hunnewell, Hollis Hunnewell, Quentin Hyder, Kenton Jernigan, Kevin Jernigan, Sam Jernigan, Jason Jewell, David C. Johnson, III, Charles T. Johnstone, Thomas Jones, Hazel White Jones, Yasser Kamel, David Kay, George Kellner, William T. Ketcham, Jr., Charlie Khan, Hashim Khan, Jahangir Khan, Latasha Khan, Shabana Khan, Sharif Khan, Charles C. Kingsley, Darwin P. Kingsley, III, Angus Kirkland, Richard Korman, Aggie Bixler Kurtz, Roland Lafontane, Bill Lane, John Lau, Barney Lawrence, Clive Leach, Sparky Lersch, John Lesko, Mark Lewis, Doug Lifford, Jane Lippincott, Katie Long, H. Hunter Lott, Jr., Colby Loud, Alex Luk, Sean M. Lynn-Jones, Malcolm MacColl, Peter MacGuire, Pierce MacGuire, Barbara Maltby, Ted Marmor, Peter Marshall, Brett Martin, Rodney Martin, Drew Mateer, G. Diehl Mateer, Jr., Alicia McConnell, Leigh McCollough, Josh McDonald, Michael P. J. McGorry, Vincent R. McGuinness, Douglas McLaggan, David McNeely, Don McPhail, James McQeenie, Ghirma Meres, Bill Miller, Patrick Miller, Richard Millman, Donald Mills, Alexis B. Miron, Albert Molloy, Jr., Paul Monaghan, Walter Montenegro, Jake Morrissey, Arnold Moss, Damian Mudge, Jeff Mulligan, John Musto, Anil Nayar, Jay Nelson, Peter Nicol, Victor Niederhoffer, Derrick C. Niederman, John G. Nimick, Edward Noll, Friday Odeh, Lucky Odeh, Jeff Osborne, Palmer Page, David Palmer, Simon Parke, Jane Parker, Bryan Patterson, Dylan Patterson, Stanley W. Pearson, Jr., Virginia Pearson, Charles Perkins, Walter F. Pettit, Deborah de Peyster, Michael J. Pierce, Michael Pirnak, Ivy Pochoda, Natalie Pohrer, Steve Polli, George Polsky, Richard Polsky, Beekman H. Pool, J. Lawrence Pool, Henry Poor, Thomas M. Poor, A. Hobart Porter, John Power, Jonathon Power, Michael Puertas, Preston B. Quick, Bill Ramsay, Gail Ramsay, Kirk Randall, Beth Rasin, Neil Reed, John R. Reese, Greg Reiss, Mike Riley, Beau Rivers, David Rosen, Michael Rothenberg, Bill Rubin, Tom Rumpler, Dicky Rutnagur, Jim Sargent, Frank Satterthwaite, Steve Scharff, Larry Sconzo, Eugene Scott, John Sears, Ed Seures, Andrew Slater, Chris Spahr, Gretchen Spruance, Jane Austin Stauffer, Gordon Steele, Ian Stewart, Gary Squires, Dick Squires, Tom Tarantino, Frank Stella, Scott Stoneburgh, Bill Sykes, David Talbott, Douglas Talbott, Mark Talbott, Hoyt Taylor, Mike Taylor, Alan Thatcher, Carol Thesieres, Taylor Thomas, Robert S. Travers, Ming Tsai, Craig Thorpe-Clark, Kim Tunney, Colleen Turner, Edward Ullman, Hugh Underhill, Dale Vargas, Anders Wahlstedt, Gary Waite, Chris Walker, Damian Walker, Edward Wallbutton, Mike Way, Peter Wendt, Ann Wetzel, Carol Weymuller, G. R. White, John White, Robert D. White, III, Ed Whitney, Virginia Whitney, Allison Danzig Whittaker, Doug Whittaker, Howard Wilkins, Melissa Winstanley, Ian Williams, Malcolm Willstrop, Bill Wilson, Peter Wood, Kim Woody, Timothy Wyant, Gregory Van Schaack, Ramsay W. Vehslage, Stephen T. Vehslage, Neal Vohr, Lisa Von Clemm and Greg Zaff.

I appreciate the editorial support of Jay Prince, Amy Boytz and Ryan Lewis at *Squash Magazine*. I also want to thank Hazel White Jones for giving me my start years ago at *Squash News,* Ian McKenzie at *Squash Player,* Amadeo Bianchetti at *International Squash Magazine,* Sherry Funston at *Squash Life,* John Nimick at *Event Engine* and Cullen Murphy at the *Atlantic Monthly.* My fellow squash journalists—Martin Bronstein, Colin McQuillan and Alan Thatcher—have, with their acerbic wit, greatly enhanced the long hours spent in the gallery. Fred Weymuller, a keen squash historian, patiently read through the manuscript, offering corrections and suggestions. I am particularly indebted to a number of people who lent me privately held materials: Charlotte Barnaby, Len Bernheimer, Robert W. Callahan, Leila Cleaves, Bob Drake, Robert Frater, Samuel P. Howe, III, John Nimick, Beekman Pool, Gary Squires and David Talbott. The following photographers kindly granted permission for me to use their excellent pictures: Richard Ashley, Ham Biggar, James A. Drake, Jr., Steve Line, Hugh McLean and Randall Scott. The offices of the United States Squash Racquets Association, under the direction of Craig Brand and with the fine leadership of Stephen Gregg, Mike Hymer, Anne Farrell and Jean McFeeley, located materials and allowed me to pick through their institutional memories.

I would like in the end to thank the person who was there from the beginning, Rebecca L. L. Zug. The nomenclature of squash is rich with metaphor, yet there is just one squash term that describes why this book exists: love.

Squash in America has a long, if intermittant, history of magazine publication.

Squash-Badminton, New York, 1933–35.
The Racquet, New York, 1951–53.
Squash Magazine, New York, 1962–74.
Squash Racquet USA, Salt Lake City, 1973–77.
Racquet Voice, Connecticut, 1978–1992.
Squash News, New York and Rhode Island, 1978–1999.
Squash Magazine, Seattle, 1997–present.

The following is a list of books on squash published in America.

Barnaby, John M. *Squash Racquets in Brief.* Lincoln, MA: privately printed, 1961.
———. *Winning Squash Racquets.* Boston: Allyn and Bacon, 1979. 2nd ed. Hope Valley, RI: Squash News, 1985.
Cooke, Richard C. *Set For Three: A Brief History of Squash Racquets in Massachusetts, 1905–1932.* Boston: privately printed, 1932.
Constable, Betty, and Norman Peck with Dan White. *Squash Basics for Men and Women.* New York: Hawthorn, 1979.
Cowles, Harry L. *A Lesson in Squash Racquets.* New York: Alex Taylor, 1934.
———. *The Art of Squash Racquets.* New York: Macmillan, 1935.
Danzig, Allison. *The Racquet Game.* New York: Macmillan, 1930.
Debany, Walter. *Squash Racquets.* New York: A.S. Barnes, 1950.
Dixon, W. Palmer. *Strokes & Tactics of Squash Racquets.* Cambridge, MA: privately printed, 1925.
Edwards, Marigold A., ed. *Tennis-Badminton-Squash Guide.* Washington, D.C.: American Association for Health, Physical Education and Recreation, 1974. See 1972, 1976 and 1980.
Feron, Stephen J. *Squash and Badminton Handbook.* New York: S. J. Feron, 1934.
Fitzgibbon, Herbert S., II, and Jeffery N. Bairstow. *The Complete Racquet Sports Player.* New York: Simon & Schuster, 1979.
Francis, Austin. *Smart Squash: Using Your Head to Win.* Philadelphia: J. B. Lippincott, 1977.
———. *Smart Squash: How to Win at Soft Ball.* New York: Lyons & Burford, 1995.
Goddard, Adrian. *Squash!: The New Player, The New Game.* New York: St. Martin's Press, 1979.
Hankinson, J. T. *Squash Racquets.* New York: Macmillan, 1946.
Khan, Hashim, with Richard E. Randall. *Squash Racquets: The Khan Game.* Detroit: Wayne State University Press, 1967.
Lindsay, Crawford W., Jr. *The Book of Squash: A Total Approach to the Game.* Dallas: Taylor, 1987.
McKay, Heather, with Jack Batten. *Heather McKay's Complete Book of Squash.* New York: Ballantine, 1979.

Bibliography

Miles, Donald. *Boast*. New York: St. Martin's Press, 1980.

Miles, Eustace. *The Game of Squash*. New York: J. F. Taylor, 1901.

———. *Racquets, Tennis and Squash*. New York: D. Appleton, 1903.

Molloy, Al, Jr., with Rex Lardner. *Sports Illustrated Book of Squash*. Philadelphia: J. B. Lippincott, 1963. Revised ed., 1971.

———. *Winning Squash*. Chicago: Contemporary Books, 1978.

———. *Contemporary Squash*. Chicago: Contemporary Books, 1978.

Potter, Arthur M. *Squash Racquets*. Annapolis, MD: U.S. Naval Institute, 1958. 2nd ed., 1966. 3rd ed., 1968.

Rowland, Jim. *Squash Basics*. New York: Methuen, 1975.

Sales, Pippa. *Improve Your Squash Game: 101 Drills, Coaching Tips and Resources*. Honolulu: Ixia Publications, 1996.

Satterthwaite, Frank. *The Three-Wall Nick and Other Angles (A Squash Autobiography)*. New York: Holt, Rinehart and Winston, 1979.

Skillman, John. *Squash Racquets*. New York: Whittlesey House, 1937. 2nd ed. New York: Ronald Press, 1964.

Squires, Dick. *The Other Racquet Sports*. New York: McGraw-Hill, 1978.

Tompkins, Frederick Charles. *Court Tennis, Racquets and Squash*. Philadelphia: J. B. Lippincott, 1909.

Toombs, Frederick R., ed. *Court Games, Racquets, Squash, Court Tennis, Hand Tennis*. New York: American Sports Publishing, 1904.

Torbet, Laura, with Doug McLaggan. *Squash: How to Play, How to Win*. Garden City, NY: Doubleday, 1978.

Truby, John O., Jr. *The Science and Strategy of Squash*. New York: Charles Scribner's Sons, 1975.

———, and Dr. John O. Truby. *The Secret of Squash: How to Win Using the 4-CRO System*. Boston: Little, Brown, 1984.

Tunis, John. *Sport for the Fun of It: A Handbook of Information on 20 Sports, Including the Official Rules*. New York: A. S. Barnes, 1940.

Varner, Margaret, and Norman B. Bramall. *Squash Racquets*. Dubuque, IA: Wm. C. Brown, 1967.

Widney, Chris, ed. *Keep Eye on Ball: Wisdom of Hashim Khan*. New York: Simon & Schuster, 1996.

Wood, Peter. *The Book of Squash*. New York: Van Nostrand Reinhold, 1972. 2nd ed. Boston: Little, Brown, 1974.

Yarrow, Phillip. *Squash: Steps to Success*. Champaign, IL: Human Kinetics, 1997.

Zuber, Cecil J. *Squash For Players and Coaches*. Englewood Cliffs, NJ: Prentice Hall, 1980.

The photograph on the cover, courtesy of Charlotte Barnaby, is of the 1951 Harvard squash team. In the front row (*l-r*) are Samuel Hoar, Jim Bacon, Henry Foster (captain), Hugh Nawn and David Symmes; in the back row are Jack Barnaby (coach), Wistar Wood, Charlie Ufford, Allston Flagg, David Watts, Jehangir Mugaseth and Larry Pierce (manager). Joe Clark is missing.

PROLOGUE

1 **Squash breeds zealots:** Lance Morrow in *Esquire*, March 1985.
2 **Piet Mondrian in an unhappy mood:** *Signature*, July 1978 and *Travel & Leisure*, December 1979.
4 **madness in an unpadded cell:** Bud Collins in the *Boston Globe*, 13 December 1970.
4 **murder in the court:** This is the title of one of the great books on the game, Jonah Barrington, *Murder in the Squash Court: The Only Way to Win* (London: Stanley Paul, 1982).
4 **winter fugue of snowfall:** "When the game is on, though, it's gut-check time. The object is to run your opponent into coronary arrest by alternating little dinky shots with deep lobs. Then, when he or she is exhausted and stands dripping against a wall, panting for breath, you stick out your hand and act sportsmanlike." Bill Mandel in the *San Francisco Sunday Examiner & Chronicle*, 21 February 1982.
    Perhaps the best description of the inner game of squash comes from Melvin Maddocks in *Sports Illustrated*, 6 January 1975: "Squash will never make it to the Astrodome. It is a game that concentrates rather than expands, moves inward rather than outward. No arena of competition is more strictly defined than a squash court: four sides, a floor, a ceiling. A little white box, like the setting of a Michaelangelo Antonioni movie. Listen— strange echoes! Sound in a squash court cannot be trusted. A laugh has volume but no mirth. The human voice doesn't seem quite human. . . . You are playing against yourself, against your limits. Body, racket and ball vs. mortality. Outside there is a corridor. At the end of the corridor there is a stack of towels, breathing the faintly disinfected air. Up the stairs behind you there is a street swarming with people and flanked with other streets swarming with other people, as far as the eye can see. And, of course, a lot further. The point is, for the moment the universe is reduced to a ball and you in a box. 'Back . . . front . . . left . . . right . . . always running, stroking, running.' Suddenly you go one notch beyond yourself and make the ball do something perhaps no man has ever made a ball do before."

I. THE JOINTS TREMBLED ON THE SPIT

7 **walked around Paris counting:** "The French enjoy the game and play with marvelous grace and dexterity," the ambassador wrote.
8 **court tennis:** In his famous diary Samuel Pepys, a regular spectator at the new court Charles II built in Lord Sandwich's garden at Whitehall, noted that the king weighed himself before and after he played; one day the king lost four-and-a-half pounds. Shakespeare described in *Henry V* the English king's answer to a present of tennis balls from the Dauphin of France: "When we have match'd our rackets to these balls,/We will, in France, by God's grace, play a set/Shall strike his father's crown into the hazard./Tell him he hath made a match with such a wrangler/That all the courts of France will be disturb'd with chases." A favorite Shakespeare quotation, from *Much Ado about Nothing*, brings a grin to every wife who has grumbled about her unshaven husband: "Don Pedro: 'Has any man seen him at the barber's?' Claudio: 'No; but the barber's man hath been seen with him; and the old ornament of his cheek hath already stuffed tennis balls.'"

Notes

8 **disemboweled a man:** Caravaggio was not his real name, but rather the name of the village in Italy from whence he came. In late May 1606, he killed Ranuccio Tomassini in campo Marzio, near the Tuscan ambassador's palace. See Peter Robb, *M—The Man Who Became Caravaggio* (New York: Henry Holt, 2001) and Helen Langdon, *Caravaggio: A Life* (New York: Farrar, Straus & Giroux, 1998). It is not clear exactly what caused the deadly argument between Caravaggio and Tomassini, but one reason often given was that Caravaggio was upset about a fault call.

8 **played at royal palaces:** When Henry VIII was informed of the beheading of Anne Boleyn, he was, legend has it, engaged in a game of tennis. In reality, this is probably untrue. He kept to his house and garden during the day of the beheading, then left by barge to see Jane Seymour upon hearing the news. The tennis connection, though, is still a part of the sad story. When the king's men found Boleyn and arrested her, she was watching tennis at Greenwich, awaiting the result of a bet on a chase. Court tennis players in the United States in the 1980s were touched by her fate and named a leading amateur women's tournament after her.

  For further investigation of the origins of tennis, the following books are the classics: Robert W. Henderson, *Ball, Bat & Bishop: The Origins of Ball Games* (New York: Rockport Press, 1947); E. B. Noel and J. O. M. Clark, *History of Tennis*, two volumes (Oxford: Oxford University Press, 1924); Julian Marshall, *The Annals of Tennis* (London: Horace Cox, 1878) and Malcolm Whitman, *Tennis Origins and Mysteries* (New York: Derrydale Press, 1932). Three recent books of interest are Heiner Gillmeister, *Tennis: A Cultural History* (New York: New York University Press, 1997); Roger Morgan, *Tudor Tennis: A Miscellany* (Oxford: Ronaldson Publications, 2001) and Lord Aberdare, *The J.T. Faber Book of Tennis & Rackets* (London: Quiller Press, 2001). See also, R. Brasch, *How Did Sports Begin: A Look at the Origins of Man at Play* (New York: David McKay, 1970).

9 **without the necessary banns:** Fleet chaplains performed six thousand marriages a year in the prison until Parliament passed an act forbidding the practice. On 25 March 1754, the day before the act came into force, 217 unions were blessed in a final burst of matrimonial bliss.

9 **this Rabelaisian life:** For history of the Fleet and London in this era, see Roger Lee Brown, *A History of the Fleet Prison, London: The Anatomy of the Fleet* (Lampeter, Wales: Edwin Mellon Press, 1996); Richard Byrne, *Prisons and Punishments of London* (London: Harrap, 1989); Anthony Babington, *The English Bastille: A History of Newgate Gaol and Prison Conditions in Britain, 1188–1902* (London: Macdonald, 1971); Thomas Burke, *English Night Life: From Norman Conquest to Present Black-out* (London: B.T. Batsford, 1941). The House of Commons closed the Fleet in 1842. Roshan Khan's club in Karachi in the 1970s was called the Fleet.

10 **supported a family of seven:** Hoskins, a Cornish man, was brought up a gentleman with a surgeon for a father. He spent thirty-eight years at the King's Bench with just a single debt held against his name. He disputed the debt and vowed he would never pay it. He ended up living in a shed sharing his food with a mouse. He died in December 1823.

11 **"highest grade of society":** The best source on nineteenth century racquets remains J. R. Atkins, *The Book of Racquets: With Original and Practical Illustrations—A Practical Guide to the Game and its History and to the Different Courts in Which it is Played* (London: Frederick Warne, 1872). See also Duke of Beaufort, editor, *Tennis, Lawn Tennis, Rackets and Fives* (London: Badminton Library, 1890); Lord Abedare, editor, *The Lonsdale Library of Sports, Games & Pastimes, vol. XVI: Rackets, Squash Rackets, Tennis, Fives and Badminton* (London: Seeley Service, 1930 and Philadelphia: J. B. Lippincott, 1930); E. B. Noel and Lord Abedare, *First Steps to Rackets* (London: Mills & Boon, 1926).

  For fives, see David Egerton and John Armitage, *Eton and Rugby Fives: A Complete Handbook of Practical Advice, Instruction and Rules* (London: Seeley Service, 1939). Fives, like racquets, was inherently social, as Egerton and Armitage explained: "Fives is very definitely fun. It is a sociable game, in which universal reputations cannot be lost or won. A Fives court is rarely remarkable for the tenseness of the silence, broken only by the clock of balls against the walls and the thud of a man's hand; it is a rather jolly place, because it is so intimate. There is time in between the rallies to admire the play of an opponent, and there is never reason to doubt that the next good shot may be one of your own. Perhaps this applies more to doubles than to singles, for singles can be very exhausting and not in the least jolly." A. C. Ainger, in 1890, also noted the garrulousness of the fives player: "It is the most sociable of games. . . . In the fives court partners and adversaries are close together, the noise of the ball does not drown the voice, and there is plenty of opportunity for talk and chaff and laughter without interfering in the least with a businesslike game. . . . There is nothing in fives, no doubt, like the joy of a fine left-handed catch or a drive to the ropes."

11 **between Hester and Canal:** Canal Street was originally called Pump Street and, when the racquets court was built there it was called Walker Street. The court was 120 feet long, with no roof, wooden floors and four stone walls.

12 **"happiest hours of my school":** Since the Corner and other places to play racquets on the old schoolyard were not bounded by four walls, Harrovians invented a new type of servant or "fag," the "racquets-fag." The fag was a younger boy who would retrieve cricket balls, light fires or do other menial jobs for upperclassmen. Sir Douglas Straight, class of 1860, wrote: "Racquet-fagging next comes under consideration, and that is the slowest of all—wretched, dreary, miserable work, without a redeeming feature of any kind of description. There you have to go and stand with your back against a wall, very often getting your toes trodden on, and being pitched into for blundering in the way. All the business you have to perform is to go round and pick up the balls that have been knocked out of court. . . . As to racquet-fagging, it really is a thing to escape if possible—not from its hardship but its excessive dullness and stupidity. And besides all that, as a general rule, the play you have to look on at is not of the highest order, for really good players would rather have fags out of the way altogether; somehow or other they are sure to spoil a good stroke if it is to be done. Occasionally, however, there are very interesting matches, especially those for the championship racquet, which contest has brought out such fine players at V. E. and R. D. Walker, Ainslie, Plowder and Maitland. Then a large crowd of spectators assemble, and there is no lack of applause, and some rare close fights have taken place. Old boys come down and look on, and make more noise than the young ones, as somehow or other they always do whenever they have the opportunity, and not infrequently chair the victor up the school steps into the yard to Sam's room." Sam was "custos," the custodian, racquets coach and general dean of the school.

12 **still playable today:** The 1865 racquets court is slightly larger than what is now the standard size.

13 **men like Charles Goodyear:** The U.S. government issued Charles Goodyear Patent No. 3633 on 15 June 1844, which granted him a short-lived reign as America's rubber monopolist. See Richard Korman, *The Goodyear Story: An Inventor's Obsession and the Struggle for a Rubber Monopoly* (San Francisco: Encounter Books, 2002) and Charles Slack, *Noble Obsession: Charles Goodyear, Thomas Hancock and the Race to Unlock the Greatest Industrial Secret of the Nineteenth Century* (New York: Theia, 2002).

13 **bastardized version of racquets:** Charles R. Read, *Squash Rackets* (London: William Heinemann, 1929). Read went up to Harrow in 1903 to work as a "boy" for Judy Stevens. The boys protected their yards as fiercely as the older boys did their courts at Old Schools. There were eleven different house yards, and as R. Stewart-Brown, class of 1891, wrote in 1938, "It was seldom that a boy went into another house, and if that involved passing through the squash yard, every effort would be made to 'cut off' (not 'cut over,' which is, I think, Etonese) the stranger and intruder. So one saw but little of other house courts." "Give a Harrow boy a wall—if a blank one so much the better—and two others,

or even one other, at right angles to it, with a clear space between, and the probability is it won't be long before he is busy at squash racquets," wrote Somerville Gibney in *The Boy's Own Paper*, 1890.

13 **continued to buy his squash balls:** Punch & Judy came from the game of racquets. Punch, known as H. B. "Cecil" Fairs, and Judy, a Mr. Stevens, were racquets pros at Prince's. Stevens then moved out to Harrow, where he was became racquets coach. He dined out on the fact he had beaten the great Peter Latham in racquets (when Latham was still young). Fairs, five foot four, became world racquets champion in 1876, beating one of the Gray brothers, Joseph, decisively at Prince's and Rugby. Two years later, though, he died. His son, H. B. Fairs, Jr., was also known as Punch and was world champion in tennis from 1905 to 1907 and 1908 to 1912. In 1915 Punch moved to New York to take charge of Harbor View Court on Clarence Mackay's estate in Roslyn, Long Island. Allison Danzig describes going out to Roslyn one spring day in 1929 and finding an elderly Punch taking his constitutional through the countryside with his collie.

14 **"sprung the idea":** Hart-Dyke opened his letter by writing that "I read with the greatest interest Lord Dunedin's letter regarding the early history of squash rackets, especially at Harrow School. That interest was much stimulated by Lord Dunedin's allusion to me as 'Billy Dykes, taken from us not very long ago.' The sadness of the situation is happily relieved by the plural, and all grief may be reserved for a departed twin brother." Hart-Dyke died in 1931 at the age of ninety-three.

16 **In 1978 Julian Marshall:** Marshall based his reasoning entirely upon one citation to "racket" in Chaucer. As Henderson pointed out, Marshall was using an error-filled edition of Chaucer, in which the spelling is normally "raket." Furthermore, the game of raket at the time of Chaucer was a dice game. See *Squash Rackets & Fives*, September 1936.

16 **no inferiority complex:** For more information on Harrow, see E. D. Laborde, *Harrow School: Yesterday and Today* (London: Winchester, 1948); Charles Wordsworth, *Annals of My Early Life, 1806–1846, With Occasional Compositions in Latin and English Verse* (London: Longmans, Green, 1891); Duke of Beaufort, *The Badminton Library of Sports and Pastimes: Tennis, Lawn Tennis, Rackets and Fives* (London: Longmans, Greens, 1890); Lord Desborough, editor, *Fifty Years of Sport: At Oxford, Cambridge and the Great Public Schools—Eton, Harrow and Winchester* (London: Walter Southwood, 1922); Sidney Daryl (Sir Douglas Straight), *School Days at Harrow* (London: George Routledge, 1867); J. G. Cotton Minchin, *Old Harrow Days* (London: Methuen, 1898); Rev. H. J. Torre, *Recollections of School Days at Harrow: More than Fifty Years Ago* (Manchester: Charles Simms, 1888); Percy M. Thornton, *Harrow and Its Surroundings* (London: W. H. Allen, 1885); Edmund W. Howson and George Townshend Warner, editors, *Harrow School* (London: Edward Arnold, 1898), especially Charles S. Roundell, "Harrow in the Forties" and M. C. Kemp, "Rackets"; and Ernest Bell, editor, *Bohn's Library of Sports and Games: Athletic Sports*, vol.1 (London: George Bell & Sons, 1890). My favorite book from this era, though, is one this publisher issued—*An Envoy Extraordinary, King Squash of Toadyland* (New York: Scribner & Welford, 1890).

II. Heaven's Heaviest Artillery

17 **was more charitable:** See A. S. Pier, *St. Paul's School, 1855–1934* (New York: Charles Scribner's Sons, 1934) and August Heckscher, *St. Paul's: The Life of a New England School* (New York: Charles Scribner's Sons, 1980).

18 **also played racquets:** The St. George Street court was sixty by thirty feet but the back wall was not at right angles—the left side was slightly obtuse, the right slightly acute. The club was highly exclusive, with only thirty-odd members. The Montreal Rackets Club moved in 1889 to its present location on Concord Street. See Christopher G. Marks, *Rackets in Canada and the Montreal Racket Club* (privately printed, 1990).

18 **cement was the norm:** For example, the racquets court at the Gymnasium Club, built by Edward La Montagne on bucolic Thirteenth Street at Sixth Avenue, was seventy feet by thirty and had a wooden floor. This club hosted the first leg of the world racquets championship in April 1866. When St. Paul's boys visited the Racquet Court Club in New York each Christmas, they found a larger court with stone rather than wooden walls, conditions quite different from their cozy little courts in Concord.

18 **"if Papa thinks":** Jean Strouse, *Morgan: American Financier* (New York: Random House, 1999), p. 203.

19 **detained for months:** *Squash Rackets, Fives, Tennis and Rackets,* 22 October 1932. In an article on "Fives in Foreign Climes" a writer tells of trouble getting fives balls through customs in Brazil, because officials thought the balls were small bombs. In 1874 the Outerbridges, bringing back from Bermuda the newfangled game of lawn tennis, also had trouble explaining their gear at customs in New York.

20 **a young sports reporter:** Allison Danzig, *The Racquet Game* (New York: Macmillan, 1930). Published in January 1930, it remains the standard work on the history of American court tennis, racquets and squash tennis. Danzig (1899–1987), was born in Waco, where his father was a timber merchant. He played football at Cornell for Gloomy Gil Dobie and joined the *Times* in 1923. He coined the tennis term the Grand Slam and was the first journalist inducted into the International Tennis Hall of Fame.

20 **at his alma mater:** Gordon also built a squash court at his eponymous boys boarding school in Garrison, New York. The court still stands today, though it is sadly not in use.

21 **"the game was started":** On squash tennis, see: John R. Tunis, *Sport$: Heroes and Hysterics* (New York: John Day, 1928) and *Sport for the Fun of It: A Handbook of Information on 20 Sports Including the Official Rules* (New York: A. S. Barnes, 1940); George M. Rushmore, *Squash Tennis* (privately printed, 1949); and Dick Squires, *The Other Racquet Sports* (New York: McGraw-Hill, 1978) and *Squash Tennis* (privately printed, 1968). For more on Dick Squires and squash tennis, see *Smoke* magazine, Summer 1998. Perhaps because of the bifurcated nature of squash tennis, its origins are up for debate. Danzig argued that it was invented in the middle eighteen nineties in a barn in West Superior, Wisconsin. Charles A. Chase, the first lawn tennis champion of the Midwest, had built a small indoor court made of pine. In 1968 Dick Squires said St. Paul's boys started it but ten years later he fingers Feron at the Harvard Club as the founder.

21 **"act like a cocktail":** See Hal Higdon, *Boston: A Century of Running* (Emmaus, PA: Rodale Press, 1995) for a history of the BAA and its Boston Marathon.

22 **behind its clubhouse:** It is believed that the court, still standing and playable today, was built in 1890. It measures thirty-one feet three inches by nineteen-and-a-half feet. See *Author Escaped, Not a History of the Dedham Polo Club: Containing Accurate Misstatements Concerning the Club from 1893–1907* (privately printed, 1907).

22 **immediately flourished:** The BAA, meanwhile, started a slow decline. Its symbol was the head of a unicorn, but the magic of its opening night soon dissipated. In 1935 it went bankrupt. Boston University bought the clubhouse, which was torn down in 1961 to make way for a new wing of the Boston Public Library. The lasting legacy of the BAA is its Boston Marathon, first run by fifteen club members in 1897 and still under its control. Ten of the fifteen runners finished the first marathon; the winning time was 2:55:10.

22 **a six-inch hole:** *The Illustrated Sporting News: Dedicated to Sport and Outdoor Life,* 30 January 1904. One hundred and fifty men, from the BAA and Racquet & Tennis Club, gave a total of $80,000 to help pay for the court. No one gave less than $100 and six men gave $5,000 each. For more on Tuxedo, see George M. Rushmore, *The World With a Fence Around It: Tuxedo Park—The Early Days* (New York: Pageant Press, 1957) and Jennet Conant, *Tuxedo Park: A Wall Street Tycoon and the Secret Palace of Science that Changed the*

Course of World War II (New York: Simon & Schuster, 2002). "Tuxedo" meant in a local Native American tongue, the place of the bear.

23 **Wheatley Hills:** His own personal full-time professional, Walter Kinsella, went on to become world champion in squash tennis from 1914 to 1926.

23 **almost every city:** Buffalo, Chicago, Baltimore, Princeton, New Haven, Hartford, Rochester, Boston, Philadelphia, Washington, Detroit, Cincinnati, St. Louis, Omaha and Denver all had squash tennis courts. Havana even had one.

23 **Merion Cricket Club:** Tucked in between the kitchen and the bowling alley, the three old squash tennis courts were the first places many of the most famous names in squash first hit a squash ball. One was lost in 1965 when Merion demolished it to make way for a doubles court, but the other two survived until 1986. As a child, I grew up playing on them. Called "junior" courts, they were small and gloomy. One had no gallery and no windows. See Eustace Miles, "Anybody's Game: Squash, and How to Play It" in *Outing* magazine, 1903.

23 **sixteen-candlepower:** *The Illustrated Sporting News: Dedicated to Sport and Outdoor Life*, 6 February 1904. "The game of squash," J. J. McNamara wrote, "is more of an exercise pastime than a sport like racquets or tennis."

24 **on its old fives courts:** When the Racquet & Tennis Club built its new clubhouse on West Forty-third Street in 1891, it installed a fives court. Bob Moore, then the head professional at the R&T, told Danzig in the late 1920s that neither squash nor squash tennis nor even fives was played on the court. Instead they were used for boxing and fencing.

25 **"than a potato":** The writer for the 1913–14 National Squash Tennis Association yearbook spoke of the usual resistance from the newcomer: "Those who have not seen squash well played are inclined to scoff at the pastime and to speak lightly of those who find pleasure in batting a ball within four walls."

26 **squash tennis was listed:** In 1933 squash tennis players challenged squash racquets players in New York to a duel. They played each other's games one afternoon at the Harvard Club. "Squash racquets players were absolutely at sea in the squash tennis court," a squash magazine reported. "The speed of the ball and the myriad of angles from which it shot out at them were as mysterious when they went off the court as when they had entered it. The squash tennis players found it relatively simple to hit the squash ball and even to keep it in play; to score a point with it was more mystifying."

26 **"force had too great a hand":** *Newsweek*, 27 March 1937.

26 **"more than ordinary endurance":** Because of the ultrafast ball, squash tennis racquets broke weekly. More than one player thought, according to Allison Danzig, that squash tennis was "the nefarious invention of professionals who found not enough racquets were being broken nor enough balls being used up at squash racquets to bring them sufficient emoluments in their role as concessionaires." Herbert Warren Wind ended his 1962 *Holiday* article on squash by repeating "the oldest and squarest of the game's special jokes, the one about the clubman who was asked if he preferred a breathtakingly pretty woman or a good squash match. The clubman frowned deep in thought for almost a minute. 'Now which do you mean?' he finally said, 'squash racquets or squash tennis.'"

27 **Norman Torrance:** *The New Yorker*, 4 August 1951. See *New York Times*, 6 February 1966 and Met SRA yearbook, 1953.

28 **nonmedal demonstration:** They were actually playing *frontenis*, a Native American version of squash tennis that was popular in Latin America. Both *frontenis* and *paleta*, another Latin American game, were the two demonstration sports. As captain, Squires appeared on the *Today Show*, the *Wall Street Journal* put a story on the team on its front page and *Saturday Night News* showed a five-minute documentary on the team. The squad included: Billy Tully, Herman Schaefer, Pedro Bacallao, Aaron Daniels, John Halpern, Al Collins, Fred Vinton and Squires. In 1970 Squires organized a team to go to the world pelota championships in San Sebastian, Spain. The team included Collins, Tully, Halpern,

Squires, Bacallao, Tom Jones, Kingman Lambert, Ted Dietrich, Dwight Lowell and Bob Ryan.

28 **the remaining heavyweights:** Bacallao and Squires also faced each other in a 1983 exhibition, in which Bacallao won in three games.

28 **come and gone:** see *Atlantic Monthly,* January 2002.

28 **moved into a home:** John J. W. F. McFadden, *The Racquet Club of Philadelphia* (privately printed, 1989).

29 **Abraham Lincoln:** David Herbert Donald, *Lincoln* (New York: Simon & Schuster, 1995), p.250.

29 **"Hand-Fives":** E. Patten, editor, *The Book of Sport,* two volumes (New York: J.F. Taylor, 1903). Bat-fives was another English public school, nineteenth-century invention similar to squash. The type of ball, racquet, size of court and scoring varied. The rules at one school, Harrenden, were as follows: There were two standard balls, a squash ball and a racquets ball; the racquets twenty-two inches long with a head six-and-a-half by four-and-a-half inches, weighing five ounces; the court was twenty-nine feet by eighteen, with a thirty-inch tin; and scoring like racquets. Some of the courts originally did not have back walls. H. B. Evington, in the February 1933 issue of *Squash Rackets & Fives,* wrote: "I am inclined to regard bat-fives as the ideal busy man's game, so long as he retains the necessary agility and quickness of eye. It is faster and more fun that Squash Racquets, as one can get real effect out of a low, hard shot down a side wall. It has another value, I think, for the young schoolboy in that it would appear to be a good introduction to Rackets."

29 **owner of the Philadelphia Phillies:** In 1905 Potter reported to the Racquet Club's annual meeting that "many squash players have moved to the more important game of racquets, the object for which squash was originally intended." Potter, a keen court tennis and racquets player, served as president of the club from 1897 to 1912 and remained on its board until his death in 1934. He once dove into the club's pool without first checking to see whether there was any water. There was not. Somehow he was not killed.

30 **at their homes:** Barclay Warburton, Thomas McKean, Jr. and Thomas Wanamaker built courts as well. The McKean court, at 1923 Walnut Street, still exists in the Catholic Philopatrian Literary Institute. Wanamaker's was on the top floor of his townhouse and reached by a separate elevator.

30 **Philadelphia Inter-Club:** The association kept the delightfully quaint "inter-club" in its official name until 1978.

30 **whether serving or not:** *Public Ledger* (Philadelphia), 16 January 1916. The article has a photograph of E. M. Spangler and G. B. Pfingst, Jr. on court at the Cynwyd Club. The article was bylined "C. L. Ubman" and headlined: 'GALLERY' IS APROPOS WHEN APPLIED TO SQUASH RACQUETS: SQUASH RACQUETS HOLDS THRILLS EVEN FOR THE UNINITIATED: SPEED AND SKILL WOULD MAKE IT POPULAR IF GALLERY WERE NOT RESTRICTED. The article discusses other unique aspects of early twentieth-century squash: some courts had ventilators in the tin; the service circle was placed outside the service box, rather than inside; netting protected the gallery; strings on the squash racquet were not as closely woven as a racquets racquet; and as for the standard squash costume, "heavy socks should be worn to protect the feet from the severe usages of the cement floor." Squash, the article concluded, was a most valuable preparatory game for future devotees of racquets and court tennis, and one could play and practice by artificial light with good results, a privilege racquets denied to its followers.

30 **In 1912:** The captains were Merion, S. H. LeBoutillier and S. V. B. Patterson; Germantown, A. G. R. White and B. S. Peacock; HVCC, George Elkins and Arthur Rush; Overbrook, S. P. Edwards and Racquet Club, Tevis Huhn. The 1913 Inter-Club teams finished the season as follows: Racquet Club went 29–7, Merion 23–13, Germantown's B team 13–23, Merion's B team 12–24, HVCC 7–19 and Overbrook 6–30.

31 **Frank White:** See the 1961–62 Met SRA yearbook for a photograph of White.

31 **"merits its obvious vogue":** Cooke, *Set for Three*.

31 **At the MSA's annual meeting:** George Morison appointed Speare, Fred Hovey and Philip Nicols to a subcommittee, with Herbert Windler of The Country Club as chair, to look into switching games.

31 **first state championship:** The Massachusetts SRA lists Quincy Shaw as state champion in 1905 and 1906 and Ray Speare in 1907 (both as members of the Boston Athletic Association), yet it appears they were still playing squash tennis at that time.

31 **three or four men:** In some years the USSRA counted as a match in the nationals when the number one players from two cities played each other during their national teams match. For example in 1913 Harold Haines, the Maryland state champion, beat Beverly Robinson, the Toronto number one (and runner up in the Canadian national championship), when Baltimore played Toronto. Likewise Mort Newhall of Philadelphia beat Constantine Hutchins of Boston in their team match. In the one-match individual tournament to determine the 1913 national champion, Newhall beat Haines 3–0. Newhall had won the 1913 thirteen-man Pennsylvania state tournament by beating Tevis Huhn 3–1 in the semis and Bill Freeland in the finals.

34 **no matter how outlandish:** See *Toronto Sun*, 20 February 1981; John Horry, *The History of Squash Rackets*, p. 70 and "130 Years of World Squash," Ted Wallbutton, 1996, www.squash.org on the web.

35 **no such brake on court:** One other explanation exists for why America had a different court size, that at some point we took the average width of all the courts in the country. Narrowness from squash tennis courts would have skewed the average. See Stewart Brauns in the program for the Australian Squash Championships, Hobart, September 1971. In 1928 the USSRA officially adopted wood as the material for all walls in a squash court. In August 1931 the USSRA further adjusted its rules by raising the back wall by two inches and the service line by six inches. This was a part of a compromise with the National Squash Tennis Association, which then agreed to make squash courts the standard for squash tennis.

35 **English let rule:** No longer did players, as *The New Yorker* wrote on 28 February 1933, "simply move to the middle after every shot and were thus assured of either a let or a chance to play a completely defensive return." See Bellamy, *Squash*, p. 23.

36 **"stale balls might":** *American Lawn Tennis*, 15 November 1911. Founded by S. Wallis Merrihew in 1907 and the official organ of the U.S. National Lawn Tennis Association, the magazine ran until 1951.

36 **flew like a bullet:** Seamless took over Hewitt and manufactured the Hewitt ball in the thirties before making their own ball.

36 **on these courts:** Brian Mutimer, *History of Squash Racquets in Canada* (Edmonton: William F. Dowbiggin, 1973), p. 15.

36 **with no back wall:** After finishing at Marlborough, Outerbridge joined his brothers in Canada and won the Canadian nationals in 1914 and 1920. Outerbridge's aunt Mary was the woman who first brought lawn tennis to America.

37 **continental friction:** A secondary reason for painted floors was that some players believed the standard crepe-soled shoe checked too abruptly on an unpainted floor.

37 **Some built courts:** Somerville Gibney and his brother, also an alum, built a court in a loft above a stable at their father's home. *The Boy's Own Paper*, 1890.

37 **long winter months:** David Milford picked up squash at the Harcourt court and later went on to become world champion in racquets from 1937 to 1947. Simon Harcourt started the Royal Automobile Club's annual tournament in 1912 and co-managed the Bath Club Cup in the 1920s and '30s.

38 **dubbed "The Long Court":** Roy McKelvie, *The Queen's Club Story, 1886–1986* (London: Stanley Paul, 1986).

38 **old coachhouses:** Atkins, *Book of Racquets*, described the game of "chamber practice" in "room courts" with the wainscoting providing the board. Atkins reminded players to wire windows in order to prevent angry parental interference. Eustace Miles told of playing squash "in many of the rooms at Lambeth Palace; and once we played out in the pool."

38 **stické and squash:** Stické was a hybrid game of court tennis and lawn tennis. It was played indoors on a wooden court tennis court. There was no standard layout, but most courts had a penthouse and galleries. None had chase lines. The ball was a large uncovered rubber ball. The Royal Artillery built the first court in 1874 at Shoeburyness. Other courts appeared across Great Britain, in India, Nova Scotia, Ottawa, South Africa and Malta. Even Buckingham Palace had a court, which was later converted into a swimming pool.

38 **"It seems almost a pity":** H. A. L. Rudd also complained of the pities of standardization in *Baily's Magazine*, March 1923.

39 **"refusing a service":** *The Games of Tennis, Rackets and Fives: A Handbook* (London: Mudie & Sons, 1912).

39 **inestimable advantages:** The Bath Club courts did, however, have steel girders that ran across the top of the court and which made lobbing a precarious proposition.

40 **New Zealand:** Even into the fifties, New Zealand maintained its own rules. Most interestingly, Kiwis could not appeal for lets, which only referees were allowed to give. Also, there was no such thing as a let point.

40 **Jeu de Paume:** Lord Fermoy's brother Francis Roche, was the founder of the Paris Squash Racquets Association and the chief financier of the Jeu de Paume courts. Danzig suggested that courts were installed in a court tennis court, rather than a racquets court. Either way, it explains the cement floor.

41 **Appalled by the two:** See 1952–53 SRA annual yearbook, for minutes compiled by H. E. Hayman. Also, the two histories of softball squash are helpful: John Horry, *The History of Squash Rackets* (Brighton, England: A. C. M. Webb, 1979) and Rex Bellamy, *Squash: A History* (London: Cassell, 1978), revised edition (London: Heinemann Kingswood, 1987).

41 **they chose the Wisden:** "It will seem an extraordinary thing that the smallest implement in the game of Squash Rackets should give so much trouble," wrote Charles Read, "but the fact remains that the ball is the point on which individual authorities disagree at the present moment. . . . prejudice dies hard and individual opinions of well-known players, prejudiced perhaps through using an old court when practicing, continue to carry weight." Charles R. Read, *Squash Rackets* (London: William Heinemann, 1929). Even as late as 1938, the pros', men's and women's associations all used different balls for their championships.

42 **least of worries:** See *Squash Rackets & Fives*, 1938. A 1938 SRA questionnaire found that 40 percent of members were in favor of switching to American scoring. Even after the Second World War, when the issue had been settled, British squash players aired their complaints. "I would say therefore that present-day Squash has departed too far from its origins," wrote Max Robertson in 1950. "The ball is very soft and is too easily returned. This encourages bad footwork and ugly shots. Squash is following the pattern of modern life, grace giving way to utility." See *British Lawn Tennis & Squash*, March 1950. In 1954 one-fifth of SRA-member clubs tried out American scoring, but nearly 90 percent of the clubs voted to keep to British scoring.

III. DON'T KEEP LATE HOURS

45 **They rented for:** See Bainbridge Bunting, *Harvard: An Architectural History*, Margaret Henderson Floyd, editor (Boston: Harvard University Press, 1985); Douglass Shand-Tucci, *Boston Bohemia: Ralph Adams Cram, Life and Architecture, 1881–1900* (Amherst: University of Massachusetts Press, 1995); *Education, Bricks and Mortar—Harvard Buildings and*

Their Contribution to the Advancement of Learning (Boston: Harvard University Press, 1949); Harold Jefferson Coolidge and Robert Howard Lord, *Archibald Cary Coolidge—Life and Letters* (Boston: Houghton Mifflin, 1932) and Wendell D. Garrett, *Apthorp House, 1760–1960* (Boston: Adams House, 1960).

45 **large athletic building:** Wetmore, ever the rival, also put in a court in Claverly, with a cement floor and wooden walls. Randolph Hall's official address was 47–57 Bow Street, while the squash courts were at 8 Linden Street. See the *Literary Digest,* 5 January 1935.

45 **Coolidge gave:** Coolidge actually exchanged Randolph for College Hall, a neglected building on Harvard Square that had housed law school students. He himself kept his room in Randolph and lived there until his death in 1928.

46 **two kegs of floor nails:** The total cost was $11,458.81. One of the new courts, court seven, was "unusually wide" according to Germain Glidden. It was remodeled to U.S. standards in 1936, and Glidden believed that the loss of a wide court was the reason why Yale beat Harvard in 1937. See *Squash Rackets Annual,* 1937–38, p. 11.

46 **gathered there in anticipation:** The *Harvard Alumni Bulletin* queried, with some irony, if the signup sheet could be moved to Appleton Chapel, so as to ensure promptness at daily church services.

47 **"snug in-door activity":** *The Bulletin* also disagreed with Geer's suggestion that squash was a desirable exercise for women, arguing that this was an entering wedge for the "insidious threat of co-education." Archibald Telesphore LaRochelle was the mainstay of the University Squash Courts. An employee of the Harvard Athletic Association, LaRochelle ran the squash courts at Randolph for fifty years. He sat at a desk at the front door and was a discerning critic of players' styles. According to Jack Barnaby, he "had a magician's knack of producing an empty court when some regular player had for once forgotten to make his reservation on time. It is whispered he borrowed from Adams House."

47 **migrated alone:** Pettitt did have a younger brother, William, who later coached tennis at the Boston Athletic Association.

47 **went for openings:** "His style on his first appearance in England was strange, wild, barbaric, untutored and apparently developed out of an inner consciousness or acquired in contests with 'the hairy-faced baboon/In the mountains of the moon,'" wrote the *Saturday Review,* 23 May 1885, after Pettitt won the world championship of tennis. "He met with but small favor from the cold eye of criticism, which was offended by the eccentricities of his play, some of which clashed irreconcilably with the pure traditions of classic canons of taste in tennis." Pettitt played in the first pro lawn tennis contest in August and September 1889, losing two out of three legs to George Kerr in Newport, Springfield and Brookline.

47 **while wearing roller skates:** Allison Danzig, who discovered winter racquet sports in the 1920s, was awed by Pettitt and by the myths surrounding him: "In America Pettitt has been a figure of almost epic proportions around whom were woven tales that spread and grew with each retelling like the folklore and chansons of the middle ages. His feats in the tennis courts had to be seen to be believed." Pettitt was the only man who had seen every national tennis championship held in Newport, from 1881 until the nationals left for New York in 1915. See *American Lawn Tennis,* 15 November 1914. An Italian word, *casino* originally meant a country house but soon was used for a building where one could dance, play sports, listen to music and gamble. In 1851 the gambling sense of the word began to gain precedence.

48 **stringing squash racquets:** See *Boston Herald,* 11 December 1958. Cowles also worked at the Tedesco Club.

48 **Cowles retired from active play:** Cowles suggested that the reason he withdrew from competitive play was that he did not want to sully the good name of Harvard by placing its varsity coach in the position where he could lose a tournament match.

48 **found the scope:** Cowles also became the varsity men's tennis coach. The Harvard Club were none too happy to see Cowles leave. "There was a feeling among some members of

the Commonwealth Avenue organization that Alma Mater was stepping over the bounds of propriety," wrote George C. Carens in the *Boston Evening Transcript*, 7 December 1931.

49 **some caveats:** Craig Lambert stated that Cowles finished with a record of 100–27–2. *Harvard* magazine, January–February 1989. Such a total included, no doubt, all national five-man team tournament matches.

49 **the varsity had just three:** The Harvard freshmen played, officially, St. Paul's School twice, Exeter and Yale once and, unofficially, Brooks School.

49 **whispered that it was St. Paul's:** *The New Yorker*, 5 March 1932.

49 **said Willing Patterson:** "The Sports Parade" by Harry Robert, in the *Philadelphia Evening Bulletin*, 13 February 1940.

49 **only pupils of Harry:** Harvard did not send a team in 1933 because the Harvard Athletic Association reduced the team's budget. *The New Yorker*, 23 February 1933. In 1934 "Cambridge" won the national teams, with such Harvard undergraduates as Germain Glidden as members.

49 **His 1925 varsity:** The team consisted of Palmer Dixon, George Debevoise, Herbert N. Rawlins, Jr., E. M. Upjohn and A. L. Smith.

49 **the USSRA banned players:** Later the rule was that no player ranked in the top twenty could play in the national teams.

50 **taught by the master:** Dixon, ever loyal, telegraphed each Harvard alum after he won the nationals. "Great Work Hearty Congratulations" read the telegram sent to Beek Pool in 1932.

51 **leapt around the court:** "One of the fastest men ever to play Squash Racquets, Baker at the top of his game drove the ball with such blistering speed that his opponents were either aced or forced into error," wrote Dick Cooke. "Baker brought to the game a new element not employed by previous champions. We refer to his intense concentration. . . ." See *Boston Globe*, 14 February 1983 and Gordon Scannell, "Myles P. Baker" in *The Tavern Club at One Hundred*, Charles B. Everitt, ed. (privately printed, 1984).

52 **"longest wallop ever made":** *Christian Science Monitor*, 30 March 1931.

52 **George Cummings:** Cummings's advice was "move your legs fast and your racquet slow."

52 **"blasted his shots":** Squash was an infrequent sidelight of Larry Pool's career. Like his father, Larry became a doctor and was head of neurological surgery at Columbia-Presbyterian; he authored nine books including a biography of Izaak Walton and a definitive history of America's early iron industry; he sailed across the Atlantic four times, raced from Newport to Bermuda in a square-rigger, flew planes, fished around the globe and was probably the only squash champion who could explain the difference between a bustle pipe, a pitchpole and a caddis fly.

53 **His rapacious rails:** Beek's furious swing was a cause of comedy, as Jack Barnaby, his classmate, remembered: "On one occasion he was playing his hardest and the ball hit a drop of sweat and the instant skid caused him to miss it completely. There was no sound of impact, but his racquet made a distinct *voove* noise as it whistled through the air, much like a violent wind in telephone wires. The gallery broke up and Beek joined in the laugh."

54 **shocking statistic:** *The New Yorker*, 5 March 1932.

54 **as proclaimed a freshman:** Like the Pools, he was the son of an alumnus, and his brother Nathaniel Glidden, Harvard 1931, had played varsity squash.

54 **terrible, dead-fish backhand:** Most lefthanders have this problem, except, of course, my wife.

56 **Glidden won the fifth game:** Germain Glidden, *The Artist and the Sportsman: Memoirs of Germain G. Glidden*, (privately printed, 1992). Even in his eighties, Glidden would dream about that match. An artist, he painted hundreds of portraits, including three presidents, sketched dozens of squash cartoons and founded the National Art Museum of Sport, now based in Indianapolis. In his studio at his house in Connecticut until his death in November 1999, Glidden used his 1937 national champion's trophy as a repository for his paint brushes.

56 **famous cricketing father:** George Stuart Patterson, a cotton broker in Philadelphia, was

considered to be the best American ever to play cricket in England. Playing for the Gentlemen of Philadelphia against first-class sides in England, Patterson led the 1889 batting figures with a 40.69 average (high score 106, not out) and bowling figures of 42 wickets for an average of 23.61. In 1897 he captained the team and batted with a 33.75 average (high score 162).

57 **that kind of player:** Patterson also believed that playing in England helped his game. "And I think it improved my squash," he said. "I developed the soft game; it's not as useful here as over there, but it helps a lot at times." *Evening Bulletin,* 20 February 1940.

57 **survived match balls against Lott:** "I was up 2–0 to Howes," remembered Lott. "I opened up the can to see if he was there and he jumped out."

58 **the game became synonymous:** *The Review of Reviews,* April 1929. Victor Niederhoffer suggested in *The Education of a Speculator* (New York: John Wiley, 1997) that Barnaby as a sophomore asked Cowles if he could play for the team. Cowles said all the positions were filled and added that Barnaby could pay for lessons, which apparently he did for a year until he could make the team. Barnaby did not recall this.

59 **Macmillan published:** Jack Barnaby was loyal to Cowles to a fault, but he did repeatedly claim, in writing and in conversation, that he ghost wrote the *Art of Squash Racquets* for Cowles. Since there is no way to corrborate or deny his claim, one can only add that Cowles ran the following acknowledgement in front of the book: "I take this opportunity to express my heartiest thanks to my assistant, John M. Barnaby, II, whose suggestions, criticisms and interest in the book were a constant stimulation to its growth."

60 **he suddenly sprung for the window:** "It was an awful scene," remembered Jack Barnaby. "We restrained him and took him to the hospital."

60 **Tennis & Squash Shop:** Cowles's partner, Everett Poeckert, continued to run the store for decades, followed by Carl and Bruce Fuller after 1965. Poeckert also assisted Jack Barnaby at Harvard and was featured in many team photographs. See *Boston Traveler,* 13 March 1958. Victor Niederhoffer, in *Education of a Speculator,* argued that "The new ways, the increasing democratization of the game, doubtless contributed to Cowles's insanity."

60 **lost its first intercollegiate match:** Harvard's closest match beforehand was in 1936 when it beat Yale 7–2.

60 **He had a frontal lobotomy:** "After that he would talk irrationally, about 'God not guard,' incessantly," remembered Jack Barnaby. Cowles was coherent enough to write an article that appeared in the *Boston Evening Transcript,* 4 February 1938.

60 **simple flat stone:** *Boston Herald,* 11 December 1958.

61 **Cowles stared straight ahead:** Barnaby, *Winning Squash Racquets,* and *Squash News,* May 1989.

IV. HOLLOW-EYED AND SQUEAKY

62 **wonderfully keen on the game:** Miles added, "Anyhow it is essential that every member of the household (if ours were a true Democracy we would include the well-fed servants) should have an opportunity for daily exercise, and not only an opportunity for it but an inducement to it. If ladies would only play Squash instead of driving and going to concerts and theatres and at-homes, and paying calls or playing cards, if they would only get some of their social life this way, they and their children would be happier and heathlier than they are, and, in the case the fact should influence them, I will not say less ugly, gauche and fat, for of course they are never this, but, if possible, more beautiful, graceful and neat in figure."

62 **the Colony Club:** Most probably it was a squash tennis court. One mother announced when the building was opened, "I've waited for this evening all my life. I've just telephoned the boys, 'Don't wait dinner. I'm dining at my club.'" In 1924, the Colony Club moved to Park Avenue. Strouse, *Morgan,* p. 521.

63 **encouraged her to play:** Bill Howe was Union Boat champion from 1927 to 1930, runner-up in the state championship in 1930 and often represented Boston at the national teams. He once came back from a 0–2, 0–14 deficit to win a national teams match against Philadelphia. Lothrop Withington falsely told Howe at match point that Boston needed his match to win the contest. His opponent was Squab Kennedy. See *Boston Globe*, 15 February 1949.

63 **with the fairer sex:** Boston women did not take no for an answer. One snowy evening around this time Abigail Adams Homans sought refuge at her husband's club in Boston (probably the Harvard Club). At the desk a clerk told her she could not check into a room unescorted. She went outside, hailed a cab on Commonwealth Avenue and had the driver escort her to her room. Sattertwhaite, *Three-Wall Nick*, p. 224.

63 **into their male sanctums:** In 1908 Merion hosted a women's club tournament. May Sayres was the winner. The Racquet Club in Chicago held a women's handicap tournament in 1924. It was won by Mrs. F. C. Lett.

63 **Margaret Howe overcame:** It was unclear whether the 1928 Round Hill tournament or the 1929 Harvard Club tournament was meant to be the first official nationals. Margaret Howe later claimed that Eleo Sears had retroactively designated the 1928 tournament as the first nationals in order to give herself a national title and that she had not been invited to the Round Hill tournament. The inscription on her 1929 trophy read "1929 Winner First Women's National Championship." See article by Susan Reed in program, 1985 national singles, Yale University.

64 **escape from Nature's provisions:** Charles Read, *Squash Rackets* (London: William Heinemann, 1929). Read concluded: "No woman can combine her natural function of tenderness with masculine characteristics, yet many women twist many men round very small fingers." "If the business-man can restrain the spread of his abdomenal dimensions by Squash, his wife or his daughter can equally retain her figure just as easily by playing Squash as by complicated exercises in the bath-room or the application of weird thinning machines." Arthur Barker, *Squash Racquets* (London: Eyre & Spottiswood, 1936).

64 **get out of the country:** Rex Bellamy, *Squash*, p. 165.

64 **broken her leg:** "Within three hours of our arrival we were practising and, after a rough voyage, the small courts seemed to close in on us like tilting biscuit tins, whilst the ball dragged like lead on light English rackets," wrote Liza Wolfe, *British Lawn Tennis and Squash*, November 1948.

65 **small, aggressive left-hander:** *Times* (London), 24 January 1998.

65 **develop stamina to keep:** Liza Wolfe agreed with Lamme's assessment. Reporting on the nationals held at Merion, she noted a semifinal match between Lytton-Milbanke and Fenwick: "This match created a great impression amongst the Americans by the pace and retrieving powers of the Englishwomen. . . . The American women play very little with men. They hit the ball less hard than the English, relying almost entirely on side wall angle shots which die off the front wall. They serve better in their own courts, but were obviously amazed by the way shots were retrieved, especially by Miss Lytton-Milbanke, who won tremendous applause in long rallies. The games were on the whole shorter than in England, and the pace of the ball varied tremendously according to the temperature of the day. The English team settled down very well to the different conditions, but had yet to find a really first-rate service." *Squash Rackets & Fives*, April 1933.

65 **"There was a dreadful commotion":** *Evening News* (London), 16 February 1953. Susan Noel believed that Mrs. John Cheney was the first woman to wear shorts. Another trick American women adopted was leaving the ball in a bowl of warm water in between games.

66 **traditional all-white:** Helen O. Mankin, *Evening Bulletin*, 7 January 1942. "'I don't suppose Americans ever will come to wearing white for squash as English girls,' said Miss Bowes. 'We like color and like to express ourselves . . .'" But Bowes said they should switch to all-white. Christine Woodall, the president of the Philadelphia Women's SRA,

disagreed: "If players get that particular they shouldn't play squash. We play squash for fun and I think we should play in anything that is comfortable and warm. Squash is a grand game to wear out our old clothes and show off our new ones. Wearing anything is part of the fun."

66 **proverbial chimney:** *Squash Rackets & Fives,* October 1934.

67 **hand-crocheted tiara:** *Evening Bulletin,* 5 February 1936. See *Sunday Bulletin,* 1 March 1959 and *The New Yorker,* 18 January 1947.

67 **the daring mermaids:** Sears knew, like all true lovers of the outdoor plunge, that it isn't swimming unless you go in twice.

68 **Hazel Hotchkiss Wightman:** One story from the 1930 finals against Eleo Sears was that during a mad scramble upfront Eleo shouted, "Get out of my way." "I can't," replied Wightman, "you're on my foot."

68 **"plays like a man":** *Squash Rackets & Fives,* February 1939.

68 **she reached the semifinals:** Page beat Peggy Scott Carrott in the fifth by two points in the 1947 finals. Of all the American women, Page seemed the most amenable to British ideas. One Mankin article in the *Evening Bulletin,* 9 December 1936, was headlined: ANNE PAGE USES MANY NEW IDEAS: NATIONAL WOMEN'S SQUASH CHAMPION ALWAYS INTRODUCING ENGLISH FADS AT TOURNEYS.

69 **sent off Barbara Williams:** Helen O. Mankin in *Evening Bulletin,* 26 February 1941. "Once the shyest of local girl athletes, Miss Bowes now has become a belle. In the past Babe's recreation consisted of going to the movies with a girl friend, now she loves parties. The champion has lost count of the number of bouquets of flowers and the congratulatory telegrams and letters she has received from folks she has never met. She arrived home wearing a spray of gardenias and carrying a corsage of orchids in a box. She regrets that the American beauty roses, a gift from an unknown New England admirer, were among the flowers she had to leave with her hostess in Boston." In the 1940 nationals at the Junior League, she was the "$20 Champion"—because her ten Cynwyd teammates had to each pay $2 to watch the tournament.

69 **"Babe Bowes possesses":** *Squash Rackets & Fives,* April 1937. Page and Bowes final match came in a playoff in 1949 to determine who would play number five on the U.S. Wolfe-Noel Cup team. Bowes won in four games. See also *New York Times,* 19 January 1938 and *Evening Bulletin,* 9 March 1946 for a Helen O. Mankin article about Babe returning from India and holding up her Christmas present: six pairs of nylon stockings.

69 **He won the last point:** Pearson joined the Racquet Club of Philadelphia in 1919 and won its club championship in 1919, 1920, 1921, 1922, 1923, 1927, 1930, 1932 and 1933. He then resigned from the club because of the Great Depression, rejoined in 1943 and died on the court tennis court in 1949.

69 **court one:** Palmer Dixon, who dethroned Peabody as state champion, described Peabody's style as "a game of extreme care, though one a trifle defensive perhaps in its concept."

70 **he captained the team:** Like most squash players at the time, Pearson found that other sports claimed his passions while at Old Nassau: he quarterbacked the Tiger's football team until a knee injury felled him in November 1940, and he played third base for the Princeton baseball team and liked to point out that in 1939 he batted in the winning run for Princeton against Columbia in the first sporting event ever broadcast on television.

70 **He won the 1948 nationals:** There were twenty-four lets in the finals against Andy Ingraham and twenty-three were because Pearson was in the way. "Father was a tough teacher," said Stan years later. "He told us never to make errors. He went crazy when you double faulted. When I came back from winning the nationals, he said, 'Now all you have to do is win five more.' He then wanted to play me in a match. And he beat me. He was that good."

70 **noted his bleary eyes:** *Squash-Badminton,* April 1935. Treddy Ketcham recalled one

evening he and a friend were coming into a club after a dinner dance. On the lawn in a snowdrift was a lump. On closer inspection the lump turned out to be Strachan. They woke him up to take him inside. Strachan stood up, walloped one of the men in the face and then fell back into the snow.

71 **hard luck smacked him down:** "It went the full distance, and the spectators choking with excitement and both contestants almost literally out on their feet," reported the *Boston Globe*, 12 February 1934.

72 **squandered four match points:** For five years in a row in the mid-1930s, he faced Strachan in the finals of the Atlantic Coasts. He reached the finals of the Pennsylvania states every year from 1929 through 1938, winning it five times.

73 **"likely to bound heavily":** *The New Yorker*, 23 February 1933. Harry Cowles wrote that Sullivan "had an eye that few can match. . . . He takes liberties with conventional tactics . . . It would be unwise for most players to imitate Sullivan."

73 **determined not to squander:** *New York Herald Tribune*, 16 February 1934.

73 **Brendon Walsh hit as hard:** *The New Yorker*, 30 December 1933.

74 **within inches of the telltale:** *New York Times*, 3 February 1933.

74 **brokerage:** The official name was Coffin, Betts & Sullivan. In August 1949 Sullivan resigned from the presidency of the USSRA.

75 **"an active American player roster":** *Literary Digest*, 20 February 1937.

75 **epitome of East Coast squash:** The 1936 Lockett Cup matches had filled the galleries at the Harvard Club because they "were open to the public, marking the first time that the Harvard Club had allowed outsiders to witness an athletic event in its quarters." *New York Times*, 11 January 1936.

76 **donated a trophy:** In 1921 Lapham, along with half a dozen other Americans, played in the Canadian nationals. They had such fun that they invited their hosts to Philadelphia the following year.

76 **Alastair Grant of Montreal:** The Grant was not played on the same weekend as the Lapham until 1953. Tevis Huhn, Johnny Smith and three father-son teams—Knox, Kingsley and Sonnabend—played in the first Grant in Montreal. Grant eventually retired to Florida.

76 **the captain slept peaceably:** See Stewart Brauns history of the Lapham-Grant in the 1983 WPSA tour program and the *History of Squash Racquets in Canada*. The Grant trophy went missing for a decade before it was discovered in the basement of the Montreal Amateur Athletic Association. Three men, David Fleming-Wood, Ian McAvity and Gordon Anderson, have played for both sides.

77 **Sam Toyne wrote:** See *Squash Rackets Annual*, 1938. The North Americans rearranged their winter schedules to accommodate the tourists, moving the nationals to Boston and delaying the Canadian nationals for a month. The USSRA allowed the English just one entry in the U.S. nationals. At the Lapham, England stacked their lineup, with Robarts and Macpherson playing at number three and four. Ralph Powers played in every nationals from 1916 through 1934 and in every international match for the United States in the 1920s.

78 **when he failed to win a single point:** W. Stewart Brauns, Jr., *The Society of United States Members of the Jesters Club: 1935–1985*; *Buffalo News*, 22 October 1940; *The Racquet*, December 1951. Strachan lost, 9–4, 9–2, 9–1, and felt terrible until he saw Wakeman lose without winning a point. Wakeman hit both his backhand and forehand with the same side of the racquet, a technique that might have served him badly on this day. Shorty Knox told the tale a bit differently in his memoirs. "We were plied with sherry and drinks by our charming hostess named Pearl and it was with great difficulty that one refused." Wakeman had invited a new lady friend down from London to watch the match. "It was without a doubt the funniest match I have ever seen," wrote Knox. Cy Polley, in a heroic fashion, beat Lionel Stubbs, 9–4, 8–10, 0–9, 9–6, 9–1. "It nearly killed him," wrote Knox. He

added that Stubbs was "a short, fat, bald, self-satisfied irritating individual." Knox, incidentally, also somehow played well and took H. M. Mellor to five games, losing, 9–3, 7–9, 9–10, 9–6, 9–7. Frank Strawson and Edward Snell played in the match, with Strawson beating Roy Coffin in three and Snell beating Patterson in four. Some of the players on the tour earned nicknames: Polley was Toots, Sullivan & Strachan were the Rover Boys and Coffin was the Reverend (the British called him Parson). In 1940 Knox hosted a reunion of the tour at his court outside Buffalo. All but Wakeman attended. Seymour H. Knox, *Other Tales in Other Years, 1922–1961* (privately printed, 1970). The Jesters made every player on the tour a member of their club that evening and one suspects that their actions that day were a sort of twisted induction ceremony.

79 **totally exhaust themselves:** *Town and Country,* January 1990.

79 **wrote Herbert Warren Wind:** *Holiday* magazine, December 1962. "Squash provides wholesome, invigorating recreation that stimulates both mentally and physically, for it is a game of brain as much as brawn, and provides it at a small cost and in fair weather and foul when athletic diversion cannot be obtained out of doors," wrote Allison Danzig in 1930.

80 **Bunny Austin shocked Wimbledon:** By the 1920s, real flannel trousers became obsolete, as players switched to white cotton.

80 **cure his insomnia:** Playing at the University Club in Toronto, it was reported, the Prince of Wales incongruously chewed gum throughout the match. One night in Vancouver, the Prince was unable to sleep and decided he wanted a game of squash. The phone soon rang at the home of Bimbo Sweeney, a leading player in Vancouver. He answered and was told that "His Royal Highness, the Prince of Wales, wants a game of squash right now." Bimbo looked at his clock. It read half past midnight. He swore at the caller, saying it was a fine joke at this hour, and hung up. The phone rang again. Bimbo swore again, but listened long enough to be convinced. He went over to Major Johnny Fordham's home and there, at one in the morning, he played the Prince.

81 **just forward of the boiler:** It owed its existence possibly to J. P. Morgan, who was a member of the board of the parent company of the *Titanic*'s owners and played squash tennis in New York. "A squash racquet court," read the notes on the *Titanic*'s blueprints, "is provided on Deck F, and is in charge of a professional player. Tickets for the use of the Court may be obtained at the Enquiry Office 2s/2d [or 50 cents; it was one dollar to use the pool] per half hour to include the services of the Professional if required. Balls may be purchased from the Professional who is also authorized to sell and hire racquets. The court may be reserved in advance by application to the Professional in charge, and may not be occupied for longer than one hour at a time by the same players if others are waiting."

81 **Wright went down with the ship:** Archibald Gracie, *The Truth about the Titanic* (1913). See *New York Times,* 7 December 1923. Charles Williams, the world champion in racquets and the racquets coach at Harrow, had a better fate on the *Titanic.* Sailing to New York to meet a challenger for the world championship, "the doughty little Scot," as the newspapers called him, spent nine hours in a lifeboat in the icy lanes of the North Atlantic before being rescued. When he reached New York, his match, to be held at the Racquet & Tennis Club, was called off due to mourning for the victims of the disaster. A year later Williams again sailed across to defend his title. This time, he made it safely to New York but lost the match. He later stayed in the United States, coaching racquets, squash and tennis at the Racquet Club of Chicago and in 1929 regained his racquets world championship. Dick Williams, the future two-time national tennis champion, was also on the ship. There was also a squash court on the *Queen Elizabeth*, a successor to the *Titanic* that maintained a regular schedule ferry service between Southampton and New York after the Second World War. Among the many amenities was a sweet-smelling cedar squash court. Unlike the *Titanic*, this one had a comfortable gallery for about fifty passengers. The pro was an Irish policeman named Bill Ashcroft.

81 **its initial infatuation:** The founding six Mass SRA clubs were the Boston Athletic Association, Tennis & Racquet Club, Harvard Club, Newton Centre, Union Boat Club and the Chestnut Hill Squash Racquets Club. Randolph joined a year later and in successive years came the Cambridge Squash Racquets Club, the Neighborhood Club of Quincy, the Milton Club and Lincoln's Inn Society, a Harvard Law School group. The University Club started its squash program in 1928. The suburbs around the city founded courts of their own: Brockton (Walkover Club), Weston (Golf Club), Newton (the Newton YMCA and the Newton Club of Newtonville), and Wellesley (Maugus Club) built courts in the late twenties and their managements, according to Dick Cooke writing in 1932, were "loud in their praise of the game as a drawing card among their members."

82 **With Otto Glockler:** Glockler beat Palmer Dixon that year in straight games in an exhibition at the club. In 1936 the University Club and the Racquet Club merged under the former's name. See Cecil J. Wilkinson, *The University Club of Washington: The First Fifty Years, 1904–1954* (privately printed, 1954).

83 **around the Windy City:** The other Chicago clubs included the Lake Shore Athletic Club, the Union League, the Harvard-Yale-Princeton Club, the Chicago Club, the Chicago Town & Tennis Club and the Winter Club in Lake Forest. The Chicago District SRA was formed in the early thirties. In the program for the 1967 nationals, Patrick Burke, chairman, wrote, "For many reasons, geographical as well as emotional, we can't help feeling Chicago is on the far distant fringe of the squash playing community."

83 **a group of Harvard men:** See the program for the 1984 nationals and the *Cleveland Plain Dealer,* 27 March 1932. George Francis, A. H. Alexander and H.W. Bosworth were among the Harvard graduates in Cleveland. Harry Cowles visited in 1932.

83 **a glass of gin:** Gordon died of cancer at age fifty-two in 1960. See the program for the 1985 national doubles and *The First Fifty Years: The Racquet Club of St. Louis, 1906–1956* (privately printed, 1956).

83 **a half-dozen other clubs:** The Detroit Athletic Club opened courts in 1906, the University Club in 1913 (in 1931 the club opened a new facility with four singles, one doubles and one racquets court), the city YMCA in 1912, the Henry Ford Hospital in 1926, the University of Michigan in 1929 (with fourteen courts), the Uptown Athletic Club in 1932 and the Detroit Tennis & Squash Club (with two courts and the most number of players in town). See Karen L. Rutkowski, *Squash Racquets: The Diffusion Process* (masters thesis in geography, Wayne State University, March 1981). See also *Squash Racquets: A Brief History of the Sport From the Monks to the Motor City* (issued at the 1995 hardball nationals).

84 **Rockaway had been playing:** Benjamin R. Allison, *The Rockaway Hunting Club* (privately printed, 1952). The two 1901 courts cost $3,300. Rockaway was led by Howes Burton, who once walked from Rockaway to the R&T in less than six hours to win a bet.

84 **the headquarters for squash:** Guy St. Clair, *A Venerable and Cherished Institution: The University Club of New York, 1865–1990* (privately printed, 1991).

85 **"quietly humorous, self-deprecatory":** "The mellowed gentleness of his 87 years shed over our sport a warmth that will be sorely missed," Lehman concluded. Met SRA yearbook, 1957–58. With the fanaticism of the convert, Lockett once wrote a nasty letter to Hugh Torrance at *The New Yorker,* after an article of his extolled the virtues of squash tennis, and challenged Torrance to meet at Madison Square Garden to "debate" the issue further. *The Racquet,* April 1953.

85 **"as esoteric as Greta Garbo's boudoir":** *The Racquet,* December 1951.

85 **dozen other squash tennis:** Clubs in the city like the Princeton, the Neighborhood and the Park Avenue Squash switched, as did clubs in outer boroughs and suburbs, like the Heights Casino in Brooklyn, Montclair Athletic Club in Montclair, New Jersey, Nassau Country Club in Glen Cove, Long Island, the Greenwich Country Club in Greenwich, Connecticut, the Staten Island Club, the Racquet & Swimming Club in Ardsley and the

Round Hill Club in Greenwich. The four teams in the Met SRA league that first year came from the Racquet & Tennis, Rockaway, University and Montclair.

87 **functioning flawlessly:** *New York Herald Tribune*, 23 January 1938. Wives and players knocked out in the early rounds played paddle tennis on the court outside in the courtyard of Chalfonte, and in the 1960s Howard Davis started a paddle tournament and provided prizes for the finalists. One night Joe Hahn was refereeing a late-night match. After one point, both players looked up to see what his decision was on an appeal for a let. He was sound asleep. His classic rejoinder to the players: "Alright, so I fell asleep. What do you think I am, a milkman?" Another player, Claude Beer, was famous for bringing two dates to an Atlantic Coast Championship in the 1960s. He ensconced each date in a separate hotel room and successfully negotiated a weekend of alternating between both rooms, the squash courts, the paddle court, the bar and the beach. It is unclear whether this fandango was busted at the Saturday evening dinner dance or whether he escaped undetected. Chalfonte-Haddon Hall hosted the 1962 U.S. Open, the 1971 U.S. Professionals and the 1991 Copa Wadsworth. After gambling came to Atlantic City, Merv Griffen bought Chalfonte-Haddon Hall, tore down Haddon Hall and renamed Chalfonte Resorts. In July 2001 the courts were closed.

87 **bundled in overcoats:** "We've got the best ventilated courts in New York," said John Jacobs. "You could hang meat out there if you wanted to." *The Racquet*, May 1952.

88 **tens of thousands of dollars:** Satterthwaite, *Three-Wall Nick*. After the Calcutta came casino games, with blackjack tables and roulette wheels placed in the North Room.

88 **How did everyone get there?:** Rumor was that one Rockaway member, so inspired by the inaugural tournament in 1928, was in the process of setting up an endowment for the tournament—reportedly with $100,000 as seed money—when the stock market crashed in October 1929. See *The Racquet* magazine, January 1953. Many Philadelphian players and Orpheus Club members stopped at a tavern near the Staten Island ferry on their way to or from the tournament. The first dues-paying member to win the Gold Racquets was Steve Vehslage in 1962, but no native-raised member has ever won the tournament.

89 **his trusty squash bat:** *Holiday*, December 1962. The father asks if his son has taken up badminton.

90 **losing effort against Harvard:** In 1932–33 Princeton played Pretty Brook (6–0), Haddon Hall in Atlantic City (4–1), the Princeton Club of New York (4–5), Yale (6–3, 2–7), Montclair Athletic Club (7–0), Penn (6–0) and Harvard (1–4).

90 **a bona fide varsity:** Dartmouth in its first season played Harvard's junior varsity (2–3), Yale (0–7), the University Club of Boston (5–4), Amherst (3–4), MIT (3–2 and 4–1), Wesleyan (3–2), Trinity (5–0) and St. Paul's (7–0).

90 **sending a team to the nationals:** In 1929 Yale's schedule contained home-and-away matches against Princeton (4–1, 2–3), a match at the Racquet & Tennis Club (2–3), Harvard (0–5) and a trip to the nationals to play in the national five-man teams (they won their first match 5–0 and lost their second 2–3).

91 **Yale became the second college:** The 1959 Yale national team champion included: Charlie Kingsley, Sam Howe, Maitland Jones, Dan Morgan and John Oettinger. In the semifinals against Toronto, the score was 2–2 when Howe beat Ernie Howard, 16–15, 13–18, 18–15, 18–16.

91 **an alumni committee:** The first alumni advisory committee for the NISRA included Honey Humpstone, Edward Herendeen, Joseph Raycroft, Arthur Lockett and Perry Pease.

91 **"particularly imposing":** Allison Danzig described the trophy as "massive." *New York Times*, 14 February 1932.

91 **increased it to nine:** Until 1971 most colleges had freshman teams. The freshman team coach, who had to deal with nervous eighteen-year-olds, struggling former tennis stars turned squash neophytes and arrogant prep-school squash phenoms, was an irregular

breed. Richard Swinnerton coached the Princeton freshman team for thirty years, retiring in 1962. British, with Popeye forearms and a glass eye, he swore like a swabber in the
Royal Navy, which he had been. Swinnie was a horror on road trips. He had an instinct
for the left side of the road and an abhorrence of maps. See Satterthwaite, *Three-Wall
Nick*.

92 **luckiest shot anyone had seen:** See Jack Barnaby in *Squash News*, July–August 1989.
Dorson also was a part of a legendary college tennis match. Dorson and a Yalie named
Stephens played an extremely close two-hour match in which each game went to deuce.
Dorson won it, 6–0, 6–0.

92 **a hoary division:** This attitude prevailed into the 1960s. In 1963 the University Club of
Philadelphia closed. Its clubhouse was taken over by the Glassblowers' Union and the
club's squash professional stayed on as an elevator operator. With union wages, his salary
actually improved.

92 **maintain this imbalance:** In 1924, when the T&RA squash committee was organizing
the first English tour of North America, they suggested a subscription to help pay for the
expenses of the touring players. The squash committee's overseers in the T&RA, afraid
these amateurs might somehow be sullied by accepting money, put the kibosh on that idea
and passed a resolution that the players had to pay for their own expenses.

93 **It was not until 1979:** The Squash Rackets Association elected the first pro to its executive in 1939.

93 **Ganley started out:** See *New York Evening Post*, 18 January 1923. Ganley coached at the
Union Boat Club, the New York Athletic Club, the Harvard Club of New York, Apawamis
and finally the Westchester Country Club.

94 **fervor with which he held:** Soutar retired from the Racquet Club in 1950. The first professional match in Great Britain was played in 1907 at the Bath Club between Charles
Read, the Queen's pro, and C. Bannister, the Bath pro. Read won, 2–0 (15–5, 15–13). Read
played three more challenge matches until 1930, when the British Open was started.

94 **small pro tournament:** Sidney Dufton beat Jack Summers in the final, 3–2. Dufton was
the pro at the BAA in the 1920s and moved to the Harvard Club in the 1930s. He was the
spitting image of James Dean.

94 **To join the association:** Its post-war, pre-WPSA presidents were as follows: Lou Ballato,
Al Chassard, Tom Byrne, Jim Bentley, Fred Weymuller and Jim McQueenie.

94 **The giants of the professional corps:** Some of the other leading, longtime pros and the
club they were most associated with were the Iannicelli brothers Frank and Tommy (Short
Hills), the Cummings brothers Allan (Apawamis), George (University) and Les (Field),
Jimmy Dunn (Racquet Club of Philadelphia) Al Molloy, Sr. (MAAA) and Jr. (Penn), Harry
Conlon, Sr., Ed Standing, Frank Lafforgue (Yale), the Dufton brothers Rowland and Sid-
ney, Harry Geidel (Nassau), Charles Costello (Princeton), Vincent Ellis (Piping Rock),
Harry King (Sleepy Hollow), Ed Stapleton, Bob Cahill (Bronxville Field), Leo Collins
(Harmonie), John Collopy (Union League), Jerry Cassidy (Racquet Club of St. Louis) and
George Armstrong (Genesee Valley).

95 **Lester Cummings:** Cummings was forty-eight years old when he won his last title in
1946.

95 **Sherman Howes:** Cummings was on the way to losing this match when Howes pushed
him accidentally, thus angering the venerable professional.

96 **speculated that the best amateur:** *The New Yorker*, 24 November 1934. The pros
seemed unable to even give a solid exhibition. *The New Yorker* reported on the opening of
new courts at the University Club in November 1934. An exhibition between George
Cummings and Skillman "was more interesting as a duel in politeness than anything else.
Both men kept trying to have lets called on themselves, even arguing these points in a
more or less illegal way with Mr. Humpstone, who was refereeing, until the Gaston-
Alphonse atmosphere became so thick that one had the horrid suspicion they were doing

it for the benefit of the gallery." Cummings was so lackadaisical that he kept one hand in his pocket while playing.

V. SEND FOR THE DRAMA CRITIC

97 **helplessly devoted characters:** Herbert Warren Wind speaks of three such men in his December 1962 article in *Holiday* magazine: Joe Hahn, Stew Brauns and Ned Bigelow, all native New Yorkers.

97 *caput mundi:* It was actually fifteen men, for a sixteenth, Archibald Montgomery, was recovering from the loss of his right arm—a saluting cannon prematurely discharged at the funeral procession of President Lincoln. Montgomery became Merion's first president.

98 **grand porch that overlooked:** During the Second World War, Merion plowed under the lawn and planted a vegetable garden. See *The Merion Cricket Club, 1865–1965: Being a Brief History of the Club for the First Hundred Years of its Existence, Together with its Roll of Officers and Members to 1965* (privately printed, 1965).

98 **launching pad:** Seixas grew up playing mostly at Cynwyd Club.

99 **like blood brothers:** William F. Talbert, *Playing for Life: Billy Talbert's Story* (Boston: Little, Brown, 1958).

99 **They played offensively:** Diehl Mateer in the *Detroit Free Press*, 12 February 1955: "There's a distinct and definite mark on squash as it is played in Philadelphia that sets it apart from the style employed elsewhere. The key is an all-out offense. We stress a strong offense designed to put the ball away and win the point rather than a 'retrieving' style that is quite prominent in other sections."

99 **give the rattlesnake half:** *Squash News*, April 1978. See *Racquet* magazine, September–October 1978.

99 **in awe of the Merion:** At least in the squash version of Yankee Stadium, aura and mystique were not the names of dancers.

100 **no coach could fix:** Lott was runner-up in the first Philadelphia & Districts.

101 **an arrow-filled diagram:** *Time*, 21 February 1949.

101 **bitterly contested:** See Met SRA yearbook 1949–50.

101 **Bill White coached:** White started his career as a ball boy at Queen's Club. He came to the United States to teach court tennis at the Mackay court in Long Island. He was working at the Yahnundasis Club in Utica, New York when Sydney Thayer, the captain of the Penn squash team, asked him to come to Merion.

101 **An avuncular presence:** "We used to hang around every afternoon watching these guys play," remembered Sam Howe, "and after they left the court, they'd see us looking all forlorn. Hunter always would come up after he played and say, 'Would you like a game?' and we'd bound into the court and he'd play with us for a while. He was the foundation of the Merion dynasty." Herbert Warren Wind, *Holiday* magazine, December 1962: "This was the way it worked at Merion, for there was always a group of players on hand at the club, oldsters who were on the verge of switching from singles to doubles and school kids who had come out by train and bus. In time, squash at Merion gained the momentum of a snowball rolling downhill, an ever-increasing number of fine players inspiriting the promising younger fellows."

103 **in his Crimson career:** Heckscher almost won a third intercollegiate title as a sophomore. In the finals against Princeton's Roger Campbell, the defending champion, he had a 2–1 lead and clawed back from being down 14–10 in the fifth to send it into overtime, which he lost, 17–14. Heckscher was also the first undergraduate player to be invited into the U.S. Open draw, in 1956; he lost in the opening round to Azam Khan by the respectable score of 3–1 and an excellent full-page photograph, taken before the match, appeared in the 1960–61 annual yearbook.

104 **both exhausted by their earlier rounds:** The Howe brothers maintained a fierce rivalry.

In 1964 in the finals of the Gold Racquets, Sam beat Ralph 18–17 in the fifth and exuberantly smashed his racquet over his knee.

105 **answer for the blackouts:** "I started to hit the ball a lot harder than ever before," said Vehslage after winning the nationals. "It started at Merion and just got better at Hartford. I used to hit it that hard when I was eighteen, but I hadn't since. I really don't know what loosened up. . . . And the fact that it was the nationals didn't seem to scare me off. I guess I'd seen Sam and Ralph win it and realized that it wasn't so sacred. Wait until next year— I'll be a jumping bean!" See Rex Lardner in *Sports Illustrated*, 22 February 1966. Vehslage died of brain cancer in 2002.

105 **pulling a crooked wisdom tooth:** *The Racquet*, February 1953.

106 **immediately excelled:** Mateer senior and junior won the highly competitive U.S. Father & Sons championship in 1947, 1949, 1950 and 1951 and were runner-up twice more. Mateer, Jr. won three Merion club grass-court tennis championships (Sam Howe won it a record eight times) and thirteen club doubles titles with eight different partners.

106 **Groomed by Hunter Lott:** Mateer told Herbert Warren Wind that Bill White had helped him as much at Lott: "Whitey had the gift of being able to instill in you the spirit and enjoyment of the game. He'd kid you after every point, but he also made you think. He would stand in the middle of the court and you would run from corner to corner until you learned to make the correct shots and understood why you had to."

106 **trying to smash his way:** Neil Sullivan took Mateer aside at the 1947 Atlantic Coasts, Mateer's first major tournament, and told him in no uncertain terms to stop hitting so many shots and go back to a basic rail and cross-court game. "That was the worst exhibition of squash I've seen in my life," Sullivan said. See Torbet, *Squash*, p. 119.

106 **he let a 2–0 lead:** During the rest period at 2–1, Strachan said to Hunter Lott, "I wish you'd tell your protégé not to be cutting across the ball when he makes a bad shot. Somebody's going to take his head off some day—and it might even be me." *Boston Globe*, 15 February 1949.

106 **a booming tin shot:** *The Racquet*, January 1953.

107 **beat the fat guys:** *The Racquet*, November 1951.

107 **lost five times in the finals:** Stew Brauns attributed Joe Hahn's bad luck in the finals of the national veterans to his 1952 match at Yale against Harold Kaese. Up 2–1, late in the fourth game, Hahn complained about noise while spectators from the national team matches settled themselves in the gallery. For two minutes he stopped play . "There is still too much noise, and I refuse to play until it is quieter," he told the referee, a twenty-six-year-old named Stew Brauns. "Furthermore, there is nothing you can do about it." "Yes, there is," Brauns boldly replied. "I can default you." Hahn played on and lost in five. See program for 1985 nationals. In 1949 he lost to George Waring in straight games in the finals. Three thousand dollars was wagered on the match, some from Joe Hahn's own pockets. See *Boston Globe*, 15 February 1949.

107 **patience of Job:** See Stew Brauns in the program for the 1983 nationals. George Cummings bet heavily on Eddie to beat Dick Rochschild in the finals of the 1950 nationals and Eddie's shock victory made the long-time professional a wealthy man.

108 **"Loose, limber and tough":** Conlon, Sr., had started in the squash industry at age thirteen as a locker-room boy at Englewood Field Club. He worked at the old Park Avenue Squash Club on East Twenty-third Street, the Crescent Athletic Club in Brooklyn, the Sidney Hill Club in Cleveland and, finally, Buffalo's University Club. Harry, Jr., was quite a phenom. In 1951 he and Lou Schafer reached the semifinals of the 1951 national doubles.

108 **lightning in a bottle:** Conlon did reach the finals of the 1963 Atlantic Coasts, losing 15–10 in the fifth to Diehl Mateer. He also won the 1953 New York states. In 1957 he reached the semifinals of the nationals, and, in 1958, he took Salaun to five games in the quarterfinals.

109 **Chateau Lafite-Rothschild:** See the program for the 1983 nationals. Harold Kaese, the

Boston Globe sports columnist, won the 1953 veterans, beating his old friend George Waring in the finals on the same court where he had lost to Brinton in the 1942 nationals. Philadelphia beat New York in the national teams 3–2, with Jim Whitmoyer clinching the final match 3–1 over Tom Kempner.

110 **sloop sailing for Plymouth:** "I was so young," he said a half century later. "I knew nothing. I never expected to get on that boat. My life, you know, it changed in ten minutes."

110 **a weaker opponent:** Salaun won eighteen straight University Club championships. After he lost, for the first time, in the finals of the 1976 tournament to Len Bernheimer, he never entered the tournament again.

111 **"it didn't come down":** Salaun remembered the ball landing in the lap of Al van der Hof, president of the University Club of Boston, who had a bet with Joe Hahn on the match. Bob Lehman thought the lob scraped the top of Salaun's head. Salaun liked his racquets strung so loosely that sometimes, like in the 1958 U.S. Open when he broke a string in the fifth game of his match against Azam Khan, he did not replace a broken racquet.

111 **he halted matches incessantly:** He did have surgery twice on his wrist and was smacked in the face twice: Ernie Howard once ripped open Salaun's cheek with his racquet (he needed thirteen stitches) and Azam Khan once bloodied his nose in the U.S. Open. In 1978 he played Heather McKay in an exhibition the night before the Viva Open. He backed out of the match with the score tied 2–2, citing a "train problem."

111 **he took a shower:** Hashim Khan, *Squash Racquets*, p. 150.

111 **He lay on his back moaning:** Francis, *Smart Squash*, p. 149.

113 **"gallery roared its approval":** Heckscher also had to overcome an early inability to beat Salaun. While a senior at Harvard he had once lost to Salaun after being up 2–0, 9–2 in the third. *Boston Herald*, 11 March 1957.

114 **threatening to quit singles:** In 1958 Mateer said he would retire after winning a third national title. He did go on to play and win more tournaments, including the Pennsylvania states in 1967. Mateer reached the finals of the Atlantic Coasts at age forty in 1969 after being down 2–0 and 6–0 in the third in the quarters to Charlie Ufford. He then went up 14–11 in the fifth against Tom Poor in the finals. A series of controversial lets and Mateer tins, including a flubbed backhand volley at 14–all, no set, ended his celebrated singles career.

115 **A Mateer-Salaun match is a sight to see:** Charlie Ufford found the aura of the two players on court quite different: "The great thing about Salaun is you're on with him and you don't even know he's on the court with you. And you're in torment, just torment. You are invariably going the extra half foot to get to the next shot. Somehow, you're always going a little bit farther than you care to go. And there's no one in your way, and you have no sense of him being anywhere on the court with you. He's just wonderful. . . . I've had less of that kind of feeling about Mateer's game because I've always thought Diehl's being stronger and being able to dominate the play, it seems sort of logical that he should dominate you and make you do most of the running and retrieving. But you're very much aware that you're in the court with Mateer, because there he is. He's a large presence in the court. There's no denying that he is largely responsible for the difficulties that you encounter. With Salaun, it's magic." Torbet, *Squash*, p. 175.

115 **He went on to win:** Salaun did play a little softball and in 1969 won the first Bermuda softball title.

116 **on the eve of the 1972 nationals:** Bob Lehman wrote that Salaun had suffered "a sudden attack of ineligibility."

117 **He casually held his racquet in his left hand:** The four-page photo spread included a number of excellent portraits of the two champions in action that appeared relatively authentic, including a nice one of Salaun outstretched on a backhand. One photograph, though, pierced the facade. It portrayed Mateer, with tongue wagging like Michael Jor-

dan, about to hit the ball off the back wall. In a real match no one, except Neil Sullivan, would ever hit such a shot with that kind of relish.

118 **in such hotbeds:** *The Racquet*, February 1952. Bigelow, for all this global interests, was not above commonplace sentiments of the time: "All these squash pros in India, Pakistan and Egypt seem to be related to each other. But that doesn't prevent them from whaling the tar out of each other—when they're in the mood."

118 **to gauge reaction:** See USSRA executive minutes, February 1953.

119 **fantastic action shots:** *Life*, 25 January 1954.

119 **neither were women:** At the 1950 nationals at the University Club, the wives of Charley Brinton and finalist Dick Rothschild tried to sneak into the club wearing men's overcoats, but they were caught.

119 **dream merchants of Hollywood:** It is common practice—unavoidable due to the amazing proliferation of successful squash players with this surname—to refer to each Khan by his first name, as I have done with the Pool and Howe brothers. For more on the Khan dynasty, see Dicky Rutnagur, *Khans Unlimited: A History of Squash in Pakistan* (Oxford: Oxford University Press, 1997) and Keith Miles with Rahmat Khan, *Jahangir and the Khan Dynasty* (London: Pelham Books, 1988).

119 **born five or more years:** Ned Bigelow even traveled to Peshawar to seek out a birth certificate but was unsuccessful.

120 **he once vanished:** *Signature* magazine, July 1978. See *The New Yorker*, 15 January 1955.

121 **"The picture he conjured up":** "Hashim Khan surprised squash followers in another way on that first visit," wrote Herbert Warren Wind in *The New Yorker*, 21 April 1973. "To an American, he looked nothing at all like an athlete, let alone a super-athlete. A round-headed, baldish man with a high-bridged nose and dark, serious eyes, he was squat in build, standing about five feet four and weighing around a hundred and forty pounds. His legs were short and on the spindly side, and, particularly since he was barrel-chested and had the suspicion of a potbelly, he seemed curiously top-heavy. When he moved, though, the whole picture changed. It was not that he was especially graceful or smooth but that he was beautifully coordinated. His strokes were sound, his reflexes were quick, he was indecently fast afoot, and no amount of exertion seemed to bring a bead of sweat to his brow." All three of Wind's major expositions on squash in *The New Yorker* started, whatever their subject, with hosannas of praise for Hashim Khan. For Wind's other squash articles, see *The New Yorker*, 10 April 1978 and 8 April 1985. Wind played squash at the Yale Club. *Time* magazine said Hashim looked "like a darker, balding version of Douglas Fairbanks, Sr." *Time*, 3 January 1955.

121 **club's service entrance:** *Signature* magazine, July 1978.

121 **legitimizing the professional game:** Hashim even changed the way the Americans finished a rally. He brought the three-wall boast, more or less dead since Glidden used it in the mid-1930s, back into use. He discovered that the working boast, what Americans called a roll corner, did not work well, so he took up the three wall and repopularized it. Satterthwaite, *Three-Wall Nick*, p. 237.

121 **Hashim solved:** After the match, Mateer counted twenty-three welts on his leg from being hit by Hashim's racquet. Hashim in 1954 apparently did not know about how lets were given in the United States and waited to be granted lets by the referee instead of asking for them.

122 **his best, pure win:** Like Hashim, Karim came from a poor family in Cairo and had learned the game from watching army officers on stone-floored, roofless courts. A professional at the famous Gezira Sporting Club along the Nile, Karim was forty-one in 1954 and in the twilight of his career. He only once made the quarterfinals of the U.S. Open after reaching the semis in 1954. Funnily enough, this aristocratic man had the nickname, at least in Canada, of "Mack."

122 **dripped off the court:** Stew Brauns told Wind about the final, that "you got the feeling that on each point Hashim was learning something more about the American game. You could practically hear his mind ticking along and filing away every new piece of information for future use." "I have surprise," said Hashim about his first time playing hardball. "This American ball wants to leap like a cat. Like a cat it has nine lives. I have to learn how to put it away." *Racquet* magazine, Summer 1979.

122 **silent as a little bird:** Barrington, *Murder in a Squash Court.*

123 **ducks in St. James's Park:** Herbert Warren Wind wrote, "Mo had a flair for the histrionic, an effervescent sense of humor, and talent to burn—and, in a way, that is what he did with it." Bob Lehman wrote that Mo "looked like a scion of the great Wallendas of circus fame."

123 **according to Stew Brauns:** One interesting import at the 1956 Open, wrote Brauns, was the Argentine squash and pelota champion Miguel Angle Filone. "He was completely ambidextrous, having two forehands and two backhands, all four terrible."

123 **Hashim won the tournament:** The Pakistani ambassador, Mohammed Ali, presented the Bigelow Trophy for the U.S. Open winner to Hashim in the Rockaway court after the match.

123 **In 1960:** During an opening-round match at the 1960 U.S. Open between Henri Salaun and Roshan Khan, a referee knocked a full box of new balls into a court during play. Buster Keaton could not have scripted the scene better. Salaun and Roshan, sometimes banging heads, collected and searched through the scattered pile, which looked like pepper blown across a white tablecloth, for a comedic few minutes trying to locate the one hot ball among the dozen cold balls. On Saturday evening during a quarterfinal match between Charlie Ufford and Al Chassard, the power went out throughout the club. The repair crew reported to the spectators huddled in the dark gallery that they would have to wait until the morning, but a janitor at the club placed a penny in the fuse box and power was restored. Chassard won twelve straight points after that.

124 **sheer velocity and excitement:** The Khans also started a long tradition of squabbling with Pakistani government officials. It started when, over their objections, they were assigned a manager. According to Stew Brauns, the manager, a lover of scotch, funneled his charges' prize money into his liquor expenses. One Sunday after the finals of the Canadian Open, he passed out cold in the Montreal airport. Whereupon he was poured onto a plane for Pakistan and never heard from again.

124 **only two clubs:** See minutes for 1961 USSRA executive.

125 **the Rockies reminded him:** On the emblem of the Colorado Squash Racquets Association was "Home of Hashim Khan." Roshan returned home to Pakistan and raised two sons destined for greatness, Torsham and Jahangir. Azam started working in 1956 at the New Grampians Club in London, which he eventually bought. Roshan's brother Nasrullah, a fine player as well, took over at the Junior Carlton Club upon Bari's unfortunate death in 1954. Naz eventually worked at Lansdowne and then at Edgbaston Priory and became one of the great coaches of the 1960s and 1970s.

125 **enlivened New England's squash community:** Mo did not age well on the court, however. In the 1982 masters at the WPSA championships, he hit Yusuf Khan in the face, leaving a six-inch gash that needed seven stitches. "He should be banned," said Yusuf afterwards. "He is always hitting people." See *Squash Monthly International,* April 1982.

VI. A CLAM IN MUD AT LOW TIDE

127 **heavy shadow:** "It was a rare game that didn't have at least two fistfights and three changes of referee," wrote Niederhoffer, *Education of a Speculator,* p. 26.

127 **one-armed forehands:** Satterthwaite, *Three-Wall Nick,* p. 65.

127 **a college sophomore:** The custom was to play the national juniors during the Christmas holidays, when prep-school boys were on vacation. The tournament that year was played

at Middlesex on 16–18 December 1961, although Niederhoffer is listed as the 1962 champion.

128 **after not being chosen:** Barnaby and Niederhoffer had an interesting relationship. Niederhoffer was very close to Barnaby, visited him often and regularly corresponded with him, and Barnaby asked Niederhoffer to write a chapter on doubles for his 1979 *Winning Squash Racquets*. Still they had their problems. In a letter to Barnaby, 24 January 1971, from Berkeley, Niederhoffer wrote that he was disappointed not being selected to the Harvard-Yale team that was touring England. Although he noted that the reasons were his "being immature and being a bad sport," he was stilll upset about it. He also criticized Barnaby of "joining in the the general level of criticism" directed at himself, instead of backing him up.

Barnaby replied from Lincoln on 18 March 1971: "First, the England trip. That trip is not a tool of education to be used to develop students in the sense we hope their Harvard experience will develop them. It is an ambassadorial affair, in which those selected represent the U.S. and Harvard abroad. Anyone considered too immature to do this job effectively is rejected. Three Yalies were rejected this year so the number six man went, to his vast surprise and joy. But the fact was you had a controversial reputation and questionable manners and the committee decided you were a bomb they didn't dare risk. I am sorry you still feel hurt. Actually, you shouldn't: you were—and are still?—a complex person who did not develop in an orthodox manner or an ordinary fashion. Such a person, in the middle of one of his 'stages,' is a poor choice for an ambassador. They must have establishment types—or they think they must. Are you angry that you didn't quite fit? Is this a compliment or a condemnation? As for the rest of it—you earned all the discredit you got. Pushing people, quarreling with referees, theatricalism in the court—all these are against the traditions of the game. You were like a 20th century dissonance thrown into eighteenth century music. I joined in the discredit—to use your word—and I'd join again. But there was a difference: many people pigeon-holed you permanently as a bad egg, a poor sport, like Ned Bigelow who wrote you off 100% in that positive way of his. I said no. I said you were sensitive and perceptive and could learn, that we should stick with you and be ready to write off the past. I thought I did this personally. At least it was my policy. Also, it was not easy. I got all kinds of pressure to throw you out—the easy solution of course. I stood on my policy. In this I thought I was very loyal to you. I took a lot of gas and refused to give way. I believe my policy paid off. Could I have done better by you? Should you reproach me or thank me? And remember: I owe loyalty to the game as well as to you boys. Last: this business about the different competitive backrounds is a crutch you should discard. Legitimate in your Freshman and Sophomore years perhaps, but not thereafter. If we believe in free will at all, then, once a man has a clear choice he is responsible. Personally, I hold seniors responsible while I am very gentle with Freshmen. As I recall, you almost behaved yourself as a senior! Ha!"

128 **That season:** "There was a lot of anticipation about this match," remembered Tom Poor, a young player who lost in the opening round that year. "It was between the wily veteran and the young upstart, and both were tough as nails. We knew there was going to be a sort of passing of the torch."

128 **"It was bedlam":** *Squash Racquets USA*, April 1974.

128 **After losing in the finals:** Niederhoffer remembered a beautiful lob that Charlie Ufford hit in the fifth game of their semifinal match in 1965 as "the finest point against me in my multifarious squash career."

129 **annual repetition:** See Lincoln Werden, *New York Times*, 14 February 1966; Al Laney, *New York Herald Tribune*, 14 February 1966 and *New York World-Telegram*, 10 February 1966.

130 **taken an extrapresentable:** Satterthwaite, *Three-Wall Nick*, p. 117.

130 **The Chicago clubs:** Niederhoffer claimed in *Education of Speculator* that, "With a great facade of hand wringing and soul searching, the officials of the squash association and my

competitors accepted my resignation with alacrity." He said he was made a hero of the Anti-Defamation League.

130 **Caesar he was not:** *Sports Illustrated*, 27 February 1975. Satterthwaite argued in *Three-Wall Nick* that the topic of Niederhoffer didn't come up much during his hiatus: "As soon as a player drops off the circuit, he's almost immediately and completely forgotten. He's no longer a factor . . . If he's not in the tournament, they don't think about him."

130 **unspoken reason for his boycott:** Six months after the 1967 nationals, the Illinois Country Club asked Niederhoffer if he wanted to join. He accepted but stayed in retirement. Niederhoffer did play some squash once he moved to the Bay Area. He reached the finals of the 1970 Northern California championships where he lost to Alex Eichmann. He also played in four national doubles tournaments during his five-year hiatus.

130 **affair grated on him:** In 1968 the USSRA issued a general statement that was widely viewed as a specific slap on Niederhoffer's wrist for bad behavior at the national doubles. "The executive committee has in mind repeated foul language, constant rebukes and criticism of the referees and judge's decisions and intentional and frequent violations of the playing rules, perhaps resulting in physical injury to his opponent. This might be particularly appropriate when there are ladies present in the gallery." USSRA minutes, 1968.

131 **Ty Cobb of squash:** Niederhoffer wrote in 1977 with faux understatement, "I found that I could not play in any of the local clubs there [in Chicago] because they didn't wish to have me as a member. I believe they found me different in several aspects from their other players." Francis, *Smart Squash*, pp. 23–24.

131 **the quizzical rictus:** Satterthwaite, *Three-Wall Nick*, p. 67.

131 **radio playing or cigarette smoke:** The radio incident happened in the finals of the 1965 nationals, and the cigarette incident happened in the quarterfinals of the 1975 nationals. See *Racquet Voice*, October 1979 and *Sports Illustrated*, 4 March 1975.

132 **struck an ice pick:** Francis, *Smart Squash*, pp. 116–122. One diary entry, dated 22 June 1975, contradicted that purported streak but also confirmed Niederhoffer's mythically analytical approach to squash: "Played well. How come? Was it that I didn't play on 6/21? Was it two-hour rest before playing? Must quantify. Will not achieve greatness if I continue to be unsystematic." In his notebook Niederhoffer talks about whirlwinds and beaver dams and the fangs of wolves. One evening, while practicing alone at the Harvard Club, the night watchman turned off the lights on that floor: "I was back in *The Pit and the Pendulum*. The four walls were slowly compressing. What a fright. What an experience. Few have known a squash court like me and yet I was lost. . . . I couldn't see. I sweated with agony. I felt along the wall, looking for the door. Couldn't find it. I was on the side wall. Looked on the back wall for the door. Then I felt it but couldn't get out. Dumb me. Tried for five minutes to get out, fooling with the latch. Gradually, the fear let go of me. I fortunately was on Court 8 at the Harvard Club which has an open gallery. Plenty of pushups finally came in handy. I jumped, grabbed, and I was free. The only time a player should be alone on a squash court with the lights turned off is with a voluptuous broad."

132 **methodical, fascinatingly self-aware:** Satterthwaite, *Three-Wall Nick*, p. 158. "Vic was always aware that he grew up in a poor section of Brooklyn, the other side of the tracks, and that he was Jewish," said his college roommate Jim Wynee. "He always had something to prove. He would chew glass to win." See *Racquet* magazine, September–October 1978.

132 **stovepipe legs:** Satterthwaite, *Three-Wall Nick*, p. 148.

132 **intercede to ensure his acceptance:** Niederhoffer, *Education of Speculator*, p. 56.

133 **"red carpet here today":** *Boston Globe*, 25 January 1976.

133 **Nayar rang the bell:** Bob Lehman wrote in the 1972–73 Met SRA yearbook: "The much awaited meeting between Nayar and Niederhoffer proved the sagacity of all the awaiters. It was brilliant. The variety inherent in the arsenal of these fine athletes surpasseth all imagining. And the speed! Usually, if Vic gets in front—forget it. Or vice versa. But not in this one. And the switches, the power, the touch, the accuracy! Oh, well."

134 **without loss of a game:** According to a history of Detroit squash, published for the 1995 nationals, Niederhoffer drilled Steve Moysey in the back three times in the third game of the finals of the 1972 nationals. "That's the third time you've hit me," Moysey said after getting nailed at 8–1. "I'll hit you seven more times if you stand in the path," Niederhoffer replied. "After that, Moysey simply seemed to give up and let balls bounce in front of him without moving for them." Niederhoffer won the match, 15–9, 15–13, 15–4.

135 **forty-five minute delay:** Gordy Anderson was watching the match through the tiny window in the back door. When the two men came out during this contact-lens delay, "Sharif just looked stunned. I wanted to shake him and say, 'Wake up.'"

135 **Word of the attack:** See the Met SRA 1964–65 yearbook for a photograph taken at Rockaway that fateful Sunday.

136 **split the atom:** See Richard Rhodes, *The Making of the Atomic Bomb* (New York: Simon & Schuster, 1986), pp. 394–442. The court, along with the stadium, was torn down in 1957. A Henry Moore sculpture marks the spot today. Although many people have claimed that the court was a squash singles or doubles court, a cursory look at the many artists' renditions of the 1942 experiment, including Gary Sheahan's well-known painting, reveals a court much larger than a squash court.

136 **bundled her up:** See Met SRA yearbook, 1980–81.

137 **Tressel hosted the national juniors:** Tressel later became president of the U.S. Lawn Tennis Association.

139 **Morris Clothier:** Art Potter, Clarence Chaffee, John Conroy, Jack Barnaby, Jack Summers, John Skillman, Red Hoehn and Harry Cowles were the coaches in the inaugural class inducted into the National Intercollegiate Squash Hall of Fame. Ed Crocker's record, 116–229, did include a 1967 season where MIT beat Princeton, Dartmouth and Trinity. Marshall's record was 233–129–1.

140 **until coming to Cambridge:** John Davis however had good lineage, as his grandfather was Dwight Davis, the donor of the Davis Cup and a top squash player in the 1920s. "There was a time when a national collegiate squash championship for the Crimson didn't mean much," wrote Peter G. Palches in the *Harvard Crimson* in 1955. "Squash, after all, was a gentleman's game, and where were there any gentlemen except at Harvard?" Many of the Harvard players were legacies—Ben Heckscher was the fourth generation of Heckschers in a row to go to Harvard.

140 **down to the fourth knuckle:** *Boston Globe*, 13 December 1970. Perhaps the greatest individual comeback was in 1959, when Dave Brechner of Princeton won against Navy after being down 2–0, 14–3.

141 **first undefeated season:** Four days later, at the national intercollegiate team tournament, Musto again went down to Baker with their teams tied at 4–4. (Other Yalies had barely won their matches—Alex Darrow won after being down 0–2 and Garrett Frank survived five match points against Jim Masland. Frank, like a rat, aced Masland at 17–all in the fifth.) This time Musto climbed back from a 2–0 deficit to win in five. Baker, demoralized, never played another intercollegiate match.

141 **help of Merion Cricket Club:** Arthur M. Potter and Arthur M. Potter, Jr., *Squash Racquets: The Server—Midshipmen Squash Racquets Manual*, 1974.

142 **1957 intercollegiate finals:** Squash did so well at the Naval Academy that in 1965 the U.S. Navy built a squash court on U.S.S. *Simon Lake*, a submarine tender.

142 **broke off relations:** In 1959 Ernie Richmond, president of the USSRA, wrote to the commandant of the Academy to seek redress. The commandant replied that Potter was only teaching his players to be aggressive. Jack Barnaby reported to the USSRA that there were many complaints against Navy. Regardless of the controversy, Potter felt compelled to warn his Navy fans about proper decorum: "Squash spectators etiquette is similar to that of tennis, in that no cheering or applauding is done during actual play. Applause is usually reserved until play of a point is completed. Spectators should refrain from cheering

an opponent's error, loud talk, or making noise during a match. When a match is played without a referee, the players will make their own decisions without spectator assistance. Remember when you wear the midshipmen uniform, you are expected to maintain the appropriate behavior for every occasion at all times."

143 **Upon retiring:** Molloy's record has also been recorded as 216–100. His first day as a professional was spent at Ardsley giving lessons. It was 7 December 1941.

143 **fancy Merion offense:** Satterthwaite, *Three-Wall Nick*, pp. 84–88. "Al gave me a lot of good squash advice that has kept me in good stead," Maurice Heckscher said. "I have always remembered to hit all my dropshots hard. Never forgot that. But he knew how to handle me. Howard Coonley and I used to smoke like chimneys. Our hotel room on the road would just be a fog bank. Once Al walked in and said, "Ok, if you lose a match, you'll have to stop smoking or I'll kick you off the team." So Howard and I proceeded to go undefeated that year. That's motivation." "All the players thought Al had a huge impact on them," said Ned Edwards who succeeded Molloy as coach in 1991. "Penn squash alums continue to play after college. Al imbued squash with a sense of mysticism. He would say, 'every time you hit the ball, you want it to come back. If you don't want it to come back, if you don't want a competitive game, play your grandmother.' He taught us how to handle the fear of losing or winning. And he knew the tiny details of the game—how to hit the lob serve with topspin, how to generate pace with the head of the racquet, little mechanical things that made a huge difference. After I took over as coach, I used to ask Al to come in and talk to the team and give us these pearls of wisdom, and we all felt that it was like a visit to the mountaintop." Molloy died in May 2000.

143 **an early proponent of softball:** Molloy wrote a manifesto for switching to softball that appeared in the February 1980 issue of *Racquet Voice*.

143 **"a stopgap thing":** Harvard-Princeton football program, 8 November 1975. Late in 1936 Barnaby planned on leaving Harvard, for he wrote to the USSRA asking to be reinstated as an amateur. See USSRA executive minutes, February 1937.

144 **"clay shoveler's fracture":** The 1950 Harvard yearbook wrote, "The Yale debacle which followed, and ended the season, was a catastrophe. The Cambridge cellmen by all rules in the prediction book should have won the game, but didn't. This tasted a little salty after the season of victory."

144 **Foster won the national intercollegiates:** The team barely got to the 1951 national teams because of a train strike and did not leave Boston until Thursday afternoon, arriving in Chicago Friday morning. Although Harvard beat Philadelphia in the final, 5–0, it was a lot closer. Foster came back from 2–0 down to beat Carter Fergusson, 15–14 in the fifth. Two other matches went to five games and a fourth was a default by John Campbell who broke his toe Saturday evening.

144 **a record of 355–95:** Barnaby's record is not entirely clear. According to *Sports Illustrated* in March 1976, it was 355–95, twenty-one Ivy League championships and twenty intercollegiates titles; according to John Powers, it was 346–95, fifteen Ivy League titles and nineteen national titles. The *Harvard Crimson* reported on 9 December 1975 on Barnaby's 350th win against Navy, at the beginning of his final season and on 4 June 1976 said he had 354 wins. The *Boston Globe* said on 25 January 1976 that he had 346 wins, with still a month left in the season. "I would have to take these [statistics] with several grains of salt," said Barnaby. "I'm not too sure of those statistics." Harvard had such a passion for squash not just because of the great enthusiasm of coaches like Cowles and Barnaby, but in part because the many squash courts in its residential houses were not bound by parietal rules, and men and their lady guests could consort there after hours.

144 **"snarling curmudgeon":** Emily Fisher, *Boston Magazine*, March 1976.

145 **"eternal sophomore":** *Boston Globe*, 13 December 1970. In 1963 Barnaby and Collins taped a tennis clinic in Boston for WGBH, a show that launched Collins's historic broadcasting career. See *TV Guide*, 11 May 1974.

145 **his tongue never faltered:** "The game can be played in so many different ways," he explained in *Winning Squash Racquets.* "This infinite variety, while not quite as sexy as Cleopatra, nonetheless offers an endless subject for conversation. Many players derive a considerable part of pleasure from analyzing, dissecting, and extolling or downgrading the efforts of others, spending far more time carrying others to inexorable verbal victory or defeat than they ever spend on the court. After all, there is no limit to the excellence of one's talking game. No shots are missed, fatigue is unknown (tongues have incredible endurance), strategy is farsighted and tactical implementation knows no bounds. Which one of us has ever failed to win a title over a beer? The Monday morning quarterbacks in squash are not outranked by those of any other sport. After being whipped by a mediocre rival, an hour of squash talk can be an unsurpassed restorative for the damaged ego."

146 **"drought kills the green grass":** *Sportscape: The Boston Sports Journal,* Summer 1982. "Jack Barnaby is to Harvard squash what Yoda was to young Luke Skywalker and the rebel force—omniscient, omnipotent, omnipresent and omniumgatherum," said George Polsky, class of 1992, in *Harvard Magazine,* March–April 1992. "He invented the double reverse Oedipus boast, which was later outlawed because it put one's opponent into an irreversible catatonic state. One evening I caught Jack levitating in the men's showers; it was then that I knew that his powers were not of this world. In a nutshell, welcome to supernature central."

146 **aimless law students:** *Harvard Crimson,* February 1959.

146 **all of whom played number one:** In 1970 the three Foster brothers and two of their sons formed a side for the national teams.

146 **polio, which paralyzed:** See Harvard-Yale football program, November 1941 for a photo of Nickerson. Nickerson later became champion of the Union Club. A coda of the story appeared in *Town and Country,* January 1990. Laurence Shames wrote that Nickerson, after winning a varsity match, received a telegram from President Franklin Roosevelt that read, "What America needs is more people like you." Legend has it that Nickerson sent back a note: "If there were more people like me, you wouldn't be sending telegrams from the White House."

146 **supple and fast:** He spent the first year after college as the John Harvard Scholar at Emmanuel College, Cambridge University. Ufford played for Cambridge and earned his blue—the first ever for an American—by defeating his man in the Oxford match. See *Harvard Alumni Bulletin,* April 1954 for photographs of Ufford looking pensively out over the Cam.

147 **Ufford redeemed himself:** A full description of this match, written by Peter Wood, appeared in the *New York Times Magazine,* 5 April 1970. See also *Sports Illustrated,* 9 March 1970.

147 **"happy as a clam":** See Princeton University yearbook, 1976. A testimonial dinner was held at the Ritz Carlton in Boston on 15 May 1976 and dozens of former players came, including Charlie Ufford, Beek Pool, Hal Baker, Herb Gross and Germain Glidden, as well as fellow coaches Clarence Chaffee, Eddie Reid and Ed Serues. The Friends of Harvard Squash sent Charlotte and Jack Barnaby on a trip to Wimbledon and England in July 1977. Jack bumped into Allison Danzig in the Members Enclosure—a conversation to which many historians would have begged to be privy.

148 **membership hovering:** In 1966 membership "increased markedly to 178 paid members."

148 **Sherlock Holmes:** *Boston Herald Traveler,* 10 March 1971.

150 **Margaret Riehl:** *Baltimore Sun,* 5 May 1971. The club was a key club, open twenty-four hours a day. Shaeffer had been an outstanding player. In 1941 he had been up 13–11 in the fifth against Lester Cummings in the U.S. Professionals, before losing in overtime.

151 **teas with the Duke:** When greeting the Queen's consort, Barbara Pilling said, "I hope we can have a match sometime." This sort of behavior was not uncommon on tours. In 1966 during a British Jester tour of America, the team visited the White House. In the Oval Office, Humphrey Truman picked up President Lyndon Johnson's beagle by the ears.

152 **"She's like a bulldog":** *Time,* 3 March 1959.

152 **smacked balls into the rears:** Satterthwaite, *Three-Wall Nick,* p. 328.

153 **meeting her gaze:** Edward Steichen famously said this about J. P. Morgan.

153 **Dilks beat Peggy Howe:** Peggy was three months pregnant at the time.

154 **"tell them once":** The motto was originally articulated by George Munger, the Penn football coach. "You taught us how to accept winning and losing with equal grace," Jane Stauffer eulogized at Bramall's funeral in April 1990. "You always said, 'If you lose I expect you to shake hands. I expect you to congratulate your opponent. It's her day. But for you, I see another day coming.' "

154 **another driver:** The first driver was charged with drunken driving and driving with a sus-pended license (it had been suspended in 1943); the second driver, who reportedly had been drinking but was not impaired, was charged with driving too fast for conditions and fined $15. The USSRA sent her an electric watch. Betty Meade died in 1990 after a fight against cancer.

155 **French tennis star Francoise Durr's:** See Jim Kaplan, *Sports Illustrated,* March 1976.

155 **"insufficient data":** See Frank Satterthwaite, *Racquet* magazine, March–April 1978.

155 **the play rough:** "When I first went on the squash court, I couldn't believe how dangerous it was. I thought I was going to lose my head. I stalled and sulked around for another year. Then I decided I had better try it again." Francis, *Smart Squash,* pp. 19–20. "I became a student of the game because I got a tremendous satisfaction from doing things right. So now when I am playing good squash it's complete fulfillment. I think, 'Oh, how marvelous this is, it's fantastic.' I just sort of sparkle." See George Bell, *Squash News,* February 1985.

156 **"beautiful women, excellent bourbon":** In 1971 St. Louis publicly challenged any city in the world to a head-to-head match. "Hey, Philadelphia, are you listening?" ran their advertisement in the USSRA yearbook. "One more thing: we're not nearly as mean off the court as on. We guarantee a weekend of wining and dining to help remove the sting of defeat."

157 **only two courts:** The Piedmont Driving Club was so exclusive, said Brian Dyson, CEO of Coca-Cola, "that ordinarily you can't get in without at least one Confederate colonel in your family." *New York Times Magazine,* 10 September 1987.

158 **factory workers played:** *Providence Journal-Bulletin,* 22 October 1997 and 1994 U.S. Open program.

158 **peculiar member clubs:** See Bill Robinson in *Squash News,* April 1986. Robinson played on average two hundred fifty times a year for forty straight years. After tearing a rotator cuff in his shoulder he switched from his right hand to left hand and soon was a B player.

158 **full-length overcoat:** *Squash News,* January 1995. The general, Tiger Jack Wood, who had built the courts at West Point, always said to players, "With your speed and my brains, we'd make a good player." Crumley died two weeks before the start of a home-and-away match series with the Olympic Club in San Francisco.

159 **at the Cate School:** The school had two courts, but the wrestling team used one and the other was filled with old bric-a-brac. Jim Murray, *Trentonian,* 27 February 1971.

159 **"more reminiscent of the NHL":** See program for 1987 softball nationals and *Squash News,* October 1978.

159 **driving force:** In 1950 twelve clubs were the charter members, and the association sanc-tioned eight tournaments that year; twenty years later it had twenty-four clubs and forty tournaments. These were member clubs of the Pacific Coast in 1951: Athens Athletic Club in Oakland, College Club in Seattle, Multonomah Athletic Club in Portland, Olympic Club in San Francisco, Pacific Union Club in San Francisco, Royal Canadian Navy in Esqumault, BC, Seattle Tennis Club, University Club of San Francisco, Univer-sity of California, Berkeley, Victoria Squash Racquets Club in Victoria, Washington Ath-letic Club in Seattle and the Seattle YMCA. At one time in the fifties, there were four

players in San Francisco who had reached the finals of the national intercollegiates and all four had lost: Walt Pettit in 1940, Dick Cooley in 1942, Larry Blair in 1946 and Larry Sears in 1957.

161 **Dick Cooley:** In the first John Jacobs in 1947, Cooley reached the semifinals. *The New Yorker,* 18 January 1947.

161 **A classic squash conundrum:** In an unprecedented move, *Squash News* devoted its October 1991 issue to a profile of Hayden-Whyte. His rails were once timed at 168 miles per hour. The paradelle is an obscure eleventh-century French form. Hayden-Whyte also wrote notable biographies of Guglielmo Baldini, the Italian composer, and Dag Henrick Esrum-Hellerup, the Danish flutist, conductor and composer. See *Oregonian,* 13 October 1991 for an article on the Whitman squash team, which included Paul Mozer, Lee Marion and Mike Alger, the brother of national champion Mark Alger.

161 **octogenarian who taught:** The illuminated scroll given to Saulson on his eightieth birthday was inscribed: "Any person who plays the game of squash racquets belongs to an elite group of men and women. They are sons and daughters of the cheetah and the whirlwind. They know and want only the best sport in the world. Most squash players play better than other squash players—at least in the locker room. A few players are legendary—always competitive, always good, always friends."

162 **"status symbol":** *New York Times,* 6 February 1966.

162 **preppy Harvard student:** In *Love Story,* Ryan O'Neal wears white clothes, but not a collared shirt. In the first scene, which lasts half a minute, he plays his college roommate who talks throughout the points: "Move your ass, preppie," and "You've got it made, you bastard, made in the shade, snug as a bug in a rug." O'Neal, a lefty, wins the first point after two hesitant backhands, but the roommate serves the next point. He lobs it out of court, much to O'Neal's chagrin. The second scene, now filmed from the front and back walls, features more movement as the players seem less afraid to take the T. The point ends with O'Neal missing on a backhand swing that looked more like someone caught in a car with angry hornets. "Hey, what's the matter, Ollie?" the friend asks. "Off day, that's all," O'Neal replies. "Off day? C'mon, you've been having an off day for two weeks now."

162 **"harnessed laziness":** Jesters in England at the time tried to defend themselves by claiming this was a private matter. John Armitage, the editor of *Squash Rackets & Fives,* commented in December 1933 on the team's composition: ". . . although its constitution has not met with universal approval, it is difficult to make out why its critics should be so positive that the matter concerns them . . . unnecessary comment is akin to stirring a nest of sleeping vipers, which once aroused, will never rest again until their hateful poison is discharged."

163 **broadcast of squash:** "Snell played beautiful squash and it was the cleverness of his tactics that forced many of his opponent's errors," wrote Allison Danzig in the *New York Times.* "His use of the drop shot, both from forehand and backhand, was masterful. So well did he disguise his direction that he frequently had Pool starting off on the wrong foot. His control was almost faultless, his position in the court was uniformly correct and so quick was he on his feet that little eluded his racquet." Amr later resigned from the Jesters and became a recluse.

163 **"roughhouse, body blocks":** *The Racquet,* December 1951.

163 **"so complicated":** *Squash Badminton* magazine, April 1934.

164 **All-American in college squash:** In 1953 Merion invited Althea Gibson to play in the Pennsylvania state tennis championships and arranged for her to spend the week at Willing Patterson's home in Radnor. Patterson was a likely choice to help break the color barrier at Merion: He was a staff member of the American Friends Service Committee, the Quaker aid organization, and a Delano kin to President Roosevelt. In 1973 the *New York Times* sent a reporter to the nationals in Princeton. The reporter asked Peter Wood whether "squash is resolving the problem of discrimination." Wood replied, "It only exists to the degree that racism and discrimination continue in the private clubs. There are no

black players now that I know of, but that's not the fault of the white players." Still, in his own book Wood notes that "within the thick stone walls and arrogant architecture of the likes of New York City's University Club and Racquet & Tennis Club, prejudice has a way of hanging on like malaria." Wood, *Book of Squash*, p. 33.

VII. SEX, SCANDAL AND CELEBRITIES

166 **favorite was an underground court:** See Monaghan's October 1972 final report to the USSRA. Showing the breadth of squash in America, he received inquires from every U.S. state but North and South Dakota, as well as from fourteen foreign countries. He also designed a court in Carmel, California, that was made of tan oak and another halfway up the Teton Mountains.

166 **a quantum leap:** Howard Butcher, III, was the leading force behind the Ringe courts.

166 **first full-length glass back:** "I took two half-inch thick panels of Pittsburgh Plate glass and put a laminate film in the middle," Monaghan said. "Al Molloy was excited. This would help him teach the game, but Penn was terribly worried the glass would shatter." See Michael Palmer, *Guinness Book of Squash* (London: Guinness Superlatives, 1984) for a detailed history of the glass court in Europe. The famous glass-back court at the Abbeydale Club in Sheffield was not built until October 1971.

167 **in a barn:** Barclay White had built his doubles court with plywood. It cost $7,000 to construct, possibly the cheapest doubles court ever made. His club was called the South Penn Woods Club.

167 **project one step further:** "It's like microwave ovens," said Stu Goldstein in *Squash News*, January 1987, in reference to Harry Saint and commercial clubs. "Now that anybody can get one, it's no big deal. Ever stop to wonder who took us from ovens to microwave ovens? Me neither."

167 **stepping out of *The Great Gatsby*:** *Signature* magazine, July 1978. See *Viva* magazine, October 1977, for a four-page fashion shoot of Saint, by Pierre Houles, in Ralph Lauren herringbone jackets; *New York Times*, 28 January 1987; *New York Post*, 2 July 1977 and *New York* magazine, 28 November 1977. In 1987 Saint wrote the bestselling novel *Memoirs of an Invisible Man*.

168 **Designed by the firm:** John Copelin was Yale, class of 1957 and also worked on the renovation of Yale's courts at Payne Whitney.

168 **"the spirit of Le Corbusier":** *Horizon* magazine, September 1977 and *Racquet* magazine, summer 1977.

168 **notorious mix of characters:** *Squash News*, April 1978. In 1978 *Squash News* serialized Peter Stephan's novel, *A Season in the C League*. Salacious extract, from June 1978: "My eyes stared into hers and found only naked lust there. . . . Forget about dykes and deadlines. He had to stop that ball from glancing off the sidewall on rail shots before he'd write another word."

168 **co-ed sessions:** Saint denied that Uptown was merely a singles bar: "The spectacle of a lot of people dressed up in white looks a lot more wholesome than a singles bar." *Viva* magazine, April 1978: "The atmosphere here is very important. We're not a singles club. People come here because they like to play squash."

168 **doggedly went on with their match:** *Dun's Review* magazine, September 1977.

168 **Woody Allen:** Shot with just one camera from behind the glass wall, the scene opens with nothing but white space and "Uptown Racquet Club" emblazoned on the tin. Woody and Murphy enter the court and play six points. Although Woody loses the first five points, he serves every time from the right side of the court, but does not stand in the server's circle. In the first point, he hits it to himself twice. In the second point, Murphy runs around his backhand (his character's name is Yale) and hits a volley over Woody's head. In the third point, Woody can't reach a drive on his backhand side. In the fourth point, Woody whiffs on a backhand. In the fifth point, Woody mishits a return of serve. Murphy apologizes for

not hitting an easier ball for him. Woody wins the last point because Murphy whiffs on the serve. Both men, although distinctly out of breath, talk throughout the match about women—which is about the only realistic part of the scene. More than anything, the match shows the truth about negative capability.

Compare this with *Wall Street*, the 1987 drama, which has a half-minute squash match between Charlie Sheen and Michael Douglas. Sheen, breathing hard, hits a topspin forehand and then crashes into a wall. "C'mon, sport," says Douglas. "You've gotta try harder. Need some exercise for Christ's sakes." Sheen tosses the ball back to Douglas and says, "I don't think I can go on, Mr. Gekko." Douglas replies like a typical squash coach: "Let's go, buddy. Push yourself. Finish out the game." He then wallops a hard overhead tennis serve.

169 **opened the Peninsula:** Alex Eichmann's father was an Olympic track star for Germany in 1920. See the *San Francisco Sunday Examiner & Chronicle*, 21 February 1982 and *Diversion: For Physicians at Leisure*, 15 September 1983.

169 **"sneaky reason for launching":** *Cleveland Plain Dealer*, 2 March 1981. See *Cleveland* magazine, April 1979.

169 **enormously spiky squash tree:** *Squash News*, October 1978.

169 **New York eventually had:** See *New York Post*, 22 June and 2 July 1977. Halpern had twenty-six angel investors. "You don't ask a squash player if he won or lost. You ask him how he feels. Invariably he'll tell you, 'I feel great,'" said Halpern, in *Dun's Review*, September 1977. Manhattan Squash had the first regulation racquetball courts in Manhattan. In 1978 Bellingham also opened the Racqueteers Club in New Haven with four squash and eighteen racquetball courts. Another club was LaRaquette, located in the Parker-Meridien Hotel. Both Park Avenue and Lincoln suffered massive flooding, the former from frozen sprinklers, the latter from a water main break. New Yorkers got so bullish on commercial squash clubs that one was planned for a spot on Second Avenue in the low Forties. Called the International Squash Club, it was to have forty courts, including softball and doubles courts.

170 **By the early eighties:** *New York Times*, 31 July 1977 and 20 July 1986. In 1977 the New York clubs started a new service, Dial-A-Court: players could call a woman, Lynne Katsafouros, who would book a caller into one of a dozen participating squash clubs.

170 **"perfect antidote":** *Cue* magazine, 24 June 1977.

170 **"neurotic, upper-middle-class":** *Forbes*, 1 August 1977.

171 **"12-meter yacht racing":** *Sports Illustrated*, 12 September 1977.

171 **"Women are finding":** *New York Post*, 22 June 1977. See *Women's Wear Daily*, 10 March 1977, for an article by Beverly Grunwald on John Knowles, president of the Rockefeller Foundation, Harvard graduate and squash player.

171 **"Daddy learned taxidermy by mail":** *Aloft*, National Airlines' magazine, September–October 1979.

171 **"Greenwich Game":** Racquetball was birthed by a series of inventive men who tinkered with racquet games: the Rev. Frank Peer Beal who created paddle tennis in Michigan in 1898; Fessenden S. Blanchard and James K. Cogswell who created platform tennis in Scarsdale in 1928 using Beal's racquets; and Earl Riskey in Michigan in the thirties who soaked a tennis ball in gasoline and used the resultant black ball for his version of Beal's game, paddleball.

171 **brash world champion:** See *Racquet* magazine, March–April 1978. Hogan earned $50,000 in prize money and endorsements in 1976 and $100,000 in 1977. See *Wall Street Journal*, 12 May 1978 for the first inkling that racquetball was going to go bust.

172 **"lace-pants game":** *Canada Racquets* magazine, April 1982.

172 **"does something for the ego":** *Horizon* magazine, September 1977.

172 **Saul Bellow:** See *Humboldt's Gift* (New York: Viking, 1975). "You collide with other player or run into the walls. You are hit in the backswing, you often catch yourself in the face with your own racquet. The game has cost me a front tooth. I knocked it out myself

and had to have a root-canal and a crown job. . . . On some mornings I am lame, hardly able to straighten my back when I get out of bed, by midday I am on the court playing, leaping, flinging myself full length on the floor to scoop dead shots and throwing my legs and spinning entrechats like a Russian dancer. However, I am not a good player. I am too tangled about the heart, overdriven. I fall into a competitive striving frenzy. Then, walloping the ball, I continually say to myself, 'Dance, dance, dance, dance!'"

172 **Elvis Presley:** The biggest knock against racquetball must be that it actually does not take care of business in a flash. The King died just a few hours after playing racquetball.

172 **"a set of Keds and sufficient motor skills":** Curt Suplee, *Washington Post Magazine*, 17 February 1985.

172 **"nine parts Bruce Jenner":** David Scorgie, *Edmonton* magazine, August 1979.

172 **"mention racquetball and bowling":** *New York Times Magazine*, 2 March 1980. See *Travel & Leisure*, June 1977.

173 **proverbial one squash court:** Perhaps it was Raul de Villafranca who built Mexico's first squash court in March 1965. Villafranca helped form the Asociacion Mexicana de Squash in 1967.

173 **marketing three lines:** Cragin had the Whipstroke, the Coronet and the Hornet. "The Cragin-Simplex bats are perfectly balanced to put extra 'whip' into every stroke," read an advertisement. "Smash hits don't bother it. And it's a racquet that never acts 'boardy' or stiff because the superb construction of the bat actually 'gives' with the ball. The grip? Cushiony. Fits your hand like a favorite glove. Never 'cramps' your hand, even after hours of hard play." The North American Professional Squash Racquets Association endorsed the Whipstroke. Montenegro served as treasurer of the association, and after 1947 he donated the trophies for the U.S. Professionals. Eddie Reid, a poker friend of Montenegro, called him "Walter Pigeon."

173 **stayed ice cold:** See USSRA executive minutes—in 1949: The doubles ball, known as 49B, bounced thirty-six inches rather than thirty-two to thirty-four inches from a height of one hundred inches; 1958: Seamless tried to slow down the ball so that it would not be so fast once it got warmed up; 1961: the six boxes of balls at the North American Open were too fast to be used.

174 **romance to an all-year affair:** It was universally acknowledged that between 1945 and 1975 Montenegro, although he never played squash, attended more American squash tournaments than any other person. In 1969 he merged Cragin-Simplex with Garcia, a gigantic sporting goods company that was traded on the New York Stock Exchange. In 1975 Garcia went bankrupt.

174 **rife with complaints:** See USSRA executive minutes—in 1961: High incidence of breakage with Cragin-Simplex balls, due to a curing problem and the doubles ball has a tendency to skid; 1964: Seamless now cooperating with the USSRA much more than in recent years and attempting to slow down its ball; 1969: Neither Seamless nor Cragin-Simplex balls meet USSRA requirements and quality control is a problem, as balls from the same box may bounce differently; 1971: Both balls have erratic bounces and the Seamless doubles ball is not in conformity.

175 **"encouraging play":** *Racquet* magazine, January–February 1977.

175 **the new ball:** Actually, the Merco blue dot, an older approximation of the seventy-plus, was used from 1975 to 1977. The USSRA changed its ball specifications to accommodate the new ball. West also sold a black dot ball for cold courts, a twin red dot for high altitude doubles courts or extremely hot singles courts and a twin orange dot for cold doubles courts.

175 **looked similar to the standard:** The seventy-plus was .68 to .76 ounces, the softball was .82 to .87 ounces and the Cragin was 1.1 to 1.5 ounces; both the seventy-plus and softball were 1.56 to 1.63 inches in diameter while the Cragin was 1.7 inches.

175 **"charm all its own":** Goddard, *Squash!*, pp.139–43. See *Forbes*, 1 August 1977.

175 **"we play horseshoes"**: USSRA Yearbook, 1972–73. See Champion advertisement in *Outside* magazine, 1990; Steuben in *The New Yorker,* 19 October 1987 and Kodel action-wear in *Women's Wear Daily*, 30 November 1977. Haggar and *Sports Illustrated* also ran ads.

176 **definitive publication**: Although no editor was ever identified in the yearbook, Howard Davis, Stew Brauns, Treddy Ketcham and Jimmy Whitmoyer were some of the men who had the thankless task of editing it. Usually it was a volunteer job, although Whitmoyer was paid $1,500 in 1965 to produce the yearbook that season.

176 **Bob Lehman**: *Squash News*, October 1983 and September 1988. Lehman captained the City Athletic Club's C team. He ran an executive gifts company and designed elevator interiors. He died at age seventy-nine in May 1988.

177 **black agate**: *Narragansett Times*, 26 December 1985 and *Providence Journal-Bulletin*, 5 June 1985. "It is utterly without any socially redeeming value, other than squash," Tom said.

177 **"The arrival of a new issue"**: *Travel & Leisure*, December 1979. Shames later wrote that *Squash News* was "a marvelously obsessive tabloid that is the hard-core squash player's bible." *Town and Country*, January 1990. Tom Jones had a good sense of humor. In the Met SRA yearbook he took out a full-page advertisement. It was a blank page with just the following in small type: "Some of the worst squash players in the world have won with Tom Jones Advertising."

178 **Boesky even sponsored**: *New York Times Magazine*, 10 September 1987.

178 **Roger Daltrey**: *Good Housekeeping*, November 1983.

178 ***Penthouse*** **cover girl**: *New York Post*, 27 August 1977 and *Beverage Retailer Weekly*, 19 September 1977. Rixon, an Australian, won 15–5. For a more licentious example of squash, see the 1974 film *Emmanuelle*. In a famous squash scene, two women play wearing sunglasses and plastic visors—as if they were playing tennis outside. As in so many films featuring squash, no one seems interested in taking the T.

178 **suffered a broken nose**: *New York Post*, 25 January 1977.

178 **Ivan Lendl**: *New York Times*, 17 July 1986.

178 **hit by a staff member**: See *New York Times*, 21 February 1985; *Washington Post*, 22 February 1984 and the *Oregonian*, 11 March 1983.

179 **"sticking to tennis"**: *W* magazine, 1–8 April 1977.

179 **"I can hardly walk"**: *The New Yorker*, 30 November 1987; *Sports Illustrated*, 10 November 1986 and *New York Times*, 30 May 1986 and 7 December 1987.

180 **got a number of matches**: Dick Polsky, Bob Campbell, Malcolm MacColl, Matt Hall, David Palmer and Peter Briggs were all subsequent chairs of this committee.

180 **slenderizing workout**: *Signature* magazine, July 1978. There was still some prejudice against women, or at least some in particular, as Austin Francis quoted Rick Rescigno in *Smart Squash*: "One thing I've noticed over the years in tennis and squash is that flat-chested women seem to run better. They are usually better squash players than more fully endowed women. There have been exceptions to this, but apparently women with smaller bosoms have less weight to counteract when starting and stopping."

181 **"brandy and comfortable shoes"**: *Savvy*, August 1980.

181 **"locker and shower facilities"**: *Town and Country*, October 1976.

181 **"squash bunnies"**: *Sunday Sun* (Toronto), 21 November 1982. There was a lecherous side to everything, as Geoffrey Wagner wrote, "old club soaks, barnacled to their bar stools for years, can now be seen admiring fast action under short skirts." *Signature*, July 1978.

182 **walking naked into the lounge**: *New York Times*, 5 November 1975. On the floor of the grill room at the club was a motto "where the women cease from troubling and the wicked are at rest." See *The New York Lawyer,* May–June 1976 and *Town and Country*, October 1976.

182 **"Long forgotten dreams of glory"**: *Squash News*, July–August 1981. James Leddy at the Yale Club had no time for the E division. "E is a joke. That must be the people that learn how to open the door." *New York Times*, 13 February 1989.

182 **allowed women to play:** *Viva* magazine, April 1978. New York men were also not terribly enthusiastic about women playing squash. "I'm not sure that women should even be allowed to play squash, because they're not strong enough to hit the ball without a huge swing and are therefore dangerous," said Kevan Pickens in *Squash News*, February 1985. "[Playing women] it's a complete waste of time. You're doing them a favor. My pet peeve is the woman who asks me to play like it's a real game."

183 **never played each other:** "It was medieval," remembered Aggie Bixler Kurtz, Smith class of 1962. "We could play during the week but on weekends we were supposed to go visit our boyfriends at Harvard. It was very informal, except for the Smith championships."

183 **rule was relaxed:** *Squash News*, January 1979.

183 **through the men's locker room:** *Yankee* magazine, November 1976. "The physics of the game are the same for males, females or neuters," Jack Barnaby said to the *Harvard Crimson*, February 1982.

184 **Princeton won:** Charter teams of the U.S. Women's Intercollegiate Squash Racquets Association: Bowdoin, Connecticut College, Penn, Princeton, Radcliffe, Smith, Trinity, Vassar, Wellesley, Wesleyan, Westminster Choir and Yale. The intercollegiate Howe Cup was played at Harvard in 1999.

184 **Encouraging hoi polloi:** "It is unlikely that the squash committees at the University or Union Clubs in New York or the Cynwood [sic] or Merion Cricket Clubs in Philadelphia will be hiring gorgeous girls in low-cut squash whites to hand out circulars on street corners," said *Town and Country*, November 1976.

185 **"mink-coated, tassel-shoed":** Some argued that the inherent nature of squash, with its dual emphasis on aggressiveness and sportsmanship, was impossibly undecipherable for the ordinary person. "Clearly, this combination of ruthlessness, chicanery and politesse is not within the emotional range of everyone. It requires a full grasp of the social graces and a top-drawer education." Laurence Shames, *Town and Country*, January 1990.

185 **whitest collars:** Curt Suplee, *Washington Post Magazine*, 17 February 1985.

187 **new tournaments appeared:** In 1958, in an effort to solve the office question, the U.S. Lawn Tennis Association agreed to give office space and the part-time assistance of one of the staff members to the USSRA. But the offer was never taken up.

188 **small office in Bala Cynwyd:** According to the 1976 annual yearbook: "Office hours: September–June 8:30–4:00. When Executive Director and secretary are out, a human answering service will take messages and these will be checked about 1 pm each day. July and August—Flexible hours depending upon vacation schedules. Answering service will be checked regularly." By way of comparison, the Squash Rackets Association had at its London headquarters in 1978 a full-time staff of nine and a budget of £200,000, half of which was supplied by the government.

188 **Bancroft agreed:** *Squash News*, January 1979. In 1978 Bancroft helped pay for a bus to ferry forty junior players from Philadelphia via New York to Montreal for the Canadian national juniors. Money also came from royalties from ball sales of the seventy-plus. See Darwin Kingsley's letter to editor, *Squash News*, May 1978.

188 **a replica of the Peace Cup:** In 1983 the Insilco trophy was stolen from a truck parked near Times Square while the driver stopped to make another delivery.

189 **greater New York City area:** *Sports Style* magazine, 12 January 1981 and 16 September 1985.

VIII. BOX OF RAIN

191 **the first to join:** Apparently the second woman to become a pro was Tati Balassis, of East Lansing.

193 **four-page memorandum:** *New York Times*, 15 November 1975 and "Why I Turned Pro," 18 November 1975.

193 **a courageous move:** Satterthwaite, *Three-Wall Nick*, p. 248.

193 **Peter Briggs:** In 1978 Briggs said, "I only turned pro as a goof. . . . Niederhoffer turned pro and I did, partly out of egoism and plus it's just part of the game, something you do." Torbet, *Squash*, p. 19. Briggs played one year on the tour before retiring from singles play.

195 **"I felt like Winston Churchill":** *Horizon*, September 1977.

195 **training certification:** The WPSA hosted ten summer conferences. From 1982 to 1987, they were held at Amherst, 1988 and 1989 at Cornell, 1990 at Princeton and 1991 in Atlanta.

196 **most lucrative prize-money:** Held at the Toronto Squash Club for five years, the Mennen moved to Valhalla for two years and then three years at Curzons.

196 **Eustace Miles advocated:** "Various men, especially those who were busy in the day-time, might easily subscribe and build a rough-and-ready Court on a vacant lot of ground. The expense for each man would be far smaller than that of a private Court, and the wives and families and friends of the men could play in the morning. A movable Court, like a movable cottage, is a possibility deserving consideration."

196 **In 1935 Harrods:** *Squash Rackets & Fives*, October 1935.

197 **took about twenty minutes:** Monaghan gave the folding court to Westtown School, the venerable Quaker boarding school in West Chester, Pennsylvania. Westtown stored the court in a gym, but rarely used it because its rollers damaged the floor. *Sports Illustrated*, 26 March 1973. In 1980 Playcon built its own folding court—"The squash court that really squashes" as their advertisements trumpeted—but also abandoned the project.

197 **World Open:** The Playcon-built court had Ellis Pearson "twin-vue" tempered glass front wall, and back walls, a clear tempered glass back wall and Fiberesin wood panel sidewalls.

197 **hanging from the ceiling:** Cummings & Sears designed the building. It cost $50,000. The French artist Dominique Philippoteaux created the opening painting. When it opened, the dome of the Cyclorama was the second largest dome in the U.S., after the Capitol Building in Washington. In the 1980s, it was a derelict place and one year amid heavy rains, Bernheimer and Poor spent their evenings moving potted plants around the hall, hoping to hide the fact that the roof was leaking badly.

198 **court placed near the blue line:** "Mixed crowd of preppies, squash junkies, Penn students and curiosity seekers. But the rink's off the beaten path location, five minutes behind Penn's Ringe courts, didn't help attendance. Until Sunday's finals there may have been more promotional banners around the court than fans." *Squash News*, November 1986.

198 **six-page ads:** The advertisements for the 1985 North American Open had a useful rules explanation section, player profiles, snappy if staged photographs with Talbott having fun with a behind-the-back trick-shot, a list of public clubs in New York and a paragraph on "How to think like a squash player."

199 **pocket handkerchief:** Donald, *Boast*.

200 **tax status:** *Squash News*, May 1978.

200 **under its aegis:** On 20 March 1979, McQueenie sent out a letter soliciting support. "There have been strong suggestions that I have 'deserted the WPSA in favor of the amateurs.' Nothing could be further from truth. . . . It is true that I have taken advantage of the past deplorable state of the WPSA to advance the Professional cause and create a Professional organization within the USSRA. This in no way detracts from, threatens or supercedes the WPSA as the governing body for Professional Squash. The USSRA Pro Division will fulfill a role that the WPSA (NAPSRA) has in the past been unable to do and has little chance of accomplishing in the near future. . . . I am asking all Squash Professionals to look beyond the limited horizons of their own selfish interests to the broad spectrum of the Squash World and recognize that it is in the best interests of the game, the players and those who make a living from the sport that the various organizations complement each other by working in harmony. There is a place for a strong united Professional Squash Association and I will continue to work toward this goal. In the mean-

time, while we await this Pro Squash Utopia, let all Squash Professionals conduct themselves with dignity, earn respect from the broad base of players from whom we earn our living and help unite the various factions by our dual membership."

200 **"slowly being eased out":** Laura Torbet, *Squash*, p. 16. Although the Pro Division folded after two years, the USSRA ran a Teaching Pro tournament at the nationals throughout the 1980s.

200 **down to a final match:** In 1987 Mexico completed the North American picture of the Loews, with teams reduced to three players each. The Loews was played for six years alternatively in the United States and Canada, with the United States winning all but the first two events.

201 **graduated and moved:** Dicky Rutnagur, in *Khans Unlimited*, had an interesting reason for Sharif's relocation.

202 **a harrowing four-game match:** "It was a pretty traumatic match, but also a proud moment," said Sharif. "One game I would be going all out like a son of a gun, trying to pretend that he was an ordinary competitor. The next one I would find myself slowing down out of the instinct of our culture." *New York Times Magazine*, 2 March 1980.

202 **before returning to Philadelphia:** Merion made him qualify into the main draw of the Whitey. Mike Pierce wrote a good account of the NAO in the 1977–78 USSRA yearbook.

203 **famously hypnotic eyes:** *People*, 19 February 1979, said it was $80,000. Sharif won twelve of fourteen events in 1977–78; sixteen of eighteen in 1978–79; fifteen of eighteen in 1979–80; nine of twenty in 1980–81 and four of twenty-four in 1981–82. He was a pro at Victoria Village Squash Club and owner of a pub in Toronto. In the late seventies, Sharif represented squash in the International Racquets Championship, a tournament at the Homowack Lodge in the Catskills. It featured the best player from each of the major racquets sport. In 1977 Sharif won the round-robin tournament, broadcast on CBS and sponsored by Bristol-Myers, beating John McEnroe in badminton, racquetball and racquets, but losing to him in table tennis. He collected $15,000. In 1979 he topped Guillermo Vilas, but Vilas was awarded the title due to nebulous tie-breaking rules.

204 **"a conspiracy against him":** *Sports Illustrated*, 14 May 1979.

204 **his socks pulled high:** Yet at least some observers thought he looked as if he sung for the Doors. See *The New Yorker*, 22 March 1974. Goldstein, always good for the bizarre quotation, said, "Tennis is slow-motion compared to squash. It's all vector analysis—you have to calculate resultants. I know it sounds corny, but the most important thing is to keep your eye on the ball."

204 **slipped on a spot of sweat:** *Rochester Times-Union*, 13 October 1980.

205 **"lost his focus and his game plan":** *Squash Magazine*, April 2002. See *Racquet* magazine, January–February 1979.

206 **"sake of being on the court":** See *Men's Wear*, 24 May 1982 and *Sports Illustrated*, 28 June 1982. Desaulniers did not play in every WPSA tournament. "I think it inspires fear in these guys if they don't know when I'm coming. Then all of a sudden they see me staring down majestically from the top of the draw." *Squash News*, May 1986: "I've never seen any reason to compliment the other guy when he hits a good shot. Why should I boost his confidence?"

207 **glory of 1982 was gone:** In the 1985 North American Open, Desaulniers double-faulted at 13–14 in the second game of his quarterfinal match against Talbott and spent the whole minute before the next game squatting motionless in the court, his hands clutching his head.

209 **never lost to Sharif again:** "When he hit me the first time, I was so stunned," Talbott said. "I was four feet behind him. It was surreal. I never flinched. After he hit me the second time, Dave was so pissed he almost throttled Sharif. But Sharif was Sharif. He never said a word."

209 **"loose-limbed kid":** "He was just a ball shagger back then," said Caldwell. Don Mills thought his strokes were "absolutely horrendous." *Dayton Daily News*, 12 March 1989.

209 **never made an error:** "He was so mentally tough, " said Neal Vohr. "Mark was incredibly intense out there. He never coughed up freebies. Not one free point. You had to hit fifteen great shots to win the game. But the deal with Mark was that he was not just a defensive type. Yes, he was terribly quick and got to everything with this uncanny ease, but he had the ability to put pressure back on you. The balls were tight on the wall, crisp, low. He never made errors. He never hit sloppy shots. It was like trying to solve the riddle of the Sphinx. He didn't seem to be doing much, but there you were, down in the fifth, dripping with sweat and Mark's over there, smiling and having a great time." "Mark was always open for advice and criticism," Peter Briggs said. "It was really quite unusual. Here's the best player on the tour and yet he wanted to learn more, to improve his game. You'd expect this with lesser players, but it was unheard of for the number one guy."

209 **twice, in major tournaments:** See *Squash News,* January and May 1983. Talbott gave back a point to Edwards in the Chivas and to Nimick in the North American Open.

210 **"singing 'Alice's Restaurant'":** *New York Times,* 21 November 1984.

211 **strung along his opponents:** The Conn College match produced a comment that Talbott relished. After innocently losing to Talbott, the Conn College player exited the court and his teammates hurriedly told him that he had been playing Mark Talbott. "Who?" he asked. In the annual Jesters versus Yale match, which was held in the spring at the Field Club in Greenwich, Dave matched the costumed Mark up against Guy Cipriano, a leading squash enthusiast well known for his competitiveness. "I told Guy that our regular varsity player was sick," said Dave Talbott, "and asked if he might play against this J.V. fellow (Mark remembered his legend was as a Yale alum) who wasn't that good—the sunglasses were because of glaucoma—but who we felt deserved a chance to play just once. Guy was pretty disappointed. He had come up from New Jersey and wanted a good game, but agreed to play Sam." Friedan, with his huge belly and sunglasses, went into the court and could barely hit the ball during warmup. Cipriano crushed him in the first game, but in the second Friedan started to improve and the score got a little closer. The third game was dead even, and somehow the hapless Friedan managed to win it. Cipriano got agitated. The fourth game went to Friedan, and Cipriano was breathing hard. In the fifth the points got longer and longer. It stretched to the tie-breaker, which Friedan won on a preposterous double-boast volley, 18–16. "Guy was furious. He stormed off the court, so angry he had lost to a lumpy J.V. guy with glaucoma."

211 **too informal at the Yale Club:** *Wall Street Journal,* 24 April 1984. Despite the outfits, they took these matches seriously. Dave beat Mark in the 1981 WPSA Championships, but in that match they wore regular squash clothes. They also dressed normally in the 1985 Chivas.

211 **"It seems that his disease":** *Village Voice,* 19 February 1985.

212 **tinning on double match point:** *Greenwich News,* 10 January 1985. Edwards said to the gallery after the match, "I can measure my personal growth largely in terms of the past two years. I have had personal difficulties that have come out on this court. Thanks for tolerating it." Talbott, meanwhile, talked about how he had gone out dancing the night before until two in the morning.

213 **a dazed Bowditch:** Derrick Niederman in *Squash News,* December 1985.

214 **toured in a Winnebago:** Once, Doucas was in a bathroom at a gas station in Auburn, Massachusetts, and Clarke, thinking Doucas was in the back sleeping, drove three hours to Greenwich before realizing he had left his wingman behind.

214 **drowned in a boating accident:** Known as Merlin or the Duke, Doucas was a finesse player, as Ned Edwards said in his eulogy: "As more and more victories in doubles went to players who could run faster and hit harder the longest, you brought to the doubles court back-bending lobs and such deceptive dropshots that sometimes other teams would be left just standing still."

215 **inaugural national boys under seventeens:** "I came home thinking I was a big shot, ranked four in the country, intercollegiate champion," said Palmer Page. "I said, 'Let's go

play,' thinking I'd give my little brother sort of a lesson. Well, we go over to Merion and we couldn't get a rally going—he was beating me so badly. He was that good. I said, 'What's happened?' and he just smiled that big smile of his."

215 **the age of forty-four:** "He will flash a boyish grin in a light moment, but it is rare. When he's not involved with a point, he will stare darkly at some distant place while walking up to the front of the court to pick up the ball. He stares so hard that you think he sees nothing at all, and maybe he just senses where to go. It's an intense gaze but not the crazed glare of Sharif Khan. He seems completely alone, existing only for the ball and the angled patterns it makes with the walls." *Racquet* magazine, Summer 1977.

216 **multiple dress code violations:** *Canada Racquets* magazine, May 1985. The WPSA fined Bowditch $150.

217 **lost in the hardball:** Talbott accidentally drilled Jahangir in the leg with a rail. It was Talbott who looked like he had been hit. He dropped his racquet and said, "I'm so sorry," clasping Jahangir's shoulders. Jahangir just said, "It hurts more with the American ball." *American Health*, January–February 1984. Jahangir earned $400,000 in 1984, *People*, 11 June 1984.

218 **four people were in the gallery:** "There was a big party that night at Skyline and so everybody had gone home to change," remembered Larry Sconzo who refereed the match.

218 **"A Game of Growth":** The board of AWPS contained every single pioneering professional woman player: Barbara Maltby was vice president, Carole Dicker was secretary, Ginny Akabane was USSRA liaison, Alicia McConnell was amateur liaison, Sue Cogswell was international liaison and the "area representatives" included: Pam Behrens, Adrienne Brandriss, Debbie Brickley, Joyce Davenport, Lisa Drake, Goldie Edwards, Sally Fields, Joyce Hogan, Dale Philippi, Cece Turner and Carol Weymuller. The symbol of AWPS was a yellow zucchini with a racquet at the end.

219 **publicly quit squash:** "The more I was traveling and playing, the emptier I felt and the more meaningless the goals became," McConnell told the *New York Times*. "Squash became a constant struggle in my head. It got to the point where the negative side began winning out. It's just too painful for me and I don't think that people understand that. I feel used by squash. Through squash, I lost my whole identity. No one knew who Alicia was . . . I'm tired of living up to other people's expectations. All along, I just wanted to play the game and have fun. But somewhere along the line the little kid in me that wanted to have fun got lost." Two anonymous donors came forward after the *New York Times* article appeared and provided money for her to play two more years overseas. *Squash News*, April 1989.

219 **eighty-one-year-old Manassa Mauler:** *New York Times*, 12 January 1977. "Did you ever play this game?" someone asked Dempsey. "No, but I will if you want me to."

219 **publisher of *Penthouse*:** See *Squash News*, April 1983. Seventies-style feminism took a further blow in San Francisco when women held the Bake-Off, a tournament with prizes not for winners but for the best pie, bread and casserole.

220 **succumbed to hometown favorite:** *Times-Union*, 13 February 1975. Maltby played a difficult game, according to the reporter: "She falls a little more often, frequently stops play for questioned rulings (sometimes that can break the momentum for opponents) and invariable emotes when she's won or lost a point."

220 **"It's disgusting and unpleasant":** *Evening Bulletin*, 16 February 1976 and *Sports Illustrated*, 4 March 1976.

220 **With the tension unbearable:** "It was my best chance for the title," said Maltby in *Women's Sports*, January 1979. "I would have hesitated to call a let point in that match. Whether it was right or wrong, I still can't say. But it was so tough. It had been such an emotional game." A month later Maltby got a small measure of revenge by beating Spruance in four tight games in the third-place playoff at the *Viva* Open at Manhattan Squash. They never played again.

221 **world's most accomplished athlete:** *Quest 80* magazine, December 1980. McKay, one of eleven children, was also a top field hockey player. See *The New Yorker,* 10 April 1978.

221 **caught her in the mouth:** Women's squash had a different flavor from old-school men's squash. A reporter noticed "an abundance of hoots, hollers, whistles and even hissing." *Majority Report,* 4–17 February 1978; *Sports Illustrated,* 7 February 1977; *New York Times,* 21, 22 and 23 January 1978 and Satterthwaite, *Three-Wall Nick,* pp. 240–45, in which he describes beating McKay 9–7 in the fifth, with twelve squandered match points, in a softball exhibition at the University Club in June 1977.

221 **began playing racquetball:** Maltby also gave squash clinics around the country: In 1976 she visited Racine and Madison; in 1977 Dayton, Chicago and Cleveland; in 1978 Denver; and in 1989 Portland, San Francisco and Washington, D.C.

221 **"a big package":** *The New Yorker,* 14 March 1983.

221 **U.S. girls team came in first:** The 1980 team included Alicia and Patrice McConnell, Kathy Castle, Diane Staley and Karen Kelso. There were nineteen nations competing in the boys division, but no U.S. boys team. Because England and Australia did not send girls teams—their excuse was that Sweden did not have a properly constituted women's association—the ISRF did not officially count the results.

222 **an instant genius:** *Women Sports* magazine, December 1981.

222 **"pouting and even some tears":** *Squash News,* January 1982. After McConnell won the 1982 Boodles, *Squash News* wrote, "if it had been a boxing match, they would have stopped it after the first game."

224 **"push somebody out of their way":** *Viva,* April 1978. It took Nyad eight hours and two minutes to swim around Manhattan. Nyad holds the record for the longest ocean swim by a man or a woman, 102.5 miles, which she set swimming from the Bahamas to Florida in 1979. See Diana Nyad, *Other Shores* (New York: Random House, 1978) and *Tennis Week,* 18 December 1976 for an article George Plimpton wrote about playing Nyad in an exhibition to open Manhattan Squash Club.

X. BAIT AND SWITCH

235 **one adamantine issue:** In 1971 Stew Brauns offered the ISRF the specifications for a compromise internationally acceptable game. Although he came up with ideas on the tin, ball, rules and even the side walls, he ignored the elephant in the court and said that no decision could possibly be made on the compromise game's standard court width.

236 **vast majority:** In 1979 John Horry suggested that more than 40 percent of the courts in the world were hardball.

236 **reasonable facsimile:** Hinkle became club champion at the Racquet Club of Washington in 1926 and 1927. "We were ill-prepared to accept an invitation to send a British team to tour the U.S.A. and Canada," wrote Sam Toyne in 1949 in the SRA annual. "We knew nothing of their standards, their courts or their balls. Little did we know then that the United States championship had been in full swing since 1907."

238 **peaceful coexistence:** In the late fifties, the Soviet Union, which had no squash courts, became a battlefield for the two squash superpowers. In 1957 Ned Bigelow traveled to Moscow and met with sports ministers in an effort to have them adopt hardball standards. Upon his return he sent over balls, racquets and squash-court blueprints and "pointed out in our communications that the American and Canadian games are particularly suited for colder climates." The USSR, despite a similarity in acronyms to the USSRA, eventually chose softball standards. See USSRA executive minutes, 1958, 1959 and 1967.

238 **After Bigelow died:** Bigelow had a rough final few years. In Mexico City in April 1965, he was attacked in his hotel room, beaten, strangled, had his arms tied behind his back and was thrown into his shower. At the 1967 nationals in Chicago, he had a massive heart

attack. Near the end of his life, Brauns himself was attacked, by a taxicab driver, on East Sixty-third Street and suffered bruised ribs and a broken thumb.

239 **hope for a compromise:** In a letter dated 12 September 1979 to Ian Stewart, Brauns detailed for six pages the past ISRF mistakes. In conclusion he wrote of "the growing cancer of administrative ineptitude combined with a flagrant disregard for official ISRF regulations and a glaring lack of intelligent fiscal management." Brauns died in 1987, disillusioned about the state of American squash. In his obituary, Robert Dinerman wrote, "Stewart was an unabashed proponent of the amateur game, of private clubs and orderly invitational tournaments. The massive expansion of the sport during the past fifteen years was a painful phenomenon to him, as he felt that the commercialization of the game was causing a loss of integrity and purity, reductions that he could not happily abide." Charlie Kingsley took over as the U.S. representative at the ISRF.

239 **exchange tours:** Cambridge University toured the U.S. in 1938, 1952 and 1979. Combined teams from Oxford & Cambridge and Harvard & Yale played each other in the spring every two years in the fifties and sixties. In 1963 pros from New York, including Tom Bryne and George Ellis, toured England and in 1964 the English pros returned the favor. In 1978 the European Squash Rackets Federation sent a team that toured the United States and Canada, playing in the Atlantic Coasts, the Harry Cowles and the U.S. and Canadian nationals.

239 **Every two years:** The 1973 team consisting of Jay Nelson, Tom Poor, Frank Satterthwaite and Dinny Adams, came in fifth out of five teams; 1976—Peter Briggs, Bill Andruss, Tom Page and Gil Mateer, ninth out of ten; 1977—eighth out of eight; 1979—Gil Mateer, Ned Edwards, Mark Alger and Jon Foster, ninth out of fourteen; 1981—Bill Andruss, Ned Edwards, Stu Goldstein and Ted Gross, seventh place of twenty; 1983 Ned Edwards, Mark Talbott, John Nimick and Kenton Jernigan, seventh out of nineteen; 1985—Ned Edwards, John Nimick, Azam Khan; 1987—Tom Page, Kenton Jernigan, Ned Edwards and Azam Khan, nineteenth; 1989—Mark Talbott, Kenton Jernigan, David Boyum and Azam Khan, seventeenth; 1991—Mark Talbott, Kenton Jernigan, Jeff Stanley and Will Carlin, nineteenth; 1993—Jeff Stanley, John Phelan, Grant Pinnington and Richard Chin, twenty-sixth; 1995—Richard Chin, Damian Walker, Anders Wahlstedt and Marty Clark, twenty-fifth; 1997—Richard Chin, Tim Long, Tony Brettkelly and Marty Clark, twenty-third; 1999—Richard Chin, Tim Long, David Ramsden-Wood and Marty Clark, twenty-second; 2001—Richard Chin, Damian Walker, Preston Quick and Tim Wyant, nineteenth.

239 **"Life is too short":** *Racquet* magazine, November–December 1978.

239 **equally bleak:** The 1979 women's team consisted of Carol Weymuller, Ginny Akabane, Barbara Maltby, Mariann Greenberg and Diana Nyad, last place; 1981—Sally Fields, Nina Porter, Nancy Gengler, Carol Weymuller and Mariann Greenberg, eleventh out of fourteen; 1983—Alicia McConnell, Nancy Gengler, Carol Weymuller, Gail Ramsay and Mary Hulbert, eighth; 1985—Nancy Gengler, Julie Harris, Karen Kelso, Nina Porter and Gail Ramsay, seventh; 1987—Alicia McConnell, Nancy Gengler and Diana Staley, twelfth; 1990—Demer Holleran, Alicia McConnell, Ellie Pierce, Julieanne Harris, tenth; 1992—Demer Holleran, Ellie Pierce, Karen Kelso and Shabana Khan, eleventh; 1994— Demer Holleran, Ellie Pierce, Karen Kelso and Shabana Khan, eighth; 1996—Demer Holleran, Alicia McConnell, Ellie Pierce and Berkeley Belknap, twelfth; 1998—Demer Holleran, Ellie Pierce, Ivy Pochoda and Louisa Hall, ninth; 2000—Ivy Pochoda, Louisa Hall, Shirin Kauffmen and Margaret Elias, eighteenth; 2002—Julia Beaver, Meredith Quick, Shabana Khan and Latasha Khan, fifteenth.

239 **stayed at the bottom of the top ten:** The U.S. girls came in ninth in 1985, eleventh in 1987, eighth in 1989, eighth in 1991, thirteenth in 1993 and eighth in 1995.

240 **Maccabiah Games:** The 1977 team included Dave Linden, Glenn Whitman, Lenny Bernheimer, Roger Alcaly, Billy Kaplan and Rick Shapiro.

240 **innately yearned to be:** "I remember when we got back from New Zealand in 1983," said Jack Herrick, nonplaying captain of the U.S. team in 1983. "We said, 'Hey, we came in seventh. Isn't that great? We've never done that well.' And people would just say, 'I thought we were the best in the world. How come we're seventh, not first?' It was a question we couldn't answer."

240 **In the spring of 1969:** The first league had teams from Downtown Athletic Club, Heights Casino, Harvard Club and New York Athletic Club. The first inter-city had teams from New York, Boston, Montreal and Pittsburgh.

241 **"whacking a dead mouse":** See program for the 1994 U.S. Open.

242 **metal racquets:** The USSRA (and the SRA) initially opposed the introduction of metal racquets, not for aesthetic reasons, but rather for safety. They were concerned with metal racquets shattering.

243 **ISANC did not merge:** *Squash News*, April 1990.

243 **refusing to communicate:** *Squash News*, June 1991.

243 **demand for softball:** *Sports Style*, 17 August 1987.

244 **"light applause":** See program, 1991 Grand Prix tournaments. The genesis of the softball U.S. Open was in a Christmas 1981 trip the Joneses took to Australia

245 **relocated after their first season:** Other émigrés of the Grand Prix generation included Philip Trueman who moved to San Antonio, Moses Olubo to Houston, Robert Graham to Santa Barbara, Angus Kirkland to Boston, Michael Porteus to St. Louis and Zac Toohey to Los Angeles.

246 **relatively inexpensive:** Some of the notable white elephants of the era, Lawrenceville, Brown, Episcopal Academy and Cornell, all opened new hardball facilities in 1988–89. Trinity built eight hardball and two softball courts in 1989.

246 **softballs overtook hardballs:** Strangely, hardball sales remained constant since 1990, suggesting either the balls were breaking more—a likely explanation—or that the growth in softball was not coming at the expense of hardball—less likely. See *Men's Journal*, December 1994–January 1995.

246 **no longer a bulwark:** Caldwell stepped down as president in 1982 and was followed by Dave Johnson (1982–85), Charlie McKnight (1985) John Nimick (1986–90) and Rob Hill (1990–92). Bob French left the WPSA in 1988. For discussion within the tour, see *Sports Illustrated*, 11 May 1990.

247 **six continents with tournaments:** In 1986 *Squash News* reported from a softball event in Toronto. "Understand I am not trying to blow my bags here, but I find it hard to take hardball seriously," said Chris Dittmar, a top Australian player. "I know that their top players get upset when we talk like that, but the scores are on the board."

247 **Marshall gave up:** The disharmony between the WPSA and the softball world reached its most absurd level in 1982. "I liken the WPSA to a group of Eskimos in the Yukon," wrote Ian Stewart, the Canadian president of the ISRF, "taking a snowball and hitting it against the wall of an igloo with a snowshoe, forming an association and calling themselves the World Squash Association." Caldwell sued Stewart. They settled out of court and Stewart apologized for his outburst.

247 **sanctioned the U.S. Pro Softball:** Fans, according to Peter Stephan, "filled bleachers with the cheerful intimacy of college students cramming into a telephone booth."

248 **"I will be out of shape":** *Racquet* magazine, April 1977.

248 **the tour switched:** "The change," one reporter wrote, "is due primarily to financial pressures. The softball event should attract greater sponsorship." *MetroSports Magazine*, April 1992.

249 **WPSA amalgamated:** On 4 December 1992, the WPSA met to vote on the merger. Twenty-one men voted yes, eight abstained and four (Robie Dinerman, Rudy Rodriguez, Octavio Montero and Alberto Nunez) voted no.

249 **a deep undertow:** "The argument was, 'if it ain't broke, why fix it?'" said Don Mills.

"There was some merit to that, but the kids really felt that if they were going to compete with other countries, they needed to learn softball. We were so isolated. We were light years behind. I led sixteen kids to Australia for a month. They were top kids and we got our asses handed to us. The purists were going to be against it, but juniors are never purists."

249 **Marmor handed in:** Marmor issued an initial report in January 1992. The committee included: Bob Callahan, Eben Hardie, Charlie Kingsley, Bart McGuire, Gene Perle, Steve Piltch, Marshall Wallach and Warren Young.

251 **association of prep schools:** "We knew this was monumental," Gallagher later said. "We sat in the room and said, 'Wow. Are we really willing to do this? Can we really go it alone?' We had one foot in the water and the question was whether we could jump in." The coaches voted 17–11 with one abstention, to allow the home school to chose the type of court for the match. See *Squash News*, April and May–June 1993.

252 **squash facilities:** In March 1990 Dave Brown, the Navy coach, and Bob Callahan, the Princeton coach, put on a clinic at Notre Dame. Like other associations, the inter-collegiates independently secured their own sponsorship, including Merrill Lynch, Marsh & McLennan and Head. Some coaches opposed the whole notion of sponsorship, afraid, as the 28 February 1986 minutes reported, "squash is losing its refinement by soliciting financial backers and that we should turn to alumni for support. We should make sure the sponsorship is in good taste." The NISRA had only three executives on its board: a president, a vice president (with no real responsibilities) and a secretary-treasurer. At one point, leadership was so lacking that the NISRA held onto its president, Chuck Kinyon of Dartmouth, for an extra year even after Kinyon had stopped coaching the Big Green's squash team.

252 **an NISRA softball tourney:** Twelve men entered, with intercollegiate champion Daniel Ezra beating Richard Chin 9–1, 9–5, 9–6 in the finals.

252 **rank in order of preference:** Some of the eight choices were fanciful: one was to break dual matches into two, with half a squad playing each other in softball, the other half in hardball.

252 **look into the matter:** The 1992–94 NISRA Ball Committee consisted of Bob Callahan, chair (Princeton), Dave Johnson (Williams), Dave Talbott (Yale), Jack Fairs (University of Western Ontario), Bob Snider (Stony Brook), George Wigton (Bates) and Dick Taylor (Hobart). The committee was also called the NISRA Committee to Study Softball Alternatives. Snider resigned from the committee in the spring of 1993 when he retired.

253 **ballot offering three proposals:** The split season proposal was disfigured beyond good taste by making the softball matches not count toward final rankings and the final softball team nationals designated for five-man teams. To vote, schools had to meet the following criteria: They had to have paid dues to the NISRA for the past three years, played in the nationals the past three years, have a coach, played at least six dual matches a year and have an athletic director that agreed with the coach's vote.

253 **needed to make the change:** Two other compromise votes were tabulated: twenty-six voted against a split season, six voted yes; and if softball didn't pass, sixteen voted for a split season, while thirteen voted for hardball only.

XI. THE INFINITELY GREATER GAME

257 **tips its hat to the person:** A manual for squash doubles has never been published, but the following books have chapters on doubles: Francis, *Smart Squash;* Torbet, *Squash;* Molloy, *Contemporary Squash;* and Barnaby, *Winning Squash Racquets.*

258 **the essence of doubles:** Almost all the court tennis balls in England were made by Alfred Tompkins, at Upper Lewes Road, Brighton. Fred Tompkins had worked at the Royal Officers Naval Court in Malta and the Army Racquets Court at Curragh Camp in Ireland.

When Jimmy Dunn arrived at the Racquet Club in 1928 as a schoolboy assistant, Tompkins took one look at him and said, "You're Irish, you're a red-head and you're a south-paw—you'll never make it." Tompkins died in 1940.

258 **shoved four men inside:** The court remained in use until 1988, when it was converted into a singles court. Tompkins got the idea for squash doubles from racquets, which had a standard open-air doubles court of eighty feet by forty. Perhaps Tompkins had also heard of the court at Wellington, an English public school. In the eighteen-nineties Wellington built a forty-eight by twenty-five-and-a-half-foot squash doubles court. The boys used a small hard ball called a "cherry." The court was converted into three fives courts in 1929. *Squash Rackets and Fives,* December 1935.

260 **Don Butcher:** Butcher also was the first person to make an instructional squash video, which he filmed on the St. John's Wood doubles court in 1938. Doubles in England was a bit unschooled. Men insisted on playing an up-and-back formation, rather than the orthodox left-and-right-wall positions. Only British women, who had played doubles in the U.S., played in the proper manner. In 1935, though, doubles orthodoxy was not imbedded in North America. Germain Glidden & Tanny Sargent won the 1935 Canadian national doubles by playing in the I formation.

260 **"admitting damsels":** This tournament was renamed after Bill O'Reilly. A few other annual midseason doubles tournaments in New York included a member-guest at the Racquet & Tennis; the Luckenbach Memorial, a handicap tournament founded in 1932 at the Nassau Country Club and made a scratch tournament in 1969 and a professional-amateur at Nassau founded in 1941 and renamed the Harry Geidel Pro-Am in 1964 (the pro-am was often a fundraiser for muscular dystrophy); the Piping Rock Invitation Doubles, run as a handicap tournament from 1933 to 1935 and as a regular tournament from 1948 to 1962; the Allan Cummings Cup at Apawamis, begun in 1967 and the Sea Bright doubles, which began in 1952 mainly for B and C players, was halted after a fire destroyed the club's locker room and singles court in 1975, resumed in 1976 and ended in 1980.

260 **white flannel trousers:** Most players wore flannels for doubles even as late at the 1970s. Bill Slack was known for wearing two pairs of trousers.

261 **"tripped by a drunken chair":** The Racquet Club of St. Louis's invitational usually involved late-night revelry as well. In 1973 Ted Simmons & Charlie Cella beat Mike & Peter Pierce in the finals. Due to some heavy arm-bending after the match, the Pierces missed their plane, and, the next morning, they woke up at Cella's racetrack in Hot Springs, Arkansas. Baltimoreans were renowned for their behavior. A couple of men once tossed a piano from a third-floor window of the University Club of New York, and another group interrupted the black-tie dinner at Rockaway by diving across tables in their tuxedos.

262 **Philadelphia's prowess:** In 1935 the Metropolitan SRA turned down a request to fund some New York players to go to Buffalo for the national doubles: "The Philadelphians so monopolize the doubles game that no New York team felt like going to the expense of traveling upstate to be put out in the first round," wrote a reporter in *Squash Badminton,* February 1935.

262 **During a frenzied melee:** See Francis, *Smart Squash,* pp. 64–65. Mateer played in one doubles tournament, the 1954 Lockett Doubles Cup, on the right wall; he and Germain Glidden teamed up to win the prestigious tournament.

264 **In a tense fifth game:** Bob Lehman described it in his unique way in the 1964–65 Met SRA yearbook: "The 5th game saw all the players at fever pitch, matched only by a screaming, frantic gallery which really went nuts, blew stacks, flipped lids and generally displayed a modicum of interest. The squash was tops, the tension topser."

265 **Cliff Sutter:** See *New York Times,* 10 May 2000.

266 **with the children's racquets:** *Squash News,* December 1980.

Notes

267 **the national junior doubles:** Beginning in 1935 the intercollegiate association held an intercollegiate doubles draw each winter at the University Club in New York. This tournament was revived in 1988 by Treddy Ketcham.

268 **an eye-opening $25,000:** "It was enough money," said Maurice Heckscher who won the Johnson six times, "to have a fine summer vacation."

269 **money to cover expenses:** A fifth member of this group of doubles specialists would be Larry Heath, a sturdy lefthander who won a number of pro doubles events and was ranked, along with longtime partner Aziz Khan, as the number two pro doubles team in 1987.

270 **tiptoed through:** "Peter just starting hitting junk, flipping shots from everywhere," said Howe. "We won a couple of points, Mo was fooling around, laughing with the crowd. When it got to 12–14, I took Peter aside and said, 'No more goofball stuff, we can win this.'"

XII. This Mollycoddled Age

275 **"landing in autogyros":** *Squash Rackets & Fives*, 22 October 1932.

276 **hardball nationals:** Dunlop sales of the fuchsia Slazenger white-dot hardball singles ball in the U.S. dropped from 10,321 dozen in 1991 (as opposed to 11,371 for softball) to 2,220 in 1993 (15,813 for softball) to 815 in 1995 (19,089 for softball). The only area of steady consumption was in high-altitude regions like Denver where the ball was used for doubles. In 1991 Dunlop produced 6,000 dozen hardball singles balls, and in 1995 they made an additional batch of 250 dozen. These balls were stored on pallets in temperature-controlled warehouses in Toronto and South Carolina. In 2000 Dunlop relocated its singles ball factory from England to the Philippines (it made the hardball doubles ball in Dublin), and the recipe for the hardball singles ball—after seventy years of continual fine-tuning—was lost in the move. In 2003 Dunlop's warehouse pallets were empty, and the company reluctantly had to come up with a new hardball singles ball entirely by scratch.

I. National Champions

Men [1]

1907 John A. Miskey
1908 John A. Miskey
1909 William L. Freeland
1910 John A. Miskey
1911 Francis S. White
1912 Constantine Hutchins
1913 Morton L. Newhall
1914 Constantine Hutchins
1915 Stanley W. Pearson
1916 Stanley W. Pearson
1917 Stanley W. Pearson
1920 Charles C. Peabody
1921 Stanley W. Pearson
1921 Stanley W. Pearson
1923 Stanley W. Pearson
1924 Gerald Roberts
1925 W. Palmer Dixon
1926 W. Palmer Dixon
1927 Myles P. Baker
1928 Herbert N. Rawlins, Jr.
1929 J. Lawrence Pool
1930 Herbert N. Rawlins, Jr.
1931 J. Lawrence Pool
1932 Beekman H. Pool
1933 Beekman H. Pool
1934 Neil J. Sullivan, II
1935 Donald Strachan
1936 Germain G. Glidden
1937 Germain G. Glidden
1938 Germain G. Glidden
1939 Donald Strachan
1940 A. Willing Patterson
1941 Charles M. P. Brinton
1942 Charles M. P. Brinton
1946 Charles M. P. Brinton
1947 Charles M. P. Brinton
1948 Stanley W. Pearson, Jr.
1949 H. Hunter Lott, Jr.
1950 Edward J. Hahn
1951 Edward J. Hahn
1952 Harry B. Conlon, Jr.
1953 Ernest Howard
1954 G. Diehl Mateer, Jr.
1955 Henri R. Salaun
1956 G. Diehl Mateer, Jr.
1957 Henri R. Salaun
1958 Henri R. Salaun
1959 Benjamin H. Heckscher
1960 G. Diehl Mateer, Jr.
1961 Henri R. Salaun
1962 Samuel P. Howe, III
1963 Benjamin H. Hechscher
1964 Ralph E. Howe
1965 Stephen T. Vehslage
1966 Victor Niederhoffer
1967 Samuel P. Howe, III
1968 Colin Adair

1969 Anil Nayar
1970 Anil Nayar
1971 Colin Adair
1972 Victor Niederhoffer
1973 Victor Niederhoffer
1974 Victor Niederhoffer
1975 Victor Niederhoffer
1976 Peter Briggs
1977 Thomas E. Page
1978 Michael Desaulniers
1979 Mario Sanchez
1980 Michael Desaulniers
1981 Mark Alger
1982 John Nimick
1983 Kenton Jernigan
1984 Kenton Jernigan
1985 Kenton Jernigan
1986 Hugh LaBossier
1987 Frank J. Stanley, IV
1988 Scott Dulmage
1989 Rodolfo Rodriquez
1990 Mark Talbott
1991 Mark Talbott
1992 Kenton Jernigan
1993 Mark Talbott
1994 Anders Wahlstedt
1995 A. Martin Clark, Jr.
1996 Mohsen Mir
1997 A. Martin Clark, Jr.
1998 A. Martin Clark, Jr.
1999 David McNeeley
2000 A. Martin Clark, Jr.
2001 Damian Walker
2002 Damian Walker
2003 Preston B. Quick

Women [2]

1928 Eleanora R. Sears
1929 Margaret Howe
1930 Hazel H. Wightman
1931 Ruth Banks
1932 Margaret Howe
1933 Susan Noel
1934 Margaret Howe
1935 Margot Lumb
1936 Anne Page
1937 Anne Page
1938 Cecile Bowes
1939 Anne Page
1940 Cecile Bowes
1941 Cecile Bowes
1947 Anne Page
1948 Cecile Bowes
1949 Janet R. M. Morgan
1950 Betty Howe Constable
1951 Jane Austin
1952 Peggy Howe
1953 Peggy Howe
1954 Lois Dilks
1955 Janet R. M. Morgan

1956 Betty Howe Constable
1957 Betty Howe Constable
1958 Betty Howe Constable
1959 Betty Howe Constable
1960 Margaret Varner
1961 Margaret Varner
1962 Margaret Varner
1963 Margaret Varner
1964 Ann Wetzel
1965 Joyce V. Davenport
1966 Betty Meade
1967 Betty Meade
1968 Betty Meade
1969 Joyce V. Davenport
1970 Nina V. Moyer
1971 Carol Thesieres
1972 Nina Moyer
1973 Gretchen V. Spruance
1974 Gretchen V. Spruance
1975 Virginia Akabane
1976 Gretchen V. Spruance
1977 Gretchen V. Spruance
1978 Gretchen V. Spruance
1979 Heather B. McKay
1980 Barbara Maltby
1981 Barbara Maltby
1982 Alicia McConnell
1983 Alicia McConnell
1984 Alicia McConnell
1985 Alicia McConnell
1986 Alicia McConnell
1987 Alicia McConnell
1988 Alicia McConnell
1989 Demer Holleran
1990 Demer Holleran
1991 Demer Holleran
1992 Demer Holleran
1993 Demer Holleran
1994 Demer Holleran
1995 Ellie Pierce
1996 Demer Holleran
1997 Demer Holleran
1998 Latasha Khan
1999 Demer Holleran
2000 Latasha Khan
2001 Shabana Khan
2002 Latasha Khan
2003 Latasha Khan

Men's Intercollegiate [3]
1931 Beekman H. Pool (Harvard)
1932 Beekman H. Pool (Harvard)
1933 William G. Foulke (Princeton)
1934 E. Rotan Sargent (Harvard)
1935 Germain G. Glidden (Harvard)
1936 Germain G. Glidden (Harvard)
1937 Richard M. Dorson (Harvard)
1938 Leroy M. Lewis (Pennsylvania)
1939 Stanley W. Pearson, Jr. (Princeton)
1940 Kim DeS. Canavarro (Harvard)
1941 Charles M. P. Brinton (Princeton)
1942 Charles M. P. Brinton (Princeton)
1943 John C. Holt, II (Yale)
1946 Glenn Shively (Yale)
1947 Peter Landry (McGill)

1948 G. Diehl Mateer, Jr. (Haverford)
1949 G. Diehl Mateer, Jr. (Haverford)
1950 Harold E. Hands (Yale)
1951 Charles H. W. Foster (Harvard)
1952 Charles W. Ufford, Jr. (Harvard)
1953 Charles W. Ufford, Jr. (Harvard)
1954 Robert L. Campbell (Princeton)
1955 Robert L. Campbell (Princeton)
1956 Benjamin H. Heckscher (Harvard)
1957 Benjamin H. Heckscher (Harvard)
1958 J. Smith Chapman (Sir George Williams)
1959 Stephen T. Vehslage (Princeton)
1960 Stephen T. Vehslage (Princeton)
1961 Stephen T. Vehslage (Princeton)
1962 Ralph E. Howe (Yale)
1963 Ralph E. Howe (Yale)
1964 Victor B. Niederhoffer (Harvard)
1965 Walter Oehrlein (Army)
1966 Howard Coonley (Pennsylvania)
1967 Anil Nayar (Harvard)
1968 Anil Nayar (Harvard)
1969 Anil Nayar (Harvard)
1970 Lawrence Terrell (Harvard)
1971 Palmer Page (Pennsylvania)
1972 Peter Briggs (Harvard)
1973 Peter Briggs (Harvard)
1974 Juan de Villafranca (Mexico City)
1975 Juan de Villafranca (Mexico City)
1976 Philip Mohtadi (Calgary)
1977 Michael Desaulniers (Harvard)
1978 Michael Desaulniers (Harvard)
1979 Edward C. P. Edwards (Pennsylvania)
1980 Michael Desaulniers (Harvard)
1981 John Nimick (Princeton)
1982 Victor Wagner (Yale)
1983 Kenton Jernigan (Harvard)
1984 Kenton Jernigan (Harvard)
1985 Paul Deratney, Toronto
1986 Kenton Jernigan (Harvard)
1987 Frank J. Stanley, IV (Princeton)
1988 Frank J. Stanley, IV (Princeton)
1989 Scott Dulmage (Western Ontario)
1990 Jon Bernheimer (Harvard)
1991 Adrian Ezra (Harvard)
1992 Jeremy Fraiberg (Harvard)
1993 Adrian Ezra (Harvard)
1994 Adrian Ezra (Harvard)
1995 Tal Ben-Shacher (Harvard)
1996 Daniel Ezra (Harvard)
1997 Marcus Cowie (Trinity)
1998 Marcus Cowie (Trinity)
1999 Peter Yik (Princeton)
2000 Peter Yik (Princeton)
2001 David Yik (Princeton)
2002 Bernardo Samper (Trinity)
2003 Yasser El Halaby (Princeton)

Women's Intercollegiate
1965 Katherine Allabough (Vassar)
1966 Susan Stephenson (Wheaton)
1967 Susan Stephenson (Wheaton)
1968 Katherine Allabough (Vassar)
1969 Jane Slocum (Smith)
1970 Beth Anders (Ursinus)
1971 Perla Hewes (Fredonia)

1972 Wendy Zaharko (Princeton)
1973 Lee Howard (Radcliffe)
1974 Wendy Zaharko (Princeton)
1975 Wendy Zaharko (Princeton)
1976 Nancy Gengler (Princeton)
1977 Gail Ramsay (Penn State)
1978 Gail Ramsay (Penn State)
1979 Gail Ramsay (Penn State)
1980 Gail Ramsay (Penn State)
1981 Jane Giammettei (Pine Manor)
1982 Alicia McConnell (Pennsylvania)
1983 Alicia McConnell (Pennsylvania)
1984 Alicia McConnell (Pennsylvania)
1985 Mary Hulbert (Harvard)
1986 Demer Holleran (Princeton)
1987 Demer Holleran (Princeton)
1988 Diana Edge (Harvard)
1989 Demer Holleran (Princeton)
1990 Jenny Holleran (Harvard)
1991 Berkeley Belknap (Yale)
1992 Jordanna Fraiberg (Harvard)
1993 Vanya Desai (Harvard)
1994 Jordanna Fraiberg (Harvard)
1995 Libby Eynon (Harvard)
1996 Jessica DiMauro (Pennsylvania)
1997 Katherine Johnson (Princeton)
1998 Ivy Pochoda (Harvard)
1999 Julia Beaver (Princeton)
2000 Julia Beaver (Princeton)
2001 Julia Beaver (Princeton)
2002 Amina Helal (Trinity)
2003 Amina Helal (Trinity)

Boy's Junior [4]

1956 Stephen T. Vehslage
1957 Stephen T. Vehslage
1958 Stephen T. Vehslage
1959 James W. Zug
1960 Ralph E. Howe
1961 William B. Morris
1962 Victor B. Niederhoffer
1963 John C. West
1964 Lawrence S. Heath, II
1965 Jose Gonzales
1966 Jose Gonzales
1967 Lawrence P. Terrell
1968 Farooq Mir
1969 Farooq Mir
1970 Craig Benson
1971 Ian Shaw
1972 Ian Shaw
1973 Ian Shaw
1974 Gilbert Mateer
1975 Michael Desaulniers
1976 Michael Desaulniers
1977 Mario Sanchez
1978 Mark Talbott
1979 Mark Talbott
1980 Edgardo Alvarez
1981 Edgardo Alvarez
1982 Kenton Jernigan
1983 Alex Doucas
1984 Gary Waite
1985 Frank J. Stanley, IV
1986 Scott Dulmage

1987 Rodolfo Rodriguez
1988 Rodolfo Rodriguez
1989 Marcos Mendez
1990 Hector Barragan
1991 Octavio Montero
1992 Ted Bruenner
1994 David McNeely
1995 David McNeely
1996 David McNeely
1997 Peter Kelly
1998 Eric G. Pearson, Jr.
1999 Richard Repetto
2000 Richard Repetto
2001 Julian Illingworth
2002 Julian Illingworth
2003 Gilly Lane

Girls' Junior

1977 Connie Pierce
1978 Connie Pierce
1979 Jane Giammattei
1980 Alicia McConnell
1981 Alicia McConnell
1982 Alicia McConnell
1983 Sophie Porter
1984 Demer Holleran
1985 Demer Holleran
1986 Shabana Khan
1987 Hope MacKay
1988 Hope MacKay
1989 Margo Green
1990 Jordanna Fraiberg
1991 Emily Ash
1992 Libby Eynon
1994 Katherine Johnson
1995 Stephanie Teaford
1996 Devon Kennedy
1997 Julia Beaver
1998 Louisa Hall
1999 Louisa Hall
2000 Louisa Hall
2001 Michelle Quibell
2002 Lily Lorentzen
2003 Lily Lorentzen

II. Tournament Champions

North American Open [5]

1954 Henri R. Salaun
1955 G. Diehl Mateer, Jr.
1956 Hashim Khan
1957 Hashim Khan
1958 Roshan Khan
1959 G. Diehl Mateer, Jr.
1960 Roshan Khan
1961 Roshan Khan
1962 Azam Khan
1963 Hashim Khan
1964 Mohibullah Khan
1965 Mohibullah Khan
1966 Mohibullah Khan
1967 Ralph E. Howe
1968 Mohibullah Khan
1969 Sharif Khan
1970 Sharif Khan
1971 Sharif Khan

1972 Sharif Khan
1973 Sharif Khan
1974 Sharif Khan
1975 Victor Niederhoffer
1976 Sharif Khan
1977 Sharif Khan
1978 Sharif Khan
1979 Sharif Khan
1980 Sharif Khan
1981 Sharif Khan
1982 Michael Desaulniers
1983 Mark Talbott
1984 Jahangir Khan
1985 Jahangir Khan
1986 Mark Talbott
1987 Edward C. P. Edwards
1988 John Nimick
1989 Mark Talbott
1990 John Nimick
1991 Mark Talbott
1992 Mark Talbott
1993 Gary Waite
1994 Marcos Mendez
1995 Rodney Eyles

Tournament of Champions [6]

1930 Jack Summers
1931 Jack Summers
1932 Jack Summers
1933 John Skillman
1934 Jack Summers
1935 John Skillman
1936 James J. Tully
1937 John Skillman
1938 Al Ramsay
1939 Lester Cummings
1940 Al Ramsay
1941 Lester Cummings
1942 Lester Cummings
1946 Lester Cummings
1947 Edward T. Reid
1948 Al Ramsay
1949 Edward T. Reid
1950 Edward T. Reid
1951 James J. Tully
1952 Edward T. Reid
1953 John Warzycki
1954 John Warzycki
1955 Hashim Khan
1956 Albert E. Chassard
1957 Mahmoud El Kerim
1958 Mahmoud El Kerim
1959 Albert E. Chassard
1960 Raymond Widelski
1961 Albert E. Chassard
1962 Albert E. Chassard
1963 Hashim Khan
1964 Hashim Khan
1965 Mohibullah Khan
1966 Mohibullah Khan
1967 Mohibullah Khan
1968 Mohibullah Khan
1969 Mohibullah Khan
1970 Sharif Khan
1971 Sharif Khan

1972 Sharif Khan
1973 Sharif Khan
1974 Sharif Khan
1975 Sharif Khan
1976 Sharif Khan
1977 Sharif Khan
1978 Stuart Goldstein
1979 Sharif Khan
1980 Clive Caldwell
1981 Michael Desaulniers
1982 Clive Caldwell
1983 Mark Talbott
1984 Jahangir Khan
1985 Jahangir Khan
1986 Mario Sanchez
1987 Mark Talbott
1988 Mark Talbott
1989 Mark Talbott
1990 Mark Talbott
1991 Kenton Jernigan
1992 Jansher Khan
1993 Jansher Khan
1994 Rodney Eyles
1995 Jansher Khan
1996 Jonathon Power
1999 Jonathon Power
2000 Jonathon Power
2001 Peter Nicol
2002 Jonathon Power
2003 Peter Nicol

Boston Open

1935 Germain G. Glidden
1949 Edward T. Reid
1950 Edward T. Reid
1951 Henri R. Salaun
1952 Roger M. Bakey
1970 Yusuf Khan
1971 Sharif Khan
1972 Sharif Khan
1973 Sharif Khan
1974 Clive Caldwell
1975 Sharif Khan
1976 Sharif Khan
1977 Clive Caldwell
1978 Clive Caldwell
1979 Sharif Khan
1980 Michael Desaulniers
1981 Sharif Khan
1982 Mark Talbott
1983 Jahangir Khan
1984 Mark Talbott
1985 Edward C. P. Edwards
1986 Edward C. P. Edwards
1987 John Nimick
1988 Mark Talbott
1989 John Nimick
1991 Edward C. P. Edwards

Canadian Open

1956 Hashim Khan
1957 Azam Khan
1958 Henri R. Salaun
1959 Azam Khan
1960 Hashim Khan
1961 Roshan Khan

1962 Hashim Khan
1963 Hashim Khan
1964 Mohibullah Khan
1985 Jahangir Khan
1986 Jahangir Khan
1987 Mark Talbott
1988 Mark Talbott
1989 Mark Talbott
1990 Greg Zaff
1991 Todd Binns
1992 Mark Talbott

United States Open [7]
1983 Mark Talbott
1984 Mark Talbott
1985 Jahangir Khan
1986 Stuart Davenport
1987 Jansher Khan
1988 Jahangir Khan
1989 Rodney Martin
1990 Jansher Khan
1991 Rodney Martin
1993 Rodney Eyles
1994 Peter Nicol
1995 Jansher Khan
1996 Rodney Eyles
1997 Jonathon Power
1998 Peter Nicol
1999 Simon Parke
2000 Jonathon Power
2001 Peter Nicol
2002 David Palmer

Carol Weymuller Open [8]
1975 Barbara Maltby
1976 Barbara Maltby
1977 Barbara Maltby
1978 Barbara Maltby
1979 Virginia Akabane
1980 Alicia McConnell
1981 Alicia McConnell
1982 Alicia McConnell
1983 Alicia McConnell
1984 Alicia McConnell
1985 Alicia McConnell
1986 Alicia McConnell
1987 Karen Kelso
1989 Karen Kelso
1990 Ellie Pierce
1991 Demer Holleran
1992 Demer Holleran
1993 Fiona Graves
1994 Cassie Jackman
1995 Michelle Martin
1996 Cassie Jackman
1997 Sarah Fitz-Gerald
1999 Michelle Martin
2000 Leilani Joyce
2001 Sarah Fitz-Gerald
2002 Carol Owens

Hyder Invitational
1968 Graham Sharman
1970 Anil Nayar
1971 Farooq Mir
1972 Mohibullah Khan

1973 Dinny Adams
1974 Jay Nelson
1975 William Andruss
1976 Thomas M. Poor
1977 Leonard Bernheimer
1978 Mo Hussain
1979 William Andruss
1980 Stuart Goldstein
1981 Doug Whittaker
1982 Doug Whittaker
1983 Robert Forde
1984 Edward C. P. Edwards
1985 Stuart Grodman
1986 Doug Whittaker
1987 Hugh Labossier
1988 Diniar Alikhan
1989 Sohail Quaiser
1990 Soli Mehta
1991 Soli Mehta
1992 John Musto
1993 Soli Mehta
1994 Nathan Dugan
1995 Philip Yarrow
1996 Richard Chin
1997 Angus Kirkland
1998 Jonathon Power
1999 Angus Kirkland
2000 Martin Heath
2001 Derek Ryan
2002 Damien Mudge
2003 Shahier Razik

Hyder Invitational
1980 Alicia McConnell
1981 Nancy Gengler
1982 Alicia McConnell
1983 Nancy Gengler
1984 Mariann Greenberg
1994 Melanie Jans
1995 Carla Venter
1996 Demer Holleran
1997 Sharon Bradey
1998 Demer Holleran
1999 Demer Holleran
2000 Toni Weeks
2001 Sharon Bradey
2002 Katie Patrick
2003 Sharon Wee

Apawamis [9]
1939 Edward C. Oelsner, Jr.
1940 Edward C. Oelsner, Jr.
1941 Donald Frame
1946 Andrew C. Ingraham
1947 Andrew C. Ingraham
1948 Andrew C. Ingraham
1949 Germain G. Glidden
1950 Germain G. Glidden
1951 Calvin D. MacCracken
1952 Germain G. Glidden
1953 Harry B. Conlon, Jr.
1954 Richard C. Squires
1955 Calvin D. MacCracken
1956 Henri R. Salaun
1957 Calvin D. MacCracken
1958 William Tully

339

1959 Calvin D. MacCracken
1960 Charles W. Ufford, Jr.
1961 Donald D. Mills
1962 Richard Stewart
1963 Harry B. Conlon, Jr.
1964 Samuel P. Howe, III
1965 Craig W. Fanning
1966 Charlton MacVeagh, Jr.
1967 Thomas M. Poor
1968 Thomas M. Poor
1969 Thomas M. Poor
1970 Anil Nayar
1971 G.H. Bostwick, Jr.
1972 John R. Reese
1973 Peter S. Briggs
1974 Juan de Villafranca
1975 Peter S. Briggs
1976 Franklin B. Satterthwaite, Jr.
1977 Peter S. Briggs
1978 Peter S. Briggs
1979 Larry Hilbert
1980 Sharif Khan
1981 Michael Desaulniers
1982 Michael Desaulniers
1983 Mark Talbott
1984 Edward C. P. Edwards
1985 Mark Talbott
1986 Mark Talbott
1987 Mark Talbott
1988 Mark Talbott
1989 Mark Talbott
1990 Mark Talbott
1991 Mark Talbott
1992 Marcos Mendez
1993 Mark Talbott
1994 Marcos Mendez
1995 Gary Waite
1996 Chris Walker
1997 Dan Jenson
1998 Paul Johnson
1999 Derek Ryan
2000 Nick Taylor
2001 Olli Touminen
2003 Shahier Razik

Gold Racquets [10]
1928 W. Jay Iselin
1929 Odgen Phipps
1930 J. Lawrence Pool
1931 Beekman H. Pool
1932 Neil J. Sullivan, II
1933 Beekman H. Pool
1934 Neil J. Sullivan, II
1935 Beekman H. Pool
1936 Germain G. Glidden
1937 Germain G. Glidden
1938 Donald Strachan
1939 H. Hunter Lott, Jr.
1940 Sherman Howes
1941 Donald Frame
1946 Stanley W. Pearson, Jr.
1947 Stanley W. Pearson, Jr.
1948 G. Diehl Mateer, Jr.
1949 Calvin D. MacCracken
1950 Henri R. Salaun

1951 Henri R. Salaun
1952 G. Diehl Mateer, Jr.
1953 G. Diehl Mateer, Jr.
1954 G. Diehl Mateer, Jr.
1955 G. Diehl Mateer, Jr.
1956 G. Diehl Mateer, Jr.
1957 G. Diehl Mateer, Jr.
1958 Calvin D. MacCracken
1959 Charles W. Ufford, Jr.
1960 Charles W. Ufford, Jr.
1961 Ralph E. Howe
1962 Stephen T. Vehslage
1963 Victor Niederhoffer
1964 Samuel P. Howe, III
1965 Victor Niederhoffer
1966 Victor Neiderhoffer
1967 Peter Martin
1968 Colin Adair
1969 Anil Nayar
1970 Colin Adair
1971 Victor Niederhoffer
1972 Colin Adair
1973 Victor Niederhoffer
1974 Victor Niederhoffer
1975 Peter Briggs
1976 Philip Mohtadi
1977 Thomas E. Page
1978 Michael Desaulniers
1979 Michael Desaulniers
1980 Gilbert Mateer
1981 Gilbert Mateer
1982 Jay Gillespie
1983 Kenton Jernigan
1984 Derrick Niederman
1985 Gordon D. H. Anderson
1986 Darius Pandole
1987 Frank J. Stanley, IV
1988 Rodolfo Rodriquez
1989 L. Robinson Hill, Jr.
1990 Jonathon R. Foster
1991 Jeremy Fraiberg
1992 A. Martin Clark, Jr.
1993 Mark Talbott
1994 Scott Stoneburgh
1995 Anders Wahlstedt
1996 Scott Stoneburgh
1997 W. Keen Butcher
1998 Edward C. P. Edwards
1999 Anders Wahlstedt
2000 Karim Yehia
2001 Daniel Ezra
2002 Ola Jangbecker

Harry Cowles [11]
1947 Charles M. P. Brinton
1948 Stanley W. Pearson, Jr.
1949 Stanley W. Pearson, Jr.
1950 G. Diehl Mateer, Jr.
1951 G. Diehl Mateer, Jr.
1952 G. Diehl Mateer, Jr.
1953 G. Diehl Mateer, Jr.
1954 Henri R. Salaun
1955 Henri R. Salaun
1956 G. Diehl Mateer, Jr.
1957 Henri R. Salaun

1958 Henri R. Salaun
1959 Henri R. Salaun
1960 Henri R. Salaun
1961 Charles W. Ufford, Jr.
1962 Stephen T. Vehslage
1963 Victor Niederhoffer
1964 Henri R. Salaun
1965 Victor Niederhoffer
1966 Samuel P. Howe, III
1967 Victor Niederhoffer
1968 Robert Hetherington
1969 Ralph E. Howe
1970 Anil Nayar
1971 Lawrence Terrell
1972 Victor Niederhoffer
1973 Victor Niederhoffer
1974 Gordon D. H. Anderson
1975 Victor Niederhoffer
1976 Peter Briggs
1977 Thomas E. Page
1978 Gilbert Mateer
1979 Edward C. P. Edwards
1980 Michael Desaulniers
1981 Edward C. P. Edwards
1982 John Nimick
1983 David Boyum
1984 Gilbert Mateer
1985 Kenton Jernigan
1986 Kenton Jernigan
1987 Darius Pandole
1988 Rodolfo Rodriguez
1989 Frank J. Stanley, IV
1990 Mark Baker
1991 Jeremy Fraiberg
1992 Jeremy Fraiberg
1993 William Doyle
1994 Adrian Ezra
1995 Daniel Ezra
1996 Tal Ben-Shacher

William White [12]
1962 Benjamin H. Heckscher
1963 G. Diehl Mateer, Jr.
1964 Stephen T. Vehslage
1965 Samuel P. Howe, III
1966 Samuel P. Howe, III
1967 Samuel P. Howe, III
1968 Samuel P. Howe, III
1969 Anil Nayar
1970 Anil Nayar
1971 Samuel P. Howe, III
1972 Samuel P. Howe, III
1973 Sharif Khan
1974 Sharif Khan
1975 Victor Niederhoffer
1976 Colin Adair
1977 Geoff Hunt
1978 Gordon D. H. Anderson
1979 John B. Bottger
1980 David Page
1981 Brad Desaulniers
1982 John Nimick
1983 John B. Bottger
1984 Kenton Jernigan
1985 Derrick Niederman

1986 Hugh LaBossier
1987 W. Keen Butcher
1988 Darius Pandole
1989 Luke Evnin
1990 Octavio Montero
1991 Hector Barragan
1992 Hector Barragan
1993 Hector Barragan
1994 Hector Barragan
1996 John Musto
1997 V. Asthana
1998 A. Giveon
1999 Damian Walker
2000 David McNeely
2001 Jamie Hickox
2002 Richard Repetto
2003 Imran Khan

Woodruff-Nee
1949 Germain G. Glidden
1950 Charles M. P. Brinton
1951 Charles M. P. Brinton
1952 J. J. Thackara
1953 A. Carter Fergusson
1954 A. Carter Fergusson
1955 Harry B. Conlon, Jr.
1956 Calvin D. MacCracken
1957 Calvin D. MacCracken
1958 Henri R. Salaun
1959 Henri R. Salaun
1960 Calvin D. MacCracken
1961 A. Carter Fergusson
1962 Christian C. F. Spahr
1963 Harry B. Conlon, Jr.
1965 G. Diehl Mateer, Jr.
1966 Charles W. Ufford, Jr.
1967 John Gay Davis
1968 Franklin B. Satterthwaite, Jr.
1969 Franklin B. Satterthwaite, Jr.
1970 Robert Hetherington
1971 Franklin B. Satterthwaite, Jr.
1972 Robert Hetherington
1973 Dinsmore Adams
1974 Lawrence Terrell
1975 Juan de Villafranca
1976 Glenn Whitman
1977 Thomas E. Page
1978 David Page
1979 Aziz Khan
1980 Robert Dinerman
1981 David Page
1982 Diderih Finne
1983 Raheil Qureshi
1984 George B. Lemmon, Jr.
1985 John Lindquist
1986 Raheil Qureshi
1987 John Lindquist
1988 Raheil Qureshi
1989 Robert Dinerman
1990 Steve Rumsey
1991 George Spahr
1992 Thomas W. Harrity
1993 Thomas W. Harrity
1994 Thomas W. Harrity
1995 W. Keen Butcher

Appendix: Record of Champions

1996 Thomas W. Harrity
1997 Robert Dinerman
1998 Thomas W. Harrity
1999 Thomas W. Harrity
2000 Jan Botha
2001 Mark Allen
2002 Ted Mathias
2003 Jahanzes Khan

Atlantic Coast Championships
1930 Neil J. Sullivan, II
1931 W. H. Baugher
1932 Donald Strachan
1933 Donald Strachan
1934 Neil J. Sullivan, II
1935 Donald Strachan
1936 Donald Strachan
1937 Germain G. Glidden
1938 H. Hunter Lott, Jr.
1939 Sherman Howes
1940 H. Hunter Lott, Jr.
1941 Sherman Howes
1942 Charles M.P. Brinton
1947 Charles M.P. Brinton
1948 Donald Strachan
1949 Charles M.P. Brinton
1958 G. Diehl Mateer, Jr.
1959 G. Diehl Mateer, Jr.
1960 Charles W. Ufford, Jr.
1961 Charles W. Ufford, Jr.
1962 Ralph E. Howe
1963 G. Diehl Mateer, Jr.
1964 Ralph E. Howe
1965 Ralph E. Howe
1966 E. Victor Seixas, Jr.
1967 Samuel P. Howe, III
1968 Thomas M. Poor
1969 Thomas M. Poor
1970 Thomas M. Poor
1971 Thomas M. Poor
1972 Lawrence Terrell
1973 Thomas M. Poor
1974 Michael J. Pierce
1975 Palmer Page
1976 David Page
1977 John Bottger
1978 Thomas E. Page
1979 Thomas E. Page
1980 Edward C. P. Edwards
1981 Michael J. Pierce
1982 Victor Wagner
1983 Kenton Jernigan
1984 Gilbert Mateer
1985 L. Robinson Hill, Jr.
1986 Thomas W. Harrity
1987 Pepe Martinex
1988 Scott Brehman
1989 Scott Brehman
1990 Scott Ryan
1991 Terry Spahr
1992 Terry Spahr
1993 Thomas W. Harrity
1994 Thomas W. Harrity
1995 Thomas W. Harrity
1996 Thomas W. Harrity

1997 L. Robinson Hill, Jr.
1998 Robert Dinerman
1999 Thomas W. Harrity
2000 Thomas W. Harrity
2001 Thomas W. Harrity
2002 Thomas W. Harrity

Western Championships
1925 F. Carpenter
1926 J.H. Douglas, Jr.
1927 R. Steven Wright
1928 B. Griggs
1929 P. Boyden
1931 R. Tinsman
1934 Andrew Ingraham
1935 Jack Gordon
1936 Leroy Weir
1937 J. Pope
1938 Leory Weir
1939 J. Pope
1940 John Reindel
1941 Jack Gordon
1946 Joseph T. Hahn
1947 Joseph T. Hahn
1948 Edward J. Hahn
1949 Edward J. Hahn
1950 Edward J. Hahn
1951 Edward J. Hahn
1952 Edward J. Hahn
1953 Edward J. Hahn
1954 Edward J. Hahn
1955 Richard D. Squires, Jr.
1956 Paul Steele
1957 Edward J. Hahn
1958 Robert H. Stuckert
1959 Edward J. Hahn
1960 Edward J. Hahn
1961 Edward J. Hahn
1962 Robert H. Stuckert
1963 Robert H. Stuckert
1964 Robert H. Stuckert
1965 Robert H. Stuckert
1966 David O'Loughlin
1967 David O'Loughlin
1968 Larry Sears
1969 David O'Loughlin
1970 David O'Loughlin
1971 Robert Hetherington
1972 David O'Loughlin
1973 Lawrence O'Loughlin
1974 Bruce Birgbauer
1975 David O'Loughlin
1976 Bruce Birgbauer
1977 George Haggarty
1978 Frank P. Giammattei
1979 Frank P. Giammattei
1980 David Talbott
1981 Thomas Shepherd
1982 Hussein Meguid
1983 David Linden

Pacific Coast Championships
1940 Ted Clarke
1941 Ted Clarke
1947 Charles M. P. Brinton
1948 Ted Clarke

1949 Ted Clarke
1950 Ted Clarke
1951 Ted Clarke
1952 Ted Clarke
1953 Bob Colwell
1954 Bob Colwell
1955 Ted Clarke
1956 Gene Hoover
1957 Gene Hoover
1958 Gene Hoover
1959 Gene Hoover
1960 Tom Owens
1961 Gene Hoover
1962 Larry Sears
1963 Larry Sears
1964 Tom Owens
1965 Sandy Robertson
1966 Dave Foster
1967 Alex Eichmann
1968 George I. Morfitt
1969 Alex Eichmann
1970 Alex Eichmann
1971 John Hutchinson
1972 Alex Eichmann
1973 George I. Morfitt
1974 Frank Satterthwaite
1975 John Hutchinson
1976 Phil Mohtadi
1977 Phil Mohtadi
1978 Pat Richardson
1979 Tom Dashiell
1980 C. Victor Harding
1981 Mark Alger
1982 Larry Franklin
1983 Christopher Burrows
1984 Hugh LaBossier
1985 John Lau
1986 Jonathan R. Foster
1987 Luke Envin
1988 Luke Envin
1989 Luke Envin

Cate Invitational
1956 K. Moore
1957 K. Moore
1958 R. Schweizer
1959 R. Torney
1960 J. Holmes
1961 J. McCormack
1962 Larry Sears
1963 B. Seymour
1964 Alex Eichmann
1965 Alex Eichmann
1966 A. Nasr
1967 Steve Gurney
1968 B. Seymour
1969 Steve Gurney
1970 Steve Gurney
1971 Steve Gurney
1972 Les Harding
1973 Alex Eichmann
1974 Alex Eichmann
1975 Alex Eichmann
1977 Ariz Sarfraz
1978 Ariz Sarfraz

1979 P. Gessling
1980 C. Jazan
1981 W. MacMillen
1982 R. Shapiro
1983 P. Gessling
1984 R. Smith
1985 D. Gordon
1986 W. Ullman
1987 Luke Envin
1988 W. Ullman
1989 W. Ullman
1990 Paul Steele, Jr.
1991 W. Fratt
1992 W. Fratt
1993 Paul Steele, Jr.
1994 Frank Huerta
1995 Ashley Kaye
1996 Paul Koehler
1997 Ashley Kaye
1998 Robert Graham
1999 J. Chilcott
2000 Robert Graham
2001 J. Chilcott
2002 Robert Graham

Canadian National Championships [13]
1912 Kenneth Molson
1913 Philip MacKenzie
1914 Leonard C. Outerbridge
1915 Gordon H. Southam
1920 Leonard C. Outerbridge
1921 Charles C. Peabody
1922 Charles C. Peabody
1923 Joseph Labrecque
1924 Gerald Roberts
1925 Ralph A. Powers
1926 Jack H. Chipman
1927 Victor A. Cazalet
1928 W. Jay Iselin
1929 Herbert N. Rawlings, Jr.
1930 Argue Martin
1931 Argue Martin
1932 Beekman H. Pool
1933 Argue Martin
1934 Edward Snell
1935 Hubert Martin
1936 Cyrus Polley
1937 Neil J. Sullivan, II
1938 Hubert Martin
1939 Hubert Martin
1940 H. Hunter Lott, Jr.
1946 Jack L. Leibel
1947 William S. Noyes
1948 Joseph T. Hahn
1949 Jack L. Leibel
1950 Edward J. Hahn
1951 Henri R. Salaun
1952 Henri R. Salaun
1953 Ernest Howard
1954 G. Diehl Mateer, Jr.
1955 G. Diehl Mateer, Jr.
1956 Henri R. Salaun
1957 Henri R. Salaun
1958 Henri R. Salaun
1959 Henri R. Salaun

1960 Benjamin H. Heckscher
1961 Donald Leggat
1962 John W. Smith Chapman
1963 John W. Smith Chapman
1964 John W. Smith Chapman
1965 Robert Hetherington
1966 Stephen T. Vehslage
1967 Samuel P. Howe, III
1968 Anil Nayar
1969 Colin Adair
1970 Anil Nayar
1971 Colin Adair
1972 Cameron Nancarrow
1973 Gordon Anderson
1974 Gordon Anderson
1975 Victor Niederhoffer
1976 Phillip Mohtadi
1977 Phillip Mohtadi
1978 Michael Desaulniers
1979 Mario Sanchez
1980 Phillip Mohtadi
1981 Jay Gillespie
1982 Doug Whittaker
1983 Jonah Barrington
1984 Dale Styner
1985 Dale Styner
1986 Jamie Hickox
1987 Dale Styner
1988 Sabir Butt
1989 Gary Waite
1990 Sabir Butt
1991 Sabir Butt
1992 Gary Waite
1993 Gary Waite
1994 Sabir Butt
1995 Gary Waite
1996 Jonathon Power
1997 Graham Ryding
1998 Graham Ryding
1999 Jonathon Power
2000 Jonathon Power
2001 Jonathon Power
2002 Jonathon Power

Montreal Amateur Athletic Association Invitational

1943 Tim O'Keefe
1944 Walter Pettit
1945 Stanley W. Pearson Jr.
1946 Stanley W. Pearson Jr.
1947 Jack L. Leibel
1948 Jack L. Leibel
1949 Tim O'Keefe
1950 Hugh Nawn
1951 John Martin
1952 Edward J. Hahn
1953 John Martin
1954 Ernest Howard
1955 John Martin
1956 Benjamin H. Heckscher
1957 John Martin
1958 John W. Smith Chapman
1959 Benjamin H. Heckscher
1960 Donald Leggat
1961 David Pemberton-Smith

1962 John W. Smith Chapman
1963 Benjamin H. Heckscher
1964 Benjamin H. Heckscher
1965 David Pemberton-Smith
1966 Colin Adair
1967 Colin Adair
1968 Colin Adair
1969 Colin Adair
1970 Peter Martin
1971 Colin Adair
1972 Colin Adair
1973 Colin Adair
1974 Gordon Anderson
1975 Sharif Khan
1976 Sharif Khan
1977 Sharif Khan
1978 Stuart Goldstein
1979 Sharif Khan
1980 Sharif Khan
1981 Mark Talbott
1982 Mark Talbott
1983 Mark Talbott
1984 Mark Talbott
1985 Mark Talbott
1986 Edward C. P. Edwards
1987 Mark Talbott
1988 Mark Talbott
1989 Mark Talbott
1990 David Boyum
1991 Gary Waite
1992 Jamie Hickox
1993 Gary Waite
1994 Oliver Rucks
1995 Jonathon Power
1996 Byron Davis
1997 John Williams
2000 Alex Gough
2001 Shawn DeLierre
2002 Matt Giuffre

III. Doubles Champions [14]

Men's National Doubles [15]

1933 Roy R. Coffin & Neil J. Sullivan, II
1934 Roy R. Coffin & Neil J. Sullivan, II
1935 Roy R. Coffin & Neil J. Sullivan, II
1936 Roy R. Coffin & Neil J. Sullivan, II
1937 Roy R. Coffin & Neil J. Sullivan, II
1938 William E. Slack & H. Hunter Lott, Jr.
1939 William E. Slack & H. Hunter Lott, Jr.
1940 William E. Slack & H. Hunter Lott, Jr.
1941 William E. Slack & H. Hunter Lott, Jr.
1942 William E. Slack & H. Hunter Lott, Jr.
1946 Charles M. P. Brinton & Donald Strachan
1947 David McMullin & Stanley W. Pearson, Jr.
1948 Charles M. P. Brinton & Stanley W. Pearson, Jr.
1949 G. Diehl Mateer, Jr. & H. Hunter Lott, Jr.
1950 G. Diehl Mateer, Jr. & H. Hunter Lott, Jr.
1951 G. Diehl Mateer, Jr. & Calvin D. MacCracken
1952 Germain G. Glidden & Richard Remsen, Jr.
1953 G. Diehl Mateer, Jr. & H. Hunter Lott, Jr.
1954 G. Diehl Mateer, Jr. & Richard C. Squires
1955 Edward J. Hahn & Joseph T. Hahn

1956 Carlton M. Badger & James M. Ethridge, III
1957 Carlton M. Badger & James M. Ethridge, III
1958 G. Diehl Mateer, Jr. & John F. Hentz
1959 G. Diehl Mateer, Jr. & John F. Hentz
1960 James H. Whitmoyer & Howard A. Davis
1961 G. Diehl Mateer, Jr. & John F. Hentz
1962 G. Diehl Mateer, Jr. & John F. Hentz
1963 Samuel P. Howe, III & R. William Danforth
1964 Samuel P. Howe, III & R. William Danforth
1965 G. Diehl Mateer, Jr. & Ralph E. Howe
1966 G. Diehl Mateer, Jr. & Ralph E. Howe
1967 Sameul P. Howe, III & R. William Danforth
1968 Victor Niederhoffer & Victor Elmaleh
1969 Samuel P. Howe, III & Ralph E. Howe
1970 Samuel P. Howe, III & Ralph E. Howe
1971 Samuel P. Howe, III & Ralph E. Howe
1972 Lawrence P. Terrell & James W. Zug
1973 Victor Niederhoffer & James W. Zug
1974 Victor Niederhoffer & Colin Adair
1975 Michael J. Pierce & Maurice Heckscher, II
1976 Peter S. Briggs & Ralph E. Howe
1977 C. Victor Harding & Peter Hall
1978 Thomas E. Page & Gilbert Mateer
1979 Thomas E. Page & Gilbert Mateer
1980 John Bottger & Gilbert Mateer
1981 C. Victor Harding & Peter Hall
1982 Lawrence S. Heath, III & John R. Reese
1983 Lawrence S. Heath, III & John R. Reese
1984 Rob Hill & Andrew MacDonald
1985 Jay Gillespie & Peter Martin
1986 Gilbert Mateer & Andrew Mateer
1987 Scott Ryan & Richard Sheppard
1988 Scott Ryan & Richard Sheppard
1989 David Proctor & Maurice Heckscher, II
1990 David Proctor & George B. Lemmon, Jr.
1991 William Ramsay & Richard Sheppard
1992 Joseph J. Fabiani & Thomas W. Harrity
1993 Jonathon R. Foster & Morris Clothier
1994 Jonathon R. Foster & Morris Clothier
1995 Jonathon R. Foster & Morris Clothier
1996 David Proctor & James Heldring
1997 Peter DeRose & Peter Maule
1998 Eric Vlcek & Morris Clothier
1999 Eric Vlcek & Morris Clothier
2000 Eric Vlcek & Morris Clothier
2001 Eric Vlcek & Morris Clothier
2002 Gary Waite & Morris Clothier
2003 Eric Vlcek & Preston B. Quick

Women's National Doubles
1933 Anne Page & Sarah Madeira
1934 Margaret Bostwick & Agnes Lamme
1935 Sheila McKechnie & Anne Lytton-Milbank
1936 Anne Page & Agnes Lamme
1937 Betty Cooke & Toby Barret
1938 Alice Bierwith & Mary Adams
1939 Alice Bierwith & Mary Adams
1940 Alice Bierwith & Mary Adams
1941 Elizabeth Pearson & Hope Knowles Rawls
1948 Peggy Scott Carrott & Margaret Vaill
1949 Janet R. M. Morgan & Alice Teague
1950 Jane Austin Stauffer & Hope Knowles Rawls
1951 Peggy Scott Carrott & Frances Bottger
1952 Anne Mattson & Ann Wetzel
1953 Louisa Manly-Power & Barbara Newlin

1954 Louisa Manly-Power & Barbara Newlin
1955 Janet R. M. Morgan & Shelia MacIntosh
1956 Barbara Clement & Ann Wetzel
1957 Louisa Manly-Power & Sylvia Simonin
1958 Louisa Manly-Power & Sylvia Simonin
1959 Ann Wetzel & Sylvia Simonin
1960 Barbara Clement & Jean Classen
1961 Jane Austin Stauffer & Frances Bottger
1962 Jeanne Classen & Bunny Vosters
1963 Sheila Speight MacIntosh & Fran Marshall
1964 Jane Austin Stauffer & Ann Wetzel
1965 Jeanne Classen & Bunny Vosters
1966 Jeanne Classen & Bunny Vosters
1967 Jeanne Classen & Bunny Vosters
1968 Betty Meade & Bunny Vosters
1969 Carol Thesieres & Joyce V. Davenport
1970 Carol Thesieres & Jane Austin Stauffer
1971 Jeanne Classen & Bunny Vosters
1972 Gretchen Spruance & Bunny Vosters
1973 Gretchen Spruance & Bunny Vosters
1974 Gretchen Spruance & Bunny Vosters
1975 Carol Thesieres & Jane Austin Stauffer
1976 Gretchen Spruance & Bunny Vosters
1977 Gretchen Spruance & Bunny Vosters
1978 Jane Austin Stauffer & Barbara Maltby
1979 Carol Thesieres & Joyce V. Davenport
1980 Carol Thesieres & Joyce V. Davenport
1981 Carol Thesieres & Joyce V. Davenport
1982 Carol Thesieres & Joyce V. Davenport
1983 Mary O'Toole & Gail Ramsay
1984 Heather McKay & Barbara Savage
1985 Heather McKay & Barbara Savage
1986 Sue Cogswell & Mariann Greenberg
1987 Barbara Maltby & Joyce V. Davenport
1988 Barbara Maltby & Joanne Law
1989 Barbara Maltby & Joyce V. Davenport
1990 Barbara Maltby & Joyce V. Davenport
1991 Julie Harris & Gail Ramsay
1992 Julie Harris & Gail Ramsay
1993 Dawn Friedly & Joanne Law
1994 Demer Holleran & Berkeley Belknap
1995 Julie Harris & Joyce V. Davenport
1996 Demer Holleran & Alicia McConnell
1997 Demer Holleran & Alicia McConnell
1998 Demer Holleran & Alicia McConnell
1999 Demer Holleran & Alicia McConnell
2000 Demer Holleran & Alicia McConnell
2001 Demer Holleran & Alicia McConnell
2002 Demer Holleran & Alicia McConnell
2003 Demer Holleran & Alicia McConnell

National Mixed Doubles
1969 Daniel Pearson & Jane Austin Stauffer
1970 Christian C. F. Spahr & Gretchen Spruance
1971 Christian C. F. Spahr & Gretchen Spruance
1972 Thomas Poor & Jane Austin Stauffer
1973 Thomas Poor & Jane Austin Stauffer
1974 Thomas Poor & Jane Austin Stauffer
1975 Palmer Page & Nina Moyer
1976 Thomas Poor & Jane Austin Stauffer
1977 Thomas Poor & Jane Austin Stauffer
1978 Ralph E. Howe & Joyce V. Davenport
1979 Gilbert Mateer & Carol Thesieres
1980 Ralph E. Howe & Joyce V. Davenport
1981 Ralph E. Howe & Joyce V. Davenport

1982 William Ramsay & Gail Ramsay
1983 William Ramsay & Gail Ramsay
1984 Peter S. Briggs & Joyce V. Davenport
1985 Neal Vohr & Gail Ramsay
1986 William Ramsay & Gail Ramsay
1987 William Ramsay & Gail Ramsay
1988 Michael J. Pierce & Barbara Maltby
1989 C. Victor Harding & Joyce Davenport
1990 William Ramsay & Gail Ramsay
1991 William Ramsay & Gail Ramsay
1992 David Proctor & Joyce Davenport
1993 Morris Clothier & Joyce Davenport
1994 W. Keen Butcher & Demer Holleran
1995 W. Keen Butcher & Demer Holleran
1996 W. Keen Butcher & Demer Holleran
1997 W. Keen Butcher & Demer Holleran
1998 W. Keen Butcher & Demer Holleran
1999 W. Keen Butcher & Demer Holleran
2000 W. Keen Butcher & Demer Holleran
2001 Gary Waite & Jessie Chai
2002 W. Keen Butcher & Demer Holleran
2003 Viktor Berg & Jessie Chai

Men's World Doubles
1981 Mohibullah Khan & Clive Caldwell
1982 Michael Desaulniers & Maurice Heckscher, II
1983 Michael Desaulniers & Maurice Heckscher, II
1986 Todd Binns & Gordon Anderson
1987 Todd Binns & Thomas E. Page
1994 Kenton Jernigan & Jamie Bentley
1996 Gary Waite & Jamie Bentley
1998 Gary Waite & Mark Talbott
2000 Willie Hosey & Jamie Bentley
2002 Gary Waite & Damien Mudge

Women's World Doubles
1994 Demer Holleran & Alicia McConnell
1996 Demer Holleran & Alicia McConnell
1998 Demer Holleran & Alicia McConnell
2000 Karen Jerome & Jessie Chai
2002 Demer Holleran & Alicia McConnell

World Mixed Doubles
1994 W. Keen Butcher & Demer Holleran
1996 W. Keen Butcher & Demer Holleran
1998 Gary Waite & Jessie Chai
2000 Gary Waite & Jessie Chai
2002 Gary Waite & Jessie Chai

David C. Johnson, Jr. Memorial Heights Casino Open
1938 George Cummings & Frank Ward
1939 Stanley Galowin & Joseph Wiener
1940 George Cummings & Thomas Iannicelli
1941 George Cummings & Thomas Iannicelli
1947 George Cummings & Thomas Iannicelli
1948 George Cummings & Thomas Iannicelli
1954 John B. Russell, III & Richard Remsen, Jr.
1955 Carlton M. Badger & James M. Ethridge, III
1956 Albert Chassard & Thomas Iannicelli
1957 Albert Chassard & Thomas Iannicelli
1958 John B. Russell, III & Richard Remsen, Jr.
1960 Albert Chassard & Frank Iannicelli
1961 Albert Chassard & Frank Iannicelli
1962 Albert Chassard & Frank Iannicelli
1963 Victor Elmaleh & David C. Johnson, Jr.
1964 Christian C. F. Spahr, Jr. & Claude Beer

1965 Christian C. F. Spahr, Jr. & Claude Beer
1966 Stephen T. Vehslage & Ramsay W. Vehslage
1967 Samuel P. Howe, III & R. William Danforth
1968 Ian M.T. McAvity & Kenneth K. Binns
1969 Mohibullah Khan & Colin Adair
1970 Mohibullah Khan & Colin Adair
1971 Mohibullah Khan & Kenneth K. Binns
1972 Mohibullah Khan & Kenneth K. Binns
1973 Mohibullah Khan & Gul Khan
1974 Michael J. Pierce & Maurice Heckscher, II
1975 Roger Alcaly & Mel K. Sokolow
1976 Michael J. Pierce & Maurice Heckscher, II
1977 Michael J. Pierce & Maurice Heckscher, II
1978 Michael J. Pierce & Maurice Heckscher, II
1979 Lawrence S. Heath, III & John R. Reese
1980 C. Victor Harding & Gordon D. H. Anderson
1981 Michael Desaulniers & Maurice Heckscher, II
1982 Michael Desaulniers & Maurice Heckscher, II
1983 David C. Johnson, III & Edward C. P. Edwards
1984 Peter S. Briggs & Gul Khan
1985 David C. Johnson, III & Edward C. P. Edwards
1986 David C. Johnson, III & Edward C. P. Edwards
1987 John Nimick & Clive Caldwell
1988 Todd Binns & Thomas E. Page
1989 Todd Binns & Thomas E. Page
1990 Kenton Jernigan & Jamie Bentley
1991 Kenton Jernigan & Jamie Bentley
1992 Todd Binns & Jose Pepe Martinez
1993 Kenton Jernigan & Jamie Bentley
1994 Kenton Jernigan & Jamie Bentley
1995 Kenton Jernigan & Jamie Bentley
1996 Gary Waite & Jamie Bentley
1997 Gary Waite & Jamie Bentley
1998 Gary Waite & Mark Talbott
1999 Gary Waite & Mark Talbott
2000 Willie Hosey & Jamie Bentley
2001 Michael Pirnak & Viktor Berg
2002 Gary Waite & Damien Mudge
2003 Gary Waite & Damien Mudge

North American Open Doubles [16]
1931 Roy R. Coffin & Neil J. Sullivan, II
1932 Roy R. Coffin & Neil J. Sullivan, II
1935 Donald Strachan & Brendon Walsh
1936 Donald Strachan & Brendon Walsh
1937 David McMullin & W. Mifflin Large
1938 William E. Slack & H. Hunter Lott, Jr.
1939 Roy R. Coffin & Neil J. Sullivan, Jr.
1940 David McMullin & W. Mifflin Large
1941 William E. Slack & H. Hunter Lott, Jr.
1942 Charles M. P. Brinton & Donald Strachan
1947 M. S. Tenny & Clifford Sutter
1948 Charles M. P. Brinton & Stanley W. Pearson, Jr.
1949 Charles M. P. Brinton & Stanely W. Pearson, Jr.
1950 G. Diehl Mateer, Jr. & H. Hunter Lott, Jr.
1951 Germain G. Glidden & Clifford Sutter
1952 Germain G. Glidden & Clifford Sutter
1953 Carlton M. Badger & James M. Ethridge, III
1954 Carlton M. Badger & James M. Ethridge, III
1955 Carlton M. Badger & James M. Ethridge, III

1956 James H. Whitmoyer & Howard A. Davis
1958 Charles M. P. Brinton & Edward W.
　　Madeira, Jr.
1959 Carlton M. Badger & James M. Ethridge, III
1960 Carlton M. Badger & James M. Ethridge, III
1961 Carlton M. Badger & James M. Ethridge, III
1962 Samuel P. Howe, III & James M.
　　Ethridge, III
1963 Christian C. F. Spahr, Jr. & Claude Beer
1964 Samuel P. Howe, III & R. William Danforth
1965 Samuel P. Howe, III & R. William Danforth
1966 Stephen T. Vehslage & Ramsey W. Vehslage
1967 Stephen T. Vehslage & Ramsey W. Vehslage
1968 Samuel P. Howe, III & Claude Beer
1969 Victor Elmaleh & Ralph E. Howe
1970 Christian C. F. Spahr, Jr. & Maurice
　　Heckscher
1971 Roger E. Alcaly & Mel K. Sokolow
1972 Anil Nayar & Thomas M. Poor
1973 Michael J. Pierce & J. Peter Pierce
1974 W. Roland Oddy & Pedro A. Bacallao
1975 Michael J. Pierce & Thomas M. Poor
1976 Peter S. Briggs & Ralph E. Howe
1977 Richard Roe & Thomas M. Poor
1978 Richard Roe & Thomas M. Poor
1979 Lawrence S. Heath, III & John R. Reese
1980 Michael J. Pierce & David C. Johnson, III
1981 Lawrence S. Heath, III & John R. Reese
1982 Peter Chester & Palmer Page
1984 Peter S. Briggs & Mark Talbott
1985 Michael Desaulniers & Brad Desaulniers
1986 Todd Binns & Thomas E. Page
1987 Todd Binns & Thomas E. Page
1988 Todd Binns & Thomas E. Page
1989 Alan Grant & Edward C. P. Edwards
1990 Alan Grant & Edward C. P. Edwards
1991 Alan Grant & Edward C. P. Edwards
1993 Kenton Jernigan & Jamie Bentley
1994 Scott Dulmage & Gary Waite
1995 Peter S. Briggs & Frank J. Stanley, IV
1996 Scott Stoneburgh & Anders Wahlstedt
1997 Gary Waite & Mark Talbott
1998 Gary Waite & Mark Talbott
1999 Gary Waite & Mark Talbott
2000 Gary Waite & Damien Mudge
2001 Gary Waite & Damien Mudge
2003 Gary Waite & Damien Mudge

Cambridge Club Doubles [17]
1973 Peter Martin & Gordon D. H. Anderson
1974 Mohibullah Khan & Gul Khan
1975 Michael J. Pierce & Maurice Heckscher, II
1976 Michael J. Pierce & Maurice Hechscher, II
1977 Peter Briggs & Ralph E. Howe
1978 Mohibullah Khan & Clive Caldwell
1979 Mohibullah Khan & Clive Caldwell
1980 Peter Briggs & Ralph E. Howe
1981 Michael J. Pierce & Thomas E. Page
1982 Michael J. Pierce & Thomas E. Page
1983 Peter Briggs & Mark Talbott
1984 Lawrence S. Heath, III & Aziz Khan
1985 Lawrence S. Heath, III & Aziz Khan
1986 David C. Johnson, III & Edward C. P.
　　Edwards
1987 Todd Binns & Thomas E. Page

1988 Todd Binns & Thomas E. Page
1989 Alan Grant & Edward C. P. Edwards
1990 Todd Binns & Thomas E. Page
1991 Alan Grant & Edward C. P. Edwards
1992 Kenton Jernigan & Jamie Bentley
1993 Scott Dulmage & Gary Waite
1994 Kenton Jernigan & Jamie Bentley
1995 Gary Waite & Jamie Bentley
1996 Gary Waite & Jamie Bentley
1998 Todd Binns & Willie Hosey
1999 Gary Waite & Damien Mudge
2000 Willie Hosey & Jonathon Power
2001 Gary Waite & Mark Chaloner
2002 Gary Waite & Stewart Boswell

The Elite
1982 Michael J. Pierce & Thomas E. Page
1983 David C. Johnson, III & Edward C. P.
Edwards
1984 Peter Briggs & David C. Johnson, III
1985 Michael J. Pierce & Thomas E. Page
1986 Michael J. Pierce & Jamie Bentley
1987 Todd Binns & Thomas E. Page
1988 Alan Grant & Jamie Bentley
1989 Edward C. P. Edwards & Alex Doucas
1990 Kenton Jernigan & Jamie Bentley
1991 Kenton Jernigan & Jamie Bentley
1992 Todd Binns & Thomas E. Page
1993 Alan Grant & Edward C. P. Edwards
1994 William Doyle & Edward C. P. Edwards
1995 Kenton Jernigan & Jeremy Fraiberg
1997 Gary Waite & Jamie Bentley
1998 Todd Binns & Jamie Bentley
1999 Scott Dulmage & Dean Brown
2001 Willie Hosey & Jamie Bentley
2002 Gary Waite & Damien Mudge
2003 Gary Waite & Damien Mudge

Gold Racquets [18]
1930 W. Jay Iselin & Hugo Fleury
1931 E. D. Pratt & Lanthrop S. Haskins
1932 D. Lee Norris & Lanthrop S. Haskins
1933 E. Maxwell & W. Stapleton Wonham
1935 D. Lee Norris & Sydney P. Clark
1936 B. Terry & M. M. MacLeod
1937 D. Lee Norris & W. Mifflin Large
1938 J. Lawrence Pool & Beekman H. Pool
1939 D. Lee Norris & Clifford Sutter
1940 D. Lee Norris & Clifford Sutter
1941 W. B. Adsit & David P. McElroy
1942 William T. Ketcham, Jr. & M. Donald Grant
1945 William E. Slack & H. Hunter Lott, Jr.
1946 W. B. Adsit & David P. McElroy
1947 W. B. Adsit & David P. McElroy
1948 William T. Ketcham, Jr. & H. Hunter
　　Lott, Jr.
1949 William T. Ketcham, Jr. & H. Hunter
　　Lott, Jr.
1950 John B. Russell & Richard Remsen, Jr.
1951 Carlton M. Badger & James M. Ethridge, III
1952 Carlton M. Badger & James M. Ethridge, III
1953 John B. Russell & Richard Remsen, Jr.
1954 John B. Russell & Richard Remsen, Jr.
1955 John B. Russell & Richard Remsen, Jr.
1956 James H. Whitmoyer & Howard A. Davis
1957 Paul Steele, Jr. and R. William Danforth

1958 G. Diehl Mateer, Jr. & John F. Hentz
1959 Paul Steele, Jr. & R. William Danforth
1960 Paul Steele, Jr. & R. William Danforth
1961 Paul Steele, Jr. & James F. Ethridge, III
1962 Christian C. F. Spahr, Jr. & Claude Beer
1963 Carlton M. Badger & James M. Ethridge, III
1964 Howard A. Davis & James H. Whitmoyer
1965 Christian C. F. Spahr, Jr. & Claude Beer
1966 Peter Martin & Kerry Martin
1967 Stephen T. Vehslage & Ramsay W. Vehslage
1968 Ian McAvity & David Pemberton-Smith
1969 Michael J. Pierce & Peter Pierce
1970 G. Diehl Mateer, Jr. & James W. Zug
1971 Michael J. Pierce & Peter Pierce
1972 Romer Holleran & Maurice Heckscher, II
1973 John Swann & Peter Hall
1974 Michael J. Pierce & Maurice Heckscher, II
1975 Michael J. Pierce & Maurice Heckscher, II
1976 Michael J. Pierce & Maurice Heckscher, II
1977 Michael J. Pierce & Jay Gillespie
1978 Lawrence S. Heath, III & John R. Reese
1979 Lawrence S. Heath, III & John R. Reese
1980 Lawrence S. Heath, III & John R. Reese
1981 Lawrence S. Heath, III & John R. Reese
1982 Michael J. Pierce & Ralph E. Howe
1983 Lawrence S. Heath, III & John R. Reese
1984 Lawrence S. Heath, III & David C.
    Johnson, III
1985 Victor Harding & Ralph E. Howe
1986 Michael J. Pierce & Jay Gillespie
1987 Hugh Labossier & William Doyle
1988 Peter S. Briggs & William Doyle
1989 Peter S. Briggs & William Doyle
1990 David Proctor & George Lemmon, Jr.
1991 David Proctor & George Lemmon, Jr.
1992 Michael J. Pierce & Richard Sheppard
1993 Lawrence S. Heath, III & Stuart Grodman
1994 Frank J. Stanley, IV & Jamie Bentley
1995 Jonathon R. Foster & Morris Clothier
1996 Frank J. Stanley, IV & J. D. Cregan
1997 Gary Waite & Andrew Slater
1998 Gary Waite & Andrew Slater
1999 Eric Vlcek & Morris Clothier
2000 Eric Vlcek & Morris Clothier
2001 Eric Vlcek & Thomas W. Harrity
2002 Steve Scharf & Thomas W. Harrity

Buffalo Tennis & Squash Invitational
1955 John B. Russell & Richard Remsen
1956 Ray Widelski & Louis Schaefer
1957 Ray Widelski & Louis Schaefer
1959 Victor Elmaleh & David C. Johnson, Jr.
1960 Paul B. Steele & R. William Danforth
1961 James H. Whitmoyer & Howard A. Davis
1962 Christian C. F. Spahr & Claude Beer
1963 Samuel P. Howe, III & R. William Danforth
1964 Samuel P. Howe, III & R. William Danforth
1965 Lorne G. Main & John Foy
1966 Victor Niederhofer & Victor Elmaleh
1967 Ian McAvity & David Pemberton-Smith
1968 Ian McAvity & David Pemberton-Smith
1969 Larry O'Laughlin & David O'Laughlin
1970 Larry O'Laughlin & Anil Nayar
1971 Thomas M. Poor & Anil Nayar
1972 Thomas M. Poor & Maurice Heckscher, II

1973 Robert Hetherington & R. William Danforth
1974 Thomas M. Poor & Peter Hall
1975 Thomas M. Poor & Peter Hall
1976 Thomas M. Poor & Richard Roe
1977 Thomas M. Poor & Alexander Martin
1978 Thomas M. Poor & Alexander Martin
1979 Thomas M. Poor & Alexander Martin
1980 Thomas M. Poor & Alexander Martin
1981 Peter Hall & Jay Gillespie
1982 Thomas M. Poor & Peter Hall
1983 Thomas M. Poor & Jay Gillespie
1984 Victor Hardin & Steven McIntyre
1985 Thomas M. Poor & Steven McIntytre
1986 Thomas M. Poor & Jay D. Umans
1987 John Boynton & Steven Hisey
1988 Charles P. Jacobs & Philip Barth, III
1989 Fred A. Reid & Alan Hunt
1990 Scott Ryan & Jay D. Umans
1991 Paul D. Assaiante & Gordon Anderson
1992 Joseph J. Fabiani & Thomas W. Harrity
1993 Paul Deratney & Taylor Fawcett
1994 D. Stevenson & W. Meek
1995 Peter DeRose & Peter Maule
1996 Peter DeRose & Peter Maule
1997 M. Costigan & A. Hunt
1998 M. Costigan & A. Hunt
1999 Tyler Millard & Ken Flynn
2000 R. Smith & D. Friedman
2001 S. Leggat & S. Belman
2002 Michael Pernak & Willie Hosey

William White [19]
1962 James H. Whitmoyer & R. William Danforth
1963 Nathan P. Stauffer & R. William Danforth
1964 James H. Whitmoyer & Edward W.
    Madeira, Jr.
1965 Victor Elmaleh & Maurice Heckscher, II
1966 Christian C. F. Spahr, Jr. & Benjamin H.
    Heckscher
1967 Maurice Heckscher, II & Benjamin H.
    Heckscher
1968 Stephan T. Vehslage & Ramsay W. Vehslage
1969 Victor Elmaleh & Ralph E. Howe
1970 G. Diehl Mateer, Jr. & James W. Zug
1971 G. Diehl Mateer, Jr. & James W. Zug
1972 Michael J. Pierce and J. Peter Pierce
1973 Hashim Khan & Ralph E. Howe
1974 Michael J. Pierce & G. Maguire
1975 Michael J. Pierce & Maurice Heckscher, II
1976 Michael J. Pierce & Maurice Heckscher, II
1977 Michael J. Pierce & Maurice Heckscher, II
1978 Michael J. Pierce & Maurice Heckscher, II
1979 Michael J. Pierce & Thomas E. Page
1980 Mohibullah Khan & Maurice Heckscher, II
1981 Lawrence S. Heath, III & John R. Reese
1982 Alexander Martin & Thomas M. Poor
1983 Lawrence S. Heath, III & John R. Reese
1984 C. Victor Harding & John R. Reese
1985 Michael J. Pierce & Jay Gillespie
1986 Michael J. Pierce & Jay Gillespie
1987 Michael J. Pierce & Jay Gillespie
1988 David Proctor & Maurice Heckscher, II
1989 Peter S. Briggs & Gordon Anderson
1990 Peter S. Briggs & Gordon Anderson
1991 Neal Vohr & Geoff Kennedy

1992 Joseph J. Fabiani & Thomas W. Harrity
1993 Edward C. P. Edwards & Gilbert Mateer
1994 Neal Vohr & Stuart Grodman
1996 W. Keen Butcher & Richard Sheppard
1997 Joseph J. Fabiani & Geoff Kennedy
1998 Eric Vlcek & Morris Clothier
1999 Eric W. Eiteljorg & Thomas W. Harrity
2000 Eric W. Eiteljorg & Thomas W. Harrity
2001 Eric Vlcek & Morris Clothier
2002 Eric Vlcek & Thomas W. Harrity
2002 Eric Vlcek & Geoff Kennedy
2003 Eric Vlcek & Geoff Kennedy

IV. Historical Data

USSRA Presidents
1920–25 Sydney P. Clark
1925–26 Lyman M. Bass
1926–27 Sydney P. Clark
1927–28 L. D. Young
1928–29 W. Candler Bowditch
1929–32 Ralph A. Powers
1932–33 Paul E. Callanan
1933–35 Adrian W. Smith
1935–37 Joseph de V. Keefe
1937–39 James D. Standish, Jr.
1939–42 Darwin P. Kingsley, Jr.
1942–48 W. Mifflin Large
1948–49 Seymour H. Knox, Jr.
1949–50 Neil J. Sullivan, II
1950–51 Andrew N. Winslow, Jr.
1951–53 Henry W. Putnam
1953–54 H. Hunter Lott, Jr.
1954–56 John P. Humes
1956–58 Braman B. Adams
1958–61 Ernest D. Richmond, Jr.
1961–63 Joseph T. Hahn
1963–65 Howard A. Davis
1965–67 William T. Ketcham, Jr.
1967–69 Seymour H. Knox, III
1969–71 W. Stewart Brauns, Jr.
1971–73 Lloyd Jacobs
1973–75 Darwin P. Kingsley, III
1975–77 E. Harmon Friel, Jr.
1977–79 A. Warren Smith, Jr.
1979–80 Thomas Wrightson
1980–82 Herbert H. Gross
1982–84 John F. Herrick
1984–86 Leonard Bernheimer
1986–88 C. Shelley Acuff
1988–90 Charles C. Kingsley
1990–93 George A. Haggarty
1993–95 Alan L. Fox
1995–97 Andre P. Naniche
1997–99 E. Taylor Quick
1999–01 Eben Hardie
2001–03 Kevin Jernigan

U.S. Women's SRA Presidents [20]
1932–33 Mrs. Edgar Arnold
1933–47 Eleanora R. Sears
1947–50 Edith Beatty
1950–53 Peggy Baker
1953–54 Barbara Clement
1954–56 Anne Page Homer
1956–57 Betty Howe Constable

1957–59 Betty Shellenberger
1959–61 Margaret Mahoney
1961–63 Mrs. Robert G. Potter, Jr.
1963–67 Caroline Haussermann
1967–69 Madelyn T. Reed
1969–71 Noel Spellman
1971–73 Laura Farnsworth
1973–75 Sally Jackson Shand
1975–79 Margaret Riehl
1979–81 Virginia Akabane
1981–83 Carol Weymuller
1983–85 Sally Ann Fields
1985–87 Mac Ryan
1987–89 Carol Dicker
1989–91 Karen Rosenberg
1991–93 Joanne Law
1993–95 Mac Ryan
1995–97 Karen Arango
1997–99 Wendy Ansdell
1999–2001 Missy Cantor
2001–03 Brenda Grossnickle

USSRA President's Cup [21]
1966 Charles W. Ufford, Jr.
1967 Joseph T. Hahn
1968 Edwin H. Bigelow
1969 William T. Kecham, Jr.
1970 John M. Barnaby, II
1974 Anthony G. Rytina
1975 W. Stewart Brauns, Jr.
1976 A. Warren Smith, Jr.
1977 James A. Traviss
1978 Hashim Khan
1979 James McQueenie
1980 E. Harmon Friel, Jr.
1981 Margaret K. Riehl
1982 Seymour H. Knox, III
1983 Thomas Wrightson
1984 Darwin P. Kingsley, III
1985 Ian Stewart
1986 Thomas B. Jones
1988 John F. Herrick
1989 Mark Talbott
1990 George A. Haggarty
1991 Charles C. Kingsley
1992 Alan L. Fox
1993 Leonard Bernheimer
1994 Fred Weymuller and Carol Weymuller
1995 Hazel White Jones
1996 The Pierce Family
1997 Craig Brand
1998 C. Howard Wilkins
2000 Demer Holleran

Achievement Bowl [22]
1955 Anne Page Homer
1956 Barbara Clement
1957 Mrs. Henry Flynt and Eleonora R. Sears
1958 Edith Beatty
1959 Betty Shellenberger and Anne B. Townshend
1960 Mrs. William Greeley
1961 Baba Lewis
1962 Mary Knapp
1963 Mrs. Robert Potter and Louisa Manly-Power
1964 Mrs. Kenneth Donaldson
1965 Noel Spellman

1966 Madelyn T. Reed	Betty Howe Constable
1967 Caroline Hausserman	Germain G. Glidden
1968 Laura Farnsworth	Anne Page Homer
1969 Jane M. Sheets	Hashim Khan
1970 Blanche Day	H. Hunter Lott, Jr.
1971 Mrs. Richard Prugh	Barbara Maltby
1972 Ann Wetzel	G. Diehl Mateer, Jr.
1973 Margaret Riehl	Alicia McConnell
1975 Lee Burling	Victor Niederhoffer
1976 Agnes B. Kurtz	Stanley W. Pearson
1977 Judy Michel	Henri R. Salaun
1978 Betty Howe Constable	Gretchen Spruance
1980 Carol Weymuller	Mark Talbott
1981 Barbara Stewart	
1982 Virginia Akabane	
1983 Carole Dicker	**2001**
1984 Mary Ellen Johnson	John M. Barnaby, II
1985 Julie Talbert	William T. Ketcham, Jr.
1986 Sally Ann Fields	Mohibullah Khan
1987 Wendy F. Lawrence	Darwin P. Kingsley, III
1988 Mac Ryan	Eleonora R. Sears
1989 Dale Walker	John Skillman
1990 Agnes B. Kurtz	
1991 Beth Rasin	**2002**
1992 Diana Lauria	Cecile Bowes
1993 Hazel White Jones	Ralph E. Howe
1994 Karen Arango	Samuel P. Howe, III
1995 Nancy Cushman	

U.S. Squash Hall of Fame

2003

Edward C. P. Edwards
Margaret Howe
Ann Wetzel

2000

Margaret Varner Bloss
Charles M. P. Brinton

NOTES

1. In November 1975 Victor Niederhoffer turned professional. Thereafter, until 1990, the best players in the U.S. were unable to compete in the nationals as they were professionals. In 1990 the USSRA started the S. L. Green, a softball tournament at the U.S. nationals open to all U.S. citizens, amateur and professional.

2. The women's hardball nationals ended after 1994. In 1995 a new open division, like the men's S. L. Green, was instituted at the softball nationals.

3. College men switched to softball in 1995; women switched in 1994.

4. After the 1992 season, the hardball junior nationals stopped, and they switched to the softball juniors, which had originally begun in 1989. The 1993 junior nationals, held at Trinity, were cancelled after completion of the second round on Saturday due to a snowstorm. In 1994 the juniors changed age groups from under 19, 17, 15 and 13 to under 19, 16, 14 and 12, and in 1997 they were closed to U.S. citizens.

5. The North American Open was founded as the United States Open in 1954. In 1966 it amalgamated with the Canadian Open and became the NAO. In 1995 it switched to softball for its final year.

6. The Tournament of Champions was originally named the United States Professionals. In 1965 it became the North America Professionals. In 1979 it became the World Professional Squash Association Championships and in 1992 switched to softball. In 1995 it became the Tournament of Champions.

7. In 1983 and 1984 a hardball U.S. Open was played at the Yale Club in New York. In 1985 it switched to softball. The 2001 U.S. Open was postponed by the September 11th attacks on the World Trade Center to January 2002.

8. It was called the Heights Casino Women's Open until 1980 when it was named after former Heights Casino professional Carol Weymuller. In 1993 the tournament switched to softball. The 2001 tournament was played in January 2002.

9. Originally named the Charles J. Hardy Invitation, the Apawamis switched in 1996 to softball.

10. In 1999 the Gold Racquets switched to softball.

11. In 1995 the Harry Cowles switched to softball.

12. In 1996 the William White switched to softball.

13. Canada started their softball nationals in 1974 and stopped their hardball nationals in 1995. Here I switch lists in 1982.

14. When recording doubles champions, it is traditional to list the left-wall player first.

15. The men's national doubles was opened to professionals in 2002.

16. Until 1984 when the tournament was opened to professionals, it was called the Greenwich Invitational.

17. In 2000 the tournament, played for the Jim Bentley Cup, split up professional doubles teams and added professional singles players.

18. The official name is the Ray Chauncey Doubles

19. The official name is the Brendan McRory–James Tully, Jr. Doubles.

20. In 1979 the USWSRA merged into the USSRA and became the Women's Division.

21. Donated by William T. Ketcham, Jr., this is highest annual award the USSRA can bestow.

22. Charlotte Prizer presented the bowl in 1955. It is awarded to the woman who makes the most notable contribution to sportsmanship and advancement of the game.

Index

Index

Niederhoffer, Victor (*cont.*)
championship, first, 1965, 128–29; North American Open, 134–35; as pro, 187, 192–95, 202; racquetball, 195; return and championships, 132–35; Sharif Khan and, 134–35, 201, 202; style of play, 131; USSRA and, 130–31
Niederman, Derrick, 217, 226–28
Nightingale, Don, 259
Nimick, John, 187, 213, 216, 249, 254
Noel, Susan, 64–65, 67
Nord, Roland, 156
Nordlie, Leif, 142
Norman, Ross, 216
North American Open (NAO), 124–25, 191, 192, 197–98, 202, 204–5, 216, 228; Bancroft sponsorship, 188; eye-protection rule and, 210; Howe-Kahn, 1967, 104; Khan-Niederhoffer, 1975, 134–35, 201; Merion champs at, 104; 1977, Hunt-Khan, 202–3; 1982, Desaulniers-Khan, 206; 1985, at Town Hall, NYC, 198–99, 201, 215; 1987, Edwards-Talbott, 212; qualifying tournament, 194; Sharif Khan record, 201–2, 204–6, 215; softball switch and demise, 275–76
North American Professional Squash Racquets Association (NAPSRA). *See* WPSA
Northeastern University, 282
Nunez, Alberto, 214
Nyad, Diana, 223–24

Oehrlein, Walter, 137, 143
O'Loughlin, Dave, 137, 240
O'Loughlin, Larry, 130, 137
Oman, Fred, 157
Olympics, 28, 245–46
Outerbridge, Sir Leonard, 36
Oxford University, 8, 80

Pacific Coast championships, 156
Pacific Coast Squash Racquets Association, 159
Page, Anne, 64, 66–69, 265
Page, Palmer, 143, 215
Page, Tom, 187, 194, 206, 214–15, 218, 271, 277
Palmer-Tomkinson, 42, 237
Pan-American Games, 245
Parke, Simon, 245
Parker, Keith, 240

Patten, Edgar, 94–96
Patterson, Bryan, 280–81
Patterson, Willing, 49, 54, 56–58, 78, 102, 143, 237
Peabody, Charles, 50, 69–70, 82n.
Pease, Perry, 85, 259
Pearson, David, 281
Pearson, Libby, 68, 69
Pearson, Stan, Jr., 57, 70, 92, 102, 114
Pearson, Stan, Sr., 69–70
Pettitt, Tom, 21, 47–48, 60, 93
Phelan, John, 245
Philadelphia, PA, 32, 69–74, 81, 172; clubs, early, 29–31, 33–34; Country Club, 29–30, 149; Cricket Club, 30, 33, 57, 102, 149; Cynwyd Club, 69, 101, 149, 153, 154, 174, 219, 221, 246, 268; doubles, 257–59, 261–62, 265, 268; Elite Doubles, 268, 270–71; Gwynedd Squash Club, 158; Inter-Club Squash Racquets Association, 30, 39, 181; league squash, 30–31; national champions, 32; Open, 215; Penn Athletic Club, 81; prep schools, 89–90; Princeton Club, 81; public courts, 167, 169, 181; Racquet Club, 28–34, 75, 80, 93, 258, 259; softball, 246; women's squash, 149, 181–82, 265. *See also* Merion Cricket Club
Philippe IV of France, 8
Phillips Andover Academy, 137, 139, 250–51
Phillips Exeter Academy, 54, 84, 89, 99–100, 137, 139–40
Phipps, Odgen, 49, 71
Pickens, Kevan, 176
Pier, A[rthur]. S., 17, 19, 20
Pierce, Ellie, 181, 223
Pierce, Mike, 200, 257, 266, 269–71
Piping Rock, Locust Valley, NY, 52
Pirnak, Michael, 272
Pittsburgh, PA: early clubs, 32; Golf Club, 95, 113; inter-city tournaments, 157; juniors, 137; nationals, 95, 113; nationals, doubles, 264; softball and, 245; U.S. Open in, 123, 156, 199
Plainfield Country Club, 86, 111, 180; DeForest-Tyler Invitation, 86, 102, 111, 266
Pleydell-Bourverie, E. O., 14
Plimpton, George, 144
Pohrer, Natalie, 282
Poletti, Chuck, 140

Printed in the United States
79023LV00004B/46-84

9 780743 229906